1987

University of St. Francis
GEN 327.73 O988r

W9-AEP-764

Eagle Resurgent?

Eagle Resurgent?
The Reagan Era in American Foreign Policy

Edited by

Kenneth A. Oye
Princeton University

Robert J. Lieber
Georgetown University

Donald Rothchild
University of California, Davis

Little, Brown and Company
Boston   Toronto

LIBRARY
College of St. Francis
JOLIET, ILL.

Library of Congress Cataloging in Publication Data

Eagle resurgent?

  Continues: Eagle defiant. © 1983.
  Includes index.
  1. United States—Foreign relations—1981–
2. Reagan, Ronald. I. Oye, Kenneth A., 1949–
II. Lieber, Robert J., 1941–   . III. Rothchild,
Donald.
E876.E232 1987   327.73   86-21429
ISBN 0-316-67733-7

Written under the auspices of
the Center of International Studies,
Princeton University

Copyright © 1987 by Kenneth A. Oye,
Robert J. Lieber, and Donald Rothchild

All rights reserved. No part of this book may be reproduced in any form
or by any electronic or mechanical means including information storage
and retrieval systems without permission in writing from the publisher,
except by a reviewer who may quote brief passages in a review.

Library of Congress Catalog Card Number 86-21429

ISBN 0-316-67733-7

9 8 7 6 5 4 3 2 1

MV

Published simultaneously in Canada
by Little, Brown & Company (Canada) Limited

Printed in the United States of America

327.73
O988r

Preface

The foreign policies of the Nixon, Ford, and Carter administrations and the policies of the Reagan administration define two sharply divergent responses to fundamental changes in the international environment. The administrations of the 1970s adapted to the secular decline of American economic and military power and to increasing international economic interdependence. Their security policies of retrenchment and international economic policies of multilateral management were part of an implicit overarching strategy of adjustment to what they saw as the end of the post-World War II era of American preeminence. By contrast, the Reagan administration initially rejected both the need to adjust and the methods of adjustment. Reagan administration security and economic policies were part of an explicit strategy of restoring the United States to a position of preeminence in international affairs. Nixon, Ford, and Carter administration rhetoric was attuned to the politics of limits and complexity, while Reagan administration rhetoric evoked the optimism and the simplicity of America in the 1950s and 1960s.

Eagle Resurgent? treats the first six years of the Reagan administration as a critical experiment in American foreign policy. The successes and failures of Reagan foreign policy may contribute, albeit inadvertently, to a redefinition of what is possible and desirable in the 1990s. Constancy and change in Reagan foreign policy may provide information on the nature of constraints and tradeoffs that are likely to shape American foreign policy in the next decade. The editors and contributors to this volume are as concerned with surveying the domain of choice open to *any* administration as with evaluating the specific choices of the Reagan administration. While drawing attention to what we see as strategic, tactical, and stylistic deficiencies of Reagan foreign policy, we seek to place the policies of the administration into structural and historical perspective.

Eagle Resurgent? is designed to provide a comprehensive assessment of the wider implications of the Reagan administration's foreign policy. Part One, "Overview," places the foreign policy of the Reagan administration in international and domestic context. The two keynote chapters present overarching themes in Reagan foreign policy and describe major constraints and tradeoffs that have affected the ability of the administration to implement its initial policies. Subsequent chapters juxtapose Reagan policies with the often inconsistent requirements of crosscutting functional and regional concerns. Part Two, "Functional Problems," examines

124/661

policies on defense, international economics, and energy. Part Three, "Regional Problems," examines policies toward the Soviet Union and Eastern Europe, China, Western Europe, Japan, Latin America, Africa, and the Middle East.

The writing of this volume has been a collaborative effort from the outset. Each regional and functional specialist proceeded with sensitivity to contradictory and correlative interests across a broad spectrum of issues. Building on the foundation provided by the precursor to this volume, *Eagle Defiant*, the contributors and editors commented on draft chapters which subsequently were further revised to treat developments in the late spring and early summer of 1986. We aimed for a publication date late enough to permit analysis of how Reagan administration foreign policy has evolved, yet early enough to contribute to the 1988 preelectoral debate over the appropriateness of these policies.

We acknowledge with gratitude the intellectual and logistical support of the Center of International Studies of Princeton University, and the encouragement of John Covell at Little, Brown and Company. The editors and contributors assume sole responsibility for the views expressed in this book.

Kenneth A. Oye, Princeton, New Jersey
Robert J. Lieber, Washington, D.C.
Donald Rothchild, Davis, California

August 1986

Contents

Part III: Regional Problems

I

Overview

1

Constrained Confidence and the Evolution of Reagan Foreign Policy

Kenneth A. Oye

Through rhetoric and action, the Nixon, Ford, and Carter administrations struggled to adjust to emerging limits of American economic and military power. By contrast, the Reagan administration initially rejected both the need to adjust and the methods of adjustment. If the 1970s were a decade of limits, the 1980s would be a decade of opportunities. The Reagan administration offered an optimistic vision, a strategy for simultaneous economic and military restoration, and economic and security initiatives that departed sharply from the directions established in the 1970s. How has the Reagan foreign policy experiment fared? Over five years, the rhetoric of restoration remained in place, but the actions of the Reagan administration reverted largely to lines established by the Nixon, Ford, and Carter administrations. With a few highly visible exceptions, most notably the Strategic Defense Initiative and the "Reagan Doctrine," American foreign policy in the late 1980s joined the rhetoric of the 1950s and 1960s to the policies of the 1970s. The essays in this volume explain and evaluate the persistence of rhetoric, the general tendency toward reversion to the economic and security policies of the 1970s, and the accentuation of exceptions to reversion.

Consider the administrations of the 1970s. Richard Nixon and Henry Kissinger spoke pessimistically of the inevitable "end of the postwar world." They formulated a narrowly realpolitik foreign policy to control America's descent into an uncertain future. Jimmy Carter spoke with mild optimism of a "new world," where "we can no longer expect that the other 150 nations will follow the dictates of the powerful," and added a

Kenneth A. Oye is an Assistant Professor of Politics at Princeton University and an editor of World Politics. *His most recent work is* Cooperation under Anarchy *(Princeton University Press, 1986). He is currently completing studies on political economy and bloc cohesion and on interwar economic diplomacy.*

soupçon of genuine idealpolitik — human rights — that increased the palatability of a fundamentally realpolitik foreign policy. Although every administration distinguishes its foreign policy from that of its predecessors, minor differences should not be permitted to obscure the fundamental continuity of American foreign policy during the 1970s. With regard to security, the Nixon, Ford, and Carter administrations narrowed the definition of American interests and commitments in peripheral regions, shifted some of the burdens of containment to allies in China, Western Europe, and the Third World, and acted on limited areas of mutual interest with the Soviet Union, particularly through strategic arms control negotiations. With regard to economics, these administrations gradually increased the scope of multilateral political management to address problems that arose as a consequence of increasing economic interdependence and decreasing American power. Their rhetoric was attuned to the politics of limits, and their actions were rooted in a strategy of adjustment.

By 1980, the strategy of adjustment had proved frustrating and alarming to a nation with expectations conditioned by a quarter century of preeminence in international relations. The 444 days of the Iranian hostage crisis crystallized these national frustrations. Mass concern was mirrored in the statements of one of the architects of the strategy of adjustment. Ten years after developing policies suited to the "end of the postwar world," Henry Kissinger spoke of a "world out of control, with our relative military power declining, with our economic lifeline increasingly vulnerable to blackmail, with hostile radical forces growing in every continent, and with the number of countries willing to stake their futures on our friendship declining."[1] The Reagan campaign repeatedly invoked this image of a weakening America in a fundamentally hostile world.

The themes of decline and restoration have been constants of Reagan administration foreign policy. In April of 1981, the then Secretary of State Alexander Haig declared,[2]

> If present trends are not arrested, the convergence of rising international disorder, greater Western vulnerability, and growing Soviet military power will undo the international codes of conduct that foster the resolution of disputes between nations.

In March 1986, President Reagan returned to these themes[3]:

> The failure to maintain our military capabilities and our economic strength in the 1970's was as important as any other single factor in encouraging Soviet expansionism. By reviving both of them in the 1980's we deny our adversaries opportunities and deter aggression. We make it easier for other countries to launch sustained economic growth, to build popular institutions, and to contribute on their own to the cause

of peace. . . . [The American people] want an effective foreign policy, which shapes events in accordance with our ideals and does not just react, passively and timidly, to the actions of others.

The administration's response to what it saw as a catastrophic erosion of American military and economic strength rested on the premise that the causes of erosion were rooted in the policies of previous administrations, not in long-term cycles of hegemonic decline. Insufficient military spending and mistaken economic ideology were the primary causes of the recession of American power. The administration's two core programs — accelerated defense spending and Reaganomics — would restore American military and economic strength simultaneously. Over the long term, these programs were expected to reverse tendencies toward international power diffusion and thereby obviate the need for adjustment and retrenchment. Over the short term, the Reagan administration explicitly repudiated the adjustments of the 1970s. The administration saw those adjustments as causes, not consequences, of the deterioration of the international position of the United States. Reagan's initial security and economic policy departed sharply from directions established in the 1970s.

The Reagan administration reversed almost every element of the 1970s security policy. The administration repudiated the very concept of conflict in "peripheral" Third World nations, rejected "social engineering" on behalf of human rights, and offered unconditional support to anti-Communist governments and unconditional opposition to radical governments. Although not objecting to a policy of shifting some of the burdens of containment to China and Europe, the administration believed that the United States had gone too far in bending American policy to fit the preferences of its allies. Initial policy on China and Europe sought to reconstruct these strategic relationships around the Reagan administration's conception of strategic interests. Finally, the administration rejected the 1970s conception of limited Soviet-American mutual interests and intensified pressure on Soviet clients, pursued counterforce escalation dominance in strategic nuclear weapons, and waged economic warfare against the Soviets. At a minimum, a more assertive United States, bargaining from a position of military strength, would wring additional concessions from the Soviet Union in such areas as strategic arms control. At a maximum, American political, economic, and military pressure would force the Soviets to choose between external retrenchment and internal collapse.

In international economic affairs, the administration initially relied, both conceptually and practically, on domestic Reaganomics. The policies of the 1970s — increasing multilateral political management of the international economy and increasing domestic buffering of the exogenous economic shocks — were seen as limiting the responsiveness of consumers, labor, and business to market incentives. The administration would trim away layers of international and domestic management. This strategy was predicated on the assumption that domestic Reaganomics would increase savings and investment, boost American productivity, and stimulate noninflationary growth. Greater American competitiveness would negate the need for governmental defense of American commercial interests, and noninflationary growth would eliminate many of the international financial and monetary problems that seemed to require multilateral management during the stagflationary 1970s. This laissez-faire economic strategy departed sharply from the managerial policies of the Nixon, Ford, and Carter administrations.

How have these programs and policies fared? The two core programs were modified on a piecemeal basis. By the start of the second term, real defense spending was frozen and the supply-side version of Reaganomics had given way to a bipartisan movement toward fiscal orthodoxy. Many elements of the administration's foreign economic and security policies, moreover, had returned to lines established in the 1970s. The administration initially embraced anticommunist authoritarian governments. Over five years, the administration returned to a policy of containment through reform. Early experiments with alliance management by unilateral assertion failed, and policies on Theater Nuclear Force negotiations, Western European participation in East-West trade, and the Taiwan question returned to those of earlier administrations. Initial Middle East and African policies were premised on the assumption that intense intra-regional and domestic conflicts could be subordinated to the extraregional Soviet threat. The administration adjusted its initial globalist policies to mesh with local circumstances. The administration's initial laissez-faire international economic policies were displaced by Group of Five efforts to manage exchange rates, German-American-Japanese efforts to coordinate interest rates, and multilateral efforts to manage the international debt crisis.

Yet the administration continued to move *away* from policies of the 1970s in two areas. First, previous administrations had learned to live, however uncomfortably, with radical nationalist governments in Third World nations. The Reagan administration targeted Soviet-backed radical regimes in small countries, codified the policy as the Reagan Doctrine, and moved this issue to center stage. Second, with reference to strategic nuclear issues, the administration turned up the heat but turned down the spotlights. The administration continued to seek counterforce escalation dominance, inaugurated the Strategic Defense Initiative (Star Wars), rejected Soviet proposals for bans on anti-satellite weapons and all nuclear testing, and announced its intention of repudiating SALT II and reinterpreting the ABM treaty. The administration, however, scrapped ballistic missile submarines to stay within SALT II limits, stopped talking about nuclear warfighting, and started proposing deep cuts in and the eventual abolition of all nuclear weapons. In brief, the administration downplayed nuclear issues by softening its initially confrontational rhetoric, emphasizing elements of continuity with previous administrations, and focusing attention on the distant future.

Why has the Reagan administration's foreign policy evolved in these directions? Explanations of the evolution of American foreign policy abound. Political scientists offer a thicket of theories, ranging from the characteristics of the international system and of domestic politics and economies through bureaucratic, organizational, group, and individual cognitive processes to the toilet training of presidents.[4] Political columnists relate twists and turns of policy to the fall of Haig, Allen, Kirkpatrick, and MacFarlane, the fluctuating fortunes of Weinberger and Buchanan, the Baker-Shultz job swap, and the diurnal rhythms of the president. To account for the precise timing and details of shifts in policy, virtually all these theories and *ad hoc* explanations might well prove necessary. To account for the direction and extent of fundamental changes in Reagan foreign policy, however, a simpler explanation may suffice.

The two introductory essays, taken together, offer a relatively parsimonious explanation of the persistence of rhetoric, the general tendency toward reversion to the economic and security policies of the 1970s, and the accentuation of exceptions to reversion. If the administrations of the 1970s were a shade too pessimistic in their assessment of limits, the Reagan administration overestimated how much room America had to maneuver. Time after time, emerging limits compelled piecemeal adjustments. This essay emphasizes the limits set by domestic resource constraints, the international distribution of power, and international configurations of interest. In the second introductory essay, William Schneider emphasizes the limits imposed by mass and elite opinion.

Behind every colorful debate over the desirability and feasibility of contemporary American foreign policy sits a corresponding dry academic discussion of the causes and consequences of change in international systems structure. The successes and failures of the Reagan administration's foreign policy experiment and the extent to which the administration persisted with its initial defense and economic programs and its initial security and economic policies hinge on the answers to two key questions.

First, what were the causes of the erosion of American economic and military power? The Reagan administration assumed that the choices of previous administrations accounted for the recession of American power and that, therefore, Reagan's military and domestic economic programs could restore the United States to a position of preeminence in international relations. Scholarly theories of hegemonic decline provide a historical and theoretical framework for explaining tendencies toward the international diffusion of power and for evaluating the Reagan programs. The next section of this essay examines the causes of American decline and the tensions between the Reagan administration's defense and economic programs.

Second, what are the consequences of the international diffusion of power? The Reagan administration believed that the gradual diminution of American preeminence was potentially catastrophic, and that view lent an understandable urgency to their military and economic programs and colored their core international security and economic strategies. An often-neglected aspect of the international environment — configurations of international interests — provides a key to assessing the consequences of power diffusion and to evaluating administration security and economic policies. When American interests conflict with those of other states, declining American power will have adverse effects on the United States. The Reagan administration's foreign policy was, of course, sensitive to this possibility. When American interests partially complement those of other states, receding American power will give rise to dilemmas of collective action. The mere existence of a mutual interest does not guarantee the realization of a common goal. Policies attuned to the multilateral pursuit of mutual interests offer hope of blunting the effects of changes in the international distribution of power. The initial Reagan administration policies toward the nations of Western Europe, and on international economic matters, were, it can be argued, insufficiently sensitive to these concerns. Finally, configurations of interest are not static. American policy can have profound effects on how other nations define their interests. The initial Reagan administration policies toward the Soviet Union and, particularly, toward revolutionary nationalist states in the Third World may have heightened conflicts and operated to the detriment of the United States. The penultimate section of this essay (p. 20) examines the configurations of international interests that have been affected by the gradual recession of American power and evaluates the Reagan administration's core security and international economic strategies in light of the structure of interests.

Hegemonic Decline and Strategies of Restoration

In the four decades since the end of World War II, American military and economic preeminence faded. Western Europe, Japan, and the upper tier of the developing world grew more rapidly than the United States, and the American comparative weight in the international economic system declined. The Soviet Union attained virtual military parity with the

United States, and the United States' relative weight in the international security system declined. The erosion of American dominance reflects the dispersion of power, as other nations' capabilities have increased relative to those of the United States. The United States is no longer the only military *or* economic superpower, but it remains the only military *and* economic superpower. And by historical standards, economic and military power remains unusually concentrated in the United States.[5] *Power*, defined in terms of the ability to influence or control events, cannot be directly measured. Imperfect surrogates can provide a crude sense of the changing American position in the international system. Before turning to the problem of explaining power redistribution, it is useful to assess the magnitude and timing of shifts.

Gross Domestic Product provides a basic measure of the resources a nation can choose to apply to military programs, consumption, and capital investment. Table 1–1 presents estimates of percentage shares of gross world product for 1950, 1960, 1970, and 1980. Discrepancies between the two overlapping series reflect the intrinsic imprecision of the exercise, and give warning of the many opportunities for chicanery in comparing disparate national incomes. Nevertheless, the trends are clear. The American share of world product declined sharply during the 1950s, and more slowly during the 1960s and 1970s. How do the shares of the two competing security blocs compare? The product of the Western advanced industrial states (60 percent) dwarfs that of the Soviet bloc (18 percent), and the ratio of Western to Eastern production has remained fairly constant for thirty years. The declining weight of the United States in international economic affairs is revealed clearly by comparing the American share (21 percent) with Japan (9 percent), the European Community (22 percent), and the developing world (15 percent). It is important to keep in mind both trends and final positions. After decades of relatively rapid growth, the nations of the Third World plus China account for less than 20 percent of world product, while the developed Western nations account for over 60 percent of world product.

Military spending and military personnel provide a crude measure of military capabilities. Barry Posen and Stephen Van Evera offer an extended assessment of the *adequacy* of American and allied military forces for varied contingencies in their chapter on defense policy. As they note, Western military capabilities have not declined relative to the capabilities of the Soviet bloc. However, the simple figures in Table 1–2 confirm perceptions of decline in the American share of world military spending between 1960 and 1980. Increases in Soviet military spending, the rapid expansion of military spending and military forces in the Third World, and increases in Western European spending are also reflected in the table. The sharp decline in the American share of world spending and military personnel between 1970 and 1980 reflects both the reallocation of

TABLE 1–1. Shares of Gross World Product (Percentages)

	Council on International Economic Policy Series			Central Intelligence Agency Series		
	1950	*1960*	*1970*	*1960*	*1970*	*1980*
Developed Countries	67.4%	65.2	64.5	66.5	65.7	62.7
United States	39.3	33.9	30.2	25.9	23.0	21.5
European Community	16.1	17.5	18.4	26.0	24.7	22.5
Japan	1.5	2.9	6.2	4.5	7.7	9.0
Other	10.5	10.9	9.7	10.1	10.3	9.7
Less Developed Countries	9.1	9.5	10.0	11.1	12.3	14.8
Communist Countries	23.5	25.3	25.5	22.4	22.0	22.0
Soviet Union	13.5	15.5	16.5	12.5	12.4	11.4
China	4.0	4.5	4.0	3.1	3.4	4.5
Other	6.0	5.3	5.0	6.8	6.2	6.1
Gross World Product in Trillions of 1980 Dollars	2.4	3.9	6.3	5.0	8.4	12.2

SOURCES: U.S. Council on International Economic Policy, *The United States in the Changing World Economy* (Washington, D.C.: GPO, 1971) Volume II, Chart 1. U.S. Central Intelligence Agency, National Foreign Assessment Center, *Handbook of Economic Statistics 1981* (Washington, D.C.: GPO, 1981), percentages calculated from Table 9. Gross World Product for CIEP Series derived by dividing U.S. GNP in 1980 dollars (*Economic Report of the President 1982*, Tables B-1 and B-3) by the CIEP estimate of the U.S. share of Gross World Product. European Community adjusted to include the United Kingdom for all years in both series. Some of the major disparities between the CIEP and CIA figures for the overlapping years of 1960 and 1970 appear to rest on the following factors: (1) European Community and Japan — Exchange rates used to value national product in dollars; (2) Less Developed Countries and China — Quantity and value of subsistence sector plus exchange rates; and (3) Communist Countries — Quantity and value of production in command economy plus exchange rates.

American resources during the 1970s and the unusually high military effort in 1970 related to the Vietnam War.

Explaining Decline

What factors account for this clear relative American decline? The pattern of economic and military changes summarized in Tables 1–1 and 1–2 are partially the product of national choices that were, in turn, conditioned by the international distribution of power. Finite economic resources create a trade-off across military spending, investment, and consumption. The priority that nations assign to guns, growth, and butter is the best single predictor of changes in economic and military strength. Table 1–3 summarizes the choices and growth rates of the United States, the United Kingdom, West Germany, Japan, and the

TABLE 1–2. United States Share of World Military Spending and Personnel

	1960	1970	1980
United States Military Spending as a Share of World Spending	51%	42%	28%
World Military Spending in billions of 1978 dollars	341	469	570
United States Armed Forces Personnel as a Share of World Personnel	13%	14%	8.3%
World Armed Forces Personnel in thousands	18,550	21,484	24,435

SOURCES: Computed from *Department of Defense Annual Report for Fiscal Year 1983*, pp. I-5 and C-3; Ruth Sivard, *World Military and Social Expenditures*, p. 24; and *Economic Report of the President*, Table B-3.

Soviet Union in the period 1960 through 1979. The Soviet Union repressed consumption to finance very high investment and very high levels of military spending and thereby attained military parity with the United States while sustaining a moderately high, but declining, growth rate. Japan opted for very high levels of investment and moderate levels of consumption, while spending little on defense, and it achieved an astonishing average growth rate of 8.5 percent per year. Germany balanced moderate investment, military spending, and consumption, and grew at 4.7 percent in the 1960s and 2.9 percent in the 1970s. Britain's high consumption, high military spending, and low investment strategy yielded an average 2.5 percent growth rate. The United States' high

TABLE 1–3. Allocation of Gross Domestic Product — Average Percentages 1960–1979

	Annual Growth Rate	Fixed Capital Formation	Military Spending	Consumption		
				Gov't +	Private =	Total
United States	3.6%	17.6	7.4	10.9	63.0	73.9
United Kingdom	2.5	18.4	5.4	13.0	62.8	75.8
West Germany	3.9	24.1	3.9	13.2	55.6	68.8
Japan	8.5	32.7	.9	7.7	55.4	63.1
Soviet Union*	4.1	28.7	14.0	—	—	54.1

SOURCES: For Western nations, see Robert DeGrasse, *The Costs and Consequences of Reagan's Military Buildup* (New York: Council on Economic Priorities, 1982). For the Soviet Union, see CIA, *Handbook of Economic Statistics 1981*, Table 37 on Fixed Capital Formation and Consumption, and Department of Defense, *Annual Report to Congress Fiscal Year 1983* for estimated military spending.
*The Soviet figures do not add to 100 because different sources were used for estimates of investment and consumption and of military spending. The CIA estimate for "R&D, inventory change, net exports, outlays and defense" over this period comes to 17.25 percent of Soviet product.

consumption, low investment, and moderately high military spending strategy yielded a growth rate of 3.6 percent. In summary, the United States could not match German and Japanese economic investments and Soviet military investments simultaneously.

The figures summarizing national allocation of resources to investment, defense, and consumption are clear and consequential, but they raise a difficult basic question. How can we explain these national choices? Robert Gilpin has developed a set of propositions to account for regularities in cycles of hegemonic rise and decline.[6] He found that external burdens of leadership, internal secular tendencies toward rising consumption, and the international diffusion of technology appear to explain gradual hegemonic recession. How well do these factors account for the American decline? Which factors bear on Soviet prospects?

Dominance often undercuts the economic bases of dominance. The United States' strategy of containment centers on the protection of Western Europe and Japan. Table 1–3 clearly indicates that the United States bears a disproportionate share of the burdens of defense. In "An Economic Theory of Alliances," Olson and Zeckhauser note that because the dominant state in an alliance has an absolute interest in offering protection, smaller allies have little incentive to contribute proportionately to their own defense.[7] Because the loss of the technologically advanced Western nations would have catastrophic effects on American interests, the United States cannot credibly threaten to retract American protection and cannot coerce increases in allied defense spending. Lesser threats and jawboning by the Nixon, Ford, and Carter administrations did succeed in raising the European share of the North Atlantic Treaty Organization (NATO) burden, but the persistent tendency of the United States to spend more on defense remains. American, Western European, and Japanese "choices" of guns, growth, and butter are conditioned by this basic aspect of alliance relations. And even with overt and covert coercion, the Soviet Union bears an even more highly disproportionate share of military spending within the Warsaw Pact.

A second burden of leadership is at least partially self-imposed. During the 1950s and 1960s, the United States guaranteed the security of anticommunist governments in peripheral regions against internal and external threats. Global containment rested on American willingness to intervene to forestall revolution under disadvantageous circumstances. The diversion of resources into military consumption undercuts both military and economic investments. It is interesting to note that the Reagan administration eliminates "South East Asian" spending from the American side of the ledger in most comparisons of Soviet and American military expenditures. Before its invasion of Afghanistan, the Soviet Union avoided direct military interventions outside Eastern Europe. The recurrent costs of controlling Eastern Europe, through invasion and occupation, and the uncertain costs of the ongoing Afghan invasion, however, must both be reckoned as costs of dominance.

The costs of bidding for allegiances and bolstering the strength of allies are a third burden of leadership. The American postwar promotion of European and Japanese recovery through direct financial assistance and tolerance of trade asymmeteries and security-supporting assistance to many Third World states are not reflected in any of the figures in Table 1–3, but they clearly entail economic costs. The Soviet Union's strategy of alternating exploitation and subsidization of Eastern Europe and of providing more modest support for Third World clients lessens its cost of dominance. The continuing instability of Eastern Europe, however, follows, at least in part, from Soviet efforts to concentrate resources on Soviet economic and military growth.

The second major factor, a secular tendency toward increasing consumption, is directly reflected in Table 1–3. A former hegemonic power, Great Britain, and a current hegemonic power, the United States, top the list in terms of proportion of national product devoted to consumption. Is the Soviet Union immune from this tendency toward rising consumption? Grumblings over the quality of life in the Soviet Union and Eastern Europe are endemic, and the recent rise of Solidarity in Poland was the result of both economic and political discontent. Even if a totalitarian state can sustain extremely high levels of investment and military spending by suppressing consumption, the ends of economic growth and perhaps even greater military capabilities may be undercut by economic discontent and inefficiency. In the period 1960–79, the Soviet Union devoted almost as great a share of its national product to investment as did Japan, but it grew at less than half the rate. In the late 1970s and early 1980s, Soviet growth was stagnant or negative.

The third major factor contributing to hegemonic decline — a tendency toward the international diffusion of technology — operates by eroding margins of technological superiority on which economic and military advantage may be based. Knowledge is intrinsically difficult to control, and the argument that technological superiority inevitably fades is substantiated by the narrowing or even nonexistent margin of the American edge over Japan. If differences in rates of growth in Table 1–3 are explained by levels of investment and technological borrowing, then more equal growth is likely to follow from technological equality.

Economic and Military Restoration

The programs and policies of the Reagan administration did not address the first cause of hegemonic decline. Burdens of leadership grew heavier under the Reagan administration. The administration's security strategy expanded American commitments, but the temporary acceleration of defense spending did not elicit matching increases from America's allies. The administration tried to address the third factor, technological diffusion, by requiring export licenses for scientific conference papers and tightening defenses against espionage. But the tension between restricting technological diffusion and eliminating freedoms of communication that may be necessary for technological advance forced a partial reversal of the policy. In any event, the narrow gap between the United States and Japan may have mooted the significance of this factor. The Reagan administration's program of military and economic restoration rests, ultimately, on managing the trade-off across defense, consumption, and investment.

The Reagan administration initially denied the need to choose among guns, butter, and growth. The administration expected its package of tax cuts and regulatory reform to evoke a vigorous supply-side response, even as it raised real defense spending by 7.4 percent per year. A rapid expansion of American economic capacity would mitigate the economic trade-offs that had bedeviled administrations in the 1970s. Reaganomics with the Laffer curve promised tax reductions without revenue reductions, rapid growth without inflation, and higher investment and defense spending without lower spending on consumption. By the autumn of 1982, a deepening recession had demolished expectations of a quick and painless expansion of economic capacity.

Reaganomics without the Laffer curve combined fiscal stimulation with monetary restraint. The indicators in Table 1–4 trace fiscal, monetary, and credit policies during the Reagan years. On the one hand, growing expenditures and declining revenues produced very large Federal budget deficits and stimulated aggregate demand. Deficits rose from an average of 1.6 percent of gross national product (GNP) during the 1970s to an average of 4.3 percent of GNP under the Reagan administration. On the other hand, Federal Reserve Chairman Paul Volcker restrained money and credit to wring inflation out of the economy. From 1975 through 1977, money stock (M2) had increased at around 12 percent per

TABLE 1–4. Macroeconomic Policy Instruments

	71–80	81–85	1980	1981	1982	1983	1984	1985
Monetary Growth (M2)	10.1	9.5	8.9	10.0	8.9	12.0	8.4	8.1
Real Interest Rates								
NY Discount − CPI	−.8	4.4	−1.7	3.0	4.9	5.3	4.5	4.1
Prime−CPI	1.0	7.8	1.8	8.5	8.8	7.6	7.7	6.3
Federal Deficit/GNP	1.8	4.3	2.2	2.1	4.6	5.3	4.6	4.9

SOURCES: U.S. President, *Economic Report of the President* (Washington, D.C.: GPO, 1986). Calculated from B-64, B-68, B-58, B-27, and B-1.

year. In 1978, Volcker slashed monetary expansion to around 9 percent per year, and he continued these policies in the Reagan years. This unorthodox combination of monetary restraint and Keynesian fiscal stimulation temporarily forced nominal interest rates well above the inflation rate. The real discount rate rose from –1.7 percent in 1980 to 5.3 percent by 1983, while the real prime rate rose from 1.8 percent in 1980 to over 8 percent in 1981 and 1982, and then dropped slowly to 6.3 percent by 1985.[8]

How did macroeconomic performance in the 1980s compare with the 1970s? The first two columns in Table 1–5 compare average performance during the stagflationary 1970s with 1981–85, and the five annual columns permit identification of trends. The conjunction of tight money and collapsing world oil prices forced inflation down from an average 7.9 percent in the 1970s to an average 5.5 percent in 1981–85 and appears to have stabilized at under 4 percent. Unemployment, however, rose from an average 6.4 percent in the 1970s to an average of 8.3 percent in 1981–85, and temporarily stabilized at about 7 percent. Growth in the 1970s averaged 2.8 percent. Under Reagan, growth fluctuated from –2.5 percent in the trough of the recession up to 6.5 percent in the midst of recovery, and down to 2.3 percent in 1985. Conclusions in mid-business cycle are, of necessity, somewhat tentative. The significant accomplishment of licking inflation is balanced against stubbornly high unemployment and surprisingly unstable growth. From 1981 to 1985, the administration's mixture of monetary and fiscal policies yielded mixed short-term macroeconomic results.

To its credit, the Reagan administration sought to develop economic policies that looked beyond short-term macroeconomic goals. As budget deficits rose, the Laffer version of supply-side economics became synonymous with wishful thinking. But the traditional notion of designing economic policies to encourage savings and investment in order to expand capacity and increase productivity became the new conventional wisdom. How has Reaganomics fared in terms of these important long-term goals?

In theory, Reaganomics would reduce consumption to finance investment and military spending. In practice, Reaganomics financed con-

TABLE 1–5. Macroeconomic Performance Measures

	71–80	81–85	1980	1981	1982	1983	1984	1985
Inflation (CPI)	7.9	5.5	13.5	10.4	6.1	3.2	4.3	3.6
Real Growth GNP	2.8	2.3	– .2	1.9	–2.5	3.5	6.5	2.3
Unemployment	6.4	8.3	7.1	7.6	9.7	9.6	7.5	7.2

SOURCES: U.S. President, *Economic Report of the President* (Washington, D.C.: GPO, 1986). Calculated from B-58, B-2, and B-38.

sumption and military spending by borrowing from abroad and by reducing investment. In theory, domestic spending cuts and tax cuts would redistribute income away from the poor, with their tendency to spend on food and shelter, toward the wealthy, with their higher savings rates. In practice, the wealthy borrowed money to purchase imported VCRs and automobiles. In theory, higher real interest rates and added tax incentives — the Individual Retirement Account and liberalized business depreciation allowances — would raise individual and business savings rates. In practice, business savings rates rose while household savings rates declined.

The sources of capital presented in Table 1–6 tell one part of the long-term story. In the first five years of the Reagan presidency, domestic savings — private and public — available for investment actually fell from the dismal 1970s average of 16.8 percent of GNP to 14.9 percent of GNP in 1981–85, and the year-by-year trend is down. Private savings of individuals and businesses averaged 17.8 percent of GNP in both the 1970s and in 1981–85, as declining individual savings were offset by rising business savings. Not all these funds are available for domestic investment. The federal budgetary deficit absorbed 10 percent of private savings in the 1970s and 25 percent of private savings in the 1980s. These federal deficits were only partially offset by increasing state and local surpluses. Net capital inflows from abroad supplemented domestic resources. As American real interest rates rose, Japanese and European capital flowed into the United States. As debtor developing nations encountered difficulty servicing their loans, international banks reduced their exposure in the Third World. Finally, American multinational corporations invested less abroad and repatriated more earnings home. As

TABLE 1–6. Sources and Uses of Capital as Percentage of GNP

	71–80	81–85	1980	1981	1982	1983	1984	1985
Domestic Savings	16.8	14.9	16.3	17.1	14.1	13.8	15.5	14.1
Private	17.8	17.8	17.5	18.0	17.6	17.7	18.4	17.5
Federal (deficit)	−1.8	−4.3	−2.2	−2.1	−4.6	−5.3	−4.6	−4.9
State and Local	.9	1.4	1.0	1.1	1.1	1.4	1.7	1.5
Net Foreign Investment	−.2	1.2	−.5	−.3	0.0	1.0	2.4	2.8
Total Domestic Investment	16.5	16.1	16.0	16.9	14.1	14.8	17.9	16.8

SOURCES: U.S. President, *Economic Report of the President* (Washington, D.C.: GPO, 1986). Calculated from B-27 and B-1. Gross Domestic Savings = Private Savings + Federal Savings + State and Local Surplus. Net Foreign Investment includes net exports of goods and services less net transfers to foreigners and interest paid by government to foreigners plus capital grants received by the United States, net. Gross Domestic Investment = Gross Domestic Savings + Net Foreign Investment. Not all columns sum to totals because of rounding errors.

a consequence, net flows of capital into the United States reversed from −.2 percent of GNP in the 1970s to +2.8 percent in 1985. Over the short term, the United States absorbed the savings of other nations to help finance domestic private investment and domestic public deficits.

The effects of Reaganomics and the Reagan defense program on the allocation of national product to investment, consumption, and defense are summarized in Table 1–7. As the totals at the bottom of the table suggest, trade-offs across these categories were temporarily mitigated by increasing imports and by increasing net borrowing from abroad. In the 1980s, investment, consumption, and defense spending added up to 98.8 percent of GNP. By 1985, spending totaled 101.9 percent of GNP. Even with foreign borrowing, the administration could not increase military spending while reversing tendencies toward declining investment and increasing consumption. Compare the averages for 1971–80 with 1981–85: Defense spending rose from 5.5 to 6.2 percent of GNP; but consumption rose from 77.1 to 78.1 percent of GNP, while investment declined from 16.6 to 16.1 percent of GNP.

The emerging trade-off across guns, butter, and growth indirectly shaped Reagan defense and economic programs. Consider the debate over defense, deficits, and the dollar. Although tax cuts, defense spending, entitlement programs, and other federal spending all contributed to deficits, in practical terms, it is fair to speak of programmed defense deficits. Under the first Five Year Defense Plan (1983–87), the military share of all federal spending was to increase from roughly 25 to 40 percent, and the military share of the "disposable" federal budget — outlays excluding trust funds and interest on national debt — was to increase from 50 to 75 percent. Budget projections were predicated on the assumption that real GNP would grow by 19.1 percent between 1981 and 1985, but real GNP expanded by a total of only 10.9 percent in those years.

TABLE 1–7. National Expenditures as Percentage Shares of GNP

	71–80	*81–85*	*1980*	*1981*	*1982*	*1983*	*1984*	*1985*
Investment	16.5	16.1	16.0	16.9	14.1	14.8	17.9	16.8
Consumption	77.1	78.1	77.6	76.5	79.0	79.1	77.4	78.5
Personal	62.7	64.4	63.4	62.7	64.8	65.5	64.2	64.7
Federal Nondefense	2.3	2.3	2.4	2.5	2.5	2.0	2.0	2.3
State and Local	12.0	11.4	11.8	11.3	11.7	11.5	11.2	11.5
Defense	5.5	6.2	5.2	5.5	6.1	6.3	6.3	6.6
Total Spending	99.2	100.3	98.8	98.9	99.2	100.2	101.6	101.9

SOURCES: U.S. President, *Economic Report of the President* (Washington, D.C.: GPO, 1986). Calculated from B-1. Total = Investment + Consumption + Defense = 100 − Net Exports. Note that transfer payments from governments to individuals are treated as *government spending* in budget statistics and as *individual consumption* in national income accounts.

Between 1980 and 1985, total revenues dropped from 19.4 to 18.6 percent of the GNP, while total federal spending rose from 22.2 to 24 percent of the GNP.[9] Revenue shortfalls and the resulting budgetary deficits forced choices on the administration. Between 1980 and 1985, spending to service the national debt rose sharply from 8.9 to 14.6 percent of all federal outlays, and conflict over all remaining categories of spending intensified. To sustain the original defense program, the Reagan administration had to raise taxes *or* cut such entitlements as Social Security and Medicare *or* decimate other non-defense spending. The administration was unwilling to raise taxes substantially and was unable to cut entitlements. Sharp reductions in other non-defense spending could not offset programmed increases in defense spending, and Congress forced defense spending off the five-year programmed trajectory. What Samuel Huntington has described as the defense budget cycle — an American tendency toward oscillation in levels of defense spending — was accentuated by the undue optimism of the administration's economic projections.[10]

By developing defense and economic programs based on the assumption that no trade-off exists, the administration inadvertently worsened the terms of the trade-off. In defending the defense program against probes from Congress, Secretary of Defense Caspar Weinberger noted that achieving defense savings in midstream has disproportionate effects on capabilities[11]:

> Because of Defense spendout patterns, outlay reductions require program reductions about four times as large. This causes serious program disruptions and impacts heavily on faster spending readiness functions.

On the one hand, stretching procurement of a weapon over time or reducing the total number of weapons procured inflates unit costs. On the other hand, trimming bread-and-butter operations and maintenance reduces readiness. In either case, reductions from planned rates of spending produce disproportionate costs. Indeed, by locking a higher proportion of defense spending into multiple year procurement, the administration may well have amplified the effects of budgetary changes on military capabilities. These actions did not deter Congress. Although real defense spending under Reagan increased substantially, defense outlays over the period 1981–85 ended up closer to Carter administration than Reagan administration projections. By projecting massive increases in defense spending and then retrenching to a lower rate of growth, the Reagan administration produced less effective defense than could have been obtained by carrying out a more modest, but sustained, defense program.

These short-term consequences of the Reagan defense and economic programs are of secondary importance. The administration's goals are long term, and the administration's programs must be evaluated with respect to the long-term compatibility of the military and economic programs. Bruce Carter Jackson of Brown Brothers, Harriman & Company found that high levels of defense spending correlated with low economic growth in seven advanced industrial democracies. He argues that military spending diverts resources and distorts their allocation, thereby hindering growth and contributing to inflation. A recent study by the Council on Economic Priorities found that among advanced industrial states in the 1970s, economic growth, growth in productivity, and gross domestic fixed capital formation were strongly and negatively associated with military spending. The American position in international trade may be expected to erode as resources are shifted from commercial to military applications. Even before the Reagan defense buildup, the United States devoted a far higher share of national resources to defense than did other advanced industrial societies. In the period 1960–76, the United States devoted well over half of each research and development dollar to defense. Over the same period, 90 percent of German, and 95 percent of Japanese, research and development was devoted to non-defense purposes. Any economy has finite resources, and spending on defense must come at the expense of consumption or investment. In practice, high rates of growth and capital formation are difficult to sustain in the face of high levels of military spending.[12]

Military spending, however, can have significant "spillover effects" for civilian sectors. Research and development spending on some weapons also can have direct civilian applications. For example, the Boeing 707 is a commercial version of a military transport. Large-scale Department of Defense purchases can provide a guaranteed market for the products of diminishing cost industries in their infancies. For example, military markets for early microprocessors were essential to the creation of that sector. Indeed, the Department of Defense may be the most important source of the implicit "industrial policy" in the United States. Governments in other nations pursue international competitive advantages directly. The government of the United States invokes the symbol of national security to legitimate sectoral intervention. For example, the Japanese government and Japanese corporations have channeled substantial resources into the development of Very Large Scale Integrated Circuits and the Fifth Generation artificial intelligence program. The United States Department of Defense funds similar research on a similar scale as part of Star Wars. Paradoxically, the importance of spillover effects may be greatest for a market-oriented administration in an economically liberal country, unable or unwilling otherwise to pursue a sectoral industrial policy.

If spillover effects are strong, defense research and development could strengthen the United States in both its economic competition with

Japan and its military competition with the Soviet Union. To what extent do spillover effects modify the trade-off between economic and military restoration? In 1985, the President's Commission on International Competitiveness reported that the increasing specialization of military research had diminished its commercial value. In the words of the report, the Department of Defense has become a "net consumer" of civilian technology.[13] As economists Wassily Leontief and Faye Duchin[14] observe:

> While some analysts claim that the civilian economy benefits from "spin-offs" from military training and infrastructure in less developed countries and from research and development in developed countries which balance the negative effects of the military burden . . . few would deny the increased potential for the civilian economy from applying these resources directly to civilian objectives.

Ultimately the trade-off across military position, international economic position, and domestic economic welfare cannot be ignored or fudged. Neither a belief in the Laffer curve nor reliance on short-term capital inflows nor accentuation of positive spillover effects provides an escape from resource constraints. Even if the administration eventually succeeds in repressing consumption to finance investment and military spending, it does not address the other causes of the international diffusion of power. The international diffusion of technology appears irreversible, and economic burdens of leadership are increased by the administration's core security policies. American policy alone cannot arrest or reverse structural tendencies toward hegemonic decline. The goal of restoring American economic and military preeminence to what it was two decades ago is alluring and unattainable.

Configurations of Interest and Strategies of Adjustment

The international diffusion of power increases the analytic significance of a frequently neglected second aspect of the international environment. As direct control over the actions of other nations becomes difficult, the prosperity and security of the United States increasingly depends on how other nations define their interests and how the United States adjusts to its changing position in the international system. When the strong can impose their will on the weak, the interests of the weak are inconsequential. As power diffuses, conflict and communality of interests often determine outcomes.

The initial security policy of the Reagan administration was based on the assumption that the scope and intensity of international conflict precluded resort to strategies of adjustment. The administration hoped that an assertive, focused security policy would weaken the position of the Soviet Union in the Third World, strengthen the anti-Soviet coalition, and ultimately force the Soviet Union to choose between external retrenchment and internal collapse. By contrast, the initial international economic policies of the administration were strangely indifferent to lines of international and domestic economic conflict. The administration adopted a minimalist foreign economic policy, which reflected the administration's commitment to classical economic liberalism at home and abroad. Paradoxically, each core policy ultimately operated to the detriment of its primary objective. Over the long term, the initial security policy increased the dependency of radical nationalist regimes on the Soviet Union, weakened the Western alliance system, and strengthened confrontationalist elements within the Soviet Union, while the initial foreign economic policy destabilized the liberal international economic order that the administration had sought to strengthen. In both security and economic affairs, 1970s policies appeared to serve Reagan administration goals better than initial Reagan administration policies, and Reagan administration policies evolved in the direction of policies of the 1970s.

International Security Policy

The Reagan administration's commitment to a strategy of restoration rested, in part, on the view that a weakening America would find itself in an increasingly hostile world. Declining relative military strength could cause international realignment toward the Soviet Union. Rising relative Soviet military strength evoked the twin specters of a "Findlandized" Western Europe and of Sino-Soviet entente. The effects of even marginal changes in the bilateral Soviet-American military balance are magnified if nations "bandwagon," that is, move from the weaker toward the stronger. The administration assigned a high priority to accelerating defense spending because it feared that international tendencies toward bandwagoning necessitated greater American military effort. By contrast, the familiar logic of the balance of power suggests that tendencies toward the international concentration of power are offset by tendencies toward the formation of countervailing coalitions. International relations remains anarchic rather than imperial because states tend to balance against the greater threat. The rise of a strong aggressive nation creates an incentive for other nations to align against the potential imperial power. The last four centuries of Western history support the view that *balancing* dominates *bandwagoning*. Again and again, rising powers seeking wider empires have conjured up opposing coalitions. Louis XIV, Napoleon, Kaiser Wilhelm, and Hitler reached for hegemony and ultimately mobilized opposing coalitions that contained or destroyed them. The security policies of the 1970s sought to capitalize on this international tendency toward balancing to lessen the American burden of military leadership.[15]

The Reagan administration rejected the modes of adjustment to diffusing power as well as the need to make adjustments. Distasteful compromises and hard choices are inherent features of a strategy of adjustment. The Reagan administration differed from the administrations of the 1970s in viewing adjustments as potentially catastrophic, not as merely distasteful.

A degree of retrenchment is the first element of a strategy of adjustment. When the interests of the United States clash with the interests of other nations, declining American power will obviously affect American interests adversely. If power is insufficient to protect all threatened interests, damage may be limited by employing policies attuned to the distinction between vital and peripheral interests. During the 1970s, the United States altered first the means and then the ends of policy toward revolution in the periphery. Under President Nixon, the United States retained the goal of controlling revolutions, but shifted from direct military intervention to the less expensive instruments of the Nixon Doctrine: security-supporting assistance, arms sales, military training programs, and covert action. Carter's policy rested ultimately on the assumption that the United States could live with revolutionary nationalist governments in the Third World and hence need not support authoritarian anticommunist governments that did not embrace programs of reform. By linking military and economic assistance to human rights, the Carter administration sought to force political and economic reforms that it believed would eventually stem revolutionary discontent while legitimizing American military aid to governments under siege. When reforms did not materialize, denial of military and economic assistance placed some distance between the United States and *anciens regimes* and facilitated the development of relations with possible successors. In either event, American policy was consonant with both narrow national interests, as defined from a realist perspective, and liberal political values.[16]

The Reagan administration viewed revolutionary change as a direct threat to American security and economic interests and as a test of American resolve. In October of 1982, former Secretary of State Haig summarized the administration perspective[17]:

> We confronted a situation where strategic passivity during the Ford administration and the excessive piety of the Carter administration's human rights crusade had sapped the will of authoritarian anticommunist governments, eroded the confidence of Western allies, and encouraged risk taking by the Soviet Union and by Soviet manipulated totalitarian regimes. Since 1975, this bipartisan policy of failure had permitted the Soviet Union to inflict disastrous defeats on the United States at regular six month intervals.

"Defeats" in the Third World were disastrous, in and of themselves, and also undercut America's global position by eroding confidence in the

United States. In 1986, President Reagan noted: "For the United States, these conflicts cannot be regarded as peripheral to other issues on the global agenda. They raise fundamental issues and are a fundamental part of the overall U.S.–Soviet relationship." By intent and in effect, the Reagan administration's reassertive policy signaled a departure from the strategy of adjustment and policies of retrenchment. The means, as well as the goals, of Third World security policy shifted. The initial Reagan Third World security policy rejected "social engineering" on behalf of human rights and offered unconditional support to anticommunist governments and unconditional opposition to radical governments.

One strand of Reagan policy was premised on the assumption that unconditional military and economic assistance to embattled authoritarian regimes would stiffen the resolve of governing elites while bolstering counterinsurgency capabilities. Statutes linking aid to economic and political reform impeded full implementation of this strategy, but the administration increased aid to many authoritarian governments after certifying progress on human rights. Initially, the administration embraced the anticommunist authoritarian governments of the military in El Salvador, of Marcos in the Philippines, and of Duvalier in Haiti. This strand of policy did not persist. Over five years, the administration returned to "social engineering." It maneuvered on behalf of centrist candidate Jose Napoleon Duarte against rightist candidate Roberto D'Aubisson in the Salvadoran presidential elections, it pushed Ferdinand Marcos for a trial and for elections following the assassination of Benino Aquino, and it linked economic aid to human rights in Haiti. By 1986, the administration had set up a "Dictators' Express" air service to facilitate eleventh-hour exits by Marcos and Duvalier. In short, the Reagan policy toward these unpopular rightist authoritarian regimes shifted back toward the Carter administration's policy of "containment through reform." Why? Human rights issues reemerged in both the United States and the Third World. In the Salvadoran case, the United States Congress insisted on political reform as the price of aid. In the Philippines, the murder of opposition leader Benino Aquino catalyzed middle-class urban opposition to Ferdinand Marcos and strengthened the insurgents in the countryside. In Haiti, long-suppressed mass resentment of the Duvalier dynasty surfaced in public demonstrations, and these public demonstrations catalyzed further popular support. In these cases, support for regimes based on economic and political repression proved fragile. Greed undermined kleptocracy and brutality undermined autocracy. The Reagan administration policy shifted after it became clear that, even with American support, Marcos and Duvalier might not be able to continue in office. The instability of dictators was the proximate cause of instability in this area of Reagan foreign policy.

Reagan policy toward South Africa also changed, though in a less dramatic manner. The early policy of "constructive engagement" rested on the assumption that American support for the white government of South Africa would encourage fundamental political and economic reforms. But black demonstrations, strikes, and violent protests against apartheid and for full political equality intensified, while the white government repressed dissent within South Africa and launched commando operations against African National Congress offices in neighboring countries. As human rights in South Africa became a matter of increasing public and Congressional concern, the Reagan administration imposed modest economic sanctions against South Africa but vetoed more stringent UN sanctions. In effect, the continuing coercive power of the South African government permitted the Reagan administration to sustain a policy of symbolic opposition to apartheid.

A second strand of the Reagan Third World policy — the Reagan Doctrine — went beyond containment to "rollback." The administration not only opposed revolutions in the making, but also moved to overthrow existing radical nationalist governments. The Reagan Doctrine was premised on the assumption that military, economic, and political pressure against radical nationalist governments might yield three benefits. At a minimum, American pressure on Soviet clients would raise the cost to the Soviets of maintaining their empire. American pressure furthermore might induce leftist governments to moderate their international behavior and attenuate their ties to the Soviet bloc. At a maximum, covert and overt intervention might bring about the overthrow of these regimes. The Carter administration had tried, at times without success, to keep relations with radical nationalist governments simmering unobtrusively on a back burner. By organizing and funding the contra insurgency against Nicaragua, by invading Grenada, by bombing Tripoli and sending a naval task force into international waters claimed by Libya, and by seeking covert assistance for the National Union for the Total Independence of Angola (UNITA) insurgency, the Reagan administration turned up the heat and turned on a spotlight. Reagan policies toward communist and noncommunist regimes in the Third World continued on a course that diverged substantially from policies of the 1970s, and the administration emphasized these actions in speeches and news conferences.

Why did the administration persist in this line of foreign policy, even as most other aspects of Reagan foreign policy returned to the positions of the 1970s? Taken apart from the Reagan Doctrine, the Grenadan intervention and Libyan confrontations were almost ideal cases for the exercise of American power. In Grenada, the administration violated national sovereignty in a clear defense of popular sovereignty. Most Grenadans feared and hated the Coard government, and the American intervention commanded overwhelming popular support in Grenada. In

Libya, the administration acted in defense of navigation rights in international waters against a regime with strong links to terrorism. Qaddafi's expansive claim to the waters of the Gulf of Sidra was, in fact, illegitimate, and, according to the administration account, Qaddafi fired first. Furthermore, Americans suffered only moderate casualties in Grenada and Libya. Both regimes were militarily weak and politically isolated. In Grenada and Libya, the administration committed modest resources for small stakes.[18] Taken apart from the Reagan Doctrine, a policy of providing overt covert aid for the contras in Nicaragua and for UNITA guerrillas in Angola were less than ideal cases for the exercise of American power. In both cases, the prospects for victory by insurgents appeared minimal, even with American support. In both cases, the insurgents were tainted. The contras were led by former officers in Somoza's National Guard and committed more than their share of atrocities against civilians. UNITA was tainted only by "guilt through association." It depended heavily on South African economic and military assistance. In both cases, most neighboring states favored diplomatic over military options. And in both cases, popular and congressional support for covert assistance was muted. By grouping the disparate Grenadan, Libyan, Nicaraguan, and Angolan policies under the label *Reagan Doctrine*, the administration sought to build support for its Nicaraguan and Angolan policies. By moving these issues from a sideshow to the center ring, the Reagan administration accentuated and publicized the most concrete difference between its foreign policy and the foreign policy of its predecessors. Indeed, as other elements of Reagan foreign policy returned to lines established by earlier administrations, the administration focused attention on the Reagan Doctrine. If strategic passivity was the principal vice of the Nixon, Ford, and Carter administrations, then the Reagan Doctrine was a symbol of the Reagan commitment to strategic activism.

The administration hoped that these two sets of policies would enhance the credibility of American security guarantees around the world, increase the difficulty and costs to the Soviets of consolidating an empire, and check direct threats against perceived American interests in the Third World. Globalist policies tend to underestimate the significance of intraregional lines of conflict. The imperfect correspondence between the administration's global images and regional realities blunted the effectiveness of initial policies toward Latin America, Africa, and the Middle East. The evolution of American policy toward these regions is examined in essays by Robert Pastor ("The Reagan Administration and Latin America"), Barry Rubin ("The Reagan Administration and the Middle East"), and Donald Rothchild and John Ravenhill ("Subordinating African Issues to Global Logic: Reagan Confronts Political Complexity") in this volume. Although the most telling criticisms of the adminis-

124,661

LIBRARY
College of St. Francis
JOLIET, ILL.

tration's regional policies are regionally specific and idiosyncratic, the premises underlying Reagan policy toward revolutionary change merit further examination on a more general plane.

First, consider the issue of credibility. Does American policy on revolutionary change in the Third World affect confidence in American core security commitments to NATO and Japan? The European allies and Japan regarded the American intervention in Vietnam as a vastly disproportionate response to a noncritical concern, and most view United States policies toward Central America with reserve or distaste. From their perspective, the American fixation on Third World revolution diverts resources to a peripheral theater, without necessarily increasing the credibility of commitments to advanced industrial societies. This view is supported by a recent study of fifty-four cases of extended deterrence from 1900 to 1980. Huth and Russett found that successful deterrence was not associated with a defender's firmness in previous crises but rather was associated with the *importance* of the possible target state to the defender as well as with local military balances of forces. Credibility of deterrence was affected by the stakes and the means, not by performance in self-imposed "tests" of credibility.[19]

Second, does the Reagan Doctrine raise the Soviet's costs of maintaining an empire and impede consolidation of empire? Surpressing insurgencies is expensive and augmenting insurgencies is cheap. The Soviets invested far less in Vietnam than did the United States, and the modest covert investment in weapons and aid to the Afghan guerrillas requires a far larger Soviet counterinvestment. By offering unconditional support to rightist governments, the United States locked itself into a strategically unfavorable position. By opposing leftist governments in Angola and Nicaragua, the Reagan administration sought to create a parallel Soviet predicament. A policy of raising the costs, however, may abet consolidation of empire and jeopardize the security interests of the United States. When revolutionary regimes permit the Soviet Union to establish bases and to use their armies as proxy forces, their actions are clearly averse to the security interests of the United States. But the Soviet's penchant for using close military relationships to penetrate and overthrow clients threatens the political autonomy of revolutionary nationalist regimes, and a number of clients have distanced themselves from the Soviet Union precisely to preserve their autonomy. The nationalism of revolutionary nationalist states is a centrifugal force that obstructs Soviet consolidation of empire. By seeking to intimidate and overthrow such regimes — whether through rhetoric, covert assistance to proxy armies, or overt assistance to regional adversaries — the Reagan Doctrine weakens this centrifugal tendency. These regimes confront a trade-off between security and autonomy. By heightening their sense of insecurity, the confrontational policies of the Reagan administration increase their perceived need for Soviet military assistance and provide openings for the military instruments of Soviet political penetration. The administration's policy toward revolutionary states simplifies the Soviets' difficult task of manipulating Third World clients and abets Soviet consolidation of empire.

Third, how great a threat does revolution pose to the economic interests of the United States? Conflict between established governments and insurgents clearly disrupts economic relations and engenders international disputes over sanctuaries and arms flows. These consequences of revolution in the making should be distinguished from the aftereffects of revolutionary change. Do the economic interests and policies of radical nationalist governments differ from those of more traditional regimes? Both revolutionary and nonrevolutionary regimes have on occasion sought to alter the terms of their relationship to the Western international economic system through complete or partial expropriation of foreign investments, renegotiation or abrogation of contracts, and threats of default on international financial obligations. Although, on balance, revolutionary states appear more likely to disrupt international economic ties, regimes of all ideological stripes appear to have an increasingly strong interest in maintaining access to Western markets, technology, and capital. To secure access to markets, capital, and technology, radical nationalist Guinea works in partnership with the Fria Mining Company. To preserve access to capital, the Sandinista regime in Nicaragua did not repudiate foreign debts incurred by their predecessors. To earn much needed foreign exchange, the Marxist government of Angola uses Cuban troops to defend Gulf Oil operations from attack by nominally pro-American UNITA insurgents. Ironically, only American neo-conservatives *and* American instrumental Marxists argue that preservation of the western capitalist order requires control over the internal political character of Third World states.

During the 1970s, American policy toward the Soviet Union was premised on the existence of limited areas of mutual interest within the context of a larger competitive relationship. A confrontationalist strategy rests on a largely zero-sum view of the Soviet-American relationship. The basic test of the appropriateness of individual actions centers on the comparison of the magnitude of *relative* gains and losses, not on the *mutuality* of possible gains. When American benefits exceed Soviet benefits, and when American costs are less than Soviet costs, the United States can advance its position relative to the Soviet Union. From the perspective of ranking members of the administration, Soviet conduct is constrained almost solely by Soviet military and economic resources. The administration's strategic nuclear policy and initial East-West trade policy, as well as the previously discussed Reagan Doctrine and defense program, were part of a coherent strategy to control Soviet conduct by reducing Soviet capabilities. Although the Soviet Union could offset any one or two elements of the strategy, the Soviets lacked the resources to respond to pressure on all fronts.

Starting from this perspective, many members of the administration rejected the existence of "limited mutual interests" in a fundamentally conflictual relationship. In their view, strategic arms negotiations had strengthened the Soviet Union and weakened the United States. SALT I, the Vladivostok Agreement, and SALT II had reduced American will to modernize and expand strategic forces while permitting the Soviet Union to open a "window of vulnerability" against American land-based missiles. The administration's strategic programs and arms control policies were designed to place the United States in a position of nuclear superiority as defined from a counterforce escalation dominance perspective. This perspective defines nuclear superiority in terms of the ratio of Soviet to American counterforce capabilities remaining after exchanges of salvos of missiles targeted against strategic forces.[20] The administration argued that this form of superiority was necessary to deter a Soviet nuclear attack because Soviet civil defense and industrial dispersion programs had limited Soviet vulnerability to countervalue retaliation and because the Soviet leadership did not value the lives of ordinary citizens. The superiority in second-strike counterforce capabilities the administration publically sought would provide an even greater degree of first-strike superiority. As a member of the administration acknowledged privately, "A missile that can be fired second can be fired first. But that doesn't mean that we would." Other members of the administration argued that such an incidental first strike counterforce capability would permit the United States to use nuclear threats to deter conventional war with more assurance. The development of an effective defensive system, such as those envisioned in optimistic projections of the Strategic Defense Initiative (Star Wars) would further enhance the credibility of extended deterrence. If the United States could mop up Soviet retaliatory forces after a first strike, then the United States could deter conventional attacks on allies by credibly threatening a nuclear response to conventional attacks.

To attain a position of strategic advantage, the administration initially followed a two-pronged approach. Offensive weapons, such as the MX and Trident II, and defensive systems such as Star Wars contribute directly to superiority as defined from an escalation dominance perspective. The *threat* to acquire such weapons provides leverage to secure strategic arms control agreements favorable to the United States. If favorable arms control agreements could not be negotiated, the United States — with its superior economic and technological base — would prevail in the ensuing arms race.

This two-pronged strategy of bargaining from strength initially commanded broad support within the administration so long as no progress seemed possible in strategic arms control talks. The administration ruled out negotiations on a Comprehensive Test Ban Treaty, on military competition in outer space, and on strategic defense, on the grounds that such agreements would inhibit American weapons development programs. In 1983, Eugene Rostow, Director of the Arms Control and Disarmament Agency, explained that the United States would not negotiate over military uses of outer space because, "Any space weapon limitation which limits the threat to United States satellites will necessarily protect threatening Soviet satellites as well." In 1985, when negotiations with the Soviets resumed prior to the first Reagan-Gorbachev summit, the administration announced that Star Wars was "nonnegotiable." In 1985, the Soviets announced a moratorium on all nuclear tests and stated that they would not resume testing if the United States refrained from testing. The Reagan administration responded by noting that the United States would not be able to proceed with Star Wars without nuclear testing. By late 1985 and 1986, progress seemed possible on arms control. The Soviets responded to the sustained pressure of the administration's strategic nuclear programs with concessions. For example, Soviet acceptance, in principle, of on-site verification, their unilateral moratorium on testing in 1985, and their call for limiting testing and banning deployment of space-based missile defenses in exchange for deep reductions in offensive nuclear weapons in the summer of 1986 may have been elicited by the strategy of bargaining from strength.

Paradoxically, the very success of the strategy in eliciting concessions from the Soviets exposed the intrinsic tension between pursuing nuclear superiority and arms control. When forced to choose between these goals, administration policy seemed to change on a bureau-to-bureau and day-to-day basis. In the first six months of 1986, President Reagan denounced the Soviet test moratorium as a propaganda ploy and conducted two tests, rejected linkages between offensive systems and Star Wars, repudiated SALT II to punish the Soviets for violations of the agreement, and termed the Soviet proposal for linking Star Wars and deep cuts in offensive systems "constructive" and "serious." Assistant Secretary of Defense Richard Perle stated that the United States would adopt a "permissive interpretation" of the Antiballistic Missile Treaty in order to proceed with Star Wars; however, presidential advisor on arms control Paul Nitze declared, "I think there is no doubt but that that is the view of Weinberger and Mr. Perle, but it is certainly not my view, and I do not believe it to have been so decided by the President."[21] At the midpoint of the second term of the Reagan administration, the contradiction between arms racing and arms control, at the heart of the Reagan strategy, was not yet resolved. No meaningful limits on Soviet-American strategic competition had yet materialized, and competing demands for resources consumed by military spending appeared as intense in the United States as in the Soviet Union. Mutual exhaustion, not bargaining, seemed likely to constrain Soviet-American strategic competition.[22]

The administration's policy on strategic nuclear issues is based on several questionable assumptions. First, the administration assumes that Soviet civil defense and industrial dispersion programs have limited Soviet vulnerability to a second-strike countervalue attack. As Van Evera and Posen note in their chapter on defense policy in this volume, 3500 United States strategic warheads would survive a Soviet surprise attack, while only 141 large warheads could destroy over half of the Soviet Union's industrial capacity. Both the United States and the Soviet Union can destroy each other's civilizations many times over *after* absorbing an attack. Second, fears of the "window of vulnerability" and desires for counterforce systems are based on the assumption that the ratio of surviving strategic forces under escalation dominance scenarios is a suitable measure of nuclear superiority or inferiority. Several important recent studies suggest that this assumption is incorrect. Even an undamaged organization with sensors and rationality intact might have difficulty distinguishing between a counterforce and countervalue attack, mounting retaliatory strikes against an adversary's strategic forces, estimating the ratios of surviving forces, and negotiating an end to the war. Can badly damaged fragments of complex organizations perform these functions while under attack? Blair argues that incurable organizational and technical weaknesses in strategic command and control make controlled nuclear warfighting impossible.[23] By playing down the strategic significance of robust second-strike countervalue weapons and exaggerating the importance of counterforce weapons and doctrines, the administration contributed to an unrealistic image of American nuclear weakness. Whatever the demerits of escalation dominance as a basis for defining degrees of strategic superiority, both the Reagan administration and the Soviet leadership allocate resources and develop strategies *as if* such wars could be won or lost. The persistence of this common delusion jeopardizes the most important Soviet-American mutual interest — the avoidance of nuclear war.

The second strand of the Reagan administration's initial Soviet strategy centered on manipulation of international trade and finance to inflict costs on the Soviet Union, Eastern Europe, and Soviet clients in the Third World. The success of economic sanctions rests on the cooperation of third parties that can provide goods, technology, credits, and markets for target states. In the absence of multilateral coordination across possible suppliers, economic sanctions will not inflict substantial tangible costs on the target nation. Japan, the nations of Western Europe, and the United States had long cooperated with each other in maintaining a strategic embargo. The Coordinating Committee for Multilateral Security Export Controls (COCOM) system limited Eastern bloc access to goods and technologies of direct military value. The Secretary of Defense believed that a strategy of broad-gauged economic warfare could reduce the capacity of the Soviet economy. Any transaction that the Soviet Union seeks alleviates, to a degree, the Soviet Union's guns-butter-growth trade-off. To the greatest extent possible, the Weinberger group sought to reduce trade between the Soviet Union and the West to exacerbate the internal economic crisis within the Soviet Union. The allies did not share Weinberger's view of the desirability of economic warfare, and the European-American clash over European purchases of Soviet natural gas became a test of wills over the economic warfare strategy. After imposing secondary sanctions against European firms participating in the project, the administration reversed its course in the face of heated opposition from allied governments.

The dispute over East-West trade reflected a more general problem with the initial Reagan administration foreign policy. In a world of declining American power, greater reliance on multilateral strategies becomes a necessity. Yet the initial Reagan administration security policies were not accepted by any other major nation, and efforts to convince other nations of the merits of the initial Reagan approach proved largely unsuccessful. In a very real sense, allied resistance influenced American foreign policy. The pattern observed in the pipeline case — departing sharply from earlier lines of policy, assuming that allies would come around to the administration position, and then reversing course when a policy failed — is characteristic of Reagan's security policy. Alliance management by unilateral assertion contributed to the early deterioration of the Atlantic and Sino-American relationships, and the administration returned to the positions of earlier administrations on Theater Nuclear Force negotiations and the Taiwan question. Initial Middle East policy was based on the assumption that the United States could subordinate intense intraregional conflicts to a common extraregional Soviet threat. When traditional enemies remained traditional enemies in the Middle East, the administration's optimistic vision of an anti-Soviet alliance spanning Israel and conservative Arab states faded, and the administration moved tentatively toward a regional policy for regional disputes. The basic fact that initial Reagan administration security strategy was at variance with the strategies of other major states rendered major elements of the initial strategy unworkable, and to its credit, the Reagan administration made necessary adjustments. The administration persisted with its initial line of security strategy only through targeting radical regimes and pursuing nuclear superiority, issues where unilateral action was possible and allied support was unnecessary.

International Economic Policy

The extent and significance of international economic interdependence during the 1950s and 1960s is often exaggerated. During the 1970s, however, American integration into the international economic system proceeded at a startling pace. Table 1–8 presents American trade in goods and services as a percentage of the GNP. Both the import and export dependency of the United States doubled during the 1970s. These developments in trade were paralleled in finance. In 1970, foreign lending amounted to 7.6 percent of total bank lending. By 1980, international lending amounted to 26 percent of total lending.[24] Even as American international economic weight declined, the importance of the international economic developments to the United States increased.

In international economic affairs, the Reagan administration departed sharply from the managerial policies of the 1970s, then moved by fits and starts to a set of policies that are almost indistinguishable from these policies. The administrations of the 1970s slowly broadened the scope of political multilateral management to address problems that arose as a consequence of increasing interdependence and declining American economic power. Equally significantly, the administrations of the 1970s gradually expanded the domain of American governmental involvement at the boundary between domestic and international economics. The federal government's role in facilitating adjustment and in fostering export development increased throughout the decade. Reagan's initial foreign economic policy departed sharply from these trends.

The initial Reagan approach to economics, domestic or international, was based on the assumption that less government is better economics. The administration's domestic economic program assumed that reducing regulations, taxes, and domestic public spending would trigger productivity and growth. By sheltering individuals and firms from the harsh realities of the marketplace, government blunts incentives to work, save, and innovate. By regulating and prohibiting economic transactions that adversely affect the environment or the health of workers, government decreases the efficiency of the private sector. By taxing, government distorts incentives and discourages work. Reagan's initial international economic policies were firmly grounded in this marketist outlook.

The Reagan administration's foreign economic policy was a logical extension of domestic Reaganomics. A Council of Economic Advisors staff member summarized the views of his colleagues: "If Federal government is bad, international government is ten times worse."[25] A former

TABLE 1–8. United States Trade in Goods and Services as a Percentage of GNP

	1950	*1960*	*1970*	*1980*
Exports/GNP	5.0	5.7	6.6	12.9
Imports/GNP	4.3	4.6	5.9	12.1

SOURCE: *Economic Report of the President, 1982*, Table B-1.

National Security Council staff member with responsibility for international economic policies observed that the Reagan perspective "rejects the notion that international conferencing can substitute for domestic policy reform." He argued, "If national economic policies promote sustained noninflationary growth, economic relations among states are unlikely to be perverse. If, on the other hand, national policies are deficient, economic interdependence among states, regardless of international arrangements, will probably produce little more than international economic malaise and instability."[26] In short, if all nations pursue stable noninflationary growth, then international economic markets rather than international political management can handle problems of coordination. Domestic Reaganomics renders international management superfluous at best, harmful at worst.

The Reagan administration targeted international management and international organizations with particular enthusiasm. The Carter administration had sought, unsuccessfully, to coordinate American macroeconomic policies with the policies of the other advanced industrial societies. Multilateral coordinated reflation might have raised growth rates and minimized international monetary instability. Initially, the Reagan administration explicitly rejected notions of macroeconomic and monetary coordination. International capital markets and floating exchange rates would reconcile divergent national macroeconomic plans. The administration departed from the directions of the 1970s in many other areas of foreign economic policy. It moved to reduce American contributions to multilateral development banks and to encourage developing states to turn to private banks and corporations for loans and investments. It rejected the draft Law of the Sea Treaty on the ground that the supranational authority created by the treaty would overregulate and overtax (American) firms that engaged in seabed mining. It opposed a UN resolution discouraging the advertising and sale of infant formula in nations with unsanitary water on the grounds that the United States should not countenance creation of a "global Federal Trade Commission." It opposed a World Bank program to fund energy conservation and exploration on the grounds that the program would create unfair competition for multinational oil companies. In each instance, the administration believed that adherence to the principles of the market and defense of particularistic American interests coincided. And the administration did adhere to its initial principles in cases that were of largely symbolic value.

The initial move away from international political management toward international deregulation, however, undervalued the significance of political structures within which markets operate and ignored the imperfections in markets. Consider international macroeconomic and monetary policy. The administration's initial rejection of a managerial approach assumed that because all advanced industrial societies desired noninflationary growth, uncoordinated national policies that aimed at noninflationary growth would be in harmony. Yet uncoordinated national policies produced exchange rates and growth rates that were unsatisfactory to the governments of all advanced industrial nations and produced global trade imbalances that threatened to trigger a resurgence of protectionism. As Michael Mochizuchi suggests in his chapter in this volume, these pressures precipitated a crisis in Japanese-American relations. In September 1985, Treasury Secretary Baker orchestrated a five-nation agreement to force the value of the dollar down through a combination of intervention on foreign exchange markets and coordination of interest rate policy. In February 1986, President Reagan faulted floating exchange rates because the strong dollar of 1983 and 1984 had devastated American agriculture. And in the period leading up to the 1986 economic summit, the Reagan administration explored ways of institutionalizing international arrangements for managing debt and exchange rates.[27]

The administration responded to emerging private dilemmas of collective action by reversing elements of its foreign economic policy. When rising real interest rates and contracting markets for exports squeezed Third World debtors, individual private banks cut back on lending to reduce their exposure. Collectively, these individually rational private actions further increased the risk of default. Furthermore, the administration had not moved to augment the abilities of the IMF and the World Bank to serve as lenders of last resort. In the face of crisis, the administration reversed direction. It pressed for increases in IMF authorizations and offered de facto guarantees to keep private banks in the game. In October 1985, the administration offered the "Baker Plan" — a classical comprehensive managerial response to private dilemmas of collective action.

The administration initially sought to bring the practices of foreign governments and the American government in line with its laissez-faire vision. In a 1981 speech before the annual meeting of the IMF, President Reagan exhorted other nations to lessen the role of government in economic management and to turn to private investment and entrepreneurial drive as vehicles for development. To support this strand of policy, the administration linked aid and trade preferences to treatment of foreign investment in its Caribbean Basin Initiative. More fundamentally, the administration sought to limit the role of the American government in foreign economic transactions. To encourage American exporters and foreign importers to turn to commercial banks for trade finance, the administration reduced the lending authorization of the Export-Import Bank. To permit market forces to spur labor's adjustment to changing patterns of international trade, the administration eliminated the income maintenance provisions of trade adjustment assistance. To permit private American manufacturers to compete more effectively in international markets, the administration sought to deregulate trade. A federal regulation discouraged American exporters from dumping unsafe toxic products onto world markets; the Reagan administration repealed this regulation one month after entering office. The Foreign Corrupt Practices Act barred American exporters and investors from bribing officials in foreign governments. The administration fought, unsuccessfuly, for repeal of this act. Antitrust laws limited the ability of American corporations and banks to develop coordinated strategies for penetrating foreign markets. The administration secured repeal of those antitrust regulations that had precluded development of coordinated export strategies. Regulations designed to limit exports of sensitive nuclear technology operated to the detriment of the American nuclear industry. The administration lifted many restrictions in an effort to assure potential suppliers of the reliability of American supplies. Specifically, it licensed the export of nuclear technology to Argentina and South Africa, neither of which had signed the Nuclear Nonproliferation Treaty. Finally, the administration considered and rejected proposals to shift responsibility for domestic monetary management from the Federal Reserve Board to gold markets dominated by South Africa and the Soviet Union. The Reagan administration worked seriously to reduce the role of government in international economic relations.

The Reagan foreign economic policy grew less coherent and more pragmatic over time. By bits and pieces, the administration addressed private and public dilemmas of collective action in commercial, financial, and monetary relations. Benjamin Cohen's chapter on economic relations with other advanced industrial states, Richard Feinberg's chapter on economic relations with the developing world, and Robert Lieber's chapter on energy describe, explain, and critique shifting Reagan policy. An overarching tension between domestic and international liberalism may account for reversals of some, but not all, of these initiatives.

The initial Reagan foreign economic policy and domestic Reaganomics were based on similar premises. Yet paradoxically, domestic laissez-faire may prove to be incompatible with international liberalism. Unrestricted participation in international commerce and finance forces substantial domestic adjustments to shifting international trade and capital flows. Free trade has uneven distributional consequences. The gains of consumers and expanding export-oriented sectors come at the expense of import-competing sectors. Inevitable political pressures from sectors and groups that bear the domestic burden of adjustment constantly threaten to undermine liberal international economic policies.

The administrations of the 1970s gradually expanded federal programs to provide financial relief and retraining for firms and labor in import-competing sectors. The Carter administration added provisions for substantial relief payments over and above normal unemployment assistance in order to buy off political opposition to trade liberalization.

When the Reagan administration slashed the expensive income mainte-nance provisions of the trade adjustment assistance program to foster adjustment and reduce domestic spending, it inadvertently increased domestic political pressures for protection. Beyond facilitating adjust-ment and buying off protectionist sectors, the government may have to play a more active role in supporting export-oriented sectors. The Reagan administration plan to slash Export-Import Bank funding eliminated leverage that the Carter administration had used to coerce France into accepting a limitation on export credit subsidization, and France reneged on the agreement. The Reagan administration restored and then in-creased the lending authorization of the Export-Import Bank in order to secure the leverage to induce France to limit export credit subsidies. Closer governmental involvement in export development and promotion, perhaps along the lines of the Japanese model, may well be a requisite of international commercial success. And explicit sectoral industrial policies may be needed to shape competitive advantage. These forms of state intervention may be both a precondition for long-term adherence to liberal international economic principles and antithetical to the precepts of domestic Reaganomics. Ironically, a larger domestic governmental role may be needed to defuse domestic opposition to international liberalism and to increase the effectiveness of liberal international economic policies.

Conclusions

Scholars commonly rely on two cyclical theories to analyze American foreign policy. Frank Klingberg and Samuel Huntington have described medium-term cycles of introversion and extroversion in American foreign policy. They argue that the United States is doomed to oscillate between withdrawal from an impure world and crusades to purify the world, as failures of crusades set the stage for withdrawal, and failures of with-drawal set the stage for crusades. The Klingberg-Huntington cycle is ultimately rooted in both the fundamental liberalism of American politi-cal culture and the fundamental imperviousness of international politics to reform. Robert Gilpin observes long-term cycles of hegemonic rise and decline in international affairs. He argues that external burdens of leader-ship, internal tendencies toward rising consumption, and international diffusion of technology account for the rise and decline of Athens, Rome, Holland, Britain, and the United States. Such international dynastic cycles are ultimately rooted in the nature of international relations and the generic characteristics of great powers.

The foreign policy of the Reagan administration unfolded at the conjunction of a short-term cycle of extroversion and a long-term cycle of decline. The initial form of the Reagan foreign policy experiment was reshaped by emerging resource constraints and by emerging limits of

American power. The Reagan administration could n
al foundation for either military or economic resto
compelled reversal of many initial security and econ
elements of the original Reagan experiment persisted.
Libyan applications of the Reagan Doctrine entailed ......
small, isolated adversaries. But by and large, external limits and internal
political processes curtailed the experiment. The Reagan administration
came to pursue an unacknowledged strategy of adjustment.

But the foreign policy of the Reagan administration is also situated in
a third cycle, a cycle of pessimism and optimism. The Nixon, Ford, and
Carter administrations, buffeted by defeat in Vietnam, energy shocks,
stagflation, and hostage crises, were acutely aware of the limits of American power. Their adjustments to emerging limits were fundamentally
sound, but their pessimistic rhetoric did not reflect America's continuing
strengths. The Reagan administration, bolstered by victory in Grenada,
energy windfalls, disinflation, and a war on terrorism, is acutely aware of
America's continuing strengths. Reagan's adjustments to emerging limits
largely paralleled adjustments made during the 1970s, but his rhetoric
remains optimistic. In an address on the Reagan economic program,
Martin Feldstein pointed to innate optimism as one of Reagan's dominant
characteristics:

> As we were reviewing a range of budget scenarios one day, the Presi-
> dent selected the optimistic projection and then told a story on himself.
> Two parents were deeply worried about their children. One child was
> unduly pessimistic, the other unduly optimistic. They placed the
> pessimistic child in a room filled with new toys and locked the optimis-
> tic child in a shed filled with horse manure. After two hours, they found
> the pessimistic child with tears streaming down his face crying, "Some-
> one will take away my toys." They found the optimistic child digging
> happily through the manure burbling, "If there's this much manure,
> there has to be a pony in here somewhere."[28]

The initial undue optimism of the Reagan administration had costs.
By basing its economic and military programs on unrealistic projections
of growth and revenues, the administration undercut its own program of
restoration. By waiting for crises to compel policy changes, the administration risked exacerbating unavoidable problems and losing opportunities for preventive diplomacy. By assuming that allies would accept the
administration's vision of relations with the Soviet Union and with radical regimes in the Third World, the administration isolated the United
States. By assuming that international financial, trade, and monetary
problems would be handled efficiently by markets alone, the administration made international economic management more difficult. By ignoring trade-offs across foreign policy goals, the administration often

sened the terms of trade-offs. In short, by persisting in its quest for storation in the face of resource limits and by maintaining its core security and economic policies until compelled to change them, the Reagan administration lost an important measure of control over the form and extent of adjustments. But perhaps this chapter has dwelt excessively on the costs of undue optimism, for confidence is also a product of optimism. And confidence facilitated the adjustments to limits and modifications of policies that have marked the Reagan era in American foreign policy.

"Constrained Confidence and the Evolution of Reagan Foreign Policy" was written for this volume. Copyright © 1987 by Kenneth A. Oye.

Notes

1. "Address before the Annual Convention of the American Society of Newspaper Editors," Washington, D.C., April 10, 1980.
2. "A New Direction in U.S. Foreign Policy," *Current Policy* Number 275, Bureau of Public Affairs, Department of State."
3. "Text of the Reagan Message to Congress on Foreign Policy," *New York Times*, March 15, 1986.
4. James R. Kurth, "A Widening Gyre: The Logic of American Weapons Procurement," *Public Policy* (Summer 1971), Vol. 19, pp. 373–404.
5. For indices of economic and military power concentration between 1830 to 1983, see Bruce Russett, "The Mysterious Case of Vanishing Hegemony; or Is Mark Twain Really Dead?" *International Organization* (Spring 1985), Vol. 39, No. 2.
6. Robert Gilpin, *War and Change in World Politics* (Cambridge: Cambridge University Press, 1981).
7. Mancur Olson and Richard Zeckhauser, "An Economic Theory of Alliances," *The Review of Economics and Statistics*, (August 1966), Vol. 48, No. 3.
8. This rise in interest rates took place after the tax cuts and defense spending increases had been announced but *before* the deficits had materialized. It is a remarkable example of the capacity of financial markets to bring the future into the present. See William H. Branson, "Causes of Appreciation and Volatility of the Dollar," in *The U.S. Dollar—Recent Developments, Outlook, and Policy Options* (Kansas City: Federal Reserve Bank of Kansas City, 1985).
9. Were the deficits unanticipated or intentional? Former Office of Management and Budget Director David Stockman suggests that the administration generated budgetary deficits as part of a strategy to secure leverage to eliminate domestic programs. Former Chairman of the Council of Economic Advisors Martin Feldstein suggests that President Reagan genuinely belived that the optimistic projections would prove correct. Martin Feldstein, Janeway Lecture, Princeton, New Jersey, March 1986.
10. Samuel Huntington, "The Defense Policy of the Reagan Administration, 1981–82," in Fred I. Greenstein, ed., *The Reagan Presidency: An Early Assessment* (Baltimore: Johns Hopkins University Press, 1983).
11. U.S. Department of Defense, *Annual Report to Congress Fiscal Year 1983* (Washington, D.C.: U.S. Government Printing Office, 1982), pp. 1–44.
12. Bruce Carter Jackson, "Military Expenditures, Growth, and Inflation in Seven Leading Industrial Countries" (New York: Brown Brothers, Harriman & Company, 1981).

Machinists and Aerospace Workers Report (New York, Council on Economic Priorities, 1982).

13. "Defense Inc." *Washington Post*, December 1, 1985.

14. *Military Spending: Facts and Figures, Worldwide Implications, and Future Outlook* (New York: Oxford University Press, 1983).

15. See Kenneth N. Waltz, *Theory of International Politics* (Reading, MA: Addison-Wesley, 1979) and Harrison Wagner, "Game Theory and the Balance of Power," *World Politics* (July 1986), Vol. 38, No. 4, for theories of balancing. See Steven Walt, "Alliance Formation and the Balance of World Power," *International Security* (Spring 1985), Vol. 9, No. 4, for evidence supporting these propositions.

16. See Robert Packenham, *Liberal America and the Third World* (Princeton: Princeton University Press, 1973) on tensions across economic, military, and ideological goals of American Third World policy and on the suspicious tendency for American policymakers to act as if "all good things go together."

17. Public Address, Princeton University, October 14, 1982.

18. Ironically, the Gulf of Sidra incidents may well have strengthened Colonel Qaddafi as well as President Reagan. Qadaffi repeatedly drew a line through international waters in the Gulf of Sidra, and Reagan repeatedly sent an American fleet across the line. In the United States, the resulting episodic low level naval and air conflict was seen as a victory over terrorism and freedom of the seas. In Libya, the conflict raised Qaddafi's visibility and standing in the Arab world and deflected domestic attention from Libya's economic woes.

19. Paul Huth and Bruce Russett, "What Makes Deterrence Work? Cases from 1900 to 1980," *World Politics* (July 1984), Vol. 36, No. 4.

20. For the seminal essay on the escalation dominance approach to defining nuclear superiority, see Paul Nitze, "Assuring Strategic Stability in an Era of Detente," *Foreign Affairs* (January 1976), Vol. 54, No. 2. For a critical review of Nitze's premises, see Gary Brewer and Bruce Blair, "War Games and National Security with a Grain of Salt," *The Bulletin of the Atomic Scientists* (June 1979), Vol. 35, No. 6.

21. "Progress Seen on Arms Control," *Christian Science Monitor*, June 25, 1986.

22. For a survey of factors that have historically affected the likelihood of arms control, see George Downs, David Rocke, and Randolph Siverson, "Arms Races and Cooperation," *World Politics* (October 1985), Vol. 38, No. 1.

23. Bruce Blair, *Strategic Command and Control and Nuclear Strategy* (Washington, D.C.: The Brookings Institution, 1985). For a wide-ranging critique of "nuclear superiority" as defined from a counterforce escalation dominance perspective, see Robert Jervis, *The Illogic of American Nuclear Strategy* (Ithaca: Cornell University Press, 1984).

24. Figures on international lending as a proportion of total lending were computed from B-63 and B-105 in *Economic Report of the President* (Washington, D.C.: U.S. Government Printing Office, 1982).

25. Background interview, Washington, D.C., July 1981.

26. Henry R. Nau, "International Reaganomics: A Domestic Approach to World Economy," Georgetown University Center for Strategic and International Studies, *Significant Issues Series* (1984), Vol. 6, No. 18.

27. For contrasting views on the importance of international institutions to realization of mutual interests in international affairs, see John Conybeare, "International Organization and the Theory of Property Rights," *International Organization* (Summer 1980), Vol. 34, No. 3; and Robert O. Keohane, "The Demand for International Regimes," *International Organization* (Winter 1982), Vol. 36, No. 1.

28. Janeway Lecture, Princeton, N.J., March 1986.

2

"Rambo" and Reality: Having It Both Ways

William Schneider

Sir, do we get to win this time?
—Asked by title character in the film *Rambo* after learning that he is
being sent back to Vietnam on a mission

Boy, I'm glad I saw *Rambo* last night. Now I know what to do next time.
—Remark made by President Reagan on June 30, 1985, following the
release of 39 American hostages in Beirut.

The American public has so far judged President Reagan's foreign policy
a success. That success, it will be argued here, was based as much on
what the administration did not do as on what it did do. What the
administration did do was restore the nation's sense of military security.
Despite the president's hard-line rhetoric, however, the first five years of
the Reagan administration saw no large-scale military intervention or
threat to world peace. Whereas Reagan's rhetoric tended to frighten
people in 1980 and 1981, his record in office reassured them. The
president's record tended to dispel the notion that he was trigger-happy,
reckless, or aggressive. In such crises as the Korean jetliner incident in
1983 and the TWA hostage crisis in 1985, the administration talked tough
but pursued a course that was exceedingly moderate and cautious. As a
result, the president managed to have it both ways, keeping the support
of the ideological hard-liners and winning the confidence of the American
people.

*William Schneider is Resident Fellow at the American Enterprise Institute in Wash-
ington, D.C. He is also a contributing editor to* National Journal *and* The Los
Angeles Times, *where his articles appear regularly, and coauthor of* The Confidence Gap: Business, Labor, and Government in the Public Mind *(Free Press,
1983). A second edition is forthcoming from Johns Hopkins University Press in 1987.
His new book on the Reagan revolution and the American electorate will be published
in late 1987.*

Between the 1980 and 1984 presidential elections, there were two discernible trends in the public's foreign policy attitudes. The first was a movement away from the hard-line views that had dominated the 1980 campaign. For example, negative views of the Soviet Union tended to diminish after Ronald Reagan took office. In 1981, a third of the public accepted the view that Russia would risk a major war to achieve global domination. That proportion was down to one-fifth in 1984. In 1980, 36 percent endorsed the view that "Russia can't be trusted and we will have to rely on increased military strength to counter them in the future." That figure had fallen by half in 1984. Moreover the feeling that the United States lagged behind the Soviet Union in nuclear strength was expressed by 43 percent in 1980 and by 27 percent in 1984. The belief that we were behind Russia in conventional military power declined from one-half to one-third over the same period. In 1980, a majority of Americans thought we were spending too little on defense (Table 2–1). That figure had fallen by one-half in 1982. In 1984, only 17 percent felt we were spending too little on defense.

In part, these trends attest to the success of President Reagan's defense buildup. The public felt a good deal more secure militarily in 1984 than it did in 1980, and this had the effect of undermining public support for the administration's program of continuing defense increases. But something else was also happening. While support for the administration's hard-line policies was diminishing, President Reagan's image as a man of peace was growing.

In 1980, for example, the public thought Jimmy Carter would do a better job than Ronald Reagan in dealing with Russia and in handling foreign relations. When the Gallup poll compared presidential candidates again in 1984, the results showed Reagan with a substantial lead over Walter Mondale on both issues. In 1980, Carter had a twenty-five-point lead over Reagan for "keeping the United States out of war." In 1984, the Democratic candidate had only a twelve-point lead on this issue. In 1980, the Democrats went into the presidential campaign with a strong peace record, and the voters had serious doubts about Reagan's commitment to peace. The polls that year suggested that Reagan was elected in spite of widespread concern over his foreign policy. By 1984, that concern had been alleviated by his record in office.

In fact, it took the public some time to gain confidence in the Reagan administration's foreign policy. The president's foreign policy ratings remained relatively low during his first three years in office. By the end of his first year, a spontaneous grass-roots movement in support of a mutual, verifiable nuclear freeze gathered momentum in various parts of the country. Freeze resolutions were approved by voters in eight out of nine states and twenty-eight out of thirty localities at the time of the 1982

TABLE 2–1. Support for Domestic and Defense Spending, 1973–1985

"We are faced with many problems in this country, none of which can be solved easily or inexpensively. I'm going to name some of these problems, and for each one I'd like you to tell me whether you think we're spending too much money, too little money, or about the right amount."

The percentages for "domestic spending" are the average of the responses for five items: "improving and protecting the environment," "improving and protecting the nation's health," "solving the problems of the big cities," "improving the nation's education system," and "welfare." The defense item was "the military, armaments, and defense."

Year	Too Little (Percent)	About the Right Amount (Percent)	Too Much (Percent)
Domestic Spending			
1973	48	29	17
1974	49	30	15
1975	48	30	16
1976	44	30	21
1977	41	31	21
1978	42	31	21
1980	42	30	21
1982	45	29	19
1983	47	31	16
1984	50	32	13
1985	46	32	16
Defense Spending			
1973	11	45	38
1974	17	45	31
1975	17	46	31
1976	24	42	27
1977	24	45	23
1978	27	44	22
1980	56	26	11
1982	29	36	30
1983	24	38	32
1984	17	41	38
1985	14	42	40

SOURCE: National Opinion Research Center, University of Chicago, General Social Surveys. Number of respondents varies between 1,468 and 1,532 for 1973–1983 surveys. The 1984 and 1985 tests were based on random half-samples (1984, $N = 490$; 1985, $N = 751$). Reprinted by permission of NORC.

midterm election. Despite major television speeches aimed at rallying public support, Americans remained profoundly skeptical of the president's policies in Central America and the Middle East. Nor could the president claim credit for a single arms control agreement.

A dramatic turnaround, however, was seen in 1984. Polls taken by the *Los Angeles Times* show that Reagan bested Mondale in all areas of foreign policy. These included military security, on which the president's record elicited a solid vote of confidence, and even keeping peace in the world, where the *Los Angeles Times* showed a small Reagan advantage. The two issues on which the Reagan administration might have been thought vulnerable, Central America and the Middle East, tended to diminish in importance over the course of the year, particularly after American troops were withdrawn from Lebanon in February. On these and other foreign policy issues, the president's advantage improved during the campaign.

The Gallup poll substantiated the finding that the president's foreign policy image improved during 1984. In January, Mondale was nine points ahead of Reagan as the candidate more likely to keep the United States out of war. In June, they were tied. In September and October, Reagan was seven points ahead. The shift was not simply a function of Walter Mondale's perceived weakness. Another Gallup question asked whether Reagan's defense policies had brought the United States closer to war or peace. Between the summer of 1983 and the summer of 1984, more people said "war" (43 to 47 percent) than "peace" (26 to 28 percent). By the fall of 1984, however, the two percentages were almost equal.

Why did the voters gain confidence in Reagan's foreign policy? The campaign had the effect of focusing attention on the administration's record. On the one hand, the Reagan administration had no foreign policy triumph comparable to Carter's Camp David peace treaty. On the other hand, there was no foreign policy disaster comparable to Iran.

The Democrats ran television advertisements suggesting that Reagan might start a nuclear war. Many voters had been worried about that in 1980. But not in 1984. For one thing, Reagan had been president for almost four years and we were still here. To an electorate that had initially been apprehensive about Reagan's foreign policy ideas, his record in office — for instance, his cautious response in September 1983 to the Soviet Air Force downing of the Korean Air Lines passenger plane — was immensely reassuring.

Many Democrats thought they could use the administration's failure in Lebanon as an issue in the campaign. After all, we lost a great many more American lives in Lebanon than in Iran. But Iran is still seen as a national humiliation and a disgrace. Lebanon is not. When it became clear that our peacekeeping mission in Lebanon was not working, President Reagan had the good sense to cut our losses and get out. That, to many Americans, is leadership — exactly the kind of leadership we did not get in Vietnam.

During the Vietnam War, pollsters regularly asked Americans if they preferred a "hawkish" or a "dovish" policy in Southeast Asia. The answer they got, over and over again, was, "We should either win or get out." What did Reagan do as president? In Grenada we won. And in Lebanon we got out. So much for the Vietnam syndrome.

As one election analyst put it, "[President Reagan] loves to display American military muscle, yet prefers to do so without there being any American victims. He supports peace from a position of American strength but is against this strength resulting in the threat of a nuclear war." That description in *Izvestia* was intended to depict Reagan's policy as inconsistent and contradictory. In fact, it turned out to be exactly the kind of foreign policy the American public wanted.

By the time of the 1984 election, the public was firmly convinced that President Reagan was sincerely committed to peace and arms control. That impression was confirmed by the Reagan-Gorbachev summit in November 1985. Even though little was accomplished on arms control, Reagan demonstrated that he could deal with the Soviets peaceably. In foreign policy, as in other areas, President Reagan managed to keep up his support among hard-liners while doing very little to implement the divisive and controversial aspects of their program. That is not deception. That is good politics. The president managed to talk like "Rambo" while demonstrating that he understood the limits imposed by political reality.

Peace and Strength, Yes; Involvement, No

The period between, roughly, 1948 and 1968, is usually depicted as one of bipartisan consensus in American foreign policy. Following World War II, despite the temptation to reject an activist role in world affairs and "return to normalcy," as the United States had done after World War I, leaders of both political parties drew together around a new internationalist consensus. "The dominant view from the late 1940s through the early 1960s," one historian of American public opinion writes, "had such powerful influence even on its critics that it may be called the Cold War consensus."[1] The foreign policy values that prevailed during this period entailed a continuity of goals — essentially containment of Soviet power — accompanied by a two-track foreign policy strategy, cooperation when possible, confrontation when necessary.

This foreign policy consensus broke down after 1968. The principal reason was ideological polarization within the activist stratum of American political life. Counterelites emerged on both the right and the left to challenge the supremacy of the old foreign policy establishment. This establishment included the traditionally moderate leaders of the two political parties, both of which endorsed the Cold War consensus. The result was a split at the elite level between conservative and liberal internationalists. The two factions have now acquired substantial influence within the major political parties.

In an earlier *Eagle* volume, Mandelbaum and Schneider analyzed data from a 1974 survey of American foreign policy attitudes in great detail.[2] The analysis revealed that certain "signals" or themes consistently divided internationalists, those generally better educated Americans who are attentive to foreign policy and supportive of an active American role in world affairs. These polarizing themes included any reference to the military, such as military aid to other nations, troop commitments abroad, and defense spending; the notion of American hegemony or world leadership; the Central Intelligence Agency (CIA), the military, and business as agents of or forces influencing American foreign policy; sympathy for Third World liberation movements; support for dictatorial regimes in countries otherwise friendly to the United States; and anticommunism as a foreign policy priority. It was possible to differentiate conservative and liberal internationalists according to their views on these issues.

Conservative internationalists were found to picture the world primarily in East-West terms: democracy versus totalitarianism, capitalism versus communism, freedom versus repression. They were supportive of military power and gave high priority to national security goals. They also showed a strong commitment to traditional anticommunist containment and were suspicious of detente as a kind of cartel arrangement whereby the two superpowers agreed to limit competition in order to stabilize the market and protect their interests.

Liberal internationalists emphasized economic and humanitarian problems over security issues and rejected a hegemonic role for the United States. They wanted leaders to think in global terms: the scarcity of natural resources, environmental and oceanic pollution, and international economic inequality. They tended to regard the common problems facing all of humanity as more urgent than the ideological differences between East and West. Liberal internationalists approved of detente as a necessary first step toward a new world order based on global interdependence. The impact of Vietnam could be seen in this group's deep suspicion of military intervention and military power as instruments of foreign policy.

Both liberal and conservative internationalists perceived foreign policy in moralistic terms, and both attacked Secretary of State Henry Kissinger for the lack of moral commitment in his diplomacy. Conservative internationalists align with the international right, which is to say that their primary moral commitment is to the free world in its confrontation with communism. Liberal internationalists align ideologically with the forces of change in world affairs — not communism, but the Third World left, including national liberation movements, such oppressed minorities as Palestinian Arabs and blacks in southern Africa and, indeed, the Third World as a whole in its claim for economic justice against the industrialized North.

Noninternationalists, who comprised almost half of the American public in the 1974 study, do not share this moralism. They are suspicious of international involvements of any kind. They tend to be poorer and less well educated and to know and care little about foreign affairs, which they see as remote from their daily concerns. This large, inattentive public is neither consistently liberal nor consistently conservative in its foreign policy views. Nor is it ideologically isolationist in the sense that many Americans were between World War I and World War II. The inattentive public is simply not internationalist minded. It is not disposed to support American involvement in other countries' affairs unless a clear and compelling issue of national interest or national security is at stake. If we are directly threatened or if our interest *is* involved in any important way, this group wants swift, decisive action but not long-term involvement.

In the pre-television era, social scientists spoke of an attentive audience for foreign affairs. This audience was better educated and followed foreign affairs regularly. It also tended to be more supportive of administration initiative and leadership in foreign affairs than the noninternationalist public was. When the attentive elite was asked about the Korean War, about American involvement in the rest of the world, about trade and treaties, it was consistently more supportive than the rest of the public.[3] Noninternationalists, however, showed a persistent strain of distrust and anti-involvement. As a rule, noninternationalists got involved in the foreign affairs debate only in election years. Between elections, the noninternationalist audience could generally be discounted.

This stratification disappeared in the late 1960s when the elite split. The issue of detente split liberal and conservative internationalists, but to the mass public, it comprised the powerfully appealing theme of *peace*. The Nixon-Ford-Kissinger detente policy was extraordinarily popular during the 1970s because it was interpreted not as a sellout to the communists but rather as a policy for keeping world peace. The peace issue draws noninternationalists and liberal internationalists together in a liberal coalition. Similarly, although liberal and conservative internationalists differ profoundly over military policy, *strength* is a sentiment that appeals strongly to noninternationalists. The desire for military security draws conservative internationalists and noninternationalists together in a conservative coalition. Peace and strength are the foreign policy values of surpassing concern to noninternationalists. As the relative salience of these two issues changes over time, so does the coalition pattern and the dominant ideological complexion of foreign policy attitudes.

Public opinion between 1964 and 1974 was preoccupied with the issue of peace. The result was to pull noninternationalists to the left. After 1968, however, the noninternationalist public turned against the Vietnam War as a wasteful, pointless, and ultimately tragic mistake. The antiwar coalition was a potent alliance between liberal internationalists and noninternationalists. The latter, however, never accepted the more extreme contentions of the antiwar activists that American motives in Vietnam were evil or corrupt.

Noninternationalists ally with the left on questions of intervention because they see no point to American involvement in most of the world. They are against foreign aid, against troop engagement, against anything that smacks of foreign entanglement. Calling this viewpoint isolationist, however, is misleading. Isolationism implies a belief system, a principled opposition to American participation in world affairs. Noninternationalists are not so much opposed in principle as they are nonsupportive. Being less well educated — that is the strongest demographic correlate of noninternationalism — this group has a limited understanding of the relevance of complex events that are remote from their daily lives. Their nonsupport is based more on practical than on ideological considerations. Noninternationalists feel that most of what the United States does for the rest of the world is senseless, wasteful, and unappreciated. And they are sometimes right.

In cases like Vietnam and, more recently, Central America, noninternationalists find a natural alliance with the left. But that alliance is neither automatic nor constant. The noninternationalist public is also oriented toward a strong military posture. After 1975, the mass public became increasingly insecure about Soviet military strength and adventurism, and public opinion began to drift to the right. Noninternationalists were pulled into an alliance with conservative internationalists because of a shared concern over the nation's military security. From 1974 to 1981, public support for increasing the size of the nation's defense budget grew monthly. Noninternationalists voted heavily for Reagan in 1980, in part because of his promise of a defense buildup and a tougher line toward the Soviet Union. This constituency likes strength and toughness in foreign affairs because they increase our independence and make us less likely to become involved in other countries' problems. No one will give us any trouble as long as we are the toughest kid on the block. The basic impulse here is defensive; the public wants to see the United States keep up its military power in order to protect itself from the Soviet threat, not in order to assume an interventionist role in world affairs. Thus noninternationalists support the conservative elite on issues having to do with defense and toughness. They support the liberal elite on issues of direct American involvement.

The public is committed to both peace and strength and does not regard them as inconsistent values. The Roper Organization, for example, asks people to choose one of three ways of dealing with the Soviet Union. In repeated tests, about one person in four prefers a tough line ("It's clear that Russia can't be trusted and we will have to rely on increased military strength to counter them in the future"). Another one in four endorses a soft line ("We should do nothing that is likely to provoke an American-Russian military conflict but instead should try to negotiate and reason out our differences"). The largest number, about one half of those interviewed, regularly prefers the "mixed" view, that "we should take a strong position with the Russians now so they won't go any further but at the same time we should try to re-establish good relations with them." In other words, the public does not favor peace over strength or strength over peace. It favors a policy that engages both values.

Asking people to choose between peace and strength is like asking people to choose between health and financial security. Both are important. But people are sometimes more concerned about one and sometimes about the other. It depends on what problems the individual, or the country, is facing. At certain times, Americans worry more over military security, at other times, over peace. These concerns have ebbed and flowed in three stages since World War II.

The first stage was the Cold War, a period in which the public became increasingly obsessed with the nation's military security vis-à-vis the Soviet Union. That obsession developed rather slowly during the late 1940s. In 1945, according to a Gallup poll, most Americans thought the Russians could be trusted to cooperate after the war. The Truman administration, privately alarmed over Soviet aggressiveness, felt it had to be cautious in its public pronouncements. President Truman and his advisors were not convinced that the American public (or Congress) would support a policy of global confrontation with the Soviet Union. After all, the American public (and Congress) had rejected an activist world role for the United States following World War I.

The turning point came with the Korean War, which had the effect of alarming Americans less about peace than about military security. The antiwar protest against Korean involvement came not from the left but from the right, from those who felt that the United States lacked the strength and determination to win a decisive victory over communism. In fact there is evidence that American leaders deliberately overstated the nature of the Soviet threat in order to obtain public support for an activist foreign policy. According to diplomatic historian Ernest R. May, "Men of the Truman, Eisenhower and Kennedy administrations doubted that the mass of voters could or would reconcile themselves to a long-term, hostile rivalry with the Soviet Union involving continual expense and danger and promising no happy conclusion at any point in the anticipatable future."[4] Given the historic American resistance to a world leadership role, leaders of this generation felt that the Cold War had to be "sold" to the American public.

It proved not to be very difficult. Anti-Soviet hostility was extremely intense during the 1950s. Some 90 percent of the public regularly reported negative attitudes toward the Soviet Union, according to Gallup polls taken at the time; fewer than 2 percent held favorable attitudes. In his 1960 presidential campaign, John F. Kennedy stressed the "missile gap" with the Soviet Union, arguing that the United States had fallen behind the Russians in military strength and global influence. That was how most voters understood Kennedy's promise to "get the country moving again."

The Cold War came to a climax with the Cuban missile crisis of 1962. What is interesting about the era of detente, which began with the nuclear Test-Ban Treaty in 1963 and lasted through the early 1970s, is that the Soviet Union virtually disappeared from the national agenda. The nuclear threat seemed much less imminent, and relations with the Soviets took on the character of a stable, competitive rivalry. The public's attitude toward Russia never became favorable, but it definitely improved. At the height of detente, between 1972 and 1975, about 19 percent said they had a favorable view of the Soviet Union, according to polls by Gallup and the National Opinion Research Center, while 36 percent had an unfavorable view. The largest number (45 to 50 percent), reported "mixed" feelings. Peace, not strength, was the public's primary concern from 1964 to 1974. As noted, the Vietnam War activated the public's traditional concern about the consequences of American involvement abroad.

The post-detente period began with the energy crisis of 1974 and the ensuing nine years of recurring recession and hyperinflation. The feeling of national weakness following American disengagement from Vietnam in 1975, plus the Soviet military buildup and Russian adventurism in Africa and the Middle East, had the effect of heightening public concern over the country's military security. The result was the trend, noted earlier, of growing support for military spending. Security consciousness reached a peak after the seizure of American hostages in Iran and the Soviet invasion of Afghanistan at the end of 1979. In the early 1980s, the preponderance of public sentiment toward the Soviet Union was once again negative, although not quite as negative as it was in the 1950s. About a third of the American public reported "mixed" feelings about the Russians, compared with only 10 percent in 1953–1956.

Thus the early 1980s saw strength replace peace as the paramount concern. It was not quite the same as the Cold War, however. Vietnam made a difference. Americans in the 1980s are less interventionist and more sensitive to the risks of foreign entanglement. The "strength" constituency is certainly larger than it was during the detente era of the late 1960s and early 1970s. But the "peace" constituency is larger than it had been in the 1950s. The nuclear freeze movement of the early 1980s, for instance, was considerably larger and more spontaneous than the "ban the bomb" movement ever was in the 1950s, even though their purposes were basically the same.

In sum, the carefully balanced, bipartisan, two-track consensus of the Cold War era has come apart, with liberal internationalists emphasizing cooperation and conservative internationalists giving priority to confrontation. The mass public, however, continues to support a two-track policy. At the same time, ordinary Americans have become increasingly impatient with and distrustful of foreign policy leadership. The long-term trend in public opinion was not right or left but rather anti-establishment, a growing hostility toward political parties and leaders as corrupt, incompetent, and ineffective. A public that was once passive about foreign policy and generally willing to grant political leaders a great deal of leeway in managing foreign affairs became increasingly suspicious and distrustful. Instead of elite consensus and mass followership, what emerged was an unstable system of competing coalitions in which the mass public swings left or right unpredictably in response to its current fears and concerns. A stable, two-track foreign policy has given way to an erratic alternation.

Internationalism

The model just presented explains some of the paradoxes associated with the American public's view of the world. For instance, the polling data reveal that although Americans are sympathetic to the problems of the Third World, and even though most Americans describe themselves as internationalists, the public's willingness to support international commitments is quite limited. We should be friendly and cooperative, the public feels. We should protect our vital interests. But we should draw the line at involvement.

This sentiment is not so much ideological as populist. The polls reveal a consistent mass-elite difference on internationalism. Educated Americans and national leaders are more willing to support all kinds of international commitments, whether they are "liberal" (detente, foreign economic assistance) or "conservative" (foreign military aid, troop intervention). Populist resistance to international involvement helps explain such diverse phenomena as the public's opposition to the Panama Canal treaties, its lack of enthusiasm for President Reagan's policies in Central America, and its deep strain of protectionism.

Since the late 1940s, the National Opinion Research Center (NORC) at the University of Chicago has been following the American public's internationalism by asking "Do you think it will be best for the future of the country if we take an active part in world affairs or if we stay out of world affairs?" Between 54 and 72 percent have always supported an active role in world affairs. The high point was reached in 1955. By 1982, only a little over 50 percent of the public favored an active role in world affairs.

That is surprising because internationalism is strongly related to education. In 1982, support for internationalism ranged from 73 percent among the college-educated to 38 percent among the grade school-educated. Educational levels have certainly risen over the past four decades. Nevertheless, the proportion of Americans taking the position that the United States should stay out of world affairs increased from one-quarter in the 1940s and 1950s to one-third in the 1970s and 1980s.

In NORC's annual surveys since 1973, foreign aid has invariably been the least popular of eleven government spending programs, and consistently less popular than "welfare." Between two-thirds and three-quarters of the public say that the government spends too much on foreign aid. Between 3 and 5 percent say the government spends too little.

It is not that Americans are unsympathetic. By two to one, Americans endorsed the view in a 1981 Gallup poll that "developed countries must share in the responsibility" for the problems of underdeveloped countries, as opposed to the view that these countries' problems are "their own responsibility." But when asked whether the United States should increase aid to underdeveloped countries "to assist them to become more self-sufficient in the future," the ratio was two to one against an increase in aid.

The strongest evidence of the gap between mass and elite opinion comes from surveys commissioned by the Chicago Council on Foreign Relations in 1974, 1978, and 1982. Each year, the same questions were asked of the general public and a sample of national leaders from government, business, labor, academia, the mass media, religion, and special interest groups. Table 2–2 shows how each sample rated a list of possible foreign policy goals for the United States.

The public rank-orders foreign policy goals in terms of self-interest. At the top of the list were protecting American jobs, keeping up the value of the dollar, and securing adequate energy supplies — all self-regarding objectives. (Protecting the interests of American business, however, was rated relatively low; the public does not seem to identify with the interests of business.) At the bottom of the list were promoting human rights, improving the standard of living in less developed countries, protecting weaker nations against foreign aggression, and bringing democracy to other nations — all "other-regarding" objectives.

The more self-interested objectives, including protecting American

TABLE 2–2. America's Foreign Policy Goals: Two Views

In 1974, 1978, and 1982, the Chicago Council on Foreign Relations surveyed a sampling of the public and of opinion leaders: "I am going to read a list of possible goals that the United States might have. For each one, please say whether you think that should be a very important foreign policy goal, a somewhat important foreign policy goal, or not an important goal at all."
Here are the percentages of those who responded "very important":

	Public			Leaders		
	1974	1978	1982	1974	1978	1982
Protecting jobs of American workers	74	78	77	—	34	43
Keeping up the value of the dollar	—*	86	71	—	73	38
Securing adequate supplies of energy	75	78	70	—	88	72
Worldwide arms control	64	64	64	—	81	86
Containing communism	54	60	59	—	45	44
Combating world hunger	61	59	58	—	67	64
Defending our allies' security	33	50	50	—	77	82
Matching Soviet military power	—	—	49	—	—	52
Strengthening the United Nations	46	47	48	—	26	25
Protecting interests of American business abroad	39	45	44	—	26	25
Promoting and defending human rights in other countries	—	39	43	—	35	41
Helping to improve the standard of living in less developed countries	39	35	35	—	64	55
Protecting weaker nations against foreign aggression	28	34	34	—	30	43
Helping to bring democratic forms of government to other nations	28	26	29	—	15	23

*Not asked.

SOURCE: Reprinted by permission of the Chicago Council of Foreign Relations.

business interests, were more highly rated by the mass public than by the leaders. The leaders tended to attach greater importance to internationalist goals. Thus the leaders were more likely to endorse such liberal goals as arms control and improving the standard of living in less developed countries. They were also more likely to support such conservative goals as defending our allies' security and protecting weaker nations against foreign aggression.

In two cases this relationship was reversed. The public was more enthusiastic than the leaders about containing communism and strengthening the United Nations (UN). These are both old ideas that date from the period of bipartisan foreign policy consensus following World War II. Thirty years ago, support for the UN and for the doctrine of containment was probably quite solid at the elite level. In recent years, however, the luster of both ideas seems to have worn thin among opinion leaders. At the mass level, support has faded more slowly.

Two relatively new foreign policy ideas that were fairly weakly endorsed by the mass public — promoting human rights and promoting democracy — have not caught on at the elite level either.

In the case of just about every international initiative tested in the 1982 Chicago Council survey, the public was reluctant to become involved. Barely 50 percent of the public, compared with 94 percent of the leaders, approved of economic aid to other nations "for purposes of economic development and technical assistance." The principal criticism of economic aid, agreed to by 75 percent of the public, was that it "gets us too involved in other countries' affairs." (Only 27 percent of leaders thought this was the case.) Military aid (defined as "arms and equipment but not troops") was even less popular. Only 28 percent of the public approved of such aid, but 59 percent of the leaders supported it.

Leaders were more likely than the public to approve the dispatch of American troops if the Soviets invaded Western Europe or Japan, if North Korea invaded South Korea, or if Arab forces invaded Israel. The leaders were also more willing to support arms control negotiations with the Soviet Union, American-Soviet trade, cultural and educational exchanges, joint efforts to solve energy problems, and negotiations to re-establish relations with Cuba. A more active role in opposing apartheid in South Africa was endorsed by 45 percent of the public and 79 percent of the leaders.

On such issues, the function of leaders is to lead public opinion in an internationalist direction. It can be difficult, as it was in the case of the Panama Canal treaties and as it still is on the issue of free trade. Sometimes it does not work. Less than half of the leaders, but almost three-quarters of the American public, agreed with the following statement in 1982: "The Vietnam war was more than a mistake; it was fundamentally wrong and immoral."

Table 2–3 shows how the American public sees the world. Respondents to the Chicago Council survey were asked to indicate their degree of favorability toward each country in a list of twenty-four countries, using a thermometer scale ranging from zero degrees (very cold or unfavorable) to one hundred degrees (very warm or favorable). A thermometer rating of fifty degrees was designated as neutral. Respondents were also asked whether they felt the United States does or does not have a vital interest in each country, where "vital interest" meant that the country is "important to the United States for political, economic or security reasons."

The public believes that the United States has a vital interest in four areas: (1) the Western Hemisphere, for reasons of geographic proximity; (2) Western Europe, where the United States has strong cultural and economic ties, as well as security interests vis-à-vis the Soviet Union; (3) Japan and China, where we have important security and economic interests; and (4) the Middle East, including Israel, Egypt, and the Arab oil-producing countries.

It is notable that, with the single exception of Taiwan, opinion leaders are more likely to see a vital American interest everywhere. That is a fact of no small importance. It helps explain why the public often resists claims that some sort of international commitment is "vital" to American interests.

As for the public's attitude toward the rest of the world, only a few countries elicit strongly positive or negative reactions: Canada and Britain are at the top of the scale; Iran, Cuba, and the Soviet Union are at the bottom. Other countries — including two communist countries, Poland and China — tend to cluster around the fifty-degree mark, which is to say, neutral. Only Canada and Britain (and, less clearly, Japan) are identified as close allies. Only Iran and the Soviet Union (and, less clearly, Cuba) are identified as enemies. Most of the rest of the world is seen as "friendly." The designation "not friendly" seems reserved for places that, for one reason or another, have caused trouble for the United States: Lebanon, El Salvador, Nicaragua, Libya, and Syria.

Despite the absence of strong feelings about many allies, there is no evidence that the public's commitment to the North Atlantic Treaty Organization (NATO) has diminished; actually, public support for NATO has tended to increase since 1974. Majorities have consistently favored maintaining or increasing the United States commitment to NATO. The size of those majorities rose from 54 percent in 1974 to 67 percent in 1978 and 1982 in the Chicago Council surveys. The proportion who wanted to decrease our commitment dropped slightly, from 20 percent in 1974 to 13 percent in 1978 and 15 percent in 1982. The public's growing security consciousness after 1974 has apparently manifested itself in a stronger commitment to the Atlantic Alliance, despite the trend of declining internationalism.

TABLE 2–3. Friend or Foe: The American Public's Choice

Here is how the American public and opinion leaders feel about other countries, based on surveys in 1982 by the Chicago Council on Foreign Relations (favorability and vital interest) and in 1983–1984 by Louis Harris and Associates Inc. (allies, friends, and enemies):

	Public favorability (scale of 0–100)	U.S. has a vital interest		Percent describing country as			
		Public	Leaders	Close ally	Friendly	Not friendly	Enemy
Canada	74	82%	95%	64	32	1	1
Great Britain	68	80	97	57	34	3	2
France	60	58	84	23	57	13	1
Mexico	60	74	98	34	56	6	1
West Germany	59	76	98	33	45	11	3
Israel	55	75	92	35	46	11	3
Italy	55	35	79	17	62	11	1
Brazil	54	45	80	—	—	—	—
Japan	53	82	97	46	44	4	2
Poland	52	43	47	—	—	—	—
Egypt	52	66	90	21	56	11	2
Saudi Arabia	52	77	93	13	47	21	8

TABLE 2–3. (Continued)

Taiwan	49	51	44	—	—	—	—
India	48	30	57	—	—	—	16
China	47	64	87	6	44	29	4
Jordan	47	41	67	9	43	24	16
Lebanon	46	55	74	5	28	40	—
South Africa	45	38	54	—	—	—	4
South Korea	44	43	66	30	44	12	—
Nigeria	44	32	53	—	—	—	—
Philippines	—	—	—	28	56	8	1
Panama	—	—	—	16	51	20	2
Colombia	—	—	—	8	50	15	3
Venezuela	—	—	—	7	44	19	4
Argentina	—	—	—	7	40	32	6
El Salvador	—	—	—	7	25	41	15
Syria	42	36	46	4	23	39	12
Libya	—	—	—	4	18	36	26
Nicaragua	—	—	—	4	16	47	22
Iran	28	51	60	1	7	34	50
Cuba	27	—	—	3	9	43	41
Soviet Union	26	—	—	2	5	36	54

SOURCE: Reprinted by permission of the Chicago Council of Foreign Relations and Louis Harris and Associates Inc.

What about policies that have caused friction among the Atlantic allies? The 1982 survey asked people whether they thought the United States should put diplomatic pressure on its allies or apply economic sanctions if they refused to go along with the American boycott of the Soviet natural gas pipeline to Western Europe. Only 15 percent of the public favored economic sanctions, but 27 percent endorsed diplomatic pressure. A plurality, 37 percent, felt that the United States should let its allies pursue whatever policies they thought best. An additional 21 percent said they did not know what the United States should do. These findings suggest that Americans are not zealous supporters of policies to pressure American allies.

Perhaps even more revealing is the scarcity of survey data concerning this country's relations with its allies. Pollsters are tireless in their efforts to probe every aspect of public opinion on timely and controversial subjects, whether or not the public really has clearly thought-out views. Hence the abundance of data on SALT II (1978–79) and on the nuclear freeze (1982–83). The fact that the Atlantic Alliance is seldom the subject of polling inquiries can be taken as evidence that it is not an issue of major interest or controversy. The few questions that have been asked about alliance policy, such as the pipeline question, do not evince strong opinions. In a 1983 Gallup poll, the public opposed the prospect of West European neutralism by the considerably less than overwhelming margin of 45 to 41 percent. By another modest margin, 45 to 31 percent, the public favored deploying medium-range nuclear missiles in Western Europe. Beyond the ranks of foreign policy specialists, alliance relationships are not matters of serious concern. This does not mean that the public does not support the Atlantic Alliance. It does, quite strongly, as the evidence showed. It is not, however, an issue of major public attention or political debate.

Interventionism

On November 4, 1979, Iranian student revolutionaries stormed the American embassy in Teheran and took sixty American hostages. Within the next few weeks, President Jimmy Carter's popularity rose almost twenty points. It was not until six months later, in June 1980, that Carter's job rating fell back to where it had been before the hostage crisis. The dual crisis in Lebanon and Grenada at the end of October 1983 — almost exactly four years after the Iranian hostage crisis — had a similar effect on President Reagan's popularity, which jumped above the 50-percent mark for the first time since 1981. Americans always "rally around the flag" during a time of military crisis. In Carter's case, the effect wore off after a few months. In Reagan's case, the effect was sustained all the way through the 1984 presidential election. If intervention is not popular, and if Reagan's aggressiveness was a cause of concern to the electorate, how did he manage to turn these issues to his advantage?

Grenada is a textbook example of the kind of foreign policy action likely to win the public's approval. If a vital national interest is at stake, Americans want to take action that is swift, decisive, and relatively cost-free. The polls all indicated strong support for the president's dispatch of American troops to Grenada (71 to 22 percent in the November 1983 ABC News/*Washington Post* poll, for example). Protecting American lives was the most widely accepted justification for the action. Respondents to a CBS News/*New York Times* poll agreed, 50 to 35 percent, that the United States had invaded Grenada "mainly to protect the Americans living there" rather than to overthrow a Marxist government. Respondents to the Gallup/*Newsweek* poll agreed by a five to four margin that American troops should leave Grenada "as soon as the safety of Americans is assured" rather than wait until "a democratic government is capable of running the country."

The principal reason for the popularity of the Grenada intervention was that it worked. The public is not eager to take similar action in Nicaragua, which President Reagan has also described as a Marxist dictatorship that threatens this country's vital interests. In the CBS/*Times* poll taken just after the Grenada episode, respondents were told that "the Reagan Administration says the United States should help people in Nicaragua who are trying to overthrow the pro-Soviet government there." The public opposed such assistance, three to one.

Grenada was an action of dubious legitimacy in terms of international law and diplomacy. It was widely criticized by other countries, including America's closest allies, as an act of aggression. The American presence in Lebanon, however, was accepted as legitimate and necessary by virtually the entire international community. In domestic politics, these evaluations were reversed. The Grenada invasion was seen by most Americans as legitimate and necessary. The American presence in Lebanon, however, was deeply controversial. Lebanon is a good example of the kind of military action Americans are likely to oppose — one that is protracted, inconclusive, and tragically costly.

A majority of the public did not feel that the American government had clear goals in Lebanon. Americans feared that the United States would become involved in a larger war in the Middle East, to the extent that, by three to two, the public opposed military retaliation to punish those responsible for the terrorist attack on American Marines "if it means risking a larger war." Although most people thought the Marines had "a worthwhile mission" in Lebanon, they did not believe the mission had been successful (62 to 29 percent said it was not) and they were skeptical that the United States could actually carry out its peacekeeping mission (46 to 42 percent felt we could not).

Americans approved of the Grenada intervention on pragmatic grounds, and they opposed keeping American troops in Lebanon on exactly the same grounds — not that it was wrong but rather that it was clearly not working. That is essentially why the American failure in Lebanon never materialized as a 1984 campaign issue. Reagan did what the public wanted him to do, namely, get out. The *Los Angeles Times* poll showed 38 percent citing the Middle East as a major foreign policy issue in February 1984, before the Marines were withdrawn. By October, only 7 percent expressed concern about the Middle East, and Reagan was rated fourteen points ahead of Mondale on the issue.

These findings suggest why public opinion on Central America has been so exasperating to policymakers. The public agrees that a communist regime in Central America represents a threat to the vital interests of the United States. But the public refuses to draw the conclusion that military support for Nicaraguan "freedom fighters" is the best way to counter such a threat. To most Americans, that kind of policy does not sound like decisive action to protect our national security. It sounds like getting involved in another country's war.

Polls taken in 1985 showed that only about a quarter of the public knew which side the Reagan administration was supporting in Nicaragua. Nevertheless a majority of Americans disapproved of helping the Nicaraguan rebels, two-thirds objected to giving them military aid and three-quarters opposed an American invasion to overthrow the Sandinista regime.

When members of Congress talk about Nicaragua, some like to bring up the example of Cuba, others of Vietnam. These two cases represent very different images of American foreign policy. The Cuban missile crisis is seen by the public as one of the proudest moments in American foreign policy since World War II, whereas Vietnam is indisputably the most shameful.

In Cuba we defined our interests clearly and forcefully and defended them with resolve. And it worked. In Vietnam, we embroiled ourselves in another country's civil war; our purposes were unclear and our methods uncertain. It was a spectacular failure. The message is, if our vital interests really are threatened in Central America, we should act forcefully and decisively to protect them, as we did in Grenada. To most Americans that does not mean giving millions of dollars in military aid to an unsavory guerrilla movement or sending a detachment of Marines to fight someone else's war.

What would happen if the United States intervened militarily in Nicaragua? First, Democratic party leaders would be shocked, just as they were in Grenada, to see how quickly anti-interventionist sentiment vanished as the public rallied behind the president. Some military leaders have expressed the view that the United States would be able to bring down the Sandinista government, control the population, and install a new government in Managua in a matter of weeks — "like falling off a log," as one of them put it. In that case, Nicaragua would be a major triumph for the administration — Reagan's Falkland Islands.

There is every reason to believe, however, that American intervention would dramatically change the political situation in Central America. The Nicaraguan population, which now appears to be highly critical of the Sandinista government because of economic shortages and the draft, would very likely turn against the foreign intruders and rally to the cause of nationalism and defense of the revolution. Moreover it would be difficult for other Latin American countries to endorse "Yankee imperialism." If the "pacification" of Nicaragua turned out to be difficult or costly, the Republicans would be shocked to see how quickly public opinion turned against the administration.

McGeorge Bundy, who has good reason to remember the lessons of Vietnam, has written, "In my view, the most effective means, for the Caribbean area, was defined by our experience in the Cuban missile crisis. It is our control of the seas that can defeat and reverse any . . . Nicaraguan choice [to move into the Soviet bloc]." Bundy's comments symbolize the difficult, perhaps impossible, problem of American foreign policy in the post-Vietnam era. We want to stop the spread of communism, but only from a safe distance offshore, without getting involved in other countries' problems.

What applies to Nicaragua applies equally to South Africa. According to the polls, Americans have two reactions to the crisis in South Africa. One is a deep aversion to that country's racial policies. The other is a deep aversion to getting involved. In August 1985, the Gallup poll asked people whether their sympathies were "more with the black population or more with the South African government." By over five to one, the public sympathized with South African blacks. Then Gallup asked, "What, if anything, do you think the United States should do next?" By far the largest number — 44 percent — said, "Don't get involved." Only 16 percent mentioned some form of sanctions.

Even though the public finds apartheid repugnant, the polls have never shown widespread support for sanctions. In a poll taken for *Business Week* in early 1985, the public resoundingly disapproved of the apartheid system. Nevertheless the majority was opposed to policies that would bar new bank loans to South Africa or prohibit new American investment there. Two-thirds opposed a trade embargo. Three-quarters did not like the idea of forcing American businesses to close their South African operations.

In June 1985, the CBS News/*New York Times* poll asked people whether the American government should do more to pressure South Africa to give up apartheid; 37 percent said yes, 43 percent said no, and

20 percent had no opinion. The poll showed a 44 to 33 percent margin against American corporations refusing to do business in South Africa to demonstrate their opposition to apartheid. Blacks favored such a policy, but only by a small margin (41 to 35 percent).

Even after the South African government declared a state of emergency in July 1985 and the violence in that country escalated, the American public remained divided. An August *Newsweek* survey found the public split over whether the United States should use economic sanctions against South Africa to increase pressure for a change in its apartheid policies (42 percent for, 39 percent against). CBS News found the same thing (37 percent for, 34 percent against, and 29 percent who "didn't know enough about it to say").

What explains the public's reluctance to back its convictions? The polls revealed some concern that sanctions would end up hurting blacks in South Africa. And many people believed that economic sanctions would not be effective in getting the South African government to change its policies.

But there is another reason. Most Americans do not support sanctions against South Africa, a right-wing regime that has been friendly to the United States. As noted, most Americans also do not favor sanctions against Nicaragua, a left-wing regime that has been bitterly hostile toward the United States. Figure 2–1 shows that the two sentiments are not unrelated: Those who favor American military aid to the anti-government rebels in Nicaragua also support American sanctions against South Africa. The much larger number who oppose aiding the Nicaraguan rebels also oppose sanctions against South Africa.

The American public opposes sanctions against South Africa for the same reason it opposes sanctions against Nicaragua — because it does not

Should the United States do more to pressure South Africa to give up apartheid?

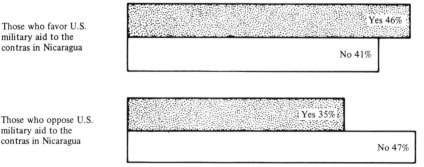

Those who favor U.S. military aid to the contras in Nicaragua — Yes 46%, No 41%

Those who oppose U.S. military aid to the contras in Nicaragua — Yes 35%, No 47%

FIGURE 2–1. Internationalism, Not Ideology

source: CBS News/*The New York Times*, May–June 1985. Copyright © 1985 by The New York Times Company. Reprinted by permission.

want to get involved. That is why President Reagan's policy of limited intervention in Central America has remained unpopular. That is also why the president's policy of constructive engagement in South Africa was surprisingly popular; by 58 to 37 percent, the public felt that "quiet diplomacy," as opposed to stronger action, was the best way to get South Africa to change its policies. The president's imposition of limited economic sanctions in September 1985 — "active constructive engagement," he called it — was enough to satisfy Congress and more than enough to satisfy the American public.

Protectionism

Protectionism is another issue on which liberal/conservative distinctions are fairly meaningless. The polls show little difference between Democrats and Republicans or liberals and conservatives on issues like tariffs and import quotas. The important difference is between informed opinion and uninformed opinion. Informed opinion tends to favor free trade, whereas uninformed opinion is more protectionist. There is evidence, however, that as a result of anger and frustration, informed opinion has been moving in the direction of trade restrictions. Free trade is not working the way it is supposed to. American business and labor are getting hurt, and the argument can be made, it is not really their fault.

The American people believe in the principle of free trade. They understand that it is the best way to organize the international economy. They also appreciate the benefits of free trade to the American consumer. At the same time, Americans support protectionist policies. The public believes that it is in the national interest to protect American business and labor from foreign competition. Americans tend to give priority to protecting the national economy over their own "selfish" interests as consumers.

Since 1973 the Roper Organization has been asking people, "Generally speaking, do you think the government should or should not place restrictions on imports of goods from other countries that are priced lower than American-made goods of the same kind?" Since 1973, people have given the same answer. They favored protectionism by 63 to 27 percent in November 1973, just before the Arab oil embargo and the beginning of the economic crisis of the 1970s. They favored protectionism by about the same margin during the recession of 1975, the recovery of 1977, the hyperinflation of 1979 (when cheap imports ought to have been very appealing), the recession of 1981–1983, and the recovery of 1984. Public support for protectionism seems to have little to do with economic conditions. It is not a matter of economic interest but rather of right and wrong: It is wrong for consumers to benefit from cheap imports at the cost of American jobs.

Over forty years ago, economist Joseph Schumpeter wrote, "The consistent support given by the American people to protectionist policy, whenever they had the opportunity to speak their minds, is accounted for not by any love for or domination by big business, but by a fervent wish to build and keep a world of their own and to be rid of all the vicissitudes of the rest of the world." That explanation still appears valid, judging from the constancy of public opinion on the subject.

On trade issues, the best informed people are typically the least protectionist. Polls of "opinion leaders" — business executives, labor leaders, journalists, politicians — have always shown them to be much more supportive of free trade than the general public. The advantages of free trade — lower prices, more jobs in the export sector — seem remote and theoretical, whereas the benefits of protecting ourselves from foreign competition are immediate, practical, and easy to understand.

Protectionism is like rent control or wage and price controls. All are shortsighted but intuitively appealing policies that are enormously popular with average voters. If rents or prices are going up, make them go down. If foreign goods are competing with American goods, keep them out. Nothing complicated about that. What is complicated is the fact that these policies do not work in the long run and have harmful side effects. But there is no reason for the average voter to understand that. To politicians interested only in the short run, these policies are a godsend. They are costless and make a politician look tough and decisive. "No more Mr. Nice Guy," said Vice-President George Bush in defending President Reagan's new trade policy announced in 1985.

What the politician has to contend with, however, is establishment opinion. Whenever a mainstream politician makes a protectionist speech, as John Connally did in 1980 and Walter Mondale did in 1983, the full force of the establishment comes down on him. He is accused by the *Wall Street Journal* and the *New York Times* of "pandering to popular prejudice" and, at the same time, "catering to special interests" (big business in the case of Connally, big labor in the case of Mondale). Politicians like George Wallace and Jesse Jackson, however, do not worry about violating received wisdom or being criticized by the *Wall Street Journal* and the *New York Times*. They are not establishment politicians; they are populists.

What happened in the 1980s is that the establishment consensus on free trade began to crack. The change was most obvious in the case of business executives. In 1980, only 15 percent of executives in a Chamber of Commerce survey favored import restrictions. By 1982, that proportion had more than doubled, to 38 percent. In 1985, 44 percent of executives polled by *Business Week* felt that the United States would have to take protectionist measures "to prevent the Japanese from completely taking over the market in many critical areas."

Moreover, the executives believed the trade deficit was not their fault. When asked to name the reason for the deficit, 64 percent said the strong American dollar. That reason far outweighed trade barriers erected by foreign governments (15 percent), inferior or noncompetitive American products (12 percent), or lack of aggressive American marketing abroad (5 percent). And 85 percent felt that American government policies were at least somewhat responsible for the trade deficit.

If American producers cannot sell their goods abroad or compete with cheap imports, it is not because American business is inefficient or poorly managed. It is because the overvalued dollar makes American products too expensive. Most of the blame lies with the federal government. By failing to control the budget deficit, the government has caused interest rates and dollar values to go up. It has also clung stubbornly to a free trade doctrine that allows other countries to take advantage of us. As Senator Bob Dole put it, "The United States cannot be the world's only free trader any more than we can unilaterally disarm."

Respectable economists are now calling for selective import embargoes, quotas, surcharges, and tariffs. Politicians who were hitherto staunch free traders have been caving in left and right. Dole is one of them, and so is Senator John Glenn, who castigated Walter Mondale for his protectionist stance in the 1984 Democratic presidential primaries.

Respected journalists are joining in. In July 1985, Theodore H. White published a cover story in the *New York Times Magazine* titled "The Danger from Japan." Its tone was bitter and alarmist, its message threatening. "The Japanese share the same peace [as we do], and under our protection, paying little for it, reserve the right to press American livelihoods to the wall. . . . The superlative execution of their trade tactics may provoke an incalculable reaction — as the Japanese might well remember of the course that ran from Pearl Harbor to the deck of the USS *Missouri* in Tokyo Bay just 40 years ago."[5]

That sort of thing was what members of Congress were hearing, not from unemployed workers, but from sophisticated business people and knowledgeable community leaders. In fact most experts agree that unfair trade practices are only a small part of the problem. It is estimated that if the Japanese government were to remove all restrictions on American imports, our balance of trade deficit with Japan would be reduced by only about one-third. Furthermore, protectionist policies by the United States would probably lead to retaliation by foreign countries, loss of jobs in export-related industries, and a resurgence of inflation.

Having failed to make a serious dent in the federal budget deficit, Congress turned to the next available target — foreign trade practices. Japan was an especially inviting target because retaliation could be justified as a defense of free trade; we are punishing the Japanese for erecting trade barriers and unfairly subsidizing their export industries. Essentially the demand for trade retaliation is an expression of frustration by business and an admission of failure by Congress. Although public opinion is sympathetic, popular pressure is not the cause of the protectionist surge.

Arms Control

Americans feel more secure than they did in 1980. That is the principal achievement of President Reagan's defense program. A perhaps unintended consequence of that achievement, however, is that Americans are in the mood for renewed detente. At the end of 1985, the public was more hopeful than it had been in many years about Soviet motives and intentions. At the same time, public confidence in President Reagan's foreign policy leadership continued to climb. The administration's defense buildup convinced Americans that the United States was reaching parity with the Soviet Union, and apprehensiveness about another arms race became widespread as a consequence.

Ironically, because little of substance was accomplished on arms control, the November 1985 summit was regarded by most commentators as a triumph for President Reagan. Gorbachev had an ambitious arms control agenda, but Reagan seemed interested only in achieving "a fresh start." The results were clearly more in line with Reagan's agenda. The most important product of the summit was probably the agreement to continue meeting. That is important for Reagan politically because it demonstrates that the Russians accept him as someone they feel they can deal with.

Just before the summit, according to the *Los Angeles Times,* 77 percent of the public felt that American leaders really wanted to reach an agreement on nuclear weapons — a marked improvement since March 1982, when only 52 percent were of that opinion. Optimism about the Soviet Union had also increased. In 1982, only 23 percent felt that Soviet leaders wanted an arms control agreement; in 1985, that figure had risen to 41 percent. Thus in the public's view, both sides were more prepared to agree in 1985 than they were during Reagan's first term.

One reason is that Americans feel the United States has been catching up to the Soviet Union in military strength. During the late 1970s and through the first year of the Reagan administration, the prevailing view was that the United States was not as strong as the Soviet Union. The Reagan military buildup apparently persuaded many Americans that the United States was getting more "bang for its bucks." The prevailing view in an October 1985 Harris/*Business Week* survey was that the United States and the Soviet Union were about equal in military strength (54 percent); 24 percent said the United States was stronger, and 18 percent said the United States was not as strong as the Russians.

The American public has two conflicting attitudes on the subject of arms control: profound suspicion of the Soviet Union and an equally profound fear of nuclear weapons. As noted, favorable views of the Soviet Union peaked in the early 1970s, when detente prevailed, and then deteriorated sharply. In a 1976 Harris poll, for example, 30 percent of Americans described the Soviet Union as an enemy of the United States. By 1982, that figure had reached 51 percent and by the end of 1984, 54 percent.

There is evidence, however, of some improvement in 1985. In a September *New York Times* poll, 53 percent felt that "the military threat from the Soviet Union is constantly growing and presents a real, immediate danger to the United States." That was down a bit from the 64 percent who felt that way two years earlier, after the Soviet Air Force shot down the Korean Air Lines passenger jet as it flew over Russian territory. By a close margin, 49 to 43 percent in the November 1985 *Los Angeles Times* poll, the public still agreed with President Reagan's characterization of the Soviet Union as "an evil empire that threatens our moral and religious values." The margin had been slightly larger, 55 to 38 percent, in January 1985.

Respondents were also asked whether they thought the United States should "get tougher with Russia, even if that means risking war" or whether we should "be more friendly, even if that means Russia may take advantage of us." The tough line was favored, 41 to 33 percent. But that is considerably closer than the 58 to 19 percent margin who favored a tougher line in November 1983.

The shift shows up most dramatically in a survey carried out just before the summit for *Time* magazine.

— The percentage of Americans who felt that the Soviet Union represents "a very serious threat" to the United States dropped from 52 percent in 1983 to 32 percent at the end of 1985.
— The percentage favoring "a cooperative policy of detente" over "a cold war approach" jumped from 45 percent in 1980 to 65 percent in 1985.

Between two-thirds and three-quarters of the American public still feel that the Russians cannot be trusted to keep their part of any arms control agreement. This does not mean that Americans are unwilling to support such agreements, however. They are clearly willing to take risks for the sake of arms control. Thus a January 1985 ABC News poll reported that, whereas a 72 to 21 percent majority felt the Soviet Union would cheat on a treaty to reduce nuclear arms, an even wider majority, 76 to 18 percent, felt that "the United States should negotiate a nuclear arms limitation agreement even if there is risk that the Soviets would cheat."

The public rejects the notion that the United States should seek military superiority. In a November ABC News/*Washington Post* poll, only 31 percent of the respondents felt that the United States should "spend whatever is necessary to achieve military superiority over the Soviet Union"; 51 percent wanted to spend enough "to be about equal" to the Soviets; and 15 percent said the United States should "limit its military spending even if it means we may fall somewhat behind the Soviet Union in military strength."

The idea of military superiority seems to have lost its attraction under conditions of "mutually assured destruction." When the *Los Angeles Times* asked people who they thought would win a nuclear war between the United States and the Soviet Union, a majority volunteered the answer, "Nobody." Thus, despite continuing distrust of the Soviet Union, those polled favored an agreement to reduce the number of American and Soviet missiles in Europe (68 to 18 percent), a ban on nuclear weapons in outer space (61 to 31 percent), a shutdown of nuclear weapons production (56 to 29 percent), and a moratorium on atomic tests (47 to 44 percent). It is worth noting that, by almost two to one, the public says it would oppose the use of nuclear weapons if the Soviet Union attacked Western Europe with conventional forces "and it looked as if they were going to conquer Europe." That, of course, is the premise behind the Atlantic Alliance.

The principal unresolved issue between the United States and the Soviet Union is Star Wars, the Reagan administration's Strategic Defense Initiative (SDI). It is difficult to say whether the public is for or against SDI. Most of the polls show public opinion closely divided and highly changeable. That is typical when people's understanding is limited and their convictions weak. On issues like this, it is easy for pollsters to sway public opinion by manipulating the wording of their questions.

By examining the polls carefully, however, one can identify the "signals" that move public sentiment one way or the other. Supporters and opponents use this information to fashion messages that will make their case most effectively. Among the findings revealed by the polls are the following:

— Americans are inclined to support SDI if it is described as a defensive system.
— However, the idea of putting nuclear weapons in space makes them very nervous.
— Americans tend to believe the system would be workable.
— But they are very concerned about the cost.
— Americans believe that SDI would make the arms race more dangerous.
— At the same time, they think it would improve the chances for arms control.
— The American public prefers a missile-based defense system to mutually assured destruction.

— But it has the greatest faith in arms control and would prefer an agreement that would ban nuclear weapons from outer space.

The public is somewhat suspicious of the view expressed by President Reagan in August 1985 that SDI offers "a way out of the nuclear dilemma that has confounded mankind for four decades." The Harris poll asked people to respond to the statement, "The only way to avoid nuclear war is to develop new weapons in space and on the ground that can shoot down all nuclear missiles." The public disagreed, 52 to 44 percent.

Several polls taken just before the summit showed a modest increase in public support for SDI. In the ABC News/*Washington Post* poll, for example, the public went from a 48 to 46 percent split on SDI in August to a 55 to 38 percent favorable margin in November. The polls agree on another point as well: Americans are willing to give up SDI in return for serious arms control. In the ABC/*Washington Post* poll, 71 percent felt it was "more important" for the United States to agree to a "substantial reduction of nuclear weapons" than to build a nuclear defense system. CBS News and the *New York Times* asked people to choose between developing the space-based defense system and negotiating arms reductions; by 53 to 33 percent, the public preferred arms reductions.

It is clear that Americans prefer arms control to advanced technology. One reason is their concern over defense spending. The public's preferred solution to the federal deficit crisis is to limit defense spending. Table 2–1 reveals that the proportion of Americans who feel we are spending too much on defense — 40 percent in 1985 — is higher than it has been since at least 1973. Only 14 percent felt we were spending too little on defense. In fact, as President Reagan has grown more popular, the drift of sentiment on spending issues has moved away from him. A new arms control agreement would create strong political pressure to cut military spending. As Reagan is undoubtedly aware, that has happened every time the United States has negotiated an arms control treaty in the past. It may help to explain the president's insistence on moving very slowly toward a new agreement.

The Two Reagans

Electing Ronald Reagan in 1980 was a departure for the United States. Americans do not usually elect ideological candidates. They are too divisive, too extreme, too threatening. We prefer "safe" centrists and compromisers like Lyndon Johnson and Richard Nixon and Jimmy Carter. But candidates like Barry Goldwater, George McGovern, George Wallace, and Jesse Jackson often elicit admiration, even if they do not get many votes. What people admire about them is that they are not typical politicians — they say what they believe. Americans took a chance with Reagan because, in 1980, the country desperately wanted leadership. His ideology gave Reagan the image of a leader, a man of strong convictions and principles (unlike, say, Jimmy Carter). The reason it has worked out is that Reagan is not a typical ideologue. He seldom acts on his ideology, and so, over the years, the public has come to feel less and less threatened by him.

The secret of President Reagan's success is his ability to have his cake and eat it too. He defines his program in bold, uncompromising terms and then proceeds to play the cautious, moderate politician, bargaining for the best deal he can get. Throughout his presidency, Reagan's failure to carry out the most controversial elements of his program has saved him politically and has allowed his coalition to hold together. Some 60 percent of the public, according to a 1985 Harris poll, approve of having a Republican president and a Democratic Congress because that prevents the president from doing all the things he wants to do. Unfortunately there is no such separation of powers in the British parliamentary system. Prime Minister Margaret Thatcher did just about everything she wanted to do and lost considerable support after her government's 1983 victory.

President Reagan has accepted budget compromises year after year and then attacked Congress for not keeping spending under control. His tax reform proposal did not go nearly as far as "supply-siders" wanted. Reagan antagonized neoconservatives by talking a tough line on foreign policy and then failing to act on it. Commentators like George Will and Norman Podhoretz were enraged by the president's cautious response to the Korean Air Lines passenger jet incident in 1983 and by his failure to retaliate after the Beirut hostage crisis in 1985.

Having characterized the Soviet Union as "an evil empire" and its leaders as willing to lie and cheat in order to gain an advantage, Reagan described Soviet General Secretary Mikhail Gorbachev after the November 1985 summit as "just as sincere as we are" in his commitment to peace. For weeks during the summer of 1985, Reagan defended the apartheid regime in South Africa and declared that his administration's policy of constructive engagement was working. Then in September, when the pressure from Congress became inexorable, the president abruptly reversed course and signed an executive order imposing sanctions against the South African government. Very few people attacked him for inconsistency. Instead it was seen as a brilliant political stroke that undercut his critics.

President Reagan also dismays Moral Majoritarians by endorsing their social issue agenda and then doing little to implement it. On such issues as abortion and school prayer, he usually lets the controversial Senator Jesse Helms of North Carolina lead the fight in Congress, a tactic that virtually ensures defeat. In the end, Reagan manages to have it both ways. Religious fundamentalists continue to support him, but he is careful not to do anything that would alienate upper-middle-class suburbanites and yuppies — constituencies that like his fiscal conservatism but feel threatened by right-wing social and foreign policies. Reagan's failure to act on the Moral Majority's social agenda, as well as on the neoconservatives' foreign policy agenda and the supply-siders' economic agenda, has been a key factor in his success.

Democrats are often confounded by the fact that there are two Ronald Reagans — one, a passionate ideologue and the other, a pragmatic politician. Many believe that his political success demonstrates the appeal of his ideology. The argument of this chapter is that, to a large extent, President Reagan has succeeded in spite of, not because of, his ideological inclinations.

President Reagan has succeeded in restoring the nation's sense of military security and in convincing the American public that he is sincerely committed to peace and arms control. There is, however, little evidence of any surge of internationalist or interventionist sentiment. American public opinion remains more or less the same as it has been for 200 years — fundamentally noninternationalist. The American public judges foreign policy by the same standards as it judges domestic policy, that is, whether it works. The principal anomaly of public opinion during the Reagan era is that, although there is little evidence of any drift to the right in the electorate's views and policy preferences, the public shows increasing confidence in President Reagan's leadership and in his party's program.[6] Americans are pragmatists; if it works, pragmatists say, it must be right.

Reagan's foreign policy has followed the principles of conservative internationalism but with more emphasis on conservatism than on internationalism. Liberals and Democrats are in the awkward position of criticizing what the president might do, or what he says he might do, more than what he has actually done. The Reagan foreign policy also faces criticism within the Republican party from those who favor a more aggressive application of the Reagan Doctrine. More often then not, these right-wing criticisms are directed at the State Department and the "pragmatists" who influence the president rather than at the president himself. Thus there is little reason to believe that the success of Reagan's foreign policy has healed the ideological division among political activists, either by pulling Democrats to the right or Republicans to the center.

It is interventionism more than any other single issue that divides liberal and conservative internationalists. On this issue, conservatives occupy the moral high ground by identifying the United States with the cause of worldwide freedom and democracy. Liberals are vulnerable to charges of isolationism and anti-Americanism because of their tendency to question American purposes abroad.[7] Liberals, however, can claim the advantage of caution and realism in appealing to an electorate that is fundamentally suspicious of all internationalist objectives.

The American public appreciates a strong dose of moralism in its foreign policy. That is why Jimmy Carter scored points in 1976 by seizing on the human rights theme to attack the cynicism and casuistry of Henry Kissinger's diplomacy. Nevertheless, Richard Nixon is still rated the best president since World War II for handling foreign affairs, and the realism of Kissinger's balance-of-power diplomacy is still widely admired. Reagan has skillfully managed to combine Carter's moralism with the kind of caution and pragmatism associated with Kissinger.

That is an unbeatable combination, but it is difficult to see the Reagan Doctrine becoming the basis of a new foreign policy consensus as the Truman Doctrine did forty years ago. The ideological forces in American politics today are too strong. Success generates popularity, but it does not convince ideologues. To an ideologue, a policy that is wrong cannot work, even if it does work. Too many activists on the left and right believe Reagan's policies are wrong, either in conception or in application. In sum, the Reagan foreign policy must be judged a political success, but not one that is likely to be institutionalized beyond the Reagan presidency.

" 'Rambo' and Reality: Having It Both Ways" was written for this volume. Copyright © 1987 by William Schneider.

Notes

1. Ralph B. Levering, *The Public and American Foreign Policy*, 1918–1978 (New York: William Morrow & Co., 1978), p. 104.
2. Michael Mandelbaum and William Schneider, "The New Internationalisms: Public Opinion and Foreign Policy," in Kenneth Oye, Donald Rothchild, and Robert Lieber, eds., *Eagle Entangled: U.S. Foreign Policy in a Complex World* (New York: Longman, 1979), pp. 40–63.
3. John E. Mueller, *War, Presidents and Public Opinion* (New York: Wiley, 1973), pp. 122–140.
4. Ernest R. May, "The Cold War," manuscript prepared for Joseph S. Nye, Jr., ed., *The Making of America's Soviet Policy* (New Haven: Yale University Press, 1984).
5. Theodore H. White, "The Danger from Japan," *New York Times Magazine*, July 28, 1985, p. 59.
6. See, for instance, R. W. Apple, Jr., "President Highly Popular in Poll; No Ideological Shift is Discerned," *New York Times*, January 28, 1986, p. A1.
7. See, for instance, Charles Krauthammer, "The Poverty of Realism." *The New Republic*, February 17, 1986, pp. 14–22.

II

Functional Problems

3

Reagan Administration Defense Policy: Departure from Containment

Barry R. Posen and Stephen W. Van Evera

During its first term, the Reagan administration embarked on the largest American military buildup since the Korean war. This chapter explores the motives behind the buildup and asks whether it was necessary and well directed.

Between 1981 and 1985, American defense spending grew by 32 percent in real terms, from $199 billion to $264 billion in constant 1986 dollars, and the administration has announced plans for another $96 billion increase in defense spending by 1990, for a net 1981 to 1990 real increase of 82 percent. The share of the American gross national product (GNP) devoted to defense grew from 5.2 percent in 1980 to 6.6 percent in 1985 and will rise to 7.5 percent by 1990 if the Reagan program is implemented.[1] Further substantial budget increases will be required after 1990 to operate and maintain the new arsenal.[2]

Thus far the debate over this buildup has focused on the merits and demerits of specific weapons and programs. By contrast, we believe that to assess the administration buildup we must first clarify and evaluate the grand strategy that guides administration programs. Basic questions must be explored: What fundamental goals does the administration seek to achieve? What specific missions must the American military be able to perform to achieve these goals? Is the strategy embodied by these goals and missions feasible and realistic? Does it adequately protect American national interests? Does it avoid unnecessary expense and danger?

Barry R. Posen is Associate Professor of Political Science at MIT. He is the author of The Sources of Military Doctrine *(Cornell University Press, 1984), which won the American Political Science Association Woodrow Wilson Foundation Award and the Edgar S. Furniss, Jr. Award.*

Stephen W. Van Evera is Managing Editor of International Security.

Once national strategy is clarified — national goals and the military capabilities required to achieve them are defined — the strategy can be evaluated by assessing its feasibility, its safety (i.e., its effect on the probabilities of war and escalation), the degree of protection it offers vital national interests, and the efficiency with which it provides this protection.

A clearly defined strategy also allows us to judge the adequacy of national military forces, to identify areas of military weakness and excess, and to establish overall defense needs. If national strategy is clear, we can measure the adequacy of national military forces by asking whether they can carry out this strategy. We can also identify areas of weakness and excess by measuring the shortfall or surplus of capability needed to execute required military missions. Without a clear strategy, however, it becomes much more difficult to establish defense requirements and to evaluate defense policies.

One shortcoming in the Reagan defense program lies with the administration's failure to specify the strategy the buildup supports. Administration policymakers have apparently developed internal agreement on strategy, but administration statements describing its strategy leave many important questions unanswered. Secretary of Defense Caspar Weinberger's *Annual Report to the Congress*, the primary public documents explaining the buildup, have not specified roles and missions required by the administration's strategy, and have failed to specify shortfalls between current American capabilities and required missions. Indeed, these reports reveal a reluctance to clarify strategy, as signified by the secretary's rejection of "arbitrary and facile" estimates of the number of contingencies for which American forces must prepare.[3]

This failure to frame the national strategy leaves Congress and the public without adequate criteria by which to judge whether the proposed buildup is necessary or appropriate. As a result, the quality of the national defense debate is diminished. This harms the overall coherence and quality of national defense policy.

A second, more fundamental problem with the Reagan defense program lies in the extravagant and dangerous nature of the hidden strategy the administration has adopted. Despite the ambiguity of administration pronouncements, the main elements of its strategy can be deduced from press leaks describing secret administration planning documents, from the shape of administration military programs, and from a close reading of official statements. This implicit strategy is the most expansive and demanding strategy adopted by any administration since Eisenhower's. Its requirements substantially exceed those suggested by the original logic of the American policy of Soviet containment, as this logic was developed by the formulators of American containment policy in the 1940s. The new Reagan strategy embraces more and harder missions than a pure containment strategy would require, and it puts more emphasis on offensive missions and tactics.

This demanding new strategy generates administration claims that American forces are dangerously weak and pushes the Reagan defense budget upward. Yet the prima facie case in favor of the new Reagan strategy seems weak. Before the buildup proceeds, therefore, its strategic foundation deserves careful scrutiny.

The next section describes the premises of the original Cold War strategy of containment and the four military missions that logically emanate from that strategy. This is followed by an assessment of the capacity of current NATO forces to execute these missions. The second section then outlines three additional missions implicit in Reagan administration statements and programs, and the third and fourth sections discuss public misconceptions about Western military strength and suggest conclusions and implications.

United States Strategy and Capabilities

Containment and United States Strategy

The United States was motivated to contain Soviet expansion after World War II largely by the same concern that had earlier drawn it into war: the need to preserve the political division of industrial Eurasia. Other concerns also affected American decision making, but were much less important. American policymakers recognized that any state controlling the entire Eurasian landmass would command more industrial power than the United States. Such a state, they feared, could distill more military power from its national economy and thus could threaten the United States, even across the Atlantic. These policymakers accordingly concluded that the United States should strive to contain any state that threatened to gain hegemony in Eurasia, as the Soviet Union appeared to do in 1946–1947. Similar considerations had impelled the United States to check German expansion in 1917 and in 1941 and had earlier drawn Britain to contain the expansion of Napoleonic France and Czarist Russia.

These concerns were voiced by the principal intellectual architects of containment, such as George Kennan and Walter Lippmann, and by other government officials.[4] Kennan summarized his thinking in these terms[5]:

> It (is) essential to us, as it was to Britain, that no single Continental land power should come to dominate the entire Eurasian landmass. Our interest has lain rather in the maintenance of some sort of stable balance among the powers of the interior, in order that none of them should effect the subjugation of the others, conquer the seafaring fringes of the landmass, become a great sea power as well as land power, shatter the

position of England, and enter — as in these circumstances it certainly would — on an overseas expansion hostile to ourselves and supported by the immense resources of the interior of Europe and Asia.

Kennan identified five important military/industrial regions: the Soviet Union, the Rhine valley, the British Isles, Japan, and the United States.[6] He advised that America strive to maintain a political division among the other four regions. In practice this suggested an anti-Soviet containment policy focused on Europe, since in the late 1940s the Soviet Union was the only plausible candidate for Eurasian hegemony, and Western Europe was the only major industrial region immediately threatened by Soviet power.

Containment and its attendant European commitment were sold to the American people through the crusading image of a battle between "slave" and "free" worlds. The logic behind containment, however, would have required American opposition to Soviet expansion even if the Soviet Union had abandoned communism for democracy. Conversely, the logic of containment did not require a general crusade against indigenous leftist forces around the world unless the success of these leftist forces would have significantly enhanced Soviet power. Containment logic specifically suggested that leftist movements be opposed (1) if they threatened to capture economic or military assets that could significantly augment Soviet power and (2) if they could be expected to subordinate their captured assets to the Soviet Union. As Kennan and Lippmann noted, however, indigenous leftist movements in the Third World seldom threatened to seize areas of much industrial importance and could often be weaned from the Soviets by accommodative Western policies. Rather, Kennan and Lippman advised, containment should focus on Europe, where the real stakes and the real threat were to be found.

The logic behind containment also suggested that the United States should pursue defensive rather than offensive goals in Europe, since the aims of containment could be achieved simply by preserving the existing Eurasian balance of power. Neither an American hegemony in Eurasia nor the destruction of Soviet power was required. Hence Kennan and Lippman opposed offensive "rollback" policies against the Soviet Union.

Lastly, containment logic suggested that the European states should help carry the weight of NATO's defense burdens. These states had to be protected precisely because their latent economic strength endowed them with great latent military power. Once European economic power was restored, with the help of the American postwar economic recovery program, Europe could meet most of its own defense requirements.

The development of large nuclear arsenals on both sides since 1945 has dramatically changed the strategic situation, but the basic logic of containment still holds. Eurasia now produces 63 percent of gross world product; the United States produces only 24 percent.[7] Therefore, as in 1946, a hegemonic Eurasian superstate could outproduce and outarm the United States. These realities require that the United States continue to prevent the formation of such a superstate. The Soviet Union remains the only plausible candidate for Eurasian hegemony and, hence, remains the object of containment.

The chief purpose of containment still resides in ensuring the independence of Western Europe and Japan from Soviet control, although now, because of Western European and Japanese dependence on Persian Gulf oil, the Persian Gulf must also be defended. The nuclear revolution now requires that these regions be defended in a manner that avoids nuclear war and that prevents any initial use of nuclear weapons from escalating to a wholesale strategic exchange. However, American security still requires their defense. The logic of sharing the military burdens of containment with Western Europe and Japan has been reinforced by their economic recovery. (As noted, the European and Japanese economies now collectively outproduce those of both the Soviet Union and the United States, giving them great potential military strength.)

Applied to current circumstances and adapted to the nuclear revolution, the logic of containment suggests a specific requirement for four principal American military capabilities. These missions were not specified by containment's formulators, but follow directly from the premises they delineated.

First, American strategic nuclear forces must be capable of inflicting unacceptable damage on the Soviet Union even after a Soviet first strike against American forces, in order to deter a Soviet nuclear attack on the United States and its allies. This capability discourages the Soviets from launching a nuclear war against NATO, and also would deter the Soviet Union from escalating a local conventional or limited nuclear war to a large-scale nuclear war.[8]

Second, NATO forces must be able to thwart a conventional Soviet invasion of Western Europe with conventional weapons. (A strategy that relied on defending Europe solely with nuclear weapons would pose an unacceptably high risk of all-out nuclear war involving the United States.)

Third, Western conventional forces must stand ready to prevent a Soviet seizure of the Persian Gulf oilfields.

Fourth, American conventional forces must be able to cope with peripheral threats to American interests while these core containment interests are protected. For instance, the United States might need to defend Israel from Arab attack, in the unlikely event that Israeli defenses fail catastrophically. The United States also might need to protect Persian Gulf oil traffic from Iranian or other regional threats, or it might need to defend South Korea from another North Korean attack. The capability to fight such peripheral wars is not specifically required by containment. The United States does have additional interests beyond containment, however, and these interests must be protected while containment is pursued.

If Japan were threatened with invasion, its defense would create a fifth mission requirement, since Japan now possesses great industrial strength. The direct Soviet threat to Japan is minimal today, so an American containment policy is left with these four principal military tasks.

United States Military Capabilities

The administration has sold its buildup to the American public by warning of serious American military weakness. During his first term, President Reagan declared that, "in virtually every measure of military power the Soviet Union enjoys a decided advantage," and he later warned that the United States is "well behind the Soviet Union in literally every kind of offensive weapon, both conventional and in strategic weapons."[9] Defense Secretary Weinberger has pointed to "serious deficiencies" and "major weaknesses" in American defenses and warned of "our collective failure to pursue an adequate balance of military strength," while the Soviets pursued "the greatest buildup of military power seen in modern times."[10]

The best evidence, however, indicates that American forces were capable of executing the four basic containment missions in the early 1980s, and can do so today. The administration's more pessimistic view of American capabilities rests on the hidden assumption that more missions are demanded or that American allies will not help to carry them out.

Given the total size of the NATO defense effort, NATO forces *should* be capable of achieving their basic missions. The NATO states have roughly as many men under arms as the Warsaw Pact (5.0 versus 5.1 million)[11] and spend more money on defense than do the Pact states. The latest American government figures show NATO substantially outspending the Pact ($440 to $340 billion in 1985, a 29 percent NATO advantage).[12] About 15 percent of the Soviet defense effort is directed toward China. If this Soviet effort is deducted, American government figures show a NATO spending lead of 49 percent. These numbers are based on rough estimates rather than precise calculations, but they suggest the approximate size of total assets invested on both sides.

Some analysts, moreover, suggest that official American figures exaggerate Soviet spending and understate allied spending. One analysis indicates that government figures underestimate Western European NATO spending by perhaps 22 percent.[13] If so, NATO outspends the Pact by 41 percent, or by 66 percent if Soviet forces facing China are deducted. Another expert has guessed that the CIA may exaggerate Soviet spending by as much as 25 to 30 percent. If so, NATO outspends the Pact by about 60 percent, and by a larger margin, if Soviet forces facing China are deducted.[14]

These figures indicate that NATO has the personnel and the resources to defend itself. If NATO forces are weak, therefore, this reflects mistaken force posture, doctrine, and choice of weapons, not inadequate defense spending. A detailed look moreover reveals that NATO forces probably can perform all their basic containment missions.

United States Strategic Nuclear Capabilities. American strategic nuclear forces consist of a triad of 1009 intercontinental ballistic missiles (ICBMs) based in the United States; 688 submarine-launched ballistic missiles (SLBMs) carried in nuclear-powered submarines; and 315 strategic bombers, which carry nuclear gravity bombs, nuclear-tipped cruise missiles, and short-range attack missiles.[15] These strategic forces consume only about one-sixth of the American defense budget, with the rest going to conventional forces, but they are the most powerful and important American military forces.

The Soviets also have a triad of 1398 ICBMs, 979 SLBMs, and 170 bombers.[16] Because more American missiles have multiple independently targetable reentry vehicles (MIRVs), which carry more than one warhead, American strategic forces carry more warheads (11,160 to the Soviets' 10,084)[17]; Soviet warheads, however, are bigger, so the Soviet force carries more total explosive power.[18]

The administration warns the public that American strategic forces are dangerously weak. President Reagan declares that Soviet strategic forces have a "definite margin of superiority" over American forces,[19] while Defense Secretary Weinberger warns that the Soviets hold a "degree of superiority and strategic edge" in strategic nuclear capability that "will last for some years through the decade, even if we pursue all the programs the president has sought."[20]

In fact, the strength of American strategic nuclear forces depends on the missions they are expected to perform. These strategic forces could easily destroy the Soviet Union as a modern society even after absorbing a Soviet first strike. An estimated 3550 American strategic nuclear warheads, carrying an explosive power of 1060 equivalent megatons,[21] could survive a Soviet surprise attack and be used against the Soviet Union.[22] These warheads carry enough destructive power to destroy Soviet society several times over.[23] This gives the United States much more than a "second-strike countervalue capability" (the capacity to inflict "unacceptable damage" on Soviet population and industry even after absorbing a Soviet nuclear first strike).

The United States, however, has much less than a "first strike counterforce capability" (the capacity to mount a first strike that leaves remaining Soviet forces incapable of inflicting "unacceptable damage" on the American population and industry). Nor do American forces have a "second strike counterforce" capability (the capacity to absorb a Soviet first strike, and then render remaining Soviet nuclear forces incapable of inflicting unacceptable damage on the remaining American population and industry). Even after a surprise American first strike, the Soviet Union could deliver an estimated 820 warheads, carrying some 540 equivalent megatons, in retaliation against American cities. Such a force could easily destroy American society several times over. The Soviets could also deliver hundreds of megatons against American cities following a Soviet first strike against American forces and an American counterstrike against Soviet forces.[24]

In sum, American forces could not prevent the Soviets from devastating the American population and industry after an American first strike, or after an American mid-war strike against Soviet reserve nuclear forces; but they could utterly destroy the Soviet Union in retaliation after a Soviet first strike. Thus overall American counterforce capability — the ability to destroy Soviet retaliatory capability — is minimal, whereas American retaliatory capability is enormous. Neither side can disarm the other, and both sides can retaliate with tremendous power.

This situation reflects the basic attributes of nuclear weapons. They are powerful, cheap, small, light, easily hidden, easily protected, and easily delivered. As a result, a second-strike countervalue capability is very cheap and easy to maintain, whereas counterforce capabilities are virtually impossible to achieve under any known technology. It is much more difficult to find new ways to destroy enemy warheads than it is for the enemy to find new ways to protect them. The "cost-exchange ratio" — the ratio of the cost of producing a capability to the cost of neutralizing it — lies very heavily in favor of second-strike countervalue capabilities and against counterforce capabilities. As a result, *neither* superpower can deny the other a second-strike countervalue capability, and the notion that either superpower could gain a militarily meaningful "margin of superiority" is an illusion.

American retaliatory forces do suffer one serious weakness: The American strategic command, control, communications, and intelligence (C^3I) apparatus is relatively vulnerable and would degrade quickly — in a matter of hours or a very few days — in a general thermonuclear war.[25] As a result, the United States could not use its strategic forces in a controlled or discriminating fashion in wartime, and American leaders would face wartime pressures to escalate before the American command apparatus disintegrated. Any general thermonuclear war would therefore be very difficult to control. The American C^3I system, however, could transmit a simple order to retaliate to a large portion of the American force, even after a Soviet surprise attack, and this force could inflict enormous damage on Soviet society.[26] The United States also could eventually reconstitute its command apparatus and could retaliate at that point. Despite the frailty of the American C³I, then, the Soviets cannot escape extreme punishment if they attack.

Other threats to American retaliatory forces also may eventually emerge, so the United States cannot afford to stand still. The Soviet Union invests heavily in counterforce nuclear forces, and American strategic forces must be continuously modernized to cope with these Soviet threats to American second-strike capabilities as they emerge. Increasingly accurate Soviet ICBMs are now threatening American ICBMs, and improving Soviet air defense capabilities may eventually threaten the penetration capability of American strategic bombers. As a result, some improvement or replacement of current ICBMs and bombers will be required to keep American second-strike capability at current levels.[27] More importantly, steps should be taken to strengthen the American C³I. These improvements should not be made in panic, however, since American forces certainly can retaliate effectively today.

Western Europe. It is commonly assumed that Warsaw Pact conventional forces could quickly overrun Western Europe in a conventional war. Admiral James D. Watkins, former Chief of Naval Operations, asserts that the Soviets have a "massive ground force advantage" against NATO in Europe, and former Secretary of State Alexander Haig has warned that the United States must "triple the size of its armed forces and put its economy on a war footing" before NATO can defend Europe successfully.[28] The Committee on the Present Danger earlier noted "a near consensus on the inadequacy of present NATO forces to defend Western Europe successfully with conventional arms."[29]

In fact, NATO conventional forces in Europe could probably thwart a Pact conventional attack today and could have done so when the Reagan administration took office in 1981. A NATO defeat would be possible, especially if NATO leaders failed to order mobilization of NATO forces promptly on receiving warning of Soviet mobilization.[30] The odds, however, favor NATO. NATO forces probably could not crush Pact attackers decisively, but they could deny the Soviets a quick victory and thereby turn the conflict into a long war of attrition.[31]

NATO would be likely to win because Pact forces probably lack the superiority in firepower and manpower necessary to overcome the natural advantage held by the defender and to compensate for the obstacles that West German geography poses. Official government statistics give the Pact only a slender manpower and material advantage in Central Europe — between 15 and 20 percent in total manpower and 20 percent in total ground firepower (that is, firepower in all NATO and Pact army formations available in the European theater).[32] These statistics, more-over, may undercount NATO firepower because they omit some NATO weapons not organized into divisions or held as reserves and because they do not take into account the greater NATO investment in division-al command, control, and intelligence hardware and staff and in logisti-cal support, which increase the effectiveness of NATO firepower. If these factors are included, the Pact advantage on the ground may disap-pear.[33]

Furthermore, NATO leads the Pact in tactical airpower, so NATO forces may hold an overall firepower advantage when tactical airpower is included in estimates. Total NATO tactical aircraft in Europe can carry vastly more payload than Pact aircraft, delivering triple the aggregate payload of Pact aircraft at distances of 100 miles and seven times the payload of Pact aircraft at distances of 200 miles, according to one study.[34] These NATO advantages reflect the much greater carrying power of NATO aircraft, which are much larger and more capable than Pact planes.

Also, NATO planes should be superior in air-to-air combat, allowing NATO to gain air superiority over the battlefield. NATO fighters are more sophisticated, NATO has better "battle-management" systems (the AWAC aircraft), and NATO pilots are much better trained than Pact pilots.[35] Overall, as Air Force Director of Plans General James Ahmann has testified, NATO fighter forces are "superior to the Warsaw Pact" and could achieve "very favorable aircraft exchange ratios" against Pact fighters.[36]

These facts are often overlooked because press accounts stress Pact advantages in unrepresentative subcategories, such as numbers of tanks or artillery or planes, where the Pact does have an advantage (150, 180, and 15 percent, respectively).[37] Such comparisons ignore NATO quality advantages (NATO planes, artillery, and antitank weapons, ordnance, and training are better than those of the Pact), and categories in which NATO leads (major warships, helicopters, logistics, and C^3I).

The advantages of the defender also favor NATO. As a rule, attack-ers require substantial material superiority for success — between three-and six-to-one at the point of attack and between one-and-one-half–to-one and two-to-one in the theater of war.[38] But the Pact could not gain advantages of this size unless NATO mobilized late. In fact, NATO could maintain theater-wide force ratios close to the premobilization ratio if NATO mobilized simultaneously with the Pact.[39] If NATO waited several days and then mobilized, the Pact briefly would gain a sizable material advantage, but quickly lose it as NATO forces reached full strength. The Pact could gain and sustain a decisive material advantage only if NATO delayed its mobilization for more than a week after receiving warning.[40]

German terrain would further complicate a Pact attack. German forests, mountains, and other obstacles would limit the Pact to four possible attack routes — the North German plain, the Hof Corridor (toward Stuttgart), the Fulda Gap (toward Frankfurt), and the Gottingen Corridor (toward the Ruhr). Because the Pact attack would be channeled by this geography, NATO could focus its defensive efforts, and Pact forces would be compressed to the point where they could not fight efficiently. Thus NATO troops could "cross the T" — chew up forward Pact units serially — while other Pact units sat idly by in the rear, since the Pact would not have room in these narrow channels to bring all its units forward at once.[41]

Moreover, three of these channels run the width of Germany, so attacking Soviet forces could not spread out even if they did break through NATO front-line defenses. The battle following such a break-through therefore would not unfold like the battle of France in 1940, when the Germans burst into open plains after crossing the Meuse. Pact forces would instead be confined by geography to a narrow area until they drove deep into Germany.[42]

Although NATO does not hold all the advantages in the European theater, NATO disadvantages are counterbalanced by Pact handicaps. The seven European NATO armies have not standardized their weapons, and therefore ammunition, spare parts, and communications gear are not fully interchangeable. As a result, NATO armies cannot easily feed on one another's supplies, a limitation that undercuts their wartime flexibility. In contrast, the Soviets have imposed Soviet arms on all the Pact armies. This advantage is offset by the fact that Pact forces are less reliable than NATO forces; in wartime, the Soviets could not be certain whether the Poles and Czechs would fight with them, sit the war out, or fight against them. This uncertainty greatly complicates Soviet planning for war in Europe, since approximately 45 percent of Pact standing ground forces in Europe are East European.

Many estimates of the European balance, especially those published during the early 1980s, are admittedly more pessimistic than ours,[43] but they fail to utilize the available information fully. Key data required for a thorough assessment are often missing from their analyses, including aggregate firepower estimates for the forces on both sides,[44] terrain factors, and estimates of troop movement and interdiction rates. Their judgment of American weakness is based instead on unrepresentative statistics and on unduly pessimistic political and factual assumptions. For example, some analysts invent an overwhelming Pact firepower advan-tage by focusing on the subcategories of weapons where the Pact has the lead. Some exaggerate the number of Soviet divisions promptly available. Some overlook Soviet weaknesses, such as the unreliability of East Eu-ropean armies. Still others neglect the NATO advantage of fighting on the defensive. Thus, pessimistic estimates, while common, are generally based on sketchy information and fragmentary analysis.[45]

The Persian Gulf. The conventional wisdom is that American forces could not block a Soviet seizure of the Iranian or even the Saudi Arabian oilfields without using nuclear weapons. One columnist has suggested that American forces "could never be a match for the Soviet juggernaut across the Iranian border."[46] Defense Secretary Weinberger has warned that American forces are "incapable of stopping an assault on Western oil supplies,"[47] while one prominent defense analyst has concluded that Iran "may be inherently indefensible."[48]

These gloomy predictions, like similar forecasts concerning Europe, are not based on the full use of available information. In fact, American forces could probably halt the Soviets short of the oilfields, chiefly because Soviet forces could not gain decisive material superiority in the battle area. The United States can probably bring as much firepower to bear in the Persian Gulf theater as can the Soviets.[49]

Proximity to the theater would seem to give the Soviets the upper hand. This appearance is misleading, however, for three reasons.

First, the United States has invested more money in mobility equipment (transport aircraft and amphibious assault ships, aircraft carriers, and airmobile and seamobile forces), which partially offsets the greater Soviet proximity.

Second, the Soviets have not tailored their military to invade the Persian Gulf, so their forces are not ready to mount such an attack on short notice. As a result, NATO would gain valuable advance warning if the Soviets chose to invade. Before the Soviets attacked, they would have to assemble and test a command and control apparatus in Transcaucasia. This activity would create telltale radio signals. They would also have to amass tens of thousands of trucks in the Caucasus to supply Soviet divisions advancing into Iran because Soviet forces near Iran do not have nearly enough trucks to support an Iranian expedition. Soviet army divisions are structured for war in Europe, with its many railroads. As a result, these divisions are designed to operate no further than 100 miles from a railhead; hence, they normally include relatively few trucks. Soviet forces invading the Gulf would be fighting hundreds of miles from any functioning railroad, however, and this would require an enormous additional complement of trucks to ferry their supplies over Iranian roads. By one estimate, all the trucks from more than fifty-five Soviet army divisions (one-third of the mobilized Soviet army) would be required to support a Soviet invasion force of seven divisions in Iran, assuming that no trucks broke down or were destroyed in fighting.[50] By another estimate, almost all the trucks in the Soviet army might be required.[51] This huge armada could not be assembled quickly or discreetly.

These preparations would give NATO at least one month's warning.[52] In the meantime, the United States could move substantial forces into the Gulf to greet Soviet attackers — perhaps 500 land- and sea-based tactical fighters, the 82nd Airborne Division, and two Marine brigades within two or three weeks. The United States could bring in much bigger forces by sea later.

Third, although the Soviets are much closer to the Gulf oilfields than is the United States, the terrain is much more difficult to traverse. Soviet invasion forces would have to move 850 miles overland to reach the oil fields, which lie in Khuzestan province, in Southwest Iran. If they attacked from the Soviet Union, they would have to cross two formidable mountain ranges — those along the Iranian northern tier and the Zagros Mountains, which separate Khuzestan from central Iran. If they attacked from Afghanistan, they would have to pass over the fierce, desolate Khorassan desert, and then the Zagros. Only a handful of roads cross the northern mountains, and only four roads and one railroad span the Zagros.[53] These mountain roads cross bridges, run through tunnels, cling to the sides of countless gorges, and wind beneath overhanging cliffs. As a result, Soviet supply arteries would be dotted with scores of "choke points" — points where these arteries could be destroyed or blocked. Such blockages could not be bypassed or easily repaired.

Soviet movements in Iran, therefore, would be exceptionally vulnerable to delaying action by American airstrikes, commando raids, or attacks by Iranian guerrillas on the scores of choke points between Khuzestan and Russia. The Soviets could not erect solid air defenses along their entire groundline of communication — the distance is simply too great — so American airpower could probably continue striking these choke points even if they were overrun by advancing Soviet forces. These air strikes could be flown from aircraft carriers; by land-based aircraft that could be moved to the Mideast after warning was received; or by B-52s based on Diego Garcia in the Indian Ocean, on Guam in the Pacific, or even in the United States.[54] Iranian forces could also slow down Soviet forces and disrupt Soviet supply lines, especially if they were organized in advance for guerrilla war.

By one estimate, American airstrikes and helicopter infantry teams working in the Zagros could slow the Soviet advance toward Khuzistan by sixty days.[55] If we assume that the United States receives and uses thirty days of warning before the Soviets launched their attack, then American forces would have ninety days to prepare for the defense of Khuzestan. In this time, the United States could move enough ground forces to Khuzestan to equal the firepower of the Soviet divisions coming through the Zagros.[56] The United States, moreover, could probably bring more airpower to bear in Khuzestan than could the Soviets,[57] giving the United States a net firepower advantage. If this were the case, American forces would have more than enough firepower to win.

Some Westerners suggest that the Soviets might seek to avoid the travails of a ground assault on Iran by mounting a surprise airborne attack, seizing key airfields and other facilities in Southern Iran with airborne units, and holding them until Soviet ground forces arrive. But such an airborne strike seems even more difficult than a ground assault, because the Soviets could not assemble the trucks they would need to support their ground forces without revealing the surprise that an "airborne grab" would require. As a result, any airborne divisions dropped into southern Iran would have to hold off American and Iranian counterattacks for weeks while the Soviets readied their follow-up invasion force in the southern Soviet Union. In the interim, these airborne units could not be easily resupplied by air, because Soviet fighter aircraft probably lack the range to provide adequate air cover over southern Iran from bases in the Soviet Union or Afghanistan, and the Soviets could not quickly seize, secure, and prepare enough air bases in Iran suitable for modern fighter aircraft. As a result, the Soviets probably could not defend their transport aircraft over southern Iran against American fighters. This would leave their airborne units stranded.

Lord Robert Salisbury once remarked, concerning British fears that Russia would sweep through Afghanistan into India: "A great deal of misapprehension arises from the popular use of maps on a small scale."[58] Similarly American fears that the Soviets could sweep through Iran spring from the dismissal of geographic and military realities. Overall, as one analyst notes, "the invasion of Iran would be an exceedingly low confidence affair for the Soviets."[59]

As with the European balance, pessimistic estimates of the Gulf conventional balance do not fully utilize available data, or they rest on dubious factual or political assumptions.[60] Again aggregate firepower estimates, geographic factors, movement tables, interdiction rates, and warning estimates are usually missing. Instead, misleading statistics are combined with unduly pessimistic political assumptions: that the Gulf states refuse American help or cooperate with Soviet invaders; that the United States loses simply because it lacks the will to fight; that America must defend *northern* Iran, which would be much harder than defending the southern oilfields; or that American leaders simply fail to use the warning they receive.

In short, public alarm about American capabilities to achieve basic missions seems exaggerated.[61] Publicly available information about American capabilities is spotty — partly because the government has published little useful information about military balances — so estimates of current capabilities must be tentative. The best evidence still indicates that NATO forces could execute the principal missions required by containment today, and could have done so when the Reagan administration took office.

The Reagan Administration's Implicit Military Strategy

If American forces can already carry out basic containment missions, what motivates the buildup now underway?

The answer lies largely in the Reagan administration's decision to adopt a demanding strategy that incorporates three additional missions beyond those required by containment: a strategic nuclear counterforce mission, an offensive conventional mission against the Soviet homeland, and an enlarged Third World intervention mission.[62] These additional missions were not widely accepted elements of American strategy a decade ago, and a case can be made that they are not now worth the costs and risks they entail.

Strategic Nuclear Counterforce

Most policy analysts agree that the United States requires a second-strike countervalue capability, but America's need for either a first-strike or a second-strike counterforce capability is much more controversial. The size and shape of American strategic forces depend on how this argument is resolved, since a meaningful American counterforce capability would require much bigger and rather different nuclear forces from those deployed today.

A disarming counterforce attack against the Soviet Union would require two operations: a strike against Soviet nuclear forces and actions to limit the damage inflicted upon American cities by surviving Soviet nuclear warheads launched in retaliation. Counterforce weapons, accordingly, include those that can destroy Soviet nuclear warheads before they are launched against the United States *and* those that can destroy retaliating Soviet warheads in flight toward American cities or that limit the damage these warheads do to American cities. Thus counterforce weapons include highly accurate ICBMs and SLBMs (which can destroy enemy ICBMs and bombers on the ground), antisubmarine ("hunter-killer") submarines and other antisubmarine warfare forces (which can destroy Soviet ballistic missile submarines), air defense systems (which can shoot down retaliating Soviet bombers), area-wide antiballistic missile systems (ABMs, which can defend cities against retaliating ICBMs and SLBMs), and civil defense (which limits the damage inflicted by Soviet warheads that get through). Such seemingly "defensive" systems as air defense, area-wide ABM, and civil defense are really "offensive" in the nuclear context, because they form a vital part of an offensive first-strike counterforce capability. Second-strike countervalue weapons include those that can ride out an enemy attack and retaliate against enemy cities or other "value" (industrial or economic) targets; they include, for example, American Poseidon SLBMs. Such weapons do not need to destroy enemy strategic nuclear forces.

In the late 1960s and early 1970s, a public consensus against counter-force was reflected in the congressional decision to constrain American ICBM accuracy improvements and in congressional hostility toward the proposed Safeguard ABM system. Some people opposed counterforce on the grounds that it increased the risk of war and the risk of wartime escalation. In their view, first-strike capabilities on both sides would create a hair-trigger dilemma — whichever side fired first would win, so both sides would be quick to shoot in a crisis.[63] They also feared that conventional war would become harder to control, since the first side to use nuclear weapons would hold the upper hand, creating a temptation to escalate if conventional war broke out.

But the clinching argument was that a counterforce capability simply could not be achieved. According to this view, the Soviets, like ourselves, could always implement countermeasures to preserve their second-strike countervalue capability because this capability is so much cheaper to maintain than a counterforce capability. Moreover the Soviets could not tolerate an American counterforce capability, so they would make sure we never got one, whatever the cost. Hence, the argument went, American spending on counterforce is futile because the Soviets will counter the counterforce America builds.

Counterforce came back in fashion in the mid-1970s and was reflected in the Ford and Carter administration decisions to build major new counterforce systems, including the high-accuracy MX and Trident D5 ("Trident II") missiles. Under congressional pressure, the Reagan administration has cut back the MX program, but it has accelerated the Trident D5 program and added new counterforce programs: a modernized continental air defense system, including new F-15 interceptors and AWACS early-warning aircraft; an enlarged civil defense program[64]; and most importantly, an ambitious new program (officially named the Strategic Defense Initiative, or SDI, but dubbed Star Wars by the press) to develop national ballistic missile defenses.[65] This emphasis on counterforce is also reflected in administration planning documents, which suggest a requirement for an American second-strike counterforce capability that could disarm the Soviet Union even after absorbing a Soviet first strike. Presumably a force with this capability could more easily disarm the Soviets if the United States struck first, so these documents also implicitly call for an American first-strike counterforce capability.[66]

Yet a counterforce capability is much more difficult to achieve today because American forces must destroy a much larger set of Soviet targets. In 1970 the Soviets had 1,800 strategic nuclear warheads[67]; in 1985 Soviets had more than 10,000, many protected in hardened shelters or invulnerable submarines. As a result, an American first strike now must be much more effective to contain the Soviet retaliation to acceptable size.

The case against the feasibility of a counterforce strategy, therefore, seems even more persuasive than it was when counterforce was un-popular.[68] Moreover, no new information has appeared to discredit ear-lier fears that a first-strike capability on either side would heighten the risk of war and escalation. The administration's commitment to decapita-tion strikes against the Soviet government leadership also seems danger-ous, since decapitating the Soviets would leave the United States with no negotiating partner while turning Soviet forces over to Soviet military officers imbued with nuclear warfighting ideas.[69] This would make it impossible to end the war by negotiation.[70]

The administration's emphasis on counterforce is also in conflict with its efforts to control the strategic nuclear arms race. Counterforce propels the arms race: Neither side can allow the other to gain a meaningful counterforce capability, so counterforce programs on both sides generate answering second-strike countervalue programs on both sides. Forces must be modernized and arsenals must be expanded because neither side can let the other achieve its goal. Nuclear arsenals on both sides far exceed overkill today partly because both sides have sought counterforce capabilities, which has led them to expand their arsenals, creating larger target sets for their opponents to cover, subsequently expanding their opponents' force requirements, and in turn, expanding once again their own force requirements. Thus the serious pursuit of counterforce is a recipe for arms racing and is incompatible with serious arms control.[71]

All these problems flaw the administration's Star Wars ballistic mis-sile defense program, which now stands as the centerpiece of its counter-force effort. Effective nationwide defenses do not seem remotely feasible. Countermeasures that could defeat current American designs for ballistic missile defenses have already been envisioned, and most scientists believe that an effective area defense cannot be deployed in the foreseeable future.[72] And if it proved successful, the Star Wars program might raise the risk of war by rewarding the side that strikes first and by shifting the world toward a more offensive form of warfare,[73] since a nationwide ABM, despite its defensive appearance, would be a fundamentally offen-sive system. An ABM also would provide a powerful stimulus to the arms race if the Soviets chose to defeat it by overwhelming it with greater numbers of missiles and warheads.

The Soviet Union devotes an even greater effort to strategic nuclear counterforce programs than does the United States, and the Soviet strategic nuclear buildup in the 1970s heavily stressed counterforce, even including an ABM research program like the American SDI. This does not argue for simple-minded American imitation of Soviet counterforce programs, however. Rather, the most effective response to Soviet coun-terforce capability is to remove it by enhancing the survivability of American forces. This negates the enormous Soviet counterforce invest-ment at a much smaller cost to the United States.

Offensive Conventional Forces and Operations

The Reagan administration's preference for counterforce reflects a general administration preference for offensive strategies[74] that shapes administration conventional force programs and strategies as well. Department of Defense planning documents reportedly endorse a new, more offensive warfighting strategy for conventional conflict, declaring that American conventional forces should be "capable of putting at risk Soviet interests, including the Soviet homeland," and endorse "offensive moves against Warsaw Pact flanks."[75] Navy Secretary John Lehman advocates "getting at the (Soviet) naval threat at its source."[76] Defense Secretary Weinberger maintains that "the principle of non-aggression would not impose a purely defensive strategy in fighting back" against an aggressor,[77] and speaks of a "counteroffensive against (Soviet) vulnerable points . . . directed at places where we can affect the outcome of the war."[78]

Most discussions concern possible air strikes against Soviet naval and air bases on the Kola peninsula (northeast of Finland, on the Barents Sea) or at Valdivostok and Petropavlovsk, in East Asia. These bases would be hit by carrier-based aircraft or possibly by long-range strategic bombers. The Navy has also announced that, in a conventional war, it would send American killer submarines into Arctic waters to seek out and destroy Soviet ballistic missile submarines.[79] By so doing, the Navy argues, it could shift the strategic nuclear balance in favor of the United States and thereby persuade the Soviet Union to call off the war. The administration has programmed new conventional forces to execute these offensive strategies, including two new nuclear-powered aircraft carriers and more hunter-killer submarines.

Two criticisms can be leveled against these strategies.

First, they require large new American forces. Only a huge fleet of carriers could safely attack the Soviet homeland because Soviet land-based aircraft could destroy a smaller American fleet as it approached. Even with two new carriers, American carrier forces would be too weak to mount such a strike. A strategy of sinking the Soviet ballistic missile submarine fleet during a conventional war would also require large new American antisubmarine forces. Overall, offensive or counteroffensive conventional strategies are a bottomless pit, because they generate demanding missions that cannot be achieved without huge expense, if they can be achieved at all. (Indeed the notion of an offensive conventional strategy does not square with administration warnings of weakness: If America is weak, these demanding new missions would seem even less feasible.)

Second, offensive strategies defeat a basic purpose of American conventional forces — the control of escalation. If it succeeds, an American counteroffensive would jeopardize assets essential to Soviet sovereignty, or appear to do so, raising the prospect of a Soviet decision to escalate from conventional to nuclear war. Thus an American campaign against Soviet ballistic missile submarines, following the strategy recently announced by the Navy, could inspire the Soviets to take desperate measures — nuclear strikes against American antisubmarine warfare (ASW) facilities or American ASW ships, for instance — to relieve American pressure. American carrier-based air strikes against the Soviet naval bases and forces at Murmansk also could threaten Soviet ballistic missile submarines (many of which are based at Murmansk and are commanded by communications facilities located in Murmansk), provoking desperate Soviet decisions — nuclear strikes against American carriers, for example — if the bases could not be defended any other way.[80] A chief purpose of American conventional forces is to provide a buffer between conventional and nuclear war, but an offensive operational strategy would use American forces in a way that defeats this fundamental aim.

Intervention Forces

When the Reagan administration took office, the United States already possessed sizable forces that were better suited for intervention in the Third World than for action against Soviet forces. If containment logic guided its policies, the administration should have reduced these intervention forces, since American Third World interventions do little to contain Soviet power, and thus contribute little to American security. Instead the administration has increased United States intervention forces and plans to increase them further.

Two attributes distinguish intervention forces from anti-Soviet forces. First, intervention forces must be relatively mobile, since the locations of interventions cannot be known in advance. By contrast, anti-Soviet forces can be less mobile, because the theaters directly threatened by Soviet forces are known, enabling the United States to put defending forces in such theaters in peacetime, as it has in Western Europe. Clearly, United States forces need some mobility to deal with Soviet threats, especially in the Persian Gulf. The question is: How much? Today the United States has more mobility forces than anti-Soviet contingencies demand, especially more aircraft carriers (unless these are used offensively against the Soviet homeland, in which case there are not enough, as noted above).

Second, intervention forces can be more lightly armed. Light forces are useful for some anti-Soviet contingencies, such as operations against Soviet supply lines in the Iranian mountains. But generally, the lightly armed forces that are best suited for fighting Third World opponents (such as guerrillas) are not appropriate for fighting heavily armed Soviet forces.

Total American mobility forces and unarmored ground forces currently include thirteen (soon to be fifteen) Navy aircraft carriers; eight Army light divisions, including its light infantry, airborne, and air-mobile divisions; Special Forces units; three Marine divisions and associated ships and air wings; airlift and sealift forces to move and supply these forces; and CIA covert operatives. A war against the Soviet Union in Europe or the Gulf would productively engage most of these forces, but not all of them. Some American aircraft carriers (perhaps ten, including those in overhaul) would be required to attack Soviet forces in Iran and guard the Atlantic and Pacific sea lanes, but some carriers would remain (perhaps three; five with the Reagan program).[81] Possibly six of the eleven American light ground divisions would be engaged in Iran or tied down in Norway or Korea, with five remaining. These remaining carriers and divisions, which represent 23 percent (soon to be 33 percent) of the American carrier fleet and 24 percent of America's twenty-one ground divisions could be classified as Third World intervention forces, since they are appropriate for intervention missions and poorly adapted for anti-Soviet contingencies. All special forces and CIA covert operatives would be similarly classified as optimized for Third World intervention, as would some American airlift and sealift capacity.

Overall, current United States forces represent a very substantial investment in Third World intervention; yet the administration is increasing this investment with new carriers, "forcible-entry" amphibious assault ships, light Army divisions, and airlift. The administration also indicates a revived interest in intervention by rejecting the requirement, endorsed by the Nixon, Ford, and Carter administrations, that American conventional forces maintain a "one-and-one-half-war" conventional capability (envisioning American conventional forces that could fight a major conventional war against the Soviet Union, while also fighting one Korean-sized "half war" against another opponent elsewhere), instead suggesting that the United States prepare to fight on "several" fronts simultaneously.[82] This represents a shift toward intervention, since additional "half wars" would be fought in the Third World.

How should this rising investment in intervention forces be evaluated? If containment criteria are applied, two questions are paramount: (1) How large is the strategic importance of the Third World? By how much would Soviet power increase if the Soviets expanded their influence in the Third World? (2) How great is the Soviet threat to the Third World? By how much would Soviet influence in the Third World increase if the United States were not prepared to intervene?

The case for maintaining large intervention forces is weak because the Third World is strategically quite unimportant and the Soviet threat to the Third World is quite small. Europe and Japan are vastly more important than the Third World, and Europe is more threatened. Current American investment in Third World intervention forces therefore seems excessive, since the stakes and the threat in the Third World are small.[83] Increased investment in Third World contingencies is clearly unwarranted.

By the principal and best measure of strategic importance — industrial power — the entire Third World ranks very low. All of Latin America has an aggregate GNP below that of Japan; all of Africa has an aggregate GNP below that of Italy or Britain. The aggregate GNP of the entire Third World, including the Persian Gulf, is less than three-fourths that of Western Europe, and barely one-half that of Western Europe plus Japan.[84] Modern military power is produced by industrial power; the Third World has very little industrial power; hence it has little military potential and correspondingly little strategic significance.

Advocates of intervention forces answer with two arguments suggesting that the Third World has strategic importance despite its paltry productive capacity. First, some analysts claim that although Third World industrial output is low, the Third World produces raw materials on which Western industry depends, making the Third World a key to Western industrial productivity. Second, some analysts suggest that basing rights in Third World areas can be militarily important, even if the area's industrial output is trivial.

The first of these arguments rests on a mismeasurement of economic dependence that confuses the scope of North-South trade with northern dependence on the South. In reality, oil is the only southern raw material on which the North depends to any degree. Northern countries import a wide range of other strategic minerals, such as chromium, cobalt, and manganese ore, from Third World areas. The industrial North, however, could adjust in several ways if it lost access to its supplies of these minerals. These include (1) developing synthetic replacements; (2) using substitutes; (3) seeking alternative Third World sources; (4) developing sources in northern countries; or (5) conserving the minerals on hand. The case of chromium is instructive: the United States imports almost all its chromium today, but it produced it during World War II from American mines, and could do so again, albeit at higher cost, if supplies were cut off.

The image of a dependent West is fostered by analysts who demonstrate Western dependence by listing the many raw materials the West imports, as if trade and dependence were one and the same thing.[85] However, what matters is not the volume of trade, but rather the cost of halting trade. American dependence on a given country or commodity should be assessed by asking how much damage the American economy would sustain (measured in lost growth, higher unemployment, and higher inflation) if trade in that commodity or with that country were cut off, and adjustments had to be made.[86]

Dependence on a given raw material can also be crudely measured by asking whether cartels can form among its producers. Cartels are possible if and only if the number of Third World producers is small and Western dependence on the product is high. Synthetic production and product substitutes would have to be expensive, and local production in Western states would have to be difficult. Otherwise the West can break the cartel by finding alternative products or sources. The presence of cartels, therefore, signals Western dependence and the absence of cartels signals Western independence.

In fact, the Organization of Petroleum Exporting Countries (OPEC) has been the only successful international cartel, which indicates that Western dependence on products other than oil is low. The West imports many other products from Third World countries, but most of these materials can be synthesized, replaced by substitutes, produced locally, or acquired from many sources. Otherwise successful cartels would exist in these materials.[87]

The second argument, that Third World bases are important militarily, is more difficult to evaluate. This argument should not be presumed valid until disproven, however; rather, it should be carefully explored on a case-by-case basis. Analysts should ask how the loss of given Western bases or the appearance of Soviet bases in given Third World areas would affect American ability to defend areas of greater intrinsic importance, such as Europe, Japan, or the Persian Gulf. When assessing the importance of United States bases, analysts should measure the cost to the United States of replacing lost bases with new bases or with new forces that can operate at greater distances from their home bases. When assessing the importance of potential Soviet bases, analysts should estimate the cost of new forces that the United States would require to neutralize new threats that the Soviets could pose from these bases.[88]

The case supporting the importance of Third World bases is seldom made this way, so it is hard to assess. Analysts should recognize, however, that the case for their importance is not made until such information is provided. Thus analysts should not assume that American bases in the Philippines are centrally important until it is demonstrated that American strategy for the defense of Japan or the Persian Gulf depends in some fashion on them and that the cost of alternatives is prohibitive. (It is doubtful that such a case can, in fact, be made.) Similar arguments for the strategic importance of Soviet bases in Central America are incomplete until the threat that such bases would pose to American wartime operations to defend Europe or the Persian Gulf is explained, and the cost of preparing effective countermeasures is assessed. (It is likely that such bases would not pose a significant threat and could be neutralized by relatively inexpensive countermeasures. Conclusions, however, must not be drawn until more data are available.)

Finally Americans should carefully assess how formidable the Soviet threat to the Third World really is. Are the Soviets really capable of significant imperial expansion in the Third World, by either direct intervention or proxy action?

The threat of direct Soviet military intervention in the Third World is often exaggerated because Soviet intervention capabilities are deemed larger than they actually are. In fact, the Soviet conventional war machine is designed for land continental warfare; it accordingly poses a very real threat to Western Europe, but little threat to Third World areas beyond the Soviet periphery. Soviet power-projection capability has grown in recent years, but it is dwarfed by Western capabilities. Soviet airlift assets are much smaller than Western assets, Soviet amphibious assault forces are a fraction the size of the American forces, and Soviet ground forces are configured primarily for combat against Western armies, not Third World guerrillas. The Soviets can move forces globally if they are not opposed, but they cannot project power over any distance against Western opposition.

This is no cause for comfort. Indeed, it means that Soviet military forces are structured to directly threaten America's most vital interests. But it also means that the Soviets pose little direct threat to the Third World. The West can therefore secure the Third World against direct Soviet encroachment with little active effort.

The threat of indirect Soviet expansion in the Third World, either by leftist revolution or by the expansion of Soviet "proxy" states, is similarly overblown. Cold War history teaches that the Soviet empire does not expand via mass revolution or by "proxy" action but rather by the direct imposition of Soviet military power. Where the Soviets can plant the jackboot of their armies — as in Eastern Europe and Afghanistan — their imperial writ can run. But elsewhere, the forces of nationalism that tear the Third World also tear Soviet imperial designs. Time and again, Soviet influence has proven ephemeral whenever its army was not introduced, even where Soviet "proxies" won control, because nationalist hatreds have overridden ideological affinities to split the Soviets from their proxy. The notion that Third World leftists are loyal Soviet minions has seldom proven correct, except when American policies helped make it true, as with Vietnam, Cuba, Nicaragua, and earlier with China. Otherwise the centrifugal power of nationalism has broken the imperial ties the Soviets sought to create.

Nationalist hatreds have been a scourge to the Third World, producing great violence and suffering. These hatreds also fuel Third World anti-Western and anti-American feeling. Such hatreds, however, vastly simplify the American strategic problem by making it more difficult for both the United States and the Soviet Union to establish a durable influence. Ultimately this serves American interests, since America's chief purpose is not to establish world dominion but rather to keep the world free from Soviet dominion. Therefore the United States should view Third World nationalism as an asset rather than a danger and should realize that the United States can usually contain the Soviets in the Third World simply by leaving things alone.[89]

The direct Soviet military threat to industrial Western regions is the principal danger confronting the West. American forces should address this threat directly while avoiding self-defeating diversions in Third World regions that do not matter and are not seriously threatened by Soviet expansionism. Indeed the United States will weaken itself — and indirectly strengthen the Soviets — if it expends its energy on less relevant Third World contingencies.

The NATO Burden Shares

Partly because it has increased American strategic requirements by pursuing these three additional missions, the administration's defense program has shifted the NATO defense burden further onto the United States. This shift raises fairness issues within the alliance and will increase intra-allied friction over burden-sharing questions as Americans complain that Europe does too little.

The United States has carried a disproportionate share of the NATO defense spending burden for many years. In 1980, the United States spent 5.5 percent of its GNP on defense, while its thirteen NATO allies only spent an average 3.4 percent of GNP, according to figures from the London International Institute for Strategic Studies.[90] Among major United States allies, only Britain spent almost as much — 5.1 percent — as the United States. These figures understate the European defense effort by failing to correct for the low salaries the Europeans pay their conscripted manpower; but even if we eliminate this bias by pricing NATO manpower at American pay scales (which adds 22 percent to European budgets),[91] average European spending in 1980 came to only 4.1 percent of GNP, or three-quarters the share of GNP spent by the United States.[92]

This unequal arrangement arose after World War II when the United States guarded against the Soviets while the Europeans repaired their war-damaged cities and industries. Americans assumed that the Europeans would eventually shoulder the primary share of the burden once their economies recovered. No one expected the United States to carry this burden indefinitely, yet Europe continued to carry a lighter burden after the European economies had recovered fully.

The Reagan defense buildup has widened the gap between American and allied defense spending, and the proposed Reagan program will widen it further. In 1984, the NATO states, excluding the United States, together spent 3.6 percent of their collective GNP on defense, barely one-half as much as the 6.9 percent of GNP spent by the United States (or about two-thirds as much if NATO manpower is priced at American pay scales).[93] If, as planned, the Reagan administration increases American spending to 7.5 percent of GNP in 1990, and if the other NATO states continue to spend 3.6 percent of GNP on defense, the average burden of the NATO allies will dwindle to less than one-half the American defense burden (or three-fifths the size of the American burden if NATO manpower is priced at American pay scales).

These growing inequities have brought angry American demands for greater effort by Europe. Many American observers assume that Europe spends less because it can "free ride" on American generosity, and call for the United States to browbeat Europe to contribute more. Some commentators even recommend that the United States withdraw forces from Europe unless the European states agree to do more, as a "shock treatment" to spur Europe into action.[94]

Before adopting such solutions, however, Americans should first study the causes of burden shares inequity. Western Europe spends less than the United States partly because it disagrees with American strategic concepts for the prosecution of containment, especially those embraced by the Reagan administration. Specifically, Western Europe prefers a more defensive military strategy than does the United States, and it views the offensive orientation of the Reagan administration with a jaundiced eye. Western Europe also prefers a Kennan-Lippmann-Morgenthau variety of containment that would defend industrially important areas from direct Soviet military expansion but would eschew a global crusade against the indigenous Third World left. This preference reflects the greater presence of socialist ideas in Western Europe, which leaves Europeans less phobic about Marxism than Americans. It also reflects the European colonial experience, which tempered the European view of the utility and feasibility of Third World colonialism and expansionism by East or West.

Much of the gap between the American and West European defense efforts reflects these strategic differences. American spending on strategic nuclear counterforce systems, offensive conventional forces, and Third World intervention forces substantially accounts for the greater size of American defense budgets. Moreover, the Reagan administration's increased investment in these missions largely explains why this differential is growing. Thus Europe spends less because Europe spends differently, on a narrower range of missions that reflect a different (and less demanding) strategic theory of containment.

The United States should not carry a heavier share of the NATO military burden indefinitely. However, if the cause of the inequity lies in American strategic extravagance, rather than European lassitude, then Americans should consider adopting a more defensive, Soviet-focused strategy along the lines favored by Europeans. If the United States and

Europe both embraced such a strategy, American-European inequities in defense burdens would diminish or disappear.

Americans' Perceptions of Their Weakness as Built on Myth

The administration's defense program has won public approval largely because it could draw on a widespread myth of American military weakness. If Western forces can, in fact, achieve their main missions today, what explains this American sense of impotence? There are three contributing causes.

First, statistical games substitute for proper measures of national military strength in the public debate over defense. Congressman Les Aspin once described the "Games the Pentagon Plays" — false measures that support Pentagon arguments for preferred policies.[95] These games still confuse and mislead the public on both the size of the Soviet threat and the best solution for defense problems.

In the "Numbers Game," the sizes of selected Soviet and American forces are compared in a manner that shows the United States lagging behind. Areas of Western numerical or qualitative superiority are ignored. Differences in the needs of each side are obscured. Thus we often hear that the Soviets have more tactical aircraft (although American aircraft are much better, and total American tactical air capability is probably greater); more attack submarines (although American submarines are much more capable); more naval warships (although American ships are much bigger, more expensive, and more capable); and so forth. The only question that really matters — "Can the United States carry out its strategy?" — is not asked. Yet such misleading analysis is abundant in Secretary Weinberger's *Annual Report to the Congress,* in the Joint Chiefs' *Military Posture* statements,[96] and in newspaper and magazine reporting on defense matters.

In the "Trend Game," alarming trends are presented without baseline figures or explanations. Thus we often hear that the U.S. Navy has fallen from 1000 ships to less than 500; it is not explained that the Navy shrank because many ships built for World War II were finally scrapped in the 1960s and 1970s and because the Navy shifted from smaller to larger ships, so it now builds fewer ships of larger tonnage. In fact, the United States has outbuilt the Soviet Union by three to one in warship tonnage since 1960, while NATO as a whole outbuilt the Soviets by nine to two.[97]

In the "Go It Alone Game," Soviet and American forces are compared head to head, as if the United States had no allies and the Soviet Union no other enemies. Thus we often hear of Soviet advantages over the United States in categories in which NATO actually holds the lead (such as total defense spending). Such comparisons dismiss the success of the entire postwar European and Japanese economic recovery programs, the express purpose of which was to build up American allies so they could defend themselves.

A proper assessment measures forces against missions, under politically realistic scenarios. Strategic nuclear capabilities on each side are measured by asking how many warheads on each side could survive an attack and how much damage these warheads could inflict on the enemy society. American second-strike countervalue capability is measured by estimating the damage that surviving American warheads could inflict on Soviet society; American counterforce capability is measured by estimating how many Soviet warheads could survive an American strike, and how much damage they could inflict on the United States in retaliation. (The less damage these forces could inflict, the greater the American counterforce capacity.) Comparing warheads, megatons, throwweights, missiles, and bombers tells us very little if these are not converted into measures of capacity to inflict harm in retaliation. The government seldom provides such measures, however, partly because they undercut official arguments for counterforce by demonstrating its futility.

A conventional theater balance cannot be measured without a thorough campaign analysis. At a minimum, such an analysis should incorporate data measuring (1) the total firepower available to both sides, (2) the rate at which both sides can mobilize this firepower and move it into the theater of action, (3) the ability of one side to interdict the other's movement, (4) the advantage that geography gives the attacker or defender, and (5) the amount of warning both sides can expect. The quality and political loyalty of commanders and troops should also be considered. Yet defense analyses in the press and popular journals almost never discuss defense problems in these terms.

A second cause of Americans' sense of impotence lies in a common tendency to search for inappropriate military solutions to political or diplomatic problems. Debates on hardware often turn on differences over the quality of American statesmanship and diplomacy. For example, pessimists often base arguments for more defense spending on scenarios that assume Western statesmen would not act on the warning they received of a Pact attack or that the United States could not persuade allies to cooperate in their own defense. In the pessimistic scenarios for war in the Persian Gulf, for instance, it is sometimes assumed that the European states would not permit American aircraft to refuel in European countries, although vital European interests would be at stake. A better answer, though, is for American leaders to provide the leadership that these scenarios assume is lacking. It often turns out, moreover, that no amount of spending can cure the problems created by weak leadership. America's defense requirements are enormous if we assume its leaders are fools and its allies are malicious or self-destructive. These are problems that more spending cannot solve easily.

A third cause of pessimism lies in the shifting of American assumptions about grand strategy during the past decade from a less demanding to a more demanding one. The drift toward counterforce, offensive conventional operations, and intervention leads to much more demanding military requirements. Western military forces have been capable of executing the basic missions required by containment throughout the past decade. Increasingly, American forces have been measured against more difficult missions, making the United States *feel* weaker than in the past because more is demanded of American forces.

Conclusion

The Reagan administration's defense program includes some praiseworthy initiatives. For example, the administration deserves credit for its efforts to increase short-term readiness, to rationalize procurement with multiyear contracts, to restructure American forces for Persian Gulf defense, and to retain more military personnel by improving living standards, salaries, and quality of life. The overall direction of administration defense policy, however, has not been adequately explained, and the scope of administration defense programs is excessive and ill-directed.

The fundamental problem with the Reagan program lies in the administration's extravagant military strategy. This strategy incorporates requirements for simultaneously performing several very demanding missions: successfully waging global conventional war against an unspecified number of adversaries, conducting offensive conventional operations against the Soviet homeland, and waging a victorious nuclear war against the Soviets. These missions simply cannot be performed at a realistic cost. In fact, both nuclear counterforce and conventional offense generate open-ended requirements, providing a recipe for huge defense budget increases.[98]

The Reagan strategy also is inconsistent with the basic goals of containment and with the American interest in controlling any war that might break out. Containment requires a defensive, Soviet-focused military strategy, not the global, offense-oriented strategy of the Reagan administration. Escalation control calls for capable defensive forces and a defensive operational strategy, whereas Reagan's emphasis on conventional offense and nuclear counterforce increases the risk that a conventional conflict could escalate to a general thermonuclear war. Thus the administration program demands expensive new capabilities that the country does not require and might be better off without.

The administration can also be criticized for spending its new defense monies inefficiently. Publicly available data do not allow refined estimates of the military effectiveness of the new forces bought in the buildup. Crude measures, however, suggest that the administration has not garnered a commensurate return on its new defense investment.

American defense outlays increased by 38 percent during Reagan's first term,[99] but American conventional force structure, which consumes most of the defense budget, hardly expanded (holding steady at sixteen Army divisions, three Marine divisions, twenty-six tactical air wings, and thirteen aircraft carrier task forces), and the force structure increases planned for Reagan's second term are modest. The production of Navy combat ships and Army weapons increased only slightly during Reagan's first term, while the production of tactical combat aircraft dropped significantly. The combat readiness of American forces has increased modestly.[100] In none of these categories do we see anything like a 38 percent increase or improvement.

In arms control, the administration has a dismal record. The administration has jettisoned the SALT II Treaty, and its Star Wars program eventually will force the abrogation of the 1972 ABM Treaty, which is the principal surviving achievement of past arms control efforts. In the meantime, the administration's commitment to counterforce works at cross-purposes with efforts to negotiate new strategic arms limits with the Soviets. Moreover in the various arms control negotiations, the administration has advanced implausible negotiating positions designed chiefly for public relations purposes. As a result, the administration has failed to reach any meaningful arms control agreements. Arms control is no panacea; at best it can help to moderate and channel the East-West military competition at the margin. The Reagan administration, however, has failed to harvest even the small gains that arms control can provide while taking steps that will eventually damage the arms control process.

Finally, the administration should be criticized for sowing the defense debate with confusion. Its failure to specify the strategy that requires the Reagan buildup deprives Congress and the public of the tools they need to analyze defense policy. As a result, the whole buildup proceeds with no clear definition of its purpose, no way to judge its necessity, no criteria by which to judge whether new forces are meeting real needs or leaving real needs unmet, and no logical stopping point. Moreover those fragments of strategy the administration offers often conflict with one another, sowing further confusion. Mutually contradictory notions appear in the same statements, as in claims that Soviet forces are so strong that the United States requires a major buildup, but also so weak that an offensive American strategy is possible.[101]

In addition, this administration has done even less than its predecessors to make basic defense information available to the public, and its publications have been even more misleading.[102] For instance, the 1983 and 1984 Defense Department Annual Reports to the Congress omitted such basic data as the relative spending of NATO and the Warsaw Pact, the aggregate tonnages of Pact and NATO fleets, and the strategic nuclear warhead inventories on both sides. They were instead filled with alarming charts that implied American weakness but did not show where the weaknesses really lay.

Public confusion about the basic facts of defense is a major American national security problem. To clarify the defense debate, better basic public information on defense is essential. Neither the government nor the major academic institutions are doing enough to make basic information available to news reporters, scholars, members of Congress, or citizens who are concerned about the defense policy. Adequate reference books do not exist, and most writing on defense policy is written by experts, for experts.

Defense matters, however, are not too complex for concerned citizens to master. Rather, defense seems complex because academic experts and government agencies fail to explain defense issues in clear terms and to make basic facts available in convenient form. The mistakes of the Reagan administration were made possible by public confusion about facts of history, hardware, and strategy. Clearing up this confusion is the first step toward a better defense policy.

The authors would like to thank Teresa Pelton Johnson, George F. Kennan, Steven E. Miller, and Lynn Page Whittaker for their thoughtful comments on earlier drafts of this chapter.

"Reagan Administration Defense Policy: Departure from Containment" was written for this volume. Copyright © 1987 by Barry R. Posen and Stephen W. Van Evera.

Notes

1. Gordon Adams, *The FY 1986 Defense Budget: The Weapons Buildup Continues* (Washington, D.C.: Center on Budget and Policy Priorities, 1985), pp. 45, 49.
2. See Adams, *The FY 1986 Defense Budget*, an analysis of these budget projections.
3. Caspar W. Weinberger, *Annual Report to the Congress: Fiscal Year 1983* (Washington, D.C.: U.S. Government Printing Office, 1982) p. I-15. This report is also available free on request from the Defense Department Public Affairs office. (Hereafter cited as *Annual Report 1983*, with later reports cited similarly by year.)

   Weinberger further suggests that the United States should "discard artificial definitions and contrived categories," and avoid "the mistaken argument as to whether we should prepare to fight 'two wars,' 'one and one-half wars,' or some other such tally of wars"; he demands a "necessary recasting of our strategy," without explaining what the old strategy was or what the new strategy would be. He also points to "serious deficiencies in our military forces," without explaining which missions cannot be met (*Annual Report 1983*, pp. I-3, I-11, I-15).

   Perhaps in response to outside criticism, the Secretary's *Annual Reports* for Fiscal Years 1984, 1985, and 1986 devoted more space to questions of strategy, and for the first time, the FY 1986 *Annual Report* included a section "U.S. National Security Objectives and Defense Strategy." Although the attempt is laudable, the report fails to relate means to ends, and to set priorities adequately. Thus the administration still has not yet explained its military buildup in terms concrete enough to allow us to measure benefits against costs.

4. See John Lewis Gaddis, *Strategies of Containment* (New York: Oxford University Press, 1982), pp. 25–88; Melvyn P. Leffler, "The American Conception of National Security and the Beginnings of the Cold War," *American Historical Review* (April 1984), Vol. 89, No. 2, pp. 346–381, especially pp. 356–358, 370, 374, and 377; Gaddis, "Containment: A Reassessment," *Foreign Affairs* (July 1977), Vol. 55, No. 4, pp. 873–887; David Mayers, "Containment and the Primacy of Diplomacy: George Kennan's Views, 1947–1948," *International Security* (Summer 1986), Vol. 11, No. 1; George F. Kennan, *Realities of American Foreign Policy* (New York: Norton, 1966); and Walter Lippmann, *The Cold War: A Study in U.S. Foreign Policy* (New York: Harper & Brothers, 1947). For an earlier discussion of American grand strategy from a similar perspective, see Nicholas John Spykman, *America's Strategy in World Politics: The United States and the Balance of Power* (Harcourt, Brace & World, Inc., 1942; reprint ed., n.p.: Archon, 1970), pp. 3–199.

5. *American Diplomacy 1900–1950* (New York: New American Library, 1951), p. 10.

6. Kennan, *Realities*, pp. 63–64; and Kennan, *Memoirs 1925–1950* (Boston: Little, Brown, 1967), p. 359.

7. These data, for 1982, are taken from Ruth Leger Sivard, *World Military and Social Expenditures, 1985* (Washington, D.C.: World Priorities, 1985), pp. 35–36.

8. The distinction between a local nuclear war and large-scale nuclear attacks on American allies may seem ambiguous. In some parts of the world, such as Europe, the use of more than a few dozen small nuclear weapons would indeed amount to a large-scale nuclear war. It is our belief that Soviet planners are strongly influenced in the direction of prudence by the fear that a local conventional or nuclear war would set in motion a chain of events that could lead to the release of the great destructive power of American retaliatory forces.

9. "Reagan's Strategic Outlook," *New York Times*, November 23, 1982, p. A12; and Hedrick Smith, " 'Star Wars' Battle: Moscow and Congress Increase the Pressure on Reagan," *New York Times*, September 26, 1985, p. A14.

10. *Annual Report 1983*, pp. I-3, I-4. Such gloomy estimates have also prevailed in the press; see the *The Wall Street Journal*'s warning that the Soviet Union "now is superior to the U.S. in almost every category of strategic and conventional force." "The Wrong Defense" (editorial), March 25, 1982.

11. Comparing total military manpower on both sides is complicated because in the West civilians do many jobs that are performed by uniformed workers in the Soviet Union. Thus there is only a rough consistency from source to source on Soviet military manpower figures; inconsistencies even appear within publications from the same source. Thus the London International Institute for Strategic Studies (IISS) now counts 1.32 million Soviet railroad workers and administrative personnel in its total count of Warsaw Pact manpower, which takes the Soviet total to 6.44 million. When these people are subtracted, which was formerly the practice in IISS publications and which is justified by the tasks that they perform, the result is the figures quoted in the text. See IISS, *The Military Balance 1985–1986* (London: IISS, 1985), pp. 21, 186.

12. These figures are drawn from Richard D. DeLauer, *The FY 1985 Department of Defense Program for Research, Development and Acquisition* (mimeo of a statement to the 98th Congress, February 27, 1984), Figure I-1, p. I-14.

DeLauer's figures apparently reflect recent downward revisions of official estimates for Soviet defense spending in 1974–81. Official figures previously held that Soviet spending increased at 3 to 4 percent per year in real terms during the 1974–81 period, as it had in 1966–74. Newer official figures suggest that the rate of growth in Soviet spending slowed to 3 percent in 1974–76, and to 2 percent in 1976–81. See *New York Times*, March 3, 1983, p. 1, November 19, 1983, p. 6; and William W.

Kaufmann, *The 1986 Defense Budget* (Washington, D.C.: The Brookings Institution, 1985), p. 6.

The IISS offers CIA estimates of Soviet spending that seem even lower than DeLauer's estimates (which reflect Defense Intelligence Agency calculations). This discrepancy has not been explained, but it suggests that NATO's defense effort relative to that of the Pact may be even greater than suggested here. See IISS, *The Military Balance 1985–1986*, pp. 17–19.

13. Ruth Leger Sivard, *World Military and Social Expenditures, 1981* (Leesburg, VA: World Priorities, 1981), p. 37, col 3.

14. Franklyn D. Holzman, "Are the Soviets Really Outspending the U.S. on Defense?" *International Security*, (Spring 1980), Vol. 4, No. 4, pp. 86–105. A summary of Holzman's views is Holzman, "Dollars or Rubles: The CIA's Military Estimates," *Bulletin of the Atomic Scientists* (June 1980), pp. 23–27. A CIA response to Holzman is Donald F. Burton, "Estimating Soviet Defense Spending," *Problems of Communism* (March–April 1983), Vol. 32, No. 2, pp. 85–93.

15. Caspar W. Weinberger, *Annual Report to the Congress, Fiscal Year 1986* (Washington, D.C.: U.S. Government Printing Office, 1985), p. 303.

16. IISS, *The Military Balance, 1985–1986*, p. 21.

17. Arms Control Association and Ploughshares Fund, *Countdown on SALT II* (Washington, D.C.: ACA, 1985), pp. 40–41.

18. IISS, *The Military Balance 1985–1986*, p. 181.

19. "President's News Conference on Foreign and Domestic Matters," *New York Times*, April 1, 1982, p. A22.

20. Theodore Draper, "How Not To Think About Nuclear War," *New York Review of Books* (July 15, 1982), Vol. 29, No. 12, p. 38.

21. A "megaton" is an explosive power equivalent to one million tons of TNT. An "equivalent megaton" is an explosive power that can do the same amount of damage as a bomb of one megaton. The concept of the "equivalent megaton" was developed to provide a unitary standard to compare the destructive power of arsenals comprised of bombs of different sizes.

22. Michael A. Salman, Stephen Van Evera, and Kevin J. Sullivan, "Analysis or Propaganda? Measuring American Strategic Nuclear Capabilities, 1969–1984," in Lynn R. Eden and Steven E. Miller, eds., *Explicating the Arms Control Debate*, forthcoming from Cornell University Press in 1987. For a concurring analysis, estimating that 3660 American strategic nuclear warheads could survive a Soviet surprise attack and be delivered against the Soviet Union, see Kaufmann, *The 1986 Defense Budget*, p. 63. Another analyst estimates that 3930 American warheads could survive such an attack and then be delivered. See Joshua M. Epstein, *The 1987 Defense Budget* (Washington, D.C.: The Brookings Institution, 1986), p. 14.

23. The Department of Defense has estimated that an American retaliatory attack of 200 equivalent megatons delivered against Soviet cities would promptly kill 21 percent of the Soviet population and destroy 72 percent of Soviet industry (Alain C. Enthoven and K. Wayne Smith, *How Much Is Enough?* [New York: Harper Colophon, 1971], p. 207). If so, American forces have five times the capability required to inflict this level of damage in retaliation.

John Duffield and Frank von Hippel more recently estimated that an American retaliatory attack of only twenty to forty equivalent megatons delivered against Soviet cities would promptly kill 21 percent of the Soviet population. John Duffield and Frank von Hippel, "The Short-Term Consequences of Nuclear War for Civilians," in Julius London and Gilbert F. White, eds., *Environmental Effects of Nuclear War* (Boulder, CO: Westview Press, for the American Association for the Advancement of Science, 1984), p. 56. If so, American forces have twenty-five to fifty times the capability required to inflict this level of damage in retaliation.

The retaliatory capabilities of American forces are also suggested by the damage that a relatively small American force could inflict if it were carefully targeted against the Soviet economy. According to one study, only seventy-three American warheads could destroy over 70 percent of Soviet petroleum production capacity. Another study suggests that only 631 small (fifty-kiloton) American warheads, totaling 86 EMT, or 141 large (one-megaton) American warheads, totaling 141 EMT, would be needed to destroy over 50 percent of total Soviet industrial capacity. See Office of Technology Assessment, *The Effects of Nuclear War* (Washington, D.C.: U.S. Government Printing Office, 1979), p. 76; and Arthur M. Katz, *Life After Nuclear War: The Economic and Social Impacts of Nuclear Attacks on the United States* (Cambridge, MA: Ballinger, 1982), p. 316.

24. For these and other data see Salman, Van Evera, and Sullivan, "Analysis or Propaganda?," which provides measures of American and Soviet first- and second-strike counterforce capabilities under a range of assumptions and scenarios.

25. The best study of American strategic C^{3}I to date is Bruce G. Blair, *Strategic Command and Control* (Washington, D.C.: The Brookings Institution, 1985). Other valuable studies of American C^{3}I include Desmond Ball, *Can Nuclear War Be Controlled?* (London: International Institute for Strategic Studies, Adelphi Paper #169, 1981); Congressional Budget Office, *Strategic Command, Control and Communications: Alternative Approaches for Modernization* (Washington, D.C.: Congressional Budget Office, 1981); Paul Bracken, *The Command and Control of Nuclear Forces* (New Haven: Yale University Press, 1983); and John D. Steinbruner, "Nuclear Decapitation," *Foreign Policy* (Winter 1981–82), no. 45, pp. 16–29.

26. American leaders, moreover, could predelegate launch authority to American military commanders if they decided that American retaliatory capabilities were otherwise too weak to deter Soviet attack. This dangerous expedient would raise the risk of accidental war, but it would preserve American retaliatory capability.

27. A good analysis of options to enhance the survivability of American ICBMs is Albert Carnesale and Charles Glaser, "ICBM Vulnerability: The Cures Are Worse Than the Disease," *International Security* (Summer 1982), Vol. 7, No. 1, pp. 70–85.

28. Admiral James D. Watkins, "The Maritime Strategy," in *The Maritime Strategy*, a supplement to *U.S. Naval Institute Proceedings* (January 1986), Vol. 112, No. 1, p. 8; and the *New York Times*, April 7, 1982, p. A8. President Reagan has similarly warned that NATO forces are "vastly outdistanced" by Pact forces in Europe, and that NATO faces a Soviet "superiority at sea" (*New York Times*, October 3, 1981, p. 12). General Bernard Rogers, the commander of NATO forces in Europe, more recently declared that NATO conventional forces were so weak that he would "face fairly quickly" a decision to use nuclear weapons if the Soviets attacked (*New York Times*, May 27, 1984, p. 3).

29. Committee on the Present Danger, *Is America Becoming Number 2? Current Trends on the U.S.–Soviet Military Balance* (Washington, D.C.: Committee on the Present Danger, 1978), p. 31.

30. A substantial percentage of both NATO and Warsaw Pact military capability becomes battle-ready only after several days of preparation, so it is critically important that NATO not allow the Pact a large head start in mobilization. NATO leaders must respond quickly when they receive warning of Pact mobilization measures. Failure to keep up with Pact mobilization would soon allow the Pact to muster sufficiently favorable force ratios to achieve a breakthrough against NATO.

31. Useful essays on the NATO conventional balance are John J. Mearsheimer, "Why the Soviets Can't Win Quickly in Central Europe," *International Security* (Summer 1982), Vol. 7, No. 1, pp. 3–39, also reprinted in Mearsheimer, *Conventional Deterrence* (Ithaca, NY: Cornell University Press, 1983), pp. 165–188; William P. Mako, *U.S. Ground Forces and the Defense of Central Europe* (Washington, D.C.: The Brookings

Institution, 1983); Barry R. Posen, "Measuring the European Conventional Balance: Coping with Complexity in Threat Assessment," *International Security* (Winter 1984–85), Vol. 9, No. 3, pp. 47–88; Andrew Hamilton, "Redressing the Conventional Balance: NATO's Reserve Military Manpower," *International Security* (Summer 1985), Vol. 10, No. 1, pp. 111–120; and Congressional Budget Office, *Assessing the NATO/Warsaw Pact Military Balance* (Washington, D.C.: Congressional Budget Office and U.S. Government Printing Office, December 1977).

32. Mearsheimer, "Why the Soviets Can't Win Quickly," pp. 7–8. This "firepower" score is a composite index that includes the killing power of all tanks, anti-tank weapons, artillery, and so on — all the significant weapons systems in the division.

33. For this argument see Posen, "Measuring the European Conventional Balance."

34. Carnegie Endowment for International Peace, *Challenges for U.S. National Security: Assessing the Balance: Defense Spending and Conventional Forces, Part II* (Washington, D.C.: Carnegie Endowment, 1981), p. 71. A similar qualitative advantage for NATO tactical air forces may be construed from figures offered by Alain C. Enthoven and K. Wayne Smith, *How Much Is Enough?* (New York: Harper Colophon, 1971), p. 145 and Weinberger, *Annual Report 1983*, p. II-18.

35. See Joshua M. Epstein, "Soviet Vulnerabilities in Iran and the RDF Deterrent," *International Security* (Fall 1981), Vol. 6, No. 2, pp. 149–150.

36. U.S. House of Representatives, *Hearings Before a Subcommittee of the Committee on Appropriations, Subcommittee on the Department of Defense, Part 4*, 95th Congress, 2d sess. (Washington, D.C.: U.S. Government Printing Office, 1978), p. 347. On deficiencies in Soviet pilot training see also Joshua M. Epstein, "On Conventional Deterrence in Europe: Questions of Soviet Confidence," *Orbis* (Spring 1982), Vol. 26, No. 1, pp. 71–88; and, acknowledging the superiority of American aircrew training, Department of Defense, *Soviet Military Power 1985* (Washington, D.C.: U.S. Government Printing Office, 1985), p. 88.

37. Mearsheimer, "Why the Soviets Can't Win Quickly," p. 4; and Carnegie Endowment, *Challenges for U.S. National Security*, p. 71.

38. These ratios represent a best estimate for average situations. There are, however, some historical cases of successful armored assaults by attackers who enjoyed less than a three-to-one force ratio at the point of attack. Therefore it is possible, though not likely, that the Pact could achieve local successes against some NATO forces with less than a three-to-one advantage at the attack point. If so, NATO might find itself without enough ground forces in the theater.

39. Mearsheimer, "Why the Soviets Can't Win Quickly," p. 9.

40. Ibid.

41. Ibid., pp. 28–29.

42. Ibid., p. 22.

43. Pessimistic estimates include John M. Collins, *U.S. Soviet Military Balance: Concepts and Capabilities 1960–1980* (New York: McGraw-Hill, 1980), pp. 291–330, 539–549; Jeffrey Record, *Force Reductions in Europe: Starting Over* (Cambridge, MA: Institute for Foreign Policy Analysis, Inc., 1980), p. 33; Joseph M. A. H. Luns, *NATO and the Warsaw Pact: Force Comparisons* (Brussels: NATO Information Service, 1982); Joseph M. A. H. Luns, *NATO and the Warsaw Pact: Force Comparisons* (Brussels: NATO Information Service, 1984); Phillip A. Karber, "The Growing Armor/Anti-Armor Imbalance in Central Europe," *Armed Forces Journal International* (July 1981), pp. 37–48; and Congressional Budget Office, *U.S. Ground Forces: Design and Cost Alternatives for NATO and Non-NATO Contingencies* (Washington: Congressional Budget Office, 1980).

44. Congressional Budget Office, *U.S. Ground Forces*, is an exception.

45. See, for instance, the 1980 Congressional Budget Office study *U.S. Ground Forces,*

which is perhaps the most thorough published pessimistic assessment, but which reaches its gloomy conclusions by exaggerating the number of Soviet divisions available to attack Western Europe, undercounting forces available to NATO, and downplaying terrain factors favoring

The Congressional Budget Office assumes that Soviet "Category III" cadre divisions can be readied and moved from the Soviet Union to Germany in 35 days, although another analyst estimates that this would take up to 4 months. See Jeffrey Record, *Sizing up the Army* (Washington, D.C.: The Brookings Institution, 1975), pp. 21–22. Soviet Category III divisions cannot be ready before 90–120 days. See also Department of Defense, *Soviet Military Power 1985*, p. 66, conceding that 60 percent of Soviet divisions, presumably Category IIIs, would take up to 60 days to mobilize for combat, exclusive of movement time. Another assessment of the readiness of Soviet Category III divisions that suggests that they mobilize slowly is found in testimony by the Defense Intelligence Agency to the Joint Economic Committee, published in "Allocation of Resources to the Soviet Union and China — 1981," *Hearings Before the Subcommittee on International Trade, Finance, and Security Economics of the Joint Economic Committee*, Congress of the United States, 97th Congress, 1st sess., Pt. 7 (Washington, D.C.: U.S. Government Printing Office, 1982), p. 199. See also William W. Kaufmann, "The Defense Budget," in Joseph A. Pechman, ed., *Setting National Priorities: Agenda for the 1980s* (Washington, D.C.: The Brookings Institution, 1980), cited hereafter as "*SNP 1981*." Kaufmann notes that the Afghanistan invasion indicates that "it takes the Soviet establishment a substantial amount of time — months rather than weeks — to organize a small operation against a weak and relatively disorganized country" (p. 30).

Because it ignores the low readiness of Category III divisions, the Congressional Budget Office (CBO) credits the Pact with a 120-division force thirty days after mobilization, instead of the 90-division force that most NATO plans assume the Soviets can field, or the 71-division force the Soviets could field if they choose not to employ any Category III divisions early in the war and relied exclusively on Category I and Category II divisions (Robert Shishko, *The European Conventional Balance: A Primer*, P-67-7 [Santa Monica, CA: Rand Corporation, 1981], p. 8.) The CBO's pessimistic conclusions depend on this unexplained assumption, since the CBO grants that NATO could halt a 90-division Pact assault (p. xiii).

Second, the CBO understates the capability of the German territorial forces. The German territorials are trained reserves that can be mobilized at least as fast as Soviet Category III divisions, to a total 750,000 men. By simply mobilizing the German territorials, NATO almost doubles the total size of NATO European forces, which would increase from 780,000 to 1,530,000 men. Yet the CBO credits the territorials with only six mechanized brigades — roughly two divisions, or about 70,000 men, a fraction of the total German territorial forces actually available to NATO.

Third, the CBO understates the advantage conferred on the defender by terrain in the North German Plain, instead repeating the conventional wisdom that the Plain is an easy invasion route for Soviet forces. In fact, this area is crossed by rivers, bogs, and urban sprawl, which make defense easier.

46. Jack Anderson, "Frightening Facts on the Persian Gulf," *Washington Post*, February 3, 1981, p. 18, quoting "top military hands."

47. Robert S. Dudney, "The Defense Gap that Worries the President," *U.S. News and World Report*, February 16, 1981.

48. Jeffrey Record, "Disneyland Planning for Persian Gulf Oil Defense," *The Washington Star*, March 20, 1981, p. 17.

49. The best assessment of the East-West balance in the Gulf is Epstein, "Soviet Vulnerabilities." For shorter assessments see Epstein, *The 1987 Defense Budget* (fn.

22), pp. 25–28; Kaufmann, *SNP 1981*, pp. 304–305; and William W. Kaufmann, "The Defense Budget," in Joseph A. Pechman, ed., *Setting National Priorities: The 1982 Budget* (Washington, D.C.: The Brookings Institution, 1981) (hereafter "*SNP 1982*"), p. 160. Also useful is Keith A. Dunn, "Constraints on the USSR in Southwest Asia: A Military Analysis," *Orbis* (Fall 1981), Vol. 25, No. 3, pp. 607–631.

50. Epstein, "Soviet Vulnerabilities," p. 144.

51. Andrew Krepinevich, *The U.S. Rapid Deployment Force and Protection of Persian Gulf Oil Supplies* (unpublished paper, Kennedy School of Government, Harvard University, 1980).

52. Epstein, "Soviet Vulnerabilities," pp. 139–140; and Kaufmann, *SNP 1981*, p. 305.

53. Epstein, "Soviet Vulnerabilities," p. 139.

54. Ibid., p. 136.

55. Ibid., p. 140.

56. Ibid., pp. 145–148.

57. Ibid., p. 146.

58. Quoted in Bernard Brodie, *War and Politics* (New York: Macmillan, 1973), p. 356.

59. Epstein, "Soviet Vulnerabilities," p. 157.

60. Pessimistic estimates include Jeffrey Record, *The Rapid Deployment Force and U.S. Military Intervention in the Persian Gulf* (Cambridge, MA: Institute for Foreign Policy Analysis, 1981), pp. 8–42, 61–68; Collins, *U.S.-Soviet Military Balance*, pp. 367–394; Albert Wohlstetter, "Meeting the Threat in the Persian Gulf," *Survey* (Spring 1980), Vol. 25, No. 2, pp. 128–188; and W. Scott Thompson, "The Persian Gulf Correlation of Forces," *International Security* (Summer 1982), Vol. 7, No. 1, pp. 157–180.

61. We have not provided measures of American capability to fight a war to defend peripheral American interests while also defending Europe or the Persian Gulf — the fourth mission that we posit that American forces must perform — because published information is too scanty to allow a careful assessment. American forces for this mission (often called the "half-war" mission) are usually sized against a possible North Korean invasion of South Korea, but detailed information on the Korean military balance is scarce. Most public sources do suggest that American forces could in fact thwart such an attack and thus could perform the mission they are measured against. (See William W. Kaufmann, "The Defense Budget," in Joseph A. Pechman, ed., *Setting National Priorities: The 1983 Budget* [Washington, D.C.: The Brookings Institution, 1982 — henceforth "*SNP 1983*,"], pp. 89–90; and Congressional Budget Office, *U.S. Ground Forces*, p. 67.)

62. For the Reagan administration's general strategic ideas see Thomas C. Reed, "Details of National Security Strategy," Speech delivered to the Armed Forces Communications and Electronics Association, June 16, 1982 (mimeo, available from the White House, Office of the National Security Advisor); *New York Times*, "Revised U.S. Policy Said to Focus on 'Prevailing' Over Russians," June 17, 1982, p. B17, summarizing Reed; Richard Halloran, "Pentagon Draws Up First Strategy for Fighting a Long Nuclear War," *New York Times*, May 30, 1982, p. A1, summarizing the secret administration five-year defense guidance document; Richard Halloran, "Weinberger Denies U.S. Plans for 'Protracted Nuclear War,' " *New York Times*, June 21, 1982, p. A5; the *Annual Report to the Congress* volumes issued yearly by Secretary of Defense Caspar Weinberger, especially his reports for fiscal years 1983 and 1984; and Caspar W. Weinberger, "U.S. Defense Strategy," *Foreign Affairs* (Spring 1986), Vol. 64, No. 4, pp. 675–697. For administration ideas about naval strategy, see Admiral James D. Watkins, "The Maritime Strategy" (fn. 28), pp. 4–17; U.S. Senate, Committee on Armed Services, Subcommittee on Sea Power and Force Projection, *Hearings on the Department of Defense Authorization for Appropriations*

for Fiscal Year 1985 (Washington, D.C.: U.S. Government Printing Office, March 14, 1984), pp. 3851–3900; and "Lehman Seeks Superiority," *International Defense Review* (May 1982), pp. 547–548. Explicating the administration defense program is Fred Charles Iklé, "The Reagan Defense Program: Focus on the Strategic Imperatives," *Strategic Review* (Spring 1982), Vol. 10, No. 2, pp. 11–18; and Fred Charles Iklé, "Strategic Principles of the Reagan Administration," *Strategic Review* (Fall 1983), Vol. 11, No. 4, pp. 13–18.

63. On preemptive war see Thomas C. Schelling, *Arms and Influence* (New Haven: Yale University Press, 1966), pp. 221–259; and Schelling, *The Strategy of Conflict* (New York: Oxford University Press, 1963), pp. 207–254.

64. See Kaufmann, *SNP 1983*, pp. 65–66. Other administration programs also enhance American counterforce capability, including enhanced nuclear "battle-management" C^3I and new nuclear hunter-killer submarines.

65. For essays and documents on the Star Wars program, see Steven E. Miller and Stephen Van Evera, eds., *The Star Wars Controversy* (Princeton, NJ: Princeton University Press, 1986).

66. Press leaks indicate that the administration's first "Defense Guidance" document, setting forth basic administration strategy, calls for nuclear forces that can "prevail" by rendering "ineffective the total Soviet (and Soviet allied) military and political power structure," even if American forces strike second. This document also reportedly envisions attacks on the whole Soviet force structure, including "decapitation" strikes against Soviet political and military leadership (Halloran, "Weinberger Denies U.S. Plan," p. A5).

67. Ground Zero, *Nuclear War: What's In It For You?* (New York: Pocket Books, 1982), p. 267.

68. In the late 1970s, the notion arose that new technologies (ICBM accuracy improvements, for example) had made counterforce easier, and that counterforce therefore made more sense than before. But this argument reflected the fallacy of counting how many warheads American forces hypothetically could destroy (which had increased), instead of counting how many could not be destroyed (which had also increased), and how much damage these warheads could do to the United States. By any measures, using the latter method counterforce is much harder now than fifteen years ago.

69. A collection of Soviet military statements about nuclear strategy is Joseph D. Douglass, Jr., and Amoretta M. Hoeber's *Soviet Strategy for Nuclear War* (Stanford, CA: Hoover Institution Press, 1979). A more comprehensive study of Soviet military thought is David Holloway's *The Soviet Union and the Arms Race* (New Haven: Yale University Press, 1983).

70. The Soviet nuclear buildup also would seem to argue against counterforce by supporting arguments that more resources now should be devoted to enhancing the survivability of American forces, if Soviet forces now threaten American forces more directly. Thus administration warnings about the size of the Soviet nuclear buildup seem to recommend against the counterforce programs that the administration propounds.

71. Indeed, the nuclear arms race is best controlled by first controlling counterforce. If the superpowers foreswore counterforce, the rationale for nuclear arms racing would largely disappear, since programs on both sides would no longer create new requirements for the other. Conversely, meaningful arms control is very difficult if the superpowers pursue counterforce seriously, because counterforce programs on both sides force both sides to keep building. Under these circumstances, arms control agreements merely ratify decisions to build ever-larger arsenals.

72. Studies criticizing the feasibility of Star Wars are Ashton B. Carter's *Directed Energy*

Missile Defense in Space (Washington, D.C.: Congress of the United States, Office of Technology Assessment, 1984); Sidney D. Drell, Philip J. Farley, and David Holloway's "Preserving the ABM Treaty: A Critique of the Reagan Strategic Defense Initiative," *International Security* (Fall 1984), Vol. 9, No. 2, pp. 51–91; and Union of Concerned Scientists, *The Fallacy of Star Wars* (New York: Vintage Books, 1984). The Carter and the Drell, Farley, and Holloway studies are also reprinted in Miller and Van Evera, eds., *The Star Wars Controversy.*

On possible countermeasures to Star Wars see Carter, *Directed Energy Missile Defense,* pp. 45–52, 69–70.

73. Arguing that the risk of war increases when offense is strong is Robert Jervis's "Cooperation Under the Security Dilemma," *World Politics* (January 1978), Vol. 30, No. 2, pp. 186–214, also excerpted in Robert J. Art and Kenneth N. Waltz's *The Use of Force,* 2nd ed. (Washington, D.C.: University Press of America, 1983), pp. 34–64. For a discussion of the dangers raised by offensive ideas and doctrines in 1914, see Steven E. Miller, ed., *Military Strategy and the Origins of the First World War* (Princeton: Princeton University Press, 1984).

74. Reagan advisor Thomas Reed, for example, has dismissed the old policy of "containment" and declared that the United States now focuses on "prevailing" over the Soviets (Reed, "Details of National Strategy," p. 17; and *New York Times,* "Revised U.S. Policy Said to Focus on 'Prevailing' Over the Russians"). Similarly, Defense Secretary Weinberger has warned against "the transposition of the defensive orientation of our peacetime strategy onto the strategy and tactics that guide us in the event of war" (*Annual Report 1983,* pp. I–16).

75. Halloran, "Pentagon Draws up First Strategy," p. 12.

76. *International Defense Review,* "Lehman Seeks Superiority," p. 547.

77. *Annual Report 1984,* p. 33.

78. Ibid., pp. I–16, III–21.

79. See Watkins, "The Maritime Strategy" (fn. 62), outlining the new Navy strategy.

80. On the risk of escalation raised by offensive conventional operations see Barry R. Posen, "Inadvertent Nuclear War? Escalation and NATO's Northern Flank," *International Security* (Fall 1982), Vol. 7, No. 2, pp. 28–54; and John J. Mearsheimer, "The Maritime Strategy and Deterrence in Europe," *International Security* (Fall 1986), Vol. 11, No. 2. Another criticism of offensive conventional strategies is Joshua M. Epstein's "Horizontal Escalation: Sour Notes on a Recurrent Theme," *International Security* (Winter 1983–84), Vol. 8, No. 3, pp. 19–31. For contrasting views, emphasizing the deterrent benefit of an offensive strategy for NATO, see Samuel P. Huntington's "Conventional Deterrence and Conventional Retaliation in Europe," *International Security* (Winter 1983–84), Vol. 8, No. 3, pp. 32–56. Defending offensive naval strategies are Watkins, "The Maritime Strategy" (fn. 28); and Captain Linton F. Brooks, "Deterrence and Defense from the Sea: An Advocate's View of the Maritime Strategy," *International Security* (Fall 1986), Vol. 11, No. 2.

81. A force of ten carriers would give the United States eight carriers for combat missions in wartime, since two carriers would normally be in overhaul. By one estimate, two carriers are required to defend the sea lanes in the Atlantic, and two to defend the Pacific sea lane. See the Congressional Budget Office's *Navy Budget Issues for Fiscal Year 1980* (Washington, D.C.: Congressional Budget Office, March 1979), pp. 41–42. This would leave four carriers for anti-Soviet missions in the Persian Gulf or the Mediterranean. The wartime requirement for carrier battle groups in the Mediterranean seems questionable, since NATO land-based reconnaisance and fighter aircraft based in Spain, Italy, and Turkey — all NATO members — could cover most of the Mediterranean. This leaves four carriers available for the Persian Gulf area, and gives the United States adequate coverage of all missions that require carriers.

82. *Annual Report 1983*, p. I-15.

83. Developments of this view are Robert H. Johnson's "Exaggerating America's Stakes in Third World Conflicts," *International Security* (Winter 1985–86), Vol. 10, No. 3, pp. 32–68; and Richard E. Feinberg, *The Intemperate Zone: The Third World Challenge to U.S. Foreign Policy* (New York: W. W. Norton, 1983).

84. Shares of Gross World Product (GWP) in 1982 were as follows: Africa, 2.9 percent; Italy, 3.0 percent; Great Britain, 4.2 percent; West Germany, 5.9 percent; Latin America, 6.3 percent; Japan, 9.3 percent; the Third World, 19.7 percent; Western Europe, 27.1 percent; Europe and Japan, 36.4 percent. The Soviet Union produced 12.2 percent of GWP, while the United States produced 23.9 percent. See Sivard, *World Military and Social Expenditures 1985*, pp. 35–37.

85. For examples see Weinberger's *Annual Report 1985*, p. 96; and General George S. Brown's *United States Military Posture for FY 1979* (Washington, D.C.: Organization of the Joint Chiefs of Staff, 1978), p. 103.

86. On measuring dependence and interdependence the classic essay is Kenneth N. Waltz's "The Myth of National Interdependence," in Charles P. Kindleberger, ed., *The International Corporation* (Cambridge, MA: MIT Press, 1970), pp. 205–223. See also Waltz's *Theory of International Relations* (Reading, MA: Addison-Wesley, 1979), pp. 138–160.

87. Moreover, OPEC has eroded with the entrance of other producers into the oil market since 1973 and the increasing effectiveness of Western conservation measures, indicating that even Western dependence on OPEC oil is not absolute.

   A useful detailed assessment of Western dependence on Persian Gulf oil is Stanley R. Sloan, *Western Vulnerability to a Disruption of Persian Gulf Oil Supplies: U.S. Interests and Options* (Washington, D.C.: Congressional Research Service Report 83-24F, March 24, 1983).

88. Wise choices about basing policy require that policymakers compare the cost of policy alternatives: What is the dollar cost of effective alternatives to American bases, compared to the cost of preserving existing bases by being prepared to intervene militarily and what would be the cost of neutralizing new Soviet bases by deploying new American forces, as opposed to preventing their appearance by military intervention? A thorough analysis of the strategic importance of Third World bases should provide data that answer these questions.

89. Advocates of intervention forces sometimes suggest that the United States needs them to halt Soviet "geopolitical momentum," a tide of Soviet influence supposedly sweeping the Third World, whose appearance allegedly demonstrates that American action is necessary to contain Soviet influence in the Third World. In fact, Soviet "geopolitical momentum" is a myth; an inventory of global alignments and realignments since 1945 reveals that over the past two decades the Soviets have barely held their ground in the Third World or have perhaps lost ground. An excellent survey of the evidence up to 1980 is Stephen Goose, "Soviet Geopolitical Momentum: Myth or Menace? Trends of Soviet Influence Around the World From 1945 to 1980," *Defense Monitor* (January 1980), Vol. 11, No. 1.

90. IISS, *The Military Balance 1981–1982*, p. 27–39, 112. Spain, which joined NATO in 1982, is excluded. The IISS estimate of American spending in 1980 differs from the estimate quoted at the beginning of this chapter (5.2 percent) because the IISS calculates its data differently than the United States government, which is the original source for the 5.2 percent figure.

91. Sivard, *World Military and Social Expenditures 1981*, p. 37, col. 3.

92. A more detailed study of burden sharing within NATO, also concluding that the United States carries a disproportionate burden, is R. William Thomas's *Burdensharing in the North Atlantic Alliance: A Preliminary Review of the Evidence* (Washington, D.C.: Congressional Budget Office, January 1985).

93. These figures are calculated from data found in IISS, *The Military Balance 1985–1986*, pp. 6, 39–60. NATO definitions of defense spending are used, and Spain is excluded for comparability to 1980.

94. Irving Kristol, "What's Wrong With NATO?" (*New York Times Magazine*, September 25, 1983, p. 71) suggests the need for such "shock treatment."

95. "Games the Pentagon Plays," *Foreign Policy* (Summer 1973), No. 11, pp. 80–92.

96. Organization of the Joint Chiefs of Staff, *United States Military Posture* (Washington, D.C.: U.S. Government Printing Office, issued annually).

97. Congressional Budget Office, *Shaping the General Purpose Navy of the Eighties: Issues for Fiscal Years 1981–1985* (Washington, D.C.: Congressional Budget Office, 1980), p. 44. See also Robert J. Murray, *Technology and Manpower: Department of the Navy Perspective* (manuscript, Kennedy School of Government, Harvard University, 1985). Murray reports that although total Navy ship numbers fell by almost 50 percent between FY 1964 and FY 1983 (from 959 ships to 490 ships), total Navy fleet tonnage fell by only 8 percent, and total Navy warship tonnage actually rose by 11 percent (pp. 138–139).

98. In fact, press accounts suggest that Reagan defense planners believe they cannot achieve their strategy without another enormous military buildup once the current one is completed. During Reagan's first term, the Joint Chiefs of Staff reportedly warned they would need an additional $750 billion to carry out the missions specified by the administration, beyond the $1.6 trillion budgeted for defense in the administration's first five-year plan (George C. Wilson, "Pentagon: $1.6 trillion will not do job," *Boston Globe*, March 8, 1982, p. 1).

99. Center on Budget and Policy Priorities, *The FY 1986 Defense Budget*, p. 44.

100. Richard Stubbing, "The Defense Program: Buildup or Binge?" *Foreign Affairs* (Spring 1985), Vol. 63, No. 4, pp. 857, 864. See also Congressional Budget Office, *Defense Spending: What Has Been Accomplished?* (Washington, D.C.: Congressional Budget Office, 1985); and William W. Kaufmann, *A Reasonable Defense* (Washington, D.C.: The Brookings Institution, 1986), pp. 41–46.

    The United States did add about thirty-two frigates and twenty-one attack submarines to its force structure during Reagan's first term (Weinberger, *Annual Report 1985*, p. 136). Most of these vessels had been ordered in previous years, however.

101. See, for example, Reed "Details of National Security Strategy" (fn. 62).

102. The Department of Defense publication, *Soviet Military Power*, in its fourth edition at this writing, has been the Reagan administration's principal vehicle for providing defense information to the American public. Early editions focused on Soviet capabilities without much reference to those of the West. Subsequent editions, especially *Soviet Military Power 1985*, do a better job of comparing Soviet and Western capabilities. This document can be a useful source, but it should be used judiciously. Its purpose is clearly advocacy; its publication each year coincides with the publication of the Secretary's *Annual Report to the Congress* and the defense budget. The document suffers from many of the deficiencies cited throughout this chapter. At the same time, however, it is now 140 pages long, and a good deal of useful information has crept into its pages. Those interested in national security questions should read *Soviet Military Power* — but with a critical eye.

4

An Explosion in the Kitchen?
Economic Relations
with Other Advanced
Industrial States

Benjamin J. Cohen

In the 1980s, the United States will continue to be subject to adverse foreign economic pressures. These pressures . . . will lead to conflict. American foreign economic policy under President Carter and his successors will be judged according to its success in keeping international conflict manageable while retaining domestic political support and maintaining U.S. influence as well as fostering prosperity at home and abroad. The foreign economic policy kitchen will be hot; success will come to those who can turn out the goodies without setting off an explosion.

—Robert O. Keohane, *Eagle Entangled* (pp. 118–119)

Robert Keohane's closing words in his contribution to *Eagle Entangled*[1] provide a useful starting point for an analysis of the foreign economic policy of the Reagan administration during its first five years in office. The test, as Keohane stressed, is not whether conflict has been absent — conflict is virtually inevitable in international economic relations — but rather whether conflict has been kept manageable. Has the United States used its resources wisely, given existing policy constraints, to promote national interests and objectives? Has prosperity been promoted? Have domestic support and foreign influence been retained?

Benjamin J. Cohen is William L. Clayton Professor of International Economic Affairs at The Fletcher School of Law and Diplomacy, Tufts University. Educated at Columbia University, he has taught at Princeton University and is a frequent consultant to United States government and international agencies. He has written seven books, including Organizing the World's Money *(New York: Basic Books, 1977),* Banks and the Balance of Payments *(Montclair, N.J.: Allenheld, Osmun, 1981), and* In Whose Interest? *(New Haven, CT: Yale University Press, 1986).*

We know that the Reagan administration has so far avoided an outright explosion. But that is no more than a *de minimus* test of success. Judged by the more discriminate criteria suggested by Keohane, the administration's record can be described as dismal at best. The purpose of this chapter is to evaluate that record in greater detail, focusing on American relations with other advanced industrial states. Relations with developing nations are discussed separately by Richard Feinberg in Chapter 5.

Traditional Objectives of Policy

Analysis of decision making in foreign economic policy may be approached in a variety of ways. For an economist, the most congenial approach views policy as a problem of "maximization under constraint." Conventional economic analysis begins with the assumption of scarcity: The things that people and societies value are limited in supply; Tin Pan Alley notwithstanding, the best things in life are *not* all free. Choices therefore are necessary. The task for economic decision makers (assuming they are rational) is to do the best they can to maximize some value or other — or several values simultaneously — under the constraint of scarcity. The task for the analyst seeking insight into such behavior is to focus on this problem of choice, to understand the trade-offs among objectives. As Walter Heller has written of the political economist: "Problems of choice are his meat and drink. His method is to factor out the costs, the benefits and the net advantage or disadvantage of alternative courses of action."[2]

In United States foreign economic policy, the choices of decision makers have traditionally focused on four main objectives: (1) national economic welfare, (2) distribution, (3) national security, and (4) system preservation. All four "target variables" reflect fundamental political and economic interests.

The first target, national economic welfare, stands for real income, the quantity of real goods and services available to the nation for final use. Although this is the traditional objective identified in conventional economic analysis, it is not a simple concept. Indeed, despite more than two centuries of development of modern economic theory, we still do not know precisely how to go about maximizing economic welfare, in good part because the target is decomposable — at the micro level identified with efficiency of resource allocation; at the macro level, with both full employment and price stability. As these three dimensions may not always be mutually compatible, policy choices necessarily involve value judgments regarding the relative weights to be attached to each and the trade-offs to be made among them. On such matters, clearly, reasonable people may reasonably disagree.

The second target variable, distribution, stands as a proxy for the set of relevant domestic political goals of policy. Being politicians and not disinterested statesmen or philosopher-kings, policymakers may be assumed to concern themselves not only (if at all) with the general interests of the nation as a whole, but also with the specific interests of certain narrower constituencies within the nation and to seek, through policy decisions, to maximize the gains of such domestic groups or to minimize their losses. In other words, they may be assumed to aim at some particular distribution of the costs and benefits of policy. This of course is the traditional objective identified in political analysis, the meat and drink of the political scientist: Whose ox is gored if one policy is chosen rather than another? It is also, like economic welfare, not a simple concept. As with economic welfare, we still do not know precisely how to go about achieving some particular distribution of the costs and benefits of policy, again in good part because the objective is decomposable. Distribution implies not only gains or losses of real income but also of relative rank, prestige, privileges, and the like; and since here too value judgments and trade-offs are necessarily involved, here too disagreements among reasonable people are possible.

The two remaining variables, national security and system preservation, embody the principal objectives that must be added when the foreign dimension, and not only the purely domestic dimensions, of economic policy are considered. National security is mainly concerned with such issues as political independence and territorial integrity, and it can logically be translated into an imperative to maximize, insofar as possible, influence abroad and autonomy of decision making at home. System preservation reflects the interest that the United States has in common with other countries to avoid disruption of the international economic relations from which everyone presumably benefits, even if unevenly. Many observers have called attention to the similarity of the system of international economic relations to a "nonzero-sum game," in which, because the interests of the players are neither entirely harmonious nor completely irreconcilable, state policies inevitably mix elements of competition and cooperation.[3] The targets of national security and system preservation express, respectively, these two elements of policy (although they may, of course, receive quite different relative weights in the policies of different governments).

Of the four objectives of American policy, national economic welfare always seems to take precedence at the level of rhetoric. On assuming office, every new administration declares America's prosperity to be its fundamental goal, defined in terms of such desiderata as full employment, price stability, and rapid growth. But then, at the level of action, every administration eventually compromises its welfare objective in some degree for the sake of the other three. Ultimately all four targets come into play in practice. Successive administrations differ only in the nature of the compromises they regard as acceptable or are willing to admit.

Thus, every American administration since World War II has emphasized this nation's commitment to an open and liberal (that is, market-oriented and nondiscriminatory) world trading system. Yet repeatedly, administrations undertake to protect specific domestic constituencies against "injury" from foreign imports, even at the expense of perpetuating an inefficient resource allocation and potentially retarding domestic growth. Similarly, all administrations have seemed prepared to pay an economic price for the sake of extending American influence overseas or preserving the international system that we were so instrumental in constructing after 1945. In postwar Europe the United States tolerated, even promoted, preferential regional trade and payments arrangements despite their inherent and obvious discrimination against American export sales, because such arrangements were thought essential to restore the health of key economic allies; similarly, America's internal market was opened to Japanese exports even when markets elsewhere remained tightly closed to goods labeled "Made in Japan." It must be assumed that policymakers are not unaware of the potential welfare costs of the compromises they make.

The reasons for such compromises are familiar. Measures to protect the interests of specific domestic constituencies have their roots in America's internal politics — our fragmented and pluralistic federal system in which disproportionate influence can be wielded by relatively narrow pressure groups. Similarly, measures to extend American influence abroad or the autonomy of decision making have their roots in America's external politics — the anarchic and insecure international system in which national interests are never entirely safe from overt or covert threat. As a major power, the United States has long enjoyed a high degree of influence over global economic events, as well as comparative freedom from external constraint on internal decision making — for so long, in fact, that what in other countries would be regarded as a privilege has come to be treated here, by many, as a right. One need only think of Washington's continued reluctance to give up the international reserve-asset role of the dollar, which grants the United States the extraordinary privilege (what Charles de Gaulle used to call the "exorbitant privilege") to finance balance-of-payments deficits, in effect, with IOUs rather than with reserve assets of its own. Few other countries enjoy a similar privilege, and none, certainly, to the same extent.

System preservation has also long figured prominently among American policy targets because of America's continuing position of leadership in international economic affairs. The story of this "hegemonic" role in shaping the institutions and structures of the postwar world economy needs no retelling here.[4] Once having fashioned an external environment largely favorable to American objectives, the United States thereby gained a vested interest in maintaining it. Other countries might act as "free riders," enjoying the benefits of a system of growing economic interdependence without contributing significantly to its preservation, but not the United States, whose support continued to be a necessary (even if now no longer a sufficient) condition of systemic survival. American policymakers have often felt obliged to make concessions to keep the system functioning without undue discord or disruption.

Thus, although national prosperity may be described as the most enduring interest served by American foreign economic policy, it is by no means either exclusive or absolute. It is not exclusive because other interests are also felt to be vital, most notably the compulsion of a great power to maintain a maximum of influence abroad and autonomy of decision making at home. It is not absolute because in order to promote economic welfare in the long term, concessions in the short term have often been felt to be necessary, most notably to safeguard the interdependent international system the coherence and viability of which continued to be identified with America's own national self-interest. In addition, since every administration feels the need to cultivate and retain domestic political support, the particular interests of key domestic constituencies are also factored into policy calculations of the interests of the nation as a whole.

For the purposes of this chapter, what is most significant about these compromises is the extent to which, over time, their costs in terms of welfare have risen as a result of the evolution of objective conditions, both domestically and internationally. In the United States, our political system has grown ever more fragmented and stalemated as a result of the historic ebb of power in recent years from the "Imperial Presidency" toward Congress, where particular regional or sectorial interests can more easily exercise effective influence over policy. Today even relatively small private groups, if well organized, can have a significant impact on public decision making. Accordingly, the price required to accommodate them seems to have steadily increased.

Abroad, too, the system has grown ever more fragmented and stalemated, as a result of the historic ebb of power away from the "imperial" United States. At the end of World War II, America could truly be described as a hegemonic world power. In international trade and finance our dominance was unquestioned; the United States could well afford the cost of aid programs and trade concessions designed to maintain its foreign influence and shore up the newly erected international economic order. But as time has passed and, as is well known, our economic position declined relative to that of our allies in Europe and Japan and, more recently, in relation to others as well, our leadership role has been increasingly challenged by other countries. Still preeminent but no longer predominant, the United States is no longer able to determine the course of events alone, at a comparatively low cost to itself. As in the domestic arena, power has become more diffused. Hence in the international arena, too, the price of accommodation has increased.

Finally, the costs of compromise have risen as the result of the sheer complexity of international economic relations today. The proliferation of issues and multiplying linkages among them have greatly magnified the uncertainties inherent in the decision-making process and limited even further the government's ability to develop an effective and coherent set of policies.

Not that the United States has therefore become a pitiful, helpless giant. Quite the contrary. As is also well known, the United States still commands impressive resources in international economic relations, based on an economy that is still the largest, most diversified, and most technologically advanced in the world. Our foreign trade is still greater than that of any other single country, our overseas investment the most extensive, our financial markets the most attractive, our currency the most widely used for international purposes. But conditions *have* changed, and as a result our ability to achieve traditional policy goals, while still considerable, is no longer what it used to be. Decision makers find their range of choice increasingly hemmed in by pressures of interest groups at home, by the growing assertiveness of governments abroad, and by the ever-greater complexity of the issues with which they have to deal. The constraints are real. How to come to terms with them has been the central dilemma of foreign economic policymaking for all recent administrations.

From Carter to Reagan

How have successive administrations tried to cope with this dilemma? At first glance, little continuity seems apparent in the historical record. As the constraints on American policy have grown, decision makers have veered often, and sharply, between efforts to adjust to the new limits of power and efforts to reassert the primacy of American interests. When Richard Nixon became president, for instance, the first inclination of his administration seemed to be to accommodate our economic allies in Europe and Japan with macroeconomic policies that would help bring the burgeoning American balance-of-payments deficit under control. But when appeals for complementary initiatives from the Europeans and Japanese, particularly with respect to exchange rates, seemed to fall on deaf ears, policy was soon shifted to a more confrontational stance, culminating in August 1971 with a 10 percent import surcharge and suspension of the dollar's convertibility into gold. The purpose of these moves, Washington made clear, was to pressure other countries into accepting an exchange rate realignment that would improve America's competitive position, whether others liked it or not: This was "economic gunboat diplomacy" at its most naked. Under the influence of his blunt and impatient Treasury Secretary, John Connally, President Nixon was not above destroying one of the key foundations of the postwar Bretton Woods system for the sake of promoting American exports.

Not that such policy swings were anything new. One need only recall the Smoot-Hawley tariff of 1930, followed four years later by the first Reciprocal Trade Agreements Act; or the generosity of our early postwar policies in Europe and Japan, followed shortly by a reversion to the narrowest sort of protection of domestic clothespin manufacturers and the like. Nor are such swings confined only to economic policy. Other dimensions of foreign policy manifest the same "oscillations," as Robert Osgood calls them, "between assertion and retrenchment, between the affirmation and restraint of national power."[5] These oscillations have deep roots in America's historical approach to the outside world, which has always reflected an uncertain tension between pretensions to America's leadership in international affairs and a gut urge to be rid of all foreign entanglements, with policy preferences switching frequently between the two. The apparent discontinuities in the historical record really constitute one of the more notable continuities in the rhythm of our external relations, political no less than economic. It is hardly surprising that other countries often accuse the United States of "incoherence" in our foreign policies, of "insensitivity," "indifference," or "lack of finesse."

In this respect, the administration of Jimmy Carter was no exception. Initially inclined toward an activist reaffirmation of America's influence over economic events, it ended by stressing the advantages of compromise and collaboration with our key allies in Europe and Japan. This trend, despite criticisms of inconsistency (or worse), was evident in both the main dimensions of our economic relations with the other industrial states, macroeconomics and trade.

In macroeconomic relations, the administration began by promoting a grand strategy of reflation by the strongest industrial states — quickly dubbed the *locomotive* strategy — to pull the world economy out of recession. When the other main locomotives, Germany and Japan, balked at introducing new expansionary measures, primarily for fear of renewing rampant inflationary pressures, the United States pressed ahead anyway. The new administration felt a heavy responsibility for renewed growth not only at home but also in the world economy as a whole, which seemed gravely threatened by slow growth, rising unemployment, and severe balance-of-payments problems; and it was determined to take the lead in fostering global recovery, on its own, if need be.[6]

The outcome is well known.[7] Inflation began to accelerate again in the United States. In addition, because of the absence of parallel stimulus elsewhere, very large deficits reemerged in the American balance of payments, which, in turn, led to severe selling pressures on the dollar and uncertainty in the exchange markets. At first Washington tended to view the dollar's decline with equanimity: "[T]he Administration does not believe it is appropriate to maintain any particular value for the dollar," President Carter's Council of Economic Advisors asserted in its first *Annual Report*.[8] But as exchange-market conditions became more chaotic, criticisms of American policy mounted, and in Europe, plans began for the construction of a new "zone of monetary stability" — the European Monetary System — to insulate currencies on the other side of the Atlantic from the vagaries of the dollar.[9] Increasingly isolated, the administration eventually shifted toward greater demand restraint at home, more active exchange intervention abroad, and closer coordination of both macroeconomic and intervention policies with other major industrial countries. The turning point came with the Bonn economic summit in July 1978, when the United States pledged to ease up on its domestic expansionary policies, and it was confirmed on November 1, 1978, when the administration announced a decisive new commitment to support the dollar in exchange markets (backed by a $30 billion "rescue package" arranged with allied governments and the International Monetary Fund). By mid-1979 it could accurately be said that "[t]he Carter Administration had conceded defeat."[10] In its last two years, the administration's emphasis was not on unilateral initiatives but rather on the need for greater international collaboration and cooperation to sustain macroeconomic and intervention policies consistent with both internal and external balance. In its last *Annual Report*, the very same Council of Economic Advisors could now speak of the merits of "consistency in economic policy objectives and cooperation in exchange-market policies . . . to ensure the smooth functioning of the international monetary system."[11]

Similarly, in the trade area the administration began — ritual declarations of adherence to traditional liberal principles notwithstanding — by reasserting the primacy of American commercial interests. Our policy was now to be "free but fair trade," according to President Carter's Special Trade Representative, Robert Strauss. In practice, this translated into a series of measures designed to protect sensitive domestic industries from the competition of lower-cost imports. During 1977 so-called orderly marketing agreements (negotiated quotas) were established to restrict, *inter alia*, imports of footwear from Korea and Taiwan and color television sets from Japan. And in early 1978, the so-called trigger-price mechanism was instituted to discourage steel imports by assuring that any shipments below the specified reference price (based on the production costs of the most efficient producer, Japan) would trigger an accelerated antidumping investigation. In effect, the device fixed a minimum price for imported steel. In addition, the administration significantly tightened the application of provisions of the 1974 Trade Act involving countervailing duties (intended to offset the price-reducing effects of foreign export subsidies) and escape clause actions.[12]

Here, too, the tide shifted in 1978, again in good part because of mounting criticisms from abroad. The Carter administration was never mercantilist in an ideological sense. Most of its protectionist initiatives were apparently taken reluctantly and only under strong domestic pressures. Not surprisingly, therefore, when similar tendencies toward increased restrictiveness became manifest in Europe and Japan,[13] threatening a snowballing of retaliatory measures that could bring down the whole edifice of international trade, the thrust of policy eventually became more conciliatory, shifting toward mutual accommodation with America's principal trading partners. In late 1978 a new National Export Policy was announced; it switched the emphasis in trade relations from import restraint to export promotion. And in April 1979 the so-called Tokyo Round of multilateral trade negotiations was brought to a conclusion, with the United States making crucial concessions on such matters as countervailing duties, agricultural subsidies, and customs valuation procedures.[14] During the administration's last two years, not one single new restriction was imposed on imports from other industrial countries, despite persistent protectionist sentiment at home (aggravated, especially, by the recession of 1980).

In effect, in both macroeconomics and trade, the Carter administration went through a kind of difficult learning process, first reasserting traditional policy goals and then gradually becoming educated to the new limits of American power. To its credit, the administration seemed to learn the lesson well. In the administration's second two years, unilateral foreign economic policy initiatives were infrequent and then taken only in response to what seemed extreme provocation; for example, the 1979 freeze of Iranian assets following the seizure of American hostages in Teheran or the 1980 grain embargo on the Soviet Union following the Russian invasion of Afghanistan.[15] For the most part, policy emphasis shifted instead to closer collaboration with our allies, in a groping attempt to find some way to manage jointly what, it was now recognized, the United States could no longer control entirely on its own. Given the evolution of objective conditions, there seemed few realistic alternatives to a stance of mutual accommodation and compromise. But to a nation long accustomed to a high degree of autonomy and influence in international economic affairs, it was a frustrating if not alarming experience; and it no doubt contributed to Jimmy Carter's defeat in November 1980.

With the arrival of Ronald Reagan the pendulum swiftly swung back, almost as if the Carter learning process had never occurred. For the new Republican administration, elected in part precisely because of the frustrations and alarms of the preceding years, it was simply inconceivable that the United States could not reclaim its accustomed autonomy and influence over economic events. President Reagan's reading of history was far different: Objective conditions had *not* fundamentally changed; American power *could* be reaffirmed. All that was needed was renewed vigor and incisive action in support of American interests. At home a new macroeconomic policy had to be initiated unencumbered by troublesome accommodation of governments elsewhere. Abroad trade policy had to be used forcefully to promote the market position of American producers. In such initiatives, it was felt, lay the real alternative to the compromises of the Carter years.

The key, according to the Reagan administration, was to be found in the "magic of the marketplace." If markets would be allowed to work, America's natural leadership would swiftly reemerge. In this respect there was no distinction at all between the administration's faith in private economic activity and its faith in the country: The two were intertwined. In the words of President Reagan's Council of Economic Advisors[16]:

> The successful implementation of policies to control inflation and restore vigorous real growth in the United States will have a profound and favorable impact on the rest of the world. . . . More generally, the Administration's approach to international economic issues is based on the same principles which underlie its domestic programs: a belief in the superiority of market solutions to economic problems and an emphasis on private economic activity as the engine of non-inflationary growth.

How well did this market-oriented approach fare during the administration's first five years?

Macroeconomic Policy: Reaganomics Rampant

Like so many administrations before it, the Reagan administration came to office proclaiming America's prosperity to be its fundamental goal. The country was to have a "New Beginning." The first order of business was to be a "Program for Economic Recovery," announced with great fanfare by President Reagan himself before Congress and a prime-time television audience on February 18, less than a month after his inauguration. The program embodied the four main pillars of Reaganomics: (1) noninflationary (tight) monetary policy, (2) slower growth of government spending, (3) reduction of federal tax rates, and (4) regulatory reform. Together, the president promised, these four steps would achieve "a full and vigorous recovery of our economy . . . and a brighter future for all our citizens."[17]

Of course, neither monetary nor fiscal policy was entirely under the president's control. Monetary policy was still the province of the independent Federal Reserve System; tax and spending policies still had to be reviewed and approved by the Congress. Yet to a remarkable degree, President Reagan was able to work his will with both institutions. Monetary growth was slowed by a willing Federal Reserve from an annual rate of 13 percent in the last quarter of 1980 to under 4 percent in the second half of 1981. In the summer, the president got his tax cuts, reducing personal income tax rates by a full 25 percent over three years. And in the fall, Congress voted his spending cuts as well, eliminating overall $95 billion from the next two fiscal years (as measured against previous spending trends) while greatly increasing military expenditures. At the year's end the president was satisfied, looking back on what he called a "substantial beginning."[18]

But what a beginning! In his February program, President Reagan predicted that economic growth would recover from the 1980 recession to a steady 4 to 5 percent annual growth path through 1986; whereas the Federal budget deficit, which had approached $60 billion in each of the last two Carter years, would gradually shrink to near balance by Fiscal Year (FY) 1984.[19] Instead, with the initiation of Reagonomics, America's economy set off on the most pronounced roller-coaster ride of the postwar period, and the budget deficit soared to heights never before seen in the United States. First came a sharp new recession, with the gross national product (GNP) dropping at an annual rate in excess of 5 percent in late 1981 and early 1982 before leveling off at mid-year. Only then came the recovery promised by President Reagan, starting in late 1982 and taking the GNP to growth rates near 4 percent in 1983 and over 6½ percent in 1984. But the boom did not last long, and it was soon followed by yet another period of sluggishness, with growth in 1985 barely topping 2 percent, unemployment still hovering near 7 percent (where it had been when Mr. Reagan took office), and with little prospect for renewed bouyancy in 1986 or beyond. The recovery turned out to be neither "full" nor "vigorous," whereas the budget deficit, far from shrinking, exploded past $110 billion in FY 1982 and some $180 billion in the next two years to reach a record $211 billion in FY 1985. Reaganomics, it seemed, had not, in fact, achieved a "brighter future for all our citizens" after all.

How could the administration have been so wrong? The best answer, ironically, was provided by President Reagan's own director of the Office of Management and Budget, David Stockman, in his celebrated *Atlantic Monthly* interviews in 1981: "The whole thing is premised on faith . . . on a belief about how the world works."[20] The belief was supply-side economics, the new religion of the Grand Old Party. Administration supply-siders, above all the president himself, assumed that the key to national prosperity lay in increasing incentives for saving and investment. If taxes could be cut, the role of the government rolled back, and money kept tight, investor confidence in the future value of money would be restored, leading to a rise of productive employment that would, in turn, help balance the Federal budget. Of little concern were charges of "voodoo economics." Disciples of the new faith were confident that taxes could be shrunk, military expenditures raised, and the budget balanced all at the same time. It took years of depressing fiscal returns to demonstrate what a false doctrine this really was. As one commentator put it, "Reaganomics proves only one thing — you *can't* do it with mirrors."[21]

In 1985, the chickens came home to roost. Hoisted on the petard of his own policies, President Reagan felt obliged to accept a congressional initiative — the so-called Gramm-Rudman amendment — designed to eliminate the Federal budget deficit entirely over a period of five years, even though this might possibly require either raising taxes once again or substantially cutting back the president's cherished defense buildup. Supply-side economics was effectively discredited. Significantly, Mr. Reagan chose to sign the new legislation in seclusion, eschewing the usual pomp and circumstance of an open White House ceremony.[22]

From an international perspective, what was most striking during this period was the way in which policy was determined in almost total disregard for the outside world. At no time during the administration's first term was there any serious attempt to moderate the external impacts of America's fiscal dilemma, either by way of collaboration with our industrial allies or by intervention in the exchange market. On the contrary, being convinced of its own rectitude, the administration accepted no responsibility at all for problems that might crop up elsewhere. Early in 1981, consistent with its belief in the superiority of market solutions, the Treasury scaled back foreign exchange operations dramatically. Henceforth, according to administration spokesmen, the United States would intervene in the exchange market only at times of extreme disturbance (such as in the event of an attempted presidential assassination). Otherwise the dollar would remain free to seek its own value. The best way to stabilize exchange rates, it was said, was for each country to restore price stability domestically. America was doing its part. If others were experiencing difficulties, they might profitably follow America's example. No compromises were called for so long as markets were free to work their magic.

This unilateral approach, authoritatively labeled "domesticism" by Henry Nau (for two years a senior staff member of President Reagan's National Security Council), was contrasted with the presumed "globalism" of the previous Carter administration.[23] The globalist view, according to Nau, traced economic problems "largely to the malfunctioning of the international economic system itself. . . . The alternative approach reverses the globalist logic and places national policymaking at the foundation of the world economy. . . . The administration's policy has consistently emphasized the primary importance and role of domestic economic policies as the key to stable and prosperous international economic relations."[24] As the president himself said at the 1981 annual meeting of the International Monetary Fund and World Bank: "The most important contribution any country can make to world development is to pursue sound economic policies at home."[25]

But would this approach *ensure* "stable and prosperous international economic relations?" No responsible official was ever likely to question the importance of "sound economic policies at home"; certainly no official of the previous administration was on record as having done so. As President Carter's former Assistant Secretary of the Treasury, C. Fred Bergsten, pointed out, Nau's "domesticist-globalist" dichotomy was in fact a strawman.[26] The real question was not whether there should be "proper" domestic policies — of course there should be — but rather whether such policies would be *enough* to promote world economic development. In Bergsten's words: "Sound national policies remain a *necessary* condition for global stability, but they are highly unlikely to be *sufficient.*"[27] The reason, simply put, is that effective national policies in an interdependent world cannot be formulated without regard for their international consequences, including the feedbacks of those consequences into the domestic economy itself. By that standard, the Reagan administration's "domesticism" could be severely criticized, and was.

Criticism focused in particular on the administration's fiscal-monetary "mix" — its combination of tight money and large fiscal deficits — that was bound to keep American interest rates high, which in turn acted as a powerful magnet for liquid savings elsewhere. After 1980, vast amounts of capital were attracted from abroad, pushing the dollar to heights not seen since the start of generalized floating in 1973. In the first four years of the Reagan administration, the average value of the dollar in terms of the currencies of other major industrial countries, as measured by the International Monetary Fund, rose by some 60 percent before peaking in the spring of 1985. Few observers doubted that this represented a sizable overvaluation of America's money in international markets.

For our industrial allies, these developments compounded an already unpleasant policy dilemma.[28] Following the run-up of oil prices in 1978–1979, inflation had once again accelerated even as growth slowed and unemployment continued to rise. In most of the industrial countries, the desire to reverse price trends kept central banks from easing up on monetary policy, despite the sluggishness of domestic output and employment. The appreciation of the dollar, which meant, of course, depreciation of their own currencies, only added to the inflationary pressures in their economies by raising import costs, while the drainage of savings attracted by America's high rates meant lost opportunities for productive investment at home. Europeans, in particular, grew increasingly vocal in their criticism of American policy, resurrecting charges of benign neglect not heard since the first two years of the Carter administration. America, they knew, was not the sole — or perhaps not even the principal — cause of their troubles. But they were understandably aggrieved by the Reagan administration's unwillingness to do anything at all to help, either in terms of domestic policy or in the exchange market. As Flora Lewis perceptively explained[29]:

> Successive U.S. governments have insisted on their sovereign right to run the economy as they think best. But it adds to Europe's sense of impotence, and resentment, when changes of policy it cannot influence aggravate its own less than satisfying attempts at economic management.

Indeed it was not very long before European officials began talking openly of a "complete breakdown" in monetary cooperation between America and Europe, describing Atlantic economic relations as now at their lowest point since President Nixon's suspension of the dollar's convertibility into gold in 1971. According to one senior official, "We have simply never before seen a United States administration that displayed this degree of indifference to the effects of its actions on its allies."[30] This was not benign neglect, wrote a British commentator: This was "an almost malign rejection of the need for a 'good neighbor' policy."[31] At the Williamsburg economic summit in 1983, according to Chancellor Helmut Kohl of West Germany, the administration's policies were "clearly opposed by everyone from the Japanese to the Canadians to us Europeans." Yet when asked if any shift of direction could be expected, he admitted ruefully "I wouldn't say I was optimistic."[32] At the London summit in 1984, Britain's Chancellor of the Exchequer labeled Reaganomics "simple-minded."[33] Yet the administration remained impervious to criticism.

Nor was the criticism exclusively foreign. At home too, questions increasingly were raised about the administration's neglect of the external dimension of its domestic policies. Exporters and import-sensitive industries, in particular, had reason to complain as they found their sales more and more severely disrupted by the dollar's unprecedented appreciation. In 1980 the United States had a trade deficit of $25 billion. Four years later, the deficit was up to $110 billion (another historic high) and still climbing; and with the resulting accumulation of foreign liabilities, America — long the greatest creditor in international finance — was on its way to becoming a net debtor for the first time since World War I. It was realized only gradually that the administration's attitude of benign neglect in the exchange markets was only adding to the difficulty of achieving a truly durable economic recovery. At least two million American jobs were estimated to have been lost during President Reagan's first term as a result of the dollar's overvaluation.[34] As Lawrence Krause of the Brookings Institution commented pointedly: "The dollar is one of the elements in our international competitiveness, but we ignore it as a matter of principle."[35] The situation was aptly summarized by investment banker Jeffrey Garten at the end of 1984[36]:

> Over the last four years America's foreign economic policy jumped its traditional track. . . . America's foreign economic policy showed little regard for the impact of U.S. fiscal and monetary policies on the rest of the world. Moreover, it was a policy which ignored the erosion of America's international competitive position. . . .
>
> The Administration should have been acutely sensitive to the open and interrelated nature of the world economy and the sophistication of the policies required to deal with it effectively. Instead it embraced a naive optimism that the unfettered market-place would handle all.

Only in 1985, after the president's triumphant reelection, did this "naive optimism" finally begin to yield to a more realistic appraisal of the costs of "domesticism." Having effectively placed autonomy of decision making above all other objectives of policy, the administration now found that it had succeeded neither in promoting a sustained economic prosperity nor in fully retaining domestic political support, while managing only to alienate most of the other industrial states. At home, the economy once again was faltering, after two years of boom, even as the budget and trade deficits continued to climb to record heights. (The trade deficit was projected to reach a new high of $148 billion in 1985.) Supply-side economics, it was evident, had been no more successful in increasing domestic savings than it had been in decreasing the federal deficit. Instead, the United States had seemingly become addicted to foreign borrowing to help finance both government and import expenditures, and was fast becoming a net debtor nation in the process. (By the year's end, America's net debt approached $100 billion — more than even Mexico's or Brazil's.) Abroad an unnecessary — and potentially perilous — strain had been placed on the Western alliance by the administration's exercise in unilateralism. Prospects for macroeconomic relations with our economic allies were the bleakest in years. Something, clearly, would have to be done to repair the damage.

What could be done? Manifestly, what was needed was a renewal of the spirit of mutual accommodation and compromise that had characterized the Carter administration in its later years — a greater sensitivity to constraints and an increased willingness to cooperate in the pursuit of common objectives. In concrete terms, this would mean (1) a revised fiscal-monetary "mix" (smaller budget deficits and somewhat less restrictive monetary policy) to permit a gradual reduction of American interest rates and (2) a resumption of coordinated currency interventions to achieve an alignment of exchange rates more consistent with both internal and external balance. In effect the Reagan administration, too, would have to acknowledge the limits of American power (*pace* all its ideological instincts to the contrary). The pendulum, after its sharp swing toward laissez-faire in Ronald Reagan's first term, would once again have to return to a degree of multilateral management of macroeconomic relations.

The turning point came with the appointment of James Baker as Treasury Secretary in January 1985, replacing Donald Regan (who took Baker's old job as White House chief of staff). Far more pragmatic than his predecessor, Secretary Baker lost no time in moving toward closer collaboration with the other industrial states on fiscal and monetary matters. In April, at a meeting of the Organization of Economic Cooperation and Development in Paris, he raised the possibility that the United States might be willing to host an international conference to review the functioning of the floating exchange rate regime, which he noted was "not without weaknesses."[37] In May at the annual economic summit in Bonn, he persuaded President Reagan, for the first time ever in this series of get-togethers, to make a formal commitment to our allies "to achieve a substantial reduction in the [U.S.] budget deficit."[38] Even more dramatically in September, he joined the finance ministers of Britain, France, West Germany, and Japan (along with the United States, the Group of Five) in announcing a major new initiative to realign and manage currency values. "Exchange rates should better reflect fundamental economic conditions than has been the case," the ministers declared, and they "stand ready to cooperate more closely to encourage this."[39] And this in turn was followed, most dramatically of all, by a call from President Reagan in his State of the Union address in January 1986 for a study to determine "if the nations of the world should convene to discuss the role and relationship of our currencies." Said the president: "Never again" should the United States permit "wild currency swings." Nothing could have been further from the "domesticism" of Mr. Reagan's first term. In the words of one New York banker: "In terms of philosophy, these are major changes."[40] Like its predecessors, the Reagan administration, too, was ultimately forced to concede defeat for a policy of assertive unilateralism.

Trade Policy: Reciprocity Redolent

The story was only a little different in the area of trade relations with our allies. Here too, as in monetary relations, unnecessary and potentially perilous strains were produced by the Reagan administration's own policies and priorities. Once again a presidency began — ritual declarations of adherence to traditional liberal principles notwithstanding — by reasserting the primacy of American commercial interests. A shift away from the generally conciliatory attitude of the later Carter years effectively placed domestic distributional goals above all other objectives of policy. Not only did this lead, once again, to a threat of snowballing retaliatory measures by our major trading partners; worse it helped to unleash — along with the dollar's unprecedented appreciation — a veritable tidal wave of protectionist sentiment in the United States that appeared to place the whole edifice of international trade in jeopardy. Here too, therefore, by the end of President Reagan's first term, it was clear that something would have to be done to repair or contain the damage. But there was also a difference. In contrast to the area of macroeconomic policy, administration officials were less prepared to concede defeat openly for their unilateralist trade policies. The possible need for greater accommodation was acknowledged, but not for any basic change of principle. Hence the outlook for trade relations with our allies still remained uncertain as the president's fifth year in office drew to a close. The pendulum in this area still had some distance to travel.

The administration's initial attitude was best summarized by President Reagan's first Trade Representative, William Brock, in a carefully crafted white paper on American trade policy released in July 1981.[41] Although free trade was pronounced essential, the white paper also contained warnings that free trade must be a two-way street and that the American market would not necessarily remain open to countries that, in the administration's view, failed to observe commonly agreed rules. "We will *insist* that our trading partners live up to the spirit and the letter of international trade agreements, and that they recognize that trade is a two-way street . . . and we *will make full use of all available channels for assuring compliance*" [italics added]. These would include both (1) strict enforcement of existing import regulations (for example, antidumping and countervailing-duty laws) designed to neutralize or eliminate "trade distortive practices which injure U.S. industry and agriculture" and (2) active pursuit of satisfactory market access for American business abroad "in a manner consistent with the goal of reducing trade barriers and trade-distorting measures." The guiding light for our policy would be the principle of reciprocity. The objective would be to "promote positive adjustment of economies by permitting market forces to operate."

Underlying the administration's policy was a perception, common in Washington, that the United States was not getting a fair shake in international trade. In part this was, supposedly, because in past multilateral bargaining, including the Tokyo Round, the United States had failed to negotiate trade rules that adequately served American interests. The American market, it was thought, had been opened up to a far greater extent than had markets elsewhere. And in part this was because other industrial states were believed to ignore systematically or to violate the framework of understandings historically championed by this country in the General Agreement on Tariffs and Trade (GATT). American manufactured and agricultural trade was handicapped by a myriad of foreign nontariff distortions; service industries and direct investments fell victim to subsidized competition or trade-related performance requirements. Hence the spotlight on reciprocity, which was generally understood to stand for "substantially equivalent market access." From now on it would be necessary not only to monitor foreign access here but also to seek unilateral concessions from other governments to provide American business with "fair and equitable" opportunities abroad. Otherwise retaliatory measures would have to be contemplated.

This was not simply protectionism in disguise. Most officials of the administration, from President Reagan on down, genuinely believed in the desirability of free trade. But it was, as *The Economist* suggested, "free-trade-tempered-by-nationalism,"[42] reminiscent of the assertiveness of Robert Strauss's "free-but-fair-trade" campaign of the early Carter years. Why, Reagan officials demanded, should the United States be forced to pay the highest price for preserving a system that seemed to them to have become increasingly discriminatory against American industry and agriculture? The time had come, they declared defiantly, to end the "free ride" of others. As Trade Representative Brock explained in a 1982 speech, "I am confident that, under this president, reciprocity will not become a code word for protectionism, but it will be used to state clearly our insistence on equity."[43]

Unfortunately the administration's policy involved two rather substantial risks. First was the danger that, in adopting such a belligerent tone, Reagan officials might actually provoke the very trade-distorting measures they were pledged to reduce. Equity, after all, is subjective: What looks to some like getting a fair shake may well appear as protectionism in the eyes of others. Many foreign governments questioned the perception that in trade relations, the United States was more sinned against than sinning. What about America's own unfair trading practices, they asked, such as "Buy American" regulations at federal or state levels or import restrictions on such agricultural commodities as sugar, meat, and dairy products? Most governments seemed prepared to resist the Reagan administration's efforts to wring unilateral concessions from them, and some made it quite clear that they would respond in kind to retaliatory measures from the United States.

Furthermore, many complained, the very concept of reciprocity could signal a retreat from the postwar system of multilateral trade relationships, a step toward bilateralism. The charge was denied by the administration, which lost no opportunity to reaffirm this country's commitment to the fundamental rule of the GATT, embodied in the most-favored nation clause, that trade should be conducted on the basis of nondiscrimination. Critics warned, however, that in practice the concept could easily degenerate into a rigid insistence on "equivalence," market by market and product by product. Barrier would be matched for barrier, concession for concession, trade balance for trade balance — all bilaterally. Nothing could be more threatening for system preservation.

The second risk was that additional protectionist pressures would be ignited at home by the administration's tough new attitude abroad. Domestic constituencies might be emboldened to think that now, after the Carter administration, they at last had friends in Washington who would move decisively to help them sustain their profits and market shares in the face of rising foreign competition. Protectionist sentiment, which was already running strong when President Reagan first took office (in particular, because of the recession of 1980), continued to build even after the end of the new 1981–82 recession and was further aggravated by the remorseless climb of the dollar in exchange markets (itself, as indicated, a by-product of the administration's own economic policies). By the end of the president's first term, with the American trade deficit soaring to record heights, the trickle of petitions for import relief had become a flood; in 1985, more than 300 bills intended to provide some form of trade protection for American producers were filed in Congress.[44] In effect, the administration had created a Frankenstein monster.

Could the monster be controlled? At the outset of President Reagan's second term, it was evident to even the most dogmatic trade officials that the open and liberal world trading system was now seriously threatened. Gradually, therefore, the administration's initial policy stance was broadened in an effort to keep home-grown protectionist pressures in check. One new element was the Group of Five exchange-rate initiative announced in September 1985, quietly orchestrated by the administration and explicitly intended to engineer a depreciation of the dollar to help ease competitive strains on American manufacturing and agriculture. A second element was a determined American campaign for a new round of multilateral negotiations in the GATT aimed, in particular, at liberalizing the movement of services such as banking, insurance, data processing, and telecommunications — all fields in which the United States, as the world's leading service-industry economy, could be expected to benefit disproportionately. Administration calls for a new trade round actually began as early as 1982. But it was only in October 1985 that the president's new Trade Representative, Clayton Yeutter (who had replaced William Brock the previous April), finally won formal assent from the other members of GATT.[45] Talks were expected to get under way sometime in late 1986.

For all their usefulness, however, from the point of view of system preservation, these additional elements remained subordinate to the main thrust of administration policy, which continued to assert the primacy of American commercial interests and to seek unilateral concessions from our major trading partners. Despite the risks of "free-trade-tempered-by-nationalism," Reagan officials were determined to pursue their own conception of economic equity. Tactically, they felt, the best way to stem the protectionist tide at home would be to keep up the pressures for fairer trade practices abroad. Strategically, the guiding light for policy must continue to be the principle of reciprocity as interpreted by the administration. This was evident as late as September 1985, when President Reagan announced new proceedings against the European Economic Community (EEC) and Japan for "unfair" barriers to American sales of such items as canned fruit, tobacco, and leather products. "We hope that . . . we will be able to convince our trading partners to stop their unfair trading practices and open those markets that are now closed to American exports," Reagan said. Otherwise, he warned, "We will take countermeasures [though] only as a last resort."[46] And later the same month, in a similar vein, the administration proposed a $300 million special fund to combat what officials described as "predatory" export financing by some foreign governments.[47] In addition, more covertly, the administration seemed almost to welcome the swelling threat of congressional action on imports as yet another form of leverage on our trading partners to coerce them into concessions — a traditional tactic of the Executive Branch in international trade negotiations. The basic belligerence of the administration's tone remained essentially unchanged.

After five years, then, it was not clear whether the damage being done by this defiant trade policy would be contained or not. What *was* clear was that the administration was playing a risky game, skating on very thin ice. Either its approach would have to produce results, in its home market as well as in opportunities to trade elsewhere, or its hand might be forced by a disappointed Congress. Ultimately reciprocity must either succeed or trigger American retaliation. Yet at the same time the United States did not want to provoke its allies into a trade war by seeming to bully them. A few examples illustrate how dangerously thin the ice really was.

Japan

Of all our allies, Japan is regarded in Washington as the most guilty of unfair trading practices. Provoked by Japan's huge and growing surplus in our bilateral trade — approaching $50 billion in 1985, more than five times the figure for 1980 — complaints address both sides of the mutual balance. On the export side, the Japanese are criticized for their habitual strategy of massive penetration of export markets in relatively narrow product lines, which severely injures local competitors. In addition, Japan's exporters are said to benefit improperly from generous government support, especially at the research and development stage. On the import side, the Japanese are criticized for a whole range of formal and informal nontariff barriers, from special product standards to time-consuming and expensive customs procedures, that limit access to their internal market. If there is any single country that is the implied target of reciprocity, it is Japan.

In many instances, the grievances against Japan appear justified — as the Japanese themselves, when pressed, have often implicitly conceded by acting selectively to restrain exports or liberalize imports. What was remarkable after the Reagan administration arrived in Washington, however, was the sharp rise in the level of acrimony in American accusations. Neither the administration nor the Congress had any tolerance for past piecemeal approaches, which, it was thought, had resulted at best in only tactical retreats by the Japanese. The feeling was that only by means of a broad, blunt assault could really significant concessions be obtained. "We needed to get their attention," one administration official said privately. "We had to use the proverbial two-by-four."[48]

The assault began on the export side, under pressure from domestic interests, with negotiation in May 1981 of a "voluntary" agreement, on the model of earlier negotiated quotas, restraining Japanese automobile sales in the United States. Having lost on a petition for escape-clause relief before the International Trade Commission in December 1980, the American automobile industry had turned instead to Congress, where supporters introduced highly restrictive quota legislation. In turn, the administration made use of this threat to persuade Japan to accept an export limit of 1.68 million units in the year beginning April 1, down from 1.82 million units the previous year, and to continue restraint each year thereafter (although with the ceiling rising to 1.85 million units in 1984 and 2.3 million units in 1985).[49] There is no question that the Japanese acceded reluctantly to these limits. Calling them "voluntary," however, allowed the administration to claim no responsibility for a protectionist agreement that it had, in fact, actively negotiated, thus ostensibly maintaining its free-trade credentials. Later those credentials were more tarnished when President Reagan, in April 1983, ordered a tenfold increase in the tariff on Japanese motorcycles — the strongest protectionist action by any administration in years — and again, in December 1984, when a fixed quota was agreed on sales of Japanese finished steel in the United States.[50]

The major focus of policy, however, was on Japanese imports. As a result of its many nontariff barriers, administration spokesmen repeatedly noted, Japan imported fewer manufactured goods as a proportion of its GNP than any other industrial country (about 1½ percent, as against 3½ percent or more in the United States and Europe); indeed the share of manufactured imports in GNP had actually declined over the previous two decades, while that of other industrial states had risen rapidly. And Japan also maintained strict controls on imports of agricultural commodities of interest to the United States, such as rice, citrus, tobacco, and beef. The Japanese furthermore were criticized for their strong "Buy Japan" ethic and their complex distribution system, which was highly dependent on long-standing social relationships; both also inhibited imports.

The assault on Japanese import practices was continued throughout the administration's first five years. In response, Japan announced no less than eight liberalization programs between December 1981 and December 1985, cutting tariffs and easing nontariff barriers on a wide array of products of interest to the United States. In April 1985, Prime Minister Yashuhiro Nakasone even went on Japan's national television to make an extraordinary appeal to the Japanese people to buy more "foreign" goods. "If we do not solve the existing trade frictions today," he said, "there is a possibility that there will arise a very serious situation affecting the life and death of our country."[51] Yet the administration was hardly mollified. In fact criticisms grew ever harsher, despite such concessions. "The mood is very strong . . . to hit the Japanese," observed a trade specialist on the Senate Foreign Relations Committee.[52] The head of a Japanese government advisory committee on trade said: "The sentiment in the United States is like that before the outbreak of a war."[53] Just one week before Prime Minister Nakasone's television appeal, President Reagan's cabinet publicly declared "equivalent access" to be its goal in trade relations with Japan — the first time that reciprocity had been formally made such a high policy goal by the entire government.[54]

In turn the Japanese, gradually abandoning their customary deference, began to lash back, citing their own grievances against this country, such as discriminatory government procurement programs, restrictions on the sale of Alaskan oil, and alleged dumping of petrochemical products. They also cited the overvaluation of the dollar, caused by the Reagan administration's fiscal-monetary "mix," as well as the lack of effort by most American businessmen to penetrate the Japanese market. "They expect to just walk in and talk to a distributor and say, 'Here's my product, the way they do in the U.S.,'" said a member of the Japan Economic Institute. "It doesn't work that way in Japan."[55] Frustration was particularly strong over Washington's threat of unilateral retaliatory measures. "If the United States does not want to trade with Japan, politics here would change," warned one high trade official in Tokyo as early as 1982. "There would be no benefit for Japan to remain a member of the free world."[56] Though perhaps an extreme example, such a statement was symptomatic of the frictions generated by the Reagan administration's demands.

Europe

In commercial relations with Europe, three issues, in particular, stood out during the administration's first five years: steel, agriculture, and trade with the Soviet bloc. Each contributed to what *The Economist* called the "rockiest patch for 30 years"[57] in the Atlantic trading relationship.

The steel issue was inherited from the Carter years. Despite the trigger-price mechanism instituted in 1978, steel imports had continued to increase their penetration of the American market (19 percent in 1981, up from 16 percent in 1980 and only 14 percent as recently as 1976), intensifying industry pressures for relief. The major culprits, the industry charged, were members of the EEC, who were accused of illegal subsidies as well as outright dumping. Reviving a tactic that had been used successfully during the Carter administration, companies such as U.S. Steel again began threatening antidumping and countervailing-duty suits against the Europeans. "The target price is simply out of control," argued the chairman of U.S. Steel in November 1981. "It is being blatantly ignored by most of the European producers. The time for patience is past. It is time for action."[58] Action finally came in early 1982, when U.S. Steel and six other companies filed more than 1900 complaints against seven EEC countries, as well as Brazil, Rumania, South Africa, and Spain.

The Reagan administration was caught in the middle, between the protectionist demands of the industry and its own free-trade pretensions. Unfortunately, its instincts seemed to place the highest priority on the interests of a powerful domestic constituency. Although there seemed much truth in industry charges against the Europeans, American companies had by no means helped their case by repeatedly raising prices in previous years, despite weak market conditions. In addition, the EEC could legitimately claim that at least some of its subsidies were legal, being tied to plans for rationalization of its own industry, and in any event were being gradually phased out. Yet the administration never hesitated to put pressure on the Europeans to restrain their sales in the United States. In October 1982, four months after Washington threatened countervailing duties ranging up to 40 percent on European steel, the EEC felt obliged to accept a three-year "voluntary" export agreement, similar to the earlier Japanese automobile pact, limiting basic steel shipments to approximately 5.5 percent of the American domestic market (reduced from 6.3 percent in 1981). In July 1983, quotas and tariffs were unilaterally imposed on European specialty steels. In early 1985, the EEC was persuaded to restrict sales of pipes and tubes. And in November 1985, after painful negotiations, the 1982 agreement was succeeded by a new four-year pact holding European shipments to roughly the same share of the American market but covering a wider range of products. "Happily we were able to maintain peace," said the EEC's commissioner for external relations after the new pact was signed.[59] But the bitterness on the European side over the Reagan administration's strong-arm tactics was palpable.

Another major irritant was agriculture. For the Reagan administration, one of the most unfair of all trading practices was the EEC's common farm policy which, with its high prices and open-ended guarantees, had turned the EEC from a net importer of food into a net exporter of such items as dairy products, beef, poultry, sugar, and wheat — thereby threatening some of the traditional overseas markets of the United States. The issue, as the administration saw it, was the EEC's aggressive use of export subsidies to gain competitive advantage. For the Europeans, however, this was a case of the pot calling the kettle black, since the United States, they pointed out, also provides broad government support for its farmers. Objecting to the administration's contentious tone, EEC officials warned that any action against European farmers would provoke countermeasures endangering America's historical markets in Europe and elsewhere. When Washington announced in early 1983 a large, heavily subsidized sale of wheat flour to Egypt, long one of the EEC's best markets, the EEC retaliated with a shipment of cheap wheat to China, where America had been the biggest outside supplier. When Washington acted in mid-1985 to restrict imports of European pasta as part of a campaign to open the EEC market to American citrus fruit, the EEC responded with higher tariffs on American exports of walnuts and lemons. The Reagan administration's attitude on farm policy "smacks of a trade war," said France's minister of agriculture in June 1985, and could lead to "a spread of protectionist measures."[60]

Finally, there was the issue of trade relations with the Soviet bloc, where early tensions developed as a result of the economic sanctions imposed by the Reagan administration on Poland and the Soviet Union following the Polish government's declaration of martial law in December 1981. As Miles Kahler points out in Chapter 9 in this volume, administration spokesmen criticized the Europeans for their failure to match America's actions, charging that Europe seemed more interested in markets than in the security of the Western alliance. The Europeans, in turn, criticized Washington for overreacting, suggesting pointedly that they might be more willing to cut their trade with the Soviet bloc if the United States were to make an equivalent sacrifice by reinstating the grain embargo that President Reagan had lifted in 1981. Throughout most of 1982, the dispute was raised to what *The Economist* described as the "hair-pulling level"[61] by administration efforts to persuade the Europeans to cancel their planned natural gas pipeline from Siberia and to restrict government-subsidized export credits to the Soviet Union, before a cooling-off was finally negotiated by Secretary of State George Shultz in November 1982. Subsequently, new tensions arose over the issue of high-technology exports to the Soviet Union, exports that Reagan hard-liners wanted to persuade European governments to restrict to the maximum extent possible. Representative was the reaction of West Germany's Economics Minister, who warned that Bonn would "not tolerate" further administration attempts to curb technology transfers to the East.[62] After five years, differences over Soviet bloc trade remained a continuing source of strain on the Atlantic alliance.

Canada

Like Japan and Europe, Canada initially was attacked by the Reagan administration for practices viewed as unfair to American commercial interests — in particular for "nationalistic" investment rules that both limited opportunities for foreign investors in Canada and imposed trade-related performance requirements on them. Such rules were anathema to Reagan officials, not only because they interfered with market forces but also because they were inherently discriminatory, contravening international undertakings regarding "national treatment" (the same treatment of foreign and domestic enterprise). For the government of Prime Minister Pierre Elliot Trudeau, restriction of foreign investment seemed essential if Canada was to preserve an independent national identity in the face of the pervasive influence of its giant neighbor, whose companies already controlled one-third of Canadian manufacturing and whose economy accounted for better than two-thirds of Canadian foreign trade. When confronted with threats of retaliation from Washington, however, Canada had few options, especially at a time of deep recession and high unemployment at home. Even before the landslide election victory of Conservative Brian Mulroney in September 1984, it was evident that Ottawa had reluctantly begun to relax enforcement of its investment rules and to retreat on other issues of bilateral commercial interest. Canada's sense of grievance could not stand up easily to American pressures. As one Canadian writer commented: "You would expect the more powerful nation to get what it wants."[63] Washington's belligerent tactics, in this case, paid off.

Indeed, under the pro-business government of Prime Minister Mulroney, the Reagan administration not only won legislation in Ottawa, in early 1985, which formally abolished many of Canada's controversial investment restrictions, Washington was even offered, in September, a commitment to begin negotiating a liberalized trade agreement between the two nations. The move was welcomed by Reagan officials still eager to demonstrate whenever possible the magic of the marketplace. What motivated Ottawa, however, was less principle than national self-interest — in particular, concern about the rising tide of protectionism in the United States. Trade talks offered a way to ensure that concessions in the future would not be all one way. "We need a better, a fairer and a more predictable trade relationship with the United States," Prime Minister Mulroney said in proposing the talks. "At stake are more than two million jobs which depend on Canadian access to the United States market."[64] Given Canadian sensibilities about national identity, it was clear that, once begun, negotiations would be long and arduous and could end up producing more trade frictions than they might resolve. For the Reagan administration, the ice still remained dangerously thin.

Conclusion

It can hardly be said that the Reagan administration's approach to international economic relations fared well during its first five years. Quite the contrary, the combination of Reaganomics at home and reciprocity abroad proved no solution at all to the central dilemma of foreign economic policy — the growing constraints on policymakers. In effect the administration tried to ignore the new limits of American power, disregarding the lesson learned by the Carter administration and thus was forced to repeat the difficult learning process of its predecessor. The return swing of the pendulum was most evident in the management of macroeconomic relations, especially after the appointment of James Baker as Treasury Secretary; it was more gradual in the trade field. America's accustomed autonomy and influence over economic events, President Reagan first believed, could simply be reasserted. The results, predictably, were disappointing. Not only was a "full and vigorous" prosperity not promoted, but relations with most other industrial states were brought to a new post-World War II low, endangering the very foundations of the Western alliance. The administration's trade-offs among policy objectives threatened to be highly costly for the nation as a whole.

Domestically the costs were evident in our exploding fiscal and trade deficits, rising protectionist pressures, and persistently long unemployment lines. Abroad the costs were potentially even more severe. By reasserting as forcefully as it did the primacy of American interests, defined in the narrowest possible terms, the administration effectively served notice that it no longer felt any special responsibility for preserving the economic system as a whole. America, too, would act as a "free rider," extracting gains where we could. In the short run, such a policy might indeed succeed in wringing concessions from our allies. But the risk was that the more often this was done, the more likely it was that these same allies would feel driven to insulate themselves from the United States in their trade and monetary relations, just as they felt driven by the chaos of the dollar in 1978 to form the European Monetary System. And this, in turn, would most certainly deprive the United States of much of the benefit of global economic interdependence. In the long run, we too would be losers. Like it or not, America still has a vested interest in avoiding undue discord or disruption in the system and this the Reagan administration clearly failed to do, particularly in the trade area. Conflict was not kept manageable. After five years, it seemed that there could yet be an explosion in the kitchen.

"An Explosion in the Kitchen? Economic Relations with Other Advanced Industrial States" was written for this volume. Copyright © 1987 by Benjamin J. Cohen.

Notes

1. Robert O. Keohane, "U.S. Foreign Economic Policy Toward Other Advanced Capitalist States," in *Eagle Entangled: U.S. Foreign Policy in a Complex World*, Kenneth A. Oye, Donald Rothchild, and Robert J. Lieber, eds. (New York and London: Longman, 1979), pp. 118–119.
2. Walter W. Heller, *New Dimensions of Political Economy* (New York: Norton, 1967), p. 5.
3. See, for example, Richard N. Cooper, "Prolegomena to the Choice of an International Monetary System"; and Lawrence B. Krause and Joseph S. Nye, "Reflections on the Economics and Politics of International Economic Organizations" — both in *World Politics and International Economics*, C. Fred Bergsten and Lawrence B. Krause, eds. (Washington, D.C.: The Brookings Institution, 1975); and Benjamin J. Cohen, *Organizing the World's Money* (New York: Basic Books, 1977), Ch. 2.
4. But see, for example, Benjamin J. Cohen, "U.S. Foreign Economic Policy," *Orbis* (Spring 1971), Vol. 15, No. 1, pp. 232–246; and Benjamin J. Cohen, "The Revolution in Atlantic Economic Relations: A Bargain Comes Unstuck," in *The United States and Western Europe*, Wolfram Hanrieder, ed. (Cambridge, MA: Winthrop, 1974).
5. Robert E. Osgood, "The Revitalization of Containment," *Foreign Affairs* (1982), Vol. 60, No. 3, p. 465.
6. For an authoritative statement of the administration's thinking at the time, see Richard N. Cooper, "Global Economic Policy in a World of Energy Shortage," in *Economics in the Public Service*, J. Pechman and J. Simler, eds. (New York: Norton, 1981). Cooper was President Carter's Under Secretary of State for Economic Affairs.
7. See, for example, Keohane, "U.S. Foreign Economic Policy," pp. 102–109.
8. Council of Economic Advisors, *Annual Report, 1978* (Washington, D.C.: U.S. Government Printing Office, 1978), p. 124.
9. Benjamin J. Cohen, "Europe's Money, America's Problem," *Foreign Policy* (Summer 1979), No. 35, pp. 31–47.
10. Andrew Shonfield, "The World Economy in 1979" *Foreign Affairs* (1980), Vol. 58, No. 3, p. 607.
11. Council of Economic Advisers, *Annual Report, 1981* (Washington, D.C.: U.S. Government Printing Office, 1981), p. 199.
12. See, for example, Marina Whitman, "A Year of Travail: The United States and the International Economy," *Foreign Affairs* (1979), Vol. 57, No. 3, pp. 543–544.
13. Ibid., p. 545.
14. See, for example, Shonfield, "World Economy," pp. 616–617; and Thomas R. Graham, "Revolution in Trade Politics," *Foreign Policy* (Fall 1979), Vol. 36, p. 55.
15. For evaluations of these two policy measures, see Robert Carswell, "Economic Sanctions and the Iran Experience," *Foreign Affairs* (Winter 1981–82), No. 60, pp. 247–265; and Robert L. Paarlberg, "Lessons of the Grain Embargo," *Foreign Affairs* (Fall 1980), Vol. 59, No. 1, pp. 144–162.

16. Council of Economic Advisors, *Annual Report, 1982* (Washington, D.C.: U.S. Government Printing Office, 1982), p. 167.
17. Presidential Message to the Congress accompanying his Program for Economic Recovery, February 18, 1981.
18. *Economic Report of the President* (Washington, D.C.: U.S. Government Printing Office, 1982), p. 4.
19. *America's New Beginning: A Program for Economic Recovery* (Washington, D.C.: U.S. Government Printing Office, 1981), pp. 12, 25.
20. As quoted in William Greider, "The Education of David Stockman," *The Atlantic Monthly*, December 1981, p. 29.
21. Tom Wicker, "Mr. Reagan's Mirrors," *New York Times*, December 11, 1981, p. A35.
22. *New York Times*, December 13, 1985, p. 13.
23. Henry R. Nau, "Where Reaganomics Works," *Foreign Policy* (Winter 1984–85), No. 57, pp. 14–37.
24. Ibid., pp. 15, 23.
25. September 29, 1981, as quoted in *IMF Survey*, October 12, 1981, p. 317.
26. C. Fred Bergsten, "Reaganomics: The Problem?" *Foreign Policy* (Summer 1985), No. 59, pp. 132–144.
27. *Ibid.*, p. 134. (Italics added.)
28. See, for example, Robert Solomon, "The Elephant in the Boat?: The United States and the World Economy," *Foreign Affairs* (1982), Vol. 60, No. 3, pp. 577–581.
29. Flora Lewis, "Alarm Bells in the West," *Foreign Affairs* (1982), Vol. 60, No. 3, p. 556.
30. *New York Times*, February 12, 1982, p. 1.
31. John Wyles, "Europe: At the Mercy of Outside Forces," *Financial Times* Supplement, December 7, 1981, p. 1.
32. As quoted in *New York Times*, May 31, 1983, p. D15.
33. As quoted in *New York Times*, June 11, 1984, p. D4.
34. The estimate was by Data Resources Inc., a private economic forecasting firm, in a report released by the Joint Economic Committee in March 1985. See *New York Times*, March 13, 1985, p. D17.
35. As quoted in *New York Times*, April 26, 1982, p. D10.
36. Jeffrey E. Garten, "Gunboat Economics," *Foreign Affairs* (1985), Vol. 63, No. 3, pp. 538, 545.
37. *New York Times*, April 16, 1985, p. 24.
38. Joint Declaration, as reprinted in *New York Times*, May 5, 1985, p. 16.
39. Statement, as reprinted in *New York Times*, September 23, 1985, p. D11.
40. As quoted in *New York Times*, September 29, 1985, Section 3, p. F1.
41. Office of the United States Trade Representative, "Statement of U.S. Trade Policy," July 8, 1981.
42. *The Economist*, July 4, 1981, p. 21.
43. Address before the European Management Forum, Davos, Switzerland, February 1, 1982.
44. See, for example, *The Economist*, September 28, 1985, p. 24.
45. *New York Times*, October 3, 1985, p. D1.
46. As quoted in *New York Times*, September 8, 1985, p. 1.
47. *New York Times*, September 24, 1985, p. 1.
48. Interview with the author, January 1982.
49. For an evaluation of these restraints, see Robert W. Crandall, "What Have Auto-Import Quotas Wrought?," *Challenge* (January–February 1985), pp. 40–47.
50. *New York Times*, April 2, 1983, p. 1; and December 7, 1984, p. D2.
51. As quoted in *New York Times*, April 10, 1985, p. D10.
52. As quoted in *New York Times*, April 4, 1985, p. D5.

53. As quoted in *New York Times*, March 14, 1985, p. A4.
54. *New York Times*, April 4, 1985, p. D5.
55. As quoted in *New York Times*, April 4, 1985, p. D5.
56. Kazuo Wakasugi, director of the trade policy bureau of the Ministry of International Trade and Industry, as quoted in *New York Times*, March 27, 1982, Business Section, p. 32.
57. *The Economist*, February 27, 1982, p. 20.
58. As quoted in *Financial Times*, November 4, 1981.
59. As quoted in *New York Times*, November 2, 1985, p. 36.
60. As quoted in *New York Times*, June 5, 1985, p. D1.
61. *The Economist*, February 27, 1982, p. 22.
62. As quoted in *New York Times*, August 11, 1984, p. 29.
63. Stephen Clarkson, author of a book entitled "Canada and the Reagan Challenge," as quoted in *New York Times*, July 18, 1983, p. D4.
64. As quoted in *New York Times*, September 27, 1985, p. D5.

5

American Power and Third World Economies

Richard E. Feinberg

Those who argued that international constraints, immutable national interests, the career bureaucrats in the Executive Branch, or the United States Congress would prevent any administration from altering the course of American policy toward the Third World were jolted during the early 1980s. Seeking to brush aside domestic and international limitations on its actions, the Reagan administration registered some impressive successes in imposing its own preferences and policies on important North-South issues. Neither the Third World — weakened by financial crises, internal strife, and internecine conflicts — nor a divided Western Europe was able to mount an effective response. By 1985 however, the Reagan administration's momentum had clearly slowed. Theoretical flaws and internal contradictions in its policies, and resource constraints, threw the Reagan administration increasingly on the defensive. Consequently the administration reversed field and returned to more tradi-

Richard E. Feinberg is Vice-President at the Overseas Development Council. He served as the Latin American specialist on the Policy Planning Staff of the Department of State from 1977 to 1979. He holds a Ph.D. in economics from Stanford University, has worked as an international economist in the Treasury Department and with the House Banking Committee, and is an Adjunct Professor of International Finance at the Georgetown University School of Foreign Service. Dr. Feinberg has held fellowships from The Brookings Institution, the Council on Foreign Relations, and the Woodrow Wilson International Center for Scholars, Smithsonian Institution. His books include The Intemperate Zone: The Third World Challenge to U.S. Foreign Policy *(New York: Norton, 1983); as editor* Central America: International Dimensions of the Crisis *(New York: Holmes and Meier, 1982); and* Subsidizing Success: The Export-Import Bank in the U.S. Economy *(New York: Cambridge University Press, 1982). He is also co-editor of ODC's U.S.-Third World Policy Perspectives series (New Brunswick, N.J.: Transaction Books); some current volumes include* Adjustment Crisis in the Third World *(1984);* Uncertain Future: Commercial Banks in the Third World *(1984); and* Between Two Worlds: The World Bank's Next Decade *(1986).*

tional policies in important matters, although the conversion was far from complete.

During its first term, the Reagan administration pursued significantly different policies from those followed during the 1970s in the key areas of macroeconomic policies, international finance and debt, North-South trade, development assistance, and diplomacy toward radical, nationalist regimes. Not all the policies followed during the Nixon, Ford, and Carter years were discarded, but the administration abandoned many inherited traditions. It did so in order to rid the global economy of the inflation and other imbalances that had characterized the 1970s and to reassert American economic and strategic power after a period of what many have perceived to have been an unnecessarily sharp decline. The administration moved boldly and forcefully to give primacy to American economic policy over macroeconomic coordination with the country's allies; to sidestep slow-moving international bureaucracies in favor of more manageable regional or bilateral accords; to transform American foreign assistance by emphasizing security rather than long-term development; and to draw sharp distinctions between friendly and hostile regimes. In each of these areas, the administration succeeded in remolding American policies and often in implementing its strategy as well. Yet as we shall see, when judged against a set of criteria different from those of the administration and when long-term interests are considered, the victories appear more fragile and the future more worrisome. By 1986, the administration was forced on more than one occasion to abandon positions in order to cut costs.

In the area of macroeconomic policy, during its first term the administration largely rejected the efforts begun in the mid-1970s to improve the coordination of policies among the major industrial countries. Previous administrations had acted on the belief that since the relative weight of the American economy had decreased, the United States should work with Western Europe and Japan to orchestrate global prosperity. The Reagan administration chose instead to concentrate on righting domestic macroeconomic policies, believing that instabilities in the international economy were less the result of the diffusion of economic power than of mistaken domestic policies in key countries.[1] According to this view, attempts at international coordination were bound to fail unless faulty domestic policies were corrected and, conversely, would be unnecessary if such corrections were made. If nations pursued inflationary fiscal and monetary policies, exchange rates and other international economic variables were bound to be volatile, but if key governments followed prudent policies, international stability would follow automatically.

Many Reagan officials believed that the "interdependence" school had exaggerated the relative decline in American power.[2] While conceding that Europe, Japan, and some developing countries had increased their share of global power, Reagan policymakers argued that the United States was still, by far, the single largest economy in the world.[3] Moreover in some areas, such as finance, the role of the United States had become relatively more important and could set the framework and tempo for other countries. And although American "openness" to international trade and financial flows had increased, the American economy was still relatively self-sufficient and, therefore, autonomous.

The administration's foreign assistance policy reflected an eagerness to reassert American power. Reversing the decade-long trend toward multilateralism in aid, the administration, in its first term, cut back sharply on new budgetary commitments to the World Bank and other multilateral development agencies, reserving new resources for bilateral aid programs. The United States Agency for International Development (AID) redirected funds toward friendly states perceived to be in jeopardy from internal (El Salvador, Sudan) or external (Honduras, Pakistan) threats, while cutting aid to governments considered unfriendly (Nicaragua, Tanzania). The bilateral aid program de-emphasized the direct provision of services and skills to the poor that had typified AID in the 1970s. Instead AID sought to emphasize reforms of national economic policies in favor of market mechanisms and private entrepreneurs.

In trade, the administration favored policies that were more in line with past administrations, and advocated trade liberalization within multilateral mechanisms. But frustration with the General Agreement on Tariffs and Trade (GATT) occasionally drove the administration to circumvent multilateral institutions and to negotiate bilateral or regional deals. Strategic concerns also motivated the administration to pursue preferential trade arrangements — in the Caribbean Basin and with Israel — that violated the most-favored-nation principle that has been the cornerstone of American (and international) trade policy since World War II. The Caribbean Basin Initiative (CBI) generously provided the small Central American and Caribbean nations with freer access to the American market without extending these concessions to other trading partners.

The debt crisis drove the administration to violate its own free-market rhetoric and many conventional practices in finance. To stabilize shaky credit markets, official institutions abandoned their traditional arms' length posture for one of close collaboration with commercial banks, thus orchestrating a quiet revolution in international finance.[4] The United States Treasury, the Federal Reserve System, and the International Monetary Fund (IMF) mobilized their own resources and coordinated the actions of the private credit markets to handle a global financial crisis. The irony is that the administration's actions resulted in a much stronger role for the public, not the private, sector in international finance.

The administration's perception of national strength also permeated its policies toward the Soviet Union. All administrations in the postwar period have, quite appropriately, sought to limit Soviet influence in the Third World. The Reagan administration, however, was more willing than previous administrations to employ economic, diplomatic, and paramilitary instruments of coercion against regimes considered too close to the Soviet Union and was, at the same time, less interested in exploring avenues for the peaceful resolution of regional conflicts. Believing that the world was rife with hostility and struggle, senior administration officials argued — sometimes even in public — that the United States ought not be constrained by some international legal and moral norms that worked to the disadvantage of its policy.[5] Covert paramilitary action assumed a prominence that it had not enjoyed since the Vietnam War. In seeking to apply pressure to unfriendly states, the administration often subordinated American economic interests to perceived strategtic objectives.

These discontinuities in American policy had their roots in strategic conceptions. The administration believed that the East-West clash was by far the greatest challenge to its foreign policy, and sought to marshal the nation's resources by injecting this paramount interest into a wide range of programs.[6] If the administration was not always clear-headed and united on tactics, it tended to maintain a straightforward vision that argued for directing resources to fortify friendly forces and to deprive seemingly hostile forces in order to weaken or destroy them.

Although the administration naturally preferred to work with cooperative allies, it was also prepared to act unilaterally when others found its strategic outlook to be too unidimensional or simplistic or its tactics too blunt and aggressive. Some administration officials had an underlying distrust of European and Third World leaders who seemed to lack the vision or will to make tough decisions. Consequently many American policies took on a decidedly anti-multilateral tenor.

Some officials believed that the United States possessed sufficient power to pursue this course. Whereas previous administrations had known that the United States had the capacity to veto the initiatives of others, the Reagan administration acted as though it could go further and impose its own solutions on recalcitrant nations, whether they were allies or not. It believed that the international correlation of forces still favored the United States if its leaders used their power more decisively and firmly than their predecessors.

The philosophy of the administration combined a belief in the free market as the most efficient and ethical mechanism for the allocation of resources with a view of Marxism as a hostile, aggressive ideology and its adherents in the Third World as inherently and irretrievably anti-American and typically pro-Soviet. This integrated world view was to some degree a reversion to earlier, Cold War attitudes. However, the magnified emphasis on the free market was more hostile to government interventions that arguably were necessary to correct for market failures or to enhance the general welfare. The administration also tended to ignore the deep rifts that had arisen among Third World radicals and between these radicals and the Soviet Union.

These views permeated the administration's approach to all aspects of relations with developing countries, including foreign assistance. Strategic and ideological perspectives combined to make the administration skeptical of multilateral development agencies — notably the World Bank — that were at least partly under the influence of Western Europe and the Third World and whose programs were seen as overly statist and redistributive. Taking a cue from their domestic agency counterparts, some Reagan appointees declared that many of the poverty-oriented programs of the 1970s "frankly, haven't worked."[7] Rather, they tried to convince official lending agencies that the economic preferences of the administration were the correct policy model for the developing countries.

Of course even during its first term, the Reagan administration continued some of the North-South policies of previous administrations. Trade policy, for example, continued to combine preferential treatment for developing countries with efforts to coax newly industrializing nations to gradually open their markets. After an initial wariness, the administration came to appreciate the value of the IMF. Moreover, some of the administration's "new directions" actually represented a return to earlier notions. Old Washington hands were quite familiar with American government programs that subsidized overseas investment, with IMF "shock treatments" that sought a rapid reduction in budget or current-account deficits, with World Bank advocacy of price mechanisms, and with AID balance-of-payments loans that were accompanied by broad policy advice. Nevertheless, these antecedents should not obscure the important changes the Reagan administration brought to its Third World policies.

As time wore on, however, circumstances increasingly forced the administration to abandon its preferred philosophy. Strategic interests sometimes convinced the administration to modify its hostility toward radical regimes, as it did in adopting a relatively low-key posture toward Iran to avoid driving Khomeini toward the Soviets. When the country in question was one of strategic interest, for example, Egypt or the Philippines, the effort to use aid to promote market mechanisms was played down. Persistent trade deficits and unemployment increased protectionist pressures, which sometimes compelled the administration to abandon its anti-statism at the water's edge. Most notably, when private financial markets patently failed, as in the chronic debt crisis, the Treasury Department pragmatically turned to government activism to stabilize the international financial system. Some of the administration's policy

revisions drew fire from its ideologically conservative allies, which complicated its ability to control the foreign policy agenda.

The Scorecard: Successes

The administration often succeeded in compelling the bureaucracy to
accept its agenda and in producing the hoped-for policy outcomes,
although in some cases, it was unable to push through its programs or to
move events in the desired direction. Overall, if judged on the basis of its
own criteria, the administration can boast of some accomplishments.
During the Reagan administration's first two years, the United States
imposed deflation and austerity on the rest of the world. The second half
of the first Reagan administration saw the domestic fruits of this strategy,
as the American economy combined rapid growth with low inflation.
Massive foreign savings flowed into the United States and helped to fund
the twin fiscal and trade deficits. The soaring dollar symbolized the
world's faith in the American economy and the apparent triumph of
Reagan's strategy. Moreover, the relatively strong performance of the
American economy, compared with that of Europe and many developing
countries, halted and marginally reversed the postwar trend toward the
diffusion of economic power away from the United States.[8]

Progress was evident in monetary policy. Largely in response to
protectionist pressures, Secretary of the Treasury James Baker, III,
convened a meeting in New York on September 22, 1985 with his
counterparts from the United Kingdom, West Germany, France, and
Japan. This Group of Five[9] announced that

> exchange rates should better reflect fundamental economic conditions
> than has been the case [and] some further orderly appreciation of the
> main non-dollar currencies against the dollar is desirable.

The Group of Five stood ready to cooperate more closely in order to
encourage realistic exchange rates. The immediate result of this philo-
sophical about-face was spectacular, as the dollar fell abruptly against
other key currencies. The announcement also called for "a more balanced
expansion" of the leading economies to reduce the American trade deficit
and the Japanese and German current account surpluses. This nod in the
direction of more coordinated macroeconomic policies essentially just
confirmed what these governments had intended to do. Neither West
Germany nor Japan committed themselves to significantly more expansionary fiscal policies, and no mechanisms or formulas were established
to ensure convergent policies in the future. Nevertheless, the Group of
Five announcement, in line with other administrative efforts, did derail
the protectionist bandwagon, at least for the remainder of 1985.

In terms of its own objectives, the administration's strategy toward
the debt crisis was a success. Large-scale defaults were avoided and the

major American banks were stabilized. With the backing of the United States, the IMF compelled banks to lend enough to keep the major debtors liquid, while advising the developing countries to adopt austerity programs. The direct financial costs to the American government of the various rescue packages were low; those official resources that were pressed into service were mostly short- or medium-term loans and were non-concessional. The debtor nations bore the brunt of the adjustment process by slashing their imports and borrowing needs with striking speed. If many nations rescheduled their outstanding principal, they nevertheless dutifully met an interest bill inflated by the sharp rise in the real cost of money on international markets.

The administration also succeeded in imposing some of its priorities on the multilateral development banks. Standing alone, the United States forced the International Development Association (IDA) to reduce sharply its future lending levels in real terms. The Europeans had proved unwilling to fund a supplemental IDA program without American participation. In addition, the administration blocked any major increase in the World Bank's capital and voted against more individual loans in the banks than had any previous administration. Closer to home, the administration systematically targeted its bilateral aid program toward political and security objectives by increasing security assistance relative to development assistance.[10]

Any assessment of the Reagan administration's trade policies depends on the criteria employed. If living up to its rhetoric and keeping American markets open to developing country products is the yardstick, then the administration's record is defensible. If opening up developing country markets to American exports is the criterion, the administration was frustrated by stalemates in the GATT and the contraction of developing country markets as the result of the global recession; in its major Third World trade innovation — the CBI — the administration beneficently granted one-way concessions. If the overall trade balance, however, is the measure, then the administration failed massively — although the widening gap was more the result of uneven global growth rates, recession in the Third World, and the high dollar than of trade policy per se.

President Reagan has claimed not to have lost "one inch of soil" to communism. No radical revolutions occured in major Third World states, no Cuban brigades appeared in new locations in Africa, and Soviet troops remained within existing parameters. It might be argued that Soviet influence did increase in several countries, either directly (Nicaragua), or via "proxies" (as through the Syrians in Lebanon), and that American influence declined elsewhere (Argentina, Morocco, Saudi Arabia). But as its handling of the withdrawal of the U.S. Marines from Beirut illustrated, the administration was adept at "rolling with the punches" and minimizing the impact of setbacks.

In sum, the administration achieved many of its objectives in macroeconomic policy, international finance and debt, and development assistance. And in its dealings with Third World radical regimes, it suffered no grievous losses.

The administration's successes can be attributed to its own strengths, the weakness of potential opponents, its pragmatism under pressure, and to plain good fortune. If the administration did not have a detailed, fully coherent strategy toward the Third World, it did maintain a set of principles and attitudes that were generally shared by its hard-liners and its moderates. In contrast, the rest of the world was chronically divided. Europe was split between conservatives, who tended to share many of the administration's sentiments, and social democrats, who were themselves fractured along ideological and national lines. The Third World was wracked by fratricidal regional conflicts; a widening gap between the more dynamic, newly industrializing states and the stagnant less developed countries; and a global recession and debt crisis that had forced many developing nations to turn inward and to adopt more cautious foreign policies. The heady days of the Organization of Petroleum Exporting Countries (OPEC) and "The New International Economic Order" were forgotten as nations scrambled to regain their creditworthiness on international capital markets, meet IMF-designed stabilization targets, and boost their manufacturing exports to industrial countries.

The Soviet Union during this period suffered from a seeming lack of direction. It was often passive in many parts of the Third World, whether because of a preoccupation with its own economic difficulties, its political succession problem, its lack of suitable opportunities, or, possibly, the fear of an American response. The Soviets did relatively little to exploit such crises as the Falklands/Malvinas war, the Iran-Iraq clash, the domestic vulnerabilities in Pakistan, or the instabilities in Southern Africa, and it pursued generally cautious policies in the Caribbean Basin.

Overall, fortune seemed to smile on Ronald Reagan. The drop in the price of oil and other commodities and the remarkable political stability maintained in many countries, despite severe economic downturns, were among the trends that made life easier for officials in Washington. Advantageous economic developments at home, recession abroad, and the absence of coherent domestic or foreign opposition provided propitious conditions for the reassertionist experiment.

The Scorecard: Setbacks

If the administration's performance was better than many of its critics anticipated, it nevertheless suffered significant setbacks. There was frustration when its ideas conflicted with reality or when its objectives proved to be incompatible. Some failures resulted from ill-conceived strategies or from the neglect of important issues, while still others emerged, ironically, out of the administration's successes.

Although the global adjustment process proceeded essentially as the administration desired, the 1980–82 recession at the same time brought serious costs. Most immediately, the contractions in developing countries — which accounted for about 40 percent of American overseas sales — cost the United States more than $18 billion in export earnings, about one million jobs in American export industries, and some $10 billion in direct investment income to American-owned firms.[11] Seemingly good loans turned bad as the creditworthiness of many debtor nations suddenly deteriorated. Banks increased their reserves against potential losses. New loans and investments slowed for many developing countries, especially in austerity-ridden Latin America and Africa.

Administration incentives to private firms — in the form of tax breaks for corporations, reduced government regulations, and low inflation — were unable to overcome the effects on the American trade account of uneven global growth rates and the high dollar. The American trade balance with all developing countries benefited from the tumbling price of oil, but the trade balance with Latin America and the Caribbean swung from a positive $1.3 billion in 1981 to a negative $17.9 billion in 1983.[12]

The uneven global growth rates — with the United States outpacing Western Europe and many developing countries — combined with the high dollar to produce a flood of imports as against a trickle of American exports. In this sense, the United States paid the price for the lack of international coordination of macroeconomic policies and exchange rates. Greater coordination might have stimulated some European countries to adopt a more growth-oriented fiscal policy. Even taking into account the strength of market forces, earlier and more forceful intervention in currency markets by central banks could have yielded a somewhat steadier, lower dollar. The fall in the dollar following the September 1985 Group of Five meeting came too late to save some American exporting or import-competing firms from severe losses and even bankruptcies. Moreover the decline was incomplete, since the intervention left the dollar still too high to make many American firms internationally competitive or to help reduce the trade deficit of the United States.

Similarly, the administration's macroeconomic successes adversely affected the trade balance by generating a faster growth in investment and consumption at home than occurred abroad. The United States trade policy was also hampered by the absence of positive measures to help workers and firms adapt to international competition. The existing programs clearly needed improving, but the administration chose to cut funds for, rather than reform, the Trade Adjustment Assistance Act. In honoring its free-market principles at home, if not offshore, the administration chose not to require firms receiving trade protection to prepare for eventual competition in open markets. These actions heightened protectionist pressures: Workers who feel vulnerable and unprotected and firms that cannot compete will press for trade barriers. At the same time, since the administration did not have plans to help phase down or restructure declining industries, it was less prepared to make concessions in bargaining with developing countries. The administration's refusal to place potentially attractive concessions on the table was one reason why many developing countries were unenthusiastic about a major new round of trade negotiations under the GATT. Paradoxically, if the United States is to continue to foster a liberal international trading regime, it may have to adopt more interventionist policies at home.

The administration's very success in passing the burden of adjustment onto the debtor nations exacerbated an already chronic debt crisis. As commercial banks virtually stopped lending money and as developing countries complied with their debt service obligations, many debtor nations were paying more to their creditors than they were receiving in new loans and investments. This perverse transfer of funds from poor to rich countries lowered consumption and investment levels in developing nations and placed additional political pressures on debtor governments to question the prevailing debt and adjustment strategies.[13]

In 1985 the administration, in effect, conceded that some of the assumptions underlying its strategy were proving to be overly optimistic: Developing country export earnings were suffering from surprisingly weak commodity prices, real interest rates remained very high, and the commercial banks were unwilling to resume voluntary lending to many debtor nations. Thus at the October 1985 annual meetings of the World Bank and IMF in Seoul, South Korea, James Baker acknowledged that insufficient funds were flowing into the major debtor nations. He urged that the multilateral development institutions and the commercial banks increase their disbursements to the major debtors, in support of adjustment policies that moved beyond austerity to a renewed emphasis on development. He argued that "there must be a commitment by the banking community — a commitment to help the global community make the necessary transition to stronger growth."[14] Specifically, he called on the banks to commit publicly to net lending in the range of $20 billion over three years, and urged the World Bank and Inter-American Development Bank to increase their disbursements to principal debtors by roughly 50 percent from the current annual level of nearly $6 billion. In return for these increases, the recipient nations would be required to agree to "comprehensive macroeconomic and structural reforms," including fiscal stringency, competitive exchange rates, higher domestic savings, more liberal policies toward trade and foreign investment, and increased reliance on the private sector.

Baker's address marked a fundamental shift for the Reagan administration in several conceptual areas. First, it was a clear public admission that, contrary to numerous previous administration statements, the existing strategy was inadequate and that not only did serious problems remain, but also that some setbacks had occurred. Second, Baker abandoned the lukewarm posture he had adopted toward the World Bank at the 1984 annual meetings, and assigned the Bank a central role in the future global adjustment process. Third, he implicitly recognized the fallacy of the earlier assumption that commercial banks would rapidly begin to lend voluntarily to debtors to improve their external accounts. In short, the United States government would have to provide more support to official financial institutions and would also have to renew efforts to coerce the banks to increase their exposure. Although to some degree Baker's proposal was a replay of the about-face made by the Treasury at the time of the first debt crisis in 1982, he was saying, in effect, that a strong public-sector role was not just a short-term emergency departure from market principles but must also be a central feature of international financial relations in the foreseeable future.

Contradictions also marked the administration's aid programs, as economic and security objectives often clashed. Confounding expectations, the administration increased aid budgets, but country allocations were increasingly based on judgments by the Departments of State or Defense that a recipient government was important to the security of the United States. Recipients of large amounts of American aid sometimes rejected AID's call for economic reforms in full confidence that their bureaucratic and congressional allies in Washington would block a cutoff of funds. Thus in many countries, AID's "policy dialogue" took a back seat to strategic ties. In other countries, AID's programs lacked leverage because of their small size.

It is more difficult to judge the administration's impact on the content of AID's programs. The administration did not formally reject the basic human needs emphasis of the aid legislation of the 1970s, although these programs sometimes conflicted with AID's renewed interest in expanding the private sector and in policy dialogue. The administration entered office with few concrete ideas on how to promote the private sector abroad and was hazy as to whether the target was indigenous firms or American companies or both. A final assessment of the impact of AID's new approaches is not yet possible, largely because most of the projects are in the early stages of implementation and results will not be available for several years. But it can be said that economic crises in many Latin American and African countries weakened their private sectors in both absolute and relative terms, as governments frequently intervened more forcefully to allocate scarce resources according to national priorities.

The administration's diplomacy in the Third World focused on containing, and if possible reversing, the radical revolutions of the 1970s. During 1985, administration officials began[15] to justify explicitly American aid — humanitarian and military, overt and covert — to

> brave people who somehow never heard that communism is the wave of the future, peoples who regret the Brezhnev Doctrine and its claims of performance for communist victory.

Although the administration suffered no glaring defeats in dealing with radical Third World states, it has so far failed to overturn earlier "losses" (except for tiny Grenada). The Ayatollah Khomeini, Muammar el-Qaddafi, Fidel Castro, the Sandinistas, and the Popular Movement for the Liberation of Angola are all still in power, while the Soviets remain in Kabul and the Vietnamese in Phnom Penh. The administration might counter that the direct costs to the American budget of its harassment of these regimes has been low. There were, however, intangible costs in the struggle for international opinion of a policy that shunned international legal norms, most notably in refusing to accept the jurisdiction of the World Court regarding Nicaragua's complaint against the United States. Whether the interests of the world's dominant conservative power are best served by legitimizing external support for rebellions against governments in power is also open to question.

It is also hard to measure the lasting effects of global economic instabilities and the handling of the debt crisis on developing country perceptions and attitudes. Certainly some Third World leaders became more wary of participating too vigorously in a highly unstable international economy, as well as less trusting that the North would seek to resolve future crises equitably. As a result, they were also less receptive to donor prescriptions for their economic ills. To some, the United States seemed more agitated by the existence of radical governments than by the development needs of the Third World. For American officials who are more interested in being feared than being respected, this outcome was not necessarily bad. But the lingering resentments seemed likely to generate more tension in North-South relations.

In sum, the administration's significant successes were clouded by the persistence of some old problems and the emergence of some new dangers, raising doubts about its lasting contribution to prosperity and peace in the Third World. The apparent progress in macroeconomic policy and international debt was brittle; some simmering problems had been ignored and new ones loomed ahead. Trade policies were incomplete and in important areas frustrated, while some aid strategies lacked coherence. Several unfriendly radical rulers checked administration parries and seemed likely to be in power at the end of the second Reagan administration.

Raising the Sights

The setbacks noted above were measured against the administration's own yardsticks. Yet these criteria themselves were rather narrow and defensive: the emphasis on bilateralism or subregionalism was born more of frustration than of promise. The programmatic emphases on deflation, financial market stability, and the avoidance of new trade protectionism amounted largely, although not exclusively, to crisis containment rather than to progressive innovation.

A shift to more ambitious criteria raises more serious questions about the results of the administration's performance. If the criteria include emphasis on the values of world order and community, a reduction in international tensions, an increased American capacity to accommodate to a politically pluralistic globe, resumption of strong economic growth, and an improved well-being for poor people in developing countries, the appraisal must be harsher.

The administration has shied away from many traditional forms of supranational cooperation. "If federal government is bad, international government is ten times worse," remarked one White House official.[16] Yet this distrust of international authority ignored the need for collective action in international relations to harmonize national economic policies, to prevent one nation from undertaking actions harmful to others, to correct for structural and cyclical market failures, and generally, to contain international tensions. Policymakers traditionally have felt that the United States, as the major power, has an important stake in a series of global political, economic, and environmental institutions and systems. The administration ignored these imperatives in adopting hostile attitudes toward the arduously negotiated Law of the Sea Treaty, the infant-formula code, the International Planned Parenthood Federation (because of its presumed abortion-related activities), the International Fund for Agricultural Development (IFAD), the World Court, several United Nations agencies, and at least initially, the international financial institutions.

The administration consciously sought to increase international tensions in regions populated by regimes considered to be antithetical to American interests. Economic sanctions and covert actions were used to "bleed" Afghanistan, Cuba, Iran and Iraq, Nicaragua, and Vietnam, and the United States seemed to acquiesce in South Africa's destructive wars against Angola and Mozambique. Such conflicts potentially hurt American economic interests, embroil regional friends, risk a direct American-Soviet confrontation, undermine development efforts, and cause human suffering. Moreover, such policies deepen the suspicion of many in the Third World that the United States is intolerant of Third World nationalism and political experimentation. In reaction, Third World radicals are more likely to anticipate American hostility and seek the security umbrella of the Soviet Union. Thus the policy risks generating the very results it seeks to prevent.

Although the administration understood the usefulness of economic ties to bolster friendly states, its assumption that radicals are incorrigible blinded it to the strategic value of economic links to radical regimes. The disinclination to use economic instruments as "carrots" to alter the behavior of radical governments left the administration more dependent on a narrower range of coercive measures. Moreover, deep hostility toward radical states sometimes clouded administration policy and prevented the Reagan team from carefully distinguishing between policies designed to unseat governments from those aimed more precisely at moderating a given regime's behavior. The administration's loss of leverage in Nicaragua clearly illustrates the incompatability of these two foreign policy goals. The administration's hostility toward Nicaragua also harmed its relations with major Latin American states, including Mexico, who forwarded peace plans that were seen as too tolerant of the Sandinistas.[17]

The Reagan administration should hardly be assigned sole responsibility for the global recession of the early 1980s. Nevertheless it did adopt a mix of fiscal and monetary policies that had grave consequences for many developing countries. Most Latin American countries will not regain pre-1980 levels of per capita income until well into the next decade. Sub-Saharan Africa is even further disadvantaged. Moreover, the administration has shown relatively little interest in helping most developing countries meet their long-term financial needs. As a result, American commercial and political interests in economic development have also suffered.

The overall impact of Reaganomics and the global recession was to produce a less integrated international economy. The boom in North-South capital markets ended, international trade contracted sharply, and many developing countries adopted restrictive trade and exchange-rate policies. (Developing countries also looked more toward each other for markets, and the relative importance of South-South trade grew markedly.) This partial de-linking of North and South ran counter to traditional American foreign policy objectives that had sought to integrate developing countries into the global economy.

The Fragility of the Current Situation and Future Challenges

The preceding analysis suggests that the Reagan administration may well have sowed the seeds of future difficulties when it carried its reassertionism and domesticism[18] too far, when it defined security too narrowly and sought to impose its philosophy too dogmatically, when it impatiently shunned international cooperation and refused to listen to the views of others, and when it allowed ends to justify means. Sometimes its focus on quickly regaining American prestige caused it to lose sight of basic American values and long-term interests.

Ultimate judgments of the North-South policies of the Reagan administration will depend on its ability during the remainder of its tenure to sustain its successes and to correct its mistakes. Especially crucial will be policy in the key areas of macroeconomics, debt, trade, foreign assistance, and diplomacy in conflictive regions.

Macroeconomic Policy

Much of the perception, and the reality, of renewed American strength is a result of the strong United States' economic performance during 1983–84. Nevertheless, the twin deficits in the fiscal and external accounts are unsustainable. The United States now finds itself in the same position as the many developing countries which, during the 1970s, enjoyed an artificial, deficit-funded expansion but are now facing international constraints that force a downward adjustment. The trick will be to manage a gradual closing of the twin deficits so as to avoid a recession that would burst the bubble of renewed American vigor, which could send the global economy into another tailspin. Greater coordination with the major industrial economies would reduce the dangers of miscalculation and actions that are collectively self-defeating. Specifically, if the American economy slows in 1986–88, other industrial nations will have to expand if global growth is to be sustained. Moreover, this expansion will have to be import-intensive in order for the developing countries to benefit in full.

The prospects for the developing countries in the period ahead will depend importantly on how the United States manages macroeconomic policy. The best American policy for the developing countries would be fiscal reforms that gradually cut the budget deficit, allowing the Federal Reserve to lower interest rates. This, in turn, would permit the Organization for Economic Cooperation and Development (OECD) expansion and, one would hope, lead to a widespread, durable global recovery. But if that sustained recovery does not come or if fears of renewed inflation or a sudden sharp fall in the dollar forces monetary authorities to drive up interest rates, the results for the Third World could be disastrous. Everything could go wrong — export demand could fall, interest payments rise, and the burden of dollar-dominated debt could increase.

Developing Country Debt

The current strategy toward Third World debt depends on a sustained recovery in the industrial countries, declining interest rates, and improvements in commodity prices for developing country exporters. Even if all the above occurs, the political problem of negative net financial flows from debtors to banks — and the consequent slower recovery of living standards — will persist. The Baker initiative properly focused attention on the key issue of inadequate capital flows and the need for the public sector to actuate more credit. But three problems remain. First, Baker's numbers simply do not approach the size of the financing gap that his address at Seoul seemed to recognize. Second, the plan was announced unilaterally, without consulting either the debtors being asked to undertake revolutionary changes in their political economies or the industrial country governments whose banks and taxpayers will be expected to contribute. Third, Baker's rhetoric is replete with supply-side phrases, emphasizing tax cuts and the free market, which if taken seriously could imply an effort by a fortified creditor cartel — this time led by the World Bank — to impose a particular, ideologically charged development model. The outcome could be a new phase of confrontation between North and South.

A broad range of mechanisms are available for further reducing the net outflow. Some focus on increasing inflows while others seek to reduce outflows.[19] The IMF, World Bank, Inter-American Development Bank (IDB), Export-Import Bank, and AID could each raise its projected contribution beyond that envisioned in the Baker initiative. Using their various formal and informal cofinancing and guarantee schemes, international financial organizations can also seek to catalyze more private credit. The Federal Reserve Board and other regulatory agencies could also stimulate private creditors to do more through their persuasive powers and the carefully crafted treatement of international loans.

Once contentious but now routine, the rescheduling of principal payments is one element in a package to reduce capital outflow. Other proposals that attack interest payments are more controversial. The President of the IDB, Antonio Ortiz Mena, has suggested, along with others, that the commercial banks agree that a certain percentage of interest payments be automatically reinvested in the debtor country. Alternatively, if market interest rates rose above a predetermined rate, a portion of the payments falling due could be postponed and rolled into principal ("capitalized"). More drastically, payments above the interest-rate "cap" could simply be canceled. An interest-rate ceiling that reduces rates on existing loans by two percentage points for the four largest Latin American debtors (Argentina, Brazil, Mexico, and Venezuela) would eliminate only an estimated 13 percent of earnings of major American banks, whereas a cut of five percentage points would reduce earnings by 33 percent.[20] Although far from negligible, neither sacrifice would force banks to dip into their essential equity base. Whether the banks might suffer a catastrophic loss of confidence would depend on the magnitude and likely duration of the concessions and on the measures taken by the regulatory agencies. Still more drastic measures, including loan writedowns, might be appropriate for some lesser debtors, including Bolivia, Nicaragua, Costa Rica, Zambia, Zaire, and the Sudan, whose export potentials seem too weak to carry existing debt.

Numerous combinations or permutations of such proposals could produce the desired result. Judgments regarding the likely direction of interest rates will be crucial: Lower rates would suggest a package more heavily weighted toward new lending; higher rates would increase the need for restructuring existing debts.

The exact formula should not be decided by the United States alone. On the contrary, involvement of the debtors in designing the program could bring several benefits. Certainly the diplomatic gains will be much greater if the debtor countries feel that they have played a meaningful role in determining their own futures. Governments are also much more likely to carry through with economic reforms they participate in formulating and are in agreement with, than with concepts imposed on them from the outside at moments of financial vulnerability.

Trade

Confronted with a tidal wave of protectionist legislation in the fall of 1985, the administration offered a package of new trade policies that tried to combine toughness toward trading partners with a continuing commitment to open markets.[21] Reagan set a new precedent by asking the United States Trade Representative, Clayton Yeutter, to investigate unfair trade practices. Two of the three initial cases were against developing nations: The United States examined a Korean law injurious to American insurance firms and a Brazilian law restricting the sale of American high-technology products. To counter the use of subsidized export credits by France and, to a lesser degree, Italy and Japan, Reagan prepared a small, $300-million "war chest" to lower the cost of credit to developing nations purchasing American goods. At the same time, he pressed for authority to reduce trade barriers through a new GATT round and warned that he would oppose blatantly protectionism legislation, a threat he honored when he vetoed a bill intended to sharply reduce textile imports from developing countries.

These disputes were minor compared to the size of the American trade deficit, which reached $53 billion with developing countries alone in 1984.[22] The administration may be hard pressed to maintain its commendable record of resisting protectionism at home if it cannot correct its two failures in trade policy: its inability to reduce protectionist barriers abroad and its huge trade deficit. Reduction of the trade deficit substantially hinges on bringing United States growth rates more into line with those in other industrial countries and our major developing country trading partners, as well as realigning the American dollar. A lessening of the Third World debt burden would also encourage American exports by freeing up funds, especially in debt-depressed Latin America, to purchase more American manufactures.

Trade liberalization would provide the administration with a major opportunity to put its preferred economics into practice, but it calls for some policy shifts. Encouraging developing countries to join a meaningful North-South trade round in the GATT will depend on American willingness to make reciprocal concessions. The administration can increase to its bargaining position in this respect by adopting a more activist policy in assisting declining domestic industries to adjust to new market forces.

Foreign Assistance

Foreign aid has always been used to achieve a broad range of goals, but current policies that emphasize political and security goals at the expense of economic development and meeting the needs of poor people run counter to long-term American goals and to the address of poverty. Reordering priorities is essential if the aid program is to be made congruent with long-term American interests in the Third World.

The United States needs to direct more development assistance to the world's poorest countries. In this respect, Africa presents the second Reagan administration with the greatest development task of the decade. The United States responded generously to the famines in Africa in 1985, and led by AID, provided a large portion of the food and other emergency supplies channeled to the hardest hit areas. But the real policy challenge is how to address Sub-Saharan Africa's chronic underdevelopment and to strengthen fragile African economies so that they can withstand natural and external economic shocks in the future. Currently sub-Saharan Africa receives just under 30 percent of total OECD aid. This share should be increased, and donors should coordinate the existing programs more effectively.

In 1982 the Treasury Department dropped its initial skepticism toward the IMF — an attitude based on an ideologically rigid rejection of international institutions per se, as well as an excessive confidence in market forces. In 1985 the administration reconsidered its hostile attitude toward the World Bank. The Baker initiative allows the World Bank a much greater role, but the modalities of that expanded role — and the funding to support it — are still unresolved. The Bank may be the most effective single institution available to assist developing countries making the transition from austerity and stabilization to structural adjustment and renewed growth. It can also help provide a framework that would inspire greater confidence in lenders and investors. If the Bank is to undertake this role, however, the resources available both to it and to IDA will have to increase.

Diplomacy

The Reagan Doctrine of paramilitary aid to counterrevolutionary forces is an ideologically charged, strategically dangerous approach to coping with social change and Soviet ambitions in the Third World.[23] Rather than relying primarily on the instrumentalities of the Central Intelligence Agency and Defense Department in cases where there is no direct Soviet military presence, the administration should give the State Department greater scope to bring its good offices to bear on resolving regional disputes. Even when American influence is limited, an activist diplomacy that engages all parties to the conflict, regardless of the regimes' professed ideologies, can often produce results. This was demonstrated in 1984 by the administration's successful efforts to improve relations between Mozambique and South Africa. Sometimes the lead should be granted to regional powers with good entrees to the parties in conflict. In Central America, the United States should assume a more positive attitude toward the peace proposals of leading Latin American powers — which address key United States security concerns in the region — even if that implies accepting a modus vivendi with the Nicaraguan government. Among other reasons, only if peace is secured in Central America will American financial aid and the opportunities offered by the CBI be able to stimulate economic recovery and long-term development.

A review of recent American policies toward radical states provides evidence that economic "carrots" and "sticks" can work — provided they are employed as part of a coherent strategy with realistic, limited objectives.[24] In the short run, economic inducements can help to moderate a regime's foreign policy, if not necessarily its internal politics. In the longer run, policies of diplomatic engagement can also encourage trends toward economic decentralization and political pluralism within revolutionary states.

In dealing with Third World debt, exchange rates, macroeconomic policies, and trade, the administration has shown some awareness that domestic and international realities limit American freedom and that a stubborn refusal to accept these limits can lead to problems and perhaps even explosive crises. The new directions proposed here imply a broadening of goals and a lengthening of the Administration's time horizon. While seeking to conserve gains, they introduce important corrections to address neglected issues and to avoid predictable dangers. Herein lie the challenges for the remainder of the Reagan presidency and beyond.

"American Power and Third World Economies" was written for this volume. Copyright © 1987 by Richard E. Feinberg. It draws heavily on the author's earlier essay, "Testing U.S. Reassertionism: The Reagan Approach to the Third World," in John W. Sewell, Richard E. Feinberg, and Valeriana Kallab, eds., U.S. Foreign Policy and the Third World: Agenda 1985–1986 *(New Brunswick, N.J.: Transaction Books, 1985), pp. 3–19.*

Notes

1. For the most coherent explanation so far of the administration's "domesticist" economic policies by a participant, see Henry Nau, "Where Reaganomics Works," *Foreign Policy* (Winter 1984–85), No. 57, pp. 14–37.
2. For example, see Paul Krugman, "U.S. Macro-Economic Policy and the Developing Countries," in *U.S. Foreign Policy and the Third World: Agency 1985–1986*, John Sewell, Richard Feinberg, and Valeriana Kallab, eds. (New Brunswick, NJ: Transaction Books, 1985), pp. 31–50. Krugman was a member of the Reagan administration's Council of Economic Advisors.
3. As described in Kenneth Oye, "International Systems Structure and American Foreign Policy," in *Eagle Defiant*, Kenneth Oye, Robert Lieber, and Donald Rothchild, eds. (Boston: Little, Brown, 1983), pp. 3–32.
4. The growing role of the public sector in international finance is discussed by Richard E. Feinberg, "LDC Debt and the Public Sector," *Challenge* (July–August 1985), pp. 27–34.
5. For example, see Jeane J. Kirkpatrick, Address Before the American Society of International Law, Washington, D.C., April 12, 1984.
6. See *Realism, Strength, Negotiation: Key Foreign Policy Statements of the Reagan Administration* (Washington, D.C.: U.S. Department of State, 1984).
7. As quoted in Christopher Madison, "Exporting Reaganomics — The President Wants To Do Things Differently in AID," *National Journal*, May 29, 1982, p. 962.
8. Krugman, op cit.
9. Statement, as reprinted in *New York Times*, September 23, 1985, p. D11.
10. See John Sewell and Christine Contee, "U.S. Foreign Aid in the 1980s, Reordering Priorities," in John Sewell et al., op cit., pp. 95–118.
11. "*Costs of Third World Recession: They Lose, We Lose,*" Overseas Development Council, *Policy Focus* (1984), No. 2.
12. *Highlights of U.S. Export and Import Trade*, U.S. Department of Commerce, December, 1981 and December 1983, Tables E-3 and I-6.
13. For a fuller discussion, see Richard E. Feinberg, "Overview: Restoring Confidence in International Credit Markets," in *Uncertain Future: Commercial Banks and the Third World*, Richard E. Feinberg and Valeriana Kallab, eds. (New Brunswick, NJ: Transaction Books, 1984), pp. 9–14.
14. James A. Baker, III, statement before the Joint Annual Meeting of the World Bank and International Monetary Fund, Seoul, South Korea, October 8, 1985, *Treasury News* (mimeo).
15. George P. Schultz, speech to the Pilgrims Society, London, England, December 10, 1985.
16. Interview cited in Oye, op. cit., p. 25.
17. See Guy Erb and Cathryn Thorup, *U.S.-Mexican Relations: The Issues Ahead* (Development Paper 35, Overseas Development Council, 1984).
18. For an explanation of the administration's "domesticist" strategy, see note 1.
19. For discussions of the many proposals to manage the debt crisis, see C. F. Bergsten et al., *Bank Lending to Developing Countries: The Policy Alternatives* (Washington, D.C.:

Institute for International Economics, 1985); Anatole Kaletsky, *The Costs of Default* (New York: A Twentieth-Century Fund Paper, Priorityu Press Publications, 1985); and Richard E. Feinberg and Valeriana Kallab, *Uncertain Future*, pp. 24–27.

20. Richard E. Feinberg, "Overview," p. 8.

21. Ronald Reagan, address before business leaders and members of the President's Export Council and Advisory Committee for Trade Negotiations in the East Room of the White House, Washington, D.C., September 23, 1985.

22. Stuart Tucker, "U.S.-Third World Deficit: Going After the Causes," Overseas Development Council, *Policy Focus* (1985), No. 7, p. 28.

23. See Robert H. Johnson, " 'Rollback' Revisited — A Reagan Doctrine for Insurgent Wars?," Overseas Development Council, *Policy Focus*, (1986), No. 1, p. 30.

24. W. Anthony Lake, *Third World Radical Regimes: U.S. Policy Under Carter and Reagan* (New York: Foreign Policy Association, Headline Series No. 272, 1985), p. 31.

6

International Energy Policy and the Reagan Administration: Avoiding the Next Oil Shock?

Robert J. Lieber

Energy-related crises occupied a predominant position on American foreign and economic policy agendas from 1973 through 1980. In the 1980s however, the Reagan administration encountered a more benign international environment. As a consequence energy did not pose security or economic difficulties of the same magnitude. Nonetheless, the issues at hand remained important. Although the dramatic development of the early and mid-1980s was a stunning reversal in the wealth and power of OPEC as a result of the oil glut, the long-term situation remains dynamic. That is, upheavals in the relative bargaining power and vulnerability of oil-producing and oil-consuming countries have been a hallmark of the years since the 1973 oil shock. The fact that the United States and the other oil-importing industrial democracies have witnessed an extraordinary improvement in their relative position does not ensure that this pattern will remain permanent. As a consequence, the basis for assessing Reagan policies in energy is whether they can minimize the long-term risks of a future oil shock.

Robert J. Lieber is Professor of Government at Georgetown University, specializing in American-European relations, American foreign policy, and energy security. Previously a professor of political science at the University of California, Davis, he has also been a visiting fellow or guest scholar at St. Antony's College, Oxford; the Harvard University Center for International Affairs; Atlantic Institute, Paris; The Brookings Institution; and the Woodrow Wilson International Center for Scholars. His books include British Politics and European Unity *(Berkeley: University of California Press, 1970);* Theory and World Politics *(Winthrop, 1972);* Oil and the Middle East War *(Cambridge, MA: Harvard Center for International Affairs, 1976); and* The Oil Decade *(New York: Praeger, 1983; and Lanham, MD: University Press of America, 1986). He was also co-editor of* Eagle Entangled: U.S. Foreign Policy in a Complex World (New York: Longman, 1979) and of Eagle Defiant: US Foreign Policy in the 1980s *(Boston: Little, Brown and Co., 1983).*

As in other foreign policy areas, the Reagan administration encountered dilemmas in the energy realm. Here too, it initially approached the subject with a Soviet-centric view of the world as well as an emphasis on the market mechanism and a reduced role for government. Periodically this approach imposed costs, both immediate and potential, for the international security of America and its allies. (Energy security here denotes a stable and reliable pattern of energy supply and demand, not seriously vulnerable to interruption or available only at excessively high prices.)

The administration did have tangible achievements in energy. These included expanding the Strategic Petroleum Reserve (SPR) — albeit under congressional prodding — from the 100 million barrels inherited after Jimmy Carter's presidency to a level of 500 million barrels at the beginning of 1986. The Reagan administration also accelerated policies to decontrol oil and, in part, natural gas prices. These measures helped reduce oil consumption and imports and thus lessened American vulnerability to international oil blackmail or embargo.

The administration also benefited from a dramatic erosion in the political and economic power of OPEC. In large measure, this followed from the long-term effects of price increases that had driven oil from $2.70 per barrel in October 1973 to $34 in October 1981. The resultant decrease in demand for OPEC oil and the increased supply of non-OPEC oil and other forms of energy reduced both the dependence and the vulnerability of the industrial democracies on Middle East oil. The effects of high prices and Western adaptation also contributed to an oil glut, disarray within OPEC, and a plunge in oil prices to a range between $10 and $15 per barrel in the first half of 1986.[1]

The administration's priorities, however, imposed trade-offs. During 1981–82, Reagan's policies brought the United States into sharp conflict with European allies over their imports of Soviet natural gas. In addition, the administration's emphasis on the market mechanism created potential conflicts with other energy security needs. These included the ability to cope with a future oil shock or to meet International Energy Agency (IEA) obligations in the event of an emergency. Free-market principles also led to opposition to a World Bank program, which was designed to stimulate energy production and conservation among non-OPEC states of the developing world.

In the military sphere, both the Carter and the Reagan administrations undertook the buildup of a Rapid Deployment Force[2] for military contingencies in the Persian Gulf. Their shared objective was to counter threats to vital allied energy supplies. Yet to the extent that American policies could result in an eventual increase in dependence on Middle East oil during the 1990s, America and its allies risked renewed vulnerability to upheavals in one of the most unstable regions on earth.

This chapter considers the context in which the international energy policy of the United States takes place. It examines the legacy of energy crises during the past decade, as well as the constraints imposed by an integrated world oil system. The chapter then analyzes the transition in policy from Carter to Reagan. It next explores the premises of administration policy and the trade-offs that resulted. It also considers how the Reagan administration was forced to adapt initial premises in response to the imperatives of coping with both energy security concerns and the need for allied cooperation. Finally, this chapter examines how another reversal in economic and power relationships between the oil-importing countries and the members of OPEC could again become a significant risk.

America and the International Oil System

The setting for international energy policy is one in which the role of oil remains overwhelmingly important. In the space of some twenty-five years, from the late 1940s to the early 1970s, North America, Western Europe, and Japan experienced a period of remarkable economic growth and sharply increased living standards. The energy source for this development was oil, available in seemingly limitless quantities and at low prices. In a mere two decades, imported oil replaced domestic coal as the dominant source of energy in most industrial countries.

The United States had long been the leading force and most important producer in the world oil market. Although America became a net oil importer as early as 1948, a substantial domestic and international reserve capacity helped to keep prices low and supplies ample. As a result, neither the Suez Crisis of 1956 nor the Arab-Israeli Six-Day War of 1967 disturbed American oil supply or oil prices. Indeed, as late as January 1970, Saudi Arabian light marker crude oil sold for a mere $1.39 a barrel.[3] In constant dollars, the price had declined by almost half over a period of two decades.

In 1971, however, American oil production peaked. Thereafter the balance between world production capacity and demand became substantially tighter. During the early 1970s, a number of additional factors combined to produce profound changes in the balance of international oil power. The hitherto unchallenged dominance of the international oil companies, the Seven Sisters, was eroded by the increased activity of the smaller independent companies and by the growing strength of OPEC. In 1970, the radical government of Libya, under the leadership of Colonel Muammar el-Qaddafi, succeeded in imposing a price increase on the Occidental Petroleum Company. Within a year, at Teheran in February 1971, the OPEC countries managed to negotiate a substantial price increase with the major oil companies. In large measure, this was made possible by the erosion of excess world oil production capacity relative to demand. The balance of bargaining power now shifted to favor the producing countries, giving them — rather than the companies — the dominant voice in setting prices and production levels.

The onset of the Arab-Israeli war on October 6, 1973 suddenly illuminated the shift in power that had taken place. An Arab oil embargo against the United States and, more importantly, Arab production cuts produced an almost fourfold increase in price over a period of several months: Saudi oil rose from $2.70 per barrel on October 4, 1973 to $10.46 by March 1, 1974.[4]

This 1973–74 oil shock seriously harmed the economy of the industrial democracies, as well as the non-oil producing, less developed countries (LDCs). The Western allies and Japan, members of the Organization for Economic Cooperation and Development (OECD), lost the equivalent of 2 percent of their gross national product (GNP). They also experienced a sharp inflationary jolt, rising unemployment, and substantial balance-of-payments problems.[5]

Equally important, the United States and its allies found themselves in serious political disarray. They faced sharp differences over Middle East policy, with individual European countries and Japan seeking individual bilateral deals with oil-producing states at the cost of cooperation on either a European or an Atlantic basis.[6] The sole positive outcome of this period was the creation of the International Energy Agency (IEA). This new body, established through American impetus in spite of the opposition of France, provided a basis for emergency consumer cooperation and oil sharing in the event of a future crisis. The trigger for such sharing would be an oil shortfall of 7 percent or more.

As the crisis receded, the international oil problem began to ease. A major Western recession in 1974–75 reduced world oil demand. To a lesser extent, because of oil price increases, a degree of conservation and fuel switching occurred. During the period from late 1974 to late 1978, the economic impact of the crisis was gradually absorbed. The looser supply and demand balance even produced a growing sense of an oil glut. OPEC prices stagnated and, in real terms, actually declined by 13 percent between 1976 and 1978.[7]

During the five years from the end of 1973 to the end of 1978, European consumption of oil declined by 3.6 percent; imports declined by 2.2 percent.[8] American consumption continued to rise, however, climbing 11.8 percent in this same period. More dangerously, American oil imports increased even faster. As a result not only of growing consumption but also of decreased domestic production, these imports rose by 28.5 percent.[9] At the same time, less oil was available from Canada and Venezuela. American dependence on both OPEC and on Arab oil producers thus soared. For example, between 1973 and 1977, OPEC's share of American oil imports rose from 50 to 73 percent, and that of Arab OPEC states from 15 to 38 percent (see Table 6–1).

American energy policy remained at a near impasse. Its chief accomplishments were legislation imposing mandatory improvement in automobile fuel economy, consolidation of the IEA, and initiation of the Strategic Petroleum Reserve (SPR) (though without substantial purchases of oil for it). Otherwise the United States experienced a stalemate. Controls on oil kept prices far below world levels and thus worked against efforts to reduce import dependence. Measures to encourage conservation, energy efficiency, fuel switching, and the development of non-oil energy sources were not given the scale of support required to effect meaningful changes. And battles over natural gas pricing pitted regions and interest groups in a bitter, inconclusive struggle.

Although a number of serious analysts warned of renewed tightening of world oil supply patterns and thus the risk of another oil shock, many observers and policymakers tended to minimize the problem. As late as the autumn of 1978, the then-Congressman from Michigan, David Stockman,[10] could write:

TABLE 6–1. U.S. Oil Imports (million barrels per day, mbd)

Year	Total Net Imports* (mbd)	Imports from			
		OPEC (mbd)	%	Arab OPEC** (mbd)	%
1973	6.0	3.0	50	0.9	15
1974	5.9	3.3	56	0.8	14
1975	5.8	3.6	62	1.4	24
1976	7.1	5.1	72	2.4	34
1977	8.6	6.2	73	3.2	38
1978	8.0	5.8	73	3.0	38
1979	8.0	5.6	70	3.1	39
1980	6.4	4.3	67	2.6	41
1981	5.4	3.3	61	1.8	33
1982	4.3	2.1	49	0.9	21
1983	4.3	1.9	44	0.6	14
1984	4.7	2.0	43	0.8	17
1985	4.3	1.8	43	0.5	11

*Includes imports for the Strategic Petroleum Reserve.
**Arab OPEC includes Algeria, Libya, Saudi Arabia, United Arab Emirates, Iraq, Kuwait, and Qatar. Non-Arab OPEC includes Indonesia, Iran, Nigeria, Venezuela, Ecuador, and Gabon.
SOURCE: Calculated from data in U.S. Department of Energy, Energy Information Administration, *Monthly Energy Review* (December 1982), pp. 31, 36–37; (May 1985), pp. 37, 42, 109; (November 1985), pp. 36–37, 42–43.

Indeed, the global economic conditions necessary for another major unilateral price action by OPEC are not likely to reemerge for more than a decade — if ever.

Suddenly in late 1978, political unrest in Iran began to disrupt oil production. That country had been OPEC's second largest oil producer after Saudi Arabia, producing 5.5 million barrels per day (mbd) as late as October 1978. As a result of revolutionary upheaval, however, the output dropped by 2 mbd in November and an additional 1 mbd in December. With the Shah's ouster in January, Iran's oil production came to a virtual halt. It then slowly began to recover, rising to 2.2 mbd in March and then fluctuating between 3 and 4 mbd for the remainder of the year.[11]

Much of the reduction was offset by increased oil production elsewhere. Saudi Arabia, however, exacerbated the situation by reducing its own output from 10.4 to 9.8 mbd in January and by a further 1.0 mbd in April. This left a net shortfall of approximately 4 percent of world oil demand for the second calendar quarter of 1979. At a time of unusually low world oil stock levels and a disruption of established oil market patterns, there was fiercely competitive bidding for oil on the international spot markets. Prices surged upward, with consuming countries unable to cooperate effectively. Ultimately, oil prices rose 170 percent over a fifteen-month period.

This rapid succession of oil crisis, oil glut, and oil crisis occurred in a highly integrated world oil system, or "regime." The functioning of this system determines the relations among producers and consumers of oil; it is based on the fact that the production or consumption of a barrel of oil, wherever it occurs, ultimately weighs as part of a world balance of supply and demand.

World oil prices are affected by political factors and by economic and market mechanisms. Before 1970, the role of the major oil companies was decisive in setting or influencing prices. Subsequently, with the emergence of OPEC and especially of Saudi Arabia as the source for meeting marginal changes in oil demand, these producers were able to make an impact even greater than their share of world oil production would suggest. Nonetheless, the overall pattern of world oil supply and demand does set the framework within which various forces contend. More importantly, the greater the margin of spare oil production capacity and the more diversified it is among oil-producing countries, the less vulnerable the system is to sudden oil shocks.

Wherever they occur, shifts in oil supply or demand affect the system as a whole. On the supply side, increases in Saudi production; the development of Alaskan, North Sea, and Mexican oil; and even small-scale increases in oil production among the LDCs all add to the potential pool of world oil. Conflict in Iran and Iraq and declines in American and Venezuelan production, however, represent real or potential reductions in world supply.

On the demand side, fuel switching from oil to any other energy source (for example, coal, natural gas, nuclear energy, or solar energy), reductions in oil consumption, energy conservation and efficiency, the drawing down of stockpiles, or the effects of recession, all decrease the demand for world oil. In turn, such factors as economic growth, development among the LDCs, and the wider spread of the automobile increase the demand pressure.

These forces shape a volatile international oil pattern. When there is little surplus production capacity, the system is especially vulnerable to oil shock, which can result from any significant disturbance to routine conditions of supply. Thus after the October 1973 war, a shortfall of roughly 7 percent created the conditions for a 300 percent increase in price. Again after the fall of the Shah, a reduction of 4 percent during the spring of 1979 led to a 170 percent price increase.

Conversely, when there is substantial spare capacity and an excess of oil production relative to demand, the system is far more resistant to change. The September 1980 outbreak of the Iran/Iraq war occurred at a time of substantial surplus capacity and record levels of world oil inventories. As a result, no oil shock occurred. During 1981 and the spring and summer of 1982, continued easing of the supply-demand balance produced a softening of world oil prices and a "glut," although the actions of OPEC in cutting production prevented a major downward price break. The burden of the cuts was borne heavily by Saudi Arabia. That country reduced its output from 10 mbd to less than 2.5 mbd by the middle of 1985. During the following winter, however, the Saudis raised production by more than 2 mbd, which intensified the oil glut and triggered dramatic reductions in price.

The implications of the integration of this oil system are profound. They impose an ineluctable interdependence on its participants, regardless of whether or not this is consciously a part of their international energy policies.

By way of illustration, the 1973–74 Arab oil embargo against the United States had little direct impact on its target. Internationally available oil was simply allocated on a pro rata basis by the oil companies. In future crises, the emergency oil sharing system of the IEA would have much the same effect.

This integrated world oil system, however, sometimes creates unwelcome trade-offs. Continued American opposition to Western European purchases of Soviet natural gas and American embargoes of equipment and technology used in the construction of the pipeline would have imposed at least a modest energy security cost through greater demand pressure on world oil markets, regardless of other foreign policy priorities.

Energy Policy: From Carter to Reagan

The Carter administration sought, in a more comprehensive way than any of its predecessors, to make energy policy a priority. Yet energy-related issues, in the form of the fall of the Shah, the second oil shock, and the Iran hostage seizure, did much to defeat the Carter administration.

President Carter sought to arouse the nation over the energy problem, but his April 1977 speech, describing the energy challenge as the "moral equivalent of war," did not have a decisive impact. The call to a massive conservation effort was more hortatory than substantive. Other major parts of his energy program, including a gasoline tax, became entangled in a congressional stalemate over natural gas decontrol.[12] The issues of costs and benefits to industries and entire regions proved particularly unmanageable, and a substantial easing of the international oil balance from 1975 to 1978 deprived a policy to conserve energy of much of its urgency.

With the overthrow of the Shah, however, energy policy once again became crucial. In April 1979 Carter used his executive authority to initiate decontrol of domestic petroleum prices over a two and one-half–year period. The new crisis also broke the deadlock over natural gas. Congress agreed on a program of phased decontrol, extending to 1985, as well as a windfall profits tax on oil.

Overall, the second crisis found the United States and the other major oil-consuming countries still ill prepared for an oil shock. In the United States, there were once again fears of shortages, problems of oil allocation, gas lines, steep price increases, and ample political recrimination. At the international level, political disarray and an inability to cooperate effectively again marked relations among Americans, Europeans, and Japanese.[13]

The difficulty was less acute than during the 1973 crisis, and consultation among IEA members did occur, which led to commitments to reduce oil consumption by 5 percent, although these and other steps were more symbolic than substantive. In any case, they were inadequate to prevent the second shock from intensifying or to ameliorate its effects substantially.

In July 1979, with the administration's overall leadership under serious criticism, President Carter announced a vast $88 billion federal program to accelerate the development of synthetic fuels over the course of a decade. The long-term objective was to produce the equivalent of 0.5

mbd of oil from coal and shale rock by 1987, and 2 mbd by 1992. These and other efforts, however, had little direct bearing on the crisis. One tangible program that might have made a difference was the use of the SPR. Yet the filling of the reserve had been slow, both for technical reasons (the need to prepare oil storage caverns and install pumps) and budgetary priorities (the cost of oil purchases). As a result, there were only 67 million barrels of oil in the SPR at the end of 1978 — the equivalent of a mere eight days of total American oil imports.[14] Indeed, SPR additions were halted in September 1979, in part because of a desire not to antagonize Saudi Arabia (which had increased production by 1.0 mbd in July). The filling of the SPR finally resumed a year later.

Reagan Administration Energy Policy: Premises and Dilemmas

The Reagan administration took office more with a set of doctrinal impulses toward energy policy than a coherent strategy. Three sets of principles shaped the administration's approach. The first of these lay outside the immediate realm of energy and economic policy: an emphasis on the Soviet threat and on East-West confrontation. To the extent that other priorities were in conflict with this, the Soviet-centric priority was likely to take precedence.

A second principle involved "a much heavier emphasis" on allowing energy decisions to be made by the free market.[15] A third, closely related principle stressed reducing the role of government and of regulatory mechanisms. Indeed, government was seen as a major cause of the energy problem. This was symbolized in a campaign pledge to abolish the Department of Energy.

These principles were accompanied by a set of beliefs about energy, typified by presidential candidate Reagan's assertion that deregulation could make the United States self-sufficient in energy within five years.[16] Emphasis on the supply side of the energy equation, rather than on demand (except insofar as the price mechanism was involved), was another characteristic. Among specific energy sources, oil, natural gas, coal, and nuclear power, were looked on favorably, whereas solar energy, other renewable sources, and energy efficiency were viewed, at best, indifferently.

The international oil crunch had eased greatly by the time Reagan took office. Oil was much less in demand as a result of earlier price increases and the most severe economic recession since the 1930s. In addition, non-OPEC oil production capacity (including Mexico, Alaska, and the North Sea) had increased by approximately six million barrels from 1978 to 1982.

These factors, together with more than 2 mbd of destocking, greatly decreased the demand for OPEC oil. Production fell from 31 mbd in 1979 to an average of 22.6 mbd in 1981, to 17.6 mbd in 1983 and 1984, and to 15.9 mbd in 1985.[17]

As a result of this drop in the demand for OPEC oil, prices softened. Anxieties over the security of oil supply eased greatly, and the balance of bargaining power between producers and consumers of oil once again shifted. This change deprived the producing countries of the unilateral advantages they had availed themselves of during and immediately after each oil shock.

The Reagan administration came into office under less pressure and with more room to maneuver than its predecessors. The president's initial step, within a week of taking office, was to end price controls on domestic crude oil. These controls were begun in 1971, but decontrol had already been initiated by Carter. At the time of Reagan's action, less than one-fourth of domestic oil was affected. In any case, controls had been due to expire on September 30th. The administration also abolished complex emergency allocation procedures for gasoline as well as regulations affecting the entitlements program. (This had required transfer payments among refineries to equalize the competitive conditions for those without access to cheap domestic oil.) Because of the soft international oil market situation, oil decontrol was completed without disruptive price increases.[18]

Another significant component of the Reagan energy policy concerned the SPR. Under congressional pressure, filling of the reserve had been resumed in the waning months of the Carter administration, and support for the SPR had also figured in the 1980 Republican platform.

Despite differences between the Reagan administration and Congress over SPR funding and the rate at which purchases would be made, additions to the reserve were accelerated. During 1981, these averaged over 300,000 barrels per day. Subsequently, the administration favored purchases of 200,000 barrels per day rather than the 300,000 sought by the Senate for the 1983 fiscal year. To lessen the impact on the federal budget deficit (which more than doubled the entire national debt during the first four years of the Reagan presidency), the administration placed the funding for the SPR off-budget. Subsequently, the administration urged a "moratorium" on filling the SPR for Fiscal year 1986.[19] It later compromised with Congress and agreed to a rate of 35,000 barrels per day. By January 1986, however, the reserve had reached 500 million barrels, and as a budgetary measure, the Reagan administration once again proposed a moratorium on further additions. During the spring of 1986, under pressure from Congress, the administration agreed to release $157 million in funds for construction of surface facilities associated with the SPR. While initially opposed to further expenditures, it agreed in

August to support a 750-million barrel target, with purchases of approximately 35,000 barrels per day.

The growing size of the SPR made the United States less vulnerable to the effects of a future oil emergency. Reductions in American oil consumption and imports — both as a result of government policies and market forces — also meant decreased dependence on foreign oil. Net oil imports, which had been 8.0 mbd in 1979, fell to 6.4 mbd in 1980 and 5.4 mbd in 1981. Imports dropped still further, to less than 5 mbd in 1982–85. Both phenomena, the growth of the SPR and the reduction in import dependence, contributed to American energy security.

East-West Priorities and Energy Tradeoffs: The Soviet Gas Pipeline

Other initial attributes of administration policy had opposite effects when judged by the criteria of oil dependence and vulnerability. The most visible of these policies concerned Soviet exports of natural gas to Western Europe. These were to be delivered, beginning in 1984, by way of a 3700 mile pipeline from Western Siberia. One reason the Reagan administration decided to oppose the project was to punish the Soviet Union for repression in Poland. There were two additional reasons: One was concern over the possibilities of Soviet leverage against Western Europe, for example, in a future opportunity for the Soviet Union to threaten to curtail natural gas supplies. (The Soviet Union had manipulated its exports of oil as a political tool in 1948 against Yugoslavia, in 1956 against Israel, in 1964 against China, and in 1968 to influence Cuba.) The other reason was to deny the Soviets hard currency earnings ($8 to $10 billion per year by its own estimates; less than $4 billion by a different estimate)[20] that West European gas exports would bring. It thereby aimed to squeeze the Soviet economy and hence make it more costly for the Soviet Union to devote scarce resources to military spending.

The specific American measures began with a December 1981 decision to prevent the General Electric Corporation from exporting turbine rotors to the Soviet Union. The restriction also applied to General Electric agreements with three European manufacturing associates: AEG-Telefunken in West Germany, John Brown in the United Kingdom, and Nuovo Pignone in Italy. In addition, the American firm of Caterpillar Tractor was prevented from selling $90 million worth of pipe-laying vehicles to the Soviet Union.

In June 1982, the administration extended the restrictions to overseas subsidiaries of American firms and to foreign companies that held General Electric licenses, in this case, the French firm of Alsthom-Atlantique, which had a contract to supply complete turbines on its own.[21] Firms in Britain, Italy, and West Germany were also affected. Reagan's decision also caused the collapse of Japanese negotiations for joint oil exploration with Russia on Sakhalin Island. However, the Japanese Komatsu firm stepped in to provide the pipe-laying equipment and the Soviets found other possibilities (albeit at additional cost) for turbine rotors.

From the perspective of the Western European countries most concerned (France, West Germany, and Italy), the gas deal appeared to be a pragmatic way of diversifying energy import sources. In this case, a reliance on the Soviets for approximately 25 to 30 percent of their natural gas supplies (but just 5 to 6 percent of their total primary energy) offered a means of lessening oil and gas dependence on the Middle East and North Africa and hence reducing European vulnerability to the effects of a crisis in that region.

Indeed, the Germans, French, and Italians already relied on Soviet gas. In 1980 the Soviet Union provided 17.5 percent of gas supply in Germany, 13.3 percent in France, and 23.7 percent in Italy.[22] Moreover, the increases in 1990 gas dependence (to 29 percent in Germany, 23 to 28 percent in France, and 29 percent in Italy) would roughly offset the decline in Soviet oil exports to Western Europe. These amounted to 1.1 mbd in 1979 and accounted for more than one-half of the Soviet Union's earnings of essential hard currency.[23] The issue, therefore, was less one of dependence on the Soviet Union per se than of whether, or at what level, these imports might pose unacceptable risks.[24]

To the extent that American sanctions had proven effective, they would have imposed a second energy trade-off — in this case, Western Europeans would have been forced to rely on the world oil market for fuel that would otherwise have been offset by Soviet gas. In addition, the June 1982 measures caused bitter recriminations with America's European allies. There was ample reason to see that the repression in Poland not be cost-free to the Soviets. Yet European skepticism about the efficacy of such sanctions (based in part on their own previous experience, for example, that of the Federal Republic in the 1950s and 1960s) was combined with a cynical view about the Reagan administration having ended the embargo on American grain exports to the Soviet Union. The Europeans were particularly irked that the Americans had not taken the occasion of the Versailles summit or of the NATO meeting in Bonn, which immediately followed, to consult over the impending increase in restrictions. Even as staunch an anti-Soviet as the Conservative British Prime Minister Margaret Thatcher protested the American actions. She did so on the grounds that it was wrong for the United States to seek to prevent existing contracts from being fulfilled.[25]

Within weeks of the American action, the governments of France, Italy, Britain, and (indirectly) Germany ordered their firms to proceed with contractual commitments for work on the Soviet pipeline project. American restrictions were rejected on the grounds that they constituted an unacceptable extension of United States' law into the internal affairs of Western Europe.[26]

Whereas discussions about increased exports of American coal or more rapid development of Norwegian oil and gas suggested long-term alternatives to dependence on Soviet gas, these sources would not be available in time to meet projected European energy needs during the last half of the 1980s. An alternative American approach, however, could have allowed the Europeans to draw on Soviet gas while minimizing the risks of Soviet leverage. Once it became apparent that it was too late for the Europeans to obtain North American or North Sea energy in the time required, and that the deal could no longer be prevented (because contracts had been signed by the early months of 1982 and because of the European jobs involved in pipeline contracts), continued American opposition was likely to be counterproductive. At this point, there would have been more purpose in promoting a comprehensive, fully funded series of gas security measures. These would have included a coordinated program of gas storage, improved integration of pipeline networks, dual capacity (gas-oil) boilers, and interruptible contracts (requiring large-scale users of fuel to switch to oil or coal in a crisis to avoid possible cut-offs for millions of individual households).

In addition, development and planning for reserve or surge capacity, based on Dutch and Norwegian gas, could have been sought systematically. Instead, many of these measures were pursued on a partial or haphazard basis, and with uncoordinated national programs.

Faced with blanket opposition from allied governments and a deep split within its own bureaucracy (essentially pitting the State and Commerce departments against the National Security Council and elements of the Defense Department), the administration sought a face-saving means of retreating. On November 13, 1982, after consultations with the Europeans, President Reagan announced the lifting of sanctions against companies taking part in the project. The action was based on "substantial agreement" among the allies on economic relations with the Soviet Union. The United States and the Europeans were to avoid trade arrangements that aided the Soviets militarily, especially in high technology projects, including oil and gas. Pending an allied study, no new Soviet gas contracts were to be signed, allied controls on transfer of strategic items to the Soviet Union were to be strengthened, and procedures to monitor and harmonize allied financial relations with the Soviet Union were to be sought.

Reagan's action at least temporarily ended an acrimonious dispute within the alliance, but not without further political cost. The French government announced it was not a party to any new agreement, the

British Foreign Minister termed it a "unilateral decision" by the Americans, and German officials described the language of the agreement as paralleling the June 1982 Versailles summit communiqué.[27] A European verdict on the American policy was offered by *The Economist*, which termed it "a catalogue of muddle of near-Carteresque proportions."[28]

The Free Market and Energy Security Externalities

The Reagan administration's National Energy Policy Plan emphasized the use of the market mechanism for making energy decisions. It held that market forces could increase petroleum investment and production. Not only was this approach to determine choices in resource allocation, it was also to prevail in times of crisis: "In the event of an emergency, preparedness plans call for relying primarily on market forces to allocate energy supplies."[29]

At the domestic level, this free-market emphasis drastically reduced the level of governmental incentives and support for conservation, fuel switching, solar energy, and renewable sources of energy. Whereas the Carter administration had encouraged solar and renewable energy, with a view to having them provide 20 percent of America's primary energy supply in the year 2000, the Reagan administration preferred that development of these sources be left to the private sector. In this, as in other areas, the administration disregarded barriers to market penetration as well as the historical role the public sector had played in providing massive subsidies and incentives for the development of coal, oil, hydroelectric, and nuclear power. The administration policy also seemed to suggest a reduction in efforts to prevent nuclear proliferation.

Emphasizing the market meant an unwillingness to promote development of synfuels. From 1981 to 1982, the oil glut had led to softening prices and left questions about long-term energy price trends unanswered. In April and May of 1982, in response to these uncertainties, as well as to rising development costs, the private firms involved in the major Colony Shale and Alsands heavy oil projects abandoned them. Meanwhile, the administration discouraged activities of the quasi-public U.S. Synthetic Fuels Corporation.[30]

As the real price for oil continued to decline, the commercial viability of most synfuel projects appeared increasingly remote. Under these conditions, the administration and Congress killed federal financing of the U.S. Synthetic Fuels Corporation in December 1985 (although not without a last minute dispute over payments to two shale oil plants supported by a number of congressional leaders and White House aides).[31]

The administration's petroleum policies were consistent with its overall philosophy. It initially rejected an increased gasoline tax, which had been proposed to reduce federal budget deficits and to reinforce long-term trends toward fuel economy. The administration also refused to maintain subsidies for fuel switching, which might have saved an additional one million barrels of oil a day. It did not discourage private company destocking, although in the first six months of 1982, these reserves were depleted at three times the SPR fill rate.[32]

Internationally, administration opposition was largely responsible for blocking expansion of a World Bank energy program. The initiative had been proposed by the Bank's outgoing president Robert McNamara. It would have increased lending by an additional $16 billion between 1982 and 1986 to stimulate oil and gas exploration and development as well as to encourage the development of other sources of energy, such as hydroelectricity and fuel wood. The plan was in response to expectations that the non-oil-producing LDCs would increase their oil demand significantly in the late 1980s. By 1990, the expanded World Bank program was to have displaced the equivalent of 1.3 mbd of oil. It also aimed to reduce LDC oil import bills by $25 to $30 billion.[33]

In opposing the program, the administration rejected arguments about the need to offset political uncertainties and to provide financing for small- or medium-scale efforts that would otherwise prove less attractive to private firms. It preferred to rely on the private sector for LDC energy development.

A clear pattern thus became evident. Apart from modest efforts to encourage the nuclear industry and to subsidize breeder reactor development, the administration would not normally employ governmental efforts and resources to decrease the country's reliance on oil. Indeed, the National Energy Plan was remarkably explicit in rejecting reductions in oil imports as a key objective. The position bears quoting, for it reflects the predominance of doctrinal consistency over both strategic considerations and a decade's experience of international energy instability:

> [A]chieving a low-level of oil imports at any cost is not a major criterion for the nation's energy security and economic health. Even at its current high price, imported oil is substantially less expensive than available alternatives.[34]

The administration's policies raised questions about its ability to meet a future oil emergency. This was not only a domestic matter. It also involved obligations to the International Energy Agency — a body created largely through the efforts of two previous Republican administrations — and relations with Europe and Japan. In the words of a former high official with responsibility for international energy security: "How can there be cooperation [with allies] if the United States dismantles almost completely its preparations to deal with emergencies."[35]

The measures that gave rise to these concerns were often highly detailed or technical in nature. The more important of them included the following:

— Virtual dismantling of the Department of Energy apparatus for handling emergencies.[36]
— President Reagan's March 1982 veto of legislation that renewed his specific authority to allocate oil supplies and set prices in an emergency.[37] (The Senate narrowly failed to override the veto.)
— Opposition to a bill, passed by a bipartisan Senate majority, seeking to fill the SPR at a rate of 300,000 barrels per day in 1983 and requiring that the president submit a plan for SPR use in an emergency. (The administration preferred a 200,000-barrel rate and opposed the provision for an emergency plan.)[38]
— Possible inability to comply with IEA emergency procedures. In the event of a general oil supply shortfall exceeding 7 percent of IEA's normal consumption, members are required to reduce consumption by 7 percent. (A shortfall above 12 percent requires a 10 percent reduction.) Yet, there appeared to be little or no effective emergency plan for such a reduction, apart from the expressed intent to rely on the market. Indeed, one proposal, to draw on oil stocks or the SPR for this purpose, could violate IEA obligations.[39]
— Initial refusal to take part in IEA discussions for coping with subtrigger emergencies. (Note that the 1973–71 and the 1979 oil shocks were both caused by shortfalls below the formal 7 percent trigger.)[40]

In short, such an overwhelming reliance on the market mechanism would often exclude consideration of energy security externalities. Whatever the virtues of the market and of simplifying or reducing an elaborate regulatory system, it was as though the Department of Defense determined to have all American combat aircraft manufactured in Japan because a firm there made the lowest bid. Indeed, skeptics, including leading Republicans in Congress and even the then-GOP governor of Texas, were concerned that the administration appeared to attach no national security premium to oil imports.[41]

Ironically, there was an inconsistency between the administration's energy and security policies. In looking toward the Persian Gulf, conventional force planning had sought to deter military threats that would reduce the flow of Middle East oil to the United States and its allies. The Rapid Deployment Force (RDF), as well as other forces capable of projecting American power, was thus bolstered for possible Gulf contingencies. These measures accounted for substantial increases in the defense budget.

Yet the security interests of the United States and its allies would be enhanced by a coherent program aimed at steadily decreasing their long-term reliance on Middle East oil and thus reducing the strategic importance of an unstable Gulf region. Although significant increases in world oil production outside the Middle East were achieved, and major reductions in dependence on the region did occur, these achievements did not eliminate the strategic dependence of the industrial democracies on Middle East oil. The point is not that preparation of the RDF was undesirable, nor that it might not be significantly useful. Deterrence of Soviet threats and support for the governments of oil-producing states threatened by outside forces may prove effective. However, these are not necessarily the most likely sources of instability and of possible oil disruption.

Internal upheavals (as in the case of Iran), as well as endemic regional conflicts (such as the Iran-Iraq war), are more likely causes of instability. Yet such problems may not be amenable to a solution by American or allied military power. In view of the likely sources of instability, there are thus limits to the utility of the RDF. In short, the Persian Gulf and the Middle East region as a whole present a series of very difficult and long-term problems. The recognition of this fact underscores the need for coherent energy policies aimed at reducing long-term Western and Japanese oil import dependence on the region.

America's Energy Security: Autonomy or Interdependence?

The Reagan administration established its energy policies at a time of increasing oil glut. Were this oil pattern to continue permanently, there would be little reason for concern. Long-term uncertainties, however, suggested the need for greater attention to energy security. While continuing to advocate reliance on the market mechanism and a reduction of governmental intervention, the administration thus found that security imperatives required it to modify a number of its initial policies. The competing pulls of non-intervention, on the one hand, and of security and other national interest externalities, on the other hand, were readily apparent in a September 1984 statement to Congress by the Secretary of Energy[42]:

> First, we seek to minimize Federal control and intervention in energy markets. . . .
>
> Our first strategy recognizes that there is a legitimate role for the Federal Government in protecting the environment and the health and safety of the public, *and in ensuring national security.*

As a practical matter, President Reagan reaffirmed the position of his predecessors in maintaining American interests in the Persian Gulf. Thus the President exclaimed that in "no way" would the United States allow the Straits of Hormuz (at the mouth of the Gulf) to be closed.[43] Consequently, when the fighting between Iran and Iraq intensified in the spring of 1984, giving rise to Western concerns about threats to Persian Gulf oil shipments, the administration was compelled to reexamine its policies toward use of the SPR and cooperation with the countries of the International Energy Agency (IEA).

Until that time, the administration had viewed the SPR as a last resort in the event of a crisis. It preferred that market mechanisms be given a free rein. It had also viewed the IEA with skepticism, as an exercise in market control and intervention writ large. In June 1984, however, the administration successfully proposed to a Western summit meeting that Europe, Japan, and the United States resolve to draw on stocks quickly in the event of an emergency, rather than wait for the 7 percent shortfall required by IEA to develop before acting. Indeed, the Reagan proposal even included asking the oil companies to limit their spot market purchases in order to avoid driving up prices in a crisis, along with other measures to discourage hoarding and panic buying.[44] A month later, the IEA Governing Board followed suit by making this official policy.[45]

There were still areas in which the administration's commitment to economic noninterventionism took precedence. Thus at the end of 1985, the administration agreed to roll back automobile gasoline mileage standards for General Motors and Ford.[46]

Averting the "Next" Oil Shock?

The realm of energy security the Reagan administration faced, especially by the time of its second term, was one in which the international crisis had eased dramatically — despite threats to the banking system posed by the plight of such oil exporters as Mexico. By the criteria of energy supply, demand, cost, and vulnerability, the United States experienced a far less difficult situation than had been the case during the Nixon, Ford, and Carter presidencies.

From 1973 to 1984, America's GNP grew by 31 percent, yet total oil consumption actually fell from 17.3 mbd to 15.7 mbd. Both the United States and the other major oil-importing countries had become significantly more efficient in their use of oil and energy. Meanwhile, OPEC had seen its production fall by half between 1979 and the end of 1985, while the price for its oil, adjusted for inflation, had plummeted. Indeed, the fall in world oil prices in early 1986 brought real oil prices down to their lowest level since 1978.

Crisis vulnerability had also eased. Between 1980 and 1984, American reliance on Arab OPEC oil had fallen from 43 percent of its imports to 17 percent. As a sign of this decreased dependence on the Persian Gulf, Saudi Arabia had dropped from second place as a supplier of oil to America (replaced by such countries as Mexico, Canada, Venezuela,

Britain, and Indonesia), although it subsequently rose again in rank. Indeed, the presence of a half billion barrels of oil in the SPR would allow the United States to do without Arab oil for nearly two years in the unlikely event of a total cut-off.

Yet despite the oil glut and the disarray of OPEC, the long-term pattern of energy security was by no means free of risk. The countries of the Middle East still possessed some 55 percent of known oil reserves, and although there are more than enough oil and gas reserves to supply the world well into the middle of the next century, their geographical distribution is very uneven: Much of OPEC's unused production capacity lies in the most unstable regions of the Middle East, and an interruption of the Persian Gulf oil supply would remove some 7 to 8 mbd from world oil markets. Yet in 1985, the available unused capacity outside the region amounted to only 3.5 mbd (Nigeria and Libya had a shut-in capacity of 1 mbd each; Venezuela, Indonesia, and Algeria had 0.5 mbd each).[47]

The effects of falling oil prices greatly benefited the oil-importing countries, including developing countries, but the long-term effects of these price changes posed potential supply and demand risks. On the supply side, sharply lower oil prices could eventually undercut the provision of both costly sources of non-OPEC oil and of competing non-oil forms of energy. Indeed, known American petroleum reserves had actually decreased by approximately one-fourth between 1972 and 1985, despite a threefold increase in the real price for oil.

On the demand side, the same price changes could also stimulate the consumption of oil and thus increase the market for OPEC oil over the long run.

Just as OPEC's apparent economic and political power proved to be unstable during the oil decade, there remained the risk of yet another reversal. Consider, for example, that American oil imports are likely to rise again in the 1990s, both in response to a slow decrease in domestic production and an increase in consumption.[48]

Much of the backup capacity for America's electricity supply consists of oil-fired power plants. Although uncertainties abound, eventual reliance on these units could drive up oil imports by as much as an additional 2 mbd in the 1990s. And even in the midst of the oil glut in 1985, the United States found itself with an annual import bill of more than $50 billion — more than one-third of the country's overall international trade deficit. Whereas the diversification of American oil import sources away from the Persian Gulf and Middle East made the United States immediately less vulnerable to an oil shock, the United States does not exist in a vacuum. Western Europe remains dependent on the region for more than 50 percent of its oil supply, and Japan for some 70 percent.

An underlying theme of this volume has been that the world of the

1980s imposes a multiplicity of issues and trade-offs. The American ability to go it alone is thus constrained — whether in terms of minimizing the impact of external events or overlooking the consequences of its actions on others. Benjamin J. Cohen observed in Chapter 4 that, on taking office, the Reagan administration found it simply inconceivable that the United States could not reclaim its accustomed autonomy and influence over events. What Cohen has identified in the economic realm is equally true for energy security, where the integration of the world oil regime and the global consequences of energy shocks imposes a tenacious interdependence. Yet just as domestic economic policy initially was made with limited regard for the outside world, so it was with energy choices.

All this suggests that the administration's concept of free world leadership is narrow, with uneven attention to issues outside East-West security. At first the approach of the United States represented a considerable break with a decade of policy, followed by both Republican and Democratic administrations, in seeking to manage interdependence rather than to ignore or transcend it. Yet in energy security, as in economic policy, defense problems, and important regional areas, the contemporary realities are those of interdependence. A policy framed with insufficient regard for these realities may, at times, succeed through luck, but this is no cause for complacency. Indeed, a gradual recognition of these realities brought about modifications in a number of the administration's original policy positions.

Any policy choice must be made under conditions of some uncertainty. This is no less true in the realm of energy. The international context of this problem, however, calls for policies that incorporate the imperatives of cooperation with allies and the security externalities of dependence on imported oil. At a minimum, the criteria for energy policy should include a recognition of trade-offs, with the aim of giving greater priority to reduced oil consumption and imports and avoiding increased dependence on Middle East oil, for even if the United States imported no oil from the Persian Gulf it would still be greatly affected by a major crisis there. The impact would be felt soon enough, whether through soaring prices for our now decontrolled oil and other forms of energy, or through the economic and political harm inflicted on the industrial democracies of Europe and Japan. The fate of these regions is inextricably linked. An energy policy based on this recognition is a matter of enlightened self-interest.

"International Energy Policy and the Reagan Administration: Avoiding the Next Oil Shock?" was written for this volume. Copyright © 1987 by Robert J. Lieber.

Notes

1. The sharpest drop in price took place in futures trading and on spot markets (oil not under long-term contract). In these markets, crude oil (for example, West Texas intermediate) fell below $11 per barrel in March 1986. Large contractual volumes of oil remained higher in price. (Technical arrangements — credit terms, "netback" deals, and other measures — did, however, result in lower effective prices than the contract prices indicated.)
2. The rapid deployment force is formally known as the U.S. Central Command.
3. Source: Exxon Corporation, *Middle East Oil*, 2nd ed. (September 1980), p. 26. For an analysis of the evolving importance of oil and subsequent shift in bargaining power, see Robert Stobaugh and Daniel Yergin, eds., *Energy Future: Report of the Energy Project at the Harvard Business School*, 3rd ed. (New York: Vintage, 1983), chs. 1 and 2.
4. Exxon, *Middle East Oil*, p. 26.
5. Organization for Economic Cooperation and Development (OECD), *Economic Outlook* (Paris) (July 1980), No. 27, p. 114.
6. For a detailed analysis of this period, see Robert J. Lieber, *Oil and the Middle East War: Europe in the Energy Crisis* (Cambridge, MA: Harvard Center for International Affairs, 1976). An invaluable inside account can be found in Henry Kissinger, *Years of Upheaval* (Boston: Little Brown, 1982), especially Chs. 16, 19, and 20.
7. The OECD figures, based on oil import prices deflated by the prices of OECD manufactured exports, showed a decline from an index figure of 271 in 1976 to 236 in 1978 (1972 = 100), OECD, *Economic Outlook* (July 1980), p. 116.
8. "European" figures for consumption are for OECD less the United States and Japan. Import figures are adjusted to exclude the United Kingdom and Norway (the North Sea oil producers). Consumption is based on total oil requirements but excludes marine bunkers. Percentages calculated from data in OECD, *Economic Outlook*, (June 1979), No. 25, p. 62.
9. Calculated from data in OECD, *Economic Outlook* (July 1979), p. 140.
10. David A. Stockman, "The Wrong War? The Case Against a National Energy Policy," *Public Interest* (Autumn 1978), pp. 3–44, at p. 20.
11. Figures from U.S. Department of Energy, Energy Information Administration, *Monthly Energy Review* (March 1980), p. 92; and (April 1981), p. 92.
12. For a thoughtful treatment of Carter's programs and problems, see Daniel Yergin's "America in the Strait of Stringency," in *Global Insecurity: A Strategy for Energy and Economic Renewal*, Yergin and Martin Hillen-brand, eds. (Boston: Houghton Mifflin, 1982), Ch. 4.
13. See Robert J. Lieber, "Cohesion and Disruption in the Western Alliance," in Yergin and Hillenbrand, eds., *Global Insecurity*, Ch. 11.
14. *Monthly Energy Review* (October 1982), pp. 31, 33. American oil imports in 1978 averaged 8.0 mbd.
15. The National Energy Policy Plan, U.S. Department of Energy (July 1981). Summarized in *Energy Insider*, August 3, 1981, p. 36.
16. *Wall Street Journal*, September 5, 1980.
17. *Monthly Energy Review* (August 1985), p. 107. Figure for 1985 from *Oil and Gas Journal*, December 30, 1985.
18. Gasoline prices rose approximately 14 cents per gallon and then drifted lower in response to the market glut.
19. *New York Times*, February 5, 1986.
20. Jonathan P. Stern, "Specters and Pipe Dreams," *Foreign Policy* (Fall 1982), No. 48, p. 23.

21. A detailed account appears in *New York Times*, July 1, 1982, p. D2.

22. *Financial Times* (London), February 25, 1982.

23. Figures for 1990 are CIA estimates. See the *International Defense Review* (January 1982), pp. 15–18. The European Economic Community estimates are somewhat higher: Germany, 34 percent; France, 26 percent; and Italy, 35 percent. Ibid. Oil import figures are from CIA, *International Energy Statistical Review*, February 22, 1982, p. 24. The total volume of Soviet gas exports to Western Europe in 1990 has been estimated as equivalent to 1.0 to 1.1 mbd.

24. For an illuminating account of allied disagreements over Soviet oil exports to Western Europe in the early 1960s, see Bruce W. Jentleson, "Krushchev's Oil and Brezhnev's Natural Gas Pipelines," in Robert J. Lieber, ed., *Will Europe Fight for Oil?* (New York: Praeger, 1983).

25. *New York Times*, July 2, 1982.

26. On June 22nd, for example, the EEC Council attacked the United States decision to prohibit the export of components and ban the use of licenses already granted and the use of components already supplied:

    > This action taken without any consultation with the Community implies an extra-territorial extension of the U.S. jurisdiction which, in the circumstances, is contrary to the principles of international law, unacceptable to the Community, and unlikely to be recognized in courts in the EEC.

    Source: quoted in "Policy statement by Chancellor Helmut Schmidt," *Federal Republic of Germany, Statements and Speeches* (June 1982), Vol. 5, No. 15, p. 4.

27. For French and British reactions, see the *Washington Post*, November 15, 1982. The text of the Reagan statement can be found in *New York Times*, November 14, 1982.

28. *The Economist* (London), November 20, 1982.

29. Summary of National Energy Policy Plan, U.S. Department of Energy, *Energy Insider*, August 3, 1981, p. 3. (Italics added.)

30. This had been established under the 1980 Energy Security Act. See the account in *Congressional Quarterly*, May 29, 1982, pp. 1249–1252.

31. See *New York Times*, December 17, 1985, and the *Washington Post*, December 19, 1985.

32. A 35-million barrel increase in the SPR was offset by a 100-million barrel reduction in private stocks. See *Business Week*, June 14, 1982. A five-cent-per-gallon gasoline tax was enacted in late 1982.

33. *Bulletin of the Atomic Scientists* (April 1982). Also see Edward R. Fried, "The World Bank and Energy Investments," in *The Future of the World Bank* (Washington D.C.: The Brookings Institution, 1982), pp. 27–31.

34. Quoted in *Energy Insider*, August 3, 1981, p. 3.

35. Private communication with the author, May 12, 1982.

36. Even emergency planning was downgraded. In the words of an administration official sympathetic to the president, "We have options but not a policy." Interview by the author, Washington, D.C., May 17, 1982.

37. The vetoed legislation was the Standby Petroleum Allocation Act. Previous legislation (the Emergency Petroleum Allocation Act) had expired on September 30, 1981. *Congressional Quarterly*, May 29, 1982. The administration argued that it already possessed sufficient legislative authority.

38. Ibid.

39. Technically this hinges on whether the stocks to be drawn upon are sufficiently in excess of the 90-day import level required by IEA. See U.S. Department of Energy, "Domestic and International Energy Emergency Preparedness," Assistant Secretary for Environmental Protection, Safety and Emergency Preparedness, DOE/EP-0027 (July 1981), pp. 4–5, 17, and 19.

40. In 1984 the administration did agree with IEA countries on a policy of early stockpile drawdown (see below).
41. *Dallas Morning News*, April 20, 1982.
42. U.S. Department of Energy, Secretary of Energy, *Annual Report to Congress* (Washington, D.C.: DOE/S-0010, 1984), p. 1 (Italics added.)
43. Quoted, *New York Times*, February 23, 1984.
44. See *New York Times*, June 5, 1984.
45. Decision by the IEA Governing Board, July 11, 1984. See *OECD Observer*, (September 1984), No. 130, pp. 28–30. Also see U.S. Department of Energy, *The National Energy Policy Plan* (Washington, D.C.: DOE/S-0040, 1985), p. 30.
46. The fuel standards were reduced from 27.5 mpg, required by law for the 1986-model year, to 26 mpg. See, for example, the *Washington Post*, January 18, 1986.
47. U.S. Department of the Interior, Geological Survey, "World Petroleum Resources — a Perspective," by Charles D. Masters, Open-File Report 85-248. Preliminary.
48. For example, the Congressional Research Service forecast a possible 50 percent increase in American oil imports by the year 2000.

III

Regional Problems

7

Reagan and the Russians: American Policy Toward the Soviet Union

Alexander Dallin
and Gail W. Lapidus

. . . Their [the Soviet leaders'] goal must be the promotion of world communism and a one-world socialist or communist state. . . . They reserve unto themselves the right to commit any crime, to lie, to cheat to obtain that. . . .

—Ronald Reagan, January 1981

I think I'm a good judge of acting. I don't think he [Gorbachev] was acting. He, I believe, is just as sincere as we are [in wanting peace and agreement]. . . . I bet the hard-liners in both our countries are bleeding when we shake hands.

—Ronald Reagan, November 1985

Alexander Dallin is Professor of History and Political Science and Director of the Center for Russian and East European Studies at Stanford University. He has served as Chairman of the National Council for Soviet and East European Research and as President of the American Association for the Advancement of Soviet Studies. His most recent books include Black Box: KAL 007 and the Superpowers *(University of California Press, 1985) and "Some Lessons of the Past" in M. Garrison and A. Gleason, eds.,* Shared Destiny *(Beacon Press, 1985).*

Gail W. Lapidus is Professor of Political Science at the University of California at Berkeley and Chair of the Berkeley-Stanford Program on Soviet International Behavior. She has served as Chair of the Berkeley Center for Slavic and East European Studies and of the Joint Committee on Soviet Studies of the Social Science Research Council and the American Council of Learned Societies. She is the author, among other works, of Women in Soviet Society *(University of California Press, 1978) and "Soviet Society in the 1980s," in R. F. Byrnes, ed.,* After Brezhnev *(Indiana University Press, 1983).*

The Promise and the Reality

The Reagan administration came into office in 1981 committed to a fundamental change in the direction of American foreign policy as well as in domestic priorities. Central to this promise was the determination to initiate a new departure in both the substance and the conduct of American policy toward the Soviet Union. The repudiation of detente and the reassertion of American primacy were the key elements of this new orientation. Alleging that previous administrations had underestimated the Soviet threat, had permitted the erosion of American political will and of economic and military strength, and had acquiesced in a dangerous expansion of Soviet power, the new administration assigned highest priority to reversing these trends and to challenging "Soviet imperialism" politically, economically, and militarily.

The Reagan administration promised major changes in the conduct of American policy as well: greater consistency of purpose; greater coherence in linking assumptions to policy instruments to goals; greater competence in the management of national affairs; and above all, strong executive leadership to eliminate the multiplicity of competing views and policies that had, it claimed, undermined the credibility of American policy under the Carter administration among friends and foes alike.

Finally the new administration held out the hope that a more assertive American approach would have a desirable impact on the Soviet Union itself, at the least modifying Soviet behavior so as to produce greater restraint and reciprocity, and at the most transforming the very nature of the Soviet system.

Five years later, the administration's record was a mixed one. Although evidence of inconsistencies and internal conflicts within the administration abounded, there was visible, over time, some modification of the initial assumption of total confrontation with the Soviet Union and some shift from bitter rhetorical warfare to limited efforts at working with the Russians. While the depth of the president's "conversion" remained unclear, and although there was nothing to preclude a reversion to the earlier confrontational rhetoric, by 1985–86 the official tone had undergone a limited shift toward civility, and the administration's policies in some areas seemed increasingly shaped by pragmatic rather than ideological considerations. The Geneva summit was the symbol of this evolution.

This shift reflected the administration's limited and reluctant recognition of and adaptation to the multiple domestic and international constraints on the conduct of a confrontational policy toward the Soviet Union. It also reflected growing confidence that international trends, including developments within the USSR itself, were more favorable to American interests than previously and that economic revival and military buildup in the United States had created more secure foundations for American policy. But domestic economic and political interests, budgetary constraints, pressures from Congress, and the role of America's allies, whose views and interests diverged from Washington's on a number of issues, also had proved to be more formidable in the conduct of foreign policy than the incoming administration had expected.

At the same time, the Reagan administration had become, if anything, even more assertive in seeking greater military and political leverage in Soviet-American relations, particularly with respect to arms control and to regional conflicts. The 'eighties have been characterized by an unprecedented combination of global activism with a shift of American policy to the political right. The Reagan administration typically viewed a whole range of international problems — from arms control, to regional conflicts to terrorism — through the prism of the worldwide struggle of the "free world" against the Soviet Union. And in that struggle, it sought to push the United States to play a more assertive and uncompromising role.

Finally, not unlike its predecessor, the Reagan team was severely hampered by sharp internal divisions and by the continued failure to reconcile contending and at times incompatible views concerning both the nature and the prospects of the Soviet system and the best policies to be adopted toward it. These differences were manifested in a most dramatic and harmful fashion over defense and arms control policy and remained largely unresolved.

American behavior toward the Soviet Union during the Reagan years thus revealed important continuities (not to say rigidities) as well as significant new departures. As the United States heads into the latter half of the 1980s, it is by no means clear where its policy toward the Soviet Union will wind up by the time the second Reagan term ends, nor what its impact is likely to be on the evolution of Soviet policy under Gorbachev.

Soviet-American Relations: The Legacy and the Options

The Perennial Problem

The Soviet Union has been the central preoccupation of American foreign policymakers since the defeat of Germany and Japan in World War II. It has been the primary cause of huge military expenditures, of a network of alliances, of a far-flung and complex intelligence effort, and of a public state of mind that has fluctuated between exaggerated optimism about the prospects of Soviet-American collaboration and obsessive anxiety about the "Soviet threat."

In dealing with the Soviet Union, every administration since World

War II has faced challenges to which there are no easy responses. These include the need to define an optimal balance between confrontation and accommodation, between competition and collaboration; to clarify American interests abroad and devise a strategy to defend them; and to assess the implications of internal and foreign policy changes within the Soviet Union for the United States. The major shifts in American policy over time may be seen as the result of several interacting and interdependent complexes: (1) changes in the nature and perception of American power, values, resources, and morale; (2) changes in the international system, above all in the strategic balance and in weapons technology, the emergence of third actors, and the loss of American hegemony; and (3) changes in Soviet capabilities, perceptions, and priorities.[1]

The United States and the Soviet Union emerged from World War II as the two new superpowers, but with widely divergent interests and priorities. Joseph Stalin's determination to use the unique opportunity to expand the area of Soviet control launched the two powers on the intense and dangerous adversary course that culminated in the Cold War.[2] For some twenty years — until well into the 1960s — there was a far-reaching American foreign policy consensus that it was essential for the United States to contain, compete with, and under crisis conditions, confront the Soviet Union. Some policymakers thought of "containment" as primarily geopolitical and intended to prevent Soviet expansion into neighboring territories and beyond. Others saw Soviet aggrandizement as primarily ideological, with "world communism" the ultimate goal.[3]

In either case, the common denominator of American policy at the height of the Cold War was set forth in a document known as NSC 68, which was drafted in 1950 by a State Department team headed by Paul H. Nitze. "The Soviet Union," it stated, "unlike previous aspirants to hegemony, is animated by a new fanatic faith, antithetical to our own, and seeks to impose its absolute authority over the rest of the world." Significant here is the perception (as of 1950!) of the Soviet challenge:

> [Recent technological developments] have greatly intensified the Soviet threat to the security of the United States. . . . In particular, the United States now faces the contingency that within the next four or five years the Soviet Union will possess the military capability of delivering a surprise attack of such weight that the United States must have substantially increased general air, ground, and sea strength, atomic capabilities, and air and civilian defenses to deter war and to provide reasonable assurance, in the event of war, that it could survive the initial blow and go on to the eventual attainment of its objectives.

In fact, "without superior aggregate military strength, in being and readily mobilizable, a policy of 'containment' — which is in effect a policy of calculated and gradual coercion — is no more than a policy of bluff."[4]

Although this assessment remained influential, in practice it was modified, in the minds of many American policymakers and diplomats, by a recognition of mutual or parallel interests of the two superpowers. Without dismissing the antagonistic strain, these actors were prepared to undertake or promote a variety of forms of cooperation with the Soviet Union. Indeed, changes in the Soviet system and in Soviet policy following Stalin's death in 1953 — and most notably under Khrushchev, a shift in perceptions of the international situation away from the previous zero-sum game assumptions — created real possibilities for such mutual efforts as the end of the Korean war, the Austrian peace treaty, and "Big Four" summits.

The acquisition of nuclear capabilities by the Soviet Union made such efforts more imperative than ever. A mutual interest in survival prompted efforts at conflict avoidance and crisis management, such as the exploration of agreements to reduce the dangers of accidental nuclear war and the establishment of the Hot Line between Moscow and Washington in 1963. More complex was the attempt to negotiate constraints on the arms race itself, with results ranging from narrow and specific agreements, such as the limited Test Ban Treaty of 1963, to protracted and wide-ranging negotiations, such as the agreements that resulted in 1972 in SALT I and the ABM Treaty and, after another seven years, in the SALT II treaty, which was never ratified by the United States.

Other areas of attempted cooperation or accommodation included such nonpolitical and functional areas of shared interests as joint space exploration (the Soyuz-Apollo mission in 1975); a sharing of information on environmental pollution; joint scientific and medical work, such as cancer research; and an exchange of scholars and graduate students.

For many protagonists of an "accommodationist" approach, these efforts were not only valuable in their own right but also served a larger purpose in contributing to the liberalization of the Soviet system. Many policymakers believed that desirable internal changes could be promoted by an appropriate American policy, and some hoped that the Soviet Union was becoming (or would become) a status quo power, which might find it in its own interest to accept and cooperate in the stabilization of the international order. It was also widely believed that the transfer of goods and services to the Soviet Union would inevitably lead to the transfer of Western ideas and values as well. Trade, technology transfer, arms control agreements, grain sales, and cultural exchanges could help weave a pervasive web of interdependence that would demonstrate to the Soviet elite that getting along with the West was a matter of Soviet self-interest and would make any departure from this system of interdependence in the future exceedingly costly.[5]

This perspective, which was most effectively formulated by Henry Kissinger and which was behind the pursuit of Soviet-American detente in the 1970s, was not only a response to objective changes in the international system, but was also congruent with emerging Soviet interests and orientations. By the late 1960s, the prospect of gross strategic parity between the United States and the Soviet Union created a foundation for meaningful arms control accords by making the consequences of reductions and limitations substantially symmetrical in impact on both sides. It also gave greater substance to the Soviet claim for recognition of its status as a coequal superpower.

The Soviet desire to benefit from imports of Western technology that might accelerate Soviet economic modernization contributed further to the USSR's stake in detente. Although this marked a fundamental departure from the traditional Soviet pursuit of autarky, or self-sufficiency, the prospect was sufficiently compelling for the Soviet authorities to acquiesce tacitly in such modifications of internal policy as permitting selective emigration, as a quid pro quo.

Finally the Soviet-American rapprochement was given additional impetus by the Sino-Soviet split: The Kremlin hoped that improved relations with the United States would further isolate the People's Republic of China and forestall Sino-American collusion against Soviet interests.

In retrospect, it is clear that both sides oversold detente, though the characteristic American swing from hostility to euphoria went well beyond Moscow's more restrained posture. The following years were to show that unsettled issues and ambiguities in agreements rapidly overtook the accords that had been reached. What particularly upset American calculations and expectations were the continued Soviet military buildup, which was perceived as an effort to achieve strategic superiority, and the effort to exploit political opportunities in Third World areas from which limited capabilities and Western predominance had previously all but excluded the Soviet Union: Angola and Ethiopia were the prime examples.

Moscow, in turn, had its own list of grievances concerning American behavior. Although some items on the list were no more than propaganda gambits, others — from impediments to trade and credit to exclusion from Middle Eastern negotiations to delays in concluding SALT II — made Moscow increasingly skeptical about the prospects and benefits of detente with the United States. The Soviet invasion of Afghanistan, at the end of 1979, destroyed the remnants of detente and accelerated a shift in American attitudes and policies already well under way.[6] The 1980s thus began with a seriously damaged Soviet-American relationship, which the Reagan administration inherited from the Carter years.

If American policy toward the Soviet Union was affected to a significant degree by Soviet behavior, it was shaped by factors inherent in the American political process and public opinion as well. The fragmentation of power between the executive and legislative branches and the rivalry between them have often had a telling effect on policymaking. The characteristics of particular administrations and the key actors within them — say a John Foster Dulles or a Henry Kissinger — have played an important part; so have such institutional arrangements as the overlapping roles of the National Security Council, the State Department, and the Department of Defense. More broadly, the policy mix has been modified by the whole range of domestic pressures and constraints that powerfully affect the conduct of foreign affairs.

Perhaps the most important yet amorphous cluster here is the world of interest groups. Lobbies for ethnic groups (Poles, Jews, Cubans), defense industries, and many other special causes (business groups, farmers, and organized labor) have a particular stake in American policy toward the Soviet Union and Eastern Europe. The four-year cycle of presidential elections and administrations adds to the difficulty of sustaining a coherent foreign policy. By their very nature, Soviet-American relations require patience and steadfastness. These are hard to come by in Washington where the pressures and temptations to resort to a quick fix are great. Bureaucratic politics, moreover, continually shapes and misshapes foreign policy, as is apparent from the record of any recent administration. Contests over "turf," jurisdiction, and resources; interagency fights; interservice rivalries; executive-legislative splits; and personal feuds often overwhelm the particular issues and policies at stake.

And in regard to the Soviet problem in particular, note should be made of a peculiar ambivalence in American public attitudes. The pervasive responsiveness of the American public, of the media, and of politicians to anticommunist and anti-Russian themes is obvious. From cartoon strips to spy novels to television screens, the Soviets are too often portrayed as villains. And American politicians will be only too cognizant of the danger of being portrayed as soft on communists, let alone appeasing the Russians. At the same time, public opinion polls consistently reveal a widespread conviction that the two peoples —American and Soviet — both want peace.

Assumptions and Mind Sets: In Search of a Typology

Underlying these shifts of American foreign policy over the postwar period it is possible to identify three distinct, relatively enduring sets of perceptions and orientations regarding the nature of the Soviet system, the character of Soviet behavior, and preferred American policy: an "essentialist," a "mechanist," and an "interactionist" approach.[7]

The essentialist approach focuses not on what the Soviet Union does but rather on what it is. This highly deterministic approach defines the Soviet system as inherently evil, sees little prospect for change, and denies the benefits of piecemeal accommodation.

The mechanist approach is concerned with Soviet behavior, not essences. It views the Soviet threat as primarily geopolitical and takes the traditional view that power can and must be checked with equal or superior power: The answer to Soviet ambitions is containment.

The interactionist approach (which has at times been labeled cybernetic or organismic) involves more recognition of the reactive aspects of Soviet behavior, and of differences, and even uncertainties, within the Soviet elite; it does not see Moscow as a unitary purposive actor. It assumes a learning process that includes significant feedback from Soviet experience abroad to the decision makers' world view. It implies the need for more fine-tuning of analysis and policy responses and generally assumes a more pervasive interdependence between the two adversary systems than would the other two approaches.[8]

Schematically we may distinguish the three approaches in terms of a number of linked assumptions about the nature of the Soviet Union and its implications for American policy.

The Sources of Soviet Behavior. The essentialists see the Soviet system as inherently evil and inherently expansionist (although they may differ on whether the reason is its Russian, communist, or totalitarian essence); they see it as substantially unchanging; and they minimize the importance of Soviet elite politics and the differences among individual actors in Moscow. The mechanists see the Soviet threat as primarily geopolitical, whereas the interactionists see the sources of Soviet-American conflict in both structural — superpower — elements and in mutual misperceptions. They are more likely to emphasize elements of diversity, if not pluralism, in Soviet elite politics and to anticipate the possibility of significant evolution in the Soviet system.

The Nature of the Soviet Threat. The essentialists view Soviet military intentions and capabilities in highly alarmist terms. Although they disagree over whether world revolution, or Russian hegemony, is the ultimate goal, they tend to see the Soviet Union as a unitary actor with a coherent long-range blueprint or master plan, and both the determination and the ability to carry it out; this perspective moves from imputed intent to outcome without much consideration of intervening constraints. Many essentialists are inclined to believe that domestic crises in the Soviet Union and Eastern Europe are apt to propel the Soviet leadership into compensatory adventures abroad. Finally they are inclined to a two-camp view of the world that tends to see conflicts anywhere in terms of the superpower relationship and minimizes the importance of local and regional factors.

The mechanists are likely to see Soviet superpower preponderance as the ultimate objective, with the quest for greater security (as defined by Moscow), influence, and status as more immediate goals. They disagree over the effect of internal Soviet strains on foreign policy, Soviet responsibility for instability the world over, and the record of Soviet caution and risk-aversion. But they differ from the essentialists in emphasizing opportunism more than a master plan as the wellspring of Soviet behavior, and in devoting more attention to capabilities and constraints than to imputed intentions.

The interactionists reject the notion of a blueprint and tend to see in Soviet foreign policy a greater reactive element to events abroad. They also see the Soviet Union as a beneficiary, and not always or necessarily as an instigator, of instability in Third World areas. And they incline toward the view that domestic difficulties are more likely to constrain Soviet foreign policy than to encourage adventurism.

The Prospects of Soviet-American Accommodation. The essentialists judge the likelihood of war, and quite possibly nuclear war, between the two powers to be high. Some have indeed argued that Moscow seriously contemplates launching an all-out nuclear strike against the United States. They believe that the Soviet Union has no interest in a stabilized world order acceptable to the United States and therefore see little purpose in limited negotiations or partial agreements. The pursuit of arms control is fundamentally misguided because the very nature of the Soviet system gives it a unilateral advantage over an open society such as the United States. Rejecting a carrots-and-stick approach as ineffective, it sees the only viable policy as one that seeks to weaken the capabilities or to affect the survival of the Soviet system itself — and that presumably is what an American military buildup and political will must aim to achieve.

The mechanists, however, take a more positive view of the possibility of useful negotiations — not as a substitute for military power but rather as a supplement to it — and see arms control as a potentially useful component of defense policy. Whereas the more militant adherents of this approach may still consider a Soviet-American conflict highly likely, more moderate adherents are likely to focus on the need, and the possibility, to "manage" the adversary relationship by means short of war.[9] They typically favor a combination of carrots and sticks to shape Soviet behavior abroad.

The interactionists share such a "managerial" perspective, emphasize the possibility of identifying areas of parallel Soviet and American interests, and favor a step-by-step approach to negotiation. They would hope that, over time, a common code of rules of the game and mutual restraint would be accepted by both sides. Because they see the climate of relations as important in affecting the Soviet elite's attitudes and at times even the balance of power within the Soviet elite, they ascribe importance to American and other foreign behavior as an influence on Soviet foreign policy and reject the notion that it is entirely internally driven. More inclined to see the loss of American hegemony as an inevitable product of secular trends, they would settle for a stable world order — including, if possible, far-reaching arms control agreements — rather than striving for American primacy.

Significant shifts in American policy toward the Soviet Union may thus be seen as products of changes in the dominant mind sets, and policy controversies are frequently seen as reflections of conflicting approaches such as those sketched above. The policy differences within the Carter administration turned on the competition between the mechanist and interactionist approaches, whereas in the Reagan administration, policy feuds — insofar as they derive from different conceptions of the Soviet Union — have shifted to the conflict between mechanists and essentialists.

These are obviously ideal types. Many factors intervene between broad assumptions and behavior under specific circumstances. Obviously political actors do not always adhere to what logic and consistency might demand. Some will change their minds; others will prefer not to commit themselves. Such systematic approaches, moreover, obviously overlap and sometimes conflict with institutional and bureaucratic cleavages.

Finally, although a Richard Pipes and a Richard Perle can be taken as archetypal exponents of an essentialist orientation, and a Marshall Shulman as an interactionist, the mechanist approach encompasses a sufficiently broad spectrum of perceptions and policy preferences that Henry Kissinger, Zbigniew Brzezinski, and George Shultz can all be identified with it. It is not always easy to assign individual administration officials to a particular camp. But the ambiguities of the Reagan administration's approach — as those of its predecessors — have clearly been, in part, the result of unresolved conflicts over assumptions and policy preferences among key officials and their advisors.

The Reagan Years

On the Eve

It was clear from the political career and rhetoric of Ronald Reagan, and from his choice of foreign policy advisors during the campaign of 1980, that his election was meant to stand, among other things, for a more confrontational approach to the Soviet Union. Candidate Reagan's speeches and press conferences had for some years been peppered with remarks more blunt in their hostility toward the Soviet Union and more sweeping in their condemnation of Marxism than those of any other recent major candidate.

Scarcely less damning was his critique of the Carter administration, and implicitly, its Republican predecessors, for their acquiescence in the decline of American power and a corresponding expansion of Soviet power. A post-Vietnam excess of guilt and breast-beating had undermined both confidence in American purposes and America's will to lead, while the wearisome sequences of negotiations and agreements epitomized by detente had conferred a one-sided advantage on the Soviet Union.[10]

Pronouncements from the Reagan camp focused particular attention on the contrast between the historically unprecedented Soviet military buildup and the alleged failure of the United States to keep pace; the president himself asserted that "in virtually every measure of military power the Soviet Union enjoys a decided advantage."[11] The alarmist scenarios to which this alleged tilt in the strategic balance gave rise were reinforced and elaborated, moreover, by the Committee on the Present Danger, a group of concerned political figures and academics who warned that the United States was becoming Number Two, that the Soviet Union remained committed to the goal of a world controlled from Moscow, and that the liberals were, in effect, practicing appeasement of the Soviet Union by seeking to prolong detente. The deteriorating international situation, in their view, required immediate and drastic action.[12]

If it was indeed easy for critics to point to a seeming American retreat from involvements and commitments abroad in the aftermath of Vietnam, there was less clarity on the causes of this decline in American power, as well as a tendency to minimize changes in the structure of the international system itself that reduced the relative power of the United States. The neo-conservative critique thus accentuated the disparity between public expectations of omnipotence fed by the unique but temporary circumstances of the postwar era and limited American capabilities to affect political developments in different regions of the world.

The ineptness of the Carter administration provided another element of obvious consensus in the Reagan camp prior to the election: the determination to avoid the naiveté, divisiveness, incoherence, and backbiting that plagued the Carter team, especially in foreign affairs. The transition teams in the foreign affairs and defense fields, appointed by President-elect Reagan in November 1980, seemed to confirm, by their composition, that the new administration would follow a clear, more militant anti-Soviet course. Yet a close student of Reagan's backers might well have recognized even before the inauguration of the new president that there were ambiguities and contradictions in the victorious team's view of Soviet power, objectives, and capabilities — in large part because of its composition. The Reagan coalition included old-line Republicans favorably oriented toward business interests; neo-conservatives hyperbolically dramatizing the options America faced between gloom and doom or newfound glory; professional politicians blithely ignorant of other than shopworn stereotypes when it came to explaining Soviet affairs; right-wing Democrats captured by — or indeed in the lead of — the Committee on the Present Danger; and retired military officers welcoming the prospect of unprecedented defense budgets. It was a coalition unlikely to find a common ground once the new administration turned from a critique of past policies to the formulation and implementation of its own program.

Key Actors and Institutions

The formulation and conduct of American foreign policy under Ronald Reagan have been shaped to a significant degree by several key individuals and institutional arrangements that should be singled out. The single most important actor has, of course, been President Reagan himself, both in setting the tone of the Soviet-American relationship and in having the authority to resolve the frequent conflicts among his advisors. But until his second term, when the decision to proceed with the Geneva summit focused his attention for a time on Soviet-American relations and gave him an intensely personal stake in the outcome, the president appeared less interested in and far less knowledgeable about foreign policy than many of his predecessors, had no clear-cut strategy for managing it, and relied heavily on subordinates to provide information, structure options, and resolve conflicts.

At the same time, Reagan was unique in possessing "the mind of both an ideologue and a politician."[13] He came to office with strong instincts, uncomplicated images, and deeply rooted prejudices about the Soviet Union; with total conviction about his views and a lack of concern about their accuracy; and with a willingness to take far-reaching and often controversial measures to implement them. Moreover, he was as bold in his retreats as he was in his initiatives, a consummate politician who instinctively knew when to compromise particular positions and when to cut his losses to achieve his larger objectives. By surrounding himself with a mixture of ideologues, who shared his convictions, and conservative pragmatists, who were effective at getting things done, he built into his administration the potential for both flexibility and continuing controversy and stalemate.

The president's reliance on a formal cabinet-style decision-making process was a further obstacle to the formulation of a coherent policy toward the Soviet Union. The effort to achieve broad consensus left key issues of interpretation and implementation on such central issues as arms control to lower-level officials in several bureaucracies, a practice that invited contradictions, confusion, or irresolution.

During the initial years of the Reagan presidency, considerable power resided in the trio of presidential assistants. Reagan's first national security advisors, Richard V. Allen and then William P. Clark, lacked either the close relationship to the president or the needed foreign policy expertise to play an influential role in foreign policymaking. The appointment of Robert McFarlane in 1983 brought to the position of national security advisor a dedicated and self-effacing professional who commanded the confidence of the president but who lacked the clear mandate needed to surmount bureaucratic divisions. His and his staff's efforts to hammer out a coherent strategy for managing the Soviet-American relationship — and an effective decision-making process — were hampered by political and bureaucratic rivalries. His resignation after the Geneva summit raised new doubts about the future effectiveness of the Reagan team.

The major institutional and political driving force behind an essentialist perspective and a confrontational stance toward the Soviet Union was the Department of Defense under Caspar Weinberger, Jr. An experienced administrator who had run a number of agencies, he had no systematic knowledge of foreign affairs. Among his major assets were the president's confidence in him and his ability to explain complicated problems in very simple terms. Insofar as the Soviet Union was concerned, Weinberger came to his job with little knowledge; no ideological fanaticism but strong convictions concerning the need for a no-nonsense massive buildup of American strength; a total lack of trust in Soviet promises or pronouncements; and a predisposition to believe alarmist, worst-case allegations. Among those whose views and information influenced Weinberger, Richard N. Perle, the assistant secretary for International Security Affairs, occupied a critical place. A long-time advisor to Senator Henry Jackson, Perle was an exceedingly effective political operator on the militant right insofar as Soviet relations were concerned, with close contacts to the neo-conservatives and easy access to many Washington influentials. Usually out of public sight, Perle, a quick mind and facile speaker, has used his superb political skills in the service of an uncompromising struggle against the Soviet Union and, as he saw it, its many dupes and stooges.

The State Department was the major counterweight to the efforts of the Pentagon civilians. The arrival of George P. Shultz, replacing Alexander Haig, enhanced the role and effectiveness of the secretary of state and brought an aura of calm, if not cohesion, to American policy. The most experienced member of the Reagan cabinet, who enjoyed a comfortable personal relationship with the president, Shultz brought to Washington a more pragmatic approach to foreign affairs, concern about managing more effectively the relations between the United States and its allies as well as its adversaries, and a preference for quiet negotiation over pressure in dealing with them.

Although the administration's initial appointments to senior positions varied in quality, few of them brought into the government individuals with a professional knowledge of Soviet affairs. Whether out of disillusionment with "expertise" or out of the conviction that loyalty to the president and managerial expertise were the primary requisites, the first Reagan administration was singularly lacking in individuals in critical policymaking or senior advisory positions who were knowledgeable about Soviet affairs. An exception was Richard E. Pipes, a Harvard professor of Russian history and the leading scholarly proponent of the "essentialist" orientation who chose to return to teaching after two years. Only from 1983 on was somewhat greater expertise and a wider diversity of views on the Soviet Union injected — almost inadvertently — into the government apparatus.

It was not surprising that no public figures associated with detente were included in the Reagan team, not even in the Arms Control and Disarmament Agency, which was now transformed from advocate to critic of the process. More surprising perhaps was the near absence from the administration of representatives of an assortment of views on the political far right. From the outset, no room was found for Major General George Keegan, formerly chief of Air Force Intelligence, or Lieutenant General Daniel O. Graham, former head of the Defense Intelligence Agency, both outspoken alarmists about Soviet capabilities and intentions. And by 1982, a new "rightist opposition" was beginning to form among publicists and others who shared a "neo-conservative anguish over Reagan's foreign policy"[14] — a trend that grew stronger as essentialists left the White House and as the administration shifted away from its initial confrontational policies and headed for the summit. Indeed, by 1985–86, full-page advertisements in major newspapers were voicing alarm over the administration's ostensible capitulation to Soviet blandishments.

Given the fragmentation of powers and the multiplicity of pressures brought to bear on policymaking, the American political system creates considerable obstacles to the conduct of a coherent foreign policy. Effective presidential leadership is critical, and it in turn depends on the development of a coherent strategy and on the establishment of an effective executive branch policy process.[15] Compared to virtually all its predecessors since World War II, with the possible exception of the Carter administration, the Reagan team has not done particularly well by these standards. The twists and turns of policy toward the Soviet Union all too often reflect not a nuanced strategy, but the uncoordinated tugging and pulling of key figures within the administration.

Issues and Policies

The Evolution of Policy

If, at the outset, the administration had produced a paper outlining in broad strokes the assumptions on which its approach to the Soviet Union was based, it would have contained an unprecedented fusion of dichotomist, globalist, unilateralist, and interventionist orientations.

Its point of departure was a dichotomous view of the world: "We" and "They." It classified people, like nations, as friends or enemies, with little room for anything in between. It tended to see neutrality as suspect and its advocates as potential dupes of communism. It tended to dismiss shadings, be they among different Soviet officials or between Soviet and other communist actors, as curiosities at best, essentially trivial and insignificant. Although ideological in origin, its political corollary was simple: "He who is not with us is against us." If the advocates of a nuclear freeze or the West European allies dissented from the official American position, they must be either infected by or vulnerable to communist propaganda or misinformation.

At the same time, a globalist "two-camp" view greatly simplified the perception of world affairs, especially in the Third World. Viewing a whole range of international problems, from regional conflicts to terrorism, through the prism of the worldwide struggle of the "free world" against the Soviet Union, the administration could dismiss regional and local concerns or needs. As Reagan remarked in an interview before his election, "Let's not delude ourselves, the Soviet Union underlies all the unrest that is going on. If they weren't engaged in this game of dominoes, there wouldn't be any hot spots in the world."[16] To be sure, this perspective made it hard to explain the differences among friends and allies, be they between Taiwan and the People's Republic of China or between the United States itself and Japan or Western Europe. The globalist perspective underlay the predictably futile idea of forging an anti-Soviet regional security pact in the Middle East that would encompass such states as Israel and Saudi Arabia. It ignored the rule that a globalism insensitive to regional needs and concerns could not be effective in drawing regional actors into a broader global alignment. In fact, such an outlook led to the dangerous temptation to identify one of the adversaries in regional conflicts with the Soviet camp — mildly, as in the case of Argentina in the Falkland Islands dispute, or more blatantly (but equally misleadingly), as in the case of the Ayatollah Khomeini.

Such an attitude also reflected a unilateralist American approach, rather than a commitment to a "multilateralist" alliance system and shared values. Perceiving alliances as constraints rather than assets, it mirrored skepticism about the steadfastness and commitment of friends and allies, and it often reflected a sense of moral righteousness. As a member of Congress declared after the proclamation of martial law in Poland, this time the United States should proceed to do "what is right" without worrying too much about its allies (or, on other occasions, about international law).

Finally, the new approach had an interventionist streak that sought to push the United States to play a more assertive and uncompromising role — and to resort to the use of armed force (albeit only when it was "safe") in selective defense of American interests.

The president revealed his underlying assumptions about the nature of the Soviet system and its leaders at his first news conference after his inauguration[17]:

> I know of no leader of the Soviet Union . . . that has not more than once repeated . . . their determination that their goal must be the promotion of world communism and a one-world socialist or communist state. . . . Now as long as they do that and as long as they, at the same time, have openly and publicly declared that the only morality they recognize is what will further their cause: meaning they reserve unto themselves the right to commit any crime, to lie, to cheat, and to obtain that and that is moral, not immoral, and we operate on a different set of standards, I think when you do business with them — even at a detente — you keep that in mind.

And yet before long, the administration, although retaining the confrontational rhetoric, began to adapt to a limited extent to political realities. A number of diplomats and senior military men had never shared the new perspective. As discussed elsewhere, on the advice of the senior military chiefs, the United States tacitly agreed to observe the key provisions of the "fatally flawed" SALT II treaty, the ratification of which Ronald Reagan had firmly opposed. Within the first two years, the fiasco over the gas pipeline led Washington to retreat and, for the sake of relations with its allies, to tolerate some of their policies on trade and technology transfer it had vigorously opposed. And after first scorning and downgrading arms control negotiations with the Soviet Union, the Reagan administration saw itself compelled to revert to the "two-track" policy adopted by the North Atlantic Treaty Organization (NATO) in 1978, namely, to modernize its missile force in Europe while simultaneously negotiating with Moscow over arms control.

This stage of adaptation was also marked by numerous inconsistencies, with abundant instances of essentialist rhetoric going hand in hand with pragmatic policies. Little was done, for instance, to implement the commitment to "destabilize" the Soviet system — perhaps because little could be done safely, cheaply, or easily — but the mind set of the policymakers was scarcely challenged. In March 1983, Reagan told an Evangelical Fundamentalist convention in Florida that the Soviet Union was the "focus of evil" in the world and that "we are enjoined by Scripture and the Lord Jesus to oppose it with all our might." Yet despite the rhetoric, it would not be unfair to say that there was, in these first years of the Reagan administration, no coherent long-term political strategy of how to deal with the Soviet Union. As Zbigniew Brzezinski remarked caustically, "A stance is not a policy."

Only in the summer of 1983 could one detect the first signs of a systematic effort — from within the State Department in particular —to elaborate a more coherent policy. Secretary of State Shultz had apparently convinced the president to explore negotiating several minor agreements with the Soviet Union. It was not until 1984 that a more comprehensive effort to articulate and then pursue a new, and less confrontational, policy began to emerge. But in the absence of sustained presidential backing and leadership, the longer-term direction of American policy remained unclear.

The overall pattern of initial confrontation and subsequent limited acquiescence in political and military realities was manifested over a broad range of issues. While in some areas, particularly those involving relations with Western and Eastern Europe, this acquiescence was relatively enduring, in others the administration sought to regain the initiative in challenging and reversing Soviet gains.

Defense Policy and Arms Control

The new administration viewed a major expansion and modernization of American military capabilities as the cornerstone of, if not actually a substitute for, an effective policy toward the Soviet Union. Its defense program had three key components: a sharp increase in defense spending, significant shifts in force posture and purposes, and a redefinition of the role of arms control in national security. Secretary of Defense Weinberger spelled out the underlying assumptions of the new administration's approach in a 1981 statement[18] before the Senate Armed Services Committee:

> It is neither reasonable nor prudent to view the Soviet military buildup as defensive in nature. It would be dangerously naive to expect the Soviet Union, if it once achieves military superiority, not to exploit their military capability even more fully than they are now doing. We must assume some rationale behind the Soviets' enormous allocation of resources to the military at the expense of basic human needs. In fact, we have clear evidence of aggressive Soviet behavior around the globe. . . .

This Soviet activity, unchallenged in recent years by the United States, has led to Soviet gains and the growing perception that the Soviets and their proxies can act with impunity. This trend must be halted and then reversed.

The priority given to a major buildup of both conventional and strategic forces was reflected in a massive increase in defense spending, by roughly 7 percent a year, which totaled over one trillion dollars from 1981 to 1985, and a request for two trillion dollars for the next five years. The Pentagon's share of the federal budget rose from 23 to 27 percent, and defense procurement authority rose by over 100 percent between Fiscal Year 1980 and Fiscal Year 1985.[19]

The redirection of budgetary priorities to sustain this military build-up was defended on several grounds. First and foremost, it was urged as a belated but vital response to a massive expansion of Soviet military capabilities — an effort to redress a "decade of neglect" of military needs that had allegedly relegated the United States to strategic and con-ventional inferiority and made American land-based missiles vulnerable to a Soviet first strike.[20] To restore a credible deterrent and especially to increase the power and survivability of the American ICBM force were the key priorities.

Quite apart from the contribution of such a buildup to the military balance, the demonstration of American determination, the administra-tion argued, would have a desirable impact on Soviet perceptions and behavior. Evidence of American resolve would strengthen the adminis-tration's bargaining position in future arms control negotiations and would also serve to deter Soviet leaders from global adventurism by raising its risks.

At the same time, the president's rigid commitment to tax reduction meant that the defense buildup could be sustained only at the expense of corresponding slashes in domestic social programs or rising deficits or both. Although the administration's exaggeration of Soviet capabilities, and corresponding understatement of American assets, raised suspicions of naiveté, if not outright distortion, it reflected a political calculus as well: To sell such a policy in peacetime to Congress and to the public required portraying Soviet intentions and capabilities in the most alarm-ing possible terms.

The unprecedented annual budgetary requests submitted by the Secretary of Defense during the Reagan administration did not reflect a coherent military strategy. Secretary Weinberger's posture statements offered only a rudimentary strategic rationale for the spending requests. These amounted to an open-ended "wish list," based on the assumption that "more is better," which offered no real criteria for assessing the adequacy or effectiveness of defense outlays. Defense spending was equated with resolve, not with combat readiness, and all proposals for cutbacks were equated with demonstrations of weakness that the USSR would exploit.

By the second Reagan term, continuing rapid increases in military spending proved impossible to sustain politically. Although Weinberger assured Congress in his annual report that substantial progress had been made in restoring American military capabilities, increasingly serious questions were raised about whether these massive expenditures, which led to unprecedented budget deficits and massive cuts in domestic programs, had actually bought a corresponding enhancement of the country's relative security.[21]

A reorientation of strategic doctrine and force posture to a more demanding range of missions constituted a second feature of the Reagan administration's defense policy. Although not initially repudiating traditional notions of deterrence, or the assumption of mutual assured destruction on which they rested, it involved a more explicit commitment to "warfighting," both conventional and nuclear, and a more assertive effort to exploit Soviet vulnerabilities. Although the Pentagon maintained that its primary purpose continued to be to deter a Soviet attack, the insistence that the United States must be in a position to "prevail" in the event of war, and to terminate a conflict "on terms favorable to the United States,"[22] reflected both an expanded definition of military objectives and the view that nuclear weapons could serve rational political goals.

The effort to neutralize the Soviet strategic buildup by reducing American vulnerability to Soviet offensive capabilities was also responsible for renewed interest in strategic defense, an interest that found its most dramatic expression in the Strategic Defense Initiative (SDI), or "Star Wars." Notwithstanding the widespread skepticism in the scientific community that a "defensive shield" was actually feasible, SDI was indeed a quintessential expression of Reagan's approach to defense. It expressed his yearning to restore American invulnerability rather than acquiescing in a "mutual hostage" posture; his unbounded faith in a technological panacea that would reaffirm American superiority, negate the Soviet buildup, and obviate the slow and painstaking search for negotiated arms control agreements; and his instinctive preference for a "solution" over indefinite management of a complex relationship. The president's vision of a defensive shield was not widely shared within the defense community itself, but SDI constituted a political umbrella that justified increased allocations for military research and development across a broad spectrum of new weapons technologies.

The third component of the administration's defense policy was a more negative approach to the role of arms control in Soviet-American relations. Earlier administrations had treated arms control as an important component of a coherent national security policy, complementing military programs by enhancing stability, predictability, and deterrence, and had viewed the arms control process as a central element in managing the Soviet-American competition. The Reagan administration tended to view arms control as fundamentally damaging to national security. For the essentialists, who charged the Soviet Union with pursuing a deliberate policy of cheating in violation of arms control agreements, the fundamental asymmetry of the American and Soviet systems — Soviet secrecy, the insulation of decision making from public pressures, the absence of moral and political constraints on cheating — made arms control inherently advantageous to the USSR.

But skepticism about arms control extended to the process itself. As with any negotiations, arms control emphasized the possibility of collaboration rather than competition, thereby undercutting, in the view of critics, public support for needed military expenditures. Moreover, the political right joined the left in its perception that arms control was a failure, leading only to constraints on the growth of arsenals but not to "real reductions." Indeed, because arms control was considered desirable only if it resulted in a fundamental restructuring of the Soviet offensive arsenal, it was difficult to imagine an achievable agreement that was also in the American interest.

Finally arms control was suspect because of the alleged failure of previous agreements to provide "effective" rather than merely adequate verification and to assure Soviet compliance with those agreements. Indeed, the exaggerated charges of massive Soviet violations of existing agreements were calculated more to undercut support for observing them, and to obstruct future arms control agreements, than to address the compliance issue constructively.

The history of Soviet-American arms control negotiations under the Reagan administration typifies the broader conflict over American policy toward the Soviet Union. In substance, the American side has been divided between essentialists hostile to all arms control accords and the "hard" mechanists seeking to strike an advantageous deal.

During its first years, the administration entered into no arms control talks. At a second stage, in 1982–83, talks were held over unpromising proposals until ended by the Soviet walkout at the end of 1983. The launching of the SDI research, on the one hand, by giving the United States unexpected leverage in negotiating with Moscow, and, on the other hand, the reassessment of Soviet priorities prompted by the accession of Mikhail Gorbachev, created a new framework for arms control talks. Finally, beginning in 1985, a series of new proposals offered by Gorbachev across the entire spectrum of weapons systems split the United States administration, with those who wanted no agreement opposing those who were prepared to accept a tradeoff of future SDI testing and deployment for major Soviet cutbacks on offensive strategic systems.[23]

Economic Relations with the Soviet Union

Having long maintained that a permissive approach toward East-West economic relations had endangered Western security without eliciting more benign Soviet behavior, the Reagan administration faced the challenge of devising new trade policies that would serve its broader political objectives. From the very beginning, its general commitment to economic deregulation and expanded, unfettered international trade conflicted with its determination to subordinate economic interests in Soviet-American relations to larger strategic concerns.[24] The desire to constrain Soviet military capabilities through the use of economic as well as political and military assets precluded a laissez-faire approach to Soviet-American economic relations and imposed instead a choice between a strategy of leverage and a strategy of denial. Both entailed enhanced government control over the flow of trade, the transfer of technology, and the availability of credits to the Soviet Union.

An emphasis on leverage, supported in particular by the Departments of State, Commerce, and the Treasury, focused on the use of economic relations to elicit more "responsible" Soviet behavior in both domestic and foreign policy. It would utilize a combination of economic incentives (the further development of mutually beneficial economic relations) and implicit threats (to reduce or cut off such opportunities) to influence Soviet policies, whether on behalf of human rights and emigration, or to deter expansion abroad.[25]

A strategy of denial, promoted by key figures in the Department of Defense as well as by neo-conservative supporters of the administration, was based on profound skepticism about the past efficacy and future prospects of efforts at leverage and sought to affect Soviet capabilities rather than Soviet behavior. Its intent was to subject the faltering Soviet economy to increased strain by reducing Soviet gains from trade, constricting the availability of technology and credits, and curtailing what was perceived as Western subsidization of Soviet economic and military development.

This strategy rested on the assessment that Soviet gains from East-West trade and technology transfer were both substantial and asymmetrically advantageous to the Soviet Union and that the Soviet economy, as it faced the prospects of long-term retardation, was highly vulnerable to external pressure. To the extent that all East-West trade made the Soviet Union a more formidable adversary by strengthening its industrial base, Western policies that deprived it of economic resources with which to pursue a buildup at home and expansion abroad would compel the Soviet leadership (in the words of Richard Pipes) to "face the consequences of its own priorities": either to divert resources from military to civilian uses or face growing social unrest as a result of declining mass consumption.[26]

Divergent assessments both within and outside the administration focused on three specific, though interrelated issues: the role of trade in

Soviet-American relations more broadly, the problem of credits, and the export of strategic goods and technologies. Trade policy toward the Soviet Union, in which American grain sales figured most prominently, was the first to demand the attention of the new administration. Here domestic political considerations quickly triumphed over foreign policy consistency. Over the objections of Haig and others, who argued that his actions would undercut both leverage and denial, President Reagan, in April 1981, honored his campaign pledge to the farm vote by not only lifting the embargo on agricultural commodities that Carter had imposed after the invasion of Afghanistan but also by pledging to refrain from reimposing one in the future.[27] The president defended his decision on the grounds that the embargo had been ineffective (thus undercutting the key assumptions of a strategy of denial) and that it had imposed excessive burdens on one segment of the American economy (thus illustrating the political constraints on the pursuit of leverage). But the major impact of his decision was to undermine the credibility of the administration's demands for greater economic sacrifices by its European allies in dealing with the Soviet Union. Despite American efforts to portray grain sales as more benign in their economic impact than European trade in industrial goods, the widespread suspicion that this was a self-serving double standard was reflected in West German Chancellor Helmut Schmidt's pointed observation that grain was also a strategic commodity.

The administration's effort to restrict the flow of credits to the Soviet Union embroiled it still further in domestic and alliance controversy. Government credits had not been available to the Soviet Union and Eastern Europe, apart from Hungary and Rumania, since 1974, when the Jackson-Vanik amendment linked such credits to emigration policies. But the flow of private credits was also criticized as an indirect subsidy of the Soviet economy: a sacrifice of national security to narrow commercial self-interest by the Western business community that was, in effect, "selling the Russians the rope" by which they would hang the West.

This view was not universally shared within the administration; whereas Richard Perle pressed an alarmist view of the military costs of economic interaction, the Department of Commerce took a more positive view of the benefits of increased trade. But it was particularly divisive within the Western alliance, given the greater stake of the West Europeans in extensive trade relations with the Soviet Union and the customary use of subsidized credits and government-backed loans to finance international economic transactions. While the allies viewed such practices as a subsidy to domestic producers rather than to the USSR, to the Reagan administration they appeared to violate free-trade principles, alliance commitments, and the canons of good sense to boot.

In both domestic and alliance policy, it was ultimately the issue of technology transfer that proved to be the most critical, enduring, and legal restrictions on technology transfer. This was an attempt not only to define the literally thousands of technologies that could not be exported directly to the Soviet bloc, but also to monitor their sale to allied and other noncommunist countries to prevent their possible re-export through a potentially infinite chain of legal and dummy intermediaries. In pressing these allies to acquiesce in its own definition of security needs, the administration transformed issues of trade, credits, and technology transfer from an East-West confrontation into a West-West one.[31]

The protracted and bitter controversy over the projected Soviet-West European natural gas pipeline project (discussed at greater length in Chapter 6) dramatized the degree to which the administration's economic policies had departed from those of its predecessors as well as its allies and had moved in the direction of outright economic warfare. Fusing as it did the issues of trade, credits, and technology transfer in one single project, the pipeline issue was a litmus test of the different assumptions held by different actors about East-West economic relations and their political and military implications. To the advocates of denial, which here included Weinberger and the president himself, the pipeline project involved the export of critical technologies that would contribute to Soviet economic, and therefore, military power; it relied heavily on Western credits, which constituted an additional indirect subsidy to the Soviet economy; it enmeshed the West Europeans even more deeply in asymmetrical trade relationships, which magnified their alleged dependence on the Soviet Union; and by alleviating its chronic shortage of hard currency, it would enable the Soviet Union to circumvent efforts to constrain its future economic growth.[32] Rejecting the advice of Haig and others, who urged acceptance of the West European commitment as a *fait accompli* and shifting the focus to improving credit terms and reducing possible risks of the undertaking, the president in June 1982 made a last-ditch effort to thwart the project by attempting to block the transfer of components manufactured by foreign subsidiaries of American firms under license from American corporations. This decision, of dubious legality and high political cost, not only helped trigger the resignation of Haig but also provoked a crisis within the alliance that French Foreign Minister Cheysson characterized outspokenly as a progressive "divorce."

The crisis itself indicated the distance the first Reagan administration had traveled in moving from the pursuit of leverage to a strategy of denial, if not outright economic warfare. Where Kissinger and Vance, as well as Schmidt and Mitterrand, had sought to enmesh the Soviet Union in a network of economic links that were viewed as mutually beneficial in their own right and as promoting a desirable interdependence, the new administration viewed such relationships as intrinsically one-sided, and costly to the West, and sought instead to isolate the Soviet Union from Western technology and trade.[33] Where earlier policies sought the dis-

controversial in the administration's efforts to frame a new strategy f(
economic relations with the Soviet bloc. Having argued that past polici
had permitted a virtual hemorrhage of advanced technologies from t
West, that these had contributed significantly to Soviet military m(
ernization, and that previous controls had been largely ineffective in t
face of a major Soviet acquisition effort, the Reagan administrat
sought to heighten public awareness of the danger and to introduce m
stringent controls over the export of all technologies that might contrit
even indirectly to the Soviet military potential.[28]

Although specific proposals were hotly contested within the adm
tration itself, with the Defense Department playing a key role in adv(
ing extreme measures, the general thrust was to broaden the sco
technologies considered strategic, to enforce export controls more
gently and give the Pentagon a greater role in the process, to st(
measures to prevent Soviet industrial espionage, and most
troversially, to reduce the scope of, and introduce closer controls
scientific communication. Alarmed that such communication migh
the Soviet Union access to ideas as well as key technologies in suc
as computers, encryption, or artificial intelligence, the adminis
pressed universities and research institutes to introduce unprece
policing of scholarship in potentially sensitive areas.

Whereas the need to bar Soviet access to technologies o
military significance was unquestioned, the new initiatives of the
administration were highly controversial on several grounds.

First, the effort to expand the definition of militarily criti(
nologies to include entire classes of advanced technology that mi
indirect military applications was fraught with difficulties, and t
controlling their export was still more so. The Defense Dep
initial (and classified) List of Militarily Critical Technologies,
1980, contained, in the words of one analyst, "a virtual roll call
contemporary techniques, including videodisc recording,
materials, and many dozens of others equally broad. If this coll(
automatically become the basis for the official Commodities C(
(as some had urged during the debate over the 1979 Export A
tion Act), the entire Department of Commerce would not have
enough to administer the export-control program."[30]

Second, the effort to subject scholarly-scientific commui
tighter governmental regulation raised grave concerns about
such restrictions to scientific and technological innovation a
the freedom of scholarly inquiry.

Third, and even more controversial, was the effort to
export controls on allies who had a significant economic stal
technology with the Soviet Union, who did not agree with t
American definition of security, and who largely lacked in

criminating use of both carrots and sticks to shape Soviet perceptions and behavior, the Reagan administration had little confidence in either the prospects of achieving such fine-tuning or its effectiveness in moderating Soviet actions. The effort to bring about greater relaxation in Soviet outlook and policy was rejected in favor of policies meant to maximize pressure on the Soviet system and to limit its capabilities. Where others had been prepared to recognize Soviet superpower status and had sought to reduce Soviet insecurities, the White House sought instead to exploit all possible Soviet vulnerabilities.

Although the merits of this approach remained untested, it soon became clear that a strategy of denial that was pursued unilaterally and that demanded major economic sacrifices from allies, while exempting American grain exports, had no prospect of success. Indeed, as Secretary Shultz soon realized, its pursuit placed far greater strain on the alliance than on the Soviet Union. The gradual realization that no effort to apply economic pressure on the Soviet Union could succeed without a concerted alliance strategy forced a shift in the American approach. By November 1982, Shultz's efforts to defuse the dispute culminated in a face-saving arrangement by which the United States lifted its sanctions against West European companies in return for Allied participation in a review of the security implications of East-West economic relations.[34]

Over the past several years, in several institutional settings and with varying degrees of success, modest progress has been made in narrowing some of the differences among the allies (as well as Japan) over the security implications of East-West trade, the use of credit subsidies to finance it, and the role of energy in Western security.[35] Some tightening of CoCom (Coordinating Committee) guidelines has been agreed upon, and allied coordination of policy has improved somewhat. American policy, however, has itself remained contradictory, with continuing struggles over policy as well as turf between key actors and agencies (Defense, Commerce, State, and the Customs Division of the Treasury) contributing to incoherence and further complicating negotiations with the allies.

Eastern Europe and the Polish Crisis

The administration's heightened preoccupation with the "Soviet threat" and its black-and-white view of world affairs made it especially difficult to develop a coherent policy regarding Eastern Europe. Although the area was typically, and traditionally, viewed through the prism of Soviet-American relations, two linked but distinct issues required clarification. The first issue was the relationship of the Soviet Union to Eastern Europe — what might be called the Yalta issue. Soviet hegemony was obviously a fact of life but had never been acknowledged as legitimate. Whereas preceding administrations had tended to acquiesce in de facto Soviet control, the Reagan administration sought to keep alive the Yalta issue by periodic challenges to its legitimacy.

The second question was whether the states of the region should be treated as an integral part of the Soviet empire — in effect, as allies of the adversary — or whether they should rather be viewed as reluctant subjects seeking to maximize their autonomy. The former approach dictated a policy of greater economic and political pressure on Eastern Europe; the latter suggested a differentiated strategy aimed at encouraging greater foreign policy independence from the Soviet Union or domestic political and economic liberalization.

Equally controversial was the question of longer term American objectives in the region. Was the maintenance of postwar stability the highest priority, even if this meant foregoing opportunities to stimulate or support resistance to communist rule? Or was the declaratory refusal to accept the consequences of Yalta — forty years later — not mere rhetoric but actual policy, and a "rollback" of Soviet control a serious political objective?[36]

These issues were hardly novel. The evolution of American policy toward Eastern Europe in the postwar period had covered a whole gamut of alternatives. At the height of the Cold War, American policy denied the legitimacy of these Soviet-sponsored regimes, treated them as mere appendages of the Stalinist system, and sought to keep alive the symbolism of Eastern European states as captive nations. But the circumstances of the Hungarian revolt in 1956 illustrated, by no means for the last time, the limits of American willingness — or ability, within reasonable costs and risks — to take effective action in the region.[37] As evidence for both pluralism and nationalism among East European political elites gradually mounted, American policy shifted toward an effort to encourage diversity and autonomy within the communist bloc. Yugoslavia provided the precedent of American support for a communist country that had become independent of the Soviet bloc; events in Hungary, Poland, Czechoslovakia, and Rumania in subsequent years raised the possibility of substantial changes within the existing political framework that the United States might welcome and support.

The effort at West European and American cultural and political bridge-building to Eastern Europe in the late 1960s was followed in the 1970s by an expansion of economic relations.[38] Despite the sweeping human rights rhetoric of the Carter administration, Eastern Europe was largely exempted from charges of violations directed at the Soviet Union.

To supporters of detente, expanding contacts between East and West in a more benign international environment and growing liberalization and diversity within Eastern Europe were among the most salient achievements, and mounting Eastern bloc indebtedness a relatively small price to pay.[39] To its critics, however, the costs of detente far outweighted its benefits: By helping ameliorate economic conditions in Eastern Europe, the West helped legitimize what were, at bottom, oppressive, Soviet-dominated regimes; by subsidizing East European economies through snowballing credits it contributed, however indirectly, to the Soviet military buildup. The West had failed to effect any visible Soviet restraint abroad. And far from increasing Western political leverage over Eastern Europe, it had had the opposite effect, creating "reverse leverage" over Western creditors who were too fearful of losing their investments to refuse requests for additional aid.

To the incoming Reagan administration, the mounting economic difficulties in Eastern Europe were further evidence of what it saw as the failure of both communism and detente. At the same time, the success of Solidarity as an independent trade union movement in Poland and its association with Polish nationalism and Christian values attracted sympathy across an exceptionally broad spectrum of American opinion, from the left to the Reagan conservatives. The overhanging threat of Soviet military intervention in Poland prompted repeated warnings by the United States to the Soviet leadership that such action would have the most serious consequences. Meanwhile the United States sought to strengthen the Polish authorities by granting them debt relief and emergency credits for the purchase of agricultural commodities. In its first year, the new administration therefore had the luxury of being able simultaneously to support Polish resistance to communist rule, a liberalization of the existing system, and a weakening of the Soviet bloc.

The imposition of martial law in Poland in December 1981 — a development that in its preoccupation with the possibility of a Soviet military intervention the administration had failed to anticipate — transformed the situation overnight, and a major controversy over policy toward Poland erupted within both the United States and the Western alliance. Some interpreted the imposition of martial law as a desperate effort by the Polish leadership to forestall Soviet military intervention, on the one hand, and a breakdown of domestic controls, on the other, and urged policies that would simultaneously maximize political pressure on Warsaw while maintaining its limited autonomy from Moscow. Others saw the events as a confirmation that political developments in Poland were entirely orchestrated in Moscow and urged the harshest possible American response directed against both the Polish and Soviet governments. Among the measures advocated were calling off all Soviet-American negotiations, the imposition of sharp economic sanctions, and the declaration of default on the Polish debt.[40]

The controversy over default crystallized the larger dilemma of American policy toward Eastern Europe. For the advocates of a more ideological and confrontational policy toward the Soviet Union, a formal declaration of default would simultaneously serve as a token of Western outrage at the suppression of Solidarity, a symbol of the bankruptcy of communism, a gesture that would end the "reverse leverage" ostensibly operating against Western creditors of communist regimes, and a measure that would further strain the Soviet system by compelling it to assume the full economic burden of a crippled Polish economy. As critics pointed out, although default might be politically gratifying, such a declaration would be an empty gesture of potentially greater cost to the West than to its intended victims, a measure that would deprive the West of whatever leverage it still had to influence the course of events in Poland, and a step that would force Poland back into the Soviet camp.[41]

The administration's response straddled the two positions. On the one hand, the president accepted the view that the Soviet Union had been centrally responsible and should be the object of serious sanctions along with Poland itself. On the other hand, the administration stopped short of imposing either a total embargo on both countries or a declaration of Polish default, holding out the possibility that economic relations and even assistance might be restored if and when three preconditions were met: an end to martial law, the release of political detainees, and a resumption of the government's dialogue with the Church and Solidarity.[42]

In backing off from an ideological to a more pragmatic decision, the administration chose a course less extreme than that advocated by a wide array of public figures, from Caspar Weinberger to Henry Kissinger. Why? First and foremost, since the effect of a declaration of default on the West European banking system was bound to be both enormous and incalculable, to have triggered default over the opposition of the West Europeans would have entailed disproportionate costs. The White House preferred to retain its freedom to opt for default later, but, in effect, it accepted the argument that to invoke it would be counterproductive in that it would (1) relieve Poland and the Soviet Union of their financial obligations, (2) destroy such leverage as the West possessed, and (3) disrupt the Western banking system. The stakes were so high and the consequences so uncertain that the balance within the Reagan cabinet tipped in favor of the business-oriented technicians, beginning with the Secretary of the Treasury, over the ideologically oriented crusaders.[43]

If the controversy over default was too arcane for much of the public, it also beclouded the basic fact that there was little the United States could or would do. There were no obvious weapons in the political or economic arsenal that the administration could wield to affect significantly the course of events in Poland — and not even the most extreme activists advocated American military action. This again became evident when, in December 1982, the Polish authorities, having banned Solidarity, now "suspended" martial law and released most of the detainees held since the crackdown a year earlier. Washington declared that the changes were insufficient to warrant lifting United States sanctions. More broadly, American incentives proved to be insufficient to bring about significant change in Poland, while the Polish government's gestures were seen in Washington as insufficient to warrant any change in United States behavior.

The dilemmas posed by developments in Poland were illustrative of the broader difficulties of American policy toward Eastern Europe. Despite the yearning for a more militant policy which would result in a "rollback of the Soviet empire," in practice the administration was forced to recognize the limited options available to the United States.

Political Warfare and Human Rights

For the more militant figures within the new administration, political warfare was to be the counterpart of economic warfare with the Soviet Union. It was intended to exploit and enhance political and social vulnerabilities within the Soviet Union, to combat Soviet ideological influence and challenge Soviet political prestige abroad, and in effect, to delegitimize and isolate the Soviet Union from the outside world.

Most novel but also unclear was the desire to promote "destabilization" in the Soviet camp. Whereas preceding administrations had focused their efforts on influencing Soviet officialdom through official channels — "from above" — the new strategy was to appeal to a target audience "from below." If this looked like intervening inside the Soviet Union, to the pragmatists this seemed to be a welcome way of getting even with the extensive Soviet propaganda campaign abroad. Officially the effort was described as giving "vigorous support to democratic forces wherever they are located — including countries which are now communist. . . . A free press, free trade unions, free political parties, freedom to travel, and freedom to create are the ingredients of the democratic revolution of the future."[44]

President Reagan chose the occasion of his address to the British Parliament on June 8, 1982, to make public his plan[45]:

> What I am describing now is a plan and a hope for the long term — the march of freedom and democracy which will leave Marxism-Leninism on the ash heap of history as it has left other tyrannies which stifle the freedom and muzzle the self-expression of the people. . . .
>
> The objective I propose is quite simple to state: to foster the infrastructure of democracy — the system of a free press, unions, political parties, universities — which allows a people to choose their own way. . . . This is not cultural imperialism: it is providing the means for genuine self-determination and protection for diversity. . . . It would be cultural

condescension, or worse, to say that any people prefer dictatorship to democracy.

The major institutional and budgetary expression of this orientation was the creation by Congress, at the administration's request, of a National Endowment for Democracy. This approach reflected a keen new interest in Washington in the nature and scope of Soviet vulnerabilities, from social cleavages to ethnic tensions to unmet consumer needs.[46] It was widely criticized at first as a "multimillion-dollar propaganda" effort and as a surrogate for American intelligence activities; later it was embarrassed by the malodorous record of some of the organizations, in third countries, who had been the beneficiaries of its financial largesse abroad. In any event, when it came to the Soviet Union, its importance was more symbolic than real.

In practical terms, radio broadcasts by the Voice of America, as well as the government-financed, but formally independent Radio Free Europe/Radio Liberty, proved a more important element in the attempted mobilization for political warfare, with increased funding for transmissions across Soviet jamming, the expansion of broadcasts in minority languages of the Soviet Union, and a more explicitly confrontational tenor of the broadcasts. While critics were concerned that the broadcasts' credibility with their putative audience would be lost if programming became more avowedly propagandistic, this militant view of the Voice's purposes was proclaimed by the deputy program director of the Voice of America, who was soon forced out after a bitter feud[47]:

> We must portray the Soviet Union as the last great predatory empire on earth, remorselessly enslaving its own diverse ethnic populations, crushing the legitimate aspirations of its captive nations. . . . We must strive to "destabilize" the Soviet Union and its satellites by promoting disaffection between peoples and rulers.

But once again militancy was no substitute for effective management. The radios continued to be plagued by unreconciled conflicts among different emigré programs and perspectives.[48]

The Carter administration had given considerable attention to the issues of human rights, globally and in the Soviet bloc, in particular. For some, the espousal of human rights abroad was a universal goal; for others, it was primarily a weapon of political warfare. Whether the demand for Soviet concessions — for instance, with regard to emigration or the fate of individual dissidents — should be linked to other issues being negotiated with Moscow was a matter of some dispute as well, and in the end the promotion of human rights, though well publicized, has generally been subordinated to "reasons of state."

In Reagan's first term in office, the question was not even posed in the same way. For one thing, there was a perception that human rights were a "soft" issue, compared to the priority needs of strengthening American posture and image. For another, to the essentialists the human-rights disaster in the Soviet Union was an organic feature of the system and the Helsinki accords were dangerously misguided for even implying that human rights could mean anything to the Soviet authorities. Human rights violations were an outrage to be publicized, not a subject over which to bargain. Moreover, negotiating over human rights presupposed an American willingness to provide suitable incentives for the Soviet Union, and until the whole climate and context of Soviet-American dealings changed in the second Reagan term, there was no willingness to provide a quid pro quo.[49]

But, as the climate began to change and preparations were made for the Geneva summit, human rights could not be omitted from the agenda, if only because of the domestic and foreign audiences. For some, moreover, their inclusion seemed to be a clever hurdle over which they expected Gorbachev to trip on the road to Soviet-American agreements.

Once removed from the realm of ideology and grandstanding and brought into the context of earnest Soviet-American dealings, the issue effectively shifted from public to private diplomacy. This marked a change of tactics and venue apparently urged on the president by Richard Nixon, Henry Kissinger, and Jewish-American leaders. It was significant both for its symbolism and for the implicit recognition of the shift that had occurred in Soviet-American relations: The object was no longer public relations or political warfare, but tangible accomplishments. The elaborate "spy trade" in February 1986 that led to the release of Anatoli Shcharansky, long the symbol of Soviet repressions in the eyes of many American-Jewish and other observers, and the visit of Elena Bonner, the wife of Andrei Sakharov, to the United States appeared to lend credence to the view that quiet diplomacy might indeed pay off.

Global Interventionism and the Reagan Doctrine

In line with the dominant "globalist" perspective, the Reagan administration was inclined to assume Soviet influence and communist activity wherever it observed social protest and revolutionary upheaval and to perceive expanding Soviet influence as a worldwide ideological and geopolitical challenge to the United States. This perspective produced a more expansive definition of vital American interests abroad than had obtained under its predecessors; it identified the Soviet Union as a key source of regional instability, be it in the Middle East or in Central America; and it made known its greater willingness both to threaten and to use military force to promote and secure its objectives there. The result of this tendency to globalize third-party conflicts into East-West issues (that is, matters contested by the superpowers) was to succumb to a new universalism that recognized — in its rhetoric, if not in practice — few limits to American power in the pursuit of similarly limitless American interests.[50]

How was the United States to deal with the various regimes, from Grenada to South Yemen, which, in the minds of some Washington analysts, amounted to an "extended empire" of the Soviet Union? Memories of Vietnam and Angola, a series of ad hoc decisions in regard to Afghanistan and Nicaragua, and United States government studies stressing the extensive use of "proxies" to promote Soviet interests in the Third World helped crystallize the new strategy. Challenged on pragmatic questions, such as funding Nicaraguan *contras*, the administration fell back on a new ideological rationale. It implied that even where they were not physically present, the Soviets were the instigators of "Marxist-Leninist" takeovers. It assumed that the indigenous surrogates were acting on Moscow's behalf, and it reflected a greater American willingness to commit resources to recruit, train, arm, and perhaps help direct insurgent forces against pro-Soviet regimes.

The result, by 1985, was what some observers labeled the Reagan Doctrine of United States support and sponsorship of such *contras*. Although varying greatly in the extent of grass roots support and authenticity, in their prospects for success, and in their own political orientations, these groups — from Angola to Kampuchea and from Nicaragua to Afghanistan — have been linked together by the president and other administration spokesmen as "freedom fighters" deserving — and presumably receiving — American aid. As Reagan declared on March 1, 1985 about the Nicaraguan "contras,"

> They are our brothers, these freedom fighters, and we owe them our help. . . . They are the moral equivalent of the Founding Fathers and the brave men and women of the French Resistance. We cannot turn away from them. For the struggle is not right versus left, but right versus wrong.

If this elevated the strategy to the strains of essentialist rhetoric, extravagant and moralistic, George Shultz[51] provided a more pragmatic if equally firm rationale:

> We must never let ourselves be so wedded to improving relations with the Soviets that we turn a blind eye to actions that undermine the very foundation of stable relations; symbolic responses to outrageous Soviet actions have their place, and so do penalties and sanctions. Experience also shows [that] . . . we can best deter or undo Soviet geopolitical encroachments by helping, in one way or another, those who are

resisting directly on the ground. . . . So long as Communist dictatorships feel free to aid and abet insurgencies in the name of "socialist
internationalism," why must the democracies — the target of this
threat — be inhibited from defending their own interests and the cause
of democracy itself?

Unlike most of the other issues we have examined where extremists
and moderates soon parted company, the Reagan doctrine, unexpectedly
for some of the policy's initial sponsors, has emerged as a happy arena in
which essentialists and mechanists have been able to converge and join in
a common policy. One consequence has been a lack of definition in the
objectives of this new strategy. For some it signaled a rollback of the
Soviet "empire"; for others it meant "harrassing the Soviets on peripheral
battlefields" or at least raising the costs for Moscow (and for its clients and
proxies) of maintaining a global presence among, and control over, its
far-flung dependencies.

Critics have hastened to point to the costs and risks of this policy. If
the element of Soviet aggression is unmistakable in the case of Afghanistan, the Soviet role is far more limited and controversial in regard to
Angola, Ethiopia, Kampuchea, or Nicaragua. By lumping together
Afghanistan and the other cases, the administration has obliterated the
distinction between direct aggression and a presumed extension of Soviet
influence by other means.

The depreciation of international law involved in the policy that
flows from the Reagan Doctrine, as well as the loss of public support
abroad, are not obviously in the American interest, either. More serious
in the eyes of many Washingtonians are the danger of uncontrolled
escalation and the identification of the United States with hopeless and at
times highly unattractive causes. It has also been pointed out that such a
strategy, rather than splitting the indigenous authorities from their Soviet
patrons, leaves them no choice but to become completely dependent on
Moscow.

It remains true that the administration has been careful not to take
undue risks. The Reagan Doctrine has not been applied against Cuba or
in Eastern Europe; American armed forces have been in action only
where the costs were sure to be slight and no risk of Soviet involvement
existed, such as in Grenada in October 1983 or Libya in April 1986.

It is precisely these areas, where the United States believes it has put
Moscow and its clients on the defensive, that Reagan has identified as loci
of regional conflict whose resolution the United States urges on the
Kremlin and makes part of the Soviet-American agenda. The United
States has nothing to lose by such a new departure. On the eve of the
Geneva summit, addressing the United Nations General Assembly,
Reagan elaborated on the regional issues, one by one, and concluded, in a
throwback to his more ideological vein[52]:

All of these conflicts, some of them under way for a decade, originate in local disputes but they share a common characteristic: they are the consequence of an ideology imposed from without, dividing nations and creating regimes that are, almost from the day they take power, at war with their own people. And in each case, Marxism-Leninism's war with the people becomes war with their neighbors.

More than one part of this statement is open to challenge. Although Washington insists that continued American support of these insurgent movements is, in 1986, by no means incompatible with an improvement in Soviet-American relations, it is a policy, which, down the road, may yet present the United States with difficult and painful choices. In any event, the effort to reduce tension has not led either side to forego its efforts to gain competitive advantages.

The Road to the Summit

The essentialists in the new administration who were committed to political and economic warfare and those who pushed for a "management" strategy for dealing with the Soviet Union soon joined battle over the question of negotiations with Moscow.

The whole strategy of political warfare implied an effort to isolate the Soviet Union; to deny it symbolic recognition, parity, or legitimacy; to cut back scientific, educational, and cultural interactions as well as trade; and, in effect, to ostracize it in the international community. The logical corollary was to refuse all negotiations with Moscow. To refrain from negotiating also fitted the pragmatic argument that at some future point the United States would be in a stronger bargaining position, thanks to the military buildup the administration had launched and to the looming crises in the Soviet system. Premature negotiations would lull American public opinion and complicate, if not inhibit, the needed military buildup.

But this hostility to negotiating was bound to go against the grain of professional diplomats and of at least some businessmen serving in the government. In a number of policy areas, it soon proved to be impossible to stick to what the militant pursuit of the new strategy would have demanded: like it or not, arms control continued to be widely regarded as the touchstone of the whole Soviet-American relationship. The pressure to negotiate with the Soviet Union over the whole complex of arms control issues, from strategic weapons to the deployment of theater forces in Europe, mounted steadily, especially in Western Europe. The commitment to negotiate had been part of the bargain that had led the European allies to accept the American program for the modernization of Theater Nuclear Forces, an essential part in their minds of the agreement to install Pershings and cruise missiles in Europe. Key figures in the administration came to realize that the arms control process was necessary to sustain the military buildup, not an alternative to it.

Public opinion, first in Europe and then in the United States, put increasing pressure on the administration to resume negotiations, and in November 1981 the White House decided to reverse course on two issues: first, to abide tacitly by the terms of the SALT II agreement, later dressed up into a public statement by the president that the United States would not undercut the terms of SALT II so long as the Soviet Union observed them; and second, to take the initiative on arms control negotiations, hoping to take the wind out of the sails of the arms control advocates and the vociferous proponents of a nuclear freeze.

At the same time, the administration dissociated itself from its predecessors' search for strategic arms limitation in favor of seeking substantial reductions — hence the change in acronym from SALT (Strategic Arms Limitations Talks) to START (Strategic Arms Reduction Talks) and a significantly altered structure of proposals. These initial proposals, it is only fair to say, were less of an effort to find a negotiable formula to deal with the Soviet Union than an effort at compromise among American bureaucracies bitterly at loggerheads over this issue. By mid-1982, the United States and the Soviet Union were engaged in arms control discussions in three different forums (although the administration refused a Soviet proposal to resume talks on a comprehensive nuclear test ban treaty).

This shift in American conduct represented only a very limited accommodation. A response to outside pressures, it did not reflect any basic shift of policy. The American proposals were no more "negotiable" than their Soviet counterparts — and American negotiators knew it — but they promptly became part of the superpower propaganda contest. Nor did the United States try to use the opportunity to cultivate broader contacts with Soviet leaders and officials. The private agenda on arms control of key administration officials amounted to choosing between American "building up" to restore parity and Soviet "building down" proportionately more to compensate for its perceived advantage.

When Leonid Brezhnev died in Moscow on November 10, 1982, the president rejected Shultz's recommendation that he go to Moscow for the funeral to meet the new Soviet leaders (just as he would abstain from attending the funeral of Brezhnev's successors, Yuri Andropov and Konstantin Chernenko, in 1984 and 1985). Vice-President George Bush and Secretary of State Shultz went instead; their public comments were upbeat and cautiously encouraging concerning the future. At the same time President Reagan reverted to his customary confrontational rhetoric. And on March 8, 1983, in addressing the National Association of Evangelicals in Orlando, Florida, he commented on the Soviet regime:

. . . While they preach the supremacy of the state, declare its omnipotence over individual man, and predict its eventual domination of
all peoples on the earth, they are the focus of evil in the modern world.

He went on to urge his audience to understand that the contest between
the two superpowers was not "a giant misunderstanding," but rather "the
struggle between right and wrong and good and evil," with the Soviet
Union demonstrating "the aggressive impulses of an evil empire."[53]

These words and the policy they informed seem, at first glance,
incompatible with the president's remarks at the summit meeting with
Mikhail Gorbachev, the new Soviet leader, in November 1985. How are
we to explain the transformation that his view of Soviet-American relations appeared to have undergone in the intervening thirty months?

One possibility is, of course, that although his words had changed,
his views had not. As he himself reminded the world after Geneva, he
was, after all, an actor. How are we to tell from his performance just what
he believes? This hypothesis is supported by his skillful adaptation to the
audiences he addresses. The "evil empire" speech was, after all, delivered, along with fundamentalist positions on abortion and school prayer,
to a fire-and-brimstone audience; to the British Parliament he spoke of
democracy; and smiles, moderate optimism, and the prospects for arms
control were appropriate for his first encounter with Mikhail Gorbachev.

But any attempt to dismiss the change in rhetoric as insignificant is
contradicted by the fact that Ronald Reagan does after all have deeply
engrained convictions — including some that concern the Soviet Union.
To be sure, they may often be based on anecdotes and gut feelings; they
may come across as one-liners and are at times wide of the mark if not
totally false (his remark that there was no word for "freedom" in Russian
was but one example of this genre); and some of his beliefs may not be
compatible with others (such as the insistence on both the seriousness of
the Soviet "threat" and the impending removal of communism to the ash
heap of history). His words, moreover, there and elsewhere, were bound
to contribute to a change of political climate that affected the substance of
Soviet-American relations. To be sure, some of the earlier stereotypes
were promptly resurrected, and private comments made clear that, if
American policy had undergone a significant change, the president's
outlook had not. This was borne out by American behavior in the months
following the Geneva summit.

If then we must accept some change in United States policy as real, it
is best explained as the result of several mutually reinforcing trends.
Among these — as we saw earlier — were public opinion in this country, pressure from Congress, and the role of America's allies. These had
already been important in reversing the initial view toward negotiating
with Moscow. Beyond this, as an astute observer has noted,[54]

> If our experience in recent years conveys one clear lesson, it is that the public will not support a policy that does not hold out the hope of improvement in our relationship with the Soviet Union, and that does not actively seek improvement. In this respect, as in so many others, there has been a marked change since the period of the classic cold war.

Moreover, 1984 was an election year, and there was a widespread perception — shared by some key figures in the White House — that the president needed to cultivate the image of a man of peace. All this, however, would suggest a reluctant and reactive accommodation rather than a change of perceptions and strategies. Certainly Reagan's opponent, Walter Mondale, had no patent recipes for dealing with the Soviet Union that would have forced Ronald Reagan to alter his stance. Interestingly, the same coalition — Congress, the Allies, some of the media, and public opinion — and some strenuous lobbying within the administration were also responsible for the shift back from the post-Geneva "hard line" policy (including the repudiation of SALT II limits, and the rejection of a moratorium on nuclear testing and of a comprehensive test ban treaty) to a seemingly more cooperative posture in mid-1986.

A second and probably more directly relevant set of changes concerned the president's entourage. As was earlier observed, the fortuitous installation of George Shultz in the State Department and, in late 1983, of Robert McFarlane as national security advisor (along with the appointment of Jack Matlock to replace Richard Pipes as senior expert on Soviet affairs in the National Security Council) exposed the president to senior foreign policy advisors who tended to view Soviet-American relations in less millennial or confrontational and thoroughly unideological terms. Although they were not known for great originality in devising grand strategy or novel initiatives, on the axis of proponents and opponents of negotiating with the Soviet Union, both tended to be proponents. Moreover, they were — each in his agency — prepared to rely on the advice of experts who, whatever their shortcomings and biases, made for a more "professional" approach to policymaking. Various observers stressed, in addition, the advice proffered by others — from Nancy Reagan to Richard Nixon — which apparently favored exploring an accommodation with the Soviets.

No less important was the impact of situational factors, both real and perceived. One was the perceived improvement in the bargaining position of the United States, in large measure thanks to the military buildup and economic recovery under the Reagan administration. Whether the relative capabilities of the American armed forces or the health of the American economy had significantly improved was a matter of some dispute, but this question was irrelevant insofar as the argument was concerned: what mattered was the psychological dimension, which allowed the White House to claim credit for the allegedly dramatic change. To be sure, the essentialists would insist that strength meant you did not need to negotiate — an argument George Shultz and other officials would refute most explicitly. And if, at the outset, one major argument by the incoming administration had been to insist that talks with the Russians must be set aside until the United States has gained the requisite power to negotiate from a "position of strength," some White House and State Department officers now argued that indeed that time had come. An unexpected but most welcome argument could now be made that it had been the president's decision to proceed with research on a strategic defense system that had scared the Russians into returning to the bargaining table.

Administration officials did, in fact, point to precisely such factors to justify their new "policy of strength and negotiation" — the two-track equivalent of the formula adopted by NATO, years earlier, in regard to arms control. President Reagan, in the first address in which he spelled out the new approach, began by positing, "I believe that 1984 finds the United States in its strongest position in years to establish a constructive and realistic working relationship with the Soviet Union." Since it came into office, George Shultz declared,[55] the administration had "begun to recover lost ground and to move ahead":

> Our own economic recovery is well underway. . . . The much-needed modernization of Western defense capabilities is on track. . . . We have restored the relations of confidence and harmony with our key allies in Europe and Asia. . . . Most important, we have restored our own confidence in ourselves. We know that we are capable of dealing with our problems and promoting our interests and ideals in a complex and dangerous world. . . .

> We hold to the principle that America should not negotiate from a position of weakness, and this Administration has ensured that we need not face such a prospect. But we reject the view that we should become strong so that we need not negotiate.

Coincidentally or not, the same years had seen a measure of restraint in Soviet foreign policy the Reagan team had not anticipated. Particularly in the Third World, where the 1970s had seen a genuine extension of Soviet influence in Ethiopia, Angola, South Yemen and a perception of greater Soviet influence in Southeast Asia and the Caribbean, "no new dominoes fell." Although the conflict in Afghanistan continued, it was seen in Washington as a source of weakness and embarrassment for the Soviet leadership, just as Poland was. For these purposes it did not matter whether such Soviet restraint was due to a lack of opportunity, to a perception of heightened risks, or to domestic Soviet constraints. Certainly there was the feeling in Washington that the succession of successions to the top position in the Kremlin — from Brezhnev to Andropov to

Chernenko to Gorbachev — had seriously weakened Soviet policymaking at a time of possible crisis.

Gorbachev's accession in March 1985 was correspondingly hailed as creating new opportunities for Soviet-American talks. (A good case could have been made that the United States had, in fact, missed opportunities under his elderly, infirm, and ineffective predecessors, unless one argues that they could not have effectively "delivered" on any agreements reached with them.) A new generation of Soviet leaders was taking over; they were, it was believed, better trained, had fewer ideological "hang-ups," were determined to get things done, and were likely to be around for a long time. They could be expected to seek a stable international environment to effect the domestic transformations to which they seemed committed: All this strengthened the sense that the time was at last ripe for a Soviet-American summit.

Finally, institutional and bureaucratic factors should be mentioned. Once a "summit" was agreed upon and announced, a logic of preparations for it imposed deadlines, the need for negotiating positions, and a climate that favored American postures that not only legitimized sitting down with the Soviets — a far cry from the initial "political warfare" assumptions — but also explored the possibilities of agreement in a variety of policy areas, big and small. Above all, it forced closure — at least momentarily — on issues over which the bureaucracy had been deeply divided and unreconciled.

The sum total of the variables just sketched helps make more plausible the evolution of United States policy from the first to the second Reagan term. By the summer of 1983, quiet and unpublicized explorations were underway — with Reagan's personal approval — between the State Department and the Soviet Foreign Ministry, involving such relatively uncritical, unpolitical issues as the renewal of cultural exchange agreements and the opening of new consulates. It is impossible to say what they might have led to, for, on September 1, they were dramatically disrupted by the shooting down of the Korean jetliner KAL 007, with all 269 persons aboard, which had strayed into Russian territory near the Soviet island of Sakhalin. The shootdown itself, the bitterness and recrimination that followed, and the propaganda battle that accompanied preparations for the deployment of new American-made Pershing-2 and cruise missiles in Western Europe, contributed to the crisis in Soviet-American relations.[56] This deterioration was marked by one of the harshest pronouncements about the United States ever issued by the Kremlin, in this case over the name of Yuri Andropov, on September 27, 1983. It stated, in part[57]:

> Even if someone had illusions as to the possible evolution for the better
> in the policy of the American administration, the latest developments

have dispelled them. For the sake of its imperial ambitions, it is going so far that one begins to doubt whether it has any brakes preventing it from crossing the mark before which any sober-minded person would stop.

. . . In their striving to justify in some way their dangerous, inhuman policies, the same people pile heaps of slander on the Soviet Union, on socialism as a social system, with the tone being set by the President of the United States himself. One must say bluntly: it is an unattractive sight when, with a view of smearing the Soviet people, leaders of such countries as the United States resort to what amounts almost to obscenities alternating with hypocritical preaching about morals and humanism.

And after making some innovative proposals in regard to the limitation of "Euromissiles," presumably to forestall the deployment of new American weapons, before the end of the year the Soviet delegation walked out of the talks in Geneva.

The freeze in Soviet-American relations continued through the winter and spring. Professor Seweryn Bialer, back from high-level conversations in Moscow, reported worriedly that the Soviet leaders had "concluded that any attempt to improve relations [with the Reagan administration] would be futile" and that they might be tempted into more dangerous gambles.[58] The mood in Moscow was "very, very negative," Brent Scowcroft reported in April 1984; the atmosphere between the two countries was "as bad as it's been in my memory." Scowcroft, a "moderate," and recently the chairman of Reagan's Commission on Strategic Forces, had been rebuffed in his effort to deliver a personal letter from Reagan to Konstantin Chernenko, by-passing Foreign Minister Gromyko, whom some Washington analysts had identified as a "hard-liner" blocking better relations.[59] The hostile Soviet stance was highlighted by their decision to boycott the Olympic Games in Los Angeles in 1984. As the United States headed for the presidential elections of 1984, there was on the American side, too, little public expectation of any change in Soviet-American relations.

All this obscured important developments below the surface on both sides. In Moscow, both practitioners and academics were engaged in earnest, albeit unpublicized debates over the future direction of American foreign policy and the durability of the Reagan orientation. In Washington, meanwhile, President Reagan on January 16, 1984, delivered an address, "The U.S.-Soviet Relationship," which, in retrospect, marked a significant new departure.

The occasion for the speech was the opening of the thirty-four-nation European disarmament conference in Stockholm, for which Washington had no high expectations. The president's address contained the customary comments about Soviet aggressiveness and America's regained strength. But he went on to declare[60]:

> Deterrence is essential to preserve peace and protect our way of life, but deterrence is not the beginning and end of our policy toward the Soviet Union. We must and will engage the Soviets in a dialogue as serious and constructive as possible, a dialogue that will serve to promote peace in the troubled regions of the world, reduce the level of arms, and build a constructive relationship.

> Neither we nor the Soviet Union can wish away the differences between our two societies and our philosophies. But we should always remember that we do have common interests. . . . There is no rational alternative but to steer a course which I would call credible deterrence and peaceful competition.

Several circumstances made it easier for the White House to adopt this posture of reasonableness — and by implication, accord Moscow the mantle of legitimacy Reagan had repeatedly denied it. First, precisely because of the Soviet stance of unmitigated hostility it was possible for Reagan to appear, even in his new refrain, at the opposite end of the spectrum from the Soviets' behavior. Second, the overwhelming presence of lesser countries — allies and neutrals — in Stockholm made them the secondary addressees of the message, presumably looking for a silver lining. And third, it was the Soviets, after all, who had walked out of the arms reduction talks, and one subsidiary argument on the American side for bringing them back, one may suspect, was the administration's desire to prove that its tactics had worked.

Once adopted, the new theme remained. And when a few weeks later Chernenko took the place of the deceased Andropov, Reagan could declare, "We should find ways to work together to meet the challenge of preserving peace. Living in this nuclear age makes it imperative that we talk to each other, discuss our differences, and seek solutions to the many problems that divide us."[61]

The notion of a summit between Reagan and whoever the Soviet leader happened to be was raised repeatedly — by West German Chancellor Kohl in April 1983, for instance, and by various voices in the press who pointed out that Reagan was the first president in half a century not to have met with his Soviet opposite number.[62] But the conventional wisdom was that, as relations deteriorated, so did the chances of holding a summit (rather than promoting one to reverse and improve matters). It was not until the following year — the election year — that the idea was successfully taken up around the White House.[63] One public step was to arrange a meeting between Reagan and Soviet Foreign Minister Andrei Gromyko in the White House, the first such meeting during the Reagan presidency. Gromyko's White House visit also seemed to confirm that

Moscow had accepted Ronald Reagan's reelection as a foregone conclusion and recognized the need to work with the incumbent administration.

When in March 1985, Mikhail Gorbachev succeeded Konstantin Chernenko, the idea of a Reagan-Gorbachev summit promptly crept up again, with official and unofficial commentary distinctly more positive about the new Soviet leadership this time around.[64]

But even as the forthcoming summit was announced and government agencies began to prepare for it, the familiar Washington divisions over policy toward the Soviet Union again arose. Thus, the day before a major Reagan address on American-Soviet relations, Richard N. Perle expressed his "personal view" that the United States should no longer observe the nuclear force limits of SALT II, a view not then shared by Secretary of State Shultz or National Security Affairs Advisor McFarlane. Reagan's speech to the European Parliament was the subject of another struggle between McFarlane and White House Communications Director Patrick J. Buchanan.[65] McFarlane and Shultz disagreed sharply on whether the ABM treaty should be "narrowly" or "broadly" interpreted — an important issue in terms of the choice between unilateral "reinterpretations" and renunciations of prior agreements, as advocated by the hard-liners, and the need either to renounce programs that would violate the treaty or renegotiate treaties if the United States proceeded with its missile defense program, as urged by others.

Though a verbal compromise was deftly struck, the differences hardly went away. In particular, during the weeks leading up to the summit Secretary of Defense Weinberger chose to occupy a role that some would describe as sentinel, others as spoiler. All the more important was the decision not to include him in the American delegation to Geneva: From the first to the second Reagan administration the balance had shifted, and now Weinberger and Perle temporarily found themselves on the losing side of each argument, though not for want of trying. Weinberger returned repeatedly to the shooting of an American officer, Major Arthur F. Nicholson, by a Soviet soldier in East Germany, declaring that this "outrageous murder really testifies to the ruthlessness of the adversaries we face" and calling it "a profound lesson" for anyone "willing to give the Soviets the benefit of the doubt." He told a group he was addressing that Soviet strategy included "a sudden, crippling first strike" on America as "one of the ways in which they would try to carry out their move toward world domination."[66]

Until literally the eve of the departure for Geneva of the president and his vast party, the lobbying over arms control continued. We have a glimpse of the continuing lobbying from a paper "leaked" just before that date. In the letter accompanying the Defense Department report on alleged Soviet violations of arms control agreements, Weinberger[67] warns the president:

In Geneva you will almost certainly come under great pressure to do three things that would limit severely your options for responding to Soviet violations:

- One is to agree to continue to observe SALT II.
- The second is to agree formally to limit SDI research, development, and testing . . ..
- Third, the Soviets may propose communiqué or other language that obscures their record of arms control violations by referring to the "importance that both sides attach to compliance."

Any or all these Soviet proposals, if agreed to, would sharply restrict the range of responses to past and current Soviet violations available to us. . . .

By then others were shaping the Geneva agenda, and Ronald Reagan himself was about to take charge.

The Geneva "summit" of Ronald Reagan and Mikhail Gorbachev, November 19–21, 1985, was a remarkable event. To be sure, Shultz and his opposite number — Foreign Minister Edvard Shevardnadze, who had replaced Andrei Gromyko — and their staffs had sought to prepare the ground in the preceding weeks and days. Still, the cordial handshake at the final, public session, after the two men had spent more than fifteen hours face to face, climaxed a change of style and rhetoric and mood that had by no means been a foregone conclusion. As it happened, both leaders wanted their encounter to be a success: Each needed the other's tacit cooperation for his own political purposes.

If the meeting was short on tangible accomplishments, it did open the door to further "summits"; to officialdom on both sides it signaled a change of rhetoric; it served to reassure both sides' allies and neutrals alike; and it prompted, in the following months, both gestures — such as the New Year's greeting by Reagan on Soviet television and by Gorbachev on the American networks — and such substantive new departures as the Soviet arms reduction proposal of January 15, 1986, the slight loosening of trade restrictions in the months following the summit, and the exchange of spies and political prisoners a month later. Before long, however, both sides fell back to sparring for competitive advantage to a degree that threatened to negate the gains made at the summit. The months following the summit made clear that in Washington the mood could speedily be reversed. Moscow seized the initiative with a series of arms control proposals, and the White House responded with a virtually unbroken chain of charges about alleged Soviet treaty violations; rejections of Soviet proposals; and unilateral moves stressing American reliance on its own capabilities, such as the bombing of Libya, a Soviet client, and the announcement that the United States would no longer be bound by the limits negotiated in the (unratified) SALT II treaty of 1979.

At the same time the White House continued to press for a second summit, whereas the Kremlin sought evidence of progress on arms control before agreeing to one.

The post-Geneva period illustrated the fragility of improved Soviet-American relations as well as the continued infighting within the administration, especially over arms control.

Conclusions

Washington

As the Reagan presidency unfolds, surprising shifts as well as compelling continuities are apparent in its policies toward the Soviet Union. There is no indication of any change in the underlying assumptions of either the president or his close associates. The commitment to a continuing buildup of American military capabilities remains firm even as its prospects dim. The Kremlin remains the number one adversary. The support — part covert, part overt — provided to various insurgent forces against regimes the Reagan entourage considers surrogates of the Kremlin suggests a continuing determination to combat what the president referred to as the empire of evil. And during a voice check, assuming his radio's microphone to be turned off, he jokes, "My fellow Americans: I am pleased to tell you today that I've signed legislation that will outlaw Russia forever. We begin bombing in five minutes."[68]

For six years after assailing the SALT II treaty as a dangerous giveaway, the administration was still observing its provisions so long as Moscow did the same. After shying away from arms control negotiations, two years later the administration was deeply involved in talks about arms reduction and force deployment abroad — negotiations that (whatever the underlying motives on either side) for years were to be the principal, if barren, arena of Soviet-American interaction. The idea of an anti-Soviet "strategic consensus" in the Middle East, including both Israelis and Arabs, was quietly dropped as palpably naive. On Poland, hyperbolic American announcements yielded, after the proclamation of martial law, to a policy of restraint. The appointment of George P. Shultz as secretary of state eliminated some idle, and counterproductive, bravado. The departure of such essentialists as Richard V. Allen, Richard Pipes, and Jeane Kirkpatrick; the transfer of such others as Edwin Meese away from the White House and the foreign policy field; and the promotion of such pragmatic conservatives as Robert McFarlane and Paul Nitze betokened a shift of balance away from extremism. So did the exclusion of Caspar Weinberger from the Geneva delegation and the Pentagon's failure to carry the day, in 1985–86.

True, this greater pragmatism need not produce a lessening of militancy in foreign policy. The Reagan doctrine and SDI represented new efforts to increase American leverage over Soviet behavior, and the logic of SDI drove the White House to renounce or violate existing arms control agreements.

The general direction in which American policy evolved from 1981 to 1986 was toward greater pragmatism, but it was a trend marked by numerous zigzags and reversals. What accounts for the evolution of policy as well as the seeming contradictions, bureaucratic conflicts, and incoherence of policy that continue to this day?

The mind sets of the new policymakers encountered the reality of the world abroad, and it turned out that some of their prior beliefs did not fit. Some were plainly wrong; more often they were too simple-minded: Reality proved to be far more complex. As we have seen, the initial White House strategy was based on a "two-camp" view of the world, which was at best obsolete and at worst primitive. It was as misleading to exaggerate Soviet power and to underestimate its limits as it was to portray the Soviet system as hovering on the brink of collapse. It was as erroneous to view Soviet expansionism as inevitable and irreversible as it would have been to ignore it. The far right (like the extreme left) is attracted to a style of unilateralist crusading that enables it to dispense with the finer points and brings little knowledge of the outside world to the policy arena —and sees little need for it.

The lack of fit between prior beliefs and present reality generates several types of outcome. One is the disjunction between the articulated world view and foreign policy behavior. Indeed it would not be the first time in American foreign policy that its bark is worse than its bite. The ideological rhetoric has its political and psychological uses at home but need not inform all policy. Thus one can frequently observe a lack of fit or proportion between the verbal exhortations, the images of dire threat, of doom and gloom, and the comparatively modest action undertaken or recommended to cope with such calamities.

The dissonance between beliefs and reality can also produce tactical adaptation. The first years, until at least mid-1983, witnessed a good many instances of precisely such retreat and reluctant accommodation. The reversal in the arms control field must be seen, in the first place, as a response to pressures — from the allies, from the public, and from the media — and, in the second place, as a product of better information. It is not clear that at least among some of the key actors — although not all — the changes in policy reflect (or cause) a genuine change in underlying attitudes and assumptions.

Finally, as a policymaker comes to grips with reality, there is apt to occur a (sometimes unwitting or unwanted) learning process. Especially since 1983, this has led to the elaboration, in at least some areas, of more systematic alternative policies. Such learning has been especially noticeable among officials with little previous experience with foreign affairs. Moreover the ideological biases contained in the essentialist mind set tend to focus on a limited number of salient issues; policy problems of lower attention may typically be handled in more pragmatic fashion and may be open to less constrained learning.

What then are the dimensions of the changes that can be observed, both in Ronald Reagan and among his policy advisors, which would help us gauge any evolution of policy outcomes? It is impossible to say with certainty, but the following appears to be a fairly clear-cut pattern:

There is every indication that Ronald Reagan's underlying *normative commitments* to ideal goals and values have remained unchanged. His view of communism remains unaltered, as does his belief that the victory of freedom, as he sees it, is both essential and inevitable.

The same is substantially true of his *assumptions about the nature of the Soviet system* and Soviet-American relations in the long run. The Soviet system, to him, is evil, a failure, and a threat, and therefore the struggle with the Soviet Union remains both a moral and a vital military-political issue. Some of these assumptions may in fact change, but we have no evidence that they have done so.

There has been a change in the estimation of the *correlation of forces* — or, more simply, the balance of power — between the two camps. The administration sees the United States "standing tall" — that is, in a far stronger and healthier position, as the result, in large part, of the perceived increase in American military capabilities and economic performance as well as an improvement in public morale and will. Although for some officials this reduces the need and the urgency to strike deals or even to negotiate with the adversary, for others it puts the United States in a particularly advantageous position to pursue desired accords.

Finally, when it comes to specific *policy preferences*, changes have been both important and numerous. Policy toward the Soviet Union has inevitably been placed in a broader context where it must fit, as a large piece of a jigsaw puzzle, among a great many other pieces. The president and, perhaps even more, some of the figures around him who have a keen sense of politics — of trade-offs and the limits of the possible — have come to recognize the many constraints within which policy options are made and the many conflicting priorities — domestic, foreign, budgetary, and sequential — among which they must choose. Over the course of the two Reagan administrations, the relative salience of visible effectiveness has grown as a goal, and this has made for an instinctive effort to tailor policies more closely not only to desired but also to realistically possible outcomes. But it must be added that this has not always made for realistic options. It has not eliminated policy incoherence, nor has it silenced essentialist sentiments — for the same actors or contending ones — on the Washington scene.

The same gap between the desired and the possible pertains to the international environment. There are elements in the structure of the international system itself that limit the exercise of American power. The tendency of the Reagan administration has been to ignore the secular trend, thus reducing the ability of the United States to play a hegemonic role. The American preponderance after World War II was an aberration, bound to be altered as other economies (including those of the loser states Germany and Japan) worked their economic miracles, as the Third World began its faltering march to development, and as other powers acquired the hydrogen bomb and harnessed nuclear energy. If in the early years the United States had its way in the UN virtually all the time, in the UN of today with over 150 members, such a prospect would be illusory. Only to a small degree has this process been the result of Soviet actions.

The Reaganites harbor a deep nostalgia for hegemony and the belief that it can be restored by an act of will. The president's rhetoric reflects an intuitive assumption of the universality of American values; in the writings of neo-conservatives, the loss of hegemony becomes virtually an indictment of past policymakers for criminal negligence, or worse.

The fact remains that one major source of problems in American foreign policy, including policy toward the Soviet Union, is the gap between aspirations and capabilities, or at least our ability to act at a reasonable cost or risk. Afghanistan and Poland both exemplify cases of frustration, in large measure because of our inability to affect the outcome without assuming undue costs. Bringing objectives and capabilities into better balance must be a major strategic objective for the United States: It requires adjustments on both sides of the equation. The Reagan administration is committed to an increase in military capabilities (the economic universe proves to be far more recalcitrant), but it has also raised its foreign policy objectives so that the gap between the desired and the possible fails to shrink. In this sense, the foreign policies of the Reagan administration reveal a striking analogy to its budget policies: by expanding commitments beyond capabilities and failing to build a program around a consensus that can be sustained, they create a "deficit" that undercuts its larger objectives.

The mind sets of the new ideologues have encountered the reality of domestic politics, and here too there grew an awareness of the costs attached to the pursuit of some of their beliefs. It is in the nature of American politics that special interests and lobbies often distort or constrain or propel foreign policy in unexpected — and often unsound — directions. At times they may encourage grandstanding; at times, as in the lifting of the grain embargo and the decision not to reinstitute the draft, they may work against a tougher foreign policy. But in either case, domestic politics tends to undercut the coherence of policy. This is particularly true when, as in the Reagan administration, the choice of particular policies (for instance, economic warfare) to be successful requires a high degree of mobilization and coordination of domestic interest groups as well as foreign allies.

The lack of fit between commitments and constituency becomes especially troublesome politically when, as in this case, the political constituency is heterogeneous. If the farm vote applauded the lifting of the grain embargo, to the neo-conservatives it was only one of many tokens of the administration's suspected downhill slide from the peak of anti-Sovietism. Policy incoherence was well demonstrated when the White House reversed itself twice on the Siberian pipeline — imposing sanctions soon after a series of representations against "creeping Haigism" on the part of the New Right, and lifting them four months later when both their futility and the cost in conflict with the NATO allies became manifest.

The flip side of the administration's sensitivity to its domestic constituency is the fact that, especially before the appointment of George Shultz, the administration's foreign policymakers lacked experience in foreign affairs. It was characteristic of the Reagan wing of the Republican party — who were largely outsiders until 1980 — to have a paucity of competent foreign policy specialists. This was, and in large measure continues to be, particularly true of experts on the Soviet Union.

Beyond these traits, the administration has suffered from the unresolved and often fundamental differences in outlook among the many actors and bureaucracies dealing with Soviet affairs. What became clear over time, as it had not at the outset, was the unsettled — and often unsettling — ambiguity between essentialist and mechanistic orientations: whether ideological preconceptions guided American policy or pragmatic considerations prevailed; whether to use American assets to apply leverage on Moscow or to negotiate in search of formal agreements or to strive to isolate, pressure, and transform the Soviet system. Ultimately, there remains the administration's ambivalence over the incompatible goals of either striving for "victory" or "managing" Soviet-American relations.

In substance all this meant that there was no single coherent policy toward the Soviet Union. All too often different departments pursued uncoordinated policies that led in different directions; all too often there was backfighting and backbiting long after basic decisions were made; all too often basic policy decisions were not made at all, and changes in policy reflected changes in personnel and in the political balance among them. Given the relative vacuum of creative and authoritative thinking on the Soviet Union, a speech writer on Patrick Buchanan's staff accidentally may "make foreign policy" in drafting a presidential pronouncement. The departure of a single actor, such as Robert McFarlane, may tip the balance in favor of the Pentagon's civilian crusaders.

Some of the causes of seeming incoherence are not specific to this administration. The cycle in turnovers of administrations and key officials has meant that there is no continuity of institutional memory, a need every four years to reinvent the wheel, and friction between the executive and legislative branches. A good case can also be made that the functional differences — say, between State and Defense departments — often make for differences in policy preferences and that oftentimes the mechanism of the National Security Council, instead of resolving them, confuses them.[69] But institutional and other sources of incoherence rooted in the American political scene can be compounded by the policy process adopted by a given president. This president has typically, if unwittingly, made a virtue of irresolution and thus magnified the problems he has faced.

Moscow

In the last analysis the crucial test of the Reagan foreign policy is its effect on Moscow. And here, for several good reasons, we cannot be sure of the effect. We face the usual problems of assessing Soviet attitudes and behavior from very inadequate information and limited access to insiders. We face the additional problem of distinguishing short-term responses from the long-term impact on Soviet elite perceptions and policies. Even if a desired change in some aspect of Soviet behavior does occur, it is methodologically next to impossible to demonstrate the extent to which American policy was a crucial precipitant or even a necessary precondition for it.

Thus if Soviet policy in the Third World has shown greater restraint in the 'eighties than in the 'seventies, it is not clear to what extent the causes of it are to be found in Moscow, in Washington, or in the Third World. If the Soviet government, after walking out on the arms control negotiations in Geneva, resumed the talks in a somewhat modified setting, we cannot tell to what extent this decision should be attributed to Soviet concern over the Reagan SDI. Initially, in launching the Star Wars program, the president surely never even envisaged using it as a tool to prompt the Soviet delegation's return to Geneva. Finally, an assessment of Soviet policy during these years is further complicated by the sequence of successions in the Kremlin, including shifts of officials who responded variously to American signals and policies, such as the replacement of Andrei Gromyko by Edvard Shevardnadze. With all due allowance, then, for the unknown and the contingent, we must set out the most plausible case the available data permit.

The Gorbachev era ushered in a far-reaching reassessment of Soviet domestic and foreign policy. It also entailed a number of new departures in substance as well as in style. It is too early to assess their total scope and impact, but not too early to inquire into their origins. In brief, although this reassessment and the implementation of the changes to which it has led have been facilitated by an international environment of which American policy is a significant part, fundamentally they are the outcome of internal Soviet developments.

This reassessment may best be seen as the product of several converging trends already visible in the last Brezhnev years but increasingly visible in the early 'eighties. Among other things, these trends served to undermine the Soviet leaders' confidence that the international "correlation of forces" continued to shift to Moscow's advantage.

First and foremost were the enormous strains produced by the slowing growth rate of the Soviet economy. Given simultaneous commitments to growth in investments, defense, and consumer welfare, the gap between perceived needs and available resources was rapidly widening, leading to painful choices among competing priorities. The economic slowdown, coupled with increasing instances of poor management, corruption, and incompetence, sharpened the widespread concern of the Soviet elite over the ultimate viability of the Soviet economic model at a time when the gap between its output and that of the West was widening instead of shrinking, when China was repudiating the Soviet model, and when Japan was overtaking the Soviet Union as "number two."

An increasingly stark perception of the extent of Soviet technological backwardness added a sense of urgency to the perceived need for change. If the pipeline controversy had highlighted the importance of Western technology, and the grain embargo the inadequacies of Soviet agriculture, the SDI was bound to sharpen the fear that the technological and communications revolution threatened to pass the Soviet Union by. The nuclear catastrophe at Chernobyl in 1986 would serve to reinforce Soviet concern.

In the 1980s, the Soviet Union also faced a less benign international environment. Events in Poland provided visible evidence of the vulnerabilities of its East European empire and the realization that reducing its costs might well threaten its stability and the certainty of control. In the Third World, the Soviet Union's military and economic support had produced dubious and transient gains in areas it could not control, while jeopardizing, in the view of some critics, the more important relationship with Washington. Events in Iran and Afghanistan increased instability and uncertainty close to Soviet borders. Even before the Reagan presidency, some Soviet scholars and analysts had expressed pessimism about Third World developments in arguing for Soviet retrenchment and reassessment of its policy.[70] Finally, the collapse of detente made it clear — or should have — that the assumptions underlying the general line of Soviet foreign policy in the 1970s were shattered along with it.

All these problems were compounded by the vacuum at the top of the Soviet power pyramid. The virtual immobilization of the late Brezhnev years and the near-paralysis during the ensuing interregnum had, in retrospect, a devastating impact on the Kremlin's ability to respond creatively and effectively to these challenges, which demonstrated the failure of previous policies. Beneath the surface there was evidence of growing anxiety, a mounting sense of urgency, and a building pressure for change; but at the top, the same old hands still controlled the key levers of policy and responded — in knee-jerk fashion — as they had been accustomed to doing over the years.

There had been evidence, for some time, that at least two different tendencies (and perhaps more) were vying for support and endorsement by academic analysts and policymakers in Moscow. They used different images to describe the United States, different adjectives to characterize American policy, and presumably also prompted different Soviet responses.

For perhaps a year, Soviet experts seemed somewhat uncertain over how to respond to Ronald Reagan's election. Soviet "Americanists" were initially divided over the likely policy of the new administration. Some invoked the Nixon precedent of an ardent anticommunist converted by pragmatic need into a partner of sorts; others welcomed an end to the unpredictability of the Carter years; not a few took the president and his spokesmen at their word and worried about the prospects.

By late 1981, the confrontational rhetoric and policies of the Reagan administration appeared to have persuaded the leading Soviet analysts that "the USA is again acting as an unreliable partner with whom one cannot have any dealings on a long-term basis."[71] There was rising concern that "the present Washington leadership . . . is trying to attain a one-sided military superiority over the Soviet Union. . . . All positive gains have been reversed."[72] Whereas some blamed the administration itself, others saw the Reagan policy as the expression of a more organic, fundamental, and perhaps more lasting orientation of American politics. By the fall of 1983, under an ailing Yuri Andropov and amidst heightened fear of a military conflict, the Kremlin professed to have reached the conclusion that serious dealings with the United States were not possible. One could no longer have any "illusions as to the possible evolution for the better in the policy of the American administration."[73]

This time, however, the confrontational Soviet foreign policy backfired. The harsh campaign against the deployment of "Euromissiles" — with the threat to erect "a palisade of missiles" across Europe — was particularly counterproductive, as was its crude interference in the West German elections. It served to antagonize and unite Europeans against it; the Soviet threat to walk out at Geneva left Moscow no alternative but to do so when the campaign failed. The new missile deployments in Eastern Europe generated tensions within the Warsaw Pact; and Soviet pressure on its clients — particularly the East Germans — dashed efforts at bridge-building with the West, much to the resentment of several East European regimes. Soviet behavior strengthened the cohesion of the Western alliance and helped to obtain additional backing for U.S. defense spending and to gain NATO acquiescence for tightening the ban on technology transfers to the East.

The belief that the Gromyko policy had led the Soviet Union into a foreign policy dead end was gaining in Moscow at a time when the succession struggle in the Kremlin was well underway and, as so frequently happens, the power contest overlapped the struggle between contending policy orientations. Though not all critics of the old line were in agreement among themselves, the growing sentiment — particularly among the younger cadres and the specialists — was that Soviet policy at home and abroad, economic as well as military, needed to be fundamentally rethought.

Gorbachev's accession — behind the scenes, in the latter part of 1984 and early 1985, and then in the open, after Chernenko's death — marked the ascendancy of this tendency. Indeed, along with a major turnover of personnel in key positions — including the replacement of the foreign minister — and new initiatives in economic policy, the period since his accession has brought significant changes in the substance as well as style of Soviet foreign policy. In Soviet-American relations, the new initiatives have marked the rejection of the Soviet essentialist position (to use the labels employed for their American analogs) by those who believed the superpower relationship had to be "managed." As if responding, belatedly, to Andropov's statement of 1983, Gorbachev declared that the existence of the United States was a fact: The Soviet Union had to live with it. Fundamental changes in economic organization and performance were critical to the effective ability of the Soviet Union to function as a superpower, for sustaining internal stability as well as its global role. A stable international environment, Gorbachev seemed to be arguing, was very much a part of the setting needed to proceed with internal reforms. And the pressure was greater than ever to avoid a further dramatic escalation of the arms race, including an exceptionally costly weapons research program requiring scarce advanced technology. It was not sheer rhetoric that made Gorbachev conclude his interview with *Time* before the Geneva summit with these words,[74] after dwelling on the reforms he wished to undertake at home,

> I don't remember who, but somebody said that foreign policy is a continuation of domestic policy. If that is so, then I ask you to ponder one thing: If we in the Soviet Union are setting ourselves such truly grandiose plans in the domestic sphere, then what are the external conditions that we need to be able to fulfill these domestic plans? I leave the answer to that question with you.

In this light, the Geneva summit was important for Gorbachev in laying the foundation for the changes he was about to introduce. It strengthened his hand in the ongoing debates within the Soviet establishment, where some members continued to oppose a policy that would eschew the habitual confrontational and ideological responses.

Where does American foreign policy fit into these developments? In all likelihood, the United States unwittingly sharpened Soviet elite commitments to overcoming technological backwardness and economic lag. The SDI may have added a military dimension to this argument by reinforcing the argument of the "reformers" that what was needed was no longer "quantitative competition" with the West — over tons of steel produced or lignite mined — but rather a "qualitative" leap in Soviet science and technology. No doubt Moscow has felt compelled to attempt both to match American efforts under the heading of the SDI and to offset or neutralize its possible effects.[75] But it is likely that the major effect was to step up the pressure in favor of effective arms reduction agreements.

More broadly, Gorbachev has brought a new dynamism to Soviet foreign policy in an effort to improve relations with a broad range of states in Europe and Asia — most notably China — and to place the United States on the defensive with a barrage of proposals aimed at the reduction of nuclear weapons. While arms agreements would benefit the Soviet Union, Gorbachev's strategy also stands to reap significant gains for the Soviet image and standing if negotiations with Reagan fail to culminate in agreement.

To date there is no evidence that the application of the Reagan Doctrine in the Third World has had any salutary impact on Soviet conduct or risk-taking. Despite claims that the "liberation" of Grenada provided an object lesson to Moscow to keep hands off, in fact, the new Soviet policy of restraint in the Third World has reflected primarily an independent appreciation of the limits of revolutionary developments there and their relative marginality to Soviet concerns. By contrast, American behavior in the Mediterranean — first intervention and then withdrawal of the Marines from Lebanon; the erratic conduct vis-à-vis Qaddafi's Libya; repeated reversals in Middle Eastern negotiations — must have raised questions in Moscow about American wisdom and resolve and may well have demonstrated to Moscow the limited predictability and rationality of American foreign policy, the limited American understanding of world affairs, and the limits of American power, at least in areas remote from the United States.

American behavior was not one of the primary inputs that produced the foreign policy outcomes under the Gorbachev regime. But it may well be that the image of firmness, power, and decisiveness — never mind the reality — emanating from Washington contributed to the atmosphere in which these, and related, changes took place.

Some public figures will no doubt propound the view that it was the administration's "toughness" that brought Moscow around. It will be well to remember that, insofar as it has rested on unrealistic assumptions about the vulnerability of the Soviet system and about the costs and limits of American power, that policy encouraged a mistaken belief that the United States was in a position to force a major reorientation of Soviet priorities or even to effect a serious breakdown of the Soviet system. To the extent that it reflected a deeply rooted American propensity to search for easy panaceas, it perpetuated costly oscillations of American foreign policy. To the extent that it widened the gap between ambitions and capabilities, it increased the risk of disillusionment and policy instability and impeded the formation of a stable domestic foreign policy consensus. And to the extent that it substituted rhetoric for policy, it risked letting slip a real opportunity to shape a strategy for managing the Soviet-American competition that — except for a nuclear showdown — will continue to be with us for decades to come.

It was not American "toughness" that brought about a shift in Soviet foreign policy; nor were earlier Soviet moves toward a more conciliatory policy (in 1959 and in 1969–72) produced by a harder American line. On the contrary, the Reagan administration unwittingly facilitated the shift in Soviet foreign policy by indicating that it was itself prepared to move toward a more collaborative stance. Such an American posture was a necessary but not a sufficient and surely not a decisive condition for the changes in the Soviet line toward the United States.

It has been painfully difficult for the Reagan administration to reconcile the diverse impulses and perspectives in its own midst on international relations, on the Soviet Union, and on arms control. It has failed to hammer out a coherent and realistic strategy to deal with the USSR. It bought time and opportunity by going to Geneva. It remains unclear how it will use them.

"Reagan and the Russians: American Policy Toward the Soviet Union" was written for this volume. Copyright © 1987 by Alexander Dallin and Gail W. Lapidus. The authors wish to express their thanks to Mathew Nosanchuk for his assistance with research for this chapter.

Notes

1. See, in particular, Stanley Hoffmann, *Primacy or World Order* (New York: McGraw-Hill, 1978).
2. Among the voluminous and controversial literature on the origins of the Cold War, see John L. Gaddis, *The United States and the Origins of the Cold War* (New York: Columbia University Press, 1972); Charles Gati, ed., *America and Russia: From Cold War Confrontation to Coexistence* (New York: Thomas Y. Crowell, 1971); Vojtech Mastny, *Russia's Road to the Cold War* (New York: Columbia University Press, 1979); Daniel Yergin, *The Shattered Peace* (Boston: Houghton Mifflin, 1980). See also Mark Garrison and Abbott Gleason, eds., *Shared Destiny* (Boston: Beacon Press, 1985); and Raymond L. Garthoff, *Detente and Confrontation* (Washington, D.C.: The Brookings Institution, 1985).
3. See Gati, op. cit.; John L. Gaddis, "Containment: A Reassessment," *Foreign Affairs*

(July 1977); and Gaddis, *Strategies of Containment* (New York: Oxford University Press, 1982).

4. On NSC 68 (which appears in *Foreign Relations of the United States, 1950*, I, pp. 237–292), see Samuel F. Wells, Jr., "Sounding the Tocsin: NSC 68 and the Soviet Threat," *International Security* (1979), Vol. 4, No. 2, pp. 116–158; also Yergin, op. cit., pp. 401ff.

5. Some approximation of it may be found in the arguments made by Secretary Kissinger at the time of the debate over the Jackson-Vanik amendment (rather than in his later comments); and in Marshall D. Shulman, "Toward A Philosophy of Coexistence," *Foreign Affairs* (October 1973). See also Lawrence T. Caldwell and William Diebold, *Soviet-American Relations in the 1980's* (New York: McGraw-Hill, 1981); and Dan Caldwell, *American-Soviet Relations From 1947 to the Nixon-Kissinger Grand Design* (Westport, CN: Greenwood Press, 1981).

6. See, e.g., Robert Legvold, "Containment Without Confrontation," *Foreign Policy* (Fall 1980), No. 40.

7. Most efforts to differentiate conflicting orientations postulate dichotomous ones. In simplest form, this is the cleavage between left and right, soft and hard, or dove and hawk. In the recent, more sophisticated versions, this is Daniel Yergin's contrast between what he calls the "Yalta school" and the "Riga school" or Robert Osgood's contrast between what he calls "Analysis A" and "Analysis B."

According to Yergin, the advocates of the "Riga axioms" saw the Soviet Union as a revolutionary state committed to a drive for worldwide mastery and to ideological warfare; the logic of their views, at the end of World War II, led to the dominant idiom of the Cold War. The "Yalta axioms," by contrast, tended to depict the Soviet Union as a great power, different only in degree from other great powers, and correspondingly played down the role of communist ideology as a source of Soviet behavior abroad, as well as the foreign policy consequences of domestic Stalinism. See Yergin, *The Shattered Peace*.

According to Osgood's "Analysis B," the Soviet Union is relentlessly expansionist, out of an inner compulsion rooted in one or more of the following: Communist ideology, which moves the Soviet elite; the totalitarian nature of the system, which requires expansion; a search for legitimacy at home, for which the regime strives by adventures abroad. According to this view, the Soviet leadership does have a grand strategic design, which it seeks to implement; it is increasingly prepared to use armed force to advance its objectives. "Analysis A," by contrast, sees the Soviet regime as pragmatic, opportunist, increasingly conservative but expansionist, seeking status and security abroad. Although Soviet and American objectives are likely to come into conflict, they can probably be compromised. In Osgood's astute analysis, "A" permits disaggregating the conflict so as to deal with issues one by one; "B" sees the relationship as a zero-sum game, a seamless web. See Robert E. Osgood et al., *Containment, Soviet Behavior, and Grand Strategy* (Berkeley: Institute of International Studies, 1981).

These labels, and similar ones used by others, do capture a real and profound split in American perceptions. Yet in our view, this dichotomous framework fails to differentiate adequately among the three distinct and significant perspectives we use, as discussed in the text. For a later, variant typology, see Graham T. Allison et al., eds., *Hawks, Doves and Owls: An Agenda for Avoiding Nuclear War* (New York: Norton, 1985).

8. For earlier variants and more detailed discussions of the characteristics of these three models, see William Welch, *American Images of Soviet Foreign Press* (New Haven: Yale University Press, 1970); William Zimmerman, "Containment and the Soviet Union," in Gati, ed., *Caging the Bear*, pp. 85–108; and Lawrence T. Caldwell and Alexander Dallin, "U.S. Policy Toward the Soviet Union," in Oye, Rothchild, and Lieber,

eds., *Eagle Entangled* (New York: Longman, 1979), especially pp. 215–219. For a sophisticated effort to differentiate several Soviet images of the United States and congruent policy preferences, see Franklyn Griffiths, "The Sources of American Conduct: Soviet Perspectives and Their Policy Implications," *International Security* (Fall 1984), Vol. 9, No. 2, pp. 3–48.

9. For an able discussion contrasting the commitment to conflict termination (either by accommodation on the left, or by victory on the right) with conflict management (again, with soft and hard variants), see John Van Oudenaren, *U.S. Leadership Perceptions of the Soviet Problem Since 1945* (Rand Corp., 1982, Doc. R-2843-NA).

10. According to one of the more imaginative publicists of the neoconservative camp, Norman Podhoretz, if the assumptions on which detente was based were not abandoned, ". . . it would signify the final collapse of an American resolve to resist the forward surge of Soviet imperialism. In that case, we would know by what name to call the new era . . . .: the Finlandization of America, the political and economic subordination of the United States to superior Soviet power." (Norman Podhoretz, *The Present Danger* (New York: Simon & Shuster, 1980), p. 12.

11. The *New York Times*, November 23, 1982.

12. In the words of Norman Podhoretz, one of the most articulate spokesmen for this approach, "I think if present trends continue, there may be a Cuban missile crisis in reverse in the Persian Gulf. . . . Then [the Soviet Union] will be in a position to dictate terms to almost everyone in the world, including us. . . ." (Podhoretz, *Book Digest* [December 1980], p. 30). Prominent members of the Committee on the Present Danger included Paul H. Nitze, Eugene Rostow, Richard Pipes, William J. Casey, Jeane Kirkpatrick, and Richard N. Perle, all of whom would join the new administration. For a fuller list, see Robert Scheer, *With Enough Shovels* (New York: Random House, 1982), pp. 144–146.

13. Leslie Gelb, "The Mind of the President," *The New York Times Magazine*, October 6, 1985.

14. Podhoretz, "The Neo-Conservative Anguish Over Reagan's Foreign Policy," *The New York Times Magazine*, May 2, 1982. See also George Will's columns, e.g., *Newsweek*, January 18 and June 21, 1982.

15. See Joseph P. Nye, ed., *The Making of America's Soviet Policy* (New Haven: Yale University Press, 1984).

16. *The Wall Street Journal*, June 3, 1980. Conscious of the fact that this statement constituted a gaffe, the presidential speech writers inserted in his address to the United Nations a different statement: "We look around the world and see rampant conflict and aggression. There are many sources of this conflict — expansionist ambitions, local rivalries, the striving to obtain justice and security." (*New York Times*, June 18, 1982.)

17. The *New York Times*, January 30, 1981. In a subsequent explanation, Reagan attributed Soviet immorality to the fact that Marxist-Leninists do not believe in an afterlife.
    For other analyses of the first years of the Reagan administration, see Strobe Talbott, *The Russians and Reagan* (New York: Vintage, 1984); and Seweryn Bialer and Joan Afferica, "Reagan and Russia," *Foreign Affairs* (Winter 1982–83), pp. 249–271.

18. The *New York Times*, March 5, 1981.

19. William W. Kaufmann, *A Reasonable Defense* (Washington, D.C.: The Brookings Institution, 1986), p. 25.

20. See, e.g., the "Decade of Neglect" controversy, in *International Security* (Fall 1985), Vol. 10, No. 2, pp. 3–83.

21. Concerns were compounded by massive cost overruns, evidence of corruption, inefficiencies in the procurement system, and interservice rivalries, so that the issue of Pentagon reform came to rival that of military spending in public attention.

22. Secretary of Defense, *Annual Report to the Congress,* FY 1986 (Washington, D.C.: U.S. Government Printing Office, 1985), p. 7.

23. See William W. Kaufmann, *A Reasonable Defense* (Washington, D.C.: The Brookings Institution, 1986); on arms control, Strobe Talbott, *Deadly Gambits* (New York: Knopf, 1984); Garthoff, op. cit.; and Michael R. Gordon, "U.S.-Soviet Arms Control Negotiations: Nuclear and Space Weapons," *AEI Foreign Policy and Defense Review* (1985), Vol. 5, No. 2, pp. 21–43.

24. As the State Department put it, "Our economic or trade relations with the Communist world, and particularly with the countries of the Warsaw Pact, have a different dimension from our economic relations elsewhere. Economic relationships with these countries cannot be divorced from our broad political-security objectives. U.S. economic policies must support the overriding foreign policy goal of deterring Soviet adventurism, redressing the military balance between the West and the Warsaw Pact, and strengthening the Western Alliance." (U.S. Congress, Joint Economic Committee, *East-West Commercial Policy: A Congressional Dialog with the Reagan Administration,* February 16, 1982, p. 22).

25. See, for example, the statement of Myer Rashish, Under Secretary of State for Economic Affairs, before the Senate Foreign Relations Committee's Subcommittee on International Economic Policy, September 16, 1981.

26. For the views of Richard Pipes, see his *Survival Is Not Enough* (New York: Simon & Schuster, 1984). See also Walter C. Clemens, "Intellectual Foundations of Reagan's Soviet Policy: The Threadbare Emperor," in Bernard Rubin, ed., *When Information Counts: Grading the Media* (Lexington, MA: Lexington Books, 1984).

    The rationale for such an approach is spelled out in Carl Gershman, "Selling Them the Rope: Business and the Soviets," *Commentary* (April 1979), Vol. 67, No. 4, pp. 35–45. Gershman's critique of leverage deserves to be cited:

    > "Economic diplomacy" is no substitute for a policy of military deterrence and common sense should dictate that anything the Russians want badly enough to forego opportunities for expansion is probably something they should not have in the first place. A policy of controls . . . would not be tied to politics, but . . . could in the long run limit the Soviet Union's ability to threaten the security of the West.

    A more sophisticated treatment is offered in Thomas A. Wolf, "Choosing a U.S. Trade Strategy Towards the Soviet Union," U.S. Congress, Joint Economic Committee, *Soviet Economy in the 1980's: Problems and Prospects* (Washington, D.C.: U.S. Government Printing Office, 1982), Pt. 2.

    Critics have argued that East-West trade occupies too limited a place in total Soviet imports to make the Soviet Union seriously vulnerable to efforts at economic warfare; that except for grain, its supplies are too diversified to make a total embargo possible; and that even if economic pressure could have an effect on Soviet performance, it is more likely to be detrimental than helpful to Western interests. See, e.g., Ed Hewett in *The Washington Post,* July 16, 1982. For an excellent analysis of leverage and denial strategies, see Abraham S. Becker, *Economic Leverage on the Soviet Union in the 1980s* (Rand Corp., 1984, Doc. R-3127-USDP).

27. In August 1981, the president announced a one-year extension of the Soviet-American grain agreement and increased the quantity the Soviet Union would be allowed to purchase. In August 1982, he extended the agreement for another year but resisted farm state pressures to negotiate a new long-term pact. In October 1982, two weeks before the mid-term elections, Reagan appealed to the farm vote by offering the Soviet Union an opportunity to purchase up to 23 million tons of grain on terms that for some

six months would be exempted from any new future sanctions against the Soviet Union.

28. Cf. Thierry Wolton, *Le KGB en France* (Paris: Grasset, 1986), and Philip Hanson, "New Light on Soviet Industrial Espionage," Radio Liberty Research Bulletin RL 36/86, January 20, 1986.

29. The effort to limit scientific contact embroiled the administration in a controversy with the scholarly community, which led to the appointment of a National Academy of Sciences panel on communication and national security. For its report, see *Scientific Communication and National Security* (New York: National Academy of Sciences Press, 1982).

30. Thane Gustafson, *Selling the Russians the Rope? Soviet Technology Policy and U.S. Export Controls* (Rand Corp., 1981, Doc. R-2649-ARPA), p. 4.

Critics have argued that the administration has overstated the degree of Soviet dependence on Western technology and that its case rests on faulty assumptions about the impact of Western technology on the Soviet economy. The diversion of dual-use technologies from civilian to military purposes is more complex than is suggested; technological imports do not necessarily free domestic resources but may require additional investments to exploit them. The Soviet system is not, on the whole, able to assimilate new technologies effectively and rapidly. And it has been argued, the costs of proposed controls far outweigh their possible benefits. Among many studies, see in particular Philip Hanson, *Trade and Technology in Soviet-Western Relations* (New York: Columbia University Press, 1981); and U.S. Congress, Joint Economic Committee, *Issues in East-West Commercial Relations* (Washington, D.C.: U.S. Government Printing Office, 1979), Pt. I.

31. See Angela E. Stent, "East-West Economic Relations and the Western Alliance," in Bruce Parrott, ed., *Trade, Technology and Soviet-American Relations* (Bloomington, IN: Indiana University Press, 1985).

32. As Senator Jake Garn graphically put it in *The Wall Street Journal*, May 20, 1982:

> The pipeline project . . . will provide the Soviet Union with a much-needed boost in foreign-exchange earnings, help the Soviets maintain their control over Eastern Europe, bail the Soviets out of serious energy and economic difficulties, expose West European banks to a heightened risk of financial ruin, and grant Moscow large-scale economic and political influence over Western European affairs that could sap the vitality from the NATO alliance. In return, the Western Europeans get the privilege of turning over to the Soviets billions of dollars in technology, goods, and equipment, paid for almost entirely by Western loans that are secured by as yet unrealized energy supplies sold at some unknowable market price in the future. All this so that our major allies can become dependent for up to 25 percent of their natural gas supplies on the country that didn't hesitate to cut off energy shipments to Yugoslavia in 1948, to Hungary and Israel in 1956, to Czechoslovakia in 1968, and that used its energy leverage over Poland in 1981.

For a more balanced treatment of the pipeline issue, see Angela Stent, *Soviet Energy and Western Europe* (Washington Papers, no. 90) (New York: Praeger, 1982), and her *From Embargo to Ostpolitik . . . 1955–1980* (New York: Cambridge University Press, 1981); John P. Hardt and Kate S. Tomlinson, "Economic Interchange with the USSR in the 1980's," *California Seminar on International Security and Foreign Policy* (April 1982); Jonathan Stern, *Soviet Natural Gas Development to 1990* (Lexington, MA: Lexington Books, 1980); and Jonathan Stern, "Specters and Pipe Dreams," *Foreign Policy* (Fall 1982), No. 48, pp. 21–36.

33. The Director of Central Intelligence, William Casey, for example, made frequent reference to a CIA study which had concluded that the gains made by Western firms from the sale of equipment and technology did not outweigh the Western military expenditures needed to overcome Warsaw Pact capabilities derived from the acquisition of Western technology. ("Soviet Acquisition of Western Technology," April 1982.) An updated version published in September 1985, "Soviet Acquisition of Militarily Significant Western Technology," did not, however, clearly differentiate between the value of technologies acquired through illegal and those acquired through legal means.

34. In May 1983, in a partial concession to the concerns of the Reagan administration, the communiqué of the seven heads of state included a statement that "East-West economic relations should be compatible with our security interests," but the expansive American definition of security continued to be resisted by the allies as excessively broad and overemphasizing the military dimension at the expense of the economic.

35. For a detailed description of the Allied studies, see John P. Hardt and Donna Gold, "East-West Commercial Relations: The Western Alliance Studies" (Congressional Research Service, Library of Congress, Issue Brief no. 83036, 1983). A summary of the findings is in Angela Stent, "Technology Transfers in East-West Trade: The Western Alliance Studies," *AEI Foreign Policy and Defense Review*, (1985), Vol. 5, No. 2.

    The issues that have remained unresolved include (1) whether to include "disembodied" as well as "embodied" technology (that is, for instance, computers only or also software and blueprints); (2) whether to tighten controls over exports to non-communist Third World countries; (3) the distribution of licences to cover multiple shipments by an American company to a foreign customer and American efforts to compel reports on such customers. Since the United States has been unable to get its allies to agree to more restrictive rules, it has begun to place more restrictions on trade with them.

36. Cf. Zbigniew Brzezinski, "The Future of Yalta," *Foreign Affairs* (Winter 1984–85); and Secretary Shultz's testimony before the Senate Foreign Relations Committee, January 31, 1985, in *Department of State Bulletin* (March 1985), p. 15.

37. Raymond L. Garthoff, "Eastern Europe in the Context of U.S.-Soviet Relations," in Sarah M. Terry, ed., *Soviet Policy in Eastern Europe* (New Haven: Yale University Press, 1984), p. 318.

38. Cf. U.S. Congress, Joint Economic Committee, *East-West Commercial Policy*, pp. 4, 13.

39. By 1981 the six East European countries of the Soviet bloc had accumulated a net debt of roughly sixty billion U.S. dollars to the West, of which just over five billion was owed to the United States. Poland accounted for some twenty-two billion of this total. (Wharton EFA, "Centrally Planned Economies Current Analysis," April 27, 1982).

40. Henry Kissinger, "Poland's Lessons for Mr. Reagan," *New York Times*, January 17, 1982.

41. Arguments in favor of default were presented in testimony before the Senate Appropriations Committee Subcommittee on Foreign Operations, among others, by Felix Rohatyn. The administration position was defended by Assistant Secretary of State Robert Hormats. A more technical analysis of the consequences of declaring the Polish debt in default is found in Wharton EFA, "Centrally Planned Economies Current Analysis," February 12 and May 17, 1982.

42. American sanctions in response to the proclamation of martial law included the suspension or cancellation of a number of exchange agreements with the Soviet Union, and the cancellation of airline landing rights and of fishing rights previously granted to Poland and the termination of Export-Import Bank insurance for credits granted to Poland. The United States did not cancel Soviet-American foreign minister talks,

arms control negotiations, or participation in multilateral conferences attended by both the United States and the Soviet Union.

43. See the discussion in S. Terry, ed., op. cit.

44. Secretary Haig's speech of April 27, 1982. See also the *New York Times*, May 30, 1982.

45. *New York Times*, June 9, 1982.

46. See also President Reagan's address before the UN General Assembly, September 24, 1984.

47. See the rather partisan account by Tom Bethell, "Propaganda Warts," *Harper's* (May 1982), pp. 19–25.

48. See, e.g., Lars-Erik Nelson, "Dateline Washington: Anti-Semitism and the Airwaves," *Foreign Policy* (Winter 1985–86), No. 61, pp. 180–196; and Josef Joffe and Dimitri Simes, "How America Backs Critics of Freedom," *Washington Post*, September 25, 1983. One set of American charges that backfired concerned the allegation that Soviet authorities tracking Americans in Moscow had used a carcinogenic chemical agent nicknamed "spy dust." Later the State Department was obliged to admit that the powder did "not pose a health hazard" (*New York Times*, February 15, 1986). Another source of embarrassment was the "yellow rain" controversy, in which the United States charged the Soviet Union with the introduction of a mysterious chemical weapon, which was ostensibly used in warfare in Southeast Asia and Afghanistan. The overwhelming weight of scientific evidence appears to be that it is "a phenomenon of nature, not of man." See, e.g., Thomas D. Seeley, "Yellow Rain," *Scientific American* (September 1985), pp. 128–137; and Peter Pringle, "Political Science," *Atlantic* (October 1985).

49. See the remarks of Deputy Assistant Secretary of State Mark Palmer to the U.S.-USSR Trade and Economic Council meeting, May 23, 1984, in *Department of State Bulletin* (July 1984), pp. 75–77. There is an implicit tension, not to say contradiction, between the view that foreign trade strengthens the Soviet system and the argument that "if the new [Soviet] leadership shows the foresight and the confidence to improve the human rights situation, our willingness to improve trade and other aspects of our relationship would be enhanced" (Under Secretary Michael Armacost, address, September 9, 1985, Department of State *Current Policy*, No. 736). On human rights policy generally, see Tamar Jacoby, "The Reagan Turnaround on Human Rights," *Foreign Affairs* (Summer 1986), pp. 1066–1086.

50. See also Alan Tonelson, "The Real National Interest," and Christopher Layne, "The Real Conservative Agenda," in *Foreign Policy* (Winter 1985–86), No. 61; Robert H. Johnson, "Exaggerating America's Stakes in Third World Conflicts," *International Security* (Winter 1985–86); Vol. 10, No. 3; and Jeremy Azrael and Stephen Sestanovich, "Superpower Balancing Acts," *Foreign Affairs* (1986), Vol. 64, No. 3, pp. 479–498.

    Under both Secretaries Haig and Shultz, the Soviet Union was charged with training, aiding, and abetting "international terrorism." Whatever the Soviet role in particular instances, especially in supporting armed "national liberation movements," the charges were so sweeping and indiscriminate that other United States government agencies were at times unable to support or substantiate them. (See, e.g., *New York Times*, February 9, 1981; *San Francisco Chronicle*, March 30 and April 27, 1981.) Yet over time the administration assumed a contradictory posture — on the one hand, recognizing full well that the upsurge of terrorism in the 1980s, such as the highjacking of aircraft and the shooting up of airports, was overwhelmingly the work of individuals and groups who were acting independently of the Soviet camp; on the other hand, quite emphatically accusing the Soviet Union of supporting and training such terrorists.

51. George P. Shultz, "Shaping American Foreign Policy," *Foreign Affairs* (Spring 1985):

p. 706. For a sensitive discussion, see Robert W. Tucker et al., *Intervention and the Reagan Doctrine* (Council on Religion and International Affairs, 1985).

52. President Reagan, "A Foundation for Enduring Peace," October 24, 1985, in *Department of State, Current Policy* No. 756.

53. The full text is in the appendix to Strobe Talbott, *The Russians and Reagan* (New York: Vintage, 1984), pp. 105–118.

54. Robert W. Tucker, "Toward a New Detente," *The New York Times Magazine*, December 9, 1984, p. 93.

55. George Shultz, "Managing the U.S.-Soviet Relationship Over the Long Term," address before the Rand/UCLA Center for the Study of Soviet International Behavior, Los Angeles, October 18, 1984, in *Department of State Bulletin* (December 1984), pp. 3–4. Note that the very terminology, "managing the U.S.-Soviet relationship," would not have been acceptable to the "essentialists" at the beginning of the first Reagan term.

56. See Alexander Dallin, *Black Box: KAL 007 and the Superpowers* (University of California Press, 1985).

57. The *New York Times*, September 29, 1983.

58. Seweryn Bialer, "Kremlin, Insecure, Might Increase Risks," *New York Times*, February 5, 1984.

59. The *New York Times*, April 18, 1984. For Soviet publications exemplifying this hostility to the United States, see e.g., Aleksandr N. Yakovlev, *Ot Trumena do Reigana* (Molodaia Gvardiia, 1984); and V. G. Shemiatenkov, *Bez peremirii i kompromissov* (Sovetskaia Rossiia, 1984).

60. Ronald Reagan, "The U.S.-Soviet Relationship," address made on January 16, 1984, in *Department of State Bulletin* (February 1984), pp. 1–4. In 1986, the government issued a collection of Reagan speeches on U.S.-Soviet Relations, which begins with the address of January 16, 1984 ([Ronald Reagan] *Realism, Strength, Dialogue* [Washington, D.C.: U.S. Government Printing Office, 1986]).

61. Ronald Reagan, "Relations with the U.S.S.R.," radio address to the nation on February 11, 1984, in ibid., April 1984, pp. 1–2. Later that year, Secretary Shultz in a carefully drafted discussion of American policy toward the Soviet Union stated: "We reject the view that we should become strong so that we need not negotiate. Our premise is that we should become strong so that we are able to negotiate. Nor do we agree with the view that negotiated outcomes can only sap our strength or lead to an outcome in which we will be the loser." In "Managing the U.S.-Soviet Relationship," loc. cit., p. 4. See also Shultz's testimony before the Senate Foreign Relations Committee, January 31, 1985, in ibid., March 1985, pp. 13–16.

62. See James Reston, "Why Not a Summit?" *New York Times*, May 1, 1983.

63. Lou Cannon, "A Summit Is Not a Summit Is Not a Summit," *Washington Post National Weekly Edition*, July 15, 1985, p. 25.

64. The *New York Times*, March 12–15, 1985.

65. Lou Cannon, "The Great Delegator Has Some Pressing Command Decisions to Make," *The Washington Post National Weekly Edition*, May 27, 1985, p. 27.

66. Bill Keller, "Weinberger's New Role: A Summit Sentinel," *New York Times*, September 21, 1985.

67. Weinberger to Reagan, with enclosure, November 13, 1985.

68. The *New York Times*, August 16, 1984.

69. For a thorough discussion, see Alexander L. George, *Presidential Decisionmaking in Foreign Policy: The Effective Use of Information and Advice* (Boulder, CO: Westview Press, 1980); I. M. Destler, Leslie Gelb, and Anthony Lake, *Our Own Worst Enemy: The*

Unmaking of American Foreign Policy (New York: Simon & Schuster, 1984); and Nye, op. cit.

70. See, e.g., Elizabeth Valkenier, *The Soviet Union and the Third World* (New York: Praeger, 1983); Jerry Hough, *The Struggle for the Third World* (Washington, D.C.: The Brookings Institution, 1986); and Francis Fukuyama, *Moscow's Post-Brezhnev Reassessment of the Third World* (Rand, 1986, Doc. R-3337-USDP).

71. S. A. Losev, "Vashington: Uzhestochenie kursa antirazriadki," *SShA* (1982), No. 2, p. 59.

72. *Izvestia*, August 30, 1981.

73. The *New York Times*, September 29, 1983.

74. Mikhail Gorbachev, in *Time*, September 9, 1985, p. 29.

75. See Stephen M. Meyer, "Soviet Strategic Programmes and the US SDI," *Survival* (November–December 1985), pp. 274–294; and David Holloway, "The Strategic Defense Initiative and the Soviet Union," *Daedalus* (Summer 1985), pp. 257–278.

8

From Nixon to Reagan: China's Changing Role in American Strategy

*Banning N. Garrett
and Bonnie S. Glaser*

President Reagan, like Presidents Nixon, Ford, and Carter before him, viewed China policy through the lens of the triangular relationship among the United States, the Soviet Union, and China. Reagan initially sought to avoid a trade-off between the imperatives of the strategic triangle and the demands of political loyalties. But when this approach threatened to result in a deterioration of Sino-American relations, he affirmed the policies of his predecessors by choosing geopolitics and national interest over conservative ideology and pro-Taiwan sympathies.

Reagan reaffirmed the strategic importance to the United States of close ties between Washington and Beijing. But the administration view of China's role in American strategy toward the Soviet Union changed during Reagan's first term in office. Reagan's first Secretary of State, Alexander Haig, sought to continue the Carter administration's triangular policy of developing an overt strategic partnership with China as part of a global coalition to counter Soviet expansion. Under Haig's successor, George Shultz, however, the Reagan administration moved away from the tactical use of relations with China to influence Soviet behavior. Shultz stressed the economic rather than the strategic underpinnings of the anti-Soviet coalition and Sino-American relations and emphasized China's regional role in Asia. Nevertheless, the administration quietly expanded military contacts and political interaction with Beijing while it publicly stressed developing bilateral ties as a solid and enduring basis of American-Chinese relations.

Banning N. Garrett and Bonnie S. Glaser are defense consultants with Palomar Corporation in Washington, D.C., specializing in American-Soviet-Chinese strategic relations. They are co-authors of War and Peace: The Views from Moscow and Beijing *(Berkeley, CA: University of California Institute of International Studies, 1984).*

The Reagan administration's China policy and geopolitical thinking is best understood in the context of American policymaking toward China and the strategic triangle since the 1971–1972 rapprochement between Washington and Beijing.

Global Realignment

For China, the rapprochement with the United States followed an assessment that the Soviet Union was a greater threat to China than the United States and that Washington was a potential strategic partner in a global strategy aimed at countering expanding Soviet military power and political influence. The Sino-Soviet split, which emerged into the open in 1960, and the Cultural Revolution that began in 1966, had left China isolated internationally and weak and divided internally as hostilities between Moscow and Beijing escalated at the end of the decade. China's decision to break out of isolation and seek a strategic counter to the Soviet Union in an American connection followed the Soviet invasion of Czechoslovakia in August 1968, the Sino-Soviet border clashes, beginning in March 1969, and veiled Soviet threats to launch surgical strikes against Chinese nuclear forces. Chinese leaders, especially Chairman Mao Zedong and Premier Zhou Enlai, judged the Soviet Union to be a greater danger to China than the United States, which they considered a declining power that would begin withdrawing from Asia.

Chinese leaders also saw their strategic realignment with the West as the underpinning of a modernization strategy that aimed at gaining access to Japanese and Western civilian and defense technology. The full extent of China's ambitions was not evident in the West until February 1978 — when Chinese leaders announced implementation of the Four Modernization's Program more than a year after Mao's death and the purge of the Gang of Four. But it was foreshadowed in the large purchases of whole plants and high technology from the West in the 1972–1975 period[1] and the goals set forth by Premier Zhou at the Fourth National People's Congress in January 1975.

The rapprochement with the United States allowed China to shift from planning for war on two fronts — against the Soviet Union in the north and the United States and Taiwan in the southeast — to concentrate their forces primarily on the Soviet threat. The American connection also raised the specter for the Soviets of possible American assistance to China in the event of a Sino-Soviet war. China was no longer isolated in the face of superior Soviet military power, however uncertain any American aid might be. The rapprochement also reduced the likelihood of American-Soviet collusion against China, although that concern continued to ebb and flow, especially at times of stagnation in relations between Washington and Beijing and improvements in relations between Washington and Moscow.

Whereas Mao and Zhou sought to end China's economic and political isolation and to establish a reliable American counterbalance to Soviet power, President Richard Nixon and his national security advisor, Henry Kissingor, sought to:

— gain Chinese support for stability in Asia as the United States scaled down its defense posture in the region;
— capitalize on the Sino-Soviet split to gain diplomatic leverage over both the Soviet Union and China and to create a new structure of global power relations that compensated for perceived American weaknesses;
— head off a possible Soviet attack on China and a Sino-Soviet war, which could become global or could lead to Soviet domination of China; and
— head off a Sino-Soviet rapprochement, which, like imposed Soviet domination, could lead once again to a coordinated Soviet-Chinese strategy against the United States.

Before the Nixon administration shifted American strategy in 1969–1970, American military posture since the early 1950s had presumed a monolithic Sino-Soviet threat and was ostensibly based on a "two-and-a-half war" strategy that envisioned fighting major wars simultaneously in Asia against China and in Europe against the Soviet Union — and at the same time meeting a "minor" contingency elsewhere, such as in Vietnam. In his memoirs, Henry Kissinger notes that the United States never had sufficient forces to implement such a strategy, and he argues that if war had broken out simultaneously against the Soviet Union and China, it would likely have escalated to the use of nuclear weapons to compensate for weakness in conventional forces.[2] The United States also secretly had planned to "swing" much of its conventional force capability — naval and air forces primarily — to the European theater in the event of a NATO/Warsaw Pact conflict.[3]

The change to a "one-and-a-half war" strategy was announced in February 1970, which Kissinger says was a signal to China that the United States publicly acknowledged the unlikelihood of Sino-Soviet cooperation and "would no longer treat a conflict with the USSR as automatically involving the People's Republic."[4] In 1972, Kissinger says, the Chinese gave the United States the assurances he and Nixon had sought that China would support stability in Asia while the United States reduced its force levels in the region.[5]

For Moscow, the Sino-American rapprochement appeared to give viability and permanency to China's split with the Soviet Union and created the possibility of a simultaneous two-front war against NATO and China. Moscow had been building up its forces in the Far East since 1965 — from fifteen to thirty-three divisions by 1969 — as its conflict with China had become more volatile. In the 1960s, however, China was isolated and the Soviets had a potential free hand to use military force against the Chinese, who were seen as adventurist and expansionist by Washington. Indeed, in the early 1960s, President Kennedy had seen China as a more dangerous enemy than the Soviet Union and had considered military action to take out China's nuclear facilities before Beijing could produce its first atomic bomb.[6] Washington's open discussions of this may have given Moscow the impression that the United States might even cooperate or at least acquiesce in a Soviet strike against China. But when Soviet officials probed the United States for such cooperation in 1969 and 1970,[7] the Nixon administration rejected the overtures and indicated Washington's disapproval of such action. This was a signal to Moscow that a triangular strategic arrangement was now operative and that the Soviets faced the prospect of Sino-American collusion against them in both peacetime and wartime.

Although wartime cooperation between Washington and Beijing seemed quite unlikely in the early 1970s, Kissinger recounts that he and Nixon were committed to preventing Soviet domination of China. According to Kissinger[8]:

> From the beginning Nixon and I were convinced — alone among senior policymakers — that the United States could not accept a Soviet military assault on China. We had held this view before there was contact of any sort; we imposed contingency planning on a reluctant bureaucracy as early as the summer of 1969. Obviously, this reflected no agreement between Peking and Washington. . . . It was based on a sober geopolitical assessment. If Moscow succeeded in humiliating Peking and reducing it to impotence, the whole weight of the Soviet military effort could be thrown against the West. Such a demonstration of Soviet ruthlessness and American impotence . . . would encourage accommodation to other Soviet demands from Japan to Western Europe, not to speak of the many smaller countries on the Soviet periphery.

During the India-Pakistan war of December 1971 — six months after Kissinger's secret trip to Beijing — Nixon and Kissinger apparently were prepared to risk war with the Soviet Union if Moscow attacked China.[9] In the decade that followed, the likelihood of American assistance to a besieged China increased as the United States and China established a "new relationship" in 1972 and moved in 1978 toward building a military and strategic dimension to Sino-American ties. Although the Chinese still could not be assured of American support, the Soviets could not rule out an American response if they attacked China. And China's strategic concern that the Soviets not succeed in achieving domination of Western Europe, through appeasement or military defeat, created the possibility of Chinese intervention to help prevent a Soviet victory in the West that could allow for a redeployment or "swinging" of Soviet forces to overwhelm China in the east. Thus by the early 1970s, the Soviets found themselves facing the prospect of a two-front war, a concern heightened by the development of American-Chinese military ties at the end of the decade. Ironically, Soviet fears of Sino-American military collusion against them had predated the idea of such collaboration within the United States government and may have contributed to its formulation.[10]

Although Nixon and Kissinger perceived strategic military benefits from the global realignment of 1969–1971, their more immediate goal was to capitalize on the Sino-Soviet split and Chinese overtures to the United States to gain diplomatic leverage over the Soviet Union on SALT, Vietnam, and other bilateral and multilateral issues. The Soviets, fearful of Sino-American collusion against them, sought to improve relations with the United States in competition with Beijing. Nixon's dramatic summitry of 1972 consolidated this new situation: Within four months, the American president formally established the "new relationship" with China and detente with the Soviet Union. The Shanghai Communiqué, signed by the president at the end of his February visit to China, set forth the principles of the new Sino-American relationship, including a declaration suggesting Washington's opposition to any effort by the Soviet Union to dominate China.[11] Nixon then went to Moscow in May, where he signed the first Soviet-American strategic arms limitation agreement (SALT I) and the principles for the conduct of Soviet-American relations, thus formalizing detente between Moscow and Washington.[12]

Nixon and Kissinger sought to use the new relationship with China to gain leverage over the Soviet Union. But the policy had an inherent contradiction in that the Chinese were seeking to pull the United States into an anti-Soviet alignment and to undermine detente, whereas the Nixon administration was seeking to further negotiations and cooperation with the Soviet Union by using Soviet fears of Sino-American collusion to pressure the Soviets to compromise. Thus if American policy toward China were successful in furthering detente, China's security would be diminished, the usefulness of the Washington connection put in doubt, and Sino-American relations would likely deteriorate.

Military Ties with China?

In the 1971–1972 period, Soviet fears of Sino-American collusion, and Chinese fears of United States-Soviet collusion produced a desire in both Moscow and Beijing to move forward in relations with Washington. But the contradiction between Chinese security interests and Soviet-American detente soon began to pose a dilemma for the United States; at the same time, a debate heated up in Washington over the viability of an American detente strategy.

By 1974–1975, the idea of developing a Sino-American military relationship began to percolate inside the United States government.[13]

The notion of Sino-American defense ties, although stimulated in part by quiet Chinese probes to the United States as early as 1973, nevertheless contradicted the conventional wisdom of China experts in the United States, who believed the Chinese would not abandon self-reliance and seek military ties with the United States. Some defense planners, however, could see the strategic logic and benefits for both the United States and China of a military relationship, and the idea received attention within the Defense Department beginning in the fall of 1973. By December 1974, Secretary of Defense James Schlesinger was briefed on the pros and cons of military ties with China, and by the fall of 1975, the outlines of a sharp debate over China's role in American strategy toward the Soviet Union had emerged with "military ties" the key issue. This debate was part of a larger struggle over detente, in which Schlesinger was pitted against Secretary of State Kissinger.

The purported benefits of a defense relationship with the "Communist Chinese" — ranging from exchange of defense attaches to sales of advanced weapons — included[14]:

— gaining leverage over Moscow to restrain its behavior internationally and to pressure the Soviets in the SALT talks and other bilateral negotiations;
— preventing a Sino-Soviet rapprochement by maintaining suspicion and tension between Beijing and Moscow while tying Chinese leaders, including senior military officers, to the policy of tilting toward the United States;
— giving Moscow reason to plan for possible American wartime aid to China in the event of a new Sino-Soviet military conflict; and
— strengthening China's military capability through the transfer of certain advanced weapons and military technology, thus helping China deter the Soviets and possibly leading Moscow to redeploy some of its conventional forces to the Far East, thereby reducing pressure on NATO in the west.

Strategic Debate

By 1975, both Kissinger and Schlesinger were attracted to the idea of military ties with China, but for different and conflicting reasons.[15] Both officials viewed China in a triangular context, but they saw China's role in the strategic triangle differently, based primarily on their conflicting views of Soviet-American relations and on their conflicting institutional concerns.

For Kissinger, detente was aimed at "strategic enmeshment" of the Soviet Union in a web of relations with the United States and the West, which could be used to constrain the extension of Soviet influence at a time when Moscow's global power, especially its military power, was growing, and American power seemed to be peaking in relative terms. Detente was intended to employ carrots as well as sticks to induce acceptable Soviet behavior by linking issues in bilateral relations with global politics; SALT was to be the political underpinning as well as the arms control foundation of detente.

Although strong American military power, including maintenance of "essential equivalence" of strategic forces in the face of a major Soviet nuclear arms buildup, was said to be a prerequisite for carrying out this strategy, it was fundamentally a diplomatic approach to the problem of coping with Soviet power. For Kissinger, the problem was strengthening the American position in the peacetime balance of power through political and economic means at a time of Vietnam war-induced defense spending cuts in the United States.

Kissinger — and Nixon in the 1969–1974 period — approached China largely in the context of their geopolitical strategy for managing the Soviet threat. Since they sought to pressure Moscow by manipulating Soviet anxiety about possible Sino-American collusion against the Soviet Union, any gestures toward military ties with China would have to be aimed at maintaining and increasing Washington's leverage over the Soviets. At the same time, such attempts to gain leverage could be counterproductive if moves toward China provoked Moscow to adopt a harder line toward the United States and engage in more aggressive international behavior, thus undermining the entire detente relationship.

For Schlesinger, coping with Soviet power was more a military than a diplomatic problem. In his view, detente had not slowed the buildup of Soviet strategic and conventional military power nor had it altered the long-term "hegemonistic" goals of Soviet leaders. The benefits accruing to the United States in the global military balance resulting from the Sino-Soviet split and then China's tilt toward the United States had become increasingly important in the effort to maintain or improve the American military position vis-à-vis the Soviet Union, especially in the Far East. As a strategic ally, China offered great potential to tie down a substantial portion of Soviet military capabilities and resources, and to greatly complicate Soviet defense planning for both conventional and nuclear war with the West. From Schlesinger's more military point of view — and his concern about the wartime balance of forces — the preservation of detente had a lower priority than did the maintenance of a favorable balance of military power.

Kissinger's Moves Toward Military Ties

Moves toward American military ties with China were first considered in the fall of 1975 as Washington's relations with both Moscow and Beijing deteriorated, and the president was under increasing domestic pressure to take strong action against the Soviet Union. At the same time, a power and policy struggle was intensifying within the Ford administration. Kissinger was facing strong opposition to his detente policies, especially from Schlesinger and from members of Congress. Kissinger's efforts to finalize the SALT II agreement based on the Ford-Brezhnev Vladivostok formula were stalled, and his strategy of "strategic enmeshment" had been seriously undermined by the December 1974 Jackson-Vanik amendment, which tied improved Soviet-American trade relations to Soviet emigration policies and led Moscow to abrogate the 1972 Soviet-American trade agreement. Soviet actions in the Middle East and Angola had eroded the credibility of Kissinger's detente strategy and further strained Soviet-American relations. Kissinger also was under attack for the Helsinki agreement, signed in July 1975 by President Ford and for his failure to criticize the Soviets directly on human rights violations. Although Kissinger was trying to defend and repair his faltering detente policy, he also was becoming increasingly disenchanted with the Soviet view of detente.[16]

Kissinger was under attack from the Chinese as well. They had begun accusing him of "appeasement" of the Soviet Union and indicating that American weakness vis-à-vis Moscow raised serious doubts about the reliability and usefulness of the United States as a strategic counter to the Soviets. Kissinger had failed to follow through on the Shanghai Communiqué and normalize relations with Beijing, and he was under pressure to do something to move Sino-American relations forward.[17] It was in this context that "administration officials" — almost certainly Kissinger or his deputy Winston Lord — expressed concern in an interview with the *New York Times* that the slippage in Sino-American relations had weakened Washington's leverage over the Soviet Union.[18] The "officials" said that in their view, Soviet fear of American-Chinese collusion against them had greatly diminished and that the Soviet concern over Sino-American ties that had moderated Moscow's behavior in the early 1970s no longer was a factor restraining Moscow's "adventurism" in Portugal and Angola.

A move toward military ties with China offered Kissinger a means of improving Sino-American relations and thereby of regaining leverage over Moscow in the SALT II talks, which were to be resumed in early 1976, as well as over Soviet actions in Angola. At the same time, a gesture toward military ties with China would allow President Ford to give the Chinese something significant at a time when he was unwilling because of a conservative challenge in the 1976 elections to compromise on Taiwan. Kissinger and Ford made that gesture in December 1975 during a trip to Beijing. They approved the British sales to China of Rolls Royce Spey jet engines — used in the British version of the F-4 Phantom fighter bomber — and a Spey factory to build engines in Xian,[19] a deal that had been under discussion since 1972. The United States had the ability to block the deal through CoCom, the Western allies' "coordinating committee" for controlling the transfer of strategic technology to the Soviet Union and other communist countries.[20]

The next move on the military-ties track followed the death of Chairman Mao Zedong on September 9, 1976, and the arrest of the Gang of Four on October 6. Kissinger was sufficiently concerned that a post-Mao power struggle could yet turn against American interests that he urged the National Security Council (NSC) on October 12 to approve the sale to China of two advanced Control Data Cyber 72 computers with military applications. Subsequently, at a news conference on October 15, he warned Moscow and reassured Beijing that "the territorial integrity and sovereignty of China is very important to the world equilibrium and we would consider it a grave matter if this were threatened by an outside power." Although Kissinger's moves may have been effective in reassuring the Chinese of American support and in signaling the Soviets that Sino-American collusion was a live option in United States policy, the secretary of state was a lame duck, and his actions did not constitute an overall policy that was necessarily to be continued by the new administration.

Carter and the China Card: To Play or Not To Play?

When Jimmy Carter assumed the presidency in January 1977, he and Secretary of State Cyrus Vance had already indicated that improving Soviet-American relations would be of paramount concern for the new administration, whereas Sino-American relations were far down the list of foreign policy priorities. Vance indicated that he would not let Washington's relations with Beijing interfere with SALT and other outstanding issues between Washington and Moscow,[21] and throughout his tenure as secretary, Vance opposed moves toward military ties with China on the grounds that they would damage Soviet-American relations.

But Vance was not the only foreign policymaker in the administration, and his desire to concentrate on improving Soviet-American relations while playing down relations with China was soon challenged by other officials — and by events. The "China card" — as it was coming to be called — was pushed to the top of the presidential options deck ten weeks after Carter was inaugurated. The president's explicit statements criticizing human rights violations in the Soviet Union quickly soured the atmosphere in Soviet-American relations, contributing to Soviet suspicions of the new administration's intentions when Vance presented a SALT "reductions proposal" during his visit to Moscow at the end of March. Soviet leaders angrily rejected the proposal and denounced Carter's human rights policy. In response, the administration considered playing the China card for the first time. The idea — which was strongly backed by National Security Advisor Zbigniew Brzezinski — was rejected at the presidential level in June after months of internal debate. Officials from the Pentagon, the NSC, and the CIA favoring military ties with the Chinese were pitted against State Department officials, who argued that such moves might be too provocative toward the Soviets.[22] The option of some sort of defense ties with China, such as transfer of military-related technology or allowing Western European arms sales to Beijing — was put on the back burner for the rest of 1977. But the issue continued to be the subject of intense debate and political struggle within the administration.

The internal debate was unresolved with the June 1977 rejection of the China card option, which represented a temporary victory for the Vance "pro-detente" faction of the administration. Besides seeking to reassure the Soviets that the United States was not moving toward a military alliance with China,[23] at Vance's urging President Carter toned down his criticisms of Soviet human rights policy and backed off from his tough SALT proposals. The administration seemed to be moving quickly toward a SALT II agreement with Moscow, and in October, President Carter erroneously predicted that an accord might be reached "within the next few weeks."[24]

In this period, the NSC concluded a major interagency study of the global balance of power — Presidential Review Memorandum (PRM) 10 — which concluded that growth in Soviet military and economic power was slowing down and that long-term trends favored the United States.[25] The comprehensive study concluded that the Soviet-American military balance was roughly equal at present but contrasted the strength and scope of the American economy and capacity for technological innovation with forecasts of impending Soviet capital and labor shortages. In addition, PRM 10 noted Moscow's problems with political succession, agricultural failures, and the continuing Sino-Soviet split as factors exacerbating Soviet long-term weakness and tilting the balance of power toward the United States. Vance and other pro-detente officials argued on the basis of the PRM 10 assessment that Soviet weaknesses and American strengths provided a basis for Soviet interest in accommodation with Washington. Brzezinski and others, however, viewed the conclusions of PRM 10 as arguing for exploitation of Moscow's vulnerabilities to diminish Soviet power, a view that did not prevail within the administration until the spring of 1978.

Chinese leaders reacted negatively to Vance's strategic assessment, based on PRM 10 and to his desire to avoid provoking Moscow by forging military ties with China and to instead deal with Sino-American relations as primarily a bilateral matter.

The Chinese conveyed their disapproval of the American strategic view and the administration's policy toward the Soviet Union during a visit to Beijing by Secretary of State Vance in August. Privately, American officials worried that the failure to move forward in relations with China resulting from Vance's trip was more a function of fundamental differences in strategic views than of a highly publicized impasse over conditions for normalization of relations. The conclusions of PRM 10 were a direct challenge to China's view of the United States as a declining superpower, with the Soviet Union as the superpower on the ascendancy. They also raised questions about the usefulness of America as an ally if Washington failed to see the need to take a strong global stand against Soviet expansion. In major press commentaries in the fall of 1977, the Chinese charged that "advocates of appeasement" in the West — apparently including Vance and some other members of the Carter administration, if not the president himself — "hope they can divert the Soviet Union to the east so as to free themselves from this Soviet peril at the expense of the security of other nations."[26] The commentaries also questioned the reliability of the United States commitment to Western Europe and, by implication, to China.[27]

Chinese leaders nevertheless hoped Washington would assume a tougher anti-Soviet posture. Their hopes for a change in American policy were raised in early 1978 as Soviet-American relations again deteriorated. President Carter was under mounting domestic pressure to take a tougher position in the SALT talks and to respond forcefully to Soviet and Cuban military intervention in Ethiopia. Carter departed sharply from his previously conciliatory approach to the Soviets in a speech at Wake Forest University on March 17. The address, which was prepared by Brzezinski and his NSC staff, took a generally harder line toward Moscow.

Although Brzezinski had won the battle to toughen up the administration's rhetoric toward Moscow, Carter rejected his proposals for a show of American military force in the Horn of Africa and for linkage of progress in the SALT talks to Moscow's international behavior. But Carter's decision to side with Vance on these issues made the "China card" a more attractive option to punish and pressure Moscow. Over Vance's objections, the president decided to send his anti-Soviet national security advisor to China in May — a signal to both Moscow and Beijing that the United States had made an important shift in its triangular policies.

Carter's new tougher line toward Moscow was well received during Brzezinski's visit to Beijing May 21–23. The White House officially denied that Brzezinski's trip was intended to send any signals to the Soviets. But administration officials said privately that the visit's primary purposes were to reassure the Chinese about American defense policies vis-à-vis the Soviet Union, to reaffirm Washington's desire to pursue parallel interests with China globally, and to keep the Soviet Union off balance by holding out the possibility of increasingly close Sino-

American cooperation if American relations with Moscow deteriorated further. Brzezinski told his Chinese hosts in his opening speech: "We approach our relations with three fundamental beliefs: that friendship between the United States and the People's Republic of China is vital and beneficial to world peace; that a secure and strong China is in America's interest; that a powerful, confident and globally engaged United States is in China's interest." He emphasized that "the United States does not view its relationship with China as a tactical expedient" but rather as "derived from a long-term strategic view" as "reflected in the Shanghai Communiqué." He added that the United States recognizes and shares "China's resolve to resist the efforts of any nation which seeks to establish global or regional hegemony." Brzezinski mentioned Africa, Europe, the Middle East, and Asia as areas where "we can enhance the cause of peace through consultations and, where appropriate, through parallel pursuit of our similar objectives."

Brzezinski and his staff added to Soviet concern about his visit by leaking to the press that the sale to China of American dual-purpose, military-related technology and Western arms had been discussed in Beijing, and that Chinese leaders had been given detailed briefings on the SALT II negotiations and on the administration's global strategic assessment PRM 10. They stressed that Soviet weaknesses and long-term American advantages should be exploited to extract greater concessions from Moscow and to contain its influence, even at the expense of possible deterioration in Soviet-American relations. This view was far more acceptable to the Chinese than Vance's strategic assessment, and it indicated a greater American willingness to pursue a potentially provocative informal alliance with Beijing against Moscow. Chinese officials, who were dissatisfied with Vance's Beijing visit, indicated that they were pleased with the Brzezinski trip. Both Deng Xiaoping and Brzezinski later said that agreement on strategic views had made possible rapid movement toward normalization of relations, which had been deadlocked since the 1972 Shanghai communiqué.

Brzezinski's visit was intended to "play the China card," and it was perceived that way in Moscow as well as in Beijing. On June 25 Soviet President Brezhnev charged that "recently attempts have been made in the U.S. at a high level, and in quite cynical form, to play the China card against the USSR." Brezhnev called Carter's China policy "short-sighted and dangerous." A week earlier, *Pravda* had stated more explicitly that American "alignment with China on an anti-Soviet basis would rule out the possibility of cooperation with the Soviet Union in the matter of reducing the danger of a nuclear war and, of course, of limiting armaments."

Some senior American officials, including the secretary of state, sought to maintain at least a public image of "evenhandedness" in Washington's dealings with Moscow and Beijing. Hoping to limit damage to Soviet-American relations, they also sought to slow if not reverse the momentum of the "new phase" in Sino-American relations. But the direction of the Washington-Beijing relationship had been set, resulting first in the normalization of relations and finally in the administration's decision, in the wake of the Soviet Afghanistan invasion, to permit sales to China of nonlethal military equipment.

Although Vance was unable to alter the direction of China policy, he managed to obtain a SALT II agreement with Moscow in the spring of 1979, even though the "China factor" continued to have a major impact on Soviet-American relations which continued to deteriorate after the winter of 1978. The December 15, 1978 announcement that the United States and China would normalize relations on January 1, and that Deng would visit Washington, was made less than a week before Vance and Gromyko were scheduled to meet in Geneva for what was billed by the United States as the final round of SALT talks before a Carter-Brezhnev summit to be held in Washington in mid-January. But those talks failed. Administration officials attributed the failure in part to a Soviet desire to put off finalization of the accord and a Carter-Brezhnev summit until after Deng's visit to Washington in order to assess how the United States dealt with the Chinese leader. Soviet officials publicly denied that Sino-American ties were the cause of the delay, apparently because they did not want to acknowledge a linkage between SALT and China.

The normalization agreement and Deng's visit to the United States January 29–February 5 were victories for those officials in the administration seeking to develop strategic ties with China. But administration debates over the strategic relationship were rekindled when the Chinese invaded Vietnam less than two weeks after Deng left the United States.[28] President Carter refrained from all-out support for China, and at Vance's urging, secretly resumed SALT discussions with Moscow during the invasion. The arms limitation agreement was finalized in the spring and signed at a Carter-Brezhnev summit meeting in Vienna. The June summit was limited to signing the SALT II accord, however, and Soviet-American relations failed to improve significantly. The Chinese, meanwhile, made new overtures in April for talks with Moscow on normalizing relations, thus keeping the Soviets off balance and showing Beijing's dissatisfaction with Washington's failure to give China all-out support for its attack on Vietnam.

Cold War with Moscow, Quasi-Alliance with Beijing

Although Sino-American relations cooled in the immediate aftermath of the Vietnam invasion and the conclusion of the SALT II agreement in

May, President Carter approved further steps toward military ties with China in the summer and fall of 1979. These began with a visit to Beijing in August by Vice-President Walter Mondale, who broadened the implied security guarantee given to China by Kissinger in 1976. Mondale stated on nationwide Chinese television that "any nation which seeks to weaken or isolate you in world affairs assumes a stance counter to American interests."[29]

By the time the vice-president returned to Washington, the United States and the Soviet Union were on a collision course over American intelligence leaks of an alleged Soviet "combat brigade" in Cuba. Although Carter's public response to the "crisis" on October 1 focused on stepped up surveillance activity and naval operations aimed at Cuba, and on a strong appeal for Senate ratification of the SALT II treaty, the president quietly approved several measures to intensify pressure on Moscow. These included moves indicating that the United States would begin to further restrict the flow of high technology to the Soviet Union and that the administration would move toward overt military ties with China. On the same day that Carter announced the measures against Cuba, the White House leaked to the press that Secretary of Defense Harold Brown would visit China.

A few days later, administration sources leaked a secret Pentagon study, "Consolidated Guidance Number 8: Asia During a Worldwide Conventional War," which concluded that in view of China's "pivotal role" in the global balance of power, it would be in the American interest "to encourage Chinese actions that would heighten Soviet security concerns."[30] "CG 8" recommended possible American military assistance to China to increase the likelihood of Chinese participation in a global war, including provision of advanced technology and intelligence data, sale of advanced arms, Chinese production of American weapons, and joint military exercises. Although Vance denied that any change had taken place in administration policy, State Department officials interviewed by the author in early December 1979 said that the "China tilters" had won the battle for military ties with China and predicted that the United States would move closer toward quasi-alliance with China, including sales of military-related technology and possibly even arms.

The Soviet invasion of Afghanistan in late December created a new crisis in Soviet-American relations and sharply weakened the position of those in the State Department, who had hoped to limit the substance of Defense Secretary Brown's upcoming trip to China to prevent further damage to the remaining shreds of Soviet-American detente. A "senior official" — probably Brzezinski — told the *New York Times* on the eve of Brown's departure for China in early January that the Soviet invasion had given Brown's mission a "new dimension" and asserted that "the Soviets have forced us and the Chinese into a posture in which we both see the world in the same way."[31] Brown received new instructions in response to the Afghanistan invasion that included informing Chinese leaders that the United States was now willing to consider the sale of nonlethal military equipment to China on a case-by-case basis.

Vance continued fighting a losing battle against Sino-American strategic ties, apparently with the hope of reversing the continuing deterioration of Soviet-American relations. But his influence within the administration had been dealt a mortal blow by the crisis over the Soviet brigade in Cuba. He finally resigned from office in April after opposing the ill-fated Iranian hostage rescue mission. With Vance's departure, the position of officials opposed to military ties with China was further weakened. Although President Carter did not lift the arms sales ban, there were indications that he would have done so had he been reelected and that American officials had already led the Chinese to believe the arms sales ban was only temporary.[32]

By the end of 1980, outgoing Carter administration officials described the pace of improvement of relations with China as remarkable. Talks with the Chinese on military matters were described as "almost like talking to an ally." Although no military equipment sales had been consummated by the end of the Carter administration, cooperation was developing in other areas — including, according to officials, agreement to set up facilities near the Sino-Soviet border for monitoring Soviet missile tests.[33]

Shifting Assessments Under the Reagan Administration

President Reagan inherited a nascent quasi-alliance with China and near Cold War tensions with the Soviet Union. Reagan's harsh anti-Soviet rhetoric and his determination to take a tough global stand against Moscow made the "China card" naturally attractive to him. And indeed, during his unsuccessful bid for the Republican presidential nomination in 1976, Reagan had said that selling arms to China to counter the Soviet Union would be a "natural development." But Reagan's fervent anti-communism also made him highly suspicious of "Chinese communists" as well as "Russian communists."

Added to this tension between viewing China as both a potential ally against the Soviet Union and a perennial communist foe was Reagan's long-time commitment to America's "old friends" on Taiwan. Reagan charged during the campaign that President Carter had made unnecessary compromises in normalizing relations with Beijing and the new president apparently hoped to retract some of those concessions. But he also sought to avoid a policy trade-off: Reagan wanted to continue the Carter administration's policy of building a strategic anti-Soviet relationship with China while resurrecting official ties with Taiwan.

The Chinese reacted sharply to what they perceived as Reagan's attempt to "roll back the clock" in Sino-American relations by upgrading Washington's relations with Taipei. But after nearly two years of tension over Taiwan, the United States and China achieved a modus vivendi that led to stabilization and then to a steady improvement in Sino-American bilateral relations.

The Reagan administration, like its predecessors since the Nixon administration, viewed China's anti-Soviet, pro-Western orientation as strategically vital to the United States. But the administration's view of China's role in American strategy toward the Soviet Union underwent a significant change between 1981 and 1983.

Alexander Haig, Reagan's first secretary of state, sought to develop strategic ties with China as part of an anti-Soviet coalition strategy similar to that pursued by Zbigniew Brzezinski.[34] Haig sought to develop strategic and military ties with Beijing to deter aggressive actions by the Soviet Union, to punish the Soviets for global expansionist activity, and to gain leverage over Moscow in Soviet-American relations. Secretary of Defense Caspar Weinberger hinted at such an administration strategy two months after Reagan's inauguration by suggesting that the United States might sell arms to China in response to a Soviet invasion of Poland. Although Haig avoided publicly acknowledging a direct linkage, he made a widely publicized announcement that the administration had lifted the American ban on arms sales to China during his visit to Beijing in June 1981. Officials in Haig's party told the press that the decision to sell arms to China was seen as a way to "get Moscow's attention." Administration officials emphasized the triangular context of the arms sales decision, noting that it signaled Moscow that a Sino-American alliance, although not yet politically feasible, had moved a step closer to realization.

George Shultz, who succeeded Haig in mid-1982 as secretary of state, saw less value in the tactical use of relations with China to influence Soviet behavior. Shultz, like Haig, supported a coalition strategy to contain Soviet power. But the new secretary of state emphasized the economic rather than the strategic underpinnings of the global coalition. Whereas Haig had viewed China through a Eurocentric lens in which Beijing's primary role was to buttress NATO deterrence of Soviet expansion in Europe and the Middle East, Shultz stressed China's regional role in Asia and the increasing economic and political significance of that region to the United States.[35]

In accordance with Shultz's world view, American officials scaled down their expectations of the role that China could play — and would be willing to play — as an active strategic partner in a global coalition. Rather, the administration viewed China's importance to the United States as stemming primarily from its passive role as a strategic counterweight to Soviet power. It was thus considered essential to long-term American objectives to maintain Beijing's pro-Western strategic posture and to strengthen China's defense capability to prevent further widening of the Sino-Soviet military gap. The administration viewed support for China's economic modernization effort through development of bilateral economic ties and the transfer of technology to China as the most effective means of achieving these goals.

Within the "new reality" in East Asia and the Pacific, as perceived by Shultz, China's role was secondary to that of Japan.[36] The administration's Pacific Basin strategy focused on Japan as the strongest economic power and as the key American military ally in the region. Japan, not China, had the potential to be the primary partner in Washington's effort to strengthen regional economic and political cooperation. Similarly Japan, not China, could provide assistance in countering growing Soviet naval and air power in the region. China continued to be important to the United States strategically in maintaining the global balance of power with the Soviet Union, but estimates of Beijing's potential contribution to American global efforts to deter the Soviet Union were lowered by a new appreciation of China's poverty, backwardness, and preoccupation with economic modernization.

The administration's de-emphasis of China's global strategic role was not only the result of its increasing focus on regional concerns in Asia. It also stemmed from perceived changes in Chinese views of the international situation and Washington's assessment that there had been a favorable shift in the Soviet-American balance of power.

The perceived improvement in the strategic situation was based on an assessment among senior administration officials that Moscow had become increasingly preoccupied with an economic slowdown, the leadership transition, and the growing challenge posed by Reagan's military buildup. In contrast with a renewed American global activism under President Reagan, the Soviets were increasingly on the defensive internationally. Secretary Shultz summarized the administration's view of the shift in the global balance in a 1985 *Foreign Affairs* article[37]:

> Today, our key alliances are more united than ever before. The United States is restoring its military strength and economic vigor and has regained its self-assurance; we have a President with a fresh mandate from the people for an active role of leadership. The Soviets, in contrast, face profound structural economic difficulties and restless allies; their diplomacy and their clients are on the defensive in many parts of the world. We have reason to be confident that the "correlation of forces" is shifting back in our favor.

In this new situation, Shultz and other American officials perceived a reduced need for an overt strategic relationship with China to compensate for Soviet advantages in the global balance of power than Brzezinski had judged necessary in the late 1970s or Haig had advocated in 1981–1982.[38]

The change in American perceptions of the Soviet Union and China followed a similar reassessment of the global balance of power in Beijing. In the 1970s, China had viewed the Soviet Union as on the offensive and as posing an increasing threat to China's security interests. The Chinese were especially threatened by Soviet support for Vietnam's invasion of Kampuchea in 1978 and the Soviet intervention in Afghanistan in 1979. At the same time, the United States was perceived as on the defensive globally and as pursuing detente with Moscow from a position of weakness.

By 1981–1982, however, Chinese perceptions of the Soviet-American balance of power had changed significantly. Beijing continued to perceive Moscow as posing the greatest threat to China's security, but judged the likelihood of conflict with the Soviets to have diminished considerably. The Chinese shared the American assessment that the Soviet Union was increasingly preoccupied with its internal economic and political problems and with consolidating its global empire, rather than with new aggressive measures to expand its influence. At the same time, the Chinese perceived the United States as overcoming the decline in its power that began with the Vietnam war and as taking new steps to counter Soviet expansion, primarily through building up its military power, strengthening its economy, and by 1983, bolstering its alliances. The Chinese concluded that the trends in the balance of power had reversed and now favored the United States. Beijing judged that a "strategic stalemate" prevailed, however, with neither superpower able to achieve superiority over the other.

On the basis of this perceived shift in the balance of power, Beijing apparently concluded that the need for Chinese participation in an overt anti-Soviet coalition had diminished. According to Chinese sources, there had been growing support in China since late 1978 for a more independent foreign policy rather than a quasi-alliance with the United States. But this shift had been postponed, partially because China needed an American counterweight to possible Soviet pressure in response to its "counterattack" against Vietnam in February 1979, and was further delayed by the Soviet invasion of Afghanistan in December 1979. By 1981, however, Beijing judged the Soviet invasion of Afghanistan to be limited in scope and to have led to a renewed American determination to oppose Soviet expansion. In this new situation, Chinese leaders readjusted China's foreign policy to a publicly more "independent" posture that was not aligned with any power, including the United States. By 1982, the Chinese had not only ceased calling for a "united front" against Moscow, but also had resumed criticizing many American — as well as Soviet — policies as "hegemonist." This policy was formally announced by Party Secretary-General Hu Yaobang at the 12th Party Congress in September 1982, which was convened on the eve of the first round of Sino-Soviet normalization talks.

Beijing's independent foreign policy was based on an assessment not only that the imminence of the Soviet threat to China had diminished but also that China's economic modernization program required a peaceful strategic environment at a lower level of Sino-Soviet tension. Chinese leaders apparently concluded that China's economic modernization program could be jeopardized if the Soviet Union stepped up political and military pressure on Beijing in response to an overt Sino-American strategic relationship. At the same time, a foreign policy that combined a degree of public distancing of China from the United States with a positive response to Soviet overtures for improved relations could produce a reduction of Sino-Soviet tensions without damaging Chinese security interests.

Chinese officials privately asserted, however, that the Soviet Union still constituted the primary long-term threat to Chinese security. They maintained that China's relations with the United States continued to play a key role in China's security strategy. And several officials privately suggested that despite the rhetoric of senior Chinese leaders, Beijing considered all forms of cooperation with the United States to be "strategic."

China's desire to emphasize its independence and to publicly play down anti-Soviet cooperation with the United States had been incompatible with Haig's goal of strengthening Washington's strategic ties with Beijing and gaining active Chinese participation in a global coalition with American allies and friends. But the new posture was consistent with and reinforced Secretary of State Shultz's inclinations and expectations. Shultz and other administration officials viewed a lower profile for American-Chinese strategic ties as an appropriate response to China's independent foreign policy that was consistent with new American priorities in Asia.

Washington and Beijing at Odds over Taiwan

Reagan's initial approach to China produced the worst crisis in Sino-American relations since the rapprochement between Washington and Beijing in 1971–1972. Not only was movement forward in strategic relations stalled, despite a Reagan administration decision to lift the ban on arms sales to China, but Beijing also repeatedly threatened to downgrade Sino-American diplomatic ties if the Taiwan issue were not satisfactorily resolved. At the same time, triangular considerations and domestic politics created pressures on President Reagan to maintain good Sino-American relations at the expense of fulfilling his campaign promises to upgrade Washington's relations with Taipei. The imperatives of triangular relations and the key role of Sino-American ties in China's security and modernization strategies also imposed limits on how far Chinese leaders would go in allowing Beijing's relations with Washington to backslide.

Even before he was elected, Ronald Reagan's statements on Taiwan led the Chinese to suspect that the new president might seek to reverse the progress achieved between Washington and Beijing with respect to Taiwan and implement a "two Chinas" policy. Reagan's Taiwan statements raised hopes in Moscow, however, that his China policy would damage Sino-American relations and reduce the threat of American-Chinese collusion.

The issue of future arms sales to Taiwan had been left unresolved by President Carter, but it did not become a focal point of Sino-American relations until after Ronald Reagan assumed the presidency. When the normalization agreement with Beijing was announced on December 15, 1978, American officials had said the United States would continue to sell "arms of a defensive character" to Taiwan on a restrained basis, although the administration suspended arms sales for the calendar year 1979. In addition, the Taiwan Relations Act (TRA) of April 1979 committed the United States to provide Taiwan with "arms of a defensive character" in order to help the island "maintain a sufficient self-defense capability."

At the time normalization was announced, Chinese Premier Hua Guofeng noted that China and the United States had "differing views" on the issue of arms sales to Taiwan, adding that "we absolutely could not agree to this" and that "it would not conform to the principles of normalization." "Nevertheless," Hua said, "we reached an agreement on the joint communiqué" announcing full normalization of relations. Washington and Beijing had thus agreed to put the arms sales issue on the back burner at the end of 1978, to be finessed and quietly resolved — or to become a source of conflict in the future.

China demonstrated a willingness to tolerate further arms sales to Taiwan under some circumstances when the Carter administration announced the resumption of sales on January 3, 1980 — on the eve of Secretary of Defense Brown's visit to China and less than two weeks after the Soviet invasion of Afghanistan. Beijing did not publicly protest the announced sales and voiced only muted criticism of the American action in private sessions with Brown, indicating a desire to avoid a confrontation with the United States over Taiwan at a time when China was primarily concerned about the strategic implications of the Soviet invasion.

The Chinese did not remain silent, however, in May 1980, when presidential candidate Ronald Reagan said he would consider restoring an "official" relationship between Taipei and Washington. A commentary in Beijing's *People's Daily* warned that "if the United States reestablished 'official relations' with Taiwan according to the policy announced by Reagan, it would imply that the very principle which constitutes the foundation of the Sino-American relationship would retrogress against the will of the two peoples." Following Reagan's victory in the November election, the Chinese refrained from sharp criticism on the Taiwan issue, apparently in the hope that Reagan's comments were campaign rhetoric that would not necessarily become Reagan administration policy.

After taking office, the new administration sent Beijing conflicting signals on Taiwan that confused and irritated Chinese officials. President Reagan sent personal, unpublicized notes to Chinese leaders, reassuring them that the new administration would abide by the normalization communiqué. The State Department publicly affirmed administration support for the normalization agreement in early February, and Secretary Haig stressed in an interview the following month that normal relations with China were "a strategic imperative . . . of overriding importance to international stability and world peace."[39] But Haig also asserted that candidate Reagan's statement of August 25, 1980, which called for resumption of "official" relations with Taiwan, represented the administration's China policy.

Within the administration, however, Haig advocated improving ties with Beijing and cautioned against taking any steps with Taipei that might endanger Sino-American relations. Haig's policy views were opposed by some White House officials, especially President Reagan's first national security advisor, Richard Allen, who supported upgrading relations with Taiwan and who was wary of closer ties with "communist" China. But no concrete moves were made toward Taipei during a policy review before Haig's June 1981 visit to Beijing.[40]

The policy review led to a decision on the eve of Haig's trip to allow sales to China of lethal weapons on a case-by-case basis. Haig apparently hoped that lifting the arms sales ban would result in Chinese tolerance of continued American arms sales to Taiwan and would provide new momentum to the Sino-American strategic relationship. Haig expressed the hope that his talks with Chinese leaders would "open a new era of strategic and economic cooperation with the PRC [People's Republic of China]," and said that President Reagan had made a "firm commitment" to advance strategic ties with China. At the time he departed from Beijing, Haig appeared to have been successful. He said, "U.S. and Chinese perceptions of the international situation have never been closer. Our common resolve to coordinate our independent policies in order to limit the Soviet Union's opportunities for exploiting its military power has likewise grown stronger." The Chinese indicated a willingness to develop closer military ties with the United States by agreeing to send Liu Huaqing, the vice-chief of staff of the People's Liberation Army (PLA) general staff to Washington in August with a shopping list for arms purchases.

Haig's mission to China was a failure, however. Liu Huaqing's trip was soon postponed indefinitely by the Chinese, who sought to dispel any notion that they had agreed to continued arms sales to Taiwan in exchange for the right to purchase American arms themselves. The warning signs had been evident at the end of Haig's stay in Beijing. Deng told Haig that arms sales to Taiwan was a sensitive issue and warned that if the United States went too far, Sino-American relations could retrogress.[41] A Chinese commentary on the same day called Washington's arms sales to Taipei the "key stumbling block" in the development of American-Chinese relations. American arms sales to Taiwan persisted as the dominant issue in Sino-American relations for over a year, while the strategic dialogue lapsed and the military relationship stalled.

No substantial progress was made toward resolving the Taiwan issue until October 1981, when Haig and Chinese Foreign Minister Huang Hua met in Washington. Huang outlined a formula for the gradual reduction of arms sales, which would provide the basis for the joint communiqué on arms sales to Taiwan reached on August 17 the following year. But Huang also insisted that the United States give China assurances that arms sales to Taiwan would cease by a specified date in the future — a condition unacceptable to the United States.[42]

While the Chinese were seeking an American commitment to end all arms sales to Taiwan, the White House was considering approval of the sale of the FX, a new jet fighter that would increase the level of sophistication of weapons provided to Taiwan.[43] Haig opposed the proposed FX sale, and in late November he sent a memo to Reagan outlining his views on the proposed sale and Sino-American relations, which, he warned, were at a "critical juncture."[44] Haig maintained that "careful management" of relations with Beijing is essential "if we are to avoid a setback which could gravely damage our global strategic policy." The secretary of state noted that the administration had given the impression to the Chinese that "we wanted to reverse normalization and pursue a 'two Chinas policy," and that this had "transformed the aircraft replacement question, which otherwise might have been manageable, into a symbolic challenge to China's sovereignty and territorial integrity." Echoing Pentagon assessments, Haig argued that "mainland capabilities and intentions do not require a level of arms sales [to Taiwan] above the final year of the Carter administration, which provided an unusually high ceiling." Haig proposed to Reagan a formula for resolving the issue: "[W]hile we cannot specify a time certain for ending arms sales, we can develop formulation linking our future actions to genuine progress on peaceful reunification."

President Reagan decided in January 1982 to reject the FX sale but to allow Taiwan to continue co-producing the less-sophisticated F-5E. Although administration officials viewed the outcome as favorable to Beijing, Chinese leaders protested the decision, complaining that it had been reached without prior consultation with China.[45] Meanwhile, negotiations over future American arms sales to Taiwan commenced in Beijing between senior American and Chinese officials that resulted in the signing of the August 17 communiqué. The crisis that had developed as a consequence of differences over the Taiwan issue led both sides to conclude that Sino-American relations were in danger of serious deterioration and that a rupture of the relationship would serve neither of their interests. Reagan sent three letters to Deng and also sent Vice-President Bush to Beijing to reassure Chinese leaders about American policy. The Chinese, in turn, adopted a more conciliatory tone toward the United States in the media.

The terms of the August 17 communiqué committed the United States not to increase arms sales to Taiwan "either in qualitative or quantitative terms" above the 1980 level, as had been recommended by Haig nearly ten months earlier. In addition, the United States pledged to "reduce arms sales to Taiwan, leading over time to a final resolution." The Chinese, although not explicitly agreeing to linkage, stated that they had a "fundamental policy of striving for peaceful reunification of the motherland."

The compromise communiqué defused and shelved the Taiwan arms sales issue. But the possibility that the dispute could return to haunt Sino-American relations was portended in conflicting interpretations of the communiqué that surfaced soon after: Washington claimed that the agreement committed the United States only to limit and reduce arms sales to Taipei, while Beijing insisted that Washington had agreed to "gradually reduce and finally stop" weapons transfers to the island. The Chinese could at any time renew pressure on the United States to further reduce arms sales to Taipei, which could reignite the Taiwan issue in Sino-American relations.

In the near term, however, Chinese leaders will likely continue to press Washington to abide by its commitments to Taiwan, yet try to avoid a confrontation with the United States over the issue that might again jeopardize the overall Sino-American relationship. This was demonstrated in the summer of 1986 when Beijing privately sought clarifaction of the August 17th communiqué. The Chinese objected to Washington's provision of advanced technology to assist Taiwan in developing its own fighter aircraft as a violation of the terms of the communiqué. Although the Chinese were dissatisfied with the American response, they continued to express their concerns privately and did not threaten retaliatory action as they had in 1981–1982.

Shultz Sets the Stage for Improved Sino-American Ties

The August 17 communiqué was finalized under George Shultz, who replaced Haig as secretary of state, in July, but it was Haig's handiwork. Shultz did not begin to put his personal stamp on China policy until his trip to Beijing in February 1983. That visit presaged a new phase in Sino-American relations that was preceeded by policy reassessments in both Washington and Beijing. Unlike earlier trips to China by senior American officials, Shultz's visit did not coincide with any policy decisions to provide the Chinese with such tangible benefits as greater access to technology or the right to buy arms. In his meetings with Chinese leaders, Shultz sought to lower expectations and develop a more realistic basis for moving the relationship forward. Shultz's discussions with the Chinese allowed for a full airing of differences and resulted in reinforcing commonly held views on security issues. Although Premier Zhao told American reporters during Shultz's trip that China "has no military relationship with the United States," Shultz discussed an agenda for renewing American-Chinese military cooperation with China's Defense Minister Zhang Aiping. In addition Chinese leaders privately reassured Shultz that Beijing's expanding contacts with Moscow — the first round of normalization talks had taken place four months earlier —would be limited and would not be at the expense of further development of Sino-American relations.

Shultz reportedly left Beijing convinced that the American failure to liberalize export restrictions on transfer of high-technology to China — promised by Haig — had become a bigger problem than Taiwan had been in 1981–1982. Shortly before Haig's China trip in June 1981, a formula for the approval of technology transfers to China had been agreed upon that provided twice the level of sophistication of advanced technology exports received by the Soviet Union before the invasion of Afghanistan. The formula was cumbersome in practice, however, and did not cover dual-use technology exports. The debate within the administration over the issue of easing restrictions on technology transfer to China pitted Haig's successor, George Shultz, and Commerce Secretary Malcolm Baldrige, who also favored loosening controls, against Weinberger and other Pentagon officials. The Defense Department wanted to tighten controls on the transfer of American technology to all countries, including not only the Soviet Union, but also American allies. Moreover, some Department of Defense officials were skeptical of Beijing's reliability and were not persuaded of China's strategic value to the United States. By spring 1983, however, administration officials had reached an agreement on easing restrictions on technology transfer to China. One of the "key players" in the administration told the *Washington Post:* "We felt at this stage of our relationships to China, if we don't do what we said we were going to do [two years ago when Haig visited Beijing] there would be a deterioration of the relationship. If we look on China as a friend, it was time to take a risk."[46] During a May visit to Beijing, Secretary Baldrige announced that the administration had agreed on new guidelines for streamlining decisions on sales to China of advanced technology, including technology with military applications. China was placed in category "V," which includes NATO countries, Japan, and Yugoslavia.[47]

The administration's steps to facilitate technology transfer to China helped ease strains in the relationship that had remained through the spring of 1983, despite the August 17 communiqué and Shultz's successful visit to Beijing. A series of disputes over the previous two years had created doubts in Beijing and Washington about the importance the other side attached to the relationship. These disputes covered a broad range of issues, including restrictions on Chinese textile exports to the United States, the defection of a Chinese tennis star, claims on the Chinese government for pre-1949 railway bonds, American opposition to the ouster of Taiwan from the Asian Development Bank, and the decision by Pan American Airlines to resume service to Taipei. Washington viewed Chinese leaders as exaggerating the importance of what it viewed as relatively minor issues to the extent that every dispute between the two countries became a "litmus test" of the entire relationship. The Chinese perceived the United States as interfering in China's internal affairs and acting in a "hegemonistic" manner toward Beijing. By mid-1983, however, many of these issues had been resolved or had receded into the background. The American decision to expedite technology transfer to China had reassured Beijing that the United States was willing to take concrete steps to assist China's modernization effort in an attempt to move the relationship forward.

American-Chinese Military Relationship Back on Track

The administration's success in regaining momentum in relations with China was demonstrated by Beijing's willingness to resume movement forward in all aspects of the relationship, including military ties. Shortly after Baldrige's trip to Beijing, the Chinese invited Secretary of Defense Weinberger to visit China, the first such high-level military contact since Carter's Defense Secretary Harold Brown went to China and Chinese Defense Minister Geng Biao came to the United States in 1980. During his September 1983 discussions in Beijing, Weinberger and his Chinese counterpart, Zhang Aiping, agreed to exchange military missions beginning in 1984 "to give American officers a better idea of China's military needs and to enable Chinese officers to see how Americans train and operate."[48] The Weinberger visit also paved the way for Premier Zhao Ziyang's visit to the United States in January 1984 and President Reagan's trip to China in April 1984. The Zhao and Reagan visits were important for strengthening, stabilizing, and institutionalizing the relationship rather than for taking major steps forward.

The military relationship was one of the major areas in which Washington and Beijing sought to routinize the Sino-American relationship. The two sides quietly began staff-level discussions to define the programs in which cooperation could be most fruitful. A series of high-level exchange visits also took place, including the chiefs of staff of the two militaries. A broad range of weapons sales were discussed and American survey teams were dispatched to China to assess the PLA's needs for modern weaponry and technology and the most appropriate weapons systems to meet those needs. A major watershed was reached when delivery of twenty-four Sikorsky helicopters began in November 1984 as part of the first Chinese arms purchase from an American company. During the visit to the United States of China's Defense Minister Zhang Aiping in June 1984, President Reagan, with little fanfare, had certified China as eligible for foreign military sales (FMS), which allowed the Defense Department to sell China weapons on a government-to-government basis. The administration notified Congress of the first government-to-government sale — $98 million in technology and equipment to modernize China's production of artillery ammunition — in September 1985. In early 1986, the administration announced the decision to sell China a $500 million avionics package to upgrade China's F-8 interceptor.

While the Reagan administration sought to expand the military contacts with Beijing, it respected China's desire to maintain a low profile in its defense ties with the United States. The measures taken by the United States and China would likely have been viewed as highly provocative by Moscow if they had occurred in the late 1970s when the Soviets were threatening "serious consequences" in response to possible American arms sales to China. In contrast with its initial policy during Haig's tenure as secretary of state, the administration no longer presented arms sales and other steps in military ties with China as a means of signaling Moscow. Rather Washington sought to advance the military aspect of Sino-American relations primarily as part of a broader American effort to build an enduring relationship with China at a pace and in areas in which the Chinese were interested. At the same time, the administration was careful to present the military relationship as nonthreatening to the Soviet Union. This was demonstrated by then Chairman of the Joint Chiefs of Staff General John Vessey, when he said during his January 1985 visit to China that Sino-American military ties "are designed to promote peace and understanding and threaten no third party."[49]

Beijing's Changing Perspective on American Policy

In their assessments of American foreign policy, the Chinese are primarily concerned with the impact of the United States on the international environment and on China's security interests. Beijing favors (1) an effective American counter to the Soviet military buildup, including growing Soviet military strength in the Asia-Pacific region; (2) American cooperation with other nations to contain Soviet influence and power; (3) Soviet-American military parity, which is viewed as minimizing the chance of war, whereas superiority by one side is viewed as destabilizing and dangerous; (4) a balanced reduction of American and Soviet military capabilities; and (5) an increasingly multipolar rather than bipolar world, in which the power gap is substantially reduced between the United States and the Soviet Union, on the one hand, and China and all other nations, on the other hand.

American policy toward the Soviet Union is perceived in Beijing as especially critical to Chinese interests. The Chinese viewed the detente policy of Presidents Nixon and Ford in the mid-1970s as a policy of weakness vis-à-vis the Soviet Union that jeopardized China's security interests by providing Moscow with advanced technology and allowing the Soviets to divert greater military assets to their buildup against China. In the late 1970s, Beijing perceived the United States under President Carter as economically weakened by the recession at home and as internationally on the defensive because of American post-Vietnam setbacks in the Third World. This American weakness, in the Chinese view, encouraged Soviet global expansion in Angola (1975–1976) and Ethiopia (1977–1978) and culminated in the 1979 Afghanistan intervention — a move that Beijing saw as posing a direct threat to China's security as well as being a possible harbinger of further Soviet moves in the Indian Ocean-Persian Gulf region.

The failure of the United States to counter Soviet power effectively engendered doubts in Beijing about the reliability of the United States as a partner in an anti-Soviet coalition, even after the nascent Sino-American strategic relationship was established during Brzezinski's May 1978 visit to Beijing. "U.S. reactions against Soviet expansionist policies," according to one Chinese analysis, "were feeble and unpredictable," and led to a decline in the "prestige and standing of the U.S. in the West."[50]

The Chinese were apprehensive in 1981–1982 about divisions within the Reagan administration over strategy toward the Soviet Union. They perceived a "unilateralist" faction, headed by Defense Secretary Weinberger, that emphasized reliance on a buildup of American military and economic strength to contain Soviet expansion. The unilateralists were seen pitted against a "coalitionist" faction, led by Haig, that stressed the necessity of strengthening anti-Soviet cooperation between the United States and its allies and friends. The Chinese viewed the unilateralist faction as downgrading the importance of allies and friends, including China, and as being less willing to compromise on bilateral issues.

Differences within the administration over strategy toward Moscow, according to the Chinese, led to inconsistent American foreign policies that damaged Washington's credibility abroad and weakened the anti-Soviet coalition. Beijing was especially critical of the administration's confrontational rhetoric toward the Soviet Union and its poor management of disputes with its NATO allies over trade sanctions against Moscow. The Chinese also charged that administration policies — especially in Central America and the Middle East — were alienating the Third World and thus increasing "the difficulty of coordinating anti-

Soviet activity." One Chinese analyst maintained, early in 1982, that the administration's foreign policies have "made people suspect that it is unreliable and has given the impression that it lacks balance in dealing with the relationships between individual problems and in distinguishing the priorities of various problems."[51]

China's initial concern about Reagan's statements on Taiwan and Sino-American relations reflected a skeptical view of the new president's strategic approach to managing Soviet power despite his anti-Soviet rhetoric and his campaign promises to rebuild American military and economic strength. On the eve of Reagan's inauguration, Yuan Xianlu, the foreign editor of the Chinese communist party paper *People's Daily*,[52] issued a prescient warning to the Reagan administration that its management of the Taiwan issue in Sino-American relations would be viewed in Beijing as a litmus test of the new administration's global strategy:

> There are those who believe that China will accept every United States action regarding Taiwan as long as Ronald Reagan is tough on the Soviet Union. Such a belief is totally erroneous. . . . [P]recisely because Sino-American relations must be viewed from a global perspective, China cannot but look upon the United States' China policy as a most important factor in evaluating the strategic measures and foreign policy of the United States government. This means that whoever truly fights hegemony must not retreat in their policy toward China. If anyone deliberately damages Sino-American relations, this certainly shows that he lacks a correct strategic point of view and also cannot really play an active role in the overall anti-hegemonistic strategy.

Over the course of Reagan's first term, Beijing gradually changed its view of the Reagan administration's effectiveness in managing the Soviet Union and American-allied relations. By mid-1983, the Chinese perceived greater unity within the administration in pursuit of a coalition strategy. Reagan's policies, from Beijing's perspective, had successfully restored the United States to a favorable position vis-à-vis the Soviet Union in the global balance of power. The Chinese viewed the American resurgence under Reagan as enhancing China's security by riveting Moscow's attention on the military competition with Washington and bolstering American credibility as a counterweight to growing Soviet military power.[53] The Chinese also perceived the administration as having strengthened relations with America's NATO allies. They viewed as especially significant the successful deployment of American intermediate-range nuclear forces (INF) in Western Europe, beginning in December 1983.

At the same time, in the Chinese view, the Soviet Union's position had been weakened by a debilitating leadership transition as well as by Moscow's intractable problems of economic stagnation, overextension abroad, and growing contradictions in its relations with Eastern Europe.

In addition, the Chinese perceived Soviet global influence to have declined, noting that many of its Third World allies and friends, including Mozambique and Angola, had sought to improve ties with the West to gain greater access to advanced technology and trade (see chapter 12). By early 1985, Beijing had concluded that the prevailing strategic environment was favorable for China and would remain so for the rest of the century. They judged that the United States had achieved the upper hand in the overall Soviet-American balance of power and predicted that Washington would retain this edge for at least the next 10–15 years, while the Soviet Union would remain in a relatively passive position. Moreover, the Chinese regarded Sino-Soviet and Soviet-American wars as unlikely and concluded that China could therefore focus its efforts and resources on economic modernization.

Beijing's assessment of Reagan's Third World policies also markedly changed during the president's first term in office. The Chinese noted that Washington had developed a coherent strategy for countering Soviet expansion in the Third World. One authoritative analysis of Reagan's diplomacy cited American gains in Latin America achieved by isolating Cuba, weakening Nicaragua, and invading Grenada; an improved American political position in Asia through greater coordination with its allies in the region; and some American success in reducing Soviet influence in southern Africa by means of quiet diplomacy.[54] The analysis also noted that the administration had increased military assistance abroad, according highest priority to countries that Washington viewed as playing "an important role in the contention with the Soviet Union." Only in the Middle East did the Chinese continue to warn that Washington was creating opportunities for Moscow to increase its influence.

The favorable international environment for Chinese security in the mid-1980s — created in part by the resurgence of American power — afforded Beijing the opportunity to pay greater attention to its objectives of enhancing China's prestige in the Third World and encouraging development of a more multipolar world that was less vulnerable to superpower intervention. Thus the Chinese stepped up their criticism of American "hegemonist" and "neo-colonialist" behavior toward Third World countries. They charged the United States with ignoring the socioeconomic roots of indigenous revolutionary movements, pursuing economic policies damaging to the interests of less developed countries, and supporting reactionary governments.

Although Beijing's concern about stepped-up Soviet-American military competition in Asia increased, the Chinese indicated tacit approval of American efforts to counter growing Soviet military activity in the region. Chinese analysts noted that Reagan's military buildup in Asia was a response to a drive by the Soviets to expand southward, tighten their encirclement of China and increase their ability to apply military pressure on Japan and the members of the Association of South and East Asian

Nations (ASEAN).* These analysts asserted that American objectives were defensive — to block Soviet expansion and to defend shipping lanes — and not aggressive.[55]

The Chinese were ambivalent about the changes in the Reagan administration strategy for managing relations with the Soviet Union. In Reagan's first term, Beijing had viewed Washington's posture toward Moscow as too confrontational, which, it claimed, increased Soviet-American tensions and accelerated the arms race. The Chinese welcomed the easing of strains between Washington and Moscow in 1985, but hinted at concern over possible Soviet-American collusion at China's expense. Following the November 1985 Reagan-Gorbachev summit, a Chinese Foreign Ministry spokesman expressed support for the resumption of the American-Soviet dialogue but warned that any American-Soviet arms control agreement should not harm the interests of "other countries."[56] The Foreign Ministry statement reflected Chinese concerns that had not been voiced publicly since 1983, when China and Japan stressed that Soviet-American accord limiting Soviet SS-20 deployments against Western Europe should prevent transfer of SS-20s from the western to the eastern part of the Soviet Union. The Chinese also privately indicated concern that the renewed Washington-Moscow dialogue could lead to Soviet-American accord on withdrawal of Soviet troops from Afghanistan on terms unfavorable to China.

Beijing was also concerned about the Reagan administration's Strategic Defense Initiative (SDI) for developing a layered ground- and space-based defense system to defend against Soviet nuclear attack. The Chinese feared that stepped-up competition between Moscow and Washington in strategic defense could disrupt Soviet-American parity, accelerate the arms race, and dangerously exacerbate tensions between the two superpowers. Deng Xiaoping publicly criticized both the United States and the Soviet Union for their plans to develop space-based anti-ballistic missile (ABM) systems and warned that extending the arms race into outer space would increase the danger of war.[57] Beijing's primary concerns were that Reagan's unwavering commitment to the SDI program would impede progress toward an agreement reducing strategic offensive arms; an expanded Soviet ABM capability could greatly diminish the effectiveness of China's deterrent force; and American and Soviet ABM research could lead to a significant widening of the superpowers' lead over China in defense and civilian technology.

Overall, the Chinese regarded the Reagan administration's tough posture toward Moscow as largely responsible for the Soviet Union's restrained international behavior and its new willingness to make concessions in various arms control fora in 1986. In addition, Beijing credited the administration with strengthening cooperation with American allies

---

*Thailand, Singapore, Malaysia, Indonesia, the Philippines, and Brunei.

and friends and resisting domestic political pressure from the pro-Taiwan right wing. The Chinese judged that although officials with ideological views remained in key administration positions, Reagan had moved toward the political center by pursuing more pragmatic policies.

Soviet Perceptions of Sino-American Relations

When the United States and China decided to forge a strategic relationship in 1978, the Soviets reacted with alarm. Moscow expressed deep concern that American-Chinese strategic ties would lead to a rapid, American-aided buildup of Chinese military capabilities and a tighter encirclement of the Soviet Union. But by 1981, Soviet fears of a large-scale provision of American military equipment to China began to diminish as Beijing cut defense spending for a second time and the United States transferred only limited quantities of dual-use technology and nonlethal military equipment. In interviews in Moscow in 1981, Soviet analysts acknowledged that Chinese defense modernization was proceeding slowly and predicted that Washington would not provide large amounts of military equipment to China.[58] They also conceded that the Soviet Union's favorable military balance with China was not likely to change and that the gap between Soviet and Chinese military capabilities would likely grow wider, even if some American military technology were transferred to China.

Nevertheless, Soviet propaganda continued to warn against the "dangerous partnership" between Beijing and Washington in the wake of Haig's June 1981 visit to Beijing. An article reflecting Soviet leadership views reacted to Haig's announcement of the American decision to sell lethal arms to China by warning that "the Soviet Union cannot remain indifferent to the dangerous new turn taken by Sino-American relations."[59]

By 1983, Soviet analysts were contending that Sino-American strategic ties would never return to the pinnacle reached in 1980. The "contradictions" between the United States and China, especially over Taiwan, will increase, and the military relationship will remain very limited or even contract. One Soviet official told the *New York Times* in March 1983 that the "silly policy of the Reagan administration" of seeking to upgrade relations with Taiwan had "taught China a lesson." "You are losing," he added, "and we are beginning to gain."[60]

The Soviets were thus caught off guard by the announcement in July 1983 that Secretary of Defense Weinberger would visit China in September and by the subsequent expansion of the Sino-American military relationship. Moscow had not expected Beijing to shelve the Taiwan issue and rapidly improve and develop the overall Sino-American relationship in the second half of 1983, leading to the exchange of visits by Premier Zhao and President Reagan in 1984.

Publicly, the Soviets reacted mildly to the warming trend in Sino-American ties, including the expansion of the military relationship. The Soviet media continued to accuse China of supporting Washington's "imperialist" policies and criticizing Soviet policies as "hegemonist," while claiming to pursue an "independent" foreign policy. But Moscow refrained from issuing threats in response to perceived Sino-American cooperation against Soviet security interests as it had in the late 1970s and early 1980s.

The Soviets' restrained public reaction to the improvement in ties between Beijing and Washington was in large part the result of a favorable turn in Sino-Soviet relations. By late 1982, public statements by Soviet leaders and Soviet press commentaries had begun to emphasize positive developments in Moscow's ties with Beijing and express hope that relations would continue to improve. Privately, however, Moscow pressured Chinese leaders to limit China's security ties with the United States.[61]

Thaw in Sino-Soviet Relations

During Reagan's first term in office, relations between the Soviet Union and China shifted from hostility and confrontation to eased tensions, dialogue, and the limited development of normal economic and state-to-state relations. At the height of Sino-American tension over Taiwan in early 1982, the Soviet Union sought to capitalize on differences between Washington and Beijing. In a speech at Tashkent in March, Leonid Brezhnev stressed that the Soviet Union, unlike the United States, had "never supported and does not now support in any form the so-called concept of two Chinas," and called for a re-opening of talks between Moscow and Beijing aimed at improving Sino-Soviet relations.

The Chinese initially responded coolly to Brezhnev's proposal, but Beijing warmed to Moscow's persistent calls for talks in the following months. A few weeks after Beijing bolstered its ties with Washington by reaching agreement on the August 17 communiqué, the Chinese publicly proposed that Moscow and Beijing hold exploratory talks on a range of state-to-state matters. China's willingness to ease tensions with the Soviet Union was primarily the result of two factors. First, Chinese leaders sought to gain leverage over the United States by indicating a softening of their position on opening a dialogue with the Soviet Union. Second, the Chinese concluded that their deepening commitment to economic modernization required the creation of a more favorable security environment, including a lower level of tension with their northern neighbor.

The first round of Sino-Soviet political "consultations" in October — which failed to produce substantive results — set the tone for subsequent twice-yearly meetings. The Chinese side presented three demands: a reduction of Soviet military deployments in the Sino-Soviet border regions; a withdrawal of Soviet forces from Afghanistan; and an end to Moscow's support for Vietnam's occupation of Kampuchea. The Soviet side refused to discuss third country issues and urged Beijing to shelve specific complaints until the two sides agreed on general principles to guide the relationship. No progress was achieved in the subsequent rounds of consultations through the eighth round of talks in spring 1986, despite occasional rumors of an impending agreement on a troop pullback. In 1983, the Chinese expanded their demand on reduction of Soviet forces along the border to include Soviet INF in the Far East.[62] The Soviets responded by claiming that its SS-20 INF were targeted at American bases in the region and not at China. In 1986, Chinese leaders hinted that Soviet use of North Korean air space to conduct reconnaissance flights against China was also being considered as part of the Soviet security threat to China that would have to be addressed by Moscow before full normalization of relations could be achieved.[63]

Soviet unwillingness to make concessions to Beijing by beginning to remove any of the three obstacles did not inhibit China from improving ties with the Soviet Union, primarily in bilateral trade and exchanges of economic, cultural, and scientific delegations. In December 1984, Soviet Vice-Premier Arkhipov, who had headed the Soviet economic assistance program in China in the 1950s, returned to an emotional welcome in Beijing, where he signed three agreements on economic, technological, and scientific cooperation. Chinese Vice-Premier Yao Yilin signed a five-year, $14 billion trade agreement in Moscow in July 1985 and that same year Chinese and Soviet parliamentary delegations exchanged visits, indicating a further normalizing of state-to-state relations.

In private discussions in 1985, Soviet analysts and officials expressed optimism over the long-term prospects for far-reaching improvements in Sino-Soviet relations. They maintained that:

1. The Taiwan problem will resurface in Sino-American relations and will result in China further distancing itself from the United States.
2. The similarity of social systems and ideologies between Moscow and Beijing will provide favorable conditions for closer Sino-Soviet ties, while limiting the development of American-Chinese relations.
3. Parallel Chinese and American interests are temporary, while the more enduring security interests of the two countries diverge — many Soviets maintain, for example, that the Chinese have hegemonic aims in Asia and eventually will threaten American interests in the region.
4. Chinese leaders who favor closer ties with the Soviet Union are likely to predominate in the post-Deng era.

5. The social unrest that has accompanied the implementation of economic reform will prompt Chinese leaders to return to a centralized planned economy.

Soviet assessments of the prospects for an extensive Sino-Soviet rapprochement do not address the issue Beijing considers fundamental: the threat the Soviet Union poses to Chinese security. Party Secretary General Hu Yaobang told interviewers in April 1985 that although China wanted to improve relations with Moscow, "the feelings of insecurity on our border . . . must be removed." Hu insisted that this is a fundamental position, "since it is bound up with the security of our country."[64]

There is little prospect that the Soviet Union will soon remove the three obstacles as demanded by Beijing. Even if Moscow were to withdraw some troops from Mongolia as announced by Gorbachev in his July 28, 1986 speech in Vladivostok and take other marginal steps to ease the Soviet military threat to China, it is unlikely that the feelings of insecurity indicated by Hu will be completely eliminated. For the foreseeable future, the Soviet Union will retain an overwhelming advantage in military power that will continue to constitute a serious threat to China's security. Under these circumstances, Chinese leaders will continue to pursue a counterbalancing strategy that includes maintaining strong ties with the United States to deter Soviet military pressure or attack on China. This does not exclude further efforts by Chinese leaders to maximize China's maneuverability within the triangle by expanding ties with the Soviet Union. But Beijing's willingness to improve relations with Moscow will be limited by Chinese leaders' concern that closer Sino-Soviet ties could undermine China's strategically vital relationship with the United States.

Conclusion

President Reagan, who had charged during the 1980 presidential campaign that President Carter had made unnecessary concessions to Beijing in the normalization agreement, two years later strongly affirmed the terms of that accord and went a step further toward resolving the issue of arms sales to Taiwan. Geopolitics and national interest had compelled the president to put aside his ideological preferences and political loyalities and reach a compromise with Chinese leaders. "Building a strong and lasting relationship with China has been an important foreign policy goal of four consecutive American administrations," Reagan said in a statement released with the August 17 communiqué. "Such a relationship is vital to our long-term national security interests and contributes to stability in East Asia."

After presiding over the worst crisis in relations between Beijing and

Washington since the 1971–1972 rapprochement, Reagan succeeded in building a more solid and enduring basis for Sino-American relations than any of his predecessors. Under Reagan, the expectations for American-Chinese ties were scaled back in both Washington and Beijing, while new steps forward were taken in all areas of the relationship. Multifaceted ties developed between the two countries entrenched the relationship in both the Chinese and American bureaucracies and provided some insulation from the vagaries of the political relationship and domestic politics. By 1983, a general agreement on China policy had been forged within the United States government. The resolution that year of the debate among senior American officials over technology transfer to China paved the way for a rapid expansion of economic and military ties. One official noted at the time, "We've got everyone on board now and realizing that a strong and modernizing China is an asset."[65]

Sino-American relations ceased to be an important domestic political issue under Reagan, although China-related issues, which were often entangled with other political issues, continued to emerge. Congressional condemnation of China's population policy for forced abortions and sterilizations, for example, was sparked primarily by domestic concern over abortion. And congressional misgivings over alleged Chinese nuclear proliferation practices that postponed approval for over a year of a Sino-American nuclear energy accord — reached by President Reagan during his visit to Beijing in 1984 — were fueled largely by general nonproliferation concerns rather than by opposition to the administration's China policy.

Reagan's anticommunist credentials enabled him in some cases to win over and in others to avoid attack from right-wing, pro-Taiwan members of Congress. To be sure, those suspicious of Beijing and supportive of closer ties with Taipei could reemerge to oppose the administration on such sensitive issues as arms sales to both Taiwan and the Mainland. And a Democratic successor to Reagan could encounter greater difficulty winning congressional support for new steps with China. But even if the forward momentum in Sino-American relations is temporarily slowed by congressional opposition under future administrations, it is unlikely to be halted or reversed.

Reagan administration officials believed that shared Chinese and American security concerns about the Soviet Union had not diminished, despite the easing of tensions between Beijing and Moscow. They maintained that improvements in Sino-Soviet relations would not inhibit the further expansion of American-Chinese political, economic, and military ties that are based on common security interests. It was clear, however, that there was a point beyond which normalization of Sino-Soviet relations would be unacceptable to Washington. Administration officials warned the Chinese that dramatically improved political ties between

Beijing and Moscow could jeopardize congressional support for the administration's China policy, especially for further liberalization of technology transfer and arms sales to China.[66]

The administration — especially after President Reagan's 1984 visit to China — increasingly played down the aspect of the Sino-American relationship most offensive to Beijing: the notion that China was a card to be played to gain leverage over the Soviet Union or to moderate Soviet behavior. Washington consented to Beijing's desire to publicly de-emphasize the strategic aspects of the relationship while quietly expanding them. Secretary of State Shultz sought to align the Reagan administration with China's priority of economic development rather than to draw Beijing into an overt global anti-Soviet coalition as his predecessor, Alexander Haig, had tried to do. The administration also concluded that China would modernize sooner or later, with or without American assistance, and that American interests would be best served by playing a positive and active role in that process.

China was no longer an integral part of the administration's policymaking toward the Soviet Union after Haig's resignation in mid-1982. China's pro-Western strategic orientation was still viewed as geopolitically vital to the United States, but day-to-day calculations of tactical moves in relations with China were no longer seen as necessary or efficacious in managing relations with Moscow. This constituted a major change in American policymaking, which, during the Nixon, Ford, and Carter administrations, had been based on careful calculations of the potential impact of China policy on Soviet-American relations and on Soviet behavior. At the same time that the Reagan administration de-emphasized the tactical coupling of China policy and Soviet policy, it also recognized the continued strategic importance of a strong Sino-American relationship to maintaining the American global position vis-à-vis the Soviet Union.

The increasing importance of economic issues and the receding emphasis on strategic considerations in Sino-American relations under the Reagan administration reflected the geopolitical realities of the mid-1980s, as well as shifting Chinese and American priorities. A resurgent Soviet Union could alter perceptions in Beijing and Washington and reignite Chinese and American interest in a "united front" to contain Soviet expansion. It is more likely, however, that the United States will maintain a strong global position and the Soviet Union will be on the defensive — at least in the short run — and that Washington and Beijing will continue quietly developing their military relationship in response to a commonly perceived long-term threat from Moscow while also expanding economic, political, and cultural ties.

"From Nixon to Reagan: China's Changing Role in American Strategy" was written for this volume. Copyright © 1987 by Banning N. Garrett and Bonnie S. Glaser.

Notes

1. Stanley B. Lubman, "Trade and Sino-American Relations," in *Dragon and Eagle: United States-China Relations: Past and Future.* Michel Oksenberg and Robert B. Oxnam, eds. (New York: Basic Books, 1978), p. 195.

2. Henry Kissinger, *White House Years* (Boston: Little, Brown, 1979), p. 222. Kissinger notes that the shift from a 2½-war to a 1½-war strategy was publicly announced in Nixon's first *Foreign Policy Report to the Congress*, February 18, 1970.

3. According to the *New York Times*, October 9, 1979, Nixon endorsed a secret "swing strategy," which had actually been the basis of American planning since the mid-1950s and which reflected the inability of the United States to achieve a 2½-war capability.

4. Kissinger, *White House Years*, p. 222.

5. Ibid., p. 1062. Kissinger says that Mao, in his conversations with Nixon during the president's February 1972 visit, gave assurances that China would not intervene militarily in Indochina and that China posed no threat to South Korea and Japan. Kissinger also says that Mao made clear that the Soviet Union was his principal security concern.

6. One strategist at the time, Morton H. Halperin, argued that the United States "might well wish to explore with the Soviet Union the possibility of joint action to halt the Chinese nuclear program or to render it politically and militarily useless. . . . The most extreme form of joint Soviet-American action (or unilateral action by one or the other) would be a military move designed to destroy Chinese nuclear facilities. . . ." *China and the Bomb* (New York: Praeger, 1965), pp. 124–125, 138. Several former government officials told the author that President Kennedy personally considered a military strike against China's nuclear facilities. Raymond Garthoff notes that he was personally involved in these internal deliberations in the mid-1960s. See his *Detente and Confrontation: American-Soviet Relations From Nixon to Reagan* (Washington, D.C.: The Brookings Institution, 1985), p. 984*n*.

7. See John Newhouse, *Cold Dawn: The Story of SALT* (New York: Holt, Rinehart and Winston, 1973), pp. 188–189; and H. R. Haldeman, *The Ends of Power* (New York: New York Times Books, 1978), pp. 89–94. Some officials interviewed by the author said they thought the Soviet overtures were a bluff to pressure the Chinese, while others believed they were serious.

8. Kissinger, *White House Years*, p. 764.

9. Ibid., p. 910.

10. For a detailed account of the origins of the idea of military ties with China, see Banning Garrett, "The United States and the Great Power Triangle," in *The China Factor: Peking and the Superpowers*, Gerald Segal, ed. (London: Croom Helm, 1982), pp. 76–104.

11. See Robert Sutter, *China-Watch: Toward Sino-American Reconciliation* (Baltimore: Johns Hopkins University Press, 1978) pp. 3, 109–112.

12. See Newhouse, *Cold Dawn*, pp. 100, 168–169, on the China factor in detente and the SALT negotiations.

13. The idea of military ties with China originated with Michael Pillsbury, then a RAND consultant, who wrote the first study exploring the subject in detail in early 1974. Pillsbury went public with his ideas in September 1975 in "U.S.-Chinese Military Ties?" *Foreign Policy* (Fall 1975), No. 20. Its publication was encouraged by high level administration officials.

14. These ideas, some of which were first proposed by Pillsbury, ibid., are outlined in Banning Garrett, "The United States and the Great Power Triangle," and in "China Policy and the Strategic Triangle," in *Eagle Entangled: U.S. Foreign Policy in a Complex World* (New York: Longman, 1979), pp. 228–263.

15. This assessment is based largely on dozens of interviews with government officials and

other informed sources. See Garrett, "The United States and the Great Power Triangle," p. 84.

16. See Robert Legvold, "Containment Without Confrontation," *Foreign Policy* (Fall 1980), No. 40.

17. According to several sources, by the fall of 1975, Schlesinger was pushing hard for a positive response to Chinese probes for military ties.

18. Leslie Gelb, "Washington Senses Loss of Leverage Against Soviets," *New York Times*, November 30, 1975. Peter Osnos, writing from Moscow for the *Washington Post*, December 7, 1975, concluded that the Soviets "apparently believe that relations between China and the United States are essentially stalled," and consequently seem relatively unconcerned about possible Sino-American collusion against them.

19. The role of the United States in "acquiescing" to the British deal was not revealed until four months later in a leak to Leslie Gelb of the *New York Times*, April 25, 1976. The leak to Gelb was itself intended to be a gesture toward a presumed pro-U.S. element of the Chinese leadership during the power struggle following the Tian An Men riots of April 5, 1976, and to provide pressure on Moscow in response to Angola and other sources of Soviet-American tension.

20. CoCom includes the NATO countries, minus Iceland, plus Japan, and was founded in 1949 to control strategic exports to communist countries. Gelb, ibid., reported and other sources have confirmed to the author that Kissinger agreed to allow the British to bypass CoCom to facilitate the sale of the Spey engines.

21. *Newsweek*, December 13, 1976. Vance writes in his memoir that normalizing relations with China was a goal of the administration "from the very outset," but that he did not expect normalization to take place before the second year of the administration. "Our first priorities were to strengthen NATO, to move toward a second SALT agreement, and to restore momentum to the Mideast and Panama negotiations." Cyrus Vance, *Hard Choices: Critical Years in American Foreign Policy* (New York: Simon and Schuster, 1983), p. 75. Vance records his consistent opposition to steps toward developing military and strategic ties with China advocated by Brzezinski for fear of provoking Moscow and damaging Soviet-American relations (see pp. 78, 101–2, 110–19, and 390–91). In his memoir, Brzezinski writes that from the beginning of the administration, he believed that improving relations with China was of strategic importance to the United States. Zbigniew Brzezinski, *Power and Principle: Memoirs of the National Security Adviser, 1977–81* (New York: Farrar, Straus and Giroux, 1983), pp. 3, 196. Brzezinski also notes that although he supported normalization of relations with China, he thought the United States might be able to "promote a strategic connection even without normalization" (p. 198).

22. See Garrett, "The United States and the Great Power Triangle," p. 88, and "China Policy and the Strategic Triangle," pp. 235–243. Brzezinski notes that Carter first indicated an interest in taking initiatives toward China in response to a harsh letter from Brezhnev at the end of February 1977 (*Power and Principle*, p. 155).

23. In a speech to the Asia Society in New York on June 29, 1977, Vance emphasized that American-Chinese relations would be dealt with primarily in a bilateral context, and that they would "threaten no one," i.e., the Soviet Union. The leak to the *New York Times* five days earlier of a major interagency review of United States-China policy, "PRM 24," also reassured the Soviets that the "China Card" had been rejected, although it also served as a warning that the option of Sino-American military ties had been considered at the highest levels of the government and could be reconsidered at a later date, as indeed it was in the spring of 1978. For Vance's account of the PRM-24 debate, see *Hard Choices*, p. 78. For Brzezinski's account, see *Power and Principle*, p. 200.

24. Speech to the United Nations, October 4, 1977.

25. See the *New York Times*, July 8, 1977 and January 6, 1978 on PRM 10's contents. Brzezinski writes that PRM-10 "reinforced my previous predisposition to push on behalf of an American-Chinese accommodation. I saw in such accommodation, together with our own enhanced defense efforts, the best way for creating greater geopolitical and strategic stability" (*Power and Principle*, p. 178).

26. "Chairman Mao's Theory of the Differentiation of the Three Worlds Is a Major Contribution to Marxism-Leninism," by the editorial department of *People's Daily*, translated in *Peking Review*, No. 45, November 4, 1977.

27. Jen Ku-ping, "The Munich Tragedy and Contemporary Appeasement," *Peking Review*, No. 50, December 9, 1977.

28. *The Washington Post*, February 1, 1979. For a detailed analysis of the Chinese invasion of Vietnam and United States policy, see Banning Garrett, "The Strategic Triangle and the Indochina Crisis," *The Third Indochina Conflict*, David W. P. Elliott, ed. (Boulder, CO: Westview Press, 1981). Also see Brzezinski's account of the Chinese invasion of Vietnam and American policy debates, in *Power and Principle*, pp. 411–414; and Raymond Garthoff, *Detente and Confrontation*, pp. 720–726.

29. *New York Times*, August 23, 1978. See also the comments by Carter National Security Council China specialist, Michel Oksenberg, "The Dynamics of the Sino-American Relationship," *The China Factor: Sino-American Relations and the Global Scene*, Richard H. Solomon, ed. (New York: Prentice-Hall, 1981), p. 53.

30. *New York Times*, October 4, 1979.

31. *New York Times*, January 3, 1980.

32. During a visit to the United States in late May, China's Defense Chief and Vice-Premier Geng Biao, when asked if China would seek to buy arms from the United States, responded: "I don't think there is such a possibility at present. But I believe there might be such a possibility in the future." *New York Times*, May 30, 1980.

33. The agreement to establish these facilities was apparently the result of the "special negotiations" Brzezinski says he initiated during his May 1978 visit to Beijing. See *Power and Principle*, p. 419; and Garthoff, *Detente and Confrontation*, p. 719*n*. The existence of the facilities was revealed by Murrey Marder, "Monitoring: Not-So-Secret Secret," the *Washington Post*, June 19, 1981.

34. In his memoir, Haig writes: "In terms of the strategic interests of the United States and the West in the last quarter of the twentieth century, China may be the most important country in the world" (*Caveat: Realism Reagan and Foreign Policy* [New York: Macmillan, 1984], p. 194).

35. George Shultz, in "New Realities and New Ways of Thinking," *Foreign Affairs* (Spring 1985), Vol. 63, No. 4, stressed the growing economic importance of the region to the United States. In a major Asia policy speech, March 5, 1983, to the World Affairs Council of Northern California in San Francisco, Shultz de-emphasized China's global role when he noted that the Sino-American relationship "can be a potent force for stability in the future of the region."

36. See Richard Nations, "A Tilt Towards Tokyo: The Reagan Administration Charts a New Course for Asian Policy," *Far Eastern Economic Review*, April 21, 1983. Nations presents an analysis of the shift in American policy toward China and the strategic triangle under Shultz. See also Robert Manning, "Reagan's Chance Hit," *Foreign Policy* (Spring 1984), No. 54.

37. Shultz, "New Realities and New Ways of Thinking."

38. Ironically, many of the phenomena — Soviet weaknesses and American strengths — pointed to by Shultz and other Reagan administration officials in the mid-1980s vindicated the assessments made in the Carter administration's study of the Soviet-American balance of power, PRM-10.

39. *Time*, March 16, 1981.

40. See Alexander M. Haig, Jr., *Caveat*, p. 204.

41. Ibld., p. 207.

42. Ibid., p. 210.

43. See A. Doak Barnett, *The FX Decision: "Another Crucial Moment" in U.S.-China Relations*, (Washington, D.C.: The Brookings Institution, 1981).

44. The November 26, 1981 memorandum was leaked to Tad Szulc, "The Reagan Administration's Push Toward China Came from Warsaw," the *Los Angeles Times,* January 17, 1982.

45. The *Los Angeles Times*, January 18, 1982, reported that Haig had promised further talks with the Chinese before a decision was made on the FX and other arms sales to Taiwan.

46. *Washington Post*, June 21, 1983.

47. A National Security Council steering group worked for six months to reach agreement among senior officials from the State, Commerce, Energy and Defense departments on guidelines on "what kinds of technology could be exported without endangering U.S. security," according to Fred Hiatt, "Role of National Security Council Again Uncertain," *Washington Post*, January 6, 1986. The specific guidelines were not announced until November 21, following Beijing's agreement to seek American approval before transferring technology to third countries. Processing of technology transfer to China was further expedited two years later, in September 1985, by the adoption of new procedures in CoCom, which were announced during a visit to Beijing in October by Vice-President Bush.

48. *New York Times*, September 3, 1983. The two sides reached agreement on exchange of logistics, training, and military medicine delegations.

49. Joseph Reeves, "China Playing Coy in U.S. Courtship," *Chicago Tribune*, January 20, 1985.

50. Huang Suan and Li Changjiu, "The U.S. Economic Recovery and Foreign Policy," *Guoji Wenti Yanjiu* International Studies No. 3, July 13, 1985, in Joint Publications Research Service (JPRS), *China Report: Political, Sociological and Military Affairs*, JPRS-CPS-85-110, October 28, 1985. See also Jin Junhui, "The Reagan Administration's Foreign Policy," *Guoji Wenti Yanjiu* No. 1 January, 1982 in FBIS-*China*, March 18, 1982.

51. Jin Junhui, "The Reagan Administration's Foreign Policy."

52. "China and Reagan," *New York Times*, January 17, 1981.

53. Chinese support for the administration's military efforts was expressed by Deng Xiaoping during Reagan's visit to China in April 1984. Deng reportedly told the president that the Soviet Union was "expansionist" and "hegemonic" and told him that China did not object to his defense buildup. David Ignatious, "Reagan's Trip Stabilizes U.S.-China Ties," *Wall Street Journal*, April 30, 1984.

54. Jin Junhui, "An Analysis of the Diplomacy of the Reagan Administration in its First Term," *Guoji Wenti Yanjiu*, No. 2, April 13, 1985, JPRS-CPS-85-067, July 3, 1985. Excerpts of the article were published in *Beijing Review*, No. 24, June 17, 1985.

55. Pei Monong, "The Situation and Existing Problems in the Asia-Pacific Region," and Xie Wenqing, "Soviet and U.S. Military Strategies in the Asia-Pacific Region," *Guoji Wenti Yanjiu*, No. 4, October 13, 1985, in FBIS-*China*, December 13, 1985.

56. Xinhua, November 22, 1985; FBIS-*China*, November 22, 1985.

57. Interview with *Liaowang*, No. 37, September 16, 1985; FBIS-*China*, September 30, 1985.

58. A more detailed analysis of Soviet views is presented in Banning Garrett, "Soviet Perceptions of China and Sino-American Military Ties," prepared for the SALT/ Arms Control Support Group, Office of Assistant Secretary of Defense (Atomic Energy), June 1981, Harold Rosenbaum Associates, Inc., Burlington, MA. The

report is based in part on extensive discussions with Soviet experts on China during a visit to the Soviet Union in February 1981.

59. I. Aleksandrov, "Escalation of Recklessness," *Pravda*, June 27, 1981; FBIS-*Soviet Union*, June 29, 1981.

60. Leslie Gelb, "Soviet Reporting a Chinese Detente," *New York Times*, March 20, 1983. For a detailed account of Soviet views of Sino-U.S. relations during this period, see Banning Garrett and Bonnie Glaser, *War and Peace: The Views From Moscow and Beijing*, Policy Papers in International Affairs, No. 20 (Berkeley: Institute of International Studies, University of California, March 1984). It is based in part on discussions with Soviet specialists on China during a visit to the Soviet Union in June 1983.

61. Soviet pressure prompted Beijing to publicly denounce Moscow's efforts to derail Sino-American relations. A *Liaowang* article noted that Moscow had rejoiced in China's squabble with the United States over Taiwan and was so "disgruntled" by the Reagan visit that it accused Beijing of "coordinating its actions with imperialism." The article asserted China's right to develop ties with the United States free of Soviet pressure, maintaining that "to develop its relations with the U.S. is in the interests of both the Chinese and the American people and is conducive to world peace." "The Chinese people do not intend to be at the beck and call of others in this matter." Michael Weisskopf, "Chinese Say Goal Is Better U.S. Ties Despite Soviet View," *Washington Post*, July 16, 1984.

62. Before the opening of the third round of normalization talks between Moscow and Beijing, *People's Daily* published a commentary indicating that China considered Soviet INF to be included in the three obstacles: "As everyone knows, the Soviet Union has already deployed large numbers of SS-20 missiles in its Asian region which pose a very serious threat to China and other Asian countries. If, as it says, the Soviet Union really hopes to reduce the danger of nuclear war, the missiles it has deployed in the Asian region must also be greatly reduced. One of the three main obstacles to the development of Sino-Soviet relations, which China has called on the Soviet Union to remove, is that of reducing military forces in the Sino-Soviet and Sino-Mongolian border regions, and this naturally includes missiles." September 17, 1983; FBIS-*China*, September 19, 1983.

63. The general secretary of the Chinese communist party reportedly expressed concern about what he termed Soviet "spying" activities to Marshal Roman Malinowski, a member of the Polish parliament. Hu apparently condemned the Soviet Union, saying that Moscow wanted to normalize Sino-Soviet relations in words only, and that it actually continued to engage in unfriendly actions against China. *Kyodo*, June 17, 1986; FBIS-*China*, June 18, 1986.

64. " 'Full Text' of Hu Yaobang's Answers to Questions from Hong Kong and Macao Correspondents," *Wen Wei Po*, April 10, 1985; FBIS-*China*, April 10, 1985.

65. Robert Manning, "Clear Air in Peking," *Far Eastern Economic Review*, September 22, 1983.

66. See Nayan Chanda, "Superpower Triangle," *Far Eastern Economic Review*, April 4, 1985; and "No Boat to China," *Far Eastern Economic Review*, May 30, 1985.

9

The United States
and Western Europe:
The Diplomatic Consequences
of Mr. Reagan

Miles Kahler

> Some day, it appeared to me, this divided Europe, dominated by the
> military presences of ourselves and the Russians, would have to yield to
> something more natural — something that did more justice to the true
> strength and interests of the intermediate European peoples themselves.
> — George F. Kennan, *Memoirs, 1925–1950* (p. 464)

> Hail Mr. President, we who are about to die, salute you!
> — Banner in a demonstration during President Reagan's visit to
> West Berlin, 10 June 1982

During the first Reagan administration, another crisis was declared in
relations between the United States and Western Europe. Some jaundiced observers yawned and asked what was novel about this latest
episode of disarray. No aspect of American foreign policy is so carefully
observed. Entire squadrons of scholars and politicians prod and poke the
alliance to see if it is still alive. Its temperature is taken so often that one is
tempted to declare it a hypochondriac.

Now many of those same professional alliance-watchers have announced the end of the crisis. Pointing to the continuing security dependence of Western Europe on the United States and the underlying bipolar
structure of the international system, they suggest that the divided European state system will persist, and with it the structures tying Western

*Miles Kahler is Professor of International Relations in the Graduate School of In-
ternational Relations and Pacific Studies, University of California, San Diego. He is
the author of* Decolonization in Britain and France *(Princeton: Princeton University Press, 1984) and the editor of* The Politics of International Debt *(Ithaca, NY:
Cornell University Press, 1986).*

Europe and the United States together.[1] Others, however, argue that the pendulum of discord and collaboration has not swung back, that certain trends in the latest crisis indicate a long-term disintegration beneath a facade of stability.

Structural Changes

Despite underlying structural stability in the security sphere, changes underway since the 1960s point to divergence in the definition of West European and American interests. The achievement of nuclear parity by the Soviet Union has had a significant impact on the perception of relative vulnerabilities and heightened the level of mistrust between Europe and the United States. Growing European weight in the world economy has been accompanied by a different pattern of economic vulnerability that reflects on European security: a more significant level of economic transactions with Eastern Europe and the Soviet Union and a higher level of dependency on imported Middle East oil.

Cumulation

The latest rifts appeared at the end of a decade of increasing friction: The Nixon "shocks" of the early 1970s were followed by divisions during the October War in the Middle East and the subsequent oil shock. Arguments after the Soviet invasion of Afghanistan took on a particularly sharp tone as a result.

Disagreement Along a Spectrum of Issues

The United States and Western Europe have had conflicts over policy outside the Atlantic area (1950s), nuclear strategy (1960s), and economic competition (1970s). With a resurgence of concern over the possibility of nuclear conflict in Europe, politicization of economic issues in the guise of economic sanctions against the Soviet Union, and divergence over strategies to ensure a stable supply of oil from the Middle East, the issue-specific debates of the past have broadened into different perceptions of Western interests in Europe and elsewhere.

European Insulation

Although European vulnerabilities may have increased in the last decade, the capabilities of the superpowers to influence events in Western Europe have declined. The United States, like the Soviet Union, can no longer count on docile proxies who will spring loyally to its bidding. High political costs are attached to appearing as a vassal, rather than an ally (as one German politician expressed it). The United States therefore finds it more difficult to reconstruct the elite solidarity that helped it to overcome earlier crises.

Democratization of Security Policy

Perhaps most important, this alliance conflict was no simple crisis of elites. Calling into question the traditional strategy and assumptions of the alliance was a broadly based, popular, and Europe-wide movement that challenged elite judgments and began a reevaluation of security policy more radical than any since the war.

Soviet Diplomacy

The Soviet Union has played on domestic political differences within Western Europe since the beginning of the Cold War. Under the leadership of Mikhail Gorbachev, Western Europe seemed to assume a new importance to the Soviets, and Soviet diplomacy seemed even more skillfully packaged for European publics. The Russian bear was no longer incompetent at public relations.

This "crisis" — whether a temporary conjuncture of events within an essentially stable set of boundaries or a reflection of deeper, irreversible changes — began in the final years of the Carter administration, as American attitudes toward the Soviet Union hardened dramatically in response to international and domestic politics. The Reagan administration has been a symbol of those domestic events, an illustration of the widening differences in perceptions on either side of the Atlantic, and a further test of the two contending views of the future: stability versus disintegration. The administration's efforts to restore American military power and to impose its concept of the Soviet threat on Western Europe, exacerbated conflict between the United States and its allies until pressures within Western Europe and in American domestic politics forced a partial revision of the administration's distaste for detente and arms control. An elite compromise was ratified at the Versailles and Bonn summits, only to come apart with renewed American efforts to overturn European economic links with the Soviet Union. The bargain was reestablished on the issues of East-West trade and deployment of long-range theater nuclear weapons, only to be threatened once again by President Reagan's Strategic Defense Initiative (Star Wars), announced in March 1983. This newest American turn in nuclear strategy threatened a future political debate even more wrenching, and more damaging to the alliance, than the one that had surrounded the Euromissiles.

The United States and Western Europe: The Historical Givens

The reality that frames and limits United States relations with Western Europe is the security dependency of Western Europe on the United States: the *separateness* and *lack of equality* in that relationship have been at the core of many of the security disputes within the "troubled partnership" since the 1950s. *Separateness:* obviously if Europe were Illinois or Wyoming (or even Canada), the American guarantee would not be questioned; much American effort has been devoted to making both the Soviet Union and Europe believe that Western Europe *is* the practical equivalent of American territory and that the United States would risk nuclear annihilation to defend its NATO allies. *Lack of equality:* since, until the construction of the British and French nuclear forces (and many would argue even after their construction), the final guarantee of Western Europe's security lay in the hands of a political class in a different country, a galling situation for a continent that once dominated the international system.

These underlying features of the security system were expressed in NATO strategy conflicts during the 1950s and 1960s: the failed European Defense Community and German rearmament, followed by Gaullist questioning of the American guarantee and the building of an independent French nuclear deterrent. Although political campaigns were mounted against the European Defense Community and German rearmament in the early 1950s, and against the stationing of tactical nuclear weapons in Germany in the latter part of the decade, these disputes remained, by and large, elite conflicts. The challenge to the alliance was never as widespread or as politically significant in Europe as it was in Japan. Also related to Europe's new security dependence was another element of conflict between the superpower and those European states that had not discovered the limited capabilities of a medium-sized power: defining the interests of the alliance outside the European theater. Sharp disagreement, over Suez and Algeria in particular, occurred because the Americans limited European action and failed to support their allies. Ironically, the positions would later be reversed, as the United States pleaded for an expansion of alliance responsibility and the Europeans resisted.

Until the late 1960s, economic conflict remained at a relatively low level among states that were basically capitalist in structure and enjoyed an international monetary regime that ensured stable exchange rates, a trading system that moved toward liberalization despite lingering protectionist exceptions, and cheap energy. The increasing prosperity of the West Europeans was related to security through the issue of burden sharing, but an expanding economic base made budgetary compromises relatively easy to negotiate. Even when serious economic conflict erupted in the early 1970s, there was little direct linkage to security questions: the years of economic disruption were also years of a mutually agreed policy of detente with the Soviet Union.

In 1973, the year of the October War in the Middle East and the first oil shock, America and Western Europe diverged on two key questions — the Middle East and energy — that had not been at the core of postwar relations but were now inextricably entwined with *both* economic well-being and national security. Although an energy program of sorts was patched together under American leadership, the American ability to ensure against an oil shortfall was gone, never to return. The Middle East question brought fundamentally different readings (influenced by domestic politics) of events in that region, producing a pro-Arab shift in Europe and a hardening of support for Israel in the United States. Less obvious, but equally important, the war had given the opponents of detente in the United States a crucial weapon to overturn the fragile domestic support for Kissinger's policies.

The election of a trilateralist, Jimmy Carter, as president might have augured well for American policies toward Western Europe, but the growing self-confidence of the Europeans in economic policy and their continuing dependence on the American security guarantee brought sharp criticism of American leadership: too much of the wrong sort in managing the international economy, too little of an erratic kind in dealing with the Soviet Union. Complaints of the first sort centered on American efforts to use the economic summits to tie together a "locomotive strategy" for lifting the world economy out of lingering recession, resisted strenuously by the West Germans. Other criticisms centered on the unsteadiness of American policy. The shifts of Carter foreign policy on the neutron bomb question demonstrated the difficulties that could arise when an American president, intending to share decision making in defense, encountered the realities of European domestic politics. Burden sharing came to mean the sharing of political costs, which no politician cares for. The bungling of the neutron bomb decision led to renewed American resolve not to waver in the future and the determination to assure the Europeans that America was commited to their defense. One result was the NATO decision in December 1979 to deploy a new generation of theater nuclear forces; a collective decision with consequences that would shake the alliance.

The early squalls of the Carter administration derived from increasing European self-confidence, a result of Europe's growing economic weight internationally, and from the American administration's dedication, at least rhetorically, to a more pluralistic view of the world and a more collegial model of alliance management. As the balance within the administration and within American domestic politics shifted toward a harder posture in relations with the Soviet Union, European complaints reversed. After 1979, the Europeans — and the use of that term globally will be qualified below — found themselves in a sort of time warp, confronting a United States whose perceptions had altered dramatically, away from the presuppositions of detente and toward those of confrontation with the Soviet Union.

The invasion of Afghanistan crystallized growing concern within the Carter administration over an "arc of crisis" around the Indian Ocean littoral and awarded victory to the opponents of detente in the administration and the country: SALT II was shelved, economic sanctions were imposed by the United States, and President Carter proposed a boycott of the Moscow Olympics. But in alliance relations Afghanistan was not to be Korea. Rather than viewing the Soviet invasion as indicative of renewed global hostility on the part of the Soviets toward the West, many Europeans refused to accept completely the American reading of the situation and its proposed strategy. They at first preferred to define Afghanistan as an "East-South" question and chose not to endanger detente in Europe (viewed as a long-term investment and a success) by following the American rhetorical lead too wholeheartedly. Pledging not to undercut American sanctions against the Soviet Union and reluctantly agreeing to support those imposed by the United States on Iran, the West European governments, including the Conservative Thatcher government in Britain (which was in accord with much of the new American analysis), were skeptical of the usefulness of economic sanctions as a means of exercising leverage over the Soviet Union and hostile to the extension of American sovereignty implied by the financial sanctions against Iran.

The invasion of Afghanistan not only brought to the fore a divergence in attitudes toward the Soviet Union and the value of perserving the fabric of detente in Europe, it also led to quarrels over the alliance's role outside the European theater, which was a question of particular sensitivity for the West Germans. The Europeans viewed the principal threat to the region and its oil supplies, not as a further military drive by the Soviet Union but rather as intraregional disputes (such as the warfare between Iran and Iraq that erupted in September 1980) or internal conflict (symbolized by the attack on the Great Mosque at Mecca). Although they accepted the need for an increased Western presence in the region, the Europeans argued for a "division of labor," which would permit them to concentrate on diplomatic and economic instruments. The United States, which thought the Soviet military threat to the region more serious, saw such a division as awarding them the military risks, in spite of the far greater dependency of the West Europeans on Middle East oil imports.[2] The regionalist perspective of the Europeans (and different domestic political givens) also influenced their judgment and implicit criticism of American policy toward the Arab-Israeli conflict.

The Carter administration witnessed the beginnings of what some called a "crisis" in relations between the United States and Western Europe, but the American administration's swing away from detente policies in the wake of the invasion of Afghanistan remained in large measure a judgment of strategy toward the Soviet Union, not a change in

America's fundamental views of the character of the Soviet regime or its foreign policy.[3] Europe and the United States disagreed over appropriate mixture of carrots and sticks in a strategy that both agreed must be, essentially, a mixed one. Questions of efficacy, such as the use of economic sanctions to influence Soviet behavior, and the separability of detente (Europe versus the Middle East) seemed to be the core of the disagreement; these were important differences, but not fundamental ones. The different givens in domestic politics on either side of the Atlantic had not yet resulted in different world views, despite the American change of line. The Carter administration had, however, introduced new sources of conflict that would only become apparent under the following administration — a mixing of the two tracks of economics and security in the form of the sanctions question, an apparent move toward a nuclear strategy that offered options for fighting nuclear wars, a tenacious defense of a Middle East peace program that failed to settle the Palestinian question. It was only when domestic politics in the United States took a further sharp turn to the right, in the presidential election of 1980, however, that the disarray in the alliance increased. This disarray was grounded in very different perceptions of the Soviet Union that were, in turn, rooted in different political givens in Western Europe and the United States. And deepening the rift, the new political givens fed into one another in a particularly perverse way.

The Reagan Administration and Western Europe

The Reagan administration from its first days confronted one element in the apparent Atlantic rift that had affected past administrations less: the consequences of cumulation. Although most administrations had had their own crises in relations with Western Europe, the positions of the new team, swinging even more sharply in the direction taken during the last years of the Carter administration, built on an existing sense in Europe of an America oblivious to the European point of view. The administration also confronted, although it took some time to become aware of it, a series of overlapping European-American disagreements that concerned not only the older and better-known questions of nuclear strategy, burden sharing, and international economic management but also the orientation of the alliance outside Europe and a growing gray area of economic issues with security implications (or, in European eyes, political manipulation of economic transactions). Finally the political and economic coalition that supported the Reagan administration was the least "Atlanticist" of any recent American presidency. Its concern for Latin America and East Asia suggested a shift in American economic and political power toward the West and the South domestically and away from traditional allies.

As it had in its policy toward the Soviet Union, the Reagan administration brought with it a very simple and coherent strategy for mending ties to Western Europe. Curiously that strategy echoed the criticisms that Europeans had made of the Carter administration, that the source of division was an absence of leadership on the part of the previous American administration and not disagreement over appropriate strategy, much less structural change. With the reassertion of a clear American line toward the Soviet Union and demonstrated American willingness to undertake a military buildup vis-à-vis the Soviets, the West European allies would respond as they had in the (distant) past.

The pursuit of this strategy pointed up the Reagan administration's initial contribution to further deterioration in relations with Western Europe. Although certain elements of the security relationship, and particularly European security dependency, remained unchanged, other features had altered, particularly Europe's greater political self-confidence (based on its greater economic weight internationally) and the greater insulation of Europe from manipulation by either superpower. Just as the Soviet Union had lost its hold over most of the West European left, so the United States could no longer play the European center and right as it had in the 1950s. Western Europe was more insulated from direct manipulation but remained highly sensitive to changes affecting its security. The Reagan administration, unwittingly, ensured that this sensitivity would grow and produce, through a democratization of the European foreign policy debate, a popular movement intensely critical of American aims and military strategy.

Sources of Conflict: Two Views of the "Giant with Feet of Clay"

The Reagan administration held a view of American relations with the Soviet Union and a preferred American and Western policy that was skeptical of negotiations and hostile toward the remnants of detente.[4] The new (or very old) views first espoused by the Reagan administration in policies toward the Eastern bloc were at the core of its conflict with the Europeans.

The position of the Carter and Reagan administrations in relation to the views of European elites and the growing "peace constituency" in Europe are outlined in Figure 9–1. Even after the shift that occurred late in the Carter administration, much common ground remained between the American political elite and the European elites. The Soviet Union might be aggressive and expansionist, but it was also ultimately a manageable threat, an opportunistic power that could be stopped with some variation of the traditional policies of containment applied to new areas of perceived threat — the Middle East and the Persian Gulf. A mixed strategy had to include many more sticks than carrots in the present phase, but the future use of positive incentives was not ruled out. The

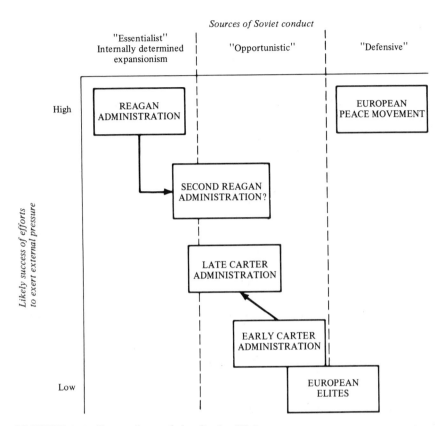

FIGURE 9-1. Perceptions of the Soviet Union.

victory of the hard-liners in the Carter administration (and divergence from the European elites) had dispelled the notion that the Soviet Union had behaved defensively (particularly in Afghanistan) and calculated Soviet vulnerability to external pressure from the West, particularly the exercise of leverage through economic sanctions.

In the first Reagan administration, an "essentialist" view of the Soviet Union seemed to hold the dominant position, at least in the early months: the Soviet Union was implacably hostile to the West for reasons of domestic ideology, militarism, nationalism, or some mix of the three. The rhetorical picture painted of the Soviet Union by the president was reminiscent of the 1950s: an inherently "evil force," a group of leaders whose morality permitted them "to commit any crime, to lie, to cheat." Soviet expansion was ceaseless, and it was global: American concern (and allied coordination) had to meet the threat wherever it presented itself. Yet the Soviet Union was also a giant with feet of clay, and the administration chose to paint different portraits of the adversary at different times. Because of the weakness of its economy, in particular, the Soviet Union *was* vulnerable to Western economic pressure. Confronting such a foe, a mixed strategy was hardly possible; rather, early Reagan policy suggested that only military buildup, coupled with resolute rhetoric and ideological confrontation, would suffice to contain the Soviet menace.

But not to strengthen the alliance, as it turned out. For elite and public opinion in Europe, however negative a view it took of the Soviet Union, still persisted in seeing the country as a state that could be bargained with, a state that *must* be bargained with, a state that the Europeans had lived with for many years. And for the building European peace movement, a defensive view of Soviet behavior, which had virtually disappeared in American political discourse, was often endorsed.

For the European elites, a mixed strategy was not dead, and however much they disagreed with the mix chosen by the Carter administration, they viewed with positive alarm the denigration of negotiation in the rhetoric of the Reagan administration. Although they made polite noises of appreciation for the clear direction now visible in Washington (and quietly asked, how long this time?) they also, in the early months of the administration, made clear that they expected the policies of arms control to continue and that they hoped for an early summit meeting between Reagan and Brezhnev. Like the Reagan administration, the Europeans often accepted a "giant with feet of clay" image of the Soviet Union, but they drew very different conclusions. The weaknesses that they perceived (perhaps they saw the feet of clay because they were closer) suggested a more manageable threat. They did not believe that Western economic pressures could change the Soviet system or Soviet foreign policy in any predictable way (the source of conflict described below). If anything, much of the European peace movement and segments of the elite saw pressures on a fragile Soviet system as leading not to collapse or conciliation but to closure and greater hostility. Ironically those who endorsed a defensive view of Soviet motivations agreed with the Reagan line on the susceptibility of the Soviets to external change. Their reading of internal Soviet dynamics, however, and their prescription — conciliatory, even unilateral policies — were radically different.

Sources of Conflict: Nuclear Strategy Enters European Politics

On October 16, 1981, in a speech to American newspaper editors, President Reagan claimed that the United States and the Soviet Union could engage in a tactical nuclear exchange without escalation into all-out nuclear war. A few weeks later, then-Secretary of State Haig claimed that NATO had plans for a low-level nuclear explosion to warn the Soviet Union of further escalation if it made a conventional attack on Western Europe. Such public statements reflected an internal debate over nuclear strategy within the administration and the increasing influence within the Department of Defense of those who believed that the United States should develop a nuclear war-fighting capability. The projection of this arcane debate into the public arena, however, could not have happened at a more inopportune time. The comments echoed and reechoed in a Europe already divided by its own debate over the proposed deployment of long-range theater nuclear forces (LRTNF), which NATO had agreed to in December 1979. That decision, meant to ease the fears of Europeans that American strategic doctrine might decouple European defense from the use of American nuclear weapons, ultimately came to be seen, under the Reagan administration, as precisely a means to such decoupling. Rather than ensuring a firmer American commitment, when combined with arguments in favor of capabilities for fighting a limited nuclear war, many Europeans saw the December 1979 decision as the first step toward a strategy of limited nuclear war in Europe.

Curiously the 1979 decision had its roots in the equivocations of the Carter administration over the neutron bomb and in the concern of some European leaders and defense analysts that nuclear parity, combined with the arms control forseen in SALT II, might lead to dangerous imbalances in nuclear forces at lower levels on the escalation ladder. It was, in fact, Chancellor Helmut Schmidt of West Germany who noted such a danger in a public lecture given in October 1977[5]:

> SALT codifies the nuclear strategic balance between the Soviet Union and the United States. To put it another way: SALT neutralizes their strategic nuclear capabilities. In Europe this magnifies the significance of the disparities between East and West in nuclear tactical and conventional weapons.

Although many would later challenge both the logic of such concerns and the breadth of European consensus on the need for countermeasures, for the Carter administration, such expressions of alarm were serious, particularly after the neutron bomb debacle.

Concern centered on Soviet deployment of a new generation of medium-range ballistic missiles, the SS-20, targeted on Western Europe (and China), which possessed larger numbers of warheads and greater mobility than the SS-4 and SS-5 systems it was replacing. More significant in the eyes of some analysts was the growing vulnerability of NATO theater nuclear forces to Soviet deployments of all kinds, not simply to the much-discussed SS-20s. Yet even those who defended the NATO decision to deploy air-launched cruise and Pershing II missiles, often conceded that the military argument in favor of that number of those systems was "not compelling," either in the reading of the consequences of parity at the strategic level or in the appropriate response to the problem of vulnerability, which could be better met by a sea-based deployment.[6]

The deployment of cruise missiles and Pershing IIs was, as had been the case with previous decisions (or nondecisions) on theater nuclear forces, a political decision. The problem addressed by the December 1979 decision was the perennial one of European and Soviet perceptions of possible decoupling of the American nuclear deterrent from the defense of Western Europe. This fear had been the original source of European claims for a countermeasure to the SS-20 deployments. As Bertram would have it, "U.S. nuclear forces *in Europe* will be a more credible and more proportionate demonstration of that link than U.S.-based strategic nuclear systems alone would be."[7] In any case, the political or perceptual argument carried the day, although the political sensitivity of the decision, even in those pre-Afghanistan days, was recognized in Europe. Germany, the most affected nonnuclear power, wanted as many other nonnuclear European countries (and at least one continental country) to accept the deployment. European sentiment also saw to it that the decision was tied, for the first time in NATO history, to an effort at arms control with the Soviet Union (the "two-track" aspect of the decision). The Germans also made certain that there would *not* be a "double key," reinforcing the "American" character of the weapons.[8] Also for the first time, the production decision on the new systems was made collectively by NATO, but, as would soon be discovered, the second track of the decision, arms control negotiations with the Soviets, remained in American hands.

As Bertram noted, the December 1979 decision was an effort to cure a problem of political trust with a military deployment: "What may be desirable today, for political reasons, may become for other political reasons less desirable tomorrow."[9] The political givens on which the NATO decision was based quickly shifted. Instead of a decision taken within a continuing, if fragile, setting of arms control negotiations, the SALT II treaty was shelved a few weeks after the decision, and serious negotiations between the superpowers became moot. With the election of Ronald Reagan on a platform rejecting SALT II and the formation of a foreign policy and defense team more skeptical of arms control than any since World War II, the second track of the NATO decision, the politically essential commitment to arms control, also seemed to be endangered.

Administration skepticism about arms control reinforced perceptions in the burgeoning European peace movement, and in a European public increasingly concerned about superpower conflict, that the new administration took a somewhat casual attitude about the danger of nuclear war. With such stimulus from Washington, the European peace movement grew enormously. Particularly in Scandinavia, in the Benelux countries, and in West Germany, pressures on political elites were enormous. Even those countries already possessing nuclear weapons (such as Britain), those previously unaffected by European disarmament movements (such as Italy), and those that were not yet members of NATO and did not confront a decision on deployment (such as Spain), witnessed major efforts at organization and demonstration. An antideployment demonstration in Bonn in April 1981 drew a crowd of 15,000; after ten months of the Reagan administration, demonstrations in October and November 1981 were attracting hundreds of thousands of demonstrators (estimates of 250,000 in Bonn, 150,000 in London, and over 200,000 in Florence). Only France seemed exempt from the marshaling of antideployment support on such a scale.

The administration's response to politicization of the Euromissile issue was twofold: a reassertion of the arms control track and the portrayal of support for deployment as a test of alliance solidarity. Reagan's speech on arms control to the National Press Club (November 18, 1981) was in large part a response to growing opposition in Europe to the deployment of new theater nuclear forces. The tone of the president's speech, meant to convey the image of a man of peace, was decidedly different from Reagan's earlier anti-Soviet rhetoric. Many of his arms control proposals remained vague, save for that on European theater nuclear weapons. Reagan endorsed the "zero option," which would commit the NATO allies to cancel their planned deployment if the Soviet Union removed all of its SS-20s (even those east of the Urals).[10] At first glance, this was a shrewd bit of politics for the European public, since the missile question was batted firmly into the Soviet court. At the same time, the American government began to emphasize the political necessity of the deployment for alliance credibility. Not stated publicly was the view that any willingness on the part of European governments to bow to the peace movement (viewed by American conservatives as the proxy of Moscow) would simply be another bit of evidence that Europe was on the road to Finlandization.

The new focus on arms control negotiations as a necessary concomitant to the planned deployment provided European politicians with an important card to play in favor of pursuing the 1979 decision, since the second track was now visible. The peace movement did not die, however. The opening of negotiations on theater nuclear forces on November 30, 1981 was only a tentative beginning, one that promised to reduce the visible dangers to Europe from a strategy based on nuclear weapons only in the distant future, if ever. Some used the burgeoning opposition to deployment of new theater nuclear forces to argue for changes in that long-standing strategy. Four of the most senior members of the foreign policy establishment — George Kennan, Robert McNamara, McGeorge Bundy, and Gerard Smith — suggested that[11]

> the events of the last year have shown that differing perceptions of the role of nuclear weapons can lead to destructive recriminations, and when these differences are compounded by understandable disagree-

ments on other matters such as Poland and the Middle East, the possibilities for trouble among Allies are evident. `

Their case in favor of a declared NATO policy that nuclear weapons would be used to retaliate only against nuclear attack challenged the imprecise, but politically useful, compromise on flexible response reached in 1967. Replies by Secretary of State Haig and German Foreign Minister Genscher suggested that, despite other disagreements within the alliance, that doctrine was still perceived as sound by both European and American elites. As deployment of the Euromissiles approached, the European elites sought, not doctrinal revision but rather a convincing American position on the second, arms control, track that would allow them to create a political coalition accepting the new nuclear forces.

Sources of Conflict: Politicization of Economic Relations — Poland and Sanctions

Nuclear strategy was an old battleground in disputes between Europe and the United States; the mirror-image fears of decoupling and becoming a nuclear battlefield were at least two decades old. What was new was the scale of politicization of these issues and the Europe-wide character of such concern. Equally grounded in divergent perceptions of the Soviet Union and in the history of the 1970s was a new source of dispute, less tied to mass politicization but deeply embedded in the contrasting patterns of economic relations that had developed over the last decade as a result of declining East-West tensions. The use of economic sanctions against Iran and the Soviet Union by the Carter administration had been endorsed by the Europeans only reluctantly, and they had made clear their resentment of the administration's extension of sovereignty to American banks in Europe in the Iranian case. The Reagan administration soon revealed assumptions about economic transactions with the East that were even further from those of the Europeans. Unlike questions of military policy, when the British and French often partially endorsed the more pessimistic American view, on the issue of economic sanctions the Europeans stood united against the American effort to burden them and their underemployed economies with a dubious foreign policy strategy.

The divergence of views stemmed from the structural place of the two economies, European and North American, in the pattern of East-West trade; from different conceptions of how to influence Soviet behavior; and from different readings of the history of detente. The contrasting stakes of American and European economies in East-West trade were clear, and proponents of sanctions in the United States saw European reluctance to exert economic pressure on the Soviet Union as further evidence that the years of detente had begun to erode the Western will to resist Soviet expansionism. Even though the Europeans were more deeply involved in East-West trade, the dependence of their economies on the East was hardly large enough to support such charges. More important than volume in determining their position on sanctions was the composition of their trade with the Soviet Union and Eastern Europe. Unlike that of the United States, which is concentrated in agricultural exports, European trade is heavily weighted toward manufactures, particularly capital goods. The Europeans argued that trade in such products, unlike trade in grain, could not be turned on and off like a tap without risking disruption to their own economies and the larger pattern of East-West economic transactions.

If the material burden of sanctions seemed heavy for the West European economies, the Europeans also disputed the notion that economic sanctions were an effective means of influencing Soviet behavior. At least three different justifications — symbolism, leverage, and economic warfare — could be found in American arguments for economic sanctions.[12] The Carter administration, had usually proposed sanctions for reasons of symbolism (to condemn the adversary, even when admitting that his behavior was unlikely to change) and as an attempt to exercise leverage (to change a specific aspect of Soviet behavior through the withholding of specific desired goods). Leverage was the typical argument of those seeking to change relatively minor aspects of Soviet behavior — the linkage of oil drilling equipment to the arrest of Soviet dissidents —while event the proponents of sanctions were forced back to arguments of symbolism in the case of Afghanistan, in which the Soviet stakes were clearly too great to be changed by the modest economic weapons at the disposal of the United States. The Reagan administration, however, took office with at least part of the administration (and a part that initially grew in influence) arguing that the Soviet economy was in dire straits and that economic warfare on the part of the West would weaken Soviet ability to pursue expansionist policies abroad and to continue its military buildup at home. In this case, the effort was not designed to change specific Soviet policies — the "essentialist' view of Soviet behavior could hardly admit that — but rather to weaken the Soviet capability to pursue policies that were unlikely to change. There was no need for fine-tuning: any denial of Western trade or credits would serve the larger purpose, and, conversely, any trade or transfer of technology was viewed as contributing to the freeing of Soviet resources for military purposes.

Europeans took a wholly different view, one that might be termed automatic destabilization. Although agreeing with restrictions of strategic technologies toward the East (a long-standing alliance policy under the Coordinating Committee for Multilateral Security Export Controls (CoCOM), they argued that Western credits, trade, and technology transfers were not easily absorbed without changing the Soviet and East

Europeans economies. The growing crisis in Poland seemed to demonstrate that detente policies had worked and that growing interdependence with the West had forced hard choices on the communist regimes. The Polish economy's dependence on a continued flow of Western credits made it unlikely that the Soviets would intervene to quell the rise of Solidarity, since, whatever the risk of Western reaction, the Soviets could not deliver what the Polish economy needed. The opening of economies produced rising and difficult-to-satisfy expectations internally and wove the "web of detente" more firmly externally, forcing all parties to move more cautiously than they would have in pre-detente days.

The European view of economic transactions with the East fitted with a third justification for resisting economic sanctions: their reading of detente in Europe. Although the Reagan administration saw the years of detente as ones in which the Soviet Union increased its military edge over the West and skillfully exploited Western divisions to win economic concessions and Third World influence, the Europeans did not see detente as a one-way street. Reagan administration statements increasingly portrayed economic transactions of any kind as a "gift" relieving the Soviet bloc's economic difficulties; the Europeans saw not only economic benefits from their trade with the East (as with other trade) but also political benefits in furthering the stabilization of political relations between East and West in Europe.

Poland provided the occasion for demonstrating the fundamental differences between Americans and Europeans on these issues. Even those who espoused the automatic destabilization view of East-West trade admitted that an overt Soviet invasion of Poland to crush the insurgent Solidarity movement would necessarily call for a unified and tough NATO response. Since military action had been ruled out, economic sanctions of some kind were necessarily on the agenda. In any event, the declaration of martial law in Poland on December 17, 1981, without Soviet military intervention, caught the alliance without a prepared position, and European, particularly German, analyses of the situation and those of the Reagan administration once again diverged sharply.

The United States announced economic sanctions against the martial law government of General Jaruszelski, which were quickly followed by a charge of Soviet responsibility and the declaration of sanctions against the Soviet Union. Even though the American sanctions were not particularly harsh, given earlier administration statements, the initial European response was less than enthusiastic: No government endorsed the American sanctions or hastened to impose its own.

The Europeans did agree not to undercut sanctions imposed by the United States, but their interpretation of that assurance was once again different from that of the Americans, particularly when the United States homed in on two questions that had caused friction since the Carter administration: the natural gas pipeline deal that was being negotiated between the Soviet Union and West European consumers and subsidized export credits in European trade with the East.

The pipeline would prove the most contentious, and no single issue better symbolized Western Europe's dogged attachment to East-West policies that ran counter to United States' views. In scale alone, the proposed pipeline was symbolic of European reliance on a minimal level of stability in East-West relations: the building of a pipeline 3500 miles long to transport natural gas from Siberia to the West European market. Plans for the Siberian pipeline had been underway for several years, and the Carter administration had expressed concern, which intensified after the Soviet invasion of Afghanistan. The worries of that administration were defined narrowly: fear that increased European dependence on Soviet natural gas would lead to increased leverage by the Soviet Union and thus allow the Soviets to exert subtle (or not so subtle) pressure on their European customers. To the Europeans, Soviet natural gas was a means of necessary diversification of their imports of energy away from the insecure Persian Gulf and Middle East; the United States refused to perceive the Soviet Union as a supplier like any other, and ultimately questioned the wisdom of any increase in dependence on the Soviet Union during a time of increasing East-West tension.[13]

Although the Carter administration had expressed concern, the dispute broadened under the Reagan administration. Even before the imposition of martial law in Poland, the pipeline had become a virtual *idée fixe* of the new administration, a potent demonstration that the Europeans did not share its overall view of East-West relations and the place of economic control in Western strategy toward the Soviet Union. The pipeline symbolized "web of detente" arguments that the Reagan administration totally rejected. For the Reagan administration, the pipeline was doubly condemned not only for the asymmetric dependency that it imposed on Western Europe (which the Europeans argued was ultimately symmetric) but also for the contribution that it made to Soviet economic well-being and ultimately to Soviet military gains. The economic warfare theme grew more and more prominent in the administration's case against the pipeline, and particularly the contribution that sales of natural gas would make in resolving Soviet shortages of hard currencies in the years ahead.

For Europeans, this new theme was even more unacceptable than the old attack via dependence, for it called into question virtually all the East-West economic ties that had been carefully constructed during the 1970s. According to this view, any gain for the Soviet Union economically was automatically a loss for the West, a zero-sum view they could not accept. The Europeans also rejected American efforts to portray the Soviet economy as a "basket case" that could be seriously damaged by restraint in Western credits and technology transfers. They had heard such predictions of Soviet economic collapse before (since 1917 in fact) and yet the Soviet system staggered on: surely the state of the economy was no worse than in the years of postwar devastation, when Western quarantine had been nearly total. The European governments also pointed to the closed character of the Soviet economy, which reduced any leverage that the "economic warriors" might hope to use. And finally it was not at all clear how foreign exchange gains contributed, except in a very indirect fashion, to Soviet military expansion: the Soviet military establishment was certainly not the most dependent on Western assistance. Politically the Europeans saw important gains for their recession-plagued economies in the pipeline deal, particularly for such hard-pressed industries as steel.

The suppression of Solidarity in Poland seemed to give the Reagan administration a final opportunity to convince the Europeans to call off the deal. As part of its economic sanctions against the Soviet Union, the American government had stopped General Electric from selling $175 million worth of components for gas turbine compressors that were to be built under license for the pipeline by three European firms. That measure did not seal off the technological loophole, however, since at least one European firm, the recently nationalized French company Alsthom-Atlantique was also capable of supplying the components, which it produced under license from General Electric. Despite this signal of American intent, the Europeans refused to budge.

At the same time, the allies were wrestling with the question of the Polish debt. After declaration of martial law, pressure mounted from the hawks in the Reagan administration to declare default on the Polish debt. It was an argument made primarily on the grounds of symbolism — to demonstrate the bankruptcy, literally, of the old regime in communist Europe — but also on the increasingly popular grounds of economic warfare. Arrayed against this position were the Treasury and State departments, who argued successfully for leverage, and therefore against default, since that would permit the Polish government and the Soviet Union to free themselves of any commitments to repay. This was, in the words of Haig, "the hard position, the more rigid position." But such arguments, made for the domestic audience, were in fact less important than the dangers that were seen to the international monetary and financial system from an abrupt declaration of default and the resistance that would be mounted by European governments, whose banks and firms were more deeply involved in Eastern Europe.[14]

Faced with European recalcitrance, the Reagan administration developed a compromise position on East-West economic relations that it hoped to sell to its allies. Although the argument was more leverage than economic warfare, it satisfied the proponents of both positions. As Assistant Secretary of State for Economic and Business Affairs Robert Hormats (who was hardly a hawk) described before a congressional committee: "The question most on our minds is 'How do we put the most pressure on the military government in Poland and therefore on the Soviet Union?' and one of our answers is 'Less hard currency.'" Less hard currency would, according to this "grand leverage" view, force not only the Poles but also the other Eastern bloc regimes to confront their economic failings. It would also lead — a crucial assumption — to the liberalization of their economic systems and ultimately of political conditions in those societies. An unspoken side benefit was that fewer economic resources would be devoted to military expenditures.

The administration beat the drum for its new course in the months before the Versailles economic and Bonn NATO summits in 1982. An implicit bargain was offered to the Europeans: no further American resistance to the gas pipeline (and more generally, a turn away from trade sanctions) in exchange for European concessions in tightening the terms and amounts of credits offered to Eastern bloc countries. It was on the basis of that bargain that the State Department thought it could find consensus at the economic summit.

Versailles to Williamsburg: A Rocky Road to Elite Reconciliation

European discontent with American economic policies early in the Reagan administration went beyond the question of economic sanctions. Recurrent trade disputes (notably over agriculture and steel) had flared up again during the recession; American macroeconomic policy, which had produced high interest rates and a robust dollar, was seen as thwarting European efforts at economic recovery. As Benjamin J. Cohen discusses in Chapter 4, the administration's model of leadership, as in other areas of alliance relations, seemed to foreclose any examination of the effects of American policies on other economies. Despite mounting discontent on these issues, however, the months before the Versailles economic summit (June 4–6, 1982) had left little doubt as to which issue would be at the top of the American agenda: economic relations between East and West. It was evidence of the changing climate under the new administration that an *economic* summit in the midst of a serious recession would devote so much time to this question.

The final bargain at the summit involved the same principals as that at the first of these summits, at Rambouillet in 1975 — France and the United States. France had won American agreement to the North-South section of the communiqué as well as a pledge of greater monetary cooperation among Europe, the United States, and Japan; the United States reiterated its willingness to intervene in the foreign exchange markets to counter "disorderly market conditions." The French relented, slightly, on the issue of East-West trade by consenting to the inclusion of the word "limits" in the final communiqué on export credits for trade with the Eastern bloc.[15] Yet, as each side — François Mitterrand for the Europeans and Donald Regan for the United States — hailed their "victories," one could detect that the summit "agreement" meant very different things to each country. In many respects, the NATO meeting of heads of state and government on June 10 was a more impressive demonstration of American-European consensus, since the Reagan administration had come much further toward the European position on arms control in its first year and because the French tended to sympathize with the American position. If the lines of division at Versailles pitted the United States against France and Germany, at Bonn the task was matching German sensibilities and desires for continuing detente policies with American hostility toward those policies.

The summits seemed to produce a consensus among the elite on some of the points at issue between Europe and the United States: a firmer commitment to arms control, while strengthening military forces; greater caution in East-West economic relations, without making clear whether that caution was simply good business sense or a strategic decision; and at least the appearance of unity, or unified floundering, in the first days of Israel's invasion of Lebanon. This tenuous reconciliation among elites appealed to, but could not incorporate, the peace movement in Europe, however. Not only were Reagan's words doubted (one movement spokesman declared, "Only when he comes here with a hammer and screwdriver to dismantle nuclear missiles will we believe one word of what he says"), the peace movement also showed few signs of slowing its momentum, with plans to move from mass demonstrations to mass civil disobedience if deployment of the missiles were attempted.[16]

An implicit bargain on East-West economic relations seemed to be sealed at Versailles: European willingness to tighten up on economic transactions with the East in exchange for American willingness to stop its efforts to thwart the pipeline. That bargain, however, was abruptly overturned on June 18, when President Reagan extended the existing American embargo on components for the pipeline to those component manufacturers that were either subsidiaries or licensees of American firms.

The West European response was swift and uniform, since the administration's action had not only reopened the question of economic relations with the Soviet bloc but added to it the equally sensitive issue of extraterritoriality. The foreign ministers of the European Community displayed a united front in opposition to the ban and to new measures that the United States had taken against European steel exports. One by one, the European governments set out to compel their firms to disobey the American ban. The United States also raised the stakes, first by threatening and then by imposing its own sanctions on those European firms that continued to participate in pipeline construction.

The new Secretary of State George Shultz, seconded by the president's economic advisors, reconstructed the overturned bargain in late 1982. Attempting to disguise its concession as part of a new and tougher joint strategy on East-West economic relations, on November 13 the administration lifted the sanctions applied to American and European firms engaged in building the Siberian gas pipeline. The French government immediately rejected any notion that the American step had been part of a bargain struck with the Europeans. Despite Shultz's claim that the French had joined in a new consensus on East-West trade in December, the Europeans had accepted no new policy commitments, apart from agreeing to avoid new natural gas contracts with the Soviet Union while studies were being completed.[17]

With the announcement by Shultz and French Foreign Minister Cheysson, the economic warfare view of East-West economic relations seemed defeated in Washington. American concerns over the export of sensitive technologies to the Eastern bloc did not diminish, however, nor did American attachment to economic sanctions as a handy symbolic device to use when force could not be used. European concern shifted to changes in the Export Administration Act, which threatened to increase the role of the Defense Department in reviewing American exports of high technology goods and to touch once again on the highly sensitive issue of extraterritoriality. European preferences were generally shared by the American business community, and those preferences were reflected in provisions to prevent the interruption of existing contracts or licenses and to make more difficult the imposition of controls for foreign policy reasons.

More important was the shift within the American administration from unilateral (and often extraterritorial) efforts toward greater use of the CoCOM, a collective mechanism that had always been acceptable to the Europeans. Successive high-level CoCOM meetings were held (the first since the 1950s), and in October 1985 the United States finally succeeded in winning agreement to establish the Security and Technology Experts' Meetings (STEM) to offer more military and technological advice to CoCOM.[18]

The continuing appeal of economic sanctions for American politicians, frustrated by the hazards of military force, remained a constant. In retaliation for alleged Libyan involvement in airport bombings at Vienna and Rome, the Reagan administration in January 1986 extended an economic embargo against Libya and froze Libyan assets in the United States. Although an American representative attempted to win support from the Europeans, all that the allies would agree on was to avoid undercutting American sanctions — a familiar position since Afghanistan. Even after the American military action against Libya in April 1986, which many Americans saw as a last resort after failing to win allied support for nonmilitary measures, Western Europe refused economic sanctions while endorsing diplomatic actions and an arms embargo. (The same spectrum of measures was later accepted by the Tokyo summit.) In regions where European economic interests were large, such as Eastern Europe and the Mediterranean, the governments of Western Europe were not likely to endorse economic sanctions as a tool of diplomacy. Their reluctance was reinforced by a firm belief that such sanctions were of dubious utility in changing the behavior of states. In this instance, and symbolic of the changed atmosphere on the use of sanctions, the Reagan administration seemed resigned to the European position and unwilling to make it a point of deeper transatlantic conflict.

The Third World: Global Anticommunism Versus Lingering Regionalism

Disputes outside the Atlantic area continued to mark the course of American relations with Western Europe, as they had since Suez and the years of decolonization. Two threads ran through these conflicts. Even in its anti-Soviet final months, the Carter administration had preserved some elements of the regionalist view on the Third World, crediting Third World politics (and the disputes between Third World nations) with a certain life of their own. The Reagan administration rejected this perspective, seeking to build up clients in Asia, Africa, and Latin America whose anticommunist credentials were impeccable. The Europeans, as they had in the case of detente, clung to the older set of attitudes and resisted fitting the world into a manichaean box.

Differences in power were as important as differences in outlook, however. While the United States had considerable means to influence events in regions outside the Atlantic area, the means possessed by the Europeans were limited, but their interest in those areas remained, often remnants of an imperial past. Frustrated, they were brought up against the disparity between their own power and that of the United States in dealing with the Third World.

The Middle East encapsulated both sources of conflict. Despite their clear disagreement with the Camp David strategy of the Carter administration, the Europeans did not press their peacemaking initiatives during the first year of the Reagan administration. As the United States set out to construct a "strategic consensus" encompassing Israel and "moderate" Arab states, the Europeans held back, in part because of the administration's own rifts with the Begin government and in part because France under its new president, François Mitterrand, definitely tilted away from the clear-cut pro-Arab position that France had followed since 1967.

The Israeli invasion of Lebanon in 1982 renewed European diplomatic activity in a country of traditional interest to France and reopened familiar disagreements with the United States. A plan offered by France at the United Nations, calling for Israeli and Palestinian withdrawal from

Lebanon, was supported by all the European members of the Security Council and vetoed by the United States. The European summit reiterated a formula for peace — that the Palestine Liberation Organization (PLO) "should be associated with negotiations" — that had angered the Carter administration two years earlier.

After massacres in the Palestinian refugee camps in September 1982, European contingents from Italy, Britain, and France joined the Americans in a multinational peacekeeping effort. Within a year, however, the Americans had redefined their mission as one of support for the beleaguered Maronite Christians (viewed as anti-Syrian and hence anti-Soviet). Such intervention resulted in the targeting of French and American troops by terrorists and a political uproar in the United States that led to American withdrawal. As Stanley Hoffmann suggested, Middle East policy within the alliance returned to a well-worn course: ineffectual calls by the Europeans for new negotiations to resolve the Arab-Israeli conflict, appeals that were backed up with little real influence in the region or over American policy.[19]

In the Western Hemisphere, the Europeans discovered even more clearly the asymmetry between their influence — even on intensely held issues — and the reach of the United States. Early in the Reagan administration, France and the United States were distinctly at odds on the administration's first "test case" of global anticommunism: Central America. The political connections of Western Europe — particularly those of the Socialists and Social Democrats — led them to a close relationship with the opposition to the Duarte government in El Salvador. In terms of past American debates, the Europeans took a distinctly regionalist position, critical of imputing all revolutionary change in the Third World to Soviet intervention, and in the French case, displaying a far more sympathetic attitude toward revolutionary movements. Disenchantment with the Sandinista government in Nicaragua and a growing awareness of the limited means they had to exercise against an adamant America apparently set on its destruction, led to diminished European activism in the region and reduced conflict with the United States.

Elsewhere, the Reagan administration's policies of polishing its relations with authoritarian regimes in the Third World and overthrowing revolutionary ones confronted, not the ideological sympathies of French socialists but rather the lingering imperial interests of Margaret Thatcher's government in Britain. The conflict between Britain and Argentina over the Falkland Islands posed enormous difficulties for the Reagan administration, not the least because it did not fit with the dominant, anticommunist world view of the American government. The embarrassment in Washington was evident, but the outcome of the internal debate was never really in doubt, particularly after the European community so surprisingly and unanimously backed the British position with economic sanctions against Argentina. The United States itself soon applied sanctions and offered its logistical support to Britain during the conflict, while, like the Europeans, pushing the British government toward a settlement of Argentine claims that would reduce damage to relations with that country and Latin America. Agreement between Britain and the United States was harder to achieve when the United States intervened against the radical government of Grenada. As the British Foreign Secretary Sir Geoffrey Howe conceded, "The extent of consultation with us was regrettably less than we wished." The Labour opposition attacked both the Thatcher government's "doormat diplomacy" and the American intervention. The "special relationship" had been bruised once again. A similar upset to the regional pretensions of a European country occurred in November 1984 when the United States government revealed that the Libyan government was violating an agreement with France on withdrawal from northern Chad. Once again, embarrassment (and the dismissal of the French foreign minister) ensued.

Such slights and disputes had long marked alliance relations; only the Reagan administration's rigid anticommunist world view and its tendency toward unilateral action set it apart from earlier administrations. The American air strikes against Libya in 1986, culmination of an escalating conflict between the Reagan administration and the Qaddafi government, illustrated the divergence between American and European approaches to the Third World in a region far more important to European interests than Central or South America. In many respects, Europeans could argue that the Mediterranean was their Central America — a region bound to them by dense economic ties, large movements of population, and geographical proximity. In the conflict between the United States and Libya, however, their conclusions were not the interventionist ones of the United States; European vulnerability to any aggravation of terrorism pointed to a lowering of the level of conflict. The United States, in an area of far less significance to it and for reasons that seemed more ideological than strategically sound, was threatening to create a backlash of violence that would probably strike Europe first and the United States only later. The Europeans resisted economic sanctions against Libya, though in the European community and at the Tokyo summit they finally consented to diplomatic sanctions. The Libyan conflict displayed the profound differences between allies in assessing "threats" in the Third World and estimating the utility of military force for dealing with them. Deeper conflict was constrained by the European realization that their global reach was limited and that their ability to sway American policy in areas of high interest (such as Central America) was equally circumscribed.

Star Wars and Alliance Conflict

The Williamsburg summit in May 1983 affirmed the new elite consensus within the alliance, declaring that "our security is indivisible" and reiterating the commitment to deploy long-range theater nuclear weapons by the end of the year if arms control talks were unsuccessful. The new consensus was also evident in the absence of East-West economic relations as a central agenda item. The subsidence of debate over the American missiles was furthered by electoral victories in Germany by the center-right coalition of Helmut Kohl (March 1983) and in Britain by Margaret Thatcher's Conservative government (May 1983). In both cases, parties critical of the deployment decision were overwhelmingly defeated. Popular acquiescence was also encouraged by an inflexible Soviet negotiating stance and by heightened anti-Soviet sentiments aroused by the Soviet downing of a Korean Airlines plane that had strayed over Russian territory in September. The Euromissiles were deployed in November 1983, in the face of large demonstrations, but not the massive disruptions that had been threatened by the peace movement.

The deployments did not bring calm to alliance security relations, however. The Soviet Union broke off all arms control negotiations, including negotiations for Mutual and Balanced Force Reductions in Europe. Domestic political stakes threatened to rise again if arms control negotiations and better United States-Soviet relations were not in view. More important, although its significance for the alliance was not immediately apparent, was the announcement by President Reagan of his Strategic Defense Initiative (SDI or, as quickly dubbed, Star Wars) in March 1983.

The threat that the SDI could pose to the alliance was slow to be perceived by the Europeans. One passage in the March speech was directed to assuaging the concerns of allies, but the SDI, a major revision in American nuclear strategy that had been advanced without allied consultation, led to some resentment on those grounds alone. (Of course most of official Washington was equally surprised by the speech.) Like many in the United States, the Europeans were also not sure how significant the SDI would be; the president's own commitment to it and its budgetary implications only became clear over time.

Reagan's reelection seems to have been a turning point, after which the doctrinal and fiscal implications of the SDI began to concern defense specialists and policymakers in Europe. European attention was drawn to Star Wars by the central, almost obsessive, attention given to SDI by the Soviet leadership, and particularly, Mikhail Gorbachev. He seems to have impressed that concern on Prime Minister Thatcher during his first visit to the West in December 1984, and she in turn impressed her worries on President Reagan later that month in Washington.[20] The four-point understanding issued following the Reagan-Thatcher meeting became a touchstone of European views on the implications of the Star Wars program: that the aim of the program was not superiority but balance; that deployment would be a matter for negotiation; that the aim of the program was the enhancement of deterrence; and finally, that arms control negotiations should seek security through reduced levels of offensive systems.[21]

Star Wars had not yet become the object of wider political debate in Western Europe; it remained, by and large, the realm of politicians and defense experts. But argument heightened in 1985, as the American administration (and particularly the Defense Department), set out to win positive European support. Rather than simply seeking verbal support, the Defense Department in March 1985 issued a formal invitation to the Europeans to join in Star Wars research and laid down a sixty-day deadline for reply. (The objectionable deadline was later withdrawn.) Weinberger's invitation marked the opening of a spring campaign to build support for the SDI before the Bonn summit and a meeting of NATO ministers in June. By bringing to the fore the issue of research and development (and potential contracts for European firms), the Pentagon seemed to have found an attractive carrot for European governments concerned about losing to the United States and Japan in the newest high-technology sweepstakes.

Raising the technology issue also produced a counterproposal by the French government, already hostile to the SDI, for a European research program, civilian in focus, that would develop some of the same technologies encouraged by Star Wars. The Eureka program, by providing a European alternative, forced difficult choices on the British and German governments, who had expressed support for the research dimension of the SDI. The French government continued to lead the opposition to European endorsement of the SDI, successfully thwarting American efforts to win such approval from NATO in June 1985. The narrower issue of research then became the center of attention, and both Eureka and European participation in SDI research gained support in Western Europe. After failing to obtain a guaranteed share of research for its signature, the British government signed an agreement to facilitate participation in the SDI by British firms in December; Germany opened negotiations on a similar pact. At the same time, the Eureka program took shape more quickly than expected, producing a list of ten initial projects, some of which were likely to receive public funding.

The hostility and skepticism that greeted the Reagan SDI in European ministries and research institutes had several sources: implications for superpower competition and conflict, likely effects on European security, impact on defense allocations, political fallout, and technological consequences. European judgments on the likely effect on relations between the superpowers resembled that of American critics of the SDI: a threat to progress on arms control and, if deployed, a certain destabilizing element in what had been viewed as a stable central nuclear balance.

The effects on European security were viewed even more negatively, affecting both the American commitment to Europe and the credibility of European nuclear forces. Arguments against the SDI have revealed the fundamental conservatism of Europeans in matters of nuclear doctrine. They remain (at least the *official* view remains) attached to nuclear deterrence and specifically Mutual Assured Destruction as the foundation of European and Western security. They do not believe, given their own position in relation to the Soviet Union, that an impenetrable defense against ballistic missiles is possible. As Colonel Jonathan Alford, Director of the International Institute of Strategic Studies, remarked, "Europeans actually tend to like nuclear weapons. They don't say we want more of them but they say it is nuclear weapons on the whole, their existence, the fear they induce which has made it impossible to contemplate war."[22] Star Wars is seen, if deployed, as reducing the willingness of the United States to defend Western Europe, with nuclear weapons if necessary: the credibility of the American guarantee would be diminished. American spokesmen argue that a defended United States would be *more*, not less, willing to defend Europe, since it would no longer "risk New York for Hamburg." Europeans, pointing to the probability of similar Soviet missile defenses, see two invulnerable superpowers producing the possibility of either limited nuclear war or conventional conflict in Europe. As Christoph Bertram argues, "The U.S. nuclear guarantee that has been so central to the Alliance becomes meaningless unless the United States is both vulnerable to nuclear attack and capable of adding its nuclear power to deter an attack on Europe. If the scenario of roughly equal superpower BMD capabilities were realized, however, the U.S. would be neither."[23]

If deployed, not only would the SDI threaten the American nuclear guarantee, superpower missile defenses would also threaten the national nuclear forces of Britain and France, viewed by many in Europe as a critical link in the deterrent threat perceived by the Soviet Union. Such defenses would endanger that deterrent threat following a costly program of nuclear modernization on the part of both countries.

The budgetary implications of Star Wars threatened to reinforce the unilateralist cast of any American defense posture based on missile defenses by draining resources from conventional forces as the program grows, a threat noted by American critics as well. If there were a deployment of anti-missile defenses in Europe, paid for by the Europeans, their resource dilemmas would mount as well.

Star Wars also threatened to reopen precisely the political debates surmounted with such difficulty before the deployment of the long-range theater nuclear forces. By undercutting arms control negotiations, it eliminated the critical corollary of any commitment to defense modernization in Europe. The SDI appeared much more an *American* initiative than the Euromissiles (which had first been urged by European leaders), and the attack on deterrence implied by the SDI undercut precisely the arguments made by the supporters of LRTNF. Since any European missile defense would have to rely on terminal missile defenses, future deployment of those defenses in Europe, as James Schlesinger remarked, would make the preceding deployments a "relative political picnic."[24] Star Wars was already opposed by those parties and groups that had mounted the previous campaign against the deployment of the Pershings and cruise missiles; if the Star Wars debate widened, those political divisions might be deepened and prolonged.

Finally as the attention to research in 1985 had indicated, Star Wars was seen as a further threat to the technological position of Western Europe. The final spin-off effects of the SDI on the United States civilian economy were difficult to predict, but the Europeans were eager to seize any opportunity to regain their technological edge. Even full-fledged participation in the American research effort might not offer a technological panacea, however: one British civil servant predicted that the trade would be "brains for crumbs."[25] Eureka's projected scale seemed far too small to offset expenditures for the SDI.

In the face of an apparently unshakable commitment by President Reagan to the SDI, European elites played for time, as John Newhouse put it, hoping that domestic budgetary pressures in the United States would force choices reducing the American commitment to Star Wars. Whatever their view of European arguments against the SDI, however, most observers agreed that, if the program continued, it would "pose a challenge of 'alliance management' at least equal to that of the 1979 INF decision," and could possibly cause "a profound rift that could break up the Western Alliance for good."[26]

The Consequences of Mr. Reagan: Conjunctural Spat or Structural Shift?

After five years, the diplomatic consequences of President Reagan for the alliance seemed slight: To many observers the 1981–82 crisis appeared to be a conjunctural ripple in an essentially stable set of relations. Conflict had resulted from mistaken Reagan administration policies and rhetoric that had diverged from the norm of previous administrations, coupled with economic recession. After those two elements changed, conflict evaporated, as it had so many times in the past. Those who espoused the conjunctural view emphasized the persistent structural conservatism in the Atlantic alliance — the enduring fact of superpower bipolarity and the fundamental dependence of Western Europe on the

United States for its security. Following the arguments of Anton De-Porte, the Atlantic alliance should continue to provide a framework for American policy toward Europe and a steady assurance of security for the Europeans. In this view, economic change — the growing weight of Western Europe in the world economy or the diverging external orientations of the European and American economies — did not significantly spill over into the security sphere. For such observers, the latest conflict was simply another example of elite division, complemented by popular concern imparted by the loose rhetoric of the Reagan administration. Popular fears of war, and particularly nuclear war, had appeared in the past in Western Europe: during the "peace campaign" of the Korean war, at the time of the *Kampf dem Atomtod* and the Campaign for Nuclear Disarmament in the late 1950s. European publics behaved rationally: Their mobilization on the issue of peace increased as the perceived risk of conflict between the superpowers increased *and* the probability grew that any war would be nuclear. In its first years, the Reagan administration had managed to increase both probabilities in the eyes of many Europeans.

The rift with Western Europe had been resolved in large measure because the Reagan administration had gradually drifted toward policies that it had previously denounced. Its rhetoric toward the Soviet Union had softened, and its willingness to negotiate had been emphasized, beginning with Reagan's address in November 1981 and continuing to the summit of November 1985. East-West economic relations were now considered principally in the multilateral forums favored by the Europeans; the deployment of the Pershing II and cruise missiles, however painful politically, had reestablished the credibility of the American commitment to defend Europe. The Reagan administration, as Figure 9-1 suggests, had not drifted completely to the stance of earlier administrations, but the gap between the United States and the European elites (whose positions had shifted much less) had narrowed.

In contrast to this optimistic conjunctural view, others pointed out that the apparently stable security relationship between the United States and Western Europe in fact masked deeper structural changes that had affected relations between the United States and Western Europe during the Reagan presidency and would continue to do so in future administrations. The achievement of parity by the Soviet Union had produced doubts of American willingness to defend Europe by nuclear means at risk to itself. But that security dependency had also created a parallel fear, fueling the European peace movement, that American nuclear weapons could be used to fight a nuclear war *in Europe*. American vulnerability had also increased the political appeal in the United States of the SDI, a program that threatened to deepen European concern over decoupling and American unilateralism. Diverging economic orientations had produced differences in stakes: Western Europe was far more dependent on an assured supply of oil from the Middle East, and the European investment in detente — economic and political — was much higher. As a result, Western Europe viewed the Arab-Israeli conflict and relations with the Soviet Union differently. Whatever the fashion in Washington, Europeans would be far more interested in the bundle of policies they continued to label detente. Throughout the Reagan administration, whatever the political coloration of the government in Bonn, ties between the two Germanies continued to develop and deepen. In similar fashion, other European countries resisted American attempts to reduce their economic dealings with Eastern Europe and the Soviet Union.

Perhaps most significant and most difficult to assess were long-term political changes. The democratization of the security debate had already influenced elite divisions; the peace movement had encompassed more European societies and put down deeper organizational roots than its predecessors. Following the missile deployments it had resisted so vociferously, the peace movement seemed to lose momentum and to fall prey to factionalism. Nevertheless its influence on mainstream politics persisted. Conservative governments disguised changes that could provide shallower support for conventional alliance policies in the future. Bertram detected "decay" in the German consensus on defense: opposition by the Social Democrats to the Euromissile deployment testified that "for the first time since the early 1960s, the Alliance argument had failed to carry the majority of the party."[27] The importance of such political forces was further demonstrated in the Netherlands, which finally agreed to missile deployment in late 1985: The decision threatened to split the Christian Democratic party, and the Dutch government reduced its nuclear tasks in NATO to balance the agreed deployment.

Other, older political distinctions seemed of less importance in defining European attitudes toward the United States. Socialist France sharply disagreed with the United States on international economic policy and the SDI, but it tended to support the American view of the Soviet threat and necessary defense measures. The French Socialists turned a deaf ear to complaints by the German Social Democrats that they were being treated like a colony by the United States.

Nevertheless, the construction of alliance consensus after 1981–1982 was assisted by governments heading conservative coalitions in Germany and Britain; the governments that replaced those of Kohl and Thatcher would be less likely to follow an American lead and accept domestic political losses in the interests of alliance unity. Across the political spectrum, including the new forces of the peace movement, the initial strategy of the Reagan administration had called forth nationalist, even Gaullist responses in unlikely quarters. These responses had taken collective European form in some instances, such as resistance to American extraterritorial demands. And that revived nationalism was likely to remain a force in future alliance relations.

The possibility that misperceptions within the alliance could flare into domestic political controversy was amply demonstrated by the president's visit to Bitburg military cemetery in Germany in May 1985. That controversy, though it seemed to leave few lasting scars, was an unexpected battle between publics in the two countries: an important segment of American opinion repelled by the honor apparently paid to the Nazi regime; a German public wishing not to forget that regime and the war it engendered, but rather to affirm that that forty years was also a significant span of history. The intensity of the debate indicated that not only future divergence but also past differences could still roil relations between the allies.

Finally some argued that changes in Soviet strategy under the new leadership of Gorbachev could be so significant as to merit the description structural. Jerry Hough pointed out that a new generation of Soviet leaders, intent on an economic modernization that requires Western technology, might break with the past Soviet fixation on superpower relations to foster more cordial relations with Europe and Japan.[28] Nothing in the early record of Gorbachev's leadership countered such a view. During his visit to France in October 1985, Gorbachev offered to open separate arms control negotiations with Britain and France; in arms control proposals presented to the United States in January 1986, the Soviets shrewdly took aim at the ambiguities of flexible response by including the elimination of all tactical and battlefield nuclear weapons in the second and third stages of the plan. The possibility was clear that Soviet efforts to play on the structural weaknesses of the alliance might have some effect over time.

For those who took these structural changes, international and domestic, seriously, three different sets of prescriptions — restoration, devolution, and transformation — have been advanced to bring policy into line with present and future realities.

Restoring American Power: Nostalgia Undefeated

The original strategy of the Reagan administration had offered a simple solution to a perceived drift of Western Europe from the Atlantic alliance: restoring American military power and economic well-being and reclaiming the role of leadership that had been lost in the years of retrenchment after Vietnam. Despite the weaknesses in this strategy (described by Kenneth Oye in Chapter 1) and the apparent victory of a less unilateralist point of view after 1982, those who backed restoration and its unilateral implications had been undefeated by the Reagan administration compromises on arms control and East-West trade. By mid-1986, Shultz's carefully constructed bargaining seemed threatened in a

Washington disenchanted by the European response to military strikes against Libya. The decision to formally cast aside the unratified SALT II treaty was the most important sign of unilateralist resurgence. It was a decision sharply criticized by the NATO allies, one taken without consultation and which created serious political problems for two of Reagan's staunchest supporters in Europe, Helmut Kohl and Margaret Thatcher.

The Defense Department, supported by conservative congressmen, still held to the original strategy in uncompromised form; and growing attention to the SDI in American strategy was only "one more expression of a shift in the American world outlook, away from coalition politics and toward an assertive, protected United States acting on its own."[29] Even staunch alliance supporters expressed their exasperation in terms that seemed to threaten a shift in American interests away from Europe. In a speech delivered in January 1984, Undersecretary of State Lawrence Eagleburger pointed to growing American economic interests in the Pacific and noted that "Western Europe [is] more and more concerned with its own problems, more and more concerned with its economic difficulties, less and less in tune with the United States as we talk about our international security interests."

Even if the State Department continues to endorse compromise with the Europeans, an appearance of continuing American concessions might once again win the president to the restorationist point of view. The winning argument could be the defense budget, which now faces cuts that will impose choices avoided up to this time. As Leslie Gelb has noted, the Reagan budgets have already embodied a strategy of globalization, with the sharpest increases for the Rapid Deployment Force (and more recently for the SDI): "This represents a growing shift in priorities toward seapower and a global maritime strategy and away from land forces and the European theatre."[30] If restorationist views on East-West strategy were not accepted by the Europeans — and there is little to suggest that they would be — the Defense Department could provide a strategic rationale and the budgetary base for a unilateralist position of disengagement from Europe. The political base for unilateralism would be the Republican right wing, now quiescent as moderation infested the Reagan foreign policy. Support could be added by those irritated over the level of European defense spending. Europeans were shocked in 1984 by proposals by two NATO supporters, Senators Sam Nunn and William S. Cohen, that proposed first a withdrawal of American troops from Europe and then a cap on United States forces, if the European members of NATO did not accelerate their defense efforts in specified ways.

Less Is More: The Temptations of Devolution

The Nunn-Cohen proposals indicate that structural change has led to recommendations that echo those of the unilateralists, although the changes would be implemented with European cooperation and not from pique over rejected leadership. Some Europeans, witnessing the democratization of the security debate and the rise of the peace movement, argue that NATO's policy of flexible response is no longer tenable. As an alternative, Lawrence Freedman has urged "a clear doctrine that both redressed the nuclear bias in NATO strategy and provided a new approach to the design and deployment of conventional forces."[31] This group of observers takes the sentiments expressed by the peace movement seriously — fear of nuclear war in Europe is real and is not likely to be dissipated by public relations techniques. What is required is a clear strategic shift away from overdependence on nuclear weapons.

Others see the need for more than a revision in NATO strategy. Rather than responding to a fear of nuclear war that has resulted from changes in the nuclear balance and in declared doctrine and military technology, the European discontent can also be seen as emerging from the relationship of security dependency itself, the resentment and sense of helplessness that it induces, and the feeling of being a "colony" of the United States. To relieve such resentment and to shift defense burdens in the face of yawning budget deficits in the United States, some have advocated a division of labor very different from that endorsed by the Europeans after Afghanistan. The United States would take on the responsibility for naval and mobile ground forces required to defend Western interests in the Middle East, while the Europeans would assume a greater share in the defense of Western Europe.[32] Henry Kissinger was only the latest to suggest a larger role for Europe in providing its own conventional defense in a *Time* essay in early 1984; his argument for devolution, like that of Nunn and Cohen had a unilateralist second stage: if the Europeans declined, the United States should respond by withdrawing up to one-half of its ground forces from Western Europe.

Such arguments are usually coupled with an enlarged role for a European defense entity, whether based on the Western European Union, a subgroup of NATO, or the European Community. Despite the appeal of such a solution, it continues to confront the same obstacles that have been apparent since the 1960s, as recently reviewed by Stanley Hoffmann.[33] The core of such a European defense entity would have to be the French and British nuclear deterrents, but Germany, as the most significant conventional power, would have to be included in decision making without having a hand in controlling or manufacturing nuclear weapons. Franco-German defense cooperation had made some progress, but its pace seemed closely correlated with French perceptions of German "neutralism." Some Europeans also feared that a move to a more independent defense posture would give the United States grounds for a withdrawal from Western Europe. Perhaps most important, a common defense presupposes a common foreign policy of which it is the instrument. Despite the proposed modest reforms within the European Community, such a level of common management of defense policy seems well beyond present capabilities.

Arguments for a different division of labor and a common European defense to relieve dependence on the vagaries of American policy can also be combined with proposals to narrow the alliance, taking into account diverging European and American interests outside the Atlantic area. These underlying tugs on the alliance could be diminished if it were restricted to a more purely military arrangement in the European theater. It is questionable, however, that a strategy of "less is more" for the alliance would satisfy the domestic political requirements of a coalition that depends on a supply of resources from increasingly hard-pressed national economies. Public support might dry up with a policy of narrowing and distancing well before European defense capability emerged to replace existing structures. The elite response in Europe to Kissinger's proposals — negative and instantaneous — suggests that devolution is unlikely to become an alternative for the alliance in the short term.

The Peace Movement and Transformation of the European Security System

Even these more radical suggestions do not meet a final set of domestic political criticisms, those advanced by the European peace movement. A nuclear Europe, under European control, would be no more satisfactory than one in which the United States controls Europe's fate. Attitudes within the movement opposing the deployment of new theater nuclear weapons are hardly monolithic; in many respects, the spectrum parallels that just described. Some challenge the Reagan administration's seriousness of intent on arms control, others seek a turn toward a denuclearized Europe through an emphasis on conventional defense; still others see the sources of European insecurity in the connection to the United States itself and argue for a denuclearized Europe between the superpowers.[34] At its core, however, the argument of the peace movement is one of skepticism about deterrence. Instead of a balance of forces that has brought Europe decades of peace and is likely to persist, its spokesmen point to the fragility of other systems of deterrence in the past and the element of chance and miscalculation in the outbreak of international conflict.

The peace movement, which seeks a unified European security sphere without nuclear weapons, confronts the old problem of national divisions, East and West: West, in the differing attitudes of the European Left toward military questions that have been evident in the last two years, and particularly the differences between French Socialists and German Social Democrats; East, in the strategy of the peace movement for confronting the irreducible hold of the Soviet Union. A similar grass roots movement of support for new security arrangements cannot exist in the East; suppression of the Solidarity movement in Poland and the tiny East German and Soviet peace movements suggests a continuing imbalance in political givens. The movement in the West is therefore forced back on some form of unilateralism or the acceptance of a purely defensive view of Soviet motivations in defense policy. The movement, particularly in Germany, has also failed to accept the paradox that movements such as Solidarity, which might provide the basis for desired grass roots change, also threatens the fabric of detente. The German response to the martial law declaration in Poland envinced a certain relief that the status quo was not endangered.

Any choice among predictions and prescriptions ultimately lies in an assessment of the permanence or transience of recent changes in the politics of Western Europe and the United States, just as the present set of disputes can be traced to the turning in American politics since 1979 and the concomitant rise of the European peace movement. It may be that the European popular mobilization will fade permanently, as other such movements have in the past, if the Reagan administration continues to offer progress on arms control and to temper its rhetoric regarding the Soviet Union. The Reagan administration may yet solidify a new political realignment that would provide the base for continuing its original policies, particularly on defense and East-West relations, or the United States may witness yet another turning, a "Europeanization" of the politics of American foreign and defense policy, as described by William Kincaide[35]:

> Increasing accuracy, shorter times to target, reduced decision or response time, large numbers of more versatile weapons, and lengthening lists of feasible targets are creating circumstances for Americans similar to those Europeans have experienced for twenty-five years: life at the epicenter of a potential nuclear battlefield where the likelihood of intentional or accidental war is remote, but never quite remote enough.

"Europeanization" could point in either of two directions, however. A sense of increasing and shared risk could prod American foreign policy toward further convergence with West Europeans. A heightened sense of risk could also reinforce tendencies toward unilateral or cooperative disengagement from Europe, as symbolized for some by the SDI. Under a veneer of renewed elite consensus, strategic choices remain in American relations with Western Europe.

"The United States and Western Europe: The Diplomatic Consequences of Mr. Reagan" was written for this volume. Copyright © 1987 by Miles Kahler.

Notes

1. The most powerful statement of this point of view is given by Anton DePorte in *Europe Between the Superpowers* (New Haven: Yale University Press, 1979).
2. For the United States, the ratio of oil imports from the AOPEC countries in the late 1970s to domestic production plus imports was about 25 percent; for the West Europeans, excluding the United Kingdom, the ratio is between 70 and 80 percent.
3. Accounts of Western disarray after Afghanistan are plentiful. A few examples: George H. Quester, "The Superpowers and the Atlantic Alliance," William G. Hyland, "The Atlantic Crisis," and Robert R. Bowie, "The Atlantic Alliance," in *Daedalus* (Winter 1981), pp. 23–70; Josef Joffe, "European-American Relations—the Enduring Crisis," *Foreign Affairs* (Spring 1981), Vol. 59, pp. 835–851; and Pierre Hassner, "Moscow and the Western Alliance," *Problems of Communism* (May–June 1981), Vol. 30, especially pp. 48–49.
4. See Chapter 7, this volume.
5. Helmut Schmidt, "The Alastair Buchan Memorial Lecture," *Survival* (January–February 1978), Vol. 20, pp. 3–4.
6. For an excellent account and criticism of the military justifications for the deployment, followed by tempered support on the ground that the deployment would contribute to strengthening deterrence and increasing survivability: Christoph Bertram, "The Implications of Theatre Nuclear Weapons in Europe," *Foreign Affairs* (Winter 1981–1982), Vol. 60, pp. 307–309; on the problem of Soviet pre-emption and survivability, Jeffrey Record, "Theatre Nuclear Weapons: Begging the Soviet Union to Pre-Empt," *Survival* (September–October 1977), Vol. 19, pp. 208–211; on the LRTNF decision, criticized by McGeorge Bundy in "America in the 1980s: Reframing Our Relations with Our Friends and Among Our Allies," *Survival* (January–February 1982), Vol. 24, pp. 24–28.
7. Bertram, "The Implications of Theatre Nuclear Weapons in Europe," p. 308. Why such systems would provide more coupling than the fate of several hundred thousand American soldiers under nuclear weapon attack remains a puzzle.
8. Josef Joffe, "German Defense Policy: Novel Solution and Enduring Dilemmas," *The Internal Fabric of Western Security*, in Gregory Flynn, ed. (London: Croom Helm, 1981), pp. 87–88.
9. Bertram, "The Implications of Theatre Nuclear Weapons in Europe," p. 309.
10. Excerpts from the speech are reprinted in *Survival* (March–April 1982), Vol. 24, pp. 87–89.
11. McGeorge Bundy, George F. Kennan, Robert S. McNamara, and Gerard Smith, "Nuclear Weapons and the Atlantic Alliance," *Foreign Affairs* (Spring 1982), Vol. 60, pp. 765–766.
12. The author is grateful to Kenneth Oye for this tripartite categorization of American justifications.
13. Hanns W. Maull, *Natural Gas and Economic Security* (Paris: Atlantic Institute for International Affairs, 1981), p. 49. Maull's account is perhaps the best defense of the pipeline decision, although combined with cautions and recommendations for measures to guard against Soviet leverage. For a more skeptical American view, see Thomas Blau and Joseph Kirchheimer, "European Dependence and Soviet Leverage: The Yamal Pipeline," *Survival* (September–October 1981), Vol. 23, pp. 209–214.
14. Leslie H. Gelb, *International Herald Tribune*, February 4, 1982, p. 2.
15. See the accounts by Hedrick Smith, *International Herald Tribune*, June 8, 1982; and John Wyles, *Financial Times*, June 7, 1982.
16. Report by Patricia Clough in *The Times* (London), June 18, 1982; John Vinocur of the *New York Times* offers a different point of view, emphasizing the divisions in the

movement over Reagan's visit and the distancing of some church groups from the demonstrations (*New York Times*, June 3, 1982, p. A10).

17. John Vinocur, "Few New Pledges in Pact, Allies Say," *New York Times*, pp. A1, A25; and Bernard Gwertzman, "U.S. and France Agree on Strategy for Handling Trade with Moscow," *New York Times*, December 15, 1982, pp. A1, A13.

18. See the review by Deputy Secretary of State Kenneth Dam, "Economic and Political Aspects of Extraterritoriality," U.S. Department of State, Current Policy No. 697; "You Know This Could Be Lethal," *The Economist*, October 19, 1985, pp. 37–38.

19. Stanley Hoffmann, "The U.S. and Western Europe: Wait and Worry," *Foreign Affairs* (1985), Vol. 63, No. 3, p. 642.

20. See the account by John Newhouse, "The Diplomatic Round," *The New Yorker*, July 22, 1985, pp. 42–43.

21. "The Strategic Defense Initiative," U.S. Department of State, Special Report No. 129, p. 3.

22. William J. Broad, "Allies in Europe are Apprehensive About Benefits of 'Star Wars' Plan," *New York Times*, May 13, 1985, p. A6.

23. Christoph Bertram, "Strategic Defense and the Western Alliance," *Daedalus* (Summer 1985), Vol. 114, No. 3, p. 294. For an American response to some of the European arguments, see Arnold Kanter, "Thinking About the Strategic Defence Initiative: An Alliance Perspective," *International Affairs* (Summer 1985), Vol. 61, No. 3, pp. 449–464.

24. James R. Schlesinger, "Rhetoric and Realities in the Star Wars Debate," *International Security* (Summer 1985), Vol. 10, No. 1, pp. 9–10.

25. Newhouse, "The Diplomatic Round," p. 40; cf. "Small Bier," *The Economist*, December 14, 1985, p. 43.

26. Kanter, "Thinking About the Strategic Defense Initiative," p. 450; Bertram, "Strategic Defense," p. 281.

27. Christoph Bertram, "Europe and America in 1983," *Foreign Affairs* (1984), Vol. 62, No. 3, p. 625.

28. Jerry F. Hough, "Gorbachev's Strategy," *Foreign Affairs* (Fall 1985), Vol. 64, No. 1, pp. 45–46.

29. Bertram, "Strategic Defense and the Western Alliance," p. 294.

30. Leslie H. Gelb, *New York Times*, February 7, 1982.

31. Lawrence Freedman, "NATO Myths," *Foreign Policy* (Winter 1981–1982), No. 45, p. 67.

32. Two contributions to the debate between advocates of traditional coalition defense and those who favor a new division of labor are Robert W. Komer, "Maritime Strategy vs. Coalition Defense," *Foreign Affairs* (Summer 1982), Vol. 60, No. 5, pp. 1124–1144; and Admiral Stansfield Turner and Captain George Thibault, "Preparing for the Unexpected: The Need for a New Military Strategy," *Foreign Affairs* (Fall 1982), Vol. 61, No. 1, pp. 122–135.

33. Stanley Hoffmann, "NATO and Nuclear Weapons: Reasons and Unreasons," *Foreign Affairs* (Winter 1981–1982), Vol. 60, pp. 327–346.

34. For the views of one wing of the peace movement, which argues for a European security system independent of the superpowers, see Edward Thompson, "Notes on Exterminism, the Last Stage of Civilization," and other contributions in *Exterminism and Cold War* (London: Verso and NLB, 1982).

35. William H. Kincaide, "Over the Technological Horizon," *Daedalus* (Winter 1981), Vol. 110, p. 125.

10

The United States and Japan: Conflict and Cooperation Under Mr. Reagan

Mike M. Mochizuki

The rapid and continuing expansion of the Japanese economy vividly illustrates the relative decline of American economic power. Some have gone so far as to argue that Japan poses a threat to the United States in the economic sphere comparable to the Soviet threat in the political-military sphere. This economic competition between the United States and Japan has stirred an acrimonious exchange across the Pacific. American business, labor, and political leaders accuse Japan of predatory trade practices and protectionism, while their Japanese counterparts cite American shortcomings in economic policy and corporate strategies.

In regards to security affairs, many Americans still feel that Japan is a "cheap rider," if not a "free rider," by not sharing the burden of maintaining world peace. The Japanese, however, loathe and continue to resist incorporation into American global military strategy and to be wary of the provocativeness of some American defense policies.

Despite the end of American economic hegemony, the frictions caused by intense economic competition, and the persisting gap in American and Japanese attitudes toward security issues, the remarkable fact is that the alliance between these two powers may be stronger today than ever before. The military link with the United States no longer ignites vehement opposition in Japan, as it did in the 1950s and early 1960s. The Japanese are now more willing to cooperate on bilateral defense. As for economic relations, American unilateralism of the early 1970s has given way to more cooperative modes of action, and Japan is taking steps to support the liberal international economic order originally established by the United States in the postwar period. Although Japanese efforts to

Mike M. Mochizuki is Assistant Professor of Political Science at Yale University. He is the author of Conservative Hegemony in Japan *(forthcoming) and a consultant to the United Nations Association of the U.S.A.*

support the American global vision may be coming too slowly to please many American policymakers, the direction of change is unmistakeable: toward the United States, not away from it.

If this trend toward convergence is correct, as the author believes it is, then the case of American-Japanese relations raises an interesting paradox about power in world politics. When the United States was strong and Japan weak, America was in a weaker bargaining position vis-à-vis Japan, and cooperation between the two nations was limited. Since the decline of American hegemony, however, American leverage over Japan and bilateral cooperation have increased.

Certainly the close relationship between President Ronald Reagan and Prime Minister Yasuhiro Nakasone has contributed to collaboration across the Pacific. The two leaders have common political values. Both are committed to economic liberalism at home and abroad. Both are staunchly anticommunist and see the importance of military power to contain the Soviet Union. Reagan and Nakasone also have similar political styles. Both are extremely skillful at appealing directly to their respective citizenries and mobilizing nationalistic sentiments in support of their policies.

But the recent trend toward American-Japanese cooperation goes beyond personalities and should continue even after the two men leave office. As American power declined relatively, Japanese began to recognize how much of a stake they have in the international order underwritten by the United States. Neither the Soviet Union nor China presented an attractive alternative to America. Japan had also learned from the Pacific War experience the dangers of international isolation. Consequently the most realistic course for Japan was to cooperate with the United States and to resolve bilateral conflicts amicably. A brief review of postwar American-Japanese relations will show how Reagan benefited from the evolution of bilateral cooperation.

Evolution of American-Japanese Relations

The Postwar Settlement

The framework for American-Japanese relations was established during the negotiations for Japan's peace settlement with the United States. Prime Minister Shigeru Yoshida calculated that the best way to end the American occupation and to ensure Japanese security was to agree to a bilateral security pact and American military bases on Japanese territory. Although John Foster Dulles, the American negotiator, asked for Japanese rearmament to contribute to America's defense efforts, Yoshida resisted the request by citing the following reasons: Japan is a weak economic power; Article 9 of the Constitution prohibits rearmament; the

Japanese have a psychological aversion to the military after the tragic Pacific War; and a rearmed Japan would affect its neighbors adversely. He agreed only to a modest National Police Reserve, which later became the Self-Defense Force. Yoshida also felt that America's assessment of the military threat from the Soviet Union and mainland China was exaggerated and that the military balance in the region was overwhelmingly in favor of the United States.

In order to gain Senate approval of the Peace Treaty with Japan, Dulles managed to persuade Yoshida to support America's China policy. Japan, as a consequence, recognized the Nationalist regime in Taiwan rather than the People's Republic of China as the sole legitimate government of China. Japan stuck to this policy even after regaining sovereignty because the United States made it quite clear that American military and economic aid to Japan was contingent on Japan remaining isolated from mainland China.[1]

All in all, the postwar bargain struck between Japan and the United States was balanced. Japan obtained an early termination of the occupation, an American security commitment, a limited burden for military expenditures, and the economic benefits of American military procurements during the Korean war and after. The United States, in turn, gained access to military bases in Japan, Japanese support of its China policy, and Japan's integration into America's containment strategy.

As beneficial as this settlement was to Japan, Yoshida was criticized by both the left and the right. The left argued that the American bases not only violated Japanese sovereignty but also risked Japan's involvement in a Soviet-American conflict. They advocated a total peace that included the Soviet Union and the People's Republic of China, and a policy of unarmed neutrality. The right attacked Yoshida's policy of slow and limited rearmament and subordination to American foreign policy. They pushed for a revision of the "peace" Constitution that was imposed by the United States. Insofar as the Yoshida-Dulles bargain survived during the 1950s, it was because of the stalemate between the left and the right rather than a broad-based consensus behind the settlement.

America as Guardian

Given its economic and military strengths, the United States naturally assumed a guardian role in its relations with Japan in the post-independence period. But American power did not necessarily mean that it had an overwhelming leverage over the Japanese. In fact, Japan's economic weakness motivated the United States to help integrate Japan into the world economy and to accept fundamental asymmetries in the economic relationship. As early as 1949 the United States unsuccessfully tried to get most-favored-nation treatment for Japan at the General Agreement on Tariffs and Trade (GATT) Annecy conference. Under

American sponsorship, Japan was admitted to the International Monetary Fund and the World Bank in May 1952 and GATT in August 1955. The United States agreed to make twice as many trade concessions as other GATT members in return for GATT approval of Japan's membership bid. It also induced several nations to make concessions to Japan in exchange for American trade concessions to them.[2]

Because Japan was running huge American trade deficits, the United States signed a bilateral trade agreement with Japan in September 1955, which opened American markets to Japanese manufactured goods while the Japanese market remained largely closed to foreigners except for raw materials, agricultural goods, and technology. American military procurements from Japan, amounting to $5.6 billion during the 1950s, played a key role in resurrecting the war-torn economy. Benefiting from this favorable trading arrangement, Japan finally managed to record its first merchandise trade surplus with the United States in 1965.

On the security front, the possibility that the Japanese peace movement could force their government to withdraw from the American security system made the United States wary of pushing bilateral defense cooperation. The security treaty was revised in 1960 to make explicit the implicit American security guarantee in the original pact, but the Japanese successfully resisted an American proposal to commit Japan to regional defense. The United States also agreed to consult with Japan before using the bases for combat operations outside of Japan and making major changes in deployments. The new treaty obligated the United States to defend Japan, but it did not require that Japan aid American forces outside of Japan. Even with these favorable terms, parliamentary deliberations on the new security agreement sparked massive protests in Tokyo.

After the 1960 Security Treaty crisis, the United States became even more sensitive to Japanese protests against the security relationship. It scheduled visits of American nuclear warships so as to minimize public opposition. And in 1969, the United States accepted Japan's request that nuclear weapons be removed when Okinawa was returned to Japan.

The End of Pax Americana

By the mid-1960s, the Japanese economy had recovered so miraculously that Japan could no longer use the excuse of weakness to avoid liberalizing its own markets. Under American pressure, Japan gradually removed its import quotas, lowered its tariffs, and liberalized its restrictions on foreign investment. All this was done strategically to minimize damage to Japanese industry. But to Japan's credit, it also responded to liberalization by promoting the development of high technology industries. While Japan's trade position was improving, the American trade surplus was shrinking, and in 1971, the American current account balance went into deficit for the first time in a century.

Symbolic of this new state of affairs was the bilateral conflict over textile trade between 1969 and 1971, which was the worst confrontation between Japan and the United States since the end of the Pacific War. After months of bitter haggling, Japan finally agreed to restrict its textile exports to the United States. But more was to come. In August 1971, President Richard Nixon unilaterally imposed a 10 percent surcharge on imports that affected 94 percent of Japan's exports to the United States.[3] His suspension of the dollar's convertibility to gold, which ended the Bretton Woods international monetary regime, forced the yen to appreciate relative to the dollar. Japan had been resisting American pressure to revalue the yen because the low yen helped Japanese exports.

Other shocks from the Nixon administration further strained bilateral relations. The surprise announcement of Nixon's intention to improve relations with the People's Republic of China without prior notification embarrassed the Japanese government, which had held firm to its support of America's China policy despite growing domestic opposition. The 1973 short-lived embargo on soybeans, directed primarily at Japan, raised serious questions about America's reliability as a source of foodstuffs. Finally during the 1973 oil crisis, Japan tilted its foreign policy dramatically toward the Arab states in order to secure oil, much to the chagrin of the Nixon administration. These developments not only bred resentment on both sides of the Pacific, they also impressed on the Japanese the notion that the era of Pax Americana had come to an end.

The Nixon years, however, had a favorable impact on American-Japanese security relations. Although the 1969 Guam Doctrine provoked some concern in Japan that the United States was withdrawing from Asia, the overall climate of detente had a positive effect on Japan. Sino-American rapprochement removed a long-standing thorn in American-Japanese relations, and the reversion of Okinawa settled a potentially contentious issue. Soviet-American detente and the American withdrawal from Vietnam eased Japanese anxieties that the security link with the United States could embroil Japan in an unwanted war. The Japanese government took advantage of this favorable international environment to foster popular support for its defense policies. It codified its adherence to a strictly defensive military policy and imposed a 1 percent of gross national product (GNP) ceiling on defense expenditures. As a result, popular attitudes about security became more relaxed, and support for the American-Japanese security treaty and the Self-Defense Force grew steadily.

Japan as a Member of the Western Alliance

By the time Jimmy Carter became president, both the United States and Japan had learned from the mistakes of the previous years regarding alliance management. Japanese opinion leaders had also gone through a lively debate about the implications of the end of Pax Americana. Some argued that Japan should become a military power commensurate with its economic might and should pursue a foreign policy independent of the United States. Others tried to win support for the old idea of unarmed neutrality. Most, however, found neither a viable choice. They believed that Japan should strengthen the Western alliance, not abandon it. This would require only an extension of the foreign policy charted by Yoshida in the early 1950s. Such a course entailed the fewest risks; it recognized that the United States was still the strongest world power, both in economic and military terms, despite its relative decline; it acknowledged that the Soviet Union and China were poor substitutes for the United States and that neutrality was unrealistic; and it affirmed Japan's commitment to liberal democracy.

Bilateral economic relations during the Carter years demonstrated that the two nations had developed an effective pattern for defusing trade tensions and that Japan was more willing to cooperate with the United States to maintain the liberal international economic order. Negotiations to restrain Japanese exports of color television sets and steel to the United States went much more smoothly than had the textile negotiations with the Nixon administration. During the Tokyo Round multilateral trade negotiations, both the United States and Japan bargained hard, but both sides also made substantial concessions to maintain the momentum of trade liberalization. At the 1978 Bonn summit, Prime Minister Takeo Fukuda even agreed to macroeconomic policy coordination by stimulating the Japanese economy as part of an American-German-Japanese locomotive strategy. Although neither West Germany nor Japan fully lived up to its side of the agreement, what remains important is that Japan seriously considered playing a role in managing the global economy as a whole.

During the oil crisis of 1979, Japanese purchases of Iranian oil from the spot market irritated American officials because the action not only raised the price of oil but also appeared to undercut the American strategy for resolving the hostage crisis. Although this episode does show that conflicts of interest and miscommunication can still mar bilateral relations, the divergence between the two nations was not as great as during the 1973 oil crisis.

In terms of security affairs, Japan was becoming more forthcoming about cooperating with the United States. Whereas Fukuda characterized Japanese foreign policy as "omnidirectional peace diplomacy," his successor, Prime Minister Masayoshi Ohira, declared that Japan must actively fulfill its responsibilities as one of the Western nations and work with the United States as a good partner and ally to achieve common goals. The "Guidelines for U.S.-Japanese Defense Cooperation," which were approved by Japan in 1978, marked a major step toward mutuality in security relations. And in 1980, the Japanese Maritime Self-Defense

Forces participated in the American "Rim of the Pacific" naval exercises for the first time. After the Soviet invasion of Afghanistan, Japan cooperated with America's economic sanctions against the Soviets to a much greater extent than the West European nations.

What explains this convergence in strategic relations? First, the period of detente and the end of the Vietnam War increased Japanese support for the security link with the United States. Second, the Soviet military buildup in East Asia, beyond what was necessary to secure the Sino-Soviet border, plus the deployment of Soviet troops on the southern Kurile Islands claimed by Japan, made the Japanese receptive to the view that the Soviet Union, not the United States, was to blame for the collapse of detente. The Japanese at last began to feel that the Soviet Union posed a serious military threat.

Consequently, when Reagan entered the Oval Office, a solid foundation for American-Japanese cooperation had already been laid. Mechanisms for managing bilateral economic conflicts, which had been developed earlier, were available to cope with the most severe trade imbalance in the nation's history. Reagan's defiant stand against the Soviet Union found some sympathy in Japan, whereas in an earlier time it surely would have strengthened Japanese neutralists. Moreover, the renewal of American military power reassured the Japanese about America's security commitment.

Economic Dimension

Trade Imbalance

Even under these favorable conditions, the growing trade imbalance still presents a formidable challenge to the Reagan administration. The American annual trade deficit with Japan more than tripled, from about $16 billion in 1981 to $49.7 billion in 1985. In the first year of the Reagan presidency, the Japanese per capita value of imports of American products was $215; the comparable American value of imports of Japanese goods was $168. By 1984, the situation had reversed itself: The Japanese per capita value of imports from the United States rose to only $224, while that of American imports from Japan grew over 50 percent to $253. Although the value of American merchandise exports to Japan increased by 6.7 percent from 1981 to 1985, the value of Japanese merchandise exports to the United States increased by 52.4 percent over the same period.[4]

These figures, however, should be placed in a global context. The American global trade balance deteriorated much more sharply than the bilateral balance with Japan: from a deficit of about $28 billion in 1981 to a record deficit of $148.5 billion in 1985. Not only has the American trade deficit ballooned but the dollar amount of American exports world-wide has also contracted since Reagan became president. Although there is no question that America's trade position relative to Japan has worsened, this trend is part of an overall decline in American trade performance. In fact the United States is doing better in Japanese markets than elsewhere. Whereas the dollar amount of American exports to Japan increased from $20.8 billion in 1980 to $23.2 billion in 1984, American exports to the European Economic Community (EEC) has declined from $53.4 to $46.5 billion. Moreover, the percentage of exports to Japan relative to total American exports has been rising during the Reagan years, while the comparable percentage of exports to the EEC has been falling.

Irrespective of the improvement in America's export performance in Japan, Japan is taking much of the heat because its individual surplus is the highest and its economy the most competitive. Congress has proposed over 300 pieces of trade-restricting legislation. In March 1985, the Senate unanimously passed a resolution calling on the president to retaliate against Japan's unfair trade practices. The House of Representatives concurred by approving a similar resolution with an overwhelming vote of 394 to 19. It went even further in May 1986 by voting for a trade bill that would require the president to force nations with "excessive and unwarranted bilateral trade surpluses" to reduce them by 10 percent per year. The Senate may pass a tough bill of its own later in the year. One public opinion poll revealed that 63 percent of the American public favored some kind of trade action against Japan.[5]

Despite all this "Japan bashing," Reagan has so far succeeded in resisting protectionism. In fact he has skillfully used the congressional threats to pressure Japan to make concessions and to pay more of the side-payments necessary to preserve the liberal international economy. Japan has responded by adopting a sophisticated strategy to keep American markets open to Japanese products. The end result of this interaction has been greater bilateral cooperation for maintaining free trade, at least in principle, while moving toward a more managed trading order.

The Reagan administration has been pursuing two direct policies to cope with the bilateral trade problem: improving American access to the Japanese market and getting Japan to restrain its exports to the United States. Japan has been cooperating with both policies.

The market access strategy rests on the belief that the trade imbalance is partly the result of Japan's closed markets. In many respects, however, Japan may be technically one of the most open markets in the world. Japanese tariff rates on manufactured items average only 3 percent, whereas those in Europe and America are about 5 and 4 percent, respectively. In 1985, tariffs were removed on computers and computer parts, one of Japan's most strategic industries. Furthermore, there are few quotas on imports outside the agricultural sector, and Japan has yet to apply the safeguard provisions of the Multifiber Agreement to shelter its textile industry.[6] Nevertheless, because American exports to Japan have not expanded as much as Japanese exports to the United States, American charges of Japanese protectionism persist. Critics of Japan blame the myriad of administrative barriers to market penetration, the bewildering distribution system, the remnants of tariffs in particular sectors, and the Japanese cultural propensity to buy domestic products. They also point out the puzzling fact that Japanese imports have not increased in many declining sectors that have lost international competitiveness.

Under American pressure, the Japanese government announced between 1981 and 1985 eight different initiatives to make the Japanese market more open to foreign goods. The most important are the last two, both of which came in 1985.

On January 2, 1985, President Reagan and Prime Minister Nakasone agreed to a "market-oriented sector-selective" (MOSS) approach to the problem of market access. According to this approach, trade barriers are to be identified and removed in specific sectors through bilateral negotiations. The MOSS discussions have so far focused on four sectors (telecommunications, electronics, medical equipment and pharmaceuticals, and forest products).[7]

As the trade conflict continued to worsen in 1985, Nakasone announced in the summer his "Action Program" to make Japan the world's most open market by 1988. The program includes sweeping tariff reductions on 1850 of the roughly 2300 industrial and agricultural products subject to duties in Japan and the relaxation of non-tariff trade barriers by accepting foreign test data and self-certification for imports.

While bold and dramatic, these measures will not mitigate the enormous trade imbalance in the short term. Although estimates vary, it is widely believed that even if Japan dismantled all its import barriers outside the agricultural sector, the American trade deficit would be reduced by only $5 to 8 billion. If the United States reciprocated to eliminate its own barriers, then this gain in trade would be canceled out.[8] Furthermore, the removal of import barriers in itself does not necessarily mean more imports. Foreign firms and governments must also make the effort to sell more abroad.

In fact, American policies are to be blamed to some extent for the failure of American producers to export more to Japan. Consider, for example, the cases of Alaskan oil and timber. In 1973 the United States banned the foreign sale of Alaskan oil. Both Reagan and Nakasone, as well as Alaskan politicians, want to permit oil exports to Japan, but the United States maritime lobby has mobilized effective resistance in Congress. The American shipping industry currently profits greatly from transporting the oil from Alaska to the Gulf of Mexico. If the ban were lifted, Japan would buy about $2 billion worth of oil.[9] Similarly, Japan is willing to buy more than the $1 billion worth of logs and wood chips it currently purchases, but a prohibition on selling much of the timber cut on federal land to foreigners prevents further sales. The purpose of this ban is to guarantee a cheap and ample supply of wood for sawmills in the Pacific Northwest.[10]

According to one analyst, America's success in the Japanese market is remarkable, given the limited effort exerted. Although American firms had over eight times as many American employees in the EEC nations as in Japan in 1982, their sales in Europe amounted to $48 billion compared to $21 billion in Japan. There are at least 25,000 to 30,000 Japanese nationals working for Japanese firms in the United States, but only some 800 Americans work in Japan. The message is clear: If the United States wants to sell more to Japan, American firms must make a greater commitment of personnel for this task.[11]

Restraining Japanese exports to the United States is the other direct policy to rectify or at least control the trade gap. Before 1981, the American government pressed Japan to restrain "voluntarily" its exports in such sectors as textiles, consumer electronics, and steel. Under Reagan, the most celebrated example of a "voluntary export restraint" (VER) is the one for Japanese automobiles. This VER originally put an annual ceiling of 1.85 million cars that could be exported to the United States from Japan for the three-year period 1981–1983. The VER has been extended annually since the original expiration year of 1983, although the ceiling was raised to 2.3 million cars in 1985. Despite five successive years of export restraints, the Japanese share of the American auto market has not declined, staying in about the 20 to 22 percent range, and automobile trade with Japan accounted for more than one-third of America's bilateral trade deficit. Under the export quotas, Japanese automakers have increased their profit margins by selling higher priced models, and their American counterparts have moved upscale leaving the subcompact market to foreign producers. American car companies have, in fact, become major importers of Japanese small cars.[12]

Although ineffective in increasing the American share of the domestic auto market, the export restraint by Japan has prevented a sharp decline in market share and more restrictive trade measures. The VERs do violate the GATT principle of non-discrimination and weaken the free trading regime, but such measures have kept the United States from abandoning the regime outright. The other norms of GATT still remain relatively intact.[13]

Financial Liberalization

Given America's competitiveness in financial services, the Reagan administration has also been pushing for greater market access in Japan's financial sector. In 1984, the United States successfully pressured Japan to negotiate and sign a "yen-dollar agreement" and commenced discussions to liberalize Tokyo's capital markets and yen transactions for foreign financial institutions. The forces for internationalization had already been set in motion in the late 1970s when the Japanese government began to deregulate its highly segmented financial system. One of the main catalysts for deregulation was the growing public budget deficit that was forcing the government to borrow more from reluctant Japanese financial institutions. American pressure helped those Japanese officials who favored quicker liberalization and internationalization.

Ironically, this push for financial liberalization aggravated the merchandise trade problem in the short term because of divergent American and Japanese economic policies and structures. Since 1981, Japan has been generating a surplus of capital for several reasons: the tight fiscal policy to control the budget deficit, the stabilization of the private sector's demand for capital in an era of moderate investment and growth, and the abundance of domestic savings.[14] This situation contrasts sharply with that of the United States, where the 1981 tax cut and increases in federal spending have produced larger federal deficits and higher interest rates. With its low rate of domestic savings, the United States has been forced to rely on foreign capital to finance the deficit and investments, making America a net debtor country. Although the outflow of Japanese capital allows the United States government and American corporations to tap into Japan's enormous financial resources, the down side has been that the dollar has appreciated relative to the yen, which hurts American exporters.

Restricting the flow of capital out of Japan is one way to check dollar appreciation, but this goes against the positive long-term trend of financial liberalization. Even the conservative Japanese Ministry of Finance now appears to favor internationalization. After much hesitation, senior Finance officials have finally come around to opening up the banking and securities sectors to foreign institutions so that Japanese banks and security firms can enjoy reciprocal rights abroad. Now that Japan is unquestionably the second largest non-socialist economy with a huge current account surplus, Japanese policymakers want to make the yen an international currency and to play a leading role in shaping the world monetary system. In exchange for liberalization, Japan has asked the United States for its support in multilateral financial organizations as well as for the removal of various barriers against Japanese banks doing business in the United States. Indicative of its new role in monetary affairs, Japan recently became second to the United States in terms of voting rights in the World Bank and hopes to move up from its number five position in the International Monetary Fund.[15]

Macroeconomic Policy Coordination

During this era of relatively free international capital flows, most economists argue that the primary cause of the large American-Japanese trade imbalance is the macroeconomic policy mix between these two countries. The combination of Japan's tight and America's loose fiscal policies has increased the American appetite for Japanese goods, permitted a Japanese strategy of export-led growth, and raised the value of the dollar.

The solution to this state of affairs would be to have Japan pursue an expansionary policy to increase its demand for imports and to have the United States lower its budget deficit and its demand for foreign capital, which would, in turn, devalue the dollar. A study by the Institute for International Economics in Washington, D.C. has calculated that a dollar depreciation to about 190 yen could pare about $17 billion from the trade deficit. This means of reducing the trade deficit would be much more than what could be achieved by getting Japan to open its markets more to foreign goods.[16] For much of the Reagan administration, the yen-dollar exchange rate fluctuated in the range of 225 to 260 yen per dollar, which is too high to make American exporters competitive in the Japanese market.

Whatever the economic logic of changing the macroeconomic policy mix, the politics in both nations have imposed a deadlock against such a solution. The Reagan administration is unwilling to cut back its defense budget increases any further and unable to force Congress to swallow more reductions in social programs. In Japan, despite pressures from his own party, Nakasone holds firm to his commitment to achieve a balanced budget in the near future.

Since the fall of 1985, however, the two nations appear to be overcoming this impasse by working out some sort of coordination through the back door. In September 1985, the finance ministers of the Group of Five nations (the United States, Japan, West Germany, Britain, and France) agreed to a coordinated intervention in exchange markets to lower the value of the dollar, especially relative to the yen. The result has been extraordinary: the yen climbed sharply soon after the announcement, and by April the dollar had fallen below the 170 yen mark. Since the September Group accord offered only an artificial stimulus, the question remains whether the United States and Japan will adjust their respective economic policies and even economic structures to make the results of the exchange rate intervention stick.

Two developments since the Group of Five initiative augur well for policy coordination. First, the passage of the Gramm-Rudman bill put the president, Congress and the American people on notice that the federal deficit will have to be cut whatever the pain involved. If America can and does pursue budget austerity, then Japan may need to reflate its economy to avoid a recession. Second, the fall in world oil prices in early 1986 has created a favorable climate in Japan for economic stimulation without fear of inflation. Although Japan raised its interest rates following the Group of Five agreement in September, the government was able to lower them in 1986. The drop in interest rates should boost Japanese domestic investment, and the cheaper oil prices will lower not only production costs but also consumer prices.[17] The result for Japan should be more economic growth without the budget balancing mission being affected.

What does all this mean for the American-Japanese trade relationship? In the short term, the Japanese trade surplus with the United States is likely to grow because the yen appreciation will increase the dollar value of Japanese exports to the United States, even as their value in yen declines. Also high prices will hurt Japanese exporters of such low-value-added products as chinaware, flatware, and textiles. In the longer run, Japanese importers of foreign goods will benefit, and American exporters should have a better opportunity to compete in both Japanese and third markets in terms of price. The impact on Japan's major export industries, such as automobiles and steel, is more ambiguous. Although the strong yen will force firms in these sectors to squeeze their profits to hang onto their overseas markets, these manufacturers in the long term may be able to convert cheap oil and a strong yen into lower input costs and thus maintain international competitiveness.

Direct Foreign Investment and Growing Interdependence

In addition to restraining exports, opening its own markets, and cooperating to raise the yen, another element of Japan's strategy to check American protectionism is direct foreign investment in the United States. Since the late 1970s, American labor leaders have encouraged such investments as a way of providing more American jobs. The Japanese response has been dramatic: Their cumulative direct investments in the United States increased from less than $5 billion in 1980 to about $16 billion in 1984.

Japan's total direct overseas investments grew from $36 billion in 1980 to about $70 billion in 1985, of which 32.2 percent was in North America compared to 22.7 percent in Asia. In 1982, Japan surpassed France as the world's fourth largest direct foreign investor, and in 1986, is likely to overtake West Germany. The United States and Britain still head the list, with shares of 45.7 percent and 16.4 percent, respectively, of the total world direct overseas investment. The comparable statistic for Japan is 6 to 8 percent.[18]

Although American direct investments in Japan have been rising steadily, Japan now invests almost twice as much in the United States as the United States invests in Japan because of the sharp upswing in Japanese investments since 1980. Nevertheless the Japanese government has changed its position from restricting to actively backing foreign investments.[19]

The growth of direct investments across the Pacific is beginning to change the politics of American-Japanese economic relations. American manufacturing firms that have invested in Japan in order to obtain components from Japanese producers have a growing stake in liberal trade across the Pacific. Many of these companies are in such high technology sectors as semiconductors and computers. The recent agreements between American and Japanese automobile firms to give American companies the exclusive right to import certain Japanese models mean that American carmakers also have an interest in keeping American markets open.[20] Furthermore, Japanese takeovers of faltering American firms are being welcomed by workers and their communities because jobs are being saved. In some regions of America, labor resentment of Japan is gradually turning to appreciation. A few American business and political leaders have warned that Japanese investments may really be a "Trojan horse," whereby Japan either acquires America's most advanced technologies or makes immense profits in the United States only to repatriate the money, depriving America of needed investment capital.[21] Nevertheless the overall reaction to mutual investment penetration between Japan and the United States has been positive. The upshot of this is that it will become increasingly difficult to forge a strong coalition in the United States in favor of abandoning the liberal trading regime.

Despite all the acrimony and threats, the Reagan administration, in cooperation with the Nakasone government, has so far succeeded in softening the bite of American protectionism. And the recent appreciation of the yen may lower the American trade deficit to a more politically acceptable level. In order to revitalize trade liberalization, the Japanese are now the leading proponents of a new round of multilateral trade negotiations.[22] If these trade talks do occur, the Japanese will certainly be hard bargainers and will not easily make concessions that go against their national interest. But what is important is that more and more Japanese political and corporate leaders realize that it is in Japan's best interest to make the necessary side payments to maintain the trading regime. Unquestionably the threat of American protectionism has forced the Japanese to come around to this view. Whether or not this protectionism remains only a threat will depend on both the speed with which Japan improves access to its markets, and the performance of the American economy.

Security Dimension

Japanese Military Buildup and Bilateral Defense Cooperation

Although Prime Minister Masayoshi Ohira stressed Japan's important role as a member of the West in his meetings with President Carter, his successor, Zenko Suzuki, was more ambiguous about Japan's strategic relationship with the United States. While upholding the bilateral security treaty and articulating Japan's policy objective of defending up to 1000 nautical miles of sea lanes, Suzuki also emphasized, in his 1981 meeting with Reagan, the severe domestic constraints against a military buildup. He even balked under Japanese media pressure about the word "alliance" that was used to describe the American-Japanese relationship in the joint communiqué. Yasuhiro Nakasone's ascension to the prime ministership in 1982 turned this uneasy dialogue into a close partnership. Reagan found in Nakasone a leader with similar views about the importance of military strength to protect national interests and to contain Soviet communism.

The Reagan approach to security relations with the Japanese differs from that of the Carter years in at least two respects. First, the administration has refrained from publicly criticizing Japan's inadequate defense efforts and has instead chosen to work privately with Japanese pro-defense politicians. Second, it shifted the center of attention from military spending levels as a percent of GNP to the roles and missions that Japan can undertake to strengthen bilateral deterrence capabilities. This approach has helped to limit opposition in Japan to the steady increase in defense expenditures, despite the overall government policy of fiscal austerity. Furthermore, the emphasis on role and missions has encouraged Japanese opinion leaders to study more seriously the problems of military strategy and has helped to change the focus of the Japanese defense debate from ideological problems to more substantive security problems.

Nakasone himself has moved in several ways to strengthen defense cooperation with the United States.

First, soon after becoming the prime minister, he forged a government consensus to permit the export of military technology to the United States. Although the Carter administration originally floated the idea of a two-way exchange of defense technology between the United States and its allies, Japan hesitated about going along. Opposition parties invoked Japan's policy of banning arms exports, while some bureaucrats feared that the United States would exploit the exchanges to raid Japanese high technology. Arguing that the American-Japanese Security Treaty supersedes the arms export ban, Nakasone used the power of his office to overcome domestic resistance; and Japan, in November 1983, signed a memorandum of understanding with the United States permitting defense technology transfers.

Second, the Nakasone government indirectly promoted the concept of collective security in parliamentary interpellations. The official interpretation of the constitution is that Japan has the right to self-defense but not to collective security, even though the latter is guaranteed by the UN charter. Nakasone, however, has made statements in the National

Diet that stretches the meaning of self-defense to embrace certain aspects of collective security. Thus, in February 1983, he noted that if the U.S. Navy were operating to defend Japan, Japanese forces could in "self-defense" protect American naval vessels near Japan before Japanese territory was attacked directly. In April 1984, the Japanese government declared that an attack on Japan alone is inconceivable as long as the United States-Japan Security Treaty is in force. Furthermore, officials maintained that because of its geostrategic location, Japan would inevitably become involved in a Soviet-American global conflict irrespective of the policy it pursues.[23] Such statements reinforce the trend toward greater mutuality in the Pacific alliance, indicated by the adoption of the 1978 Guidelines for United States-Japan Defense Cooperation, the commencement of joint planning exercises in the Far East outside of Japan, and Japanese participation in joint military training exercises.[24]

Third, Nakasone attempted, in the summer of 1985, to rescind the defense spending limit of 1 percent of GNP imposed by Prime Minister Takeo Miki's Cabinet in 1976. By the fall, however, he was forced to back down because other leaders in the ruling Liberal Democratic party took a more cautious stance. Nevertheless, because the current defense budget is at the brink of the spending barrier, a slight dip in the GNP or routine increases in personnel costs could push military spending beyond the 1 percent ceiling without a government decision. In any case, Nakasone definitely wants to remove this artificial limit during his tenure. His cabinet did approve the Japan Defense Agency's mid-term estimate for 1986–90 defense procurements, which, if met, should require annual defense expenditures beyond 1 percent.[25] In the meantime, Japan is likely to continue to increase its defense outlays by 4 to 5 percent annually in real terms, a rate higher than the NATO objective of 3 percent.

Nuclear Arms Control and the Strategic Defense Initiative

Considering that the Japanese have what many observers call an "allergy" to nuclear weapons, it is remarkable that the United States has avoided provoking a sharp conflict in Japan about the nuclear question similar to the one that arose in Western Europe. This is, in part, the result of America's long-term sensitivity to Japanese opposition to nuclear weapons. The United States respected Japan's three non-nuclear principles by removing its nuclear weapons in Okinawa on returning the Ryukyu Islands to Japan. Since the 1960s, the U.S. Navy and the American Embassy in Tokyo have taken great care to time visits by American nuclear warships into Japanese harbors to minimize public protests. Furthermore, in contrast to the European theater, there has not been any American talk of a limited nuclear war in Northeast Asia and the United States has not deployed intermediate-range ballistic and cruise missiles on Japanese territory to counter Soviet SS-20s.

Nevertheless the Japanese antinuclear movement has been quite mild. Protests against the deployment of nuclear capable sea-launched cruise missiles (the Tomahawk) by the U.S. Seventh Fleet have been muted, and demonstrations against nuclear ship visits have fewer and fewer participants. Even the New Zealand government's decision to prohibit the transit of American nuclear warships did not inspire the Japanese opposition forces to press for a stricter application of the non-nuclear principles.

In addition to the sensitive handling of the nuclear problem by both the Japanese and American governments, there may be two additional factors to explain the absence of a strong antinuclear movement. First, although most Japanese oppose both the acquisition of nuclear weapons by Japan and their deployment on Japanese territory, they also recognize that America's nuclear arsenal works to deter a Soviet nuclear threat against Japan. Second, because the conventional military balance is still generally favorable to the United States and Japan in the Northwest Pacific, the Japanese do not have to rely on American nuclear forces to deter a Soviet conventional attack. Put differently, unlike the situation in the European theater, the United States does not have to rely on a first use of nuclear weapons to buttress deterrence in East Asia. Consequently, the prospect of a nuclear conflict limited to the Northeast Asian theater is remote, and the Japanese need for reassurance does not approach that of America's West European allies.[26]

A further difference between Japan and Western Europe is the different reactions of their respective security specialists to the Soviet SS-20 and other theater nuclear force (TNF) deployments. European strategists fear that Soviet superiority in TNFs would make Western Europe vulnerable to a Soviet nuclear threat without a credible American response. They are not reassured by the American strategic nuclear arsenal because the onus of escalation would be on the side of the West, and the Soviet Union now has parity with the United States at the strategic level. Given NATO's conventional weakness in Europe, an additional imbalance in TNFs amplifies the feeling of insecurity. In contrast, Japanese defense specialists generally feel that American strategic nuclear forces are adequate to counter Soviet nuclear threats against Japan. It does not matter whether the Soviet threat comes by way of intermediate-range ballistic or intercontinental ballistic missiles; American strategic forces are effective against both of them. In fact, Japanese strategists do not see much substantive difference between the two. Contrary to the situation in Europe, the onus of nuclear escalation in East Asia is on the Soviet side. Because Japan is surrounded by water and the conventional balance still favors the American-Japanese alliance, the most effective Japanese response to the Soviet military buildup in the region is to strengthen its conventional capabilities and to promote American-Japanese defense cooperation. There is no need to deploy theater nuclear forces on Japanese territory.[27]

Although the Soviet SS-20s have not caused much Japanese concern, the American-Soviet arms control negotiations on intermediate-range nuclear forces (INFs) have. The Japanese favor arms control as a way of reducing Soviet-American tensions, but they do not want an agreement that will downgrade Japanese interests in the Western alliance. Consequently, at the 1983 Williamsburg summit, Nakasone pressed for global limits on SS-20 missiles so that the Soviet Union could not move its European SS-20s to East Asia as part of an arms control deal on INFs in Europe. Reagan supported Nakasone's position, and the summiteers issued a statement of Western solidarity. The Japanese government also opposes an agreement that would require the Soviet Union to destroy its SS-20s in Europe, while the existing missiles in Asia would be allowed to remain. Thus far the Reagan administration has resisted such a bargain for the sake of trilateralism.

The response to the Reagan Strategic Defense Initiative (SDI), or Star Wars, also reveals major differences between Japan and Western Europe. Although European defense analysts feel that the SDI would weaken the credibility of the American nuclear guarantee, Japanese mainstream strategists see the initiative in a more positive light. First, they recognize that the SDI was instrumental in bringing the Soviets back to the arms control talks. Second, noticeably absent from the initial Japanese discussions about the SDI is the European concern about decoupling. Many Japanese defense experts, in fact, believe that the SDI will strengthen the American nuclear guarantee, not weaken it.[28] At this point, they do not view the SDI as a program that will shield most of the American population centers from nuclear attack. Rather the SDI will be useful in making American land-based missiles less vulnerable to a Soviet preemptive strike and therefore make more credible an American nuclear response. In other words, the SDI reduces the utility of ballistic missiles as counterforce weapons while enhancing their value as instruments of deterrence.

In addition to support from Japanese military experts, several firms in high technology fields are actively considering participation in the SDI program. For them, the initiative suggests a technological opportunity, not a technological threat. In fact, the agreement on defense technology transfer, signed by Nakasone in 1983, opens the way for Japanese private sector involvement.[29]

Although Japanese policy elites are more favorably disposed to the SDI than their West European counterparts, public opposition to the program may be just as strong, if not stronger, in Japan than in Europe. A smaller percentage of Japanese (11 percent) support the SDI than Americans (30 percent) and Europeans (between 20 and 25 percent), according to an April 1985 Gallup-Yomiuri poll.[30] No matter how sympathetic the Japanese government may be to the SDI, a 1969 Diet resolution opposing the militarization of space may prevent Japan from officially endorsing the program. The opposition will undoubtedly use the resolution to block such a move and to reinvigorate the antinuclear movement. If the government does not act cautiously, it could destroy the fragile consensus on defense policy that has been emerging in Japan since the 1970s. The government's greatest challenge is how to convince the media and public to support the arguments of its top security experts. In the meantime, however, Japanese private firms are likely to participate discreetly in SDI research.

Relations with the Soviet Union

Because Soviet leaders have been singularly inept at managing relations with Japan, the Japanese share Reagan's dislike of the Soviet Union. After Japan concluded a Peace and Friendship Treaty with China in 1978, the Soviet Union added insult to injury by deploying troops on the southern Kurile Islands claimed by Japan. The dramatic increase in Soviet military activity near Japanese territory and the 1983 Korean airline tragedy have only reinforced their traditional distrust of the Soviets. Even Japanese socialists are now expressing concern about the Soviet military buildup in Northeast Asia.[31]

The animosity toward the Soviet Union notwithstanding, there are some limits to how far Japan is willing to go toward embracing all of Reagan's Soviet policy. One limit involves the use of economic sanctions. After the Soviet invasion of Afghanistan in 1979, Japan, under Prime Minister Ohira, decided to sacrifice its economic interests in the Soviet Union to demonstrate that it was a staunch ally of the United States. Japan supported American sanctions against the Russians by tightening credit and restricting exports of capital machinery and high technology, in addition to boycotting the Moscow Olympics. But the lack of similar cooperation by Western Europeans irritated many Japanese officials and business leaders. As a consequence, Japan's position as the number two noncommunist trading partner of the Soviet Union (after West Germany) slipped to fifth place after 1980, and Japanese firms watched helplessly while major contracts were lost to European competitors.

When Reagan called for another round of economic sanctions in response to martial law in Poland in December 1981, the Japanese were understandably much less eager to join in. After two months of waffling, the Japanese government decided to terminate science and technology exchanges and official trade consultations. The June 1982 Reagan decision to prohibit the export of energy development equipment produced by American-owned or American-controlled technology and licenses angered the Japanese and the Western Europeans. The ban would have harmed the Soviet-Japanese oil and gas development project off the coast of Sakhalin, which was approved in 1972 and began in 1976. Japanese officials protested that the sanctions would hurt Japan more than the Soviet Union and referred to the unfairness of America's earlier decision to lift its Soviet grain embargo because of American farm pressure. As soon as it became apparent that the Europeans were going to defy Reagan's policy, Japan decided to go ahead with the Sakhalin project irrespective of the ban.[32]

From Japan's point of view, the ban on energy-related exports was ineffective and unfair, and the lack of any prior consultation was especially galling. But it is still important to note that Japan has supported economic sanctions against the Soviet Union more actively than the Western European countries. Two factors explain this difference. First, compared to Europe, Japan's economic interdependence with the Soviet Union is more limited. Although resources in Soviet Asia remain attractive, Japan has successfully diversified its supply of raw materials from many other nations. Moreover, China holds the promise of becoming a major market for Japanese capital goods, compensating for the loss of any opportunities in the Soviet Union. Second, given the important stake that Japan has in the American market and its sensitivity to American charges of unfairness and free-riding, the Japanese generally put greater priority on solidarity with the United States than on any economic interests in the Soviet Union.

The other limit to how far Japan is willing to cooperate with American policy toward the Soviet Union is the basic character of American defense policy: Does American policy deter or provoke Soviet military expansionism? Given its close physical proximity to the Soviet Union, Japan wants to stress the strictly defensive character of its alliance with the United States and would be loath to cooperate with an American strategy that it felt was provocative. Despite the adversarial nature of Reagan's Soviet policy, there has been little open criticism of it from the Japanese. One obvious reason for this is that Japanese officials do not want to debate Reagan about the merits of his policy toward the Soviets when bilateral economic tensions pose enough of a problem for American-Japanese relations. The other reason is that, in the eyes of most Japanese, it has been the Soviet Union rather than the United States that has sparked the intense arms race now underway in the Northwest Pacific. Consequently Japan accepted America's 1982 decision to deploy two squadrons of F-16 interceptors in the Misawa Air Force base, in northern Japan, with very little opposition. By augmenting Japan's air defense capabilities, this decision symbolized America's renewed commitment to Japanese security in the face of a dangerous Soviet military buildup in the region.

There is, however, another aspect to the F-16 deployments that could cause some problems in alliance relations in the future. Statements by Reagan's defense officials of the possibility of "horizontal escalation" during a war with the Soviet Union have begun to seep into Japanese strategic discussions. According to this strategy, the United States would open up a front in the Northwest Pacific where it is in a relatively strong position if a Soviet-American war broke out over Europe or the Middle East. The American F-16s in Misawa could be used in a counteroffensive operation against Soviet bases on the Sea of Japan coast, while the Seventh Fleet could bottle up the Soviet Pacific Fleet in the Sea of Japan and possibly engage the Soviets in a key naval battle. Although such scenarios probably appear much too surreal for most Japanese to take seriously, some of the most influential Japanese security experts see how the notion of horizontal escalation could rekindle Japanese pacifism and feelings of opting out of the Soviet-American conflict. With this consideration in mind, one of Nakasone's closest foreign policy advisors has recently written that the best way of preventing American unilateral military actions near Japan is to build up Japan's defense capabilities to such an extent that America cannot escalate horizontally without the cooperation of the Japanese Self-Defense Force.[33]

Since Soviet General Secretary Mikhail Gorbachev's rise to power, there have been a series of diplomatic overtures from the Soviet Union to improve relations with Japan. A Soviet-Japanese rapprochement that is not disadvantageous to Japan would clearly be a major political coup for Nakasone or his successor, but the Japanese government is suspicious of the latest Soviet peace offensive. Officials suspect that Gorbachev wants access to Japanese high technology and would like to weaken the solidarity of the Western alliance.

The January 1986 visit by Soviet Foreign Minister Eduard Shevarnadze to Tokyo, the first by a Soviet foreign minister since Gromyko's visit in 1978, improved the atmosphere of Soviet-Japanese relations but accomplished little of substance. The Soviets still refuse to recognize the very existence of a territorial dispute concerning the southern Kuriles. Even in the improbable event that the Soviet leadership agreed to negotiate the territorial question in the future, Japan would not accept an accommodation that would jeopardize the Western alliance, such as the removal of American bases in Japan in exchange for the islands. Moreover, Soviet leverage over the Japanese has weakened significantly since the 1970s because the Japanese no longer have an acute need for Siberian raw materials. If Gorbachev's strategy is in fact to weaken the Western alliance, it is not likely to succeed, at least for the Pacific wing of the alliance, because Japanese have found that strong ties with the United States strengthens their bargaining position vis-à-vis the Soviets.

Linkage of Economic and Security Dimensions

Although this chapter has treated the economic and security dimensions of American-Japanese relations separately, the two are in reality inextricably linked.

In the United States, there are complaints that the nature of the security relationship gives Japan an unfair advantage in bilateral economic competition. To be simplistic, because Japan spends only 1 percent of its GNP on defense compared to 6 percent for the United States, Japan can allocate more resources into its civilian economy and improve productivity. Admittedly, America has profited from the commercial spin-offs of defense technologies in industries like aviation, aerospace, and telecommunications; some American officials, however, note that Japan has also benefited from some of these same spin-offs through bilateral co-production agreements on military equipment. Furthermore, whereas practically all of Japan's many engineers work in civilian industries, much of America's engineering talent goes to the defense sector.

It is therefore not surprising that politicians from areas hardest hit by Japanese imports are the ones who are most critical of Japan's minimal defense efforts. A few have taken this argument to its extreme by stating that if Japan does not do more to mitigate bilateral economic tensions as well as contribute more to global security, then America should do less for Japan's defense. This kind of negative linkage of security and economic issues will seriously jeopardize the Pacific alliance if translated into concrete policy. Nothing could provoke Japanese xenophobic nationalism and neutralism more than the feeling of insecurity that would result from a withdrawal of America's security guarantee.

Because Reagan has stressed America's global strategy to contain the Soviet Union, Japanese fears of American abandonment have been minimal. Moreover, Americans who talk of withdrawing from Japan have lost their persuasiveness, since the Reagan administration has emphasized the importance of Japan to America's own forward deployment strategy.

The Japanese link security and economic dimensions differently. Since the postwar period, the priority has been on economics rather than security, and they prefer to separate economic from political considerations. For example, before Sino-American rapprochement, the Japanese developed economic ties with the People's Republic of China while continuing to support America's cold war policy of recognizing the Taiwan regime. If the Japanese thought about security at all, it was usually in terms of economic security, such as access to raw materials and foreign markets. Consequently, when the United States pressured Japan to do more for global security, most Japanese preferred to expand its economic assistance programs rather than its military forces. Some even proposed a division of labor whereby the United States would contribute to the military component of security while Japan would mainly contribute economically. Such an arrangement found little support in Congress, but Japan has steadily enlarged its foreign aid budget and now ranks only behind the United States in absolute amount of aid.

Since the late 1970s, however, the Soviet military buildup and activity in the region have made Japan more aware of the military aspects of security. But the Japanese do not intend to extend its defense obligations down to southeast Asia or to replace American military power in the region. They are well aware that such a course would threaten neighboring countries and ultimately endanger their economic interests in Asia. A more prudent response would be to strengthen Japan's capability to defend its own territory and to contribute to American deterrence in the Northwest Pacific. Although economic concerns constrain security policy, there is now a reverse relationship as well. Since the security link with the United States has become more important because of the growing Soviet threat, Japan is more likely to make concessions on economic issues with the United States so as to preserve the alliance.

This same logic also applies to the United States. Now that Japan is so critical for American security interests, the United States is less likely to adopt foreign economic policies that will undermine the pro-American coalition in Japan. In other words, the end of Soviet-American detente has had the unforeseen consequence of making more manageable the American-Japanese economic conflict.

"The United States and Japan: Conflict and Cooperation Under Mr. Reagan" was written for this volume. Copyright © 1987 by Mike M. Mochizuki.

Notes

1. J. W. Dower, *Empire and Aftermath: Yoshida Shigeru and the Japanese Experience, 1878–1954* (Cambridge, MA: Harvard University Press, 1979), pp. 369–414.

2. Charles Lipson, "The Transformation of Trade: The Sources and Effects of Regime Change," in *International Regimes*, Stephen D. Krasner, ed. (Ithaca: Cornell University Press, 1983), pp. 250–251.

3. F. C. Langdon, *Japan's Foreign Policy* (Vancouver: University of British Columbia, 1973), pp. 166–169; and I. M. Destler, Haruhiro Fukui, and Hideo Sato, *The Textile Wrangle: Conflict in Japanese-American Relations, 1969–1971* (Ithaca: Cornell University Press, 1979).

4. Figures based on Keizai Koho Center, *Japan 1982: An International Comparison* (Tokyo: Keizai Koho Center, 1982), pp. 1, 26, 29; and *Japan 1985: An International Comparison* (Tokyo: Keizai Koho Center, 1985), pp. 6, 36–38.

5. Susan Chira, "Poll Blames U.S. on Japan Trade," *New York Times*, August 13, 1985.

6. Kent E. Calder, "The Emerging Politics of the Trans-Pacific Economy," *World Policy Journal* (Fall 1985), Vol. 2, No. 4, p. 612.

7. Charles Smith, "More Action, More Talk," *Far Eastern Economic Review*, January 23, 1986, pp. 53–54.

8. "America v. Japan: Case Dismissed," *The Economist*, November 2, 1985, p. 73; and Calder, p. 613.
9. "Alaskan Oil — A Drop for Japan," *The Economist*, November 9, 1985, p. 38.
10. Lee Smith, "What the U.S. Can Sell Japan," *Fortune*, May 13, 1985, p. 95.
11. Bernard K. Gordon, "Truth In Trading," *Foreign Policy* (Winter 1985–86), No. 61, pp. 105–106.
12. William J. Hampton and James B. Treece, "Why Tokyo's Quotas Don't Do Detroit Any Favors," *Business Week*, March 3, 1986, pp. 38–39.
13. Lipson, pp. 246–247, 267–268.
14. Kiyohiko Fukushima, "Japan's Real Trade Policy," *Foreign Policy* (Summer 1985), No. 59, pp. 26–27.
15. Anthony Rowley, "The Supermarket Is Ready to Open," *Far Eastern Economic Review*, November 1, 1984, pp. 54–58.
16. "America v. Japan: Case Dismissed," *The Economist*, November 2, 1985, p. 73.
17. "Who's Afraid of the Big Bad Yen?" *The Economist*, February 22, 1986, pp. 61–62; and Larry Armstrong, "Is Japan Finally Ready to Pump Up Its Economy?" *Business Week*, February 17, 1986, pp. 48–49.
18. Bruce Roscoe, "Getting Round Protectionism by the Direct Route," *Far Eastern Economic Review*, June 13, 1985, p. 82.
19. Charles Smith, "The Sad Story of the West's Singular Lack of Success," *Far Eastern Economic Review*, June 13, 1985, p. 84.
20. Calder, pp. 600–601.
21. Winston Williams, "Japanese Investment, a New Worry," *New York Times*, May 6, 1984.
22. C. Michael Aho and Jonathan David Aronson, *Trade Talks: America Better Listen!* (New York: Council on Foreign Relations, 1985), pp. 87–88.
23. *Yomiuri Shimbun*, April 26, 1984.
24. Richard L. Sneider, *U.S.-Japanese Security Relations: A Historical Perspective* (New York: Columbia University, Occasional Papers of the East Asian Institute, 1982), pp. 81–89.
25. Charles Smith, "A Shot in the Foot," *Far Eastern Economic Review*, September 26, 1985, pp. 52–53.
26. Michael Howard, "Reassurance and Deterrence: Western Defense in the 1980s," *Foreign Affairs* (Winter 1982–83), Vol. 61, No. 2, pp. 309–324.
27. Okazaki Hisahiko, *Senryaku-teki shikō to wa nani ka* [What is strategic thinking?] (Tokyo: Chūō kōron sha, 1983), pp. 206–209.
28. Nishimura Shigeki, *SDI — Senryaku bō'ei kōsō* [SDI — the Strategic Defense Initiative] (Tokyo: Kyōikusha, 1985), pp. 155–159.
29. Richard Nations, "Star-Wars Dilemma," *Far Eastern Economic Review*, February 13, 1986, pp. 32–33.
30. *Yomiuri Shimbun*, April 29, 1985.
31. Masanori Tabata, "JSP Official Casts Wary Eye on Soviet Motives," *The Japan Times*, October 23, 1985.
32. Hikaru Kerns, "An Outfall in the East," *Far Eastern Economic Review*, July 23, 1982, pp. 43–46.
33. Satō Seizaburō, "Naze, soshite dono yō na gunji ryoku ka" [Why and what kind of military power?], *Chuo Koron*, November 1985, pp. 96–98.

11

The Reagan Administration and Latin America: Eagle Insurgent

Robert A. Pastor

Clearing Away the Complexity

To some Americans, the failure to prevent the Soviet Union from establishing a foothold in Cuba was not just a violation of the hallowed Monroe Doctrine, it was also the first of a series of humiliating reverses. Next came the agonizing defeat of the United States by a small Asian nation; revolutions in Iran, Nicaragua, and Grenada, which seemed targeted as much against the United States as against the rulers in each country; and the manipulation of oil prices by relatively small, weak nations. These and other developments left Americans feeling frustrated with the world and impatient with their leaders, who explained their inability to translate American power into effective influence by describing a complex world rather than admitting their own weaknesses.

No one articulated the frustration and impatience better than Ronald Reagan. His campaigns for the presidency in 1976 and 1980 were ringing declarations that the United States could once again take charge of its destiny and the world's. By 1980 the American people were ready for Reagan's message. The United States, according to two public opinion analysts[1]

Robert A. Pastor is Professor of Political Science at Emory University in Atlanta and the Director of the Latin American and Caribbean Program at the Carter Center of Emory. In 1985–1986, he was a Fulbright Professor at El Colegio de Mexico. Dr. Pastor was the Director of Latin American and Caribbean Affairs on the National Security Council, 1977–1981. He received his Ph.D. in Government from Harvard University and is the author of Congress and the Politics of U.S. Foreign Economic Policy *(Berkeley: University of California Press, 1980) and* Migration and Development in the Caribbean: The Unexplored Connection *(Boulder, CO: Westview Press, 1985).*

felt bullied by OPEC, humiliated by the Ayatollah Khomenei, tricked by Castro, out-traded by Japan, and out-gunned by the Russians. By the time of the 1980 Presidential election, fearing that America was losing control over its foreign affairs, voters were more than ready to exorcise the ghost of Vietnam and replace it with a new posture of American assertiveness.

Ronald Reagan offered a vision of the world that was uncluttered with the complexities that had distracted previous presidents. All one needed to know was that the United States was engaged in a global struggle against Soviet communism. "The inescapable truth," Reagan stated, "is that we are at war, and we are losing that war simply because we don't or won't realize we are in it . . . [and] there can only be one end to the war we are in. . . . War ends in victory or defeat."[2] During a war, all interests and concerns are subordinated to a single overriding security interest. Trade-offs between competing values and objectives only become difficult during times of peace.

Other policies or events were interpreted and became significant only through this organizing prism: Terrorism was manipulated from a single source, the Soviet Union[3]; human rights was a fight against communism; economic development could only succeed if the state was removed from the path of businessmen. And in no region of the world was Reagan's world view applied with more clarity, consistency, and vigor than in Latin America.

Although popular in the United States, Reagan's "reassertionism" faced a different world than the one on which it was premised.[4] First, in the 1970s, Latin American governments had begun to play important and independent roles in influencing world affairs. Second, Latin America had rejected Reagan's crystalline vision of a bipolar world in favor of one in which its global economic concerns had the highest priority. Reagan's predecessor recognized Latin America's desire to open the hemispheric envelope first sealed by the Monroe Doctrine. Carter also was prepared to respond to Latin America's international economic agenda rather than just insist on the traditional North American security agenda.

The question, as Reagan took office, was whether the United States could succeed in imposing its vision and strategy on an assertive Latin America or whether the Reagan administration would be forced to recognize and adapt to the complexities and changes that had occurred in the previous two decades? A related question was whether the new administration could maintain its classic realist hierarchy of objectives — all interests subordinated to the war against communism — in the face of competing values and interests?

The origins of the administration's approach toward Latin America will first be described, followed by an explanation of how the vision was transformed into policy. Central America — the region perceived to be the most threatened by communism — remained the administration's principal concern, and many of its other Latin American policies were designed to reinforce or facilitate its approach to Central America. Reagan's second term permitted the administration to solidify this approach, take credit for the wave of democratization, and address the urgent debt crisis. The last section will return to the questions above, and also evaluate the policy's successes and failures.

Background

The Reagan administration's new approach to Latin America and the Caribbean was the product of (1) the views of the president and his key advisors; (2) the ideological tendencies of the Republican party at that time; (3) the reaction of the president and his party to his predecessor; and (4) the problems and issues on the administration's agenda as it took office. Each of these factors reinforced the others in a way that made Reagan's clear vision even clearer and his determination to combat communism even sturdier.

Reagan is one of the few presidential candidates in history who projected his world view before the American people by using Latin American issues during his campaign. The Panama Canal treaties offered him his first and best vehicle. In a debate with William F. Buckley, Reagan argued that if the United States accepted the Canal treaties, "we would become a laughingstock by surrendering to unreasonable demands." Then putting the issue into a broader context, Reagan said that the world would not see the treaties as a magnanimous gesture "not in view of our bug-out in Vietnam, not in view of an administration that is hinting that we're going to throw aside an ally named Taiwan. I think the world would see it as, once again, Uncle Sam put his tail between his legs and crept away rather than face trouble."[5]

Reagan, in fact, took positions on many issues in inter-American relations, and disagreed with much of what the Carter administration was doing. Reagan defended both Pinochet's Chilean government and the Argentine military regime in its war against "a well-equipped force of 15,000 terrorists."[6] He criticized Carter's human rights policy, writing that it was "little wonder that friendly nations, such as [the military governments of] Argentina, Brazil, Chile, Nicaragua, Guatemala, and El Salvador have been dismayed by Carter's policies." And for similar reasons, he opposed Carter's policies on nonproliferation and arms sales.[7] On Cuba, Reagan proposed a blockade as a way to pressure the Soviet Union: "Suppose we put a blockade around that island and said, 'Now buster, we'll lift it when you take your forces out of Afghanistan?' "[8] He also advocated releasing the Central Intelligence Agency (CIA) from its many congressional restrictions.

The Republican party embraced and developed Reagan's themes. Jeane Kirkpatrick, a Georgetown University professor, wrote two articles that argued that Carter's policy had "positively contributed . . . to the alienation of major nations, the growth of neutralism, the destabilization of friendly governments, the spread of Cuban influence, and the decline of U.S. power in the region."[9] Kirkpatrick did not offer an alternative prescription except by implication. By her criticism of Carter's alleged destabilization of Nicaraguan dictator Anastasio Somoza and other military governments, and her distinction between friendly authoritarian and unfriendly totalitarian governments, she implied that the only valid criterion for making United States policy should be if the regime is friendly. No matter how tenuous its legitimacy or how repressive its actions, a friendly regime should receive American support, since the alternative is, at best, uncertain and, generally, worse.

As a rebuttal to the Linowitz Commission on United States-Latin American Relations, which had influenced the Carter administration, several conservatives formed a group called the Committee of Santa Fe to recommend a new policy for the incoming Reagan administration. A number of the group's members found positions in the new administration. Their report began with a dramatic warning of impending doom:

> America is everywhere in retreat. . . . Even the Caribbean, America's maritime crossroad and petroleum refining center, is becoming a Marxist-Leninist lake. Never before has the Republic been in such jeopardy from its exposed southern flank. Never before has American foreign policy abused, abandoned, and betrayed its allies to the south in Latin America.[10]

Unlike Kirkpatrick, the Committee of Sante Fe did offer some clear recommendations for United States policy. It called for the revitalization of the Monroe Doctrine and urged strengthening security agreements in the region and renewing military assistance agreements with military governments. It directly confronted the trade-off between human rights and security, and concluded that the human rights policy:

> . . . must be abandoned and replaced by a non-interventionist policy of political and ethical realism. . . . [The human rights policy] has cost the United States friends and allies and lost us influence. . . . The reality of the situations confronted by Latin American governments that are under attack . . . must be understood not just as a threat to some alleged oligarchy, but as a threat to the security interests of the United States.[11]

The 1980 Republican party platform adopted similar positions. It deplored "the Marxist Sandinista takeover of Nicaragua"; recommended the end of the aid program to Nicaragua; and called for closer cooperation with Mexico. But the principal theme of the platform and of Reagan's campaign for the presidency was that Soviet-Cuban power was advancing in the world and the United States must devote all its energies to stopping and then rolling back the communists.[12]

On taking office on January 20, 1981, Reagan based his policy toward the region (and the world) on this central theme.

The Centrality of Central America

"The morning of an administration," Alexander Haig noted in his memoirs of the first eighteen months of Reagan's administration, "is the best time to send signals." To Haig, the Carter administration had sent so many signals that its message was blurred and confused. The Reagan administration, in contrast, would send just two clear signals[13]:

> Our signal to the Soviets had to be a plain warning that their time of unresisted adventuring in the Third World was over, and that America's capacity to tolerate the mischief of Moscow's proxies, Cuba and Libya, had been exceeded. Our signal to other nations must be equally simple and believable: once again, a relationship with the United States brings dividends, not just risks.

The administration chose to send the Soviets the first signal by drawing a line in Central America; it sent the second signal by embracing the military governments of South America.

On February 23, 1981, the State Department issued a White Paper, presenting "definitive evidence of the clandestine military support given by the Soviet Union, Cuba, and their communist allies to Marxist-Leninist guerrillas" trying to overthrow the Salvadoran government. President Reagan later explained the rationale for United States policy in an interview[14]:

> What we're actually doing is offering some help against the import or the export into the Western Hemisphere of terrorism, of disruption, and it isn't just El Salvador. That happens to be *the target* at the moment. Our problem is this whole hemisphere and keeping this sort of thing out.

Alexander Haig defined the problem in a way that offered the administration a framework for addressing it: ". . . it is our view that this is an externally managed and orchestrated interventionism, and we are going to deal with it *at the source.*" Haig gained early agreement in the administration to increase military aid (by $25 million) and advisors (by forty) to El Salvador, but his suggestions for more direct military actions against Cuba and Nicaragua met resistance.

Frustrated, Haig decided to submit a specific plan "to lay down a marker on the question of Cuba," which included a blockade and other military actions. He presented his proposal to the National Security Council in early June 1981, again in November 1981, and finally in February 1982, but it was rejected for four reasons. First, Secretary of Defense Caspar Weinberger feared another Vietnam and the Joint Chiefs of Staff feared that the Soviets might respond forcefully in another part of the world. Second, the rest of the administration doubted that Congress or the public would accept such action without some provocation on the part of Cuba. Third, some in the State Department doubted that a blockade would affect Castro's support for revolutions in Central America. And finally, the White House political advisors wanted to keep the president and the public focused on domestic economic issues, especially a tax cut, and not dissipate his popularity on too many controversial issues so early. Haig, by his own admission, was "virtually alone" in arguing at that time to bring "the overwhelming economic strength and political influence of the United States, together with the reality of its military power, to bear on Cuba in order to treat the problem at its source."[15]

Whatever the impact of the administration's signals on the Soviet Union, its initial impact on El Salvador was nearly disastrous. The struggle in that country was not, at that time, between the Marxist guerrillas and the government; the Marxists had been defeated soundly in their January 1981 offensive. The struggle was between the government and rightist elements, and the latter interpreted statements by the president and Haig as indicating support for their war against the Christian Democrats.[16]

One of the Reagan administration's first decisions was to authorize the Milgroup Commander to negotiate a new aid agreement directly with the military. In bypassing Duarte, the administration undermined his authority,[17] and it is conceivable that this may have been intentional, since there is evidence that some in the administration viewed him as too far to the left to be effective against the Marxists. National Security Advisor Richard Allen had met Duarte during the transition and criticized the land reform as socialistic.[18] Aware of this and buoyed by the strong anticommunist rhetoric of the new administration, the right perhaps thought its approach was favored in Washington. On March 3, 1981, Salvadoran rightist leader Colonel Roberto D'Aubisson told the press that, based on his meetings with "members of Reagan's group [including Allen's Latin American advisor, Roger Fontaine], . . . the Reagan administration would not be bothered by a takeover" that eliminated the Christian Democrats from the government.

The Embassy quickly recognized the seriousness of D'Aubisson's threat. In response to questions raised the next day, the White House equivocated ("We just don't have a view on that"), but the State Department offered a strong statement of support for Duarte and said a coup would have "serious consequences" for the continuation of American aid to El Salvador.[19] This stopped the plot, but according to Duarte's close friend and his ambassador in Washington, Duarte felt his position was weakened and that he did not enjoy the support of the administration until the fall of 1981.[20]

The major priority of the administration's policy toward El Salvador was to help modernize the military's counterinsurgency program. After Duarte announced elections in November 1981 for a constituent assembly, the administration added this component to its policy. It firmly opposed negotiations with the left and showed no interest in pressuring the right until late in 1983. Nonetheless Congress forced the administration to assign a higher priority to human rights and negotiations by setting explicit conditions on the use of aid.[21]

When the Christian Democrats won 40 percent of the vote in the elections in March 1982, the various rightist parties united to prevent them from taking power. By this time, the administration had recognized the importance of the Christian Democrats — if for no other reason but that Congress was unlikely to provide aid without them — and the Embassy played a leading role, negotiating a moderate rather than a rightist into the presidency.

But as the war in El Salvador grew worse, the administration returned to the "source" — Nicaragua. The Carter administration had suspended aid to the Nicaraguan government in January 1981 because of evidence that it was transferring arms to the Salvadoran guerrillas.[22] The new administration was expected to terminate the aid, but United States Ambassador Lawrence Pezzullo convinced Haig to use the aid as leverage to negotiate an end to the arms trafficking.[23] He was correct that the Nicaraguans would stop their material support for the Salvador guerrillas, but he was wrong that the administration, in the light of Reagan's campaign statements, would continue aid. On April 1, 1981, the State Department announced that it was terminating aid even though Nicaragua had ceased military support for the guerrillas. To encourage "favorable trends," the administration did "not rule out the eventual resumption" of aid.[24]

Between August and October 1981, Assistant Secretary of State Thomas Enders visited Managua to determine the willingness of the Sandinistas to reach an agreement. Negotiations between and within the two governments were pursued feverishly but ultimately unsuccessfully. The reasons for the failure are unclear, except, of course, to the State Department, which blames the Sandinistas, and to the Sandinistas, who blame the United States.

Enders offered a five-point plan that included an end to Nicaraguan support for the insurgency in El Salvador as well as to Nicaragua's military build-up, a pledge of United States nonintervention in Nicaragua's internal affairs and enforcement of U.S. neutrality laws, renewal of economic aid to Nicaragua, and an expansion of cultural relations.[25] Hard-liners in the Reagan Administration phrased the proposal in a "peremptory" manner so that it sounded to Arturo Cruz, who was Nicaragua's Ambassador to Washington at the time and participant in the negotiations, "like the terms of [a] surrender."[26] While the Nicaraguans were considering the proposal, the administration launched its first large military exercise off the Caribbean coast of the Honduras.

The Sandinistas failed to respond adequately to the proposal, and the Reagan administration chose not to explore the nature and the depth of the Sandinistas' concerns or try to negotiate an alternative formulation. The author's interviews in Managua and Washington in 1983 led him to conclude that both governments were constrained by officials who felt the other side was untrustworthy.[27] The Sandinistas interpreted the Reagan administration's pledges to enforce its domestic laws and international obligations as disengenuous, since the United States should have been enforcing them in the first place. And the administration interpreted the lack of an official response from the Sandinistas as an indication that they could not be diverted from their revolutionary goals. Instead of negotiating seriously, each side for its own reasons preferred to rest on the preconception that the other side was not serious.

Having "tried" negotiations, the administration was pressed again by Haig to go "to the source." A meeting of the National Security Council on November 16, 1981 made two pivotal decisions, which were formalized in National Security Decision Directive #17 signed the next day by President Reagan.[28] First, rather than reject entirely Haig's proposal for a blockade, Reagan ordered contingency planning for the use of North American military forces, including "a petroleum quarantine and/or retaliatory air reaction against Cuban forces and installations," but this would only be taken in *response* to "unacceptable military actions by Cuba" rather than as part of a United States-initiated pressure campaign. Oberdorfer cites one participant, who described this decision "as a way of letting Al [Haig] down easily." (There is no evidence that the group reached agreement on what constituted "unacceptable" actions.)

The second decision — for the CIA to fund and direct a secret anti-Sandinista guerrilla force — was of greater consequence for the future course of the administration's policy. In briefing the Intelligence Committees in Congress in December, the administration reportedly described its proposal as a $19 million program to set up a 500-man force aimed largely at the "Cuban infrastructure" in Nicaragua that was allegedly training and supplying arms to the Salvadoran guerrillas.

The groundwork for such a proposal came earlier in 1981, when the administration decided not to enforce the neutrality laws against the Nicaraguan and Cuban exiles who were training in Florida and California to overthrow the Nicaraguan government. The administration initially saw these camps as bargaining chips to be used in negotiations with the Nicaraguan government and indeed subsequently admitted that during the negotiations with Nicaragua in 1981, it offered "to enforce laws pertaining to exile activities in the United States" if the Sandinistas were responsive to American concerns.[29]

On March 9, 1981, Reagan signed a "Presidential Finding," authorizing the CIA to undertake covert actions in Central America to interdict arms trafficking to Marxist guerrillas.[30] Perhaps using the authority provided by that finding, CIA agents began to organize disaffected Nicaraguans. Edgar Chamorro, who was selected by CIA agents in November 1982 to be a member of the Directorate of the Nicaraguan Democratic Force (FDN), was first asked in August 1981 to participate in "an important meeting in Guatemala with U.S. officials, the National Guardsmen [the core of the contras at that time], and their Argentine military advisors." The issue was whether those Nicaraguans who had grown disenchanted with the revolution should merge their efforts with the National Guardsmen. Chamorro indicated that the CIA controlled everything from the budget to the propaganda — some of which was an attempt to influence Congress.[31]

Congress, led by the House Permanent Select Committee on Intelligence, raised questions about the program from the beginning. The committee approved of the need for interdicting arms flows from Nicaragua, but based on remarks by the contra leaders, questioned whether that was the administration's objective. On February 14, 1982, the *Washington Post* disclosed the $19 million covert action program and indicated that the money had been used to support about 1000 fighters and to help middle-class leaders in Managua.[32] The Sandinistas responded to the report by arresting a number of leading moderates and accused them of complicity with the contras.

Repairing Relationships for the Common Struggle

Although Central America remained at the center of its Latin American policy, the Reagan administration also embraced military governments that had had cool relations with the Carter administration for reasons of human rights, conventional arms restraint, or nuclear nonproliferation. In doing so, the Reagan administration chose to give higher priority to its interest in forging a common front against communism than to any other interest.

In its first months, the Reagan administration deliberately made a number of decisions to demonstrate its distance from Carter's policies.

Secretary Haig stated he had replaced the Carter administration's linkage with human rights with a new linkage to the East-West struggle. But he captured the change best in his statement: "International terrorism will take the place of human rights in our concern."[33]

There were other signs of disinterest in human rights. On February 27, 1981, plainclothes police captured three of Argentina's most prominent human rights activists, held them incommunicado, and seized their files. A State Department official said "there would be little reason to criticize these arrests since they were carried out in connection with a judicial order concerning the seizure of certain documents."[34] Nor did the arrests have any effect on President Reagan's decision to receive Argentina's President-elect General Roberto Viola as his first Latin American visitor. Indeed, in announcing the visit, State Department spokesman William Dyess publicly underscored the break from the immediate past: "We want good relations with Argentina. Any abnormality in relations is due to a large extent to the public position this country took regarding human rights practices in the country." Dyess said that public criticism of human rights violations would be reserved for such "totalitarian" countries as the Soviet Union.[35] The administration considered its policy vindicated when Argentina agreed to advise the contras in Honduras.[36]

On March 1, the administration also announced its intention to improve relations with Chile by restoring normal Export-Import Bank financing and inviting them to participate in joint naval exercises.[37] United States Ambassador to the United Nations Jeane Kirkpatrick visited Chile in August 1981, and at a press conference, she said that the United States intended "to normalize completely its relations with Chile in order to work together in a pleasant way." She declined comment when asked about Chile's human rights record, and refused to meet with Jaime Castillo, President of the Chilean Commission on Human Rights and former Minister of Justice. Two days after Kirkpatrick departed, security agents beat up Castillo and dumped him and three other prominent opposition politicians on the Argentine frontier. Claudio Orrego, a Christian Democratic leader, said that the arrests had occurred because Pinochet viewed Kirkpatrick's visit as offering him "enthusiastic and unconditional support."[38]

General Vernon Walters visited Guatemala in May, 1981 to make clear that Guatemala's friendship with the United States was more important than its human rights violations: "It is not difficult to see which countries are our friends and which are not." The next month, the administration approved the sale of fifty military trucks and one hundred jeeps and, by an administrative act, provided an additional $3.2 million of arms sales.[39] Congress resisted the administration's efforts to provide other military aid to the Guatemalan government, but on January 7, 1983, the Reagan administration lifted the five-year embargo on arms sales to that country.

On July 1, 1981, President Reagan sent a letter to Congress indicating that his administration would support development loans to Chile, Argentina, Paraguay, and Uruguay. Although the Carter administration had voted against or abstained from voting on 118 loans to twenty different countries for human rights reasons, the Reagan administration, using the same criteria, in its first two years, only abstained or voted against five loans — to the communist countries Angola, Yemen, and Laos.

Actually, the Reagan administration did use its vote in the international development banks, but mostly for the purpose of opposing public sector loans.[40] Whereas the Carter administration had sought ways to be responsive to the Third World, the Reagan administration refused to acknowledge its existence. In his confirmation hearings on January 9, 1981, Haig referred to the "so-called Third World" as "a myth — and a dangerous one."[41]

The Reagan administration also discarded its predecessors' efforts to curb arms sales and nuclear proliferation. United States arms sales to South America had been on a secular plunge even before Carter took office. As a proportion of South American arms purchases, United States sales amounted to 75 percent in 1960, 25 percent in 1970, and 7 percent in 1980. Although the United States had shown restraint, Europe, Israel, and the Soviet Union promoted sales, and Brazil became a major exporter. The Reagan administration reversed this course. During its first two years, the United States sold more than twice as much (in dollars) as were sold during the Carter administration in four years.[42]

During the 1980 presidential campaign, Reagan said that the United States should not stand in the way of a country that wanted to develop its own nuclear weapons: "I just don't think it's any of our business."[43] Nonetheless, the Reagan administration declared its intent to curb nuclear proliferation, but it also claimed — as in the arms sales policy — that its predecessor's restraint only antagonized friends and diminished American influence; therefore it relaxed the policy. In 1982, in a reversal of Carter's policy, the Reagan administration authorized the export of 143 tons of heavy water and a computerized control system for Argentina's nuclear program, without demanding safeguards. The administration claimed that the sale would permit it to influence Argentina to stop completion of an enrichment plant, but as it turned out, the sales facilitated the completion of the plant one year later.[44]

President Reagan's efforts to improve relations with Mexico did not involve a trade-off of any United States interests or a change from Carter policy. Because the relationship between both countries is so important, both Mexican President Jose Lopez Portillo and President Reagan had a stake in smoothing the strains that had developed in previous years.[45] With a good eye for symbols and a readiness to meet with his counterparts more frequently than any other president, Reagan improved the tone of the relationship at the beginning of his administration. Moreover, the Reagan administration responded quickly and effectively on the two occasions that Mexico was in genuine need — in August 1982 during the first phase of the debt crisis and in September 1985 after the earthquake. Still, the important differences — on foreign policy, immigration, the border, trade, narcotics — that have long separated Mexico and the United States continued, and in some cases worsened. By mid-1986, the deterioration of the Mexican economy, combined with an openly aggressive posture by the administration, threatened to undermine the stability of the Mexican government and seriously injure the bilateral relationship.

Coping with Constraints

Within a month of President Reagan's inauguration, the Assistant Secretary of State for European Affairs Lawrence Eagleburger was dispatched to Europe to consult on policy toward El Salvador. Vernon Walters made a similar tour to Latin America, and other administration officials consulted on Capitol Hill. They found more opposition than support for the administration's strategy.[46] The administration never deviated from its principal objective, but it did show a willingness to compromise on the edge of its policy and to concede some rhetoric or symbol to its critics in order to gain support for its program. Most of its concessions occurred as Congress debated its requests for foreign aid.

To counter the impression, however accurate, that the administration only viewed the region's problems in an East-West military framework, Haig consulted with the foreign ministers of Mexico, Venezuela, and Canada on an economic program for the small nations of the Caribbean. When Jamaican Prime Minister Edward Seaga first suggested the idea, the administration intended to rely strictly on private investment.[47] When that proved inadequate for dealing with the economic crises in Central America, Reagan maintained the rhetoric extolling the "magic of the market," but he announced an innovative one-way free trade arrangement, the Caribbean Basin Initiative (CBI) in February 1982, with a sizable foreign aid package — $350 million of economic aid and a substantial amount of military aid.

In response to the sharp criticism of Ernest Lefever, its first designee as Assistant Secretary of Human Rights, the administration withdrew his nomination and modified its approach. It issued a memorandum that ironically not only affirmed Carter's policy, but rebutted the Kirkpatrick critique of it. "A human rights policy means trouble," the memo noted, "for it means hard choices which may adversely affect certain bilateral relations. There is no escaping this without destroying the credibility of our policy, for otherwise, we would be simply coddling friends and criticizing foes."[48] Although this memorandum did not lead to a complete change in the administration's policy, it did diffuse the criticism of it.

The political dimension of Reagan's Salvador policy was elections, and by the middle of 1982, the administration broadened this interest into a global program for promoting democracy. As with many of the administration's new ideas, it was motivated in part by its interest in responding to what the Soviets were doing. In a speech to the British Parliament on June 8, 1982, President Reagan announced a program "to foster the infrastructure of democracy," acknowledging that one of the sources of the idea was the Soviet Union, which "has given covert political training and assistance to Marxist-Leninists" since 1917.[49] Reagan's proposal included a major propaganda campaign called Project Democracy and the establishment of a number of institutions associated with the National Endowment for Democracy to assist political parties, labor unions, and business.

Despite these initiatives, the administration continued to have difficulty obtaining the support of Congress. Led by House Democrats, Congress became increasingly wary of the administration's intentions in El Salvador and Nicaragua. Congressional uneasiness was reinforced by public opinion polls and by warnings against military intervention issued by senior military officers on their retirement.[50]

In addition to internal opposition, the most potent restraint on the administration's strategy in Central America emerged from a meeting of the foreign ministers of Mexico, Venezuela, Colombia, and Panama on the island of Contadora off Panama in January 1983. The "Contadora Initiative" soon gained nearly universal support, and it began to negotiate treaties within Central America aimed at the demilitarization of the region and the reconciliation between warring factions in each country.

At this time the Reagan administration became anxious about the war in the region. The guerrillas in El Salvador had launched a series of coordinated actions, which culminated with the seizure in January 1983 of the town of Berlin. On February 22, 1983, the United States Ambassador to the UN Jeane Kirkpatrick returned from a trip to Latin America with a tale of doom unless the administration demonstrated the political will to reverse the gains of the leftists.

Reagan turned his attention to the region. In a speech on March 10, 1983, Reagan asked Congress for a $298 million emergency assistance package, with $110 million earmarked for El Salvador. Central America, Reagan argued, "is simply too close, and the strategic stakes are too high, for us to ignore the danger of governments seizing power there with ideological and military ties to the Soviet Union." For the first time, Reagan placed his approach in a bipartisan mold — alluding to his predecessor's efforts "to stop the advance of communism in Central America." Reagan assured his audience that he had no intention of sending United States troops; rather, his objectives were "reform, human rights, and democracy" to be pursued through aid and negotiations. He also condemned the communist countries for using Grenada to build "a naval base, a superior air base, storage bases and facilities for the storage of munitions, barracks, and training grounds for the military."[51]

When Congress rebutted his arguments and blocked his program, Reagan responded with strident rhetoric in another speech on March 23. At the same time, the president explored compromises. In exchange for the support of Representative Clarence D. Long, Chairman of an influential House Appropriations Subcommittee, Reagan agreed to appoint a Special Envoy, Richard Stone, to begin negotiations in Central America.[52] To announce this compromise and to mobilize public support to assure passage of Central American aid and to preclude efforts to stop funding the contras, Reagan decided to address a joint session of Congress on April 27. He repeated some of the arguments he had made on March 10 but concluded with a jab at Congress: "The national security of all the Americas is at stake in Central America. . . . Who among us would wish to bear responsibility for failing to meet our shared obligation?"

In arguing for the covert program, Reagan stressed the Sandinista threat but assured Congress that his objective was not the overthrow of the government. Many congressmen remained skeptical, and on May 3, the House Permanent Select Committee on Intelligence banned covert aid to the rebels. The administration worked through the Senate and tried to enhance its credibility by supporting ARDE, an anti-government group led by the independent revolutionary Eden Pastora.[53] Supporting Pastora may have helped to obtain a compromise that permitted funding of the contras until April 1984, albeit with a number of restrictions. Funding to Pastora stopped, however, when Congress reduced the amount.

To achieve the compromise on the covert program as well as to obtain 75 percent of the aid he had requested for El Salvador, Reagan endorsed the Contadora Group, appointed Richard Stone as a Special Envoy, accepted a limit of fifty-five military advisors for El Salvador, took the first tough steps of his administration to curb the death squads in El Salvador, and also approved an idea for a bipartisan commission to try to draft a long-term policy for the region. On July 18, he asked Henry Kissinger to chair the commission and report to him in the new year. The administration not only hoped to obtain a bipartisan boost to its policy but also to remove this issue from the presidential campaign.

But these compromises were less important to the administration's strategy in Central America than the expansion of military aid, training, joint exercises, and the construction of several airfields in the south of Honduras to support the contras and provide a contingency option for the U.S. Air Force to attack Nicaragua if provoked. Reagan's speeches and his personal involvement emboldened those in the administration, who began talking openly about military victories in Central America.[54]

Still, despite the compromises, the effort to persuade Congress appeared stalemated until late October 1983, when United States military forces joined with token forces from six Caribbean nations to invade the island of Grenada and overthrow the Marxist regime. One faction of the regime had arrested Maurice Bishop, the popular Prime Minister, on October 13. When several members of his Cabinet freed Bishop several days later, they tried to secure a fort, but were captured and executed by the military. The Caribbean, one of the few genuinely peaceful and democratic regions in the developing world, was shocked by the assassinations and violence, and several neighboring governments invited the United States to join them to remove the regime. Although the invasion was condemned by the vast majority of states in the Organization of American States (OAS) and the UN, its popularity in Grenada and the Caribbean helped its popularity in the United States and offered Reagan a campaign theme, which he first articulated in a speech two weeks later: "Our days of weakness are over. Our military forces are back on their feet and standing tall."[55]

On January 10, 1984, the Kissinger Commission presented its report to the president. Its analysis of the indigenous causes of the crisis differed from the administration's, as did its conclusion that indigenous revolutions did not pose a threat to the United States. The administration, however, deftly chose to agree with its other conclusion that Soviet-Cuban involvement required a strong United States response. On February 3, claiming bipartisan support, Reagan asked Congress to fund a five-year, $8 billion aid program to Central America.

In an election year and with a widening budget deficit, many in Congress tried to avoid the aid issue, but the president forced it to a vote. The election of Napoleon Duarte as president of El Salvador in mid-May helped Reagan's lobbying considerably, as Duarte enjoyed widespread support from Democrats in Congress. Congress's attention then shifted to the contra program, which was jeopardized by a series of disclosures in the spring of 1984 of CIA supervision for the destruction of the oil refinery in Corinto and the mining of Nicaraguan harbors.[56] In a radio address on April 14 and a television address on May 9, Reagan appealed for more funding for the contras, but he failed to persuade either Congress or the public.

With the economy doing well, public opinion surveys suggested that the only issue standing in the way of Reagan's reelection was the peace issue. Reagan therefore sent Secretary of State George Shultz to Managua for talks on June 1, and the administration also opened negotiations with Cuba (on returning Mariel prisoners). By opening these negotiations, the Reagan administration succeeded in defusing the argument made by Democratic presidential candidate Walter Mondale that Reagan's reelection would mean United States involvement in war in

Central America. In the end, Central America played a small part in the voters' calculations, and President Reagan won by a landslide.

Reagan's first term therefore concluded on an uncharacteristic note of ambiguity. No one doubted his determination to confront communism in Central America; the question was whether his 1984 peace initiatives were serious or just campaign ploys.

Reagan's Second Term: Consolidation and Advance

An administration requires at least a year to transmit credible signals to foreign governments so that they can calculate American policies as they formulate their own. If foreign governments dislike the orientation of American policies, they can wait for a change, but few would wait through a second term. Ronald Reagan, one of the few American presidents who sustained a high level of interest in the region throughout his first term, therefore had a unique opportunity to impose his vision on Latin America. As he began his second term, he faced a continuing crisis in Central America, a breath-taking opportunity as democracy swept across the hemisphere, and a worsening problem as the burden of debt threatened to undo two decades of economic progress.

Those who were uncertain whether Reagan's reelection would mean pursuing peace initiatives or confrontation had their answer on election night. Moments before Reagan's acceptance statement, White House sources told CBS news that the Soviet Union was sending MIG-23 jets to Nicaragua and that this might provoke an air strike by the United States or even an invasion. A few days later, the Soviet ship docked in Nicaragua, and helicopters — not MIGs — were unloaded.

That crisis passed, and so the administration chose to send two other signals when Reagan's National Security Advisor Robert McFarlane visited the region just before the inauguration. To reassure the contras and the Hondurans of continued North American support, the administration ended talks with the Sandinistas begun by Shultz the previous June and withdrew from the World Court's case on Nicaragua.[57]

Just as Reagan generalized his support for elections in El Salvador into a program for democracy, similarly, in his 1985 State of the Union address, he transformed his contra program into a policy on national liberation movements: "We must not break faith with those who are risking their lives on every continent from Afghanistan to Nicaragua to defy Soviet-supported aggression and secure rights which have been ours from birth. . . . Support for freedom-fighters is self-defense." At a press conference on February 21, Reagan candidly described his goal as seeing the Sandinista government "removed in the sense of its present structure," and he said his support for the contras would stop when the Sandinistas "say uncle." In a radio address on March 30, 1985, Reagan described the contras fight as "morally right and intimately linked to our own security," and he announced that he intended to ask Congress to release $14 million for the contras.[58]

Congressional opposition, however, persuaded the administration to request humanitarian rather than military aid. Also, the president presented the request in the form of a proposal: He would suspend the aid if the Sandinistas engaged in a dialogue with the contras — or Nicaraguan Democratic Resistance — under the auspices of the Bishops Conference.[59] The Sandinistas rejected the proposal and so did Congress. One of the arguments made in the Senate for rejecting aid to the contras was that the United States ought to consider such other steps as economic sanctions before contributing to groups whose aim was to violently overthrow a government. The administration accepted the argument, and on May 1, Reagan decreed a trade embargo by signing an executive order that read: "I, Ronald Reagan, . . . find that the policies of the Government of Nicaragua constitute an unusual and extraordinary threat to the national security and foreign policy of the United States, and hereby declare a national emergency to deal with that threat."[60]

The administration was then handed a cogent talking point by Daniel Ortega, Nicaragua's president, who left for a visit to Moscow days after Congress's vote. By June, the administration found the votes to pass $27 million in "non-lethal" humanitarian aid to the contras. This was the first time both branches of the American government openly debated and approved support for a movement whose aim was to overthrow a government with which the United States had diplomatic relations. This was a significant step but hardly the last.

The Sandinistas had received sophisticated military equipment and, by the end of 1985, were beginning to use it effectively against the contras. Reagan stepped up the propaganda barrage against the Sandinistas, and on February 25, 1986, he formally requested Congress to approve $100 million in aid for the contras — 75 percent of it military aid. Once again, he combined strident attacks against the Sandinistas and congressional opponents with a willingness to make small concessions. He accused his opponents in Congress of being partial to communists, but at the same time he appointed Phillip Habib as a Special Envoy and resumed funding of the independent revolutionary Eden Pastora.[61] The Reagan administration also continued and expanded its military exercises in Honduras and began construction of its sixth airfield in the southern part of the country near the Nicaraguan border.[62]

Reagan's determination to change the Nicaraguan government was clear, but there were other initiatives in the region, and it was uncertain which would ultimately prevail. The Contadora Group, expanded to include a four-nation support group (Argentina, Brazil, Uruguay, and Peru), met with Secretary of State George Shultz on February 10, 1986 to request that the United States open talks with the Sandinistas and stop funding the contras. Reagan ignored their request and refused to meet them, but the Contadora Group continued to pursue their negotiations.

A second set of initiatives emerged from the newly elected Democrats in Central America. Guatemalan Christian Democratic President Vinicio Cerezo invited his Central American colleagues to a summit meeting at Esquipulas, Guatemala on May 25, 1986 to discuss peace in the region and the establishment of a Central American Parliament. In Costa Rica, President Oscar Arias pledged to prevent contras from using his country as a base for attacking Nicaragua, and Costa Rica reached an agreement with Nicaragua that would permit the Contadora countries to monitor the border jointly.

Nonetheless, the Sandinistas and the Reagan administration showed little flexibility and appeared headed for a prolonged confrontation. It remains to be seen whether the Contadora Group or the Central American initiatives can prevent such a collision.

Because the contra program did not enjoy public support, each time the administration requested funding from Congress, it had to intensify its rhetoric. Increasingly, the administration sought to justify its support for the contras by stressing its global commitment to democracy. Although that commitment was debated, there was no question that democracy was sweeping through the hemisphere with unprecedented force. By 1986, 94 percent of the people of Latin America were living under civilian constitutional governments. In 1985, democratic government returned to Brazil, Guatemala, Grenada, and Uruguay; a peaceful transfer of power from one civilian government to another occurred in Peru for the first time in forty years and in Bolivia for the first time in twenty-five years. Argentine democracy was strengthened by a successful mid-term election.

Two long-standing Caribbean dictatorships also collapsed, raising hopes that democracy might emerge from the ruins. Forbes Burnham, who had ruled Guyana for twenty years, died in 1985, and Jean-Claude Duvalier, whose family ruled Haiti for almost thirty years, fled the country on February 7, 1986. The United States stopped aid to Duvalier in the closing moments of his regime, and although some believed that American pressure was decisive in forcing Duvalier to leave, Reagan denied that during a press conference.[63]

To enhance its credibility in attacking the human rights violations of the Sandinistas, the administration changed its policy and began to criticize the remaining right-wing regimes publicly; indeed, it began to pair its positions on Nicaragua with those on Chile. Thus in February 1985, while trying to stop a loan to Nicaragua in the Inter-American Development Bank, the administration abstained on a loan to Chile. On March 12, 1986, while lobbying Congress for aid to the contras, the administration introduced a resolution in the UN condemning the human rights situation in Chile, after having either voted against or abstained on such anti-Chilean resolutions before. Then it issued a "major policy statement" on March 14, 1986 that indicated that it "opposed tyranny in whatever form, whether of the left or the right."[64]

But while using the spread of democracy as a justification for its assaults on the Sandinista government, the Reagan administration did not try to formulate a joint approach with these new democracies on Central America or on the debt. To the contrary, its approach to both issues seemed partly aimed at undermining any regional cooperation.[65]

With the exception of its CBI, the Reagan administration tried to avoid economic issues in inter-American relations. When Mexico informed the United States in August 1982 that it would no longer be able to pay its debt, the Reagan administration fashioned an ad hoc emergency package, but at the same time, it recommended adjustment for the other Latin American countries. As regards the need for future capital, Assistant Secretary Enders said: "This is basically a question between borrowing governments and the markets themselves."[66]

By 1985 it was impossible to ignore the debt problem: Latin America owed $368 billion. Annual debt service payments consumed nearly 44 percent of the region's foreign exchange. In just three years — 1983 to 1985 — Latin America transferred over $100 billion of capital to the United States and other industrialized countries in payment of its debt, making it a larger exporter of capital to the United States in this short period than the United States was to Latin America in the entire decade of the Alliance for Progress.[67] Debt affected the region's political stability and American economic growth, and it appeared as if Latin America might form a debtors' cartel. Therefore, at the Seoul World Bank/ International Monetary Fund meeting in October 1985, Secretary of Treasury James Baker, III, proposed that the private banks and the international development institutions increase funding to the major debtor countries if the latter implemented a series of reforms to remove distortions and subsidies and privatize inefficient parastatal corporations.[68]

In mid-December the eleven-nation Cartagena Group met in Montevideo and welcomed the initiative as "a first step" but said it was not sufficient. They called for more loans and reduced interest rates. But in an important shift from previous efforts to press for a new international economic order in the 1970s, most Latin American governments recognized that the principal solution to their debt problem would have to be internal. While renegotiating their external debts, many governments also revised their national strategies: the newly elected president of Peru, Alan Garcia, announced that his government would only pay 10 percent of its export earnings to service its debt; Argentina instituted a dramatic new austerity program in June 1985 with the beginning of a new currency, the Austral; and Brazil followed in February 1986 with a similar plan

and a new currency, the Cruzado. The two major oil producers —
Mexico and Venezuela — had avoided such drastic prescriptions, but the
precipitous drop in oil prices in late 1985 and early 1986 placed both
economies in an extremely precarious position. As before, the Reagan
administration signaled both its willingness to help Mexico (even while
seeking changes in Mexico's economic and foreign policies) and its reluctance to address the longer term, broader issues related to the debt and
American-Latin American economic relations.

The Legacy of Ronald Reagan: Eagle Insurgent

On assuming the presidency in 1981, Ronald Reagan viewed his mandate
in Latin America as confronting and defeating the communists and
reassuring the "friendly" military governments that had been alienated by
the Carter administration's policies. The administration, therefore,
emphasized defending El Salvador, confronting Grenada, and destabilizing Nicaragua; but it also moved early to dismantle its predecessors'
policies on human rights and arms control.

By March 1986, five years later, the administration's approach had
broadened and deepened: it professed a bipartisan commitment to human
rights, democracy, and negotiations; it implemented a one-way free trade
plan for the Caribbean Basin; it proposed a plan to address the debt crisis;
and it elaborated a unique, revolutionary strategy to pursue its central
objective — to confront and overcome communism. Yet the evolution in
the administration's policy should not obscure the tenacity with which it
held to its initial objective. First, the changes in policy can be explained
partly in terms of the concessions the administration made to Congress or
to international public opinion in order to further its objective. Second, in
a process not dissimilar to that of an arms race, the administration's policy
toward Central America grew increasingly belligerent as both a cause and
a consequence of Cuban and Nicaraguan efforts to expand their military
capacities.

In this section the administration's revolutionary strategy will first be
described, and then four sets of questions will be addressed: First, did
Reagan succeed in imposing his vision on the region, or did he adapt to
take into account the changes in the world as well as in the United States?
Second, to what extent did his policy resemble those of his predecessors
and in what way was it new? Third, was his policy successful or not?
And fourth, what will be the long-term impact of the Reagan administration's policies on United States-Latin American relations?

A North American Doctrine of National Liberation

The administration's case against the Soviet Union, Cuba, and
Nicaragua is multifaceted. First, the communists try to export their

revolution, believing in a "revolution without borders." Second, they organize, train, and support guerrillas struggling to overthrow regimes friendly to the United States. Third, they use covert actions to exploit every "target of opportunity" to weaken the United States. Fourth, the communists use negotiations as they use propaganda — as swords to defeat their rivals rather than as instruments of communication. And fifth, they are internally repressive.

As the administration struggled to convince Congress and change the regime in Nicaragua, its strategy gradually came to resemble the communist strategy against which it was directed.

First, President Reagan enunciated a clear doctrine of supporting national liberation movements against communist oppression. Like communist revolutionaries, the Reagan administration failed to see the way the tactics of *its* revolutionaries resembled those of the government it aimed to overthrow. It condemned terrorism aimed at itself or its friends but promoted terrorism against its enemies (as in Nicaragua). The double standard was explained away because, as Jeane Kirkpatrick wrote, "force that liberates is not the same as force that enslaves."

Second, the administration played a direct role in organizing, training, and providing medical and military material for the insurgents. As Cuba united the Sandinista factions in 1978–79, the Reagan administration used its aid to encourage unity among the separate Nicaraguan contra groups. The CIA also wrote a manual for the contras that borrowed much from Che Guevara. The administration offered political support for the contras and maintained a propaganda offensive that resembled in quantity (Radio Marti) and style ("communist thugs") communist propaganda. Reagan used words as jackhammers to undermine the legitimacy of his adversaries and as trumpets to mobilize his supporters; he did not take his words as seriously as his friends wished or his critics feared.

Third, like Cuba, the administration sought "targets of opportunity," the weakest links of the communist system like Grenada and Nicaragua, to keep its global adversary off balance. During the Reagan administration, the eagle was insurgent.

Fourth, the administration developed a long-term political program to promote democracy, providing aid and training to young cadres in Latin America and a massive educational exchange program. The administration expanded the program with the express purpose of trying to catch up to the Soviet program.[69]

Fifth, the administration's intense concern over security had its internal as well as external side. Lie-detector tests, loyalty oaths, and restrictions on visas of foreign critics of the administration; although these instances of internal security cannot be compared to the repression of the communist system, they did reflect a fear of dissent and a need to control that is unusual for a democracy in a time of peace. Externally, the administration effectively lobbied a reluctant Congress to train police forces in Central America. Congress prevented the administration from giving military aid to such repressive regimes as Argentina and Guatemala, but when democratic governments replaced these regimes, the administration's first gesture was to offer military aid, despite the publicly stated reluctance by both governments to receive military aid.[70]

Sixth, the administration viewed negotiations as a tool for defusing allied or domestic criticism or improving its propaganda position; it did not view "negotiations" as an effective means for pursuing American interests with its adversaries. In April 1982, the National Security Council recommended that the United States "step up efforts to co-opt the negotiations issue to avoid congressionally mandated negotiations, which would work against our interests."[71] Another council document, leaked in November 1984, described how the United States successfully blocked a Contadora Treaty.[72] Administration officials often described American options in Nicaragua in a way that avoided the mention of negotiations.[73] Undersecretary of Defense Fred Ikle was the most candid: "The idea that you can strike a deal with them [the Sandinistas] seems unrealistic."[74] The administration was similarly disinterested in negotiating with revolutionary Grenada. Despite repeated statements of concern about the possible use of the airport, the Reagan administration never tried to negotiate with the Grenadians, despite considerable evidence that the Grenadians were prepared to discuss American concerns on this issue.[75]

Finally, the seventh element in the administration's strategy was its relentless unilateralism, which took the form of (1) reducing support for multilateral institutions; (2) undermining efforts at regional cooperation; and (3) dismissing international law, organizations, or public opinion. One of its first decisions was to reduce American contributions to international development banks by 25 percent and to increase bilateral aid, and especially military aid. In the administration's 1986 budget, bilateral aid accounted for 92 percent of total foreign aid, and the total foreign aid devoted to military and security aid increased from 25 percent in 1980 to 40 percent.[76]

Rather than use the multilateral Caribbean Group, the administration preferred to structure the CBI as a bilateral program in which each government would have to negotiate with the United States. When the Central American nations united to seek aid for the whole region from Europe, the administration tried to undermine their efforts.[77] Unlike its predecessors, who viewed the Caribbean Development Bank as a vital development tool in the Caribbean, the Reagan administration denied aid to the bank when the nations refused to exclude the revolutionary government of Grenada.[78] When Europe tried to help Central America as a unit, the administration tried, unsuccessfully, to have Nicaragua excluded.[79]

When a draft of the Contadora Treaty appeared to receive region-wide support, the United States urged the nations most dependent on it for aid to reject it.[80] And only when Latin America seemed on the verge of forming a solid front to demand fundamental changes in its external debt did the administration offer a proposal, which had the effect of dividing the region.

The Reagan administration listened to its friends less and sought to divide regional efforts more than any other administration in the postwar period. The administration showed a blatant disregard for international law and organizations. Instead of bringing evidence of Nicaraguan subversion to the OAS, the Reagan administration released it as a White Paper. Instead of confronting Nicaragua in the World Court, the administration withdrew. By 1985, the administration had stopped pretending to seek a multilateral approach to the region's problems, and the assistant secretary of state[81] began defending unilateralism:

> We can't abdicate our responsibility to protect our interests to a committee of Latin American countries . . . the notion that if we have interests at stake we should ask Latin Americans what to do about it is wrong. . . . They want to know what we are going to do. They want to know if we have the guts to protect our interests, and if we don't, then they are going to walk away, and that is the way it should be.

Considered together, these seven elements constituted a radical departure for American foreign policy. To be sure, the United States had supported coups in Latin America before but had never publicly acknowledged its support for an army of insurgents dedicated to overthrowing a government in the region. Nor did it ever support as large an insurgency for so long or incorporate that policy into a presidential doctrine.

Imposition or Adaptation?

There is no disputing the significant changes that occurred in the region during Reagan's tenure. The assertiveness of many Latin American governments appeared a permanent fixture in international relations in the late 1970s, but in the early 1980s, the assertiveness disappeared, to be replaced by national self-preoccupation. This change was less the result of external American pressure than of internal pressure derived from debt and democracy. Concerned about reelection and coping on a daily basis with financial crises, Latin America's leaders were more moderate and realistic, with less time, interest, and resources to pursue abstract international objectives or to unravel the tangle of Central American politics.

The United States did not persuade, nor did it impose its vision on the region. Nor did the Reagan administration, so certain of its vision, adapt to the region's concerns. Instead, both Latin America and the United States concentrated on their own priorities.

But this does not mean that Latin America did not influence the Reagan administration. The administration's determination to change the regimes in Grenada and in Nicaragua was clear almost from the beginning. The administration, however, only took action in Grenada when the silent veto of the Caribbean was transformed — by the self-destruction of the Grenada revolution — into an invitation. Similarly the administration watched the Contadora Group with both anxiety and hope. At a minimum, the administration wanted to make sure the group did not defend or legitimize Nicaragua; at a maximum, it hoped that the group would further isolate Nicaragua and join with the United States to change the regime. Contadora did not change the Reagan administration's objective, but it did constrain the administration — making some options too costly to undertake.

Continuity and Change

Every administration's policy reflects some continuity and some change from that of its predecessor's. The change seems most stark at the beginning of an administration when its mandate is clear and the desire to distinguish its approach from that of its predecessor's is most compelling. As the mandate weakens, and the administration's desire for effectiveness overtakes its quest for uniqueness, it begins to seek the appearances — and, if necessary, the reality — of bipartisanship.

The Reagan administration conformed to this pattern, first flagellating its predecessor, and then by 1983, stressing the bipartisan character of its policies. And there was a thread of continuity connecting both administrations. Both gave an unprecedented amount of high-level attention to the region, and both pursued the full range of American interests, including security, human rights and democracy, and economic development.

On further analysis, however, the differences seem much more significant than the similarities. Those differences stem from different perceptions of the threat to the United States and the different weight each administration attached to each national interest. The Carter administration was relatively relaxed about the threat in the region to the United States and therefore gave much greater weight to human rights and development and less to traditional security concerns than its successor.[82]

In addition to giving a different weight to each interest, the two administrations used different instruments. The Carter administration relied on negotiations (Panama Canal treaties; Nicaragua mediation) and multilateral cooperation (Caribbean, Andean), whereas the Reagan administration downplayed these instruments and stressed military aid, covert actions, military exercises, and unilateralism.

Evaluating the Reagan Administration

It is only fair to begin an evaluation of an administration's policy by reviewing its values and objectives. How successful has the Reagan administration been in undermining communism in the Caribbean Basin? By that criteria, there is no disputing its success in Grenada: the rapid and effective use of force replaced a Marxist regime with a democratic government.

Beyond that the record is either poor or equivocal. In the administration's first five years, increasing American military involvement in Central America did not intimidate its adversaries; it fueled an arms race, with Nicaragua and Cuba receiving more military aid from the Soviet Union than in any previous period. Both governments were more militarized and tied to the Soviets in 1986 than in 1981. In January 1981, Nicaraguan armed forces were about 31,000; four years later, they had increased to 120,000. In 1980, Nicaragua received 850 tons of armaments from the Soviet bloc; in 1985, after five years of intimidation, the Nicaraguans received 18,000 tons.[83] The region also became more militarized. Even Costa Rica was impelled to risk its civilian consensus by accepting military aid.[84]

One could argue that the Salvadoran government became stronger over the same five-year period, but so too did the guerrillas, although they were weaker in 1986 than in 1983. At the same time the land reform, the effort to curb death squads, and the dialogue with the left — the only possible exits from the civil war — all stalled. The administration gave high priority to counterinsurgency operations, and while the Salvadoran military became more mobile and professional, their war against the left was no closer to success.

How does the administration fare using criteria weighted in favor of human rights, democracy, and development? In every Central American country except Nicaragua, the primary struggle for democracy in the last decades has been against the right, which dismissed everyone arguing for reform or change as communists. Although some in the Reagan administration recognized the problem of the right, few were willing to risk dividing the noncommunist forces. Only in El Salvador, for a brief moment in December 1983, did the administration deliver a clear message to the right. Except for that, the administration sometimes delivered *Congress's* message on human rights, which was better than no message, but no substitute for a policy.

The administration's efforts to improve American relationships with military regimes backfired in a most ironic way, as many of these regimes were replaced by democracies. Although the administration tried to take credit for the wave of democracy sweeping the region, most of the newly elected presidents in South America risked the displeasure of the Reagan administration to acknowledge the contribution of Reagan's predecessor and to question Reagan's commitment.[85] Chile's Augusto Pinochet made the same point from the opposite direction, telling a *New York Times* reporter in 1984 that "relations with the United States under the Reagan administration were better than at any other time in Chilean history."[86]

By a rather convoluted route, the administration did deserve some of the credit for bringing democracy to Argentina. In its effort to warm relations with the Argentine generals, the Reagan administration sent them an unintentional signal: If Argentina helps the United States in Central America, then the United States would help — or at the least, acquiesce — when Argentina seized its strategic prize. However, when Argentina invaded the Falklands/Malvinas in the spring of 1982, the United States first negotiated as a neutral, and then supported the British, leaving the generals feeling betrayed.[87] Their disastrous defeat finally forced the military to transfer power to the civilians in a free election.

In justifying its confrontation with Nicaragua, the administration discovered and then elaborated on a commitment to democracy. It created the National Endowment for Democracy and promoted elections. Most important, it informed the military throughout Latin America that American support depended on their acceptance of civilian, democratically elected governments. When the Panamanian military forced the resignation of President Nicolas Ardito-Barletta, the administration reduced aid to the country. Even though the administration disliked the radical approach of Peruvian President Alan Garcia, it was careful not to antagonize him or to give a green light to the military to overthrow him. Although the administration was unwilling to apply the kind of pressure that might have transformed military acquiescence for democracy into genuine civilian control over the military, at least, the administration insisted that the military permit nominal control by civilians. This represented the first time that conservative Republicans had demonstrated a willingness to work with both Christian and Social Democrats in Latin America in preference to stable, military regimes. Therefore, although the administration does not appear to deserve the credit for the transitions toward democracy in the region, it does deserve some credit for preventing the new democracies from being overthrown.

Other than Central America, the administration did as little as was absolutely necessary. Latin American democracies have come of age, and American neglect should no longer disturb the region as it once did. The issue is whether American national interests are better served by doing as little as possible with the debt crisis or as much as possible. The CBI remains one of the administration's most important programs, and although, it is too soon to judge its effectiveness, the early signs are favorable. In Central America, the economic task is the more difficult, but American aid undoubtedly kept the region from further economic decline.

Legacy

The Reagan administration's approach first appeared to be a simple repetition of the anticommunist crusade of John Foster Dulles. But in order to surmount internal criticism and international constraints, a determined administration broadened its approach to include a moralistic emphasis on democracy, the anti-statism of nineteenth-century liberals, and the zealousness of revolutionaries to use "all means necessary." The administration's readiness to compromise with Congress to further its objective, however, coincided with an unyielding resistance to negotiate seriously with its adversaries. Its approach remained unilateral without apologies, in the evident belief that leadership on moral issues requires strength, not compromise.

The Reagan administration is unlikely to be remembered for its economic policies, as it sidestepped the debt issue, and the CBI had only a limited effect. The verdict on its contribution to democracy will be positive but not outstanding. Most of all, the administration will be remembered for its "reassertionism," and its determination to confront communism. The cost of that legacy is that Latin America will continue to believe that "communism" is the only issue that matters to the United States and that the United States is reluctant to deal with Latin America on its own terms.

The legacy of the administration will ultimately come to rest on the issue it chose to place its greatest weight — Nicaragua. Whether or not the administration attains its objective, it has succeeded in changing the terms of the debate, inducing even liberal Democrats to ask when and how to use covert actions to overthrow unfriendly governments.[88] Whether the new strategy is a contribution or a costly mistake for American interests will ultimately be judged by whether it fails or succeeds in Nicaragua. If the war further binds the Sandinista government to the Soviet Union and Cuba, and the contras fail to effect a change, then it can be considered a failure, even if American troops intervene to remove the regime. In either case, the costs — human, economic, and political — to American interests will be substantial, if not exorbitant.

The Reagan administration's pursuit of United States security interests in Latin America, but especially in the Caribbean Basin, has been relentless and singular of purpose. It is unusual for a powerful democratic nation to sustain such a campaign in peacetime. In many ways, the administration has forged a policy that more nearly reflects the revolutionary style of Cuba than that of earlier administrations. That may be the ironic legacy of this administration. At a moment of unprecedented opportunities for inter-American cooperation among democracies, the United States chose to pursue this single issue alone, gradually adopting the tactics of its enemies.

While accepting responsibility for any remaining flaws, the author wishes to thank Robert Lieber, Donald Rothchild, Bernardo Mabire, Sergio Aguayo, and Eliot Disner for their comments on an earlier draft.

"The Reagan Administration and Latin America: Eagle Insurgent" was written for this volume. Copyright © 1987 by Robert A. Pastor.

Notes

1. Daniel Yankelovich and Larry Kaagan, "Assertive America," *Foreign Affairs: America and the World, 1980*, p. 696.
2. Cited by Ronnie Dugger, *On Reagan: The Man and His Presidency* (New York: McGraw-Hill, 1983), p. 351.
3. In an interview with the *Wall Street Journal* in 1980, Reagan stated this view without reservations: "The Soviet Union underlies all the unrest that is going on. If they weren't engaged in this game of dominoes, there wouldn't be any hotspots in the world." [Cited in Dugger, *On Reagan*, p. 353.]
4. See the excellent essay by Richard E. Feinberg, in "Testing U.S. Reassertionism: The Reagan Approach to the Third World," *U.S. Foreign Policy and the Third World: Agenda, 1985–1986*, John Sewell, Richard Feinberg, and Valeriana Kallab, eds. (New Brunswick, NJ: Transaction Books, 1985), pp. 3–20.
5. The debate was reprinted in the *Washington Post*, January 24, 1978. For a good description of how conservatives used the issue to their advantage, see William J. Lanouette, "The Panama Canal Treaties: Playing in Peoria and in the Senate," *National Journal*, October 8, 1977, pp. 1556–1562. With considerable prescience, Gary Jarmin of the American Conservative Union told Lanouette that the Canal treaties offered "an excellent opportunity for conservatives to seize control of the Republican party."
6. Dugger, *On Reagan*, pp. 382–383.
7. Ronald Reagan, "The Canal As Opportunity: A New Relationship with Latin America," *Orbis* (Fall 1977), pp. 551–561.
8. Dugger, *On Reagan*, p. 360.
9. Jeane Kirkpatrick, "U.S. Security and Latin America," *Commentary*, January 1981, p. 29. Her other article was "Dictatorships and Double Standards," *Commentary*, November 1979.
10. The Committee of Santa Fe, *A New Inter-American Policy for the Eighties* (Washington, D.C.: Council for Inter-American Security, 1980), p. 2.
11. Ibid., pp. 20–21.
12. Republican National Convention, *Republican Platform* (Detroit, Michigan), July 14, 1980, pp. 68–69.
13. Alexander M. Haig, Jr., *Caveat: Realism, Reagan, and Foreign Policy* (New York: MacMillan, 1984), pp. 96–97.
14. Office of the Press Secretary, The White House, "Interview with the President by Walter Cronkite," March 3, 1981. (Italics added.)
15. The principal source for this summary of the debate within the administration was Haig's *Caveat*, pp. 98–100, 117–140, but three other articles cast light on other positions: Don Oberdorfer, "Applying Pressure in Central America," *Washington Post*, November 23, 1983; Roy Gutman and Susan Page, "Central America: The Making of U.S. Policy," *Newsday*, July 31, 1983; and Leslie H. Gelb, "Haig Is Said to Press for Military Options for Salvadoran Action," *New York Times*, November 5, 1981. The Oberdorfer article describes three separate occasions in which Haig tried to persuade the National Security Council to accept a blockade of Cuba.

16. In an interview with *Time* on January 5, 1981, Reagan suggested postponing the land and banking reforms in El Salvador, and the right in El Salvador rejoiced. An article by Viera Altamirano in Salvador's *El Diario de Hoy* the same day praised Reagan: "The U.S., having rejected a policy of appeasement toward Communism is finally going to confront and conquer the terrorism which has bathed Central America in blood. . . . Reagan is aware of the need . . . to re-establish market mechanisms. . . . Significantly, Reagan rejected the idea that 'changes' should be made when a country is facing subversive attack."

17. Interview with Napoleon Duarte, July 26–27, 1983, San Jose, Costa Rica. Duarte said he had no choice but to accept the plan, although he did convince the Minister of Defense to set a ceiling of fifty-five military advisors, rather than seventy-five, as had been recommended by the U.S. Military Group. For an analysis of the two policies, see Robert Pastor, "Continuity and Change in U.S. Foreign Policy: Carter and Reagan on El Salvador," *Journal of Policy Analysis and Management* (Winter 1984), Vol. 3, No. 2.

18. Allen recalls telling Duarte that he "wasn't much impressed with land reform . . . I didn't think land reform was such a key to stability" (Roy Gutman and Susan Page, "Central America: The Making of U.S. Policy," *Newsday*, July 31, 1983). The author talked to Duarte after his meeting with Allen, and recalls that Duarte was shaken by the interview. It's worth noting that in an interview on television on February 27, 1982, before the elections in El Salvador, Senator Jesse Helms offered the ultimate conservative Republican insult to Duarte, saying he was "far to the left of McGovern."

19. Juan de Onis, "Haig Opposes a Coup by Salvador's Right," *New York Times*, March 5, 1981, p. A9.

20. According to Salvadoran Ambassador Ernesto Rivas Gallont, Duarte was initially viewed with suspicion by the administration, and that changed only after Duarte condemned the Franco-Mexican initiative of August 1981, which recognized the left as a "legitimate political force." "The Reagan administration then believed Duarte was honest, a true democrat," said Gallont. (Joanne Omang, "Progress Made in Face of Five-Year Civil War," *Washington Post*, June 2, 1985, pp. A1, 20.)

21. For a good description of the congressional debate in 1981, see U.S. House of Representatives, Committee on Foreign Affairs, *Congress and Foreign Policy, 1981*, 1982, pp. 115–131. Congress appropriated $290 million in economic and $117 million in military aid to El Salvador in Fiscal Years 1981 and 1982.

22. Some of this evidence was released in the White Paper in February 1981, but the most credible and important proof was not released until September 1985. See U.S. Department of State, *Revolution Beyond Our Borders*, September 1985, No. 132, pp. 7–10.

23. Interview with American Ambassador Lawrence Pezzullo, New York City, July 30, 1985. Pezzullo, however, was not consulted when the administration made its final decision to terminate aid to Nicaragua.

24. U.S. Department of State, *American Foreign Policy: Current Documents, 1981*, p. 1298.

25. United States Department of State, *"Revolution Beyond Our Borders": Sandinista Intervention in Central America*, September 1985, Special Report No. 132, pp. 21–23.

26. Cited in Roy Gutman and Susan Page, "A Fumbled Chance for Accord," *Newsday*, August 1, 1983.

27. These interviews in Managua, held in July and August 1983, were with Minister of the Interior Tomas Borge, numerous officials from the FSLN International Relations Department, and United States embassy personnel; and in addition, periodic and confidential meetings were held with various officials from the Reagan administration.

28. The authoritative reference to NSDD No. 17 of November 17, 1981 is in the National Security Council document, "U.S. Policy in Central America and Cuba Through FY

'84," which was written in April 1982, but leaked to the press and published in the *New York Times* on April 7, 1983. The request for contingency options in advance of the meeting generated its apparently desired leak. (See Leslie Gelb, "Haig Is Said to Press for Military Options for Salvador Action," *New York Times*, November 5, 1981, p. 1.) Haig's memoirs refer to the discussion without identifying the date. The best, most credible account of the meeting is by Don Oberdorfer, who cited government records. (See his "Applying Pressure in Central America," *Washington Post*, November 23, 1983, pp. A1, 10.)

29. United States Department of State, *Revolution Beyond Our Borders*, September 1985, p. 23. Hector Fabian, the leader of an exile training camp in Florida, confirmed the Reagan administration's decision not to enforce the law in an interview in December 1981. Fabian admitted that the FBI brought charges before grand juries seventy times between 1973 and 1980, but "December 5, 1980 was the last time the FBI bothered me. . . . Under the Carter and Nixon administration, what we were doing was a crime. With the Reagan administration, no one has bothered us. . . ." (Jo Thomas, "Latin Exiles Focus on Nicaragua As They Train Urgently in Florida," *New York Times*, December 23, 1981, pp. 1, 14.)

30. A presidential finding is required for a covert action. The reference to the March 9, 1981 finding is in the NSC document of April 1982. That document noted that $19.5 million had been allocated for the covert interdiction program and recommended an increase to $22 million to cover an expanded program in Guatemala that would begin in 1982.

31. Edgar Chamorro and Jefferson Morley, "Confessions of a 'Contra': How the CIA Masterminds the Nicaraguan Insurgency," *The New Republic*, August 5, 1985, pp. 18–23.

32. Don Oberdorfer and Patrick E. Tyler, "Reagan Backs Action Plan for Central America: Political, Paramilitary Steps Included," *Washington Post*, February 14, 1982, p. 1. For a history of congressional objections, see U.S. House of Representatives Permanent Select Committee on Intelligence, "Report 98-122: Amendment to the Intelligence Authorization Act for Fiscal Year 1983," May 13, 1983; and Nina Serafino, "U.S. Assistance to Nicaraguan Guerrillas: Issues for the Congress," Congressional Research Service of the Library of Congress, November 26, 1984.

33. The reference to linkages was in a *Time* cover story on Haig on March 16, 1981, "How a Policy Was Born," p. 15. Haig's statement about terrorism was in a press conference on January 28, 1981, reprinted in the *New York Times* the next day.

34. Terri Shaw, "Argentine Police Raid Human Rights Office, Seizing Leading Activists," *Washington Post*, March 1, 1981, p. A16.

35. *Washington Post*, March 12, 1981, p. A16.

36. Jackson Diehl, "State Department Official Sees Role for Argentina in Central America," *Washington Post*, March 10, 1982, p. A18.

37. *Washington Post*, March 12, 1981, p. A23.

38. John Dinges, "Kirkpatrick Trip Upsets Opposition in Chile," *Washington Post*, August 13, 1981, p. A25; and Raymond Bonner, "Chilean Exiles Appeal to Mrs. Kirkpatrick for Help," *New York Times*, September 22, 1981, p. A16.

39. Warren Hoge, "Repression Increases in Guatemala As U.S. Tries to Improve Relations," *New York Times*, May 3, 1981, p. 1; Christopher Dickey, "Haig's Emissary, in Guatemala, Discounts Charges of Rights Abuse," *Washington Post*, May 14, 1981, p. A16; and John Goshko, "Military Truck Sale to Guatemala Backed," *Washington Post*, June 19, 1981, p. 1.

40. Dana Priest, "Nicaraguan Loan Splits Inter-American Development Bank," *Washington Post*, January 20, 1985; Clyde H. Farnsworth, "U.S. Votes No At World Bank More Often Under Reagan," *New York Times*, November 26, 1984, p. A1.

41. For the overall approach of the administration, see Ronald Reagan's speech on "U.S. Policy Toward Developing Countries," *New York Times*, October 16, 1981, p. A12.

42. Sam Dillon, "U.S. Arms Sales to Latin America Skyrocket," *The Miami Herald*, November 28, 1982.

43. Terence Smith, "U.S. Frames Policy on Halting Spread of Nuclear Arms," *New York Times*, July 8, 1981, p. 1.

44. Milton R. Benjamin, "U.S. Is Allowing Argentina to Buy Critical A-System," *Washington Post*, July 19, 1982, pp. A1, 4; and "Argentina's Blow to U.S. Nonproliferation Policy," letter by John Buell to the *New York Times*, November 29, 1983, p. A30.

45. The two main reasons for the deterioration related to the natural gas agreement signed in 1977, but not approved by the United States, and the decision by the Mexican president not to permit the reentry of the Shah of Iran despite his prior pledge to do that. For more discussion of these decisions, see Robert Pastor, "The Carter Administration and Latin America: A Test of Principle," in *U.S. Foreign Policy Toward Latin America: Quarter Century of Crisis and Challenge*, John D. Martz, ed. (University of Nebraska, forthcoming).

46. Alexander Haig, *Caveat*, p. 130.

47. Juan de Onis, "U.S. Caribbean Plan to Stress Private Investment," *New York Times*, June 14, 1981, p. 23.

48. Barbara Crosette, "Strong U.S. Human Rights Policy Urged in Memo Approved by Haig," *New York Times*, November 3, 1981, p. 1.

49. "Reagan's Address to Parliament on Promoting Democracy," was reprinted in the *New York Times*, June 9, 1982, p. A16.

50. In April 1986, a *New York Times*/CBS News poll found 62 percent of Americans opposed to aid to the contras ("American Opinions on Aid to the Contras," *New York Times*, April 20, 1986, p. 3). In response to the question whether a communist government in Nicaragua or United States troops intervening in Nicaragua is of greater concern, 54 percent indicated that United States intervention was of greater concern, and 34 percent said a communist government. (Gallup poll, *Newsweek International*, April 7, 1986, p. 11.) On retiring, Army Chief of Staff General Edward Meyer said: "I don't know how to design right now a U.S. military solution to the [Central American] problem" (cited in *Newsweek*, June 20, 1983). General Wallace Nutting, head of Southern Command, was even more candid on his retirement, saying that he strongly opposed an American invasion of Nicaragua (Richard Halloran, "General Opposes Nicaragua Attack," *New York Times*, June 30, 1985, p. 3).

51. Department of State, President Reagan's "Strategic Importance of El Salvador and Central America," address to the National Association of Manufacturers, March 10, 1983.

52. Patrick E. Tyler, "American Special Envoy to El Salvador in Works," *Washington Post*, April 17, 1983, p. 1.

53. Pastora later admitted that he received $300,000 to 400,000 per month from the CIA from October 1983 to February 1984, although he didn't understand why the funding was cut (Edward Cody, "Pastora's Lonely Battle," *Washington Post*, January 18, 1985, p. A25).

54. See, for example, the speech by Undersecretary of Defense Fred Ikle, Baltimore Council on Foreign Relations, September 12, 1983; Fred Hiatt, "Weinberger Calls Military Effort in Central America Vital to U.S.," *Washington Post*, September 7, 1983; and especially "Heat on Central America: The Three Big Words around Washington These Days are 'Whatever is Necessary'," *Newsweek*, June 20, 1983, pp. 18–19.

55. Juan Williams, "President Defends Using Force," *Washington Post*, December 13, 1983, p. 1.

56. David Rogers and David Ignatius, "How CIA-Aided Raids in Nicaragua in '84 Led Congress to End Funds," and "CIA Internal Report Details U.S. Role in Contra Raids in Nicaragua Last Year," *Wall Street Journal*, March 6, 1985. The latter article cites an internal CIA report that documents direct CIA involvement in nineteen separate operations from January 1–April 10, 1984.

57. Robert J. McCartney, "McFarlane Ends Trip to Five Nations," *Washington Post*, January 20, 1985, p. A19; Philip Taubman, "U.S. Says It Has Halted Talks With Nicaragua," *New York Times*, January 19, 1985, p. 4; and "Text of U.S. Statement on Withdrawal from Case Before the World Court," *New York Times*, January 19, 1985, p. 4.

58. Cited in Loretta Tofani, " 'Contra' Cause is Just, Reagan Says," *Washington Post*, March 31, 1985, p. A22.

59. Reagan made this proposal on April 5, 1985, and it was reprinted in the *Washington Post* that day.

60. For a good description of the embargo's origins, see Joanne Omang, "Sanctions: A Policy By Default," *Washington Post*, May 8, 1985. For the Executive Order, see Bernard Weinraub's "Reagan, Declaring 'Threat', Forbids Nicaraguan Trade and Cuts Air and Sea Links," *New York Times*, May 2, 1985.

61. Doyle McManus, "U.S. Resumes Funding for Rebel Leader Pastora," *Los Angeles Times*, March 12, 1986, p. 1; and Gerald M. Boyd, "Reagan Sees a 'Moral Obligation' by U.S. to Aid Nicaraguan Rebels," *New York Times*, March 11, 1986, p. 1. Aid to Pastora stopped again after the vote by Congress. See Stephen Kinzer, *New York Times*, May 17, 1986, p. 3.

62. James Lemoyne, "U.S. Army Says G.I.s Will Begin to Build Sixth Airfield in Honduras," *New York Times*, March 3, 1986, p. 4.

63. In a press conference on February 11, 1986, the president said that the United States provided an airplane for Duvalier, but when he was asked if he gave "him any strong advice to leave," the president responded: "No. And he never asked us for any." (Reprinted in the *New York Times*, February 12, 1986, p. 10.)

64. Bernard Gwertzman, "U.S., In Reversal, Faults Chileans Over Rights Issue," *New York Times*, March 13, 1986, p. 1; and Bernard Weinraub, "The U.S. and Dictators: Reagan's Vow to Oppose All Despots Offers a Rationale for His Efforts to Aid Contras," *New York Times*, March 15, 1986, p. 1. Reagan's message to Congress is printed in the same issue, pp. 4–5.

65. For a discussion of the administration's apparent lack of interest in exploring the opportunity presented by the spread of democracy and the challenge of the debt, see Abraham F. Lowenthal, "Threat and Opportunity in the Americas," *Foreign Affairs: America and the World, 1985* (1986), Vol. 64, No. 3.

66. Thomas Enders, Address to the Inter-American Press Association, Chicago, September 30, 1982, printed by U.S. Department of State.

67. The data are from Naciones Unides Comision Economia Para America Latina y El Caribe, "Notas Sobre La Economia y El Desarrollo," Diciembre de 1985, pp. 16–18. George Shultz cites the figure of 44 percent of foreign exchange in his speech to the OAS, December 2, 1985.

68. The Latin American presidents first met in Ecuador in January 1984 to discuss a regional strategy on the debt. Their finance ministers met six months later in Cartagena, Colombia, and again in September 1984 at Mar del Plata, Argentina. Discussions in early 1985 seemed pointed toward finally taking the leap toward a regional strategy, but the Baker Plan headed that off. For a discussion of the debt crisis and the origins of the Baker plan, see Christine Bogdanowicz-Bindert, "World Debt: The U.S. Reconsiders," *Foreign Affairs* (Winter 1985–86), Vol. 64, No. 2.

69. The administration initially tried to end the exchange programs, including the Ful-

bright and Humphrey programs, but by 1983 the administration discovered how insignificant these were as compared to those of the Soviet bloc, and therefore sponsored the largest expansion of educational exchanges in American history. (See Barbara Crossette, "Budget Cuts Threaten Cultural Exchange Projects," *New York Times*, October 24, 1981, p. 3; for a comparison of American and Soviet-bloc scholarships, see the table on p. 10, of U.S. Departments of State and Defense, *The Soviet-Cuban Connection in Central America and the Caribbean*, March 1985; and for a list of the new exchange programs, see U.S. Department of State, *Sustaining a Consistent Policy in Central America*, Report to the President No. 124, April 1985, p. 7.)

70. See James Lemoyne, "Latin American Police Get Some Pointers from Washington," *New York Times*, February 16, 1986, p. E2; Douglas Tweedale, "Buying Arms Not a Priority, says Dante Caputo [new Argentine Foreign Minister]," *Buenos Aires Herald*, November 13, 1983, p. 1; and Shirley Christian, "New Guatemalan Leader Wary on U.S. Military Aid," *New York Times*, December 18, 1985, p. 8.

71. "National Security Council Document on Policy in Central America and Cuba," April 1982, reprinted in *New York Times*, April 7, 1983.

72. Alma Guillermoprieto and David Hoffman, "Document Describes How U.S. 'Blocked' a Contadora Treaty," *Washington Post*, November 6, 1984, p. 1.

73. In a background briefing in January 1983, Robert McFarlane made the case for covert actions as the only option between going to war or doing nothing. Similarly, Elliott Abrams described three options: support the contras, go to war, or surrender. (Shirley Christian, "Administration Awaits a Signal from Congress on Aid to Contras," *New York Times*, January 3, 1986, p. 5.)

74. Cited in "Nicaragua and the U.S. Options: An Invasion Is Openly Discussed," *New York Times*, June 5, 1985, p. A8.

75. See Robert Pastor, "Does The U.S. Push Revolutions To Cuba? The Case of Grenada," *Journal of Inter-American Studies and World Affairs*, Spring 1986.

76. Robert S. McNamara, "The Role of the Multilateral Finance Institutions in Development Assistance," statement before the House Subcommittee on International Development Institutions, Banking and Currency Committee, September 9, 1985.

77. Marlise Simons, "Central American Nations Refuse to Join U.S. Boycott of Nicaragua," *New York Times*, September 26, 1983, p. A10.

78. John M. Goshko, "U.S. Rebuffed in Move to Bar Aid to Grenada," *Washington Post*, June 23, 1981, p. A9. American aid to the CDB had grown from $7.2 million in 1977 to $45.1 million in 1980, before the Reagan administration stopped contributions. (See General Accounting Office, Report to the Administration, GAO/ID-83-50, July 22, 1983, pp. 6–19.)

79. Edward Cody, "W. Europeans to Aid Central Americans," *Washington Post*, September 30, 1984, p. A28.

80. Robert J. McCartney, "U.S. Urges Allies to Reject Contadora Plan," *Washington Post*, September 30, 1984, p. 1.

81. An interview with Elliott Abrams, "Big Sticks and Good Neighbors," *The Detroit News*, September 12, 1985. For the underlying intellectual rationale of the Reagan administration's unilateralism, see Charles Krauthammer, "The Multilateral Fallacy," *The New Republic*, December 9, 1985, pp. 17–20.

82. Of course, one has to adjust this point to take into account the different, not entirely comparable periods. By the end of the Carter administration, the changes in the region led it to give greater weight to security concerns, but this was still insignificant as compared to the Reagan administration. (See Robert Pastor, "The Carter Administration and Latin America: A Test of Principle," in *U.S. Policy Toward Latin America*, John D. Martz, ed.)

83. For graphic evidence of the Soviet-sponsored military buildup in Cuba and Nicaragua

during the Reagan administration — unprecedented according to the Defense Department since the missile crisis — see U.S. Department of State and Defense, *The Soviet-Cuban Connection in Central America and the Caribbean* (Washington, D.C.: March 1985).

84. Joel Brinkley, "Costa Ricans at Odds over U.S. Army Advisers," *New York Times*, May 19, 1985, p. 16.

85. For example, Julio Sanguinetti, who in March 1985 became the first civilian president of Uruguay in twelve years, described "Carter's efforts" as "very important," particularly as compared to Reagan's policy ("We Fought in a Great Silence: Interview with Sanguinetti," *Newsweek*, December 10, 1984, p. 17). Argentine President Raul Alfonsin made a similar point publicly and in his conversations with the Reagan administration.

86. Edward Schumacher, "Chile's Leader, Belittling Foes, Vows to Stay On," *New York Times*, August 8, 1984.

87. In a revealing interview with Oriana Fallaci, General Galtieri described in great detail the "excellent" rapport established with the Reagan administration and the "deception . . . bitterness . . . [and] betrayal" he felt when Reagan didn't support him ("The Argentina General Who Never Fought in a War," an interview with Oriana Fallaci, *Washington Post*, June 13, 1982, p. C5). During the crisis, President Reagan wrote to General Galtieri that "it has never been more important to reaffirm the common interests and values that unite Argentina and the United States." Galtieri released that letter to the press, criticizing it for being incoherent and "incomprehensible. . . . If our government and people were surprised by the unexpected move of the U.S. to take sides with Great Britain . . . today, on receiving your greeting . . . I could not be more shocked." (Cited in *Washington Post*, May 28, 1982, p. A1, 19.)

88. See, for example, Stephen Solarz, "Six Questions for the Reagan Doctrine: Next Stop, Angola," *The New Republic*, December 2, 1985, pp. 18–21; and Lloyd N. Cutler, "The Right to Intervene," *Foreign Affairs* (Fall 1985), Vol. 64, No. 1.

12

Subordinating African Issues to Global Logic: Reagan Confronts Political Complexity

Donald Rothchild
and John Ravenhill

By the end of 1985, the Reagan administration appeared to have little to show for the few major initiatives it had taken in Africa. Its efforts to broker Namibia's independence had been stalemated, and its policy of "constructive engagement" toward South Africa had brought few significant changes. In 1985 the president suffered a major foreign policy setback when congressional pressure forced him to introduce economic sanctions against South Africa, a tacit admission of the futility of the "constructive engagement" approach. Elsewhere the administration seemed to have been concerned primarily with damage limitation — ensuring that American interests were not threatened by radical and revolutionary forces on the continent. As Africa emerged as a major locus for superpower rivalry and as the struggle for black majority rule in the continent's southern tip intensified, the United States has become a more active player on the African stage.

Donald Rothchild is Professor of Political Science at the University of California, Davis. He has lectured at universities in Uganda, Kenya, Zambia, and Ghana. His books include Racial Bargaining in Independent Kenya *(London: Oxford University Press, 1973), (coauthor)* Scarcity, Choice and Public Policy in Middle Africa *(Berkeley: University of California Press, 1978), (coeditor)* Eagle Entangled *(New York: Longman, 1979), (coeditor)* Eagle Defiant *(Boston: Little, Brown and Company, 1983), and (coeditor)* State Versus Ethnic Claims: African Policy Dilemmas *(Boulder, CO: Westview, 1983).*

John Ravenhill is Senior Lecturer in international politics at the University of Sydney, Australia. He previously taught at the University of Virginia. He is the author of Collective Clientelism *(New York: Columbia University Press, 1985) and editor of* Africa in Economic Crisis *(New York: Macmillan and Columbia University Press, 1986).*

Policies adopted by successive administrations have differed according to whether African issues were viewed from a regionalist or a globalist perspective. Regionalists have generally perceived African problems with a sympathetic eye, emphasizing the uniqueness of the African environment and attempting to accommodate the aspirations of African peoples. Globalists, however, tend to view African issues from the perspective of an all-encompassing East-West conflict in which there can be no neutral parties. The simplicity of the globalist perspective gives it a certain inner consistency. This perspective, however, may entail high costs in terms of both misperceptions of the issues at stake in regional conflicts and the misallocation of scarce resources from the point of view of national interest. Whereas the Carter administration adopted a rather complex and low-profile regionalist orientation, the Reagan team has moved decisively to embrace a globalist view in which the unrelenting Soviet threat is emphasized.

The Reagan administration claims to have an enhanced sense of priorities dictated by the "national interest." At the top of that list is a determination to counter the threat of "Soviet hegemony" in African states. But it is not altogether clear what Soviet hegemony means in the African context, particularly given the evidence of a continued economic hegemony of the West over some of Moscow's closest allies in the region. American interests in Africa are real but limited. High on the list are such objectives as promoting trade and investment, obtaining raw materials, and encouraging economic development; other important interests include securing African diplomatic support at the United Nations (UN) and other multilateral bodies, gaining strategic advantage and a rough power equilibrium vis-à-vis the Soviets, and furthering human rights and racial justice. These interests are, of course, interrelated: The United States cannot expect to secure the long-term trading and strategic advantages that it desires unless it heeds the development needs of the continent.

Africa plays a relatively minor role in American total foreign trade and investment. Over the last decade, the United States has accounted for less than one-quarter of Africa's total exports (but close to 40 percent of those of oil-exporting states) and only 10 percent of Africa's imports (15 percent of those of South Africa). Africa (excluding South Africa) accounts for only 2 percent of the cumulative total of American foreign direct investment (FDI) (about 8 percent of the total American investment in developing countries); a further 1 percent of the total American FDI is in South Africa. Africa is, however, a significant source of strategic metals for the American economy — especially such metals as cobalt, chromium, manganese, platinum, vanadium, and zirconium, which are essential for the production of specialty steels. Mica is imported from Malagasy; cobalt from Zaire, Zambia, and South Africa;

tantalum (used in light bulb filaments) from Nigeria and Zaire; chromium from Zimbabwe and South Africa; and oil from Angola, Nigeria, Gabon, Algeria, and Cameroon. Nigeria, by the end of the 1970s, had become the second most important supplier of oil to the United States, accounting for 13 percent of the total imports; by 1983 it had slipped to seventh place — a position that it currently holds — contributing only 6 percent of the total.

South Africa in the years 1980–1983 supplied the United States with 55 percent of its imports of chromium, 49 percent of platinum, 44 percent of vanadium, 39 percent of manganese, and 61 percent of total cobalt (although much of the cobalt was mined in Zaire and Zambia and processed in South Africa). South Africa also has a large percentage of total known world reserves of many of these metals, which has led some conservatives to argue that the interests of the United States are best served by supporting the policies of the present South African regime. Their assumption appears to be that black majority government in South Africa would threaten the supply of these metals. There is nothing in the behavior of other independent African states, however, to suggest that this would be the case. Even countries like Angola, in which the socialist government has not been recognized by the United States, are happy to sell oil and minerals to Americans to increase their foreign exchange earnings. Any regime in South Africa, and this would include any future black majority government (as it would likely encounter increased popular expectations for public distributions after coming to power) would have no alternative but to sell its minerals to the West, given its heavy dependence on revenue from this source. The conservative position also discounts the prospect that a greater threat to security of supplies may come from instability in South Africa, arising from the intransigence of the white minority government in the face of demands for political change. The possibilities of diversifying sources of supply, including exploiting seabed nodules, stockpiling, substituting, and recycling, make grave apprehensions over a minerals' cutoff seem overstated.

The economic and security interests of the United States in the region are not confined to the Republic of South Africa. Any tilt toward the South African regime — as practiced by the Reagan administration in its policy of constructive engagement, discussed below — tends to alienate black African leaders and to jeopardize American interests in other parts of the continent. An enlightened view of long-term national interest (including the promotion of American egalitarian values, domestic racial harmony, and security ties, as well as trade relations with the continent) would indicate the desirability of accommodating black Africa's reasonable goals and aspirations. To a considerable degree, however, the Reagan administration's globalist outlook has led to a narrower interpretation of the American national interest in the region: the containment of what it has perceived as communist expansionism. Too often the administration has been insensitive to the differences between self-proclaimed "African socialist" regimes and their Eastern European and Soviet supporters. The administration has neglected to see that the success of the Soviet Union in southern Africa in the last decade has been, to a considerable extent, the result of its support for African struggles against white minority regimes. Similarly the continued presence of Cuban troops in Angola is the result of perceptions of the South African threat to Angolan security. American lack of sympathy with the aspirations of the Angolan government has driven its leaders toward greater dependence on the Soviet Union.

Due to a number of factors — the perceptions of the United States of southern Africa, and American resistance in the last decade to the demands of less developed countries for reforms in the international economic order — the political capital enjoyed by the United States in contemporary black Africa is not as high as it was in the early 1960s. Thus American motives are often regarded with great suspicion. At the same time, it is apparent that American capabilities are more circumscribed than was once assumed.

The American role in sub-Saharan Africa must not be overstated. Not only is the United States not a major trading partner for the majority of African states, but the American share of bilateral development aid to Africa (with the exception of Egypt) is also relatively small and has decreased under the Reagan administration. In most of black Africa, the European Economic Community is by far the most significant economic partner, and former European colonial powers often have better contacts and greater influence in many African capitals than has the United States. The United States has access to few military facilities in Africa and maintains only a small number of military advisors to African governments. When it was decided in the past to intervene militarily in support of friends, intervention had taken the form of providing transport facilities and logistical support for European forces, for example, in the case of the rebel invasions of the Shaba Province of Zaire in 1977–1978. Yet the United States alone is in a position to exert significant pressure on South Africa to modify its apartheid policies and to provide the wherewithal for African states to resist unwanted incursions by such Soviet-backed aggressors as Libya. These are the major parameters within which current American policy must operate. How the United States arrived at this position and how American policymakers perceive and respond to these parameters are the subjects of this chapter.

Minimal Engagement, 1946–1976

By current standards, all the American administrations in the 1946–1976 period adopted a low-profile stance toward Africa.[1] In the late 1950s, as independence neared for many new African countries, American spokes-men, anxious to avoid disruptions in the world system, encouraged African leaders to retain close ties with Europe after the transfer of power. The themes of moderation, orderly transition, and international stability were reiterated during this period and were sometimes accorded a higher priority than African desires for rapid independence (for ex-ample, the Eisenhower administration's abstention at the UN on the 1960 vote on the Declaration on the Granting of Independence to Colonial Countries and Peoples).

As the trauma of independence came and went, American policymakers began to adjust to the new world of African states. Presi-dent Kennedy, who did not hesitate to bypass European capitals, in-creased American bilateral assistance and built effective relations with African nationalist leaders. Although African nonalignment was no lon-ger viewed as immoral, the fundamental thrust, competition with Soviet expansion, remained unaltered. The United States continued to seek to contain Soviet expansion in the area, in particular supporting the UN initiative in the Congo. If the Kennedy administration made conscious efforts to establish personal ties with radical as well as with moderate African leaders, the Johnson administration moved steadily toward the center, both in its policy positions and in its preference for reformist leaders. And with material and psychic resources heavily committed to Vietnam, it was little inclined to become embroiled in other regions or issues that could, it seemed, be safely left to future administrations.

It is possible to distinguish two periods in African policy during the ensuing Nixon and Ford administrations: Kissinger phase I, which lasted from President Nixon's inauguration in 1969 until the spring 1976 change in policy, and Kissinger phase II, which followed. Preoccupied with the Vietnam war and predisposed toward "benign neglect," Kissinger was only minimally engaged with African issues during much of phase I. Nevertheless a policy tilt to the right became manifest. Not only did Kissinger prefer alignment with moderate and conservative African lead-ers during the first phase, but he also pursued policies that had the effect of identifying the United States with white racist regimes in southern Africa. Kissinger, in phase I, accepted the major premise of National Security Study Memorandum 39[2] that "the whites [of southern Africa] are here to stay and the only way that constructive change can come about is through them." Following from this premise, NSSM 39's option 2, which Kissinger embraced, called for a "selective relaxation of our stance toward the white regime." Thus in 1971 Nixon failed to offer resolute leadership to Congress in opposition to the Byrd amendment, which permitted the United States to import Rhodesian chromium and other strategic minerals in direct violation of UN sanctions. The United States cast its first veto in the UN Security Council in 1970 on a resolution that condemned Britain for failure to overthrow by force the illegal white minority regime in Rhodesia. This and other negative votes on arms embargoes aimed at South Africa isolated the United States from the mainstream of African and liberal public opinion.

Kissinger clearly conceived of global stability in terms of a relative equilibrium between major international actors. Hence when the Soviet Union moved outside its immediate orbit and intervened in mineral-rich Angola — sending to the Popular Movement for the Liberation of Angola (MPLA) support teams of military technicians and advisors, some $200 million in military equipment, and some 11,000 Cuban combat troops — Kissinger saw it as necessary for the United States, as the leader of the noncommunist states, to counter the spread of Soviet influence in Angola. Senate liberals, drawing analogies to earlier defense appropriations for Vietnam, effectively resisted Kissinger's arguments for confrontation. No one seriously questioned Angola's importance as a supplier of raw materials or its strategic significance, but unlike Kissinger and the global confrontationists, the Senate liberals did not believe that American interests required a strong response to Soviet-backed MPLA power. The paralysis of will argument advanced by neoconservatives to explain congressional opposition to direct intervention by the United States seemed unconvincing. More important was the feeling that the limits of accommodation with Africa and the Soviet Union had not yet been reached. Two forms of realpolitik were engaged head-on, and in this instance, the confrontationists failed.

Accommodations with Black Africa: Kissinger II and Carter

With the failure of a confrontationist stance in Angola, Kissinger recognized that minimal engagement with a tilt toward white Africa was increasingly counterproductive. As he declared in early 1976, "The radicalization of the Third World and its consolidation into an antagonistic bloc is neither in our political nor our economic interest." Thus was born phase II of Kissinger's African policy and its rationale, in North-South relations, of a movement from confrontation to cooperation. In a speech at Lusaka, Zambia, in April 1976, Kissinger set forth a ten-point program aimed at facilitating southern African negotiations and blocking external encroachment in the area. He called for the establishment of majority rule prior to independence in Rhodesia and outlined a program of action that included direct diplomatic pressures on the Salisbury regime, repeal of the Byrd amendment, and political and economic support of Rhodesia during the transition to majority rule. As regards Namibia, the former German colony illegally administered by South Africa, Kissinger sought to promote movement toward a peaceful settlement while an opportunity for bargaining still existed. He called on the South Africans to announce a timetable for self-determination acceptable to the international community and promised that once progress toward a settlement was apparent, the United States would ease its restrictions on trade and investment.

Stressing that South Africa's independence set it apart from Namibia and Rhodesia (still technically a colony), Kissinger contended that the South African regime "represents a legitimate government which carries out practices with which we disagree," which therefore required a different type of American response. He refused to intervene openly in the struggle against South Africa's institutionalized racism, preferring to rely on domestic pressures in the Republic of South Africa, assisted by a quiet external diplomacy. Kissinger's handling of South Africa was predicated on a need to secure Prime Minister John Vorster's cooperation in achieving accommodationist objectives in southern Africa. In something of a tacit exchange, Kissinger held out the possibility of respectability, even international legitimacy, to South Africa while attempting to secure critically needed support for his objective of black majority rule in Rhodesia and Namibia. In linking South Africa to the wider strategy of accommodation, Kissinger redefined the southern African question. Although early responses to Kissinger's proposals were encouraging, final agreement on Namibia proved elusive. On the Rhodesian issue, nationalist leaders and front-line presidents refused to agree to terms that allowed the ministries of defense and law and order to remain in white hands. The gulf between white and black Africa remained as wide as ever, and the Kissinger package came apart.

Carter's advent to power marked something of a shift in American foreign policy style. Highly moralistic in tone and pro-black in inclination, the Carter administration sought to fashion a "liberal" American approach that would shun mechanical cold war responses to African issues and put the United States more in step with black aspirations at home and abroad. If, in substance, there was considerable continuity with the policy outlined in Kissinger II, the "principled pragmatism" of the Carter team meant a more concerted effort to reconcile the symbols of idealism with effective restraints on Soviet expansionism. Carter policymakers sought to deal with African problems in their African context. Rather than ignoring the Soviet global factor, they believed that the best way to confront it was by trying to resolve the problems the Soviets were exploiting for their own purposes. In this sense, Carter's accommodation joined liberal purposes with considerations of national self-interest.

Both domestic and international pressures pushed the Carter administration to a sensitivity toward African aspirations. On the domestic side, a liberal bloc, including intellectuals, professional Africanists, church groups, and black Americans (who contributed in no small part to Carter's close electoral victory), emerged as an important element influencing his policies on African-related issues. The appointment of Andrew Young, the black civil rights leader, as ambassador to the UN was more than symbolic. Young's highly accommodative style was supported by many professional policymakers at the State Department's Africa Bureau and Policy Planning Staff, the National Security Council, and the UN, who were determined to eradicate all traces of the Kissinger I tilt on southern Africa.

Developments in economic relations with Africa reinforced Carter's accommodation stance. Trade with black Africa was increasing, although South Africa remained a significant export market. Nigeria, which replaced South Africa as America's largest African trading partner, was courted as one of the administration's "new influentials," key regional actors who could be expected to play major stabilizing roles. For Nigeria, southern African racism was deemed a nonnegotiable issue on which there could be no straddling by Western interests, a position the Carter administration could well understand. It responded by rhetorically disavowing the Kissinger strategy of dividing the Rhodesian, Namibian, and South African issues into distinct negotiating tracks. Carter's opposition, in principle, to all compromises with white racism in southern Africa led to an improvement in United States-Nigerian relations, one of the major successes of his liberal internationalist approach.

How successful was an accommodative policy style when applied to southern African issues? Accommodation meant a generally similar game plan in all three conflicts: to come to terms with moderate elements and thus preclude a radical takeover. What was desired were regimes acceptable to black Africa and linked to the global economy through Western capital and technology. In the case of Rhodesia, the accommodation stance led to a major symbolic achievement soon after Carter took office, when Congress moved swiftly to overturn the Byrd amendment. With its support of all-party negotiations and its efforts at mediation, the Carter administration contributed substantially to a successful resolution of the conflict. But the eventual settlement of the Rhodesian issue occurred with the Americans limited to a behind the scenes role. Carter's consistent support for independence under black majority rule had, however, successfully identified the United States with progressive forces in Africa.

The course pursued on Namibia paralleled that on Rhodesia but without the same success. Again a white-backed administration, under severe military pressure from the South West Africa People's Organization (SWAPO) liberation movement and from African nationalist and world opinion generally, recognized the need to transfer power to a majority-backed regime. A South African-sponsored solution, based on ethnic representation in the legislature, was opposed by American officials, who maintained that no settlement was likely to endure in the face of intense SWAPO resistance. To secure a comprehensive settlement, a "contact group" of five Western UN Security Council members (the United States, Britain, France, Canada, and West Germany) met separately in 1977 and 1978 with SWAPO and South African representatives. On various occasions, the contact group presented a package plan to the two sides and managed, in July 1978, to reach an understanding with SWAPO leader Sam Nujoma that included a wide measure of agreement on UN-supervised elections, the release of political prisoners, South African troop levels, and the size of the UN peacekeeping force. But the accord, as the American negotiator predicted, proved a "fragile souffle." In September outgoing South African Prime Minister Vorster rejected the UN Namibia plan, and despite strong UN opposition, South African authorities went ahead with a December election for a constituent assembly. The SWAPO liberation movement and two other nationalist parties boycotted this exercise, leaving the Democratic Turnhalle Alliance a winner by default.

New UN and contact group initiatives to find an internationally acceptable accord followed. The United States carried on discussions in the summer of 1979 with Angola's President Agostinho Neto, which produced a proposal for a demilitarized zone on both sides of the Namibia-Angola border. Throughout this frustrating period, the various parties had little difficulty finding new problems at every stage; the central difficulty was less one of specific provisions than of a general lack of confidence in the other side's intentions: The SWAPO liberation movement feared that South Africa would deny it political power based on genuine majority backing, and South Africa worried that UN favoritism would prejudice the results. In all this the Carter team played an important facilitative role, supporting an all-party agreement embracing the principles of majority rule and minority protection.

If an accommodative stance remained a reasonably steady guide to strategy in Rhodesia and Namibia, it was applied less consistently to South Africa. In line with its accommodative stance, the United States curtailed official sports contacts; reacted harshly to violations of civil liberties; suspended nuclear cooperation unless South African authorities agreed to adhere to the nonproliferation treaty; endorsed the Sullivan code on fair labor practices; and voted favorably on UN resolutions condemning apartheid, imposing a mandatory arms embargo, and criticizing South Africa's continued attack against its neighbors. Vicepresident Mondale asserted, following talks with Vorster in Vienna in May 1977, that without "evident progress" toward ending apartheid, the United States would have to take "actions based on our policy . . . to the detriment of the constructive relations we would prefer with South Africa." Although these actions were considered evidence of good intentions in the Third World, African leaders urged more forceful and effective measures. During Carter's trip to Nigeria, then-head-of-state

General Olusegun Obasanjo expressed his government's "strong disappointment" over the continued pursuit of "policies of outright collaboration with South Africa." In practice, the American arms embargo still did not eliminate all gray areas, and the Carter administration continued to extend Export-Import (EX-IM) Bank loan guarantees to South Africa until October 1978, when Congress, despite administration opposition, overturned the policy. Moreover, faced with a bitter South African attack on Mondale's call for full political participation, American officials stressed that they offered no blueprint or timetable for South Africa's democratization.

The administration's efforts appeared even less satisfactory in middle Africa. Given the American low-profile involvement in black Africa's struggle for independence, nonintervention and deference to African preferences seemed a logical framework for Carter policy. In line with Young's formula, "African solutions for African problems," the early Carter team limited its involvement in middle African struggles, declining in 1977 to be drawn directly into a series of conflicts of questionable concern to the United States: the April invasion of Zaire's Shaba Province by 2000 former Katanga gendarmes (Shaba 1), the growing conflict in Western Sahara, and the Ethiopian-Somali and Ethiopian-Eritrean disputes. If the parties to inter-African disputes were unable to resolve their differences among themselves, the standard American prescription was Organization of African Unity (OAU) mediation, not great-power interference.

By November 1977, the effectiveness of an accommodative stance on such issues was called into question. That the Soviets would become involved in a large buildup of the Somali army and would establish an extensive military complex in Berbera was of concern to those who had assumed a more conciliatory Soviet Union. This concern increased as the Soviets dispatched massive military assistance to the new Marxist-oriented government in Ethiopia. For a time it seemed just possible that the Soviets might be able to reduce tensions between these two self-proclaimed socialist regimes, but President Siyad Barre's determination to include all ethnic Somalis in an enlarged Somali state proved to be at cross purposes with Mengistu Haile Mariam's efforts to maintain a shaky Ethiopia against all challengers — Somali, Eritrean, or other-nationality dissidents. Inevitably the Soviet straddle failed, and in October, the Soviets cut off further arms shipments to Somalia. The Somalis, meanwhile, invaded Ethiopia's Ogaden region. The United States retreated from any assurances it may have given the Somalis on arms shipments, viewing such assistance as intensifying the conflict and as violating OAU findings on changing the border by force. The Soviet Union provided Mengistu with all the human and material support needed to defeat the Somalis in the Ogaden, thereby consolidating its alliance with Ethiopia, which subsequently signed a Treaty of Friendship with Moscow. Decisive Soviet intervention in the Horn demonstrated its capabilities and resoluteness to Africa.

National Security Advisor Zbigniew Brzezinski, a prominent conservative internationalist, warned Moscow that its activities in Africa would "inevitably complicate" the SALT negotiations. Another indication of a tougher Carter stance on Africa was the refusal to extend diplomatic recognition to the MPLA government unless Cuban troops were withdrawn from Angola. With another invasion of Shaba Province in May 1978 (Shaba 2), Washington seized the initiative and responded quickly to a request from Zaire, France, and Belgium for logistical support. This invasion of Zaire by Katangan exiles from Angola (allegedly trained and equipped by East German and/or Cuban forces) involved a violation of OAU principles on respect for sovereignty of member states.

With the departure of Young and Cyrus Vance from government service, a more traditional approach to global competition became apparent. Growing concern regarding American interests in the Middle East had brought about a noticeable hardening of attitude toward Soviet activities in Africa. In August 1980 a United States-Somali agreement was signed permitting American forces to make use of the Berbera facilities in exchange for $45 million in credits for defensive equipment. Despite firm assurance from the Siyad Barre government that American equipment would not be used in the Ogaden,[3] the political costs of military identification with a Somali regime intent upon incorporating kinsmen and territory in a neighboring land might prove high. Clearly the optimistic, initial visions of the Carter policymakers on the possibilities of accommodation in Africa were shaken as they came up against the cold realities of global competition, domestic pressure, African demands, and South African intransigence.

The New Administration's African Guidelines

A new administration in Washington frequently means a change in the country's approach to world issues, as the incoming team seeks to distinguish itself from its predecessors. Although the basic perceptions of American interests in Africa shifted little from the late Carter-Brzezinski period, there was a change in how these interests might best be pursued. President Ronald Reagan stressed the importance of rooting foreign policy "in realism, not naivete or self-delusion."[4] The essential element of Reagan's realism was the restoration of America's military "credibility," its economic dynamism, and its psychological vigor. Administration representatives castigated policies they saw as responsible for a decreasing American influence or for uncertainty over the country's future, including a supposed failure to recognize the global Soviet threat, an attempt to accommodate Soviet client states, and a neglect of Third World allies on the grounds of human rights violations. Taking a more traditional view of the role of power in international relations than the Carter administration had, the Reagan team concentrated more single-mindedly on resisting "Soviet adventurism" in Africa and elsewhere. Such a predisposition toward globalism carried with it a lower priority on accommodating African claims as well as a more independent American effort to arrest the general decline in the power of the West.

Guidelines for African policy, which were followed in the first five years of the Reagan administration, were set out in a series of articles by Chester Crocker, the Assistant Secretary of State for African Affairs.[5] Four key areas of focus for American policy were identified: the Horn, where the objective should be to contain Soviet-inspired damage to American interests by supporting clients in the Sudan and Kenya; Zaire, where a joint Western effort should be made to preserve the integrity of the country and the survival of an acceptable government; West Africa, where the objective should be to contain the spread of radical Arab influence; and southern Africa, where an internationally acceptable solution to the Namibian question should be sought. In the crucial southern African subregion, Crocker had initially supported the internal settlement in Rhodesia and criticized the "utopian" nature of proposals for a UN-administered transition to majority rule. He later reversed himself to applaud "British diplomatic virtuosity" in negotiating the settlement. On Namibia he argued that only an agreement backed by the UN would bring an opportunity for peaceful transition in the subregion. Although normalization of relations with Angola was desirable, recognition should result in increased American leverage within the subregion and should be timed to ensure some quid pro quo.

Shortly before taking office, Crocker had published a major statement in *Foreign Affairs* that provided a number of insights into his thinking on American policy toward South Africa. Noting the need to strengthen the "fragile centrist consensus" in American political circles, Crocker criticized the policies of previous administrations for either acquiescing to Pretoria or for sending false signals. The objective of American policy toward South Africa would be to promote the emergence "of a society with which the United States can pursue its varied interests in a full and friendly relationship, without constraint, embarrassment or political damage." The present apartheid system precluded this. But American influence would be achieved only if South Africa's internal dynamics (including the importance of Afrikaner nationalism) were appreciated. Crocker stressed the necessity of sympathy "for the awesome political dilemma in which Afrikaners and other whites find themselves" (without suggesting that this dilemma might be largely of their own making).

Crocker's prescription was for constructive engagement. He ruled out economic warfare or even more moderate economic instruments of foreign policy against the South African system and contended that the United States should not judge the legitimacy of a sovereign South Africa's rules and regulations. Crocker did argue, however, that there should be no support for the independent homelands unless a "meaningful" test of opinion of those affected by the policy was obtained. Moreover the United States should encourage those changes that would enable blacks to acquire the economic and organizational base from which they could effectively demand a larger share of political power. Noting that the "political and attitudinal preconditions for significant change have emerged in recent years," Crocker asserted that American interests might best be pursued by encouraging evolutionary change: The United States should maintain consistent pressure on Pretoria, but there must be a recognition that "the power to coerce Pretoria is not in America's hands." In taking this position, Crocker appears to have underemphasized the ability of the United States to wield the stick against South Africa.[6] Curiously, Crocker's initial realism regarding the prerequisites for bargaining with the Soviet Union contrasts with his kid-glove, all-carrot-and-no-stick approach to South Africa — that is, until the policy shift on this issue in the summer of 1985.

Reagan's Strategic Globalism

On African security issues, the assertiveness of the Reagan administration distinguished it from that of the preceding administration. As Crocker told the Council on Foreign Relations on October 5, 1981, "It is . . . time to recognize . . . that the solution to regional disputes does not lie in Western abstinence at a time when Libyan, Soviet, and Cuban policies seek actively to exploit and fuel the fires of instability." The Reagan administration stated clearly that it would not remain on the sidelines, allowing its Soviet adversary a free hand. Rather, it asserted its intention to counter Soviet involvement with American involvement. This included the provision of bilateral aid and military assistance to "proven African friends" to enable them to resist possible aggression — whether in the form of direct Soviet expansion or indirect expansion through the agency of local "proxies." The effectiveness of such a globalist posture appears questionable, however. To the extent that the administration stresses military solutions to political problems, it tends to overplay the force variable and to underestimate Africa's commitment to nonalignment and to the New International Economic Order.

The American commitment to identify openly with friends and to shun adversaries appears at first glance to be consistent with the Reagan team's focus on East-West rivalries. Yet the costs of such an orientation seem relatively high in terms of grappling effectively with complex intraregional issues. An emphasis on globalist issues has brought the United States into dangerously close proximity with regimes disliked by the majority of their own populations for their racialism (South Africa) or for their corrupt and arbitrary practices (Zaire), whereas an open commitment of support has at times been embarrassing to friends who are sincerely pledged to nonalignment (Kenya, Nigeria, and Zambia). Although the targets of Reagan's displeasure are likely to be perceived as embracing a hostile "Marxist" ideology and having a substantial number of communist-bloc troops stationed on their territories, a more pragmatic stance did become evident toward Soviet-supported Mozambique by 1982 and reached a high point with President Samora Machel's visit to Washington in September 1985.

In addition to Libya, those radical states most frequently identified by Reagan spokesman as Soviet surrogates are Ethiopia, Angola, and until recently, Mozambique. Namibia's independence movement, SWAPO, and the regimes in Tanzania and Zimbabwe have also evoked administration ire for the way they have distanced themselves from American purposes. Not surprisingly, as is discussed below, these states have tended to fare poorly in the allocation of foreign aid under the Reagan administration. Nevertheless the geopolitical importance of such countries as Ethiopia and Mozambique has led the Reagan team to move at times to improve relations with the incumbent regimes. Not only are such initiatives in line with American stability objectives, they can also be interpreted as attempts to deny these countries to their Soviet backers.

In Ethiopia, the Mengistu regime has proclaimed its commitment to Marxist-Leninist principles and established a formal communist party. Links with the Soviet Union, however, have been based on perceptions of common interest as well as ideology. Soviet support was decisive in helping Mengistu repel the Somali invasion in 1977, and subsequently, Soviet and Cuban troops, in addition to Soviet arms, have provided important support to the Addis Ababa regime in its wars with secessionist forces in the provinces of Eritrea and Tigre and in the continuing struggle against Somali-backed rebels along the country's southeastern borders. In exchange the Soviet Union has been granted access to strategically important air and naval facilities. The continuing presence of Soviet and Cuban troops, the signing of a twenty-year friendship treaty between Ethiopia and the USSR, and Ethiopian backing for the Soviet invasion of Afghanistan have all generated considerable unease in Washington. Yet the Reagan administration has acted cautiously in its policy toward the Horn. Diplomatic relations with Ethiopia have been maintained and substantial famine relief has been extended to its people. Military assistance for the Somali government has been moderate — amounting to only $35 million in Fiscal Year 1985. Similarly there have been only modest expenditures on modernizing the naval facilities at the Somali port of Berbera, to which the United States has access. The only American troops in the region — 250 sent to Berbera to participate in the "Bright Star" exercises of November 1981 — were quietly withdrawn at the conclusion of the exercises.

In Mozambique, President Samora Machel signed a treaty of friendship with Moscow, transformed the Mozambique Liberation Front (FRELIMO) from a national liberation movement into a Marxist-Leninist vanguard party, and applied for membership in the Council for Mutual Economic Assistance (COMECON). United States-Mozambique relations deteriorated dramatically in the initial Reagan years, when Mozambique's leaders expelled four American diplomats for alleged espionage. Subsequently a gradual rapprochement has taken place between the United States and the FRELIMO leaders. In part this is explained by the effort made by American diplomats to place limits on the South African effort to destabilize the region; it is also explained, in part, by Machel's apparent disappointment over Soviet bloc aid and his country's limited economic progress under state socialist policies. The result has been the difficult Mozambique decision to sign a nonaggression treaty (the Nkomati Accord) with South Africa in 1984 and to move toward closer economic relations with the West. The United States, which played a critical mediatory role in the negotiations leading up to the accord, has favorably accepted the agreement, restored its economic assistance to Mozambique, and welcomed its president, Samora Machel, to the White House in 1985.[7]

Clearly there have been significant divisions within the Reagan administration on how to deal with the self-proclaimed socialist regimes of Africa. Globalists have tended to respond in a knee-jerk manner, advocating the isolation of such regimes. Others, however, have emphasized the salience of regional factors to these regimes and the differences that often exist between them and their Soviet backers. Although the Reagan administration appears to have undergone a learning process in its dealings with Ethiopia and Mozambique, there is less evidence of this process in its relations with the self-proclaimed Marxist-Leninist regime in Angola. Here the advent of the Reagan administration brought a more combative stance.

Angola had been pivotal in changing Kissinger's perceptions of Soviet behavior. Soviet and Cuban support for the MPLA was on an unprecedented scale and decisively altered the course of the Angolan civil war in 1975–1976. Soviet intervention was not welcomed by many African states: A meeting of the OAU split evenly between supporters of the MPLA and the states that wished to see a coalition government of the three independence movements — the MPLA, UNITA (the National Union for the Total Independence of Angola), and the FNLA (National

Front for the Liberation of Angola). With South African intervention in support of UNITA, a movement enjoying substantial support from the Ovimbundu and Chokwe peoples of southern Angola, its legitimacy and that of its leader, Jonas Savimbi, were undermined in the eyes of black Africa. The MPLA was quickly recognized as the legitimate government by African heads of state, and Angola was admitted to the OAU.

Even though the Carter administration had refused to establish diplomatic relations with Angola on the grounds that the MPLA regime came to power by forcible means and was maintained by some 20,000 Cuban troops, it had nonetheless pursued a hands-off policy toward the country's internal affairs. The Reagan administration, however, has attempted to exert greater pressure on the MPLA regime to force it to agree to a broad-based coalition government at the political center, the withdrawal of Cuban troops, and a settlement of the Namibian issue. In February 1984, American diplomats played a key role in brokering the Lusaka agreement between Angola and South Africa under which South Africa agreed to halt the fighting and to "disengage" its forces from Angolan territory (which it failed to deliver on in the months that followed). Then in 1985, after Congress had resisted the move for four years, the administration succeeded in repealing the 1976 Clark Amendment, which had banned American assistance to forces opposed to the MPLA government. Black African opinion viewed administration attempts to repeal the amendment and to provide American support for the South-African–backed forces of UNITA as a destabilizing act, helpful only to South African desires for regional hegemony. This perception was reinforced by the administration's failure to voice strong criticism of South African raids into southern Angola in support of UNITA forces. Although the Reagan administration initially adopted a pragmatic approach to Angola, pressured not only by black African opinion but also by the executives of American multinational companies that have extensive Angolan investments,[8] frustration at the lack of success in reaching a settlement of the Namibian issue (see below) and the continued presence of 1,200 Soviet and East European advisors and 35,000 Cuban troops led to a decision in February 1986 to intervene directly in the Angolan civil war by covertly providing the UNITA rebel forces with some $15 million in military assistance.

Even in support of "proven friends," Reagan administration motives are mixed. In addition to a desire to back allies (Morocco, Tunisia, Zaire, and Angola's UNITA), to stabilize what are perceived as critically important countries (Zaire, Zimbabwe, Namibia, and South Africa), and to counterbalance Soviet-Cuban involvement on the continent, there are two related globalist objectives: to secure naval and air facilities for use by the U.S. Navy and the U.S. Central Command (Somalia, Kenya, Diego Garcia, Morocco, and Egypt), and to resist Libyan adventurism (Liberia, Chad, Sudan, and Somalia). Colonel Muammar el-Qaddafi's messianic anti-American style, his close military links with the Soviet Union, his support of international terrorism, and his apparent penchant for intervening abroad are profoundly repugnant to the Reagan team. As part of a get-tough policy, then-Secretary of State Alexander Haig ruled out a "business as usual" relationship with a regime he accused of distorting the rules of international behavior. The Libyan People's Bureau in Washington was closed, Americans living in Libya were asked to return home, an embargo was put on American imports of Libyan oil, curbs were placed on the sale of American technology to Libya, and an aerial encounter took place off the Libyan coast. Then as terrorist units carried out near-simultaneous assaults against civilians in the Rome and Vienna airports in January 1986, the United States, accusing Libya of sponsoring the violence, retaliated by imposing trade and commercial sanctions and ordering American citizens and companies to leave Libya by February 1. The conflict took a turn for the worst in March. As American planes crossed Qaddafi's "line of death" and carried out operations in the Libyan-claimed but international waters of the Gulf of Sidra, Libyan forces fired antiaircraft missiles. American warplanes returned the fire, damaging several patrol boats and shoreline missile sites. Soon after this engagement had passed and quiet had resumed, new tensions emerged in the relations between Libya and the United States. The immediate cause was the explosion of a bomb in a West Berlin nightclub, killing an American soldier and a Turkish woman and injuring 230 others. The United States, blaming Libya for masterminding this and other terrorist attacks against Americans, retaliated on April 15 with a direct air raid, sending British-based F-111s and carrier-based A-6 and A-7 bombers against military targets in the Tripoli and Benghazi areas.

This get-tough policy has also included pledges of American military assistance to African states resisting Libyan interventionism, including major increases in military assistance to such Libyan neighbors as Tunisia, Morocco, Egypt, and the Sudan; an allocation of $12 million to help the OAU peacekeeping force, which arrived in Chad in 1981 following the withdrawal of Libyan troops (and subsequent support for Hissan L. Habre's regime against its Libyan-backed rivals in 1982); joint military exercises with Egyptian and Sudanese forces; and an extensive economic and military aid program, including the dispatching of a one hundred-man Green Beret unit, to bolster the Liberian military regime. Qaddafi's much publicized adventurism had indeed provoked the United States to respond; questions, however, remain as to whether such wide-ranging American sanctions, only partially supported by its European allies, effectively raise the costs of sponsoring terror or engaging in adventurist activities and whether they serve American national interests, since possibly they may strengthen the underdog Qaddafi internally and externally as a champion of extreme Arab causes.

If the United States sought to counter Qaddafi's actions as destabilizing to his subregion, it attempted to play the role of peacemaker in southern Africa, again in pursuit of the greatest stability. Such a status quo approach follows logically from the Reagan administration's perceptions of economic and political interests. Seeing the United States as the hub of the world economic system, Reaganites naturally place great emphasis on buttressing a global order that contributes to American strength and well-being. Thus a September 1980 working paper prepared for Reagan observed, with continued access to southern Africa's mineral resources plainly in mind, that "we can't afford to de-stabilize such an important region."[9] Although the administration has subsequently played down a sense of urgency over access to these minerals (since a South African embargo is most unlikely in any event), the unresolved question remains: What is the main cause of instability in southern Africa — racial inequality and poverty or Soviet-inspired subversion? To stress the latter, as the Reagan team is all too prone to do, is to miss the genuine African grievances that give the Soviets opportunities for intervention.

The Reagan team's conciliatoriness toward the South African regime is largely the product of its perceptions on how to resolve the complex problems of Namibia and South Africa itself. In the latter instance, the Reagan administration, assuming that the Afrikaner-dominated regime shared Western values on good-faith bargaining and mutually beneficial solutions, urged reform on the government of Pieter W. Botha; its methods to this end included a mixture of sympathetic encouragement and quiet, behind-the-scenes diplomacy. However, constructive engagement was ineffective in the face of South African intransigence and soon encountered strong opposition by Congress and the general public. Then as violence spread across South Africa in the summer of 1985, this rather passive administration approach lost whatever credibility it still possessed for the concerned American public. A *Business Week*/Harris poll, conducted in January 1985, had previously underscored the growing impatience of Americans with any tacit support for the Botha regime; 68 percent of those interviewed favored continued American and Western pressure on South Africa.[10] The public had become quite vocal in its denunciations of South African racial discrimination and alleged American collusion in white domination through its policy of constructive engagement. Demonstrations took place daily outside the South African Embassy in Washington, and demands for change, including divestment, were heard on campuses throughout the country. The divestment movement became a central issue around which these events gathered momentum, with proponents arguing that universities, churches, and pension funds should seek to influence policy by selling off their South-African–related stocks. This powerful expression of a long pent-up feeling on this issue raised public consciousness and contributed to congressional determination to push ahead with legislation providing for economic sanctions against the Republic of South Africa.

Then as information surfaced about an attempted sabotage mission by South African forces against American-owned oil facilities in Cabinda, Angola, and a subsequent raid by South African military units against alleged African National Congress safe houses in quiet, multiracial Botswana, the Reagan administration, spurred by the growing public pressures at home, recalled its ambassador from Pretoria and began a general review of its Southern Africa policy. The Cabinda raid brought a chill in high administration circles, especially as it raised serious doubts about South Africa's good faith in its American-mediated negotiations with Angola. In August the administration was further embarrassed as Botha, following high level consultations between American and South African officials in Vienna, dashed all hopes of major reforms in his much-heralded Durban speech by defiantly ruling out any significant concessions to black demands. The Reagan administration policy of constructive engagement appeared to be at a dead end; if persuasion and sympathetic support had proved ineffectual, tougher action would not be long in coming.

By the summer of 1985, the Reagan administration had little alternative but to reexamine constructive engagement and to take a stronger stance on white dominance in South Africa. Therefore, despite his administration's continuing opposition to formal economic sanctions and its effort to put a good face on Botha's "reformist" moves, his spokesmen noticeably stiffened their tone toward the Pretoria government, telling these officials bluntly that it was their policy of apartheid that was "largely responsible for the violence" in South Africa.[11] The American ambassador was recalled to protest the military raids into Angola and Botswana, and then, in an effort to fend off pending sanctions legislation in Congress, Reagan imposed limited economic sanctions of his own in September 1985 "designed and aimed against the machinery of apartheid without indiscriminately punishing the people who are victims of that system."[12] Even though the Reagan team persisted with the policy of constructive engagement long after it ceased to hold out hope of bringing about change, a toughening of stance did occur as a reluctant administration came to recognize that Congress would likely override its veto of a sanctions bill.

The provisions of the Reagan executive order included a ban on computer exports to government agencies involved in the enforcement of apartheid, a prohibition on virtually all exports of nuclear goods and technology, and a ban on loans to the government, except for those intended for specified humanitarian or social purposes. The president instructed his secretary of state and American trade representative to consult with other trading partners about a possible ban (subsequently enacted) on imports of Krugerrands, and called for a halt on further United States government assistance to American firms employing more than 25 people in South Africa that failed to adhere to the Sullivan principles on fair and nondiscriminatory employment practices. He also called on the secretary of state to establish an advisory committee of distinguished Americans to make recommendations on peaceful change in that country. Although these measures were largely "after the fact" ones (most banks had already pulled back from such loans and few large computers were being offered for sale by American companies to the South African government and its agencies), and although they fell considerably short of the provisions of the 1985 Anti-Apartheid bill in Congress, the president's executive order nonetheless was symbolically important in its firm rejection of apartheid as "wrong" and in its application of sanctions against a former "ally." Clearly, as South Africa's Progressive Federal party spokesman on foreign affairs, Colin Eglin, stated following Reagan's speech, "The tragedy for South Africa is that the government has squandered the borrowed time previously given to it by President Reagan's low-key approach to the South African situation."[13] Events in the United States and abroad had forced a reluctant reversal of policy on the Reagan administration; the move to "active constructive engagement" indicated, at the least, that a more assertive public policy would follow. Moreover the more decisive developments in private sector involvement (in particular the unexpected decision of the Chase Manhattan Bank to end further loans to private borrowers in South Africa in August 1985), left Botha with reduced options and limited time. The deteriorating economic situation in South Africa made external financial and business linkages indispensable, yet the possibility of a white backlash against any significant dismantling of apartheid placed political limits on his ability to create conditions conducive to the foreign ties that were so important. In the face of increasing external and domestic economic pressures (many members of Congress have continued to press for effective sanctions, and a number of West European and Commonwealth countries have sought strong measures), it remains to be seen whether Botha will enter into direct negotiations with the legitimate leaders of black opinion or whether he will allow the ship of state to drift toward an uncertain and possibly dangerous future.

The Reagan administration's efforts to negotiate Namibian independence have appeared to be a kind of high-risk diplomacy that has yet to display conclusive results. Reagan had to deliver both on Namibian independence and South African internal reform, or constructive engagement would be seen as diplomatically damaging. Delivering on Namibia, in the sense of hammering out a settlement minimally satisfactory to both black and white interests, was a risky undertaking at best. If in 1981, Crocker found Nigeria and the front-line states adamant on the need for Western pressure to support an unchanged Security Council Resolution (SCR) 435 of 1978 (providing for the withdrawal of South Africa's illegal administration, a cease-fire, and free elections under UN supervision), he found the South Africans equally unyielding in their opposition to UN-administered elections and the prospect of a SWAPO government in Windhoek. Perhaps inevitably, the mediator became part of the problem.

For all the assurances Haig made to Nigerian Foreign Minister Ishaya Audu in March 1981 that United States policy "would not change substantially" on Namibia, the American role in the peacemaking process shifted noticeably.[14] The new administration's refusal to send an observer to the Geneva conference on Namibia in January 1981 suggested the possibility of a separate American initiative. Its policy appeared to be closer to the South African position; this perception was reinforced by hard-line Reagan administration statements on convergent United States-South African political, economic, and strategic interests in countering Soviet influences in southern Africa and the Indian Ocean. Further indications of a policy tilt followed as the Reagan team took hold — the call, early in the administration's tenure, for a repeal of the Clark Amendment; the welcoming to Washington of UNITA's Savimbi, leaders of Namibia's ruling Democratic Turnhalle Alliance, and even South African military officers; the linking of Namibian independence to the withdrawal of Cuban troops from Angola; and a reference to SCR 435 as a basis for a transition to Namibian independence rather than as a final settlement.

If further evidence of a change of policy were necessary, there were revelations in several leaked documents. While backing SCR 435, Crocker called for "Pretoria's cooperation in working toward an internationally acceptable solution to Namibia which would . . . safeguard U.S. and South African essential interests and concerns." Provided the South Africans cooperated on this and the domestic reform issue, Crocker saw no difficulty in pledging to work toward ending that country's "polecat status" in the world.[15] The African response was sharply critical. At the Eighteenth Summit Conference of the OAU in Nairobi in June 1981, resolutions were passed criticizing the abandonment of SCR 435 and denouncing "the emerging unholy alliance between Pretoria and Washington."[16] The conflict in Namibia was described as a colonial one, not "one of global strategic consideration."

In the fall, intensive American discussions with the South Africans and the front-line leaders on revised American proposals rekindled hopes of ending the Namibian deadlock. These proposals provided the foundation for a revised Western plan released in Lagos in late October. This Western plan outlined the principles to be used by the constituent assembly in drawing up the constitution (Phase I); the implementation of the cease-fire, the positioning of the UN force, the withdrawal of SWAPO and South African forces, the arrangements for the election (Phase II); and the holding of the election and adoption of the constitution (Phase III). The constitutional principles under Phase I called for establishing a unitary state under a constitution adopted by a two-thirds vote of all the members of the constituent assembly. Elections would be monitored by UN troops drawn largely from the forces of the five contact group countries, wearing their national uniforms (a concession to South African charges of UN partiality toward SWAPO). The SWAPO forces would be confined to bases in Angola under UN supervision during the elections, and Cuban troops would be kept in northern Angola. South African armed forces would be removed from Namibia before the elections; and SWAPO pledged not to use Namibian territory as a base for future terrorist attacks. South Africa would retain Walvis Bay temporarily; after independence, it would be the subject of separate negotiations.

Initial reactions to the Western plan were cautiously positive. Although SWAPO spokesmen expressed a great reluctance to tamper with SCR 435, Nujoma indicated a willingness to include provisions on minority rights in the independence constitution. South Africa's Prime Minister Botha said the plan could open the way to a settlement, and Namibia's Democratic Turnhalle Alliance, though not joined by the extreme right-wing whites, expressed a readiness to participate in elections under the proposed guidelines. By December 1982 agreement had been reached on many of the Phase I and Phase II principles: a voting system on the basis of either proportional representation or single-member constituencies but not both, a UN force to guarantee free elections for an assembly to work out Namibia's independence constitution, and four of the seven countries to make up the supervisory force (Sudan, Bangladesh, Yugoslavia, and Panama).

With agreement reached by 1983 on "virtually all of the pieces of the Namibian negotiation concerning [Security Council] Resolution 435,"[17] what stood in the way of a settlement? The impasse was accounted for by three interrelated factors. First, the issue of linking a withdrawal of Cuban troops from Angola to a Namibian independence settlement was a Reagan administration initiative that made the negotiations more complicated. Clearly, as Crocker has insisted, the linkage issue had been raised earlier during the negotiations, but it was the Reagan team that made linkage a formal part of the negotiating process. Crocker admitted as much under persistent probing before the House Subcommittee on Africa: "Our effort to relate Namibia to Angola was our effort. I am not denying that," he declared.[18] The effect of this deliberate action has been to stymie the negotiations, for Angola's ruling (MLPA) regime looks on the presence of Cuban forces on their territory not as an intrusion but rather as a protection against South African efforts to overthrow their government, either alone or in alliance with UNITA military units. Only if the Luanda government feels more secure from internal and external attack will it be willing to order the Cuban troops to leave. By repealing the Clark amendment and by deciding to provide covert assistance to the resistance forces in Angola, the Reagan administration achieved the opposite result. As the United States has come to be perceived as siding with UNITA, it has complicated the peacemaking process and, unwittingly, "promot[ed] South Africa's foreign policy agenda."[19] The effect is almost certain to prolong the Cuban presence in Angola.

Linkage became intertwined with the second and third factors — that is, the South African government's perceptions both of its own strategic insecurity and of its ability to retain a hold on internal state power in the event of a SWAPO takeover in Namibia — because it was a convenient means of avoiding difficult choices on the latter issues. From an official American standpoint, linkage was described, in part, as an incentive designed to assist the South Africans to sell a Namibian settlement to their own constituency.[20] If taken at face value, this represents a recognition of Botha's dilemma in pressing change on an essentially conservative domestic constituency. For the South Africans, linkage seemed an opportune means of stalling, when no other equally powerful obstacles to a negotiated settlement were at hand. Determined South African resistance itself is explained more by their view on the implications of a SWAPO victory in Namibia for themselves than by the presence of the Cubans in Angola. For many South African officials, the possibility of SWAPO control was regarded as a matter that gravely threatened their country's well-being, for they viewed it as putting a hostile, African-nationalist regime on their border. As Robert S. Jaster observed, South African officials are convinced "that a future Namibia dominated by SWAPO would pose an unacceptable risk to the security of the Republic."[21] Hence in light of these seeming risks, inaction, rather than concerted movement toward a negotiated settlement acceptable to the international community, is seen as a preferable strategy.[22] In addition conciliatoriness on Namibia is perceived by the Botha regime as potentially risky, in terms of domestic politics, because conservative politicians within the white community, playing on prevalent fears of a sellout, are quick to point to any sign that the regime is inclined to placate foreign interests as opposed to standing firm in upholding the interests of their own constituents. As a consequence, the practical, cautious side of Botha tends to remain uppermost, inclining him toward toughness on the Namibian issue, to the embarrassment of his sympathizers in the Reagan administration.

The result has been an extended period of hopeful signs with little in the way of solid accomplishments. The modalities of a peace settlement have been hammered out; moreover in February 1984, a cease-fire and disengagement agreement was signed between Angola and South Africa (but not SWAPO) at Lusaka, with the United States acting as mediator. The modalities did not extend to the deeper issues at stake in regional politics, however, and the Lusaka accord was undercut by South African intransigence, that is, an unwillingness to withdraw all troops from

Angolan territory, a determination to use the military option to carry out further deep penetrations into Southern Angola, and in Namibia, a move to install a new, multiracial administration with power over foreign affairs and defense. Through constructive engagement, then, the United States had become deeply enmeshed in a regional problem, only to be embarrassed by the seeming embrace of a white minority regime intent on using the negotiating process for its own ends to create a zone of dependent states on its borders that have no option but to accept the right of South Africans to manage their own internal affairs as they see fit.[23] In this the 1984 nonaggression treaty between South Africa and Mozambique (the Nkomati Accord) is a prototype of what a "dominant" Pretoria has in mind for its relationship with Angola. Thus, despite a formal agreement to respect one another's territorial integrity, South Africa admitted in 1985 that it has continued to resupply Renamo, the opposition group responsible for much of the violence carried on in Mozambique in recent years. For Washington, Pretoria, and Luanda, then, agreement on Namibia's independence appeared to be stymied by basic differences as to their objectives; for Namibia, the impasse in the negotiations seemed to represent a lost opportunity for peace after years of warfare and illegal occupation.

Reagan's Economic Policies and Africa

The accession of Reagan to the presidency coincided with the onset of Africa's most serious economic crisis since independence. The most dramatic manifestation of Africa's problems has been widespread famine, in which drought played a significant role. Africa's malaise is more deep-rooted than climatic factors alone, however; ineffective government development strategies and unfavorable international economic conditions have contributed significantly to poor economic performance. Africa is the only region in the world in which per capita food production declined during the last decade, the result of inappropriate government policies toward agriculture and of the continent's high birthrate.

Like all Third World countries (see Chapter 5), those of the African continent have been adversely affected by the Reagan administration's subordination of international economic policy to the needs of supply-side and monetarist domestic economic policies. Enormous budget deficits have produced unprecedentedly high real interest rates. Other industrialized countries inevitably have had to defend the value of their currencies by raising their own interest rates, which has contributed to worldwide recession. This has severely reduced the markets for many of the raw material exports on which African economies depend heavily, with consequent falls in price; the International Monetary Fund's (IMF) composite commodity price index reached its lowest level ever in 1982.

Although there has been marginal improvement in subsequent years, many of Africa's exports are currently being sold at prices close to their historical lows. Most African countries have experienced severe balance of payments difficulties, with exports covering only one-half of the cost of often severely curtailed imports; the remainder has been financed by foreign aid and overseas borrowing. High interest rates have added to the debt servicing burden of African countries, which, according to the World Bank, will rise to "alarming" levels for the remainder of this decade. To be sure, interest rates have moderated slightly and oil prices have declined, but given the dimensions of the problem it is not clear that this will have a significant impact over the long term. Moreover such oil-producing states as Nigeria, Algeria, and Angola must pay off earlier contracted debts at a time of declining oil revenues.

One dimension of what can be termed the "new unilateralism"[24] of the Reagan administration has been the emphasis on bilateral aid at the expense of assistance through multilateral organizations. This has been particularly disadvantageous for African countries, which, constituting the majority of the countries designated as least developed by the UN, are major recipients of multilateral aid. Although there were signs in 1985 that the Reagan administration was having second thoughts on its hostility toward the World Bank, its reluctance to fund multilateral organizations in its first six years in office had already had a severe negative impact on Africa. This is particularly true of the World Bank's soft-loan affiliate, the International Development Association (IDA). The IDA has been the largest single source of development assistance for African states, the majority of which are ineligible, as a result of their debt servicing problems, for regular World Bank loans. Refusal by the Reagan administration to pay its share of the seventh IDA replenishment was responsible for a 25 percent reduction in the Association's funding, in nominal terms, and 40 percent, in real terms. Although Congress, in appropriating funds for IDA, stipulated that the Association's loans to Africa be maintained at existing levels, it is difficult to see how this will be possible, given the overall funding reductions; the World Bank estimates that IDA assistance to Africa will be cut by 21 percent, in real terms.

In 1984 the Reagan administration refused to contribute to the World Bank's special emergency aid fund for Africa, which consequently was cut back from the proposed $6 billion level to $1.1 billion. Similarly in 1985, the future of the UN International Fund for Agricultural Development, an organization that has significantly contributed to African agriculture, was placed in doubt by the refusal of the administration to agree to a new financing arrangement. By the fall of 1985, however, the administration appeared to be undergoing a partial change of heart when it announced, at the annual meeting of the World Bank and IMF, a proposal for a new joint World Bank/IMF fund to reschedule the debts owed by the poorest countries. Here the apparent concern was that the debt servicing problems of some African countries were so severe that they would be unable to meet their IMF repayments and would consequently be declared in default — a problem the administration apparently feared might spread to Latin America. Although the total debt of *all* African countries is less than that of Brazil, many countries are experiencing severe difficulties in meeting their debt repayment as a result of the current economic crisis. Thus even the relatively successful Ivory Coast has had to devote more than one-third of its export earnings to meeting interest payments and capital repayments on outstanding debt. In this instance, the administration has been forced to reverse course as a result of confronting constraints exerted by the international economic system. Despite its relative decline in economic power, the United States remains by far the most important and powerful actor in international economic relations. No American administration can afford to abdicate its responsibility for leadership and management of the system.

Within its own program of bilateral aid to Africa, the Reagan administration, to a considerable extent, has followed the ideas put forward by Undersecretary of State for African Affairs Crocker, before he assumed office. Crocker had written that the United States had tied its own hands in Africa by adopting an aid program that lacked "coherence of purpose and focus of effort." Not only was the American aid program too small, its focus on meeting basic human needs also "almost rules out using aid as a tool for the promotion of *any* U.S. interest — either developmental or political." Crocker also criticized the distribution of American aid, observing that "a relatively large chunk of aid is sent routinely to socialist Tanzania," whereas pro-West, capitalist Ivory Coast received virtually nothing. He concluded that "Washington needs to stop thinking of African policy as a philanthropic venture and start defining *U.S. interests* in the economic relationship with Africa." After chiding American aid givers for running "rural welfare programs," he urged attention to "more mundane tasks," including export promotion, investment incentives, and regional infrastructure aid projects. Not only should greater assistance be given to the American private sector but military assistance to such long-standing American clients as Zaire and Morocco should also be given priority. Determination of which African governments to aid, he suggested, should depend on their past and current attitudes on issues of direct importance to the United States, postures on foreign investment and nationalization, potential contributions to regional and international peacekeeping, and estimates of the likely durability of the governing groups.

Crocker's priorities were reflected in the administration's moves to effect a significant shift away from development aid toward general economic assistance through the Economic-Support Fund (ESF) and toward military assistance (a movement reversed in 1984–1985 largely by the increase in emergency funds for famine relief). In the years 1981 to 1983, military assistance to Africa was increased more than threefold. Of the other categories of assistance, funds under the ESF program increased much more rapidly than development aid. The ESF, in the words of the *Congressional Quarterly*, "aims to help friendly nations with their economic troubles so they can spend more on defense."[25] Support under the ESF is determined by such security considerations as a country's strategic location, provision of military facilities, and pro-Western stance. The Library of Congress estimated that 82 percent of ESF for Africa in Fiscal Year 1983 and 77 percent in Fiscal Year 1984 would be employed for purposes not directly related to rural development and meeting basic needs.[26]

Resistance to this redirection of funding has come from liberal Democrats in Congress, ably led by the chairman of the House Subcommittee on Africa Howard Wolpe. According to the House Subcommittee:

> Excessive increments of military assistance have been given to selected African countries while development assistance has remained relatively low. Africa's alarming economic crisis and the resultant political-social problems cannot be given a quick fix by means of larger and larger military expenditures. Indeed, to the extent that our policies encourage African governments to divert resources away from pressing economic needs, we exacerbate already worsening circumstances . . . it is in our national interest to help Africa overcome its economic problems by giving greater emphasis to developmental criteria, not military ones; to encourage Africa to strengthen its agricultural and industrial productivity, not its military capacity; and to support Africa in securing its legitimate aspirations for self-determination and racial justice in southern Africa.[27]

Congressional action succeeded in cutting back administration requests for arms and military assistance for Morocco, when Congress had become concerned that American assistance had encouraged King Hassan's intransigent position on the Western Sahara issue; for Somalia, whose support for irredentist forces in Ethiopia had caused Congress to voice displeasure; and Zaire, where human rights abuses and rampant corruption led Congress to call on the administration to distance itself from the regime of President Mobutu Sese Seko. Congress also resisted the administration's attempts to lift the restriction limiting to six the number of American military advisors in countries receiving military assistance. But the failure of the Senate and the House to agree on foreign aid and appropriations bills between 1981 and 1985 meant that Congress had exercised less control over aid expenditure than would otherwise have been the case. And by 1985, with the repeal of the Clark amendment, it appeared that Congress was more willing than in the past to go along with the administration's emphasis on military aid.

Aid has been given to reward "proven friends" and withdrawn from those states deemed either to have been insufficiently supportive of the foreign policy objectives of the United States or whose domestic policies were regarded as hostile to private enterprise or both. "Security interests" have been given top priority, with particular attention directed toward assisting countries regarded as vulnerable to Libyan adventurism. Sudan, threatened by Libyan destabilization, was the largest single beneficiary of the administration's aid until February 1985 when support to the government of then-President Numeiri was frozen in an effort to pressure it to introduce economic reforms. Kenya and Liberia have been the other principal beneficiaries of ESF support, both receiving over $30 million annually, as well as military assistance.

In contrast, the aid program to Kenya's southern neighbor, Tanzania, was terminated because of the Nyerere government's socialist economic policies and its vociferous pursuit of a nonaligned foreign policy. Aid to Zimbabwe was similarly cut back in 1985 in an expression of the administration's anger at Zimbabwe's criticism of the United States in the UN and its votes there on such issues as the Grenada intervention and the shooting down of a Korean jetliner by the Soviet Air Force.[28] Later, when provoked by the refusal of Zimbabwe's prime minister, Robert Mugabe, to apologize for an insult to the United States made in the presence of former President Carter at a July 4, 1986 reception, the Reagan administration, hearing new criticism of American policy at the nonaligned summit meeting in Harare, responded by announcing a cancellation of aid to that country. Mozambique, another socialist pariah, had been treated more favorably by the administration following its signature of the Nkomati Accord with South Africa. But conservatives in Congress succeeded, in 1985, in stipulating conditions for aid in Mozambique similar to those that liberals had attempted to impose on further assistance for El Salvador: a reduction in the number of foreign military advisors, demonstrated respect for human rights, and economic reforms to give greater weight to the private sector. Congress and the administration appear to have gambled that, given the present weakness of African countries, a curtailment of aid will either be sufficient to convince governments to change their policies or contribute to their overthrow and that this course of action is preferable to an attempt at dialogue with countries that adamantly assert their sovereignty and nonalignment. Whether this lack of sympathy with African aspirations will be to the disadvantage of the United States over the long term remains to be seen.

The action of Congress in making aid more conditional on the introduction of economic reforms by African governments has supported the administration's objective of promoting the private sector. This has not fallen entirely on deaf ears among African leaders. Many governments appear to be disillusioned with the performance of the parastatal sector (public enterprises that operate on a commercial basis) and increasingly sympathetic toward both local and international private enterprise. An emphasis on market forces and on cutting back the "overextended" state in Africa was endorsed by an important policy paper issued by the World Bank in 1981. Although the Reagan administration applauded this paper, it has disregarded the report's other principal conclusion — that there will be no significant economic progress in African countries unless there is a substantial increase in development assistance (the Bank recommended that aid to Africa be doubled in real terms in the 1980s).[29]

Even though the Reagan administration's position that "the most important contribution any country can make to world development is to pursue sound economic policies at home" cannot be faulted on strictly logical grounds, the administration has failed to acknowledge sufficiently that the worldwide recession to which its policies have contributed in the short term has further strained African economies. Insistence on the "magic of the marketplace" has too often appeared to be an excuse for refusing aid requests. African leaders have been alienated by the failure of the administration to appreciate the difficult economic circumstances that they face and by the refusal to provide the development assistance necessary to reduce the heavy economic (and political) costs of introducing the types of reforms that both the White House and the World Bank favor. The one attempt made by the administration to provide funding to promote economic reform — the Economic Policy Initiative for Africa — was killed in 1984 by the Senate, which remained unconvinced of the criteria to be used in allocating the assistance and feared that it would be turned into a "slush fund." The $75 million to have been appropriated for the program was added to Africa's allocation under the ESF.

Another of the administration's stated objectives on coming into office was to promote the activities of the American private sector in Africa. Studies commissioned by the State Department showed that the principal trading rivals of the United States — the European Economic Community and Japan — had increased their share of African markets at the expense of the United States in the 1970s. As a result, the United States trade deficit with Africa (even when oil-exporting states like Nigeria were excluded) had grown dramatically. The United States had been particularly ineffective in penetrating the markets of black Africa — including the most significant, Nigeria — and had become more dependent on sales to South Africa. And whereas its competitors were enjoying success in expanding their sales of capital equipment and machinery, the most rapidly growing category of American exports was foodstuffs, much of it financed by American aid. Given the political instability of the continent and its economic problems, the situation faced by private enterprise — regardless of its origin — has been a difficult one. Here governments can play a particularly important role by promoting exports through suppliers' credits (provided for American exporters by the EX-IM Bank) and by subsidizing export insurance to reduce the risk that exporters face. The studies found that American exporters received far less government assistance than their overseas rivals.[30] Despite the administration's pledge to promote the American private sector, its actions in its first five years, for example, cutting back funds for the EX-IM Bank and for the Foreign Commercial Service, were directly contrary to this objective. Again a change of heart appeared to be forced on the administration by economic realities — in 1984 the deteriorating trade balance led the administration to reverse its policy and to request increased assistance for the EX-IM Bank.

The American response to the famine that swept parts of Africa in 1984 and 1985 was generous, although one in which Congress took the lead and pressured a reluctant administration to allocate more assistance than it had originally intended to provide. Indeed Democrats and some private relief agencies criticized the administration for being slow to react to the unfolding disaster in Africa and, in particular, for allowing its distaste for the Ethiopian regime to interfere with the provision of humanitarian assistance. Ethiopia had asked for famine relief in October 1982, but the United States did not respond until May 1984. The horrifying television pictures from Ethiopia galvanized congressional and public support for a substantial American aid effort and caused the administration to reverse its previous policy of attempting to exclude Ethiopia from PL 480 assistance. Critical delays in authorizing emergency appropriations occurred, however, in both 1984 and 1985, when the bills became entangled with contentious political issues. In 1984, delays arose when administration-backed Senate attempts were made to attach provisions for military assistance to Central America to the emergency appropriation. This led House Speaker Tip O'Neill to charge that the administration had "shown that it is ready to starve Africans so that it can kill Central Americans."[31] In 1985, it was the Democrats' turn to delay emergency relief by attempting to attach provisions for additional assistance to American farmers; Reagan had to use his emergency powers in order to continue the flow of aid.

Although delayed, the American response to Africa's needs was substantial. In Fiscal Year 1984, sub-Saharan Africa received $172 million in emergency Title II grants, $117 million in regular Title II grants, and $127 million in Title I and III loans. In April 1985, Congress passed a bill appropriating an additional $784 million for emergency African relief — more than three times the amount the administration had requested. Of this amount, Congress appropriated $609 million for food aid and $175 million in international disaster assistance and emergency relief for such purposes as providing seeds for farmers and clothing and shelter for refugees.

Conclusion

Globalism and regionalism are two prominent perspectives on how American foreign policy objectives in contemporary world arenas might be secured. On African policy, globalists and regionalists may well agree as to basic American interests and capabilities, as well as to the gravity of superpower rivalries on the current global scene. Within the Reagan administration, as was the case with the Carter administration before it, a wide spectrum of opinion is present, ranging from unrestrained globalist thinking to various shades of regionalist thinking. It is also evident that this entire spectrum shifted with the advent of the Reagan administration. Thus Crocker, before taking office, criticized the Carter team for underestimating America's global strategic concerns. In power, however, he fell near the regionalist side of the Reagan administration's continuum — perhaps reflecting his institutional role as assistant secretary of state for African affairs. In true globalist fashion, former Secretary of State Haig pointed to the Soviet Union's "ominous objective" of positioning itself on the Horn to strike against countries near vital Western resource lines,[32] yet Haig also spoke with the sensitivity of a committed regionalist regarding the implications of Soviet military aid to Africa. "Many are very free," he wrote, "about labeling these recipient states as Marxist. Some have suggested they will be Marxist or democratic depending on their assessment of which label will bring them the progress for their people that they seek. And I am one that shares that view."[33]

The globalist-regionalist distinction is situational and relative, not fixed. On certain issues, proponents of African policies have distinctive overviews with respect to their ranking of priorities on strategic, economic, and social concerns. Nevertheless it is unwise to overemphasize the significance of these distinctions. Individuals, even factions within the bureaucracy, are likely to display different tendencies on diverse policy questions, and these may vary as the time, or the place, shifts. During his first year in office, Reagan acted in a cautious and pragmatic manner in his dealings with the Somali government; his early relations with the Nimeiry regime in the Sudan seemed less guarded and judicious, no doubt reflecting his determination to respond forcefully and effectively to perceived Libyan threats in the area. Hence globalist and regionalist foreign policy perspectives, long employed by Washington participant-observers themselves, can be said to be generally useful for analytical purposes, provided it is recognized that these labels are intended to represent no more than overarching perspectives, not fixed or necessarily opposed policy positions.

The principal features of the Reagan administration's African policies that distinguish them from those of the Carter administration may be summarized as follows:

1. In general the Reagan administration has given African issues a lower priority except insofar as they affect East-West rivalries or economic concerns. In part this reflects a conscious choice to restrict the foreign policy agenda.[34]
2. Regional problems are perceived as arising not so much from local sources but from a planned and organized Soviet global threat. For Haig, Libya's pressures against Sudan and Tunisia were part of a broader external challenge and suggested a central point: *"the interrelationships between threats and events in different theatres."*[35] Thus Soviet penetration in the Horn and southern Africa has been perceived as not restricted to the Soviet Union's own regionalist goals but rather as also involving such broader globalist objectives as the possible denial of strategic minerals or sea lanes to Western adversaries.
3. The Reagan administration is unwilling to suffer criticism, hostility, and adventurist actions on the part of radical African states and has been determined to raise the costs when it believes that such states are engaging in antagonistic or reckless behavior. Thus Libya's expansionist moves directed at such American allies as Chad, Sudan, and Tunisia brought a strong American response. Foreign critics and adversaries were to be alerted to a changed attitude on the part of the American government that was intentionally more assertive. In reckoning on gaining respect commensurate with its status as a superpower, the United States seems to be acting in line with its perception of what has made Soviet practices successful in the Third World in recent years (for example, extensive military support to Ethiopia, Libya, and Angola). The tentativeness that marked the post-Vietnam era is gone; the administration is resolved to take the rhetoric of their African critics at face value and to treat them as the opponents they claim to be.
4. Reagan policymakers firmly insist on an explicit linkage between a Cuban troop withdrawal from Angola and a settlement of the Namibian conflict.
5. Human rights have not been high on the administration's agenda. The Reagan team has explicitly proclaimed its support for "proven friends," despite their human rights and development records. To be sure, this stance brought the Reagan administration an improved working relationship with such African regimes as the corrupt dictatorship in Zaire. The identification of American interests with regimes such as Mobutu's, however, may well prove costly in the

future, should conditions deteriorate further and a shift in power occur.

6. General economic support and military transfers have been assigned higher priorities than has development assistance. There has been a marked reluctance to work through multilateral aid agencies, indicating a tendency on the part of the Reagan administration toward a new unilateralism.

The policy preferences of the Reagan administration are clearly different from those of the Carter administration. American interests and capabilities remain much as they were, but the objectives of policy and the manner of securing these objectives have changed. Although it is apparent that trade-offs may be present in each type of policy orientation, how is one to assess the realism of the Reagan administration's current Soviet-centric orientation as it affects American relations with Africa? It is concluded that such a Reagan-style globalist thrust tends to be dysfunctional for broader United States-African interests for the following reasons:

1. As a superpower, the United States has, of course, to be concerned with the global strategic balance. But the globalist approach to Africa exaggerates the importance of the continent to vital American interests, overestimates the threat from the Soviet Union and its perceived military allies, and fails to understand the reasons behind Soviet successes on the African continent in the past decade. Soviet experience in Africa has not been a particularly happy one; over the past twenty-five years the Soviet Union has suffered a number of significant diplomatic defeats there. The reason for its successes in the mid-1970s was its ability to supply armaments to African movements, often in the context of a struggle against white minority regimes. Subsequently, however, Moscow's closest allies in black Africa — Angola, Ethiopia, and Mozambique — have openly expressed their disillusionment with the failure of the Soviet Union to meet their development needs. Since African trade with the Soviet Union must be conducted primarily through barter, African countries have had few opportunities to increase their exports. And Soviet development aid has been miniscule. As a result, the Soviet Union's African friends have increasingly looked to the West. Even African states that proclaim their allegiance to socialism are often better characterized as nationalist rather than Marxist-Leninist: Socialist rhetoric has been adopted as a means of creating a new national identity, of distancing regimes from their colonial predecessors, and of asserting a nonaligned position in international affairs.

   A globalist approach, which tends to perceive these states as "enemies" and to punish them, is counterproductive, since it closes off opportunities for the West to exert influence. Irrational, self-defeating policies may result (the covert assistance to UNITA, for example), which are not the most effective means of containing Soviet influence. Indeed Soviet influence is likely to be increased by such policies, since it tends to be directly proportional to the security threat these regimes face. By acting in terms of a Soviet-centric perspective, then, Reagan administration policymakers run the risk of increasing American involvements and of making American prestige dependent on events they are unable to manage.[36]

2. A globalist approach, with its primary concern for East-West competition, may cause the United States to be insensitive to African goals and priorities. The uniqueness of Africa tends to be overlooked, even dismissed, and a kind of new paternalism, which places the ultimate responsibility for policy in non-African (that is, Western and Soviet) hands, is adopted. Those who hold such a view refuse to accept Africa's primary responsibility for its own security and well-being; instead they assume that the United States and its allies can best decide Africa's true interests and that these interests in time will be seen as identical with those of the West. Such a view inclines the United States toward a status quo orientation that may prove counterproductive. To the extent that the United States ceases to be in rapport with African leaders and ideas, it may well frustrate the achievement of its most critical objectives in Africa.

3. Globalism, with its emphasis on strategic factors, tends to lead to false priorities being set in dealings with African states. Thus the stress on the protection of sea lanes; access to strategic minerals; the right to make use of military facilities, bases, and so forth, complicates dealings with those African host countries who find themselves identified with American purposes. Thus in acceding to American wishes with respect to the use of naval facilities in Mombasa, the Moi government in Kenya has been placed somewhat on the defensive in its relations with domestic political opponents.[37] More serious, perhaps, the desire to protect sea lanes and access to minerals contributes to the special American treatment given to certain resource-rich African lands, as witness the policy of constructive engagement with South Africa and the conciliatory stance toward Mobutu's Zaire. Unless these approaches bring demonstrable progress toward majority human rights, and, in the case of Namibia, independence, they will likely identify the United States with racism and reactionary impulses in Africa for a long time to come.

4. A high-risk policy in regard to a Namibian settlement may jeopardize the long-term position of the United States in the view of other governments, should it fail. External mediation is a risky undertaking under the best of circumstances, and given the high stakes, as well as

the evidence of Soviet interference and South African intransigence, steady progress toward an internationally accepted settlement seems unlikely. The Reagan administration's decision to give military aid to Savimbi's UNITA, a guerrilla movement fighting against the Angolan government, has, moreover, gravely complicated its self-chosen role as a mediator in southern Africa.[38] Hence, by focusing attention on the American initiative in resolving the Namibian dispute, the Reagan administration risks major embarrassment in the event that its policy package unravels completely.

5. Globalism, by its very nature, lacks a vision of future objectives in Africa. In the case of Namibia, even if a settlement is hammered out, what program will follow? Constructive engagement with South Africa, even though modified and updated in response to the events of 1985, is likely to remain unacceptable to African states throughout the continent. African states are, quite rightfully, to be expected to continue to strive for majority African rule in the rest of southern Africa and will not be diverted for long by internal "reforms" in South Africa or by signs of progress on Namibian independence. A globalist orientation seems of little help in understanding the forces for self-rule and equality at work here or in setting long-range priorities in line with Africa's values and expectations.

6. Globalist influences on aid priorities may work against American objectives on the long-term stability of the African state system. Anti-American populism arose in such friendly countries as Ghana precisely because economic deterioration led to a sense of desperation in the populace at large. With its tendency to direct an increasing proportion of its assistance in Africa to defense-related purposes, the United States is courting further economic, political, and social breakdown, with all its attendant effects on United States-African relations.

The new Reagan "realism" on Africa must be examined in terms of its near- and longer-term consequences. To the extent that the qualitative costs seem to outweigh the benefits, a reappraisal of policy seems imperative. "As a matter of fact," writes Arnold Wolfers, "the moral dilemmas with which statesmen and their critics are constantly faced revolve around the question of whether in a given instance the defense or satisfaction of interests other than survival justify the costs in other values."[39] Genuine realism, then, eschews an ideological mind set and requires an accurate assessment of both the global and regional forces at work. An anti-Soviet orientation *not grounded in regional reality* is not likely to prove effective in the long run. Hence an enlightened realism that balances these interrelated regional-global perspectives seems to hold out the greatest promise for achieving various American purposes in a constructive and morally fulfilling manner.

"Subordinating African Issues to Global Logic: Reagan Confronts Political Complexity" was written for this volume. Copyright © 1987 by Donald Rothchild and John Ravenhill.

Notes

1. For further information on the points covered in this section, see Donald Rothchild, "U.S. Policy Styles in Africa: From Minimal Engagement to Liberal Internationalism," in *Eagle Entangled* (New York: Longman, 1979), pp. 304–335.
2. See the documents in Colin Legum, ed., *Africa Contemporary Record 1975–1976* (New York: Africana Publishing Co., 1976), pp. C97–106.
3. See the letter from President Siyad Barre to Ambassador John L. Loughran, April 23, 1978, as quoted in U.S. Congress, House Subcommittee on Africa, Committee on Foreign Affairs, *Hearings on Reprograming of Military Aid to Somalia*, 96th Cong., 2d sess., August 26, 1980, p. 15.
4. President Reagan's State of the Union Message, as reprinted in the *New York Times*, January 27, 1982, p. 8.
5. Crocker's positions were outlined in a series of articles including "Lost in Africa," *New Republic*, February 18, 1978, pp. 15–17; "Making Africa Safe for the Cubans," *Foreign Policy* (Summer 1978), Vol. 31, pp. 31–33; "Missing Opportunities in Africa," coauthored with W. H. Lewis, *Foreign Policy* (Summer 1979), Vol. 35, pp. 142–161; "Voila, Zimbabwe!" *New Republic* December 22, 1979, pp. 10–13; and, with Mario Greszes and Robert Henderson, "Southern Africa: A U.S. Policy for the '80s," *Freedom at Issue* (November–December 1980), Vol. 58, pp. 11–18. See also the article, quoted below, which appeared shortly after Crocker's nomination, "South Africa: Strategy for Change," *Foreign Affairs* (Winter 1980–81), Vol. 59, No. 2, pp. 323–351.
6. See Michael Clough, "Why Carrots Alone Won't Work," *African Index* (June 30, 1980), Vol. 4, No. 10, pp. 1–14.
7. See Winrich Kuhne, "What Does the Case of Mozambique Tell Us About Soviet Ambivalence Toward Africa?" *CSIS Africa Notes*, No. 46, August 30, 1985.
8. On this, see the statement of the president of Gulf Oil Exploration and Production Co., in U.S. Congress, House Subcommittee on Africa, Committee on Foreign Affairs, *Hearings on United States Policy Toward Angola—Update*, 96th Cong. 2d sess., September 17, 1980, pp. 10–13.
9. Nora Olmsted, "Africa Viewed from the Reagan Camp," *West Africa*, November 17, 1980, p. 2285.
10. See Stuart Jackson, "Business Week/Harris Poll: Fight Apartheid, But Don't Close up Shop," *Business Week*, February 11, 1985, p. 39.
11. Gerald M. Boyd, "Apartheid Blamed by U.S. for Unrest in South Africa," *New York Times*, July 23, 1985, p. 1.
12. Ronald Reagan, "South Africa: Presidential Actions," September 9, 1985 (Washington, D.C.: Department of State, Bureau of Public Affairs, 1985), PR 735, p. 2.
13. *Cape Times* (Cape Town), September 10, 1985, p. 4.
14. On a reported threat by Nigerian leaders to use their "oil weapon" as a last resort if they felt the Reagan administration tilted too far toward South Africa, see *Weekly Review* (Nairobi), April 10, 1981, p. 16.
15. Several of these leaked documents appear in *Counterspy* (August–October 1981), Vol. 5, No. 4, pp. 48–57.
16. Quoted in *Africa Research Bulletin* (July 1981), Vol. 18, No. 6, p. 6069.
17. Statement by Chester A. Crocker, U.S. Congress, House Committee on Foreign Affairs, Subcommittee on Africa, *Namibia and Regional Destabilization in Southern Africa*, 98th Cong., 1t sess., February 15, 1983, p. 32.
18. Ibid., p. 33.
19. Statement by Rep. Ted Weiss when introducing a bill to prohibit military or para-

military operations in Angola (H.R. 3690). *Congressional Record* (November 6, 1985), Vol. 131, No. 152, P.E. 5036.

20. Statement by Chester A. Crocker, U.S. Congress, House Committee on Foreign Affairs, *Namibia and Regional Destabilization*, p. 34.

21. Robert S. Jaster, *South Africa in Namibia: The Botha Strategy* (Lanham, MD: University Press of America, 1985), p. 31. Also see Robert I. Rotberg, "Namibia's Independence: A Political and Diplomatic Impasse?" *CSIS Africa Notes*, No. 13, May 5, 1983, p. 5.

22. Jaster, *South Africa*, p. 105.

23. Winrich Kuhne, *Sudafrika und seine Nachbarn: Durchbruch zum Frieden?* (Baden-Baden: Nomos Verlagsgesellschaft, 1985), pp. 163–165.

24. John Ravenhill and Donald Rothchild, "Reagan's Africa Policy: A New Unilateralism," *International Journal* (Winter 1982–1983), Vol. 38, No. 1, pp. 107–127.

25. *Congressional Quarterly Weekly Report*, November 14, 1981, p. 2231.

26. Cited in Colin Legum, ed., *Africa Contemporary Record 1982–1983* (New York: Africana Publishing Company, 1984), p. C19.

27. "Foreign Assistance Legislation for Fiscal Years 1984–1985 (Part 9): Markup Before the Committee on Foreign Affairs, House of Representatives, Ninety-Eighth Congress" (Washington, D.C.: U.S. Government Printing Office, 1983), p. 22.

28. Michael Clough, "The UN: A Not So Dangerous Place?" *CSIS Africa Notes*, No. 45, July 24, 1985, p. 1.

29. International Bank for Reconstruction and Development/The World Bank, *Accelerated Development in Sub-Saharan Africa: An Agenda for Action* (Washington, D.C.: World Bank, 1981); for a discussion of the Bank's proposals and their alternatives see John Ravenhill, ed., *Africa in Economic Crisis* (New York: Columbia University Press, 1986).

30. Joanna Moss and John Ravenhill, *Emerging Japanese Economic Influence in Africa: Implications for the United States* (Berkeley: Institute of International Studies, University of California, 1985); and Pauline Baker, "Obstacles to Private Sector Activity in Africa" (Washington, D.C.: Department of State, mimeo, 1983).

31. Quoted in *Congressional Quarterly Weekly Report*, December 1, 1984, p. 3042. Also see Jack Shepherd, "Ethiopia: The Use of Food as an Instrument of U.S. Foreign Policy," *Issue* (1985), Vol. 14, pp. 4–9.

32. U.S. Congress, House Subcommittee on Foreign Operations and Related Agencies, Appropriations Committee, *Hearings on Foreign Assistance and Related Programs Appropriations for 1982*, Part 2, April 28, 1981, p. 91.

33. U.S. Congress, Senate Subcommittee on Foreign Operations, Appropriations Committee, *Hearings on Foreign Assistance and Related Programs Appropriations, FY 1982*, Part 1, 97th Cong., 1t sess., March 26, 1981, pp. 32–33.

34. See Thomas L. Hughes, "Up from Reaganism," *Foreign Policy* (Fall 1981), Vol. 44, p. 9.

35. House Appropriations Committee, *Hearings on Foreign Assistance*, Part 2, April 28, 1981, p. 102.

36. Christopher Layne, "The Real Conservative Agenda," *Foreign Policy* (Winter 1985–86), Vol. 61, p. 92.

37. Expressing a radical Kenyan viewpoint, one newspaper noted: "They [Moi's Kenya African National Union] have finally given our entire country over to U.S. imperialism to use as a political and military base." *Pambana* (Nairobi) (May 1982), Vol. 1, p. 1.

38. Significantly, on April 8, 1986 the six front-line states issued a communiqué declaring that the United States had lost its credibility as a mediator in southern Africa by backing the rebels in Angola. See *Africa Research Bulletin* (Political Series) (May 1986), Vol. 23, No. 4, p. 8031.

39. Arnold Wolfers, "Statesmanship and Moral Choice," *World Politics* (January 1949), Vol. 1, No. 2, p. 190.

13

The Reagan Administration and the Middle East

Barry Rubin

In the Middle East, more than in any other part of the world, the Reagan administration's policy was constrained by regional forces and long-standing American commitments. Paradoxically then, although local opportunities and crises resulted in periodic shifts of American policy, there was a broader thread of continuity and a narrower margin of choice for policymakers in the Middle East.

Although the Arab-Israeli conflict tended to be the single most important issue for American involvement, Washington was also concerned over the Iran-Iraq war, the security of the oil-rich Persian Gulf states, terrorism, and a range of bilateral relationships.

Corresponding to these factors — multiple problems, apparently conflicting relationships, lack of maneuverability, and primacy of regional developments — the administration's policy went through four distinct phases:

1. From January 1981 to August 1982, the Middle East was a low priority for the administration. In dealing with the region, it emphasized efforts to safeguard the security of the Persian Gulf.
2. From September 1982 to April 1983, there was intensive American activity in the Middle East. Israel's invasion of Lebanon and other events created new, high priority conditions. The administration's diplomatic interventions in Lebanese civil war and the Arab-Israeli conflict failed. In Lebanon, terrorism, Syrian opposition, and bitter mistrust among Lebanese factors stymied American efforts. On the Arab-Israeli front, President Reagan's plan was rejected by all sides, although it became the basis for his new diplomacy.

Barry Rubin is a Fellow at the Foreign Policy Institute of the Johns Hopkins School of Advanced International Studies. His recent books include Secrets of State: The State Department and the Struggle over U.S. Foreign Policy *(New York: Oxford University Press, 1985) and* Modern Dictators *(New York: McGraw-Hill, 1987).*

3. From May 1983 to February 1985, in response to these failures Washington decided to await openings from local forces, and the Middle East again became a low priority.
4. Promising events early in 1985 — a more conciliatory government in Israel and a Jordan-Palestinian Liberation Organization (PLO) accord — seemed to offer a way out of the impasse, and the administration undertook a new initiative. The PLO's intransigence, however, stymied this initiative, and the experience produced a new period of relative inactivity for the Reagan administration.

Overall it is certainly difficult to formulate clear and successful policies for the Middle East. This region presents the United States with many conflicts and problems the mere listing of which leaves one breathless. They include the war in the western Sahara between Morocco and Algerian-backed guerrillas, the ambitions and activities abroad of the Libyan government in supporting terrorism and subverting other states, the desire to maintain Egypt-Israel relations in the post-Camp David era, the Arab-Israeli conflict, the Palestinian question and the future of the West Bank, the Lebanese civil war and the lack of an effective government in that country, the demands of local countries for increasingly larger amounts of arms from the United States, the Iran-Iraq war, the rapid economic development of Gulf oil producers with their social and political problems and threat of instability, the aftermath of the Iranian revolution and the breakdown of American-Iranian relations, the Soviet invasion of Afghanistan and the struggle of Afghan guerrillas against Soviet occupation, and the threat posed to Pakistan by Afghan events. The fact that the four largest recipients of American aid (Egypt, Israel, Pakistan, and Turkey), as well as the main purchasers of American arms, are in the region indicates its centrality in American foreign policy.

Past Policies: Consistency of American Interests

The Middle East has become a focus of American foreign policy in recent years. Not only has the region increasingly been the site of major international crises, it has also been significant in setting the tone of overall American diplomacy. Developments in the region also played an important role in shaping American public opinion toward international affairs, in general, and in influencing domestic politics, including the 1980 election.

American interests in the Middle East are simply stated, but the way of best ensuring them can be defined only with difficulty in the face of tremendous controversy. Different politicians, administrations, and government departments agree more often on the ends than on the means of American Middle East policy.

The first of these interests, which is of particular significance since

1973, is the continued flow of oil. The argument can be made that a reliable oil supply is relatively independent of the regime ruling any country, since the export of oil is usually that state's only major economic asset. This is truer than many policymakers realize; yet during a war or crisis, the supply of oil may be governed by factors contrary to those of normal trade and commerce. Further, control over oil could be used by unfriendly forces for political leverage against Western Europe and Japan, who are still more dependent on Middle East oil than is the United States.

A second American interest is to keep Soviet influence in the area at the lowest possible level. The Soviet Union and its allies must not be allowed to control the oil fields. The region's strategic location at the crossroads of three continents and vital shipping lanes also makes it critical in the East-West conflict. Furthermore, the huge amounts of capital the oil-producing countries hold is another asset that must also be kept from the Soviet Union's control.

Regional stability is a third American interest, as access to oil will be more reliable if countries in the area are not disrupted by internal and external strife. Revolutions might cause nonaligned states to move closer to the Soviet Union or disrupt states that maintain close relations with the United States. Radical change may also produce regimes more hostile to their neighbors — eager to fight or subvert them. Finally, wars between Middle Eastern countries might create significant problems for the United States in the event that it has good relations with both sides.

A fourth interest is the maintenance of close contacts with friendly states, especially Egypt, Israel, Saudi Arabia, Turkey, and Pakistan, and to a lesser extent, Jordan; the small Arab sheikdoms of the Gulf; Tunisia; Sudan; and Oman. Before the Iranian revolution, the Shah's regime was also included in the former category. These ties provide the United States with political allies in the regional and international arenas and, in turn, keep them from the Soviet Union and its allies.

Many of the debates over the American Middle East policy revolve around how to weigh these four main interests. Both stability and alliance are concepts whose promotion and delineation is subject to many different interpretations. Political change is sometimes inevitable, the Carter administration argued, and the problem for the United States sprang not so much from the fact of change itself as from Washington's decision to maintain the status quo. Such an approach encouraged or even forced opposition parties, once they came to power, to look on the United States as an adversary. Is support for allies necessarily the best way to deter Soviet influence? Will American pressure on or accommodation with friends help maintain greater stability? Despite the American-Soviet rivalry in the area, the question remains how high a priority to place on these aspects of American concern. Would the East-West conflict be regarded as primary in all circumstances, or would American influence be best served and Soviet leverage most effectively circumscribed by a proven American ability to cope with regional problems?[1]

During the 1950s, the United States dealt with the Middle East as a Cold War area. This policy addressed the existing Arab tensions between traditionalist states and radical military regimes allied with Moscow. With the 1967 war, Israel emerged as a major regional military power and American-Israeli relations improved, given their often parallel enmities and global alignments. After the 1973 war, Secretary of State Henry Kissinger emphasized the policy of building bridges to Egypt and oil-rich Saudi Arabia. Given America's interests on both sides of the Arab-Israeli conflict, the United States government sought to maintain good relations with all the combatants. Not surprisingly, this resulted in an effort to defuse the points of conflict as much as possible.

The Carter Administration

The Carter administration's approach to the region emphasized local problems rather than the East-West conflict and stressed political relations rather than military/security considerations. At the same time it continued the Nixon Doctrine and the "two-pillar" Gulf policy; this policy eschewed direct American involvement in that subregion, relying on Saudi Arabia and Iran to maintain stability there. The Shah's fall made the policy obsolete and undermined much of the thinking behind it.

Within this framework, Carter set out in the first half of his term to make progress in resolving the Arab-Israeli conflict. The Soviet Union, lacking a similar standing with the two sides, could not compete in this effort. Washington initially explored possibilities of a broader settlement, including contacts with Palestinian groups, but finally, after President Sadat's trip to Jerusalem, turned to the best achievable option, the Camp David accords. Although two major goals were achieved — peace between Egypt and Israel and a complete Israeli withdrawal from the Sinai — the talks on autonomy for the residents of the West Bank and the Gaza strip bogged down. Significantly, other Arab states did not enter this negotiating process or propose a realistic alternative.

The regional position of the United States was later affected by the great traumas of 1979: the Iranian revolution, the taking of American hostages in Teheran, and the Soviet invasion of Afghanistan.[2]

The two Iranian crises had very different psychological effects in the United States. Many Americans saw the revolution as retribution for American support of an unpopular and repressive dictatorship: American actions in that country may have led to Iranian anti-Americanism. The Carter administration was slow throughout 1978 to recognize the extent of the upheaval in Iran; by late December, however, the White House decided to try to negotiate a moderate transition from the Shah's regime. The interim government that followed was unable to mobilize significant support from monarchists or Islamic fundamentalists, and, in February 1979, Khomeini came into power.

The revolution's strategic and political impact was enormous. The collapse of a regime previously thought to have been a pillar of regional stability created doubts about every government in the Gulf area. The Islamic nature of the revolution led many American observers to expect a series of similar explosions, and Carter's national security advisor, Zbigniew Brzezinski, dubbed the area the "arc of crisis."

The taking of American diplomats as hostages by Khomeini-supported student militants in November 1979 intensified the crisis. In addition, it negated the earlier, "liberal" interpretations of the Iranian revolution that traced it to the Shah's violations of human rights, excessive arms buildup, the indulgence of the United States for the Shah's regime, and other similar causes. Instead, the Islamic republic's "irrationality" and extreme hatred and contempt for America were seen as characteristic of the revolutionary change. The revolution had, in the eyes of most Americans, greatly harmed the interests of both the American and Iranian people.

In short, the hostage crisis accelerated or created the victory of a "conservative" interpretation of Iranian events. According to this interpretation, Khomeini dared to act as he did only because the United States was weak or at least seemed to be weak. Other foreign leaders watching the American handling of the crisis would conclude that Washington did not really support its own allies and was not a reliable friend. The failure of the April 1980 hostage rescue mission further undercut public confidence in the Carter administration. This image of Carter's weakness was consistent with the thinking of Ronald Reagan and his supporters. Thus the hostage crisis reinforced the ideological perspective of this group and made it far more acceptable to the general public.[3]

Former Secretary of State Henry Kissinger provided an influential version of this critique of weakness. American failings, presumably arising after he left office, had transformed "inchoate unrest into a revolution. . . . To my mind," he explained, "the combination of Soviet actions in Ethiopia, South Yemen, Afghanistan, plus the general perception of an American geopolitical decline, had the consequence of demoralizing those whose stock in trade was cooperation with the United States, undermining their resolution towards potential revolutionaries." The Shah did not resist the revolt more forcefully "because he must have had doubts about our real intentions," but concessions could not stop revolutions and should come only when order is restored. "Whether we like it or not," Kissinger concluded, "the Shah was considered our close ally in that area for thirty-seven years. He left office under the visible urging of the

United States. Other local rulers might fear similar treatment by America and would seek alliances elsewhere."[4]

The idea of White House responsibility for the collapse of the Shah's regime was as irresistible as it was erroneous. The then vice-presidential candidate George Bush accused Carter of "pulling the rug out from under the Shah." The president's "on-again, off-again statements . . . did much to hasten his departure," and the administration's policy of "splendid oscillation" severed the links between the United States and its allies.[5]

The Shah's fall forced changes in American strategic thinking on the Middle East. Ironically, as in the case of detente, the challenged theory had been formulated by the Nixon rather than the Carter administration. The Iranian revolution was taken to show that the indirect approach favored by the Nixon Doctrine did not work. If the United States wanted something done, it must do it itself.

Such conclusions were further reinforced by the Soviet invasion of Afghanistan in December 1979. President Carter's statement that this was the greatest crisis since World War II was generally taken as exaggeration, but the occupation of Afghanistan was a shock to American policymakers. Speaking of the Middle East in the 1950s, veteran diplomat Raymond Hare once commented, "It's hard to put ourselves back into this period. There was really a definite fear of hostilities, of an active Russian occupation of the Middle East physically, and you could practically hear the Russian boots clumping down over hot desert sands." In the early 1980s, the psychology of American Middle East policy reverted to that of the 1950s.

The invasion's impact was particularly strong, given its echo of the events that first began the Cold War in the post-World War II period. The United States was generally prepared to accept an Eastern Europe friendly toward the Soviet Union, but it also assumed that those states would be independent of Moscow's control — a "Finlandized" but sovereign Eastern Europe. The subsequent brutal suppression of all opposition and democracy convinced American policymakers that the Soviets, whether through their appetite for security or aggressive design, would continue to extend their power unless stopped.

The same framework was applied to Afghanistan, long a neutralist country, but somewhat under Soviet influence. Precisely because Kabul had made such efforts to appease Moscow, the takeover was seen as a sign of Soviet insatiability; political accommodation as a way for neighboring states to maintain good relations with the Soviet Union was deemed unsafe. Whatever the reasons for Moscow's action, whether "offensive" or "defensive," whether a step toward the Gulf or to the maintenance of a pro-Soviet Marxist government, objectively the new situation marked a major advance for Soviet forces and a possible stepping stone for more expansion.

In January 1980, National Security Advisor Brzezinski called for the United States to establish a "cooperative security framework" of Middle East nations against the Soviet Union.[6] A few days later, President Carter's State of the Union message outlined the approach that later became known as the Carter Doctrine. "The steady growth and increased projections abroad of Soviet military power," he said, had combined with "the overwhelming dependence of Western nations, which now increasingly includes the United States, on vital oil supplies from the Middle East" to become a serious threat to American interests.

"The pressure of change in many nations of the developing world," and particularly the possibility of internal upheavals in the Gulf states, provided "some of the most serious challenges in the history of this nation," Carter continued. "The denial of these oil supplies — to us or to others — would threaten our security and provoke an economic crisis greater than that of the Great Depression fifty years ago, with a fundamental change in the way we live."[7] This situation required, he concluded, an increase in American military strength and the ability to project it through a Rapid Deployment Force, a regional security framework, some covert aid to Afghan guerrillas, and a warning to Moscow that aggression in the Gulf would be met by a strong American response.

Thus the conclusions drawn by the Carter administration from these experiences were, first, that the East-West conflict must be given a more central place in any consideration of the Middle East and particularly of Gulf security and, second, that the ability to project American forces into the area must play a more important role in American military thinking. These ideas were both accepted and extended by the Reagan administration.

The Reagan Administration: Policy Premises and Phase I

It became fashionable, both in the United States and the Middle East, to say that the Reagan administration had no Middle East policy. This misconception arose because the Reagan policy was not comprehensive. The administration consciously ignored the regional problems it considered unimportant. Emphasis on the necessary incompleteness of policy diverted attention from its fundamental change in approach. The Reagan administration, rejecting the view that changes in international politics limited the ability of the United States to shape regional developments, asserted that American power should and could be used to determine the course of events. The refusal to do so rather than an inability to do so was at fault, they argued. The Shah's incompetence, the shortcomings of Nixon-Kissinger policy, and socioeconomic changes in Iran were not regarded as responsible for the revolution's success; rather the fault lay with a failure of will and toughness on the part of the Carter administration.

The incoming Reagan administration's view of the region was based on three premises that broadly defined its strategy. The first premise was the primacy of the Gulf as an area for American concern and activity. This resulted from changes in regional financial power and strategic importance (with the rise of the oil exporting countries) and from the crises in Iran and Afghanistan. Hence the Gulf was to become the focus of the administration's "strategic consensus" — a broad regional alliance against the Soviets, pivoted on Saudi Arabia. The implications of this new emphasis included an increased arms sales program, a theater for the training of American troops, and a network of support facilities.

Obviously this emphasis on the Gulf meant less attention to the Arab-Israeli conflict in general and the autonomy negotiations between Egypt and Israel in particular.[8] From the administration's point of view, this was no oversight. The limits placed on Camp David (caused by the intransigence of the PLO and Israel and the refusal of more Arab regimes to join the talks) made a breakthrough seem unlikely. Also since the Camp David agreements were the Carter administration's creation, Reagan felt much less commitment to them.

Further, the Reagan team saw no attractive plan in sight. The PLO was considered a terrorist and pro-Soviet group, which defined it as an enemy in the Reagan administration's book. A Palestinian state was seen as destabilizing for the region. A "Jordanian solution" involving a Jordan-West Bank federation was preferable and was indeed later taken up in the September 1982 Reagan plan, but it required Jordanian support and possibly even PLO acquiescence. Finally the Israeli annexation of the territories, which the permanent settlements seemed headed toward, would carry high costs for American interests in the Arab world and was also opposed by the administration. Given the complexity of the issue and the difficulty in making progress, it was more expedient to focus on other questions.

The second main premise was that the Soviet Union posed the greatest clear and present danger to the region. The invasion of Afghanistan lent credence to this view. With the exception of Pakistan, however, this perspective did not correspond to regional perceptions. Middle Eastern countries, including the Arab states of the Gulf, were far more worried about regional and domestic problems than they were about the external Soviet threat.

In this context the administration emphasized, and sometimes overstated, the capabilities of Moscow's prospective and real regional allies. Richard Allen, then national security advisor, explained in September 1981, for example, that the threat to the Gulf "could come from a destabilized Iran, from Ethiopia, from Yemen or elsewhere. . . . The situation has changed dramatically in the last four years."[9]

Given the unexpected explosion in Iran, American leaders believed anything was possible in the Middle East, a belief that was conducive to panic. Thus when the Sudanese government claimed that Libya was about to launch a cross-border attack — an unlikely contingency on logistical, military, and political grounds — Senator Richard Lugar, an administration ally, said, "It seems to me . . . invasion is imminent." Even Senator John Glenn, who expressed concern about White House commitments on Gulf intervention, added that the Libya-Ethiopia-South Yemen pact was "probably under Soviet leadership."[10]

As Gulf Arabs remained uninterested in an anti-Soviet alliance, however, and as Iran won victories in its war with Iraq, American concern shifted to Teheran. By mid-1982, Washington, while ostensibly remaining neutral in the Iran-Iraq war, gave some covert aid to Iraq and its Arab allies against an Iranian invasion or a possible revolution by radical Islamic forces in the Gulf.[11]

The third premise, based on the emphasis on Gulf security and on a Soviet threat, led to the conclusion that American regional policy must be primarily military and unilateralist. If the greatest danger was from the Soviet Union, only the United States could confront it successfully. If local states could not ensure regional security against the Soviets or Soviet-backed aggressors, then the United States would have to respond directly. On this point, analysts often misunderstood the administration's attitude as a revival of 1950s regional alliance policy. The United States, however, was serious about the use of its own forces; local states were mainly expected to supply bases or facilities.[12] Thus while Egypt, Israel, and Saudi Arabia sometimes competed for the position of America's best friend and favored ally in the region, Washington was not looking for a regional policeman. This job would, in principle, be reserved for the United States.

At the same time, the United States, as part of its military posture, continued and increased its large-scale arms sales programs in the area. These, it should be remembered, came at the insistence of local governments. Failure to provide such equipment could carry political costs with it. As the *Washington Post* correctly noted in regard to the sale of intelligence and surveillance aircraft: "The Saudis evidently asked for AWACS not so much to prepare for either a Soviet or an Israeli attack, although both contingencies continually bob up and down in their minds, as to test the strength of their American connection."[13] In many cases, there were legitimate defensive requirements. For example, Saudi oil fields were relatively unprotected, and keeping these assets safe was not only in Saudi interests but also those of the West. As in Iran, however, the equipment purchased was not always the most effective for preserving internal stability; the most advanced, sophisticated armaments for international warfare were provided instead.

The United States Rapid Deployment Force (RDF) and a whole

network of support facilities were explicitly designed to oppose any Soviet attack on the region. The RDF might also be used in state-to-state or internal conflicts, and this led to much distrust of American intentions in the Gulf. President Reagan hinted at additional missions for the force in an October 1981 press conference, "Saudi Arabia we will not permit to be an Iran."[14] The implication of American willingness to intervene in internal Saudi upheavals was of extraordinary significance, but Secretary of Defense Caspar Weinberger had some difficulty defining this pledge. What the president had in mind, he said, "is that we would not stand by and allow in the event of Saudi requests . . . a government . . . totally unfriendly to the United States and the Free World to take over."[15] By failing to define the RDF role clearly, the administration invited major controversy in the United States and abroad should it ever be used.

Both the Carter and Reagan administrations had little success in securing European cooperation for Gulf security; most local countries, including those friendly to the United States, were reluctant to be publicly involved or to provide bases. Some facilities were found, however, on the region's periphery in Kenya, Somalia, Oman, and the Indian Ocean island of Diego Garcia. In June 1980, a United States-Kenya agreement provided for the use of Mombasa port and an adjacent airfield in exchange for military and economic aid; a United States-Oman accord at the same time allowed for access to bases, including the air force base on Masirah island. Two months later an arrangement was made with Somalia for use of facilities in Mogadishu and Berbera.

All these facilities required large-scale spending to make them usable and none of them were close to the Gulf. But the maintenance of naval units in the Arabian Sea with stored supplies supplemented these efforts. The presence of AWACS, first under complete American control and then to be sold to the Saudis, provided intelligence information to the United States on the activities of a variety of potentially inimical forces in the region. Despite their public criticism of any American military involvement in the region, there was ample evidence that the Saudis and other Gulf Arab states were overbuilding their own bases in case American forces would ever need to use them. Much of the local military cooperation, including the new Gulf Cooperation Council, was also consistent with American objectives.

Saudi Arabia played a central role in administration policy as the region's most important oil producer and as a potential leader of the Arabian nations.[16] The main controversy of American Middle East policy in 1981 was over the sale of AWACS to the Saudis. The request to buy AWACS was accompanied by orders for Sidewinder air-to-air missiles, auxiliary fuel tanks, and bomb racks for already purchased American-built F-15s, as well as for refueling planes able to extend those fighter-bombers' range. In 1978 the Carter administration, to gain Israeli acquiescence on the original sale, promised Israel that such equipment would not be sold; this policy was reversed two years later, however.

Advocates of the $2 billion sale argued it would enhance Saudi security, help protect the oil fields and the Gulf against aggression by Soviet or local radical forces, aid American military and intelligence efforts, and strengthen bilateral relations. Failure to deliver the AWACS would severely undermine American credibility in the Gulf.[17] Opponents saw this step as endangering America's secret technology; as threatening to Israel's security; and as entangling the United States with a regime whose fall might be hastened by excessive military transfers. After a heated congressional debate, the Senate narrowly supported the sale.[18]

As for the political side of American-Saudi relations, President Reagan himself succinctly explained American goals: "Moderate Arab states like Egypt want peace, and Israel wants peace. Together they can be a force to keep the biggest troublemaker in the world, the Soviet Union, from making mischief in the Mideast. . . . Saudi Arabia is a leader of the moderate Arab states. I believe the Saudis are the key to spreading the peace throughout the Mideast instead of just having it confined to Israel and Egypt."[19]

Any hope the administration might have had of Saudi Arabia as a catalyst for the peace process, however, was doomed. Saudi Arabia's great wealth made it more a hostage to political and military weakness than a regional leader. The kingdom would never risk angering radical states like Syria. The oil glut and the rise of new, non-OPEC producers undermined Riyadh's economic leverage. Consequently Saudi Arabia became a secondary consideration in the administration's overall regional policy, though not in its Gulf security approach.

Phase 2: September 1982–April 1983

Despite the administration's initial emphasis on the issue of Persian Gulf security, a series of events nonetheless tended to highlight the Arab-Israeli conflict. These developments included the movement of Syrian antiaircraft missiles into Lebanon; an artillery battle between Israel and the PLO on the Israel-Lebanon border; the June 1981 Israeli raid that destroyed Iraq's nuclear reactor; the July Israeli air attack on PLO offices in Beirut, which resulted in civilian casualties; the controversy over AWACS sales to Saudi Arabia; Israel's step toward annexing the Golan Heights in December; the firing of West Bank mayors in March and April 1982; and the Israeli invasion of Lebanon in June 1982.

The Reagan administration was at first tolerant of the Begin government's assertive policies. Washington's prime goal was to preserve quiet on the Arab-Israeli front; its fear was that trouble there might lead to war or weaken Gulf cooperation. The United States government alternated between the view that the Begin regime was endangering that balance and the concern that pressure on Israel might only encourage precipitate action by Jerusalem.

Israel's policies were based on expectations of continued Arab hostility and a mistrust of foreign allies, seen as inevitably selling out Israeli interests. Although the country tended to rally against outside pressure, the government's ability to work with and maintain the American connection remained an important domestic asset. In the fight for survival, words were far less important than the military balance of forces and the situation on the ground. Foreigners saw Israel as all-conquering, but Israelis were conscious of security dangers; they would make concessions on security issues only if offered acceptable alternatives. In line with these priorities, the Begin government claimed that safety lay in continued West Bank settlement and permanent Israeli control over the occupied territories.

American vacillation over bilateral relations affected Israel's political culture adversely. Since Israel was afraid of what the United States might do, it repeatedly acted quickly to grab any possible advantage during periods of apparent American support. The September 1981 strategic understanding was a good example of the effect of administration policy shifts, which inspired neither concessions nor restraint from Israel. As Shlomo Avineri, former Director-General of Israel's Foreign Ministry, wrote, "It just does not reflect seriousness of purpose when the United States hastily signs a strategic memorandum of understanding with Israel merely to placate the Israelis in the wake of the AWACS sale to Saudi Arabia and then, just as hastily, voids the understanding after Israel's de facto annexation of the Golan Heights."[20]

The main conflict between the United States and Israel came during Jerusalem's invasion of Lebanon in the summer of 1982. Early in the administration, the anti-Syria and anti-PLO stance of the United States seemed to support strong Israeli measures. Thus former National Security Advisor Richard Allen contended that "to the extent that one reaches to the source of terrorism, then, of course, there's ample justification . . . for taking actions. . . . I'm just saying that reaching to the source is generally recognized as a 'hot pursuit' of a sort and therefore justified."[21]

Later, however, Haig realized that Lebanon was the most likely place for a general war to break out in the Middle East; although the State Department had no particular blueprint for dealing with this situation, he set a high priority on ending the civil war there. Simultaneously, the United States worked hard to restrain Israel from invading Lebanon. More than once, these pressures worked, but they finally failed in June of 1982.

Even though the United States had strongly opposed any Israeli invasion, Washington was slow and confused in responding to the attack. The military success of the Israeli move seemed to prompt Haig's acceptance of the idea that a defeat for the PLO and Syrians was a setback for forces inimical to the United States and might end Lebanon's civil war. But Haig soon resigned, and despite Ambassador Philip Habib's strenuous labors, Israel's demand for Lebanese political concessions before it would withdraw its troops increased Washington's frustration and anger.[22]

President Reagan's September 1 proposals further strained United States-Israel relations, since Israel was not consulted and did not agree with the new initiative. To a great extent, the carefully worded speech reiterated past American thinking. Reagan called for a solution based on a federated Jordanian-Palestinian state ruling the occupied territories under King Hussein. Border adjustments might be made for Israel's security, but construction of Jewish settlements on the West Bank should be frozen as soon as possible. The United States would not accept either Israeli annexation of the territory or an independent Palestinian state under PLO leadership.

There were several reasons for the timing and shape of this proposal. Israel's invasion of Lebanon provided opportunities for American policy by weakening Arab hard-liners, demonstrating the lack of a viable Arab military option, and forcing them to seek protection from Israeli power. The United States clearly held the cards for any diplomatic settlement. But to take advantage of these developments, Washington had to dissociate itself from the policy of Israel's government and effect a reconciliation with the Arabs. A moderate solution could for the first time build a consensus in the United States over how to resolve the conflict. Finally, the administration became convinced that a slow and confused response to the Lebanon crisis was damaging its credibility and prestige at home.

In response to these dramatic developments, President Reagan, in a speech on September 1, 1982, prescribed an American approach to resolving the Arab-Israeli conflict. He described his position as the "next step" in the Camp David "autonomy talks to pave the way for permitting the Palestinian people to exercise their legitimate rights." The Lebanon war, "tragic as it was, has left us with a new opportunity for Middle East peace," he said. "The military losses of the PLO have not diminished the yearning of the Palestinian people for a just solution of their claims. . . . While Israel's military successes in Lebanon have demonstrated that its armed forces are second to none in the region, they alone cannot bring just and lasting peace to Israel and her neighbors." The question is "How to reconcile Israel's legitimate security concerns with the legitimate rights of the Palestinians?" This must be done through diplomacy rather than on the battlefield and would involve concessions by both sides.

The United States, Reagan continued, had a "special responsibility

. . . . No other nation is in a position to deal with the key parties to the conflict on the basis of trust and reliability." Israel deserved Arab recognition and, Reagan implied, some changes in the pre-1967 boundaries. Up to that point, he said, Israel had lived in narrow borders, within artillery range of hostile Arab armies: "I am not about to ask Israel to live that way again."

He advocated, in line with the Camp David accords, a five-year transition period after the election of a self-governing Palestinian authority, and in addition, "the immediate adoption of a settlement freeze by Israel, more than any other action, could create the confidence needed for wider participation in these talks." But what specifically was Reagan proposing? "Peace cannot be achieved," he stated, "by the formation of an independent Palestinian state . . . nor is it achievable on the basis of Israeli sovereignty or permanent control over the West Bank and Gaza." The preferred American solution was "self-government by the Palestinians of the West Bank and Gaza in association with Jordan."[23]

The Reagan plan grew out of the belief that the United States had to show that progress was being made in solving the Arab-Israeli issue — or at least that there were attempts in that direction — to retain American influence in the Arab world. The policy was meant to show the Arabs that America was trying to respond to their grievances. There was also an important domestic component, since dramatic action was deemed necessary to prove that the administration had the Middle East situation under control. It was hoped that a broad consensus at home could be built on behalf of the proposals.

The second element of Reagan's policy at this point was the dispatch of U.S. Marines to Beirut. At first, the 1400-man force was to supervise the PLO retreat from the city, but it then returned after the Sabra and Shatila massacres of Palestinians by the Christian militia. American leverage and the Marine presence was now to be used for more ambitious goals: securing the removal of all foreign troops from Lebanon, helping to end the civil war, and assisting in the formation of a new political accord around President Amin Gemayel.

Secretary of State George Shultz accepted the State Department's analysis that if arrangements were made for an Israeli withdrawal, the Syrians would quickly follow suit.[24] In addition, the State Department also suggested that King Hussein was eager to accept the Reagan Plan but could not act until Israeli troops left Lebanon. Hence American negotiators emphasized this issue rather than internal negotiations or pressure on Syria at a time when Damascus was most vulnerable. Both premises, however, were wrong. If it had been possible to accomplish anything in Lebanon — and this is not altogether clear — the administration's priorities were in error, and the opportunity was lost.

After months of negotiations, an Israel-Lebanon treaty was mediated.[25] What followed, however, was an accelerated Syrian buildup, and all-out opposition to the accord from Damascus. To make matters worse, King Hussein rejected the Reagan Plan on April 11, 1983, largely because of strong PLO opposition and the lack of support by other Arab leaders.[26]

Phase 3: May 1983–February 1985

The Arab failure to deliver on either Lebanon or the Reagan Plan was a disillusioning experience for the Reagan administration. At the same time, a period of relatively strained American-Israeli relations ended. Continued problems in Lebanon persuaded the White House that the Middle East was an area in which potential political trouble greatly outweighed any opportunity for productive effort or diplomatic progress.

During the second half of 1983, the U.S. Marines and the American Embassy in Lebanon came under attack from terrorists who were apparently assisted by the Syrians, and the resulting casualties led to growing pressure at home to withdraw American forces. Having earlier pressed Israel to withdraw from Lebanon, Washington now urged it to stay in order to keep the pressure on Damascus. The failure to make progress in securing a Syrian withdrawal, however, helped Washington accept an Israeli pullback in August.

Artillery and sniper fire against the Marines increased during July and August, 1983, and a dozen American soldiers were killed. At the same time, Syrian-backed Druze and Shiite Moslem militias launched offensives against the Gemayel government. The administration, concerned that Syria intended to replace Gemayel with a radical government, perceived a critical challenge to United States power.

In reaction to this political and military problem, President Reagan stationed an additional 2000 Marines on American ships just off Lebanon's coast and ordered that the naval guns and the Marine artillery ashore be used to wage "aggressive defense" tactics against Druze artillery positions harassing the Marines or supporting offensives against Lebanese government forces.

The continuing Marine casualties and this escalation provoked much debate in Congress. After some heated exchanges, a compromise giving the president eighteen months to keep American forces in Lebanon was reached. The timing of this accord was important, since only two weeks later, on October 23, 1983, a suicide truck-bomber destroyed the Marines' barracks and killed 241 soldiers. This disaster increased domestic political opposition to the administration's effort; a congressional commission criticized military security arrangements and the administration's lack of political direction. Reagan's difficulties only increased when an American plane was shot down in a December 1983 air attack against Syrian positions that had fired on reconnaissance flights.

The problem was not, as was generally held, that the Marines lacked a mission, but rather that American diplomacy lacked a strategy for achieving success. It was impossible to mediate among Lebanese factions because Damascus forbade its clients to compromise while any Americans or Israelis remained in Lebanon; the Gemayel government was also reluctant to make any concessions to its enemies. The alternative position for Washington, to intimidate Syria into backing down, was not realistic, since Damascus knew that the United States lacked the necessary forces and staying power to carry through any threats.

With a presidential election coming up, with results in Lebanon disappointing, and with domestic opposition increasing, the Reagan administration decided to pull out the Marines in early February 1984. Domestically this move was quite successful, for although American efforts in Lebanon seemed to have failed, the political fallout was limited: once the Marines had been withdrawn, the issue largely disappeared from the ensuing presidential campaign. Although there was much talk of damage to American credibility in the Middle East, there seemed to be no long-range negative effect, nor did Lebanon come entirely under Syrian or radical control as the administration had earlier warned.

But the failure of the Reagan Plan to gain Arab and Israeli support, plus the failure of American intervention in Lebanon, had a major effect on administration thinking. King Hussein's criticism of American policy stirred real resentment in the White House and Congress. High officials, including Secretary of State Shultz and National Security Advisor Robert McFarlane, who entered office willing to press Israel toward a settlement, were now skeptical of Arab willingness to negotiate seriously.

American-Israeli relations, which had been marked by friction when there had been policy differences over Lebanon, now improved. In November 1983 there had been a bilateral strategic cooperation agreement. American aid levels continued to climb, the United States dropped objections to providing aid for building Israel's new Lavi plane, and there were other signs of improving relations.

Phase 4: February 1985–February 1986

A conjunction of regional developments — Hussein's seeming success in establishing a joint Jordan-PLO bargaining position and a new, more flexible government in Israel — set the stage for the fourth phase of American policy in the opening months of 1985. Washington sought to encourage the formation of such a joint delegation, nudge it toward recognition of Israel, and create a framework for direct negotiations that would produce a solution within the general context of the 1982 Reagan Plan.

The changing fortunes and policy shifts of earlier periods had never altered Reagan's policymakers' continued preference for some form of

Jordanian solution. As Deputy Secretary of State Kenneth Dam expressed this view in a May 1985 speech, American policy was that self-government by the Palestinians of the West Bank and Gaza, in association with Jordan, offered the best chance for a durable, just, and lasting peace. The key barriers remained the conditions for PLO involvement in negotiations, the framework for talks, and the extent of American participation to move the process forward.

The prospects for renewed American diplomatic efforts in early 1985 seemed promising in several respects: In Israel, Labor party leader Shimon Peres had become prime minister as the head of a national unity government. Peres was friendly to the Reagan Plan concept and eager to negotiate with Jordan. Further, one of the new cabinet's first actions was to withdraw Israeli forces from Lebanon (from January through June 1985), a step that Jordan had earlier made a precondition for pursuing negotiations.

A further important consideration was that, under the terms of the coalition agreement, Peres was scheduled to hand over his office to Yitzhak Shamir of the Likud bloc in October 1986. Although Labor favored territorial compromise with Jordan on the West Bank (indeed, Peres and other party leaders had been meeting secretly with Hussein to discuss these matters) the Likud was more skeptical about the possibility of successful negotiations and more interested in permanently retaining the territories captured by Israel in the 1967 war. Thus time became a central factor.

This incentive applied especially to Jordan's King Hussein, who saw 1985 as a window of opportunity for seeking a political settlement. On the one hand, Hussein knew that Peres was more open to compromise than Shamir, his predecessor and his scheduled successor. On the other hand, he feared that Israel was becoming permanently entrenched on the West Bank. Hussein warned the November 1984 Palestine National Council meeting (held, significantly, in Amman) that time was not on the Arab's side. In this danger, Hussein noted an opportunity for himself. A PLO weakened by being driven out of Lebanon and split by pro-Syrian forces was easier for Jordan to influence and perhaps even to control.

Hussein thus sought to adapt the Reagan Plan approach to his own needs and constraints, incorporating the PLO as a subordinate partner. By seeking Yasir Arafat's consent to a joint Jordan-PLO negotiating delegation, Hussein hoped to develop a series of talks with the United States leading to some form of negotiations with Israel. The object was a peace agreement based on mutual recognition between the Arab side and Israel and on the establishment of a Jordan-West Bank confederation with Amman as senior partner. The first step was the February 11, 1985 communiqué between Hussein and Arafat.

This agreement, apparently drafted by the Jordanian side, was to provide for and regulate bilateral cooperation. It called for a solution involving an exchange of "land for peace"; the acceptance of conditions "cited in UN resolutions," total Israeli withdrawal from the West Bank; a Palestinian "right to self-determination" but only within the framework of a confederation between Jordan and Palestine; and an international conference that would include the PLO within a joint Arab delegation.

Almost as soon as the Jordanian government announced the communiqué, however, both individual PLO leaders and the PLO Executive Committee threw doubt on its contents and demanded further amendments, including a joint delegation of all the Arab governments plus the PLO, independence for a PLO-led Palestinian state, criticisms of the "land for peace" formula, insistence on their refusal to recognize Israel or to accept UN Resolutions 242 and 338, and refusal to cede representation (even temporarily) to non-PLO Palestinians (even those willing to follow Arafat's orders). Hani al-Hassan, a close advisor to Arafat, said, "Frankly and clearly, I say that we reject [UN] Resolution 242. We rejected it in the past and will reject it in the future."

The PLO's obduracy resulted from several factors. Having barely escaped Syrian domination, Arafat was not about to accept Jordanian hegemony. And rather than freeing him from the need to appease his most hard-line colleagues, the split in the PLO only added credibility to the threats of the remaining rejectionists. In short, although Arafat was eager to keep open all his options, he was not willing to commit himself seriously to negotiations or to peace with Israel.[27]

The February 11 accord, at least as interpreted by Jordan, was generally in line with American policy. But it lacked vital clarifications and principles, including an unambiguous expression of the PLO's intentions and a clear framework for the implementation of any diplomatic effort. These two issues made the task for Reagan policymakers both difficult and complex.

PLO Policy and Intentions. The United States' objective was now to determine whether the PLO was really willing to accept UN Resolutions 242 and 338, negotiate seriously with Israel, abandon the use of terrorism, and agree to recognize Israel. Previous experience, reinforced by Arafat's behavior in 1985, showed that the PLO leader was too constrained by internal PLO conflicts, Syrian threats, fear of Jordanian domination, historical ideological commitments, and lack of control over his own organization to take such major steps. He might simply be maneuvering for American recognition without making any concomitant concessions or seeking a stronger position — a military presence in Jordan or even control over the West Bank — from which to continue a long-term revolutionary and terrorist campaign against Israel.

Successive American administrations had preferred a Jordanian option precisely because they deemed an independent Palestinian state under Arafat's leadership to be against American national interests. Policymakers asked such questions as: Would such a state really be a stabilizing force in the region or would it have revanchist ambitions against Israel or even Jordan that would lead to further, chronic violence? Would the PLO's long alliance with the USSR and the radical stance of many of its leaders seriously threaten American regional standing?

For these reasons, Hussein's approach appealed to the Reagan administration.[28] But by the same token, the administration wanted to be sure that Hussein could deliver the PLO along the promised lines, which, it was hoped, would lead to a successful diplomatic process and a lasting peace.

Framework for Negotiations. Hussein and Arafat insisted on an international conference that would include the members of the UN Security Council and all relevant Arab states. Washington and Jerusalem wanted direct negotiations, arguing that an all-inclusive international conference would be doomed to failure. Damascus could be expected to try to wreck the meeting by pushing the Arab side toward intransigence, and Moscow would try to seek Arab favor and subvert the moderates by raising maximalist demands. These considerations had led both the Carter and Reagan administrations to abandon a Geneva conference framework in which the United States and USSR would be co-chairs.

During the six months after the February 11 communiqué, the United States stressed diplomatic explorations with Jordan and Israel on solving the question of Palestinian participation. After failing to find an acceptable joint delegation, Washington shifted its emphasis to gaining a compromise over the diplomatic framework for talks. The fundamental American approach on the representational issue was to give the PLO a choice. Either Arafat could find some format to indicate his willingness to recognize Israel or he could designate pro-Arafat but non-PLO Palestinians to represent his interest during the preliminary exchanges.

But the administration also expected a resolution to the problems of the joint delegation, the recognition of Israel by the PLO, linkage between the steps Hussein proposed, and direct negotiations rather than an international conference. This required a better offer from Hussein and Arafat. As Assistant Secretary of State Richard Murphy put it in late June, "If 1985 is the year of opportunity, as Arab leaders say, then the Arabs themselves are going to have to make some hard decisions."[29]

By July, the Arab failure to produce a list acceptable to either the United States or Israel dimmed hopes for success. Building on its experience with the Reagan Plan, the administration put the onus on the regional actors for ensuring progress. Certainly, explained Murphy, there had been a "sea change" in the attitudes of some Arabs but the timing for "a big push" was "not an exclusive American calendar."

King Hussein's visit to the United States in September provided a last chance for a breakthrough in 1985. Hussein stated his willingness "to negotiate, under appropriate auspices, with the government of Israel, promptly and directly, under the basic tenets of Security Council Resolutions 224 and 338," yet he could not deliver the PLO or agree to direct negotiations.

Hussein's position, then, was disappointing. His statements did not convince Congress to vote for a large American arms deal with Jordan. After eight months of effort, the peace process was stalled because the actual stance of Jordan and the PLO did not correspond with their optimistic hints.

Terrorism

In 1981 the Reagan administration proclaimed that combating terrorism was one of its highest priorities. But on several subsequent occasions, it had found terrorist violence as difficult to cope with as had its predecessors. Although the White House had courted a reputation for toughness, in fact it did not carry out reprisals, or even attempt missions to rescue hostages, in various terrorist incidents.

Both the political entanglements that terrorism could create and the cautious American policy underlying the hard-line rhetoric were vividly illustrated when, in June 1985, a TWA airliner was seized by Shiite fundamentalist hijackers and flown to Beirut. One American passenger was murdered and thirty-nine others were held for seventeen days in a seige of terror.

The administration faced a complex situation. On the one hand, although the hijacking was carried out by pro-Iranian fundamentalists, a large element of control over the situation quickly passed into the hands of Nabih Berri, leader of the Amal Shiite group. Berri, an ally of Syria and a communal nationalist, had little interest in Islamic revolution or in war with the United States or Israel as ends in themselves. The crisis, then, had more to do with Lebanese politics — with each group trying to prove its militancy and effectiveness — than it did with American policy or interests. The hijackers' main demand was that Israel free Shiite militiamen and terrorists captured in southern Lebanon. But Israel was already in the process of freeing them, and the real issue became which Shiite group could claim the credit for this achievement.

The official American position continued to be a refusal to negotiate with terrorists or to meet their demands. The administration, however, urged Israel to release the prisoners. Syria, worried about any spread of pro-Iranian Islamic revolution in Lebanon, used its leverage with the Shiite groups. The hostages were finally released safely.

Despite the apparent national fixation on the TWA hostage crisis, American media coverage reached saturation levels. The affair had little or no lasting political impact, nor did it affect American-Syrian rapprochement or produce any serious American-Israeli friction. Specific terrorist incidents attract a great deal of attention for a short period of time, but they rarely alter political circumstances.

At the same time, the TWA affair showed how uncertain American political leaders and the general public were on how to deal with terrorism. Polls showed that most Americans wanted the hostages to be released even if this required giving in to terrorist demands. An American attempt to organize an international boycott of Beirut's insecure airport gained almost no support, even from allies. In a major speech, President Reagan attacked Iran and Libya, but not Syria or Iraq, as countries supporting terrorism; the debate within the American government, however, on what, if anything, to do about such behavior continued.

Also, once again, some observers claimed that the situation had lowered American credibility. One of the terrorists jeered, "The American war machine is nothing but a child's toy" and argued that the hijacking demonstrated the "ability of the oppressed to confront America." Yet even after the fall of the Shah, the American withdrawal from Lebanon, and numerous other policy setbacks, few Middle Eastern leaders seemed to believe that America was weak. Rather they complained of American bullying while clamoring for American aid, arms, technology, support, and mediation on a range of issues.

The series of events in September–October 1985 revived some of these controversies. A number of attacks against Israeli civilians culminated in a brutal September 25 murder of three people in Cyprus. Israel blamed the PLO and bombed the PLO offices in Tunisia on October 1. Six days later, Palestinian terrorists, whose close links with the PLO were later revealed, hijacked an Italian cruise ship, the *Achille Lauro*, and murdered an elderly, crippled American. Three days later, an Egyptian airliner carrying the three terrorists was forced by American fighter planes to land in Italy where the three men were tried and convicted.

A number of apparent, but ultimately short-lived, problems for the United States arose from these developments. Much was made of conflicting statements between President Reagan and State Department officials over Israel's raid against PLO facilities in Tunisia. The President said that Israel and other nations had the right to strike back at terrorism, "If they can pick out the people responsible." Shultz's more critical statement stressed regret over the Tunisian casualties. The United States abstained on a UN resolution that condemned Israel for the attack without mentioning the foreign-backed terrorist attacks that had motivated it. Although the ambiguity could have been handled better, it did reflect diverse American positions. The United States, although an ally of Israel and an enthusiastic supporter of counterterrorism, was also an ally of several Arab states, including Tunisia, and a mediator in the Arab-Israeli conflict.

Relations were also strained with Italy, which refused American requests to extradite the terrorists, while letting the PLO leader Abu Abbas, the affair's apparent mastermind, flee the country, and with Egypt, which resented the American action against one of its planes despite President Hosni Mubarak's central role in securing the release of the *Achille Lauro* passengers. These tensions should not be overstated. The Italians were soon forced to admit that Abu Abbas had been behind the *Achille Lauro* attack; the Egyptians later used American assistance when terrorists hijacked one of their planes to Malta in November. When the heat of specific terrorist incidents dissipates, tempers cool as well.

As for the peace process, which was already in *significant* trouble, the *Achille Lauro* affair made the PLO seem less attractive as a negotiating partner and less credible as a moderate force. A planned meeting between a joint Jordan-PLO delegation and Great Britain, which seemed almost like a dress rehearsal for the long-awaited American conference with that group, fell through after the PLO refused to authorize signing a statement that would imply willingness to recognize Israel. Amman sided with London in criticizing Arafat.[30]

But the greatest international impact of the terrorism issue on American policy was in Washington's relations with Libya. Colonel Muammar el-Qaddafi's support of terrorism made him, in the Reagan administration's view, a test case to show that the United States would not be bullied by petty dictators.

The administration had often considered the possibility of overthrowing Qaddafi, although it never made any all-out attempt to effect a coup. In May 1981, the United States expelled Libyan representatives from Washington; six months later, the State Department ordered Americans out of Libya; and in March 1982, the United States barred the import of Libyan crude oil. The only direct confrontation had taken place in August 1981, during American naval exercises in the Gulf of Sidra, which Qaddafi claimed as Libyan territorial waters. When Libyan planes approached the American ships, two of them were shot down.

After the apparent Libyan involvement in terrorist murders at the Vienna and Rome airports in December 1985, Reagan banned all trade with Libya and invoked strong measures against the continued presence of American oil technicians there.[31] The problem, however, was in determining some action that could affect Libyan behavior.

In March 1986 United States naval forces on maneuvers in the contested Gulf of Sidra were ineffectively attacked by Libya's armed forces. Some observers concluded that the American naval operations were designed to provoke Libyan reprisals. After all, the administration had run out of sanctions against Qaddafi, European allies refused to cooperate, and domestic public opinion and Congress only supported direct action against Qaddafi as a self-defense measure. After Libya fired missiles at the ships, American forces replied by bombing Libyan ships and shore installations.

In the following weeks American intelligence discovered, through breaking Libya's code and other means, that Qaddafi was involved in a new terrorist offensive. The most publicized incident was the bombing of a West Berlin discotheque in April that killed three people, including two American soldiers. American planes based on aircraft carriers and in Britain staged a surprise raid on Libyan military bases and on Qaddafi's personal compound. One American plane was shot down and a number of Libyan civilians, including Qaddafi's adopted child, were killed by the bombs. Although American public opinion supported the raid, it was widely criticized in Western Europe and in the Arab world. Nevertheless, America's European allies were prompted to put their own pressures on Libya, seeking to avoid escalation; the Arab states did not match their rhetoric with action, because of their own dislike and distrust of Qaddafi.

Despite the inevitable vicissitudes and uncertainties, the overall strategic and political situation in the Middle East was not unfavorable to American interests at the end of 1986. Terrorism, often aimed against Americans, hypnotized the media and caused terrible losses in human terms, but it hardly destabilized the region. Islamic fundamentalism had been incapable of mounting successful or even serious revolutionary challenges to any of the region's regimes. The Lebanese civil war still raged, but it was equally clear that neither Syria nor radical anti-American forces could really dominate Lebanon. A bloody Iran-Iraq war remained indecisive but showed no sign of spreading or endangering the level of Gulf oil exports, which were falling at any rate, due to the oil glut.

Significantly, the United States retained a wide variety of allies while the USSR's influence remained extremely limited. Moscow's achievement of diplomatic relations with Oman and the United Arab Emirates only showed the weakness of the Soviet regional position. Soviet problems stemmed from the USSR's inability to supply aid and modern technology, to broker peace negotiations, or to support their own clients. Since some of these shortcomings stemmed from Moscow's leadership vacuum, the ascent of Gorbachev to power might prove the basis for a new Soviet activism in the region.

If the Iranian revolution and the failure of American leverage in Lebanon demonstrated the limits of American power, especially military power, in the region, 1985 provided a lesson on the continuing importance of America's political and diplomatic role. American attempts to mediate — or failure to resolve — the Arab-Israeli conflict often seemed to produce acrimonious reactions in the area, yet it was still universally acknowledged that only Washington could further any peaceful conclusion.

A second lesson was that regional forces had to take the lead in seeking to solve their own conflicts. The United States could help this process but would not be able to break through the resistance of those directly involved in the dispute. But within this framework, the controversy concerned the right balance of American activism and initiative.

Many experts hold the well-worn view that the close American-Israeli relation constantly jeopardizes all these policy goals. They predict imminent Marxist or fundamentalist revolt and the compromise of America's whole regional position unless policy is drastically changed to incorporate a quick solution to the Arab-Israeli conflict on traditional Arab terms. But nearly four decades' experience demonstrates the fallacy of this argument and has led American policymakers to reject it, although its appeal for some academics and analysts has not been reduced.

Washington's relative edge in the East-West competition rests on an ability to maintain good relations with a variety of Middle Eastern countries — Israel, Egypt, Jordan, Saudi Arabia, and even Iraq. This ability, in turn, is based on America's unique military, political, economic, and technological resources. Whether the issue is mediating the Arab-Israeli conflict or providing the needed training, equipment, and guarantees to further Persian Gulf security, the United States enjoys powerful advantages.

But given the very real ideological and domestic political constraints, nationalism, and conflicting objectives of Middle East leaders, the United States can neither dictate terms nor produce magical solutions to the region's passionate rivalries and problems. The ambiguous nature of regional attitudes can be seen in the Arab world's reaction to the Reagan-Gorbachev summit: that the superpowers paid little attention to Middle East questions. But the Arabs would have been equally — or more — upset if they had detected some "new Yalta" (a phrase popular in the region) purporting to partition or order the area.

The American role is even more pivotal because the Middle East lacks reliably consistent alliance systems or internationally recognized leaders. As Arab states have implicitly and explicitly developed their separate identities, pan-Arabism has become a less tenable ideology. The willingness of Egypt to sign the Camp David accords, of Lebanese Maronite Christians to ally themselves with Israel, or of Syria and Algeria to support Iran against Arab Iraq, all point to this disarray. Although Islamic fundamentalism's rise signals dissatisfaction with existing regimes, the fundamentalists have been unable to seize power anywhere outside of Iran and have also proved to be divisive — through the Iran-Iraq war, terrorism, and heightened communal tensions.

Egypt cannot play a leadership role in the region because of its continuing penalization over the Camp David accords, Iraq is tied up with an expensive war effort, Syria's obvious ambitions have isolated it, and Saudi Arabia's economic leverage has steadily declined as the price of oil and its production fell. In this situation of every state for itself, American leverage becomes more important. Several rulers seek an American *deus ex machina* to help them realize their political dreams.

The conflict, search for security, and disunity that invites American involvement also make such involvement complex and frustrating.

First, there are conflicting state objectives, not only between Arabs and Israel but also among the Arab nations. Syria, for example, is determined to sabotage negotiations that would allow a Jordanian role on the West Bank, Egypt's return to the Arab fold, or the emergence of an independent PLO. King Hussein and Yasir Arafat, will compete to dominate any future Jordan-West Bank federation, and so on.

Second, there are internal contradictions in the bargaining position and goals of each state. Jordan would like to have the West Bank back but does not want to pay the price of recognizing Israel. Israel wants peace, but some political groups want to retain the occupied territory and almost all of them are determined to prevent PLO participation. Arafat would like to have his own West Bank state but will neither recognize Israel nor designate stand-ins to negotiate because he fears Jordanian domination, Syrian revenge, and a split in his own ranks.

Third, all these difficulties are interlocked. It is hard to envision a diplomatic solution without Syrian participation but almost impossible to see any framework or outcome that would please Damascus and still be acceptable to Israel, Jordan, or the PLO. Hussein cannot step forward to negotiate without Arafat and, apparently, cannot persuade the PLO leader to make concessions either.

The American government consequently has tended to focus on other more pressing — or promising — areas of the world, except when developments in the region itself has forced action or given some reason to hope for success.

Finally the Reagan administration performed about as well as could be reasonably expected in the Middle East because it was generally able to adjust policies to the realities of regional problems. This assessment, ironically, rests on rejection of the administration's fondly held view that American power was so overwhelming that great advances could be achieved if only there was the willpower to use it. In fact, the Middle East has amply demonstrated the real constraints and limits of American influence and leverage in resolving the Arab-Israeli conflict, the Iran-Iraq war, and the problem of international terrorism.

"The Reagan Administration and the Middle East" was written for this volume. Copyright © 1987 by Barry Rubin.

Notes

1. Harold Saunders, *The Middle East Problem in the 1980s*, American Enterprise Institute (Washington, 1981) is one attempt to analyze American regional interests. See also John Campbell, "The Middle East: A House of Containment Built on Shifting Sands," Foreign Affairs, *America and the World 1981*, pp. 593–628.

2. Barry Rubin, *Paved with Good Intentions: The American Experience and Iran* (New York: Oxford University Press, 1980); and "American Relations with the Islamic Republic of Iran, 1979–1981," *Iranian Studies* (1980), Vol. 13, Nos. 1–4, pp. 307–326.

3. On the effect of the Iranian crisis on the elections, see the *New York Times*, November 16, 1980.

4. Interview in *The Economist* (London), February 10, 1979.

5. *Washington Post*, January 26, 1979.

6. The *New York Times*, January 21, 1980.

7. *Washington Post*, January 22, 1980.

8. On Washington's low profile on the autonomy negotiations, see the *New York Times*, December 16, 1981.

9. Interview on "The Today Show," September 23, 1981.

10. Interview on "The Today Show," October 14, 1981.

11. Barry Rubin, "The Iranian Revolution and Gulf Instability," in Shirin Tahrir-Kheli et al., *The Iran-Iraq War—Old Conflicts, New Weapons* (New York: Praeger, 1982).

12. Christopher Madison, "U.S. Balancing Act in the Middle East," *National Journal*, November 28, 1981; and Christopher Joyner and Shafqat Ali Shah, "The Reagan Policy of 'Strategic Consensus' in the Middle East," *Strategic Review* (Fall 1981).

13. *Washington Post*, September 4, 1981.

14. The *New York Times*, October 2, 1981.

15. "Face the Nation," October 4, 1981.

16. *Washington Post*, November 3, 1981; the *New York Times*, December 16, 1981; William Quandt, *Saudi Arabia in the 1980s* (Washington: The Brookings Institution, 1981); Department of State, "Saudi Arabia and U.S. Security Policy," *Current Policy*, No. 320, September 25, 1981; and Alexander Haig, "Saudi Security, Middle East Peace and U.S. Interests," *Current Policy*, No. 323, October 1, 1981.

17. On the debate, see the *Washington Post*, September 27, 1981; the *New York Times*, September 28, October 1, October 6, 1981; and *The Economist*, October 3, 1981.

18. Polls showed that 56 percent of Americans were against and only 29 percent were in favor of the sale, *Los Angeles Times*, October 8, 1981.

19. *Washington Post*, November 1, 1981.

20. Shlomo Avineri, "Beyond Camp David," *Foreign Policy* (Spring 1982): 35–36. Text of accord in *Department of State Bulletin* (January 1982).

21. Interview, April 2, 1981, in Congressional Research Service, *Documents and Statements on Middle East Peace 1979–1982* (Washington, 1982), p. 229.

22. Zeev Schiff charges, in his book *Israel's Lebanon War* (New York: Macmillan, 1984), that the United States gave a "green light" for the invasion. This author's own observations at the time and later research make him doubt this. It is more likely that Defense Minister Ariel Sharon presented the American position to his own government in a manner calculated to convince them to proceed with a project he strongly favored. See also Alexander Haig, *Caveat* (New York: Simon & Schuster, 1984) and Itamar Rabinovich, *The War for Lebanon* (Ithaca, NY: Cornell University Press, 1984).

23. For the text of Reagan's speech see Walter Laqueur and Barry Rubin, *The Israel-Arab Reader* (New York: Viking, 1984), pp. 650–52.

24. For Shultz's views on taking office, see his July 12, 1982, testimony in Laqueur and Rubin, *The Israel-Arab Reader*, pp. 656–663.

25. The May 17 agreement negotiated by Israel and Lebanon with American assistance never went into effect. See Laqueur and Rubin, *The Israel-Arab Reader*, pp. 691–695.

26. Ibid., pp. 686–91.

27. On the course of the 1985–1986 peace process and its problems, see Barry Rubin, "The PLO's Intractable Foreign Policy," Washington Institute for Near East Affairs (Washington 1986).

28. As Assistant Secretary of State, Murphy put it in April 4, 1985 testimony to the

House Foreign Affairs Committee, "The parties in the region have imparted a new momentum to the search for peace. We strongly support King Hussein's efforts to move toward negotiations, but only time will tell whether the agreement will ultimately enable him to do so." U.S. State Department, Current Policy No. 683.

29. U.S. State Department, Current Policy No. 726, June 27, 1985.
30. Shultz commented, "Those who perpetrate violence deal themselves out of the peace process" (*Washington Post*, September 7, 1985).
31. On the economic sanctions against Libya, see *Congressional Quarterly*, January 11, 1986, pp. 59–60.

Index

ABC News/*Washington Post* poll, 59, 67–69
ABM systems, Chinese view of, 284
ABM treaty, interpretation of, 234
Adjustment strategies
  configurations of interest and, 20–36
  Reagan view of, 22–23
  and U.S. decline, 4
Afghanistan invasion, 50, 272
  and European alliance, 302
  grain embargo following, 123
  shock of, 436
African famines (1985), 162, 422–423
African National Congress, commando operations against, 24, 411
African policy
  of Carter, 399–403
  Kissinger II phase of, 398–399
  minimal engagement phase, 396–398
African policy, of Reagan, 393–396, 403–427
  Crocker exposition of, 404–405
  economic, 416–423
  globalism of, 405–416, 423–427
  and Namibia negotiations, 412–416
  sanctions imposed on South Africa, 411–412
Ahmann, James D., 84
AID (U.S. Agency for International Development), 147
  in African famine relief, 162
  allocation of, 155
Alford, Jonathan, 323
Allen, Richard V., 205, 236, 275, 364, 438, 442

American decline
  exaggeration of, 146–147
  factors in, 10–13
  Reagan view of, 4–5, 7–8
  and strategies of restoration, 8–20
Americans' perceptions of their weakness, 100–102
Andropov, Yuri, 231–232, 241
  death of, 227
Angola, 24–25
  disengagement agreement with South Africa, 415–416
  Gulf Oil operations in, 27
  Soviet-Cuban intervention in, 407–408, 414
Apartheid
  as cause of violence, 411
  protests against, 24, 410
  public opinion on, 54, 61–63, 410
Aquino, Benino, assassination of, 23
Arab-Israeli conflict
  Carter efforts to resolve, 434
  and European alliance, 300–301
  and oil embargo, 170
  Reagan approach to, 443–444
Arafat, Yasir, 447–449
Argentina
  human rights record of, 368
  Falklands war, 319–320
  nuclear exports to, 35, 369
  public attitude toward, 57
Arms control
  and counterforce, 91
  and Geneva summit, 235
  and Japan, 350–353
  pressure to negotiate, 226–227
  public support for, 66–69

459